Frommer's

Los Angeles 2003

It's not just any downtown…the palm trees lining the streets show you're in Los Angeles—in this case, across the street from the Central Library. © Richard Cummins Photography.

L.A.'s vast concrete web of freeways can be intimidating to the visitor. For a detailed overview of the freeway system (and getting around), see chapter 2. © Chad Ehlers Photography/Photo Network.

Hollywood's biggest stars—past and present—have left their marks at Mann's Chinese Theatre, on Hollywood Boulevard. See chapter 7. © Mark E. Gibson Photography.

Hollywood's late great stars might have taken up residence in a celebrity-studded cemetery (see chapter 7), but there's no shortage of admirers and look-alikes to keep legends alive. © A. Ramey Photography/Woodfin Camp & Associates, Inc.

Manhattan Beach, just south of LAX, has some of the best surfing and body boarding around. See chapter 7.
© *Robert Landau Photography.*

Pretty Santa Catalina Island is a favorite weekend getaway for busy Angelenos. For information on this and other side trips from the city, see chapter 11. © *Robert Landau Photography.*

Encounter, a restaurant located in the former control tower at LAX, has a science-fiction feel to it—inside and out. See chapter 6. © Richard Cummins Photography/Photophile.

Locals love the Tail O' the Pup hotdog stand. For a list of other great and/or bizarre architecture in L.A., see chapter 7. © Nik Wheeler Photography.

The Peterson Automotive Museum is a wonderful tribute to that icon of California culture. See chapter 7. © Nik Wheeler Photography.

The much-hyped J. Paul Getty Museum at the Getty Center has become L.A.'s biggest cultural attraction. See chapter7 for information about parking reservations (required) and the times when it is least crowded. © Maxine Cass Photography.

The famous Tower Records on the Sunset Strip claims to have L.A.'s largest selection of CDs. See chapter 9. © Nik Wheeler Photography.

The Hollywood Bowl, a natural outdoor amphitheater, is a great place to hear a concert under the stars. See chapter 10. © Nik Wheeler Photography.

A boy and his dog in Malibu. © Sunstar/INSTOCK.

A New Star-Rating System & Other Exciting News from Frommer's!

In our continuing effort to publish the savviest, most up-to-date, and most appealing travel guides available, we've added some great new features.

Frommer's guides now include a new star-rating system. Every hotel, restaurant, and attraction is rated from 0 to 3 stars to help you set priorities and organize your time.

We've also added **seven brand-new features** that point you to the great deals, in-the-know advice, and unique experiences that separate travelers from tourists. Throughout the guide, look for:

Finds	Special finds—those places only insiders know about
Fun Fact	Fun facts—details that make travelers more informed and their trips more fun
Kids	Best bets for kids—advice for the whole family
Moments	Special moments—those experiences that memories are made of
Overrated	Places or experiences not worth your time or money
Tips	Insider tips—some great ways to save time and money
Value	Great values—where to get the best deals

We've also added a **"What's New"** section in every guide—a timely crash course in what's hot and what's not in every destination we cover.

Here's what the critics say about Frommer's:

Other Great Guides for Your Trip:

Frommer's Irreverent Guide to Los Angeles
Los Angeles & Disneyland® For Dummies
Frommer's California
California For Dummies

Los Angeles

with Disneyland®
& Palm Springs

2003

by Matthew Richard Poole

based on the previous edition by
Stephanie Avnet Yates

Wiley Publishing, Inc.

About the Author

Matthew R. Poole, a native Californian, has authored and contributed to more than 20 travel guides, including *Frommer's California, ACCESS Hawaii,* and *Berlitz Las Vegas.* Before becoming a full-time travel writer and photographer, he worked as an English tutor in Prague, ski instructor in the Swiss Alps, and scuba instructor in Maui. He currently lives in Marin County, but spends most of his time on the road doing research and avoiding commitments.

Published by:

Wiley Publishing, Inc.

909 Third Ave.
New York, NY 10022

ISBN 0-7645-6672-5
ISSN 1528-6673

Editor: John Vorwald
Production Editor: Ian Skinnari
Cartographer: John Decamillis
Photo Editor: Richard Fox
Production by Wiley Indianapolis Composition Services

For information on our other products and services or to obtain technical support, please contact our Customer Care Department within the U.S. at 800-762-2974, outside the U.S. at 317-572-3993 or fax 317-572-4002.

Wiley also publishes its books in a variety of electronic formats. Some content that appears in print may not be available in electronic formats.

Manufactured in the United States of America

5 4 3 2

Contents

10 Los Angeles After Dark   247

by Bryan Lane

11 Side Trips from Los Angeles   268

Appendix: Useful Toll-Free Numbers & Websites   319

Index   322

List of Maps

Acknowledgments

The editor would like to thank Karen Quarles for her contribution to this edition.

I would like to acknowledge the following people for their time and effort in helping me complete this 2003 edition: Bryan Lane, Trisha Clayton, Tohnia Miller, Susan Bejeckian, Patrick Connolly, Dean Fox, Carol Martinez, Linda Adams, Robert Deuel, Melissa Centeno, and my ever-patient editor, John Vorwald.

—Matthew R. Poole

An Invitation to the Reader

In researching this book, we discovered many wonderful places—hotels, restaurants, shops, and more. We're sure you'll find others. Please tell us about them, so we can share the information with your fellow travelers in upcoming editions. If you were disappointed with a recommendation, we'd love to know that, too. Please write to:

Frommer's Los Angeles with Disneyland® & Palm Springs 2003
Wiley Publishing, Inc. • 909 Third Ave. • New York, NY 10022

An Additional Note

Please be advised that travel information is subject to change at any time—and this is especially true of prices. We therefore suggest that you write or call ahead for confirmation when making your travel plans. The authors, editors, and publisher cannot be held responsible for the experiences of readers while traveling. Your safety is important to us, however, so we encourage you to stay alert and be aware of your surroundings. Keep a close eye on cameras, purses, and wallets, all favorite targets of thieves and pickpockets.

New! Frommer's Star Ratings & Icons

Every hotel, restaurant, and attraction listing in this guide has been ranked for quality, value, service, amenities, and special features using a star-rating scale. In country, state, and regional guides, we also rate towns and regions to help you narrow down your choices and budget your time accordingly. Hotels and restaurants in the Very Expensive and Expensive categories are rated on a scale of one (highly recommended) to three stars (exceptional). Those in the Moderate and Inexpensive categories rate from zero (recommended) to two stars (very highly recommended). Attractions, towns, and regions are rated according to the following scale: zero stars (recommended), one star (highly recommended), two stars (very highly recommended), and three stars (must-see).

In addition to the rating system, we also use seven icons to highlight insider information, useful tips, special bargains, hidden gems, memorable experiences, kid-friendly venues, places to avoid, and other useful information:

(*Finds* (*Fun Fact* (*Kids* (*Moments* (*Overrated* (*Tips* (*Value*

The following abbreviations are used for credit cards:

AE	American Express	DISC	Discover	V	Visa
DC	Diners Club	MC	MasterCard		

FROMMERS.COM

Now that you have the guidebook to a great trip, visit our website at www.frommers.com for travel information on nearly 2,500 destinations. With features updated regularly, we give you instant access to the most current trip-planning information available. At Frommers.com, you'll also find the best prices on airfares, accommodations, and car rentals—and you can even book travel online through our travel booking partners. At Frommers.com, you'll also find the following:

- Online updates to our most popular guidebooks
- Vacation sweepstakes and contest giveaways
- Newsletter highlighting the hottest travel trends
- Online travel message boards with featured travel discussions

What's New in Los Angeles

L.A. and Madonna have a lot in common—they're always one step ahead of the trends. Trying to keep up with the constant changes in this amorphous metropolis is a full-time job, because what was *in* last year is most definitely *out* the next. But fear not, fellow adventurers, because we've crammed this new edition with dozens of new clubs, restaurants, hotels, and insider tips. Heck, we've even included a whole new section to Catalina Island.

ACCOMMODATIONS It seems like wherever you turn, L.A.'s hotels are upping the ante with stylish facelifts and new personalities. At the **Century Plaza Hotel & Spa,** 2025 Avenue of the Stars, Century City (© **800-WESTIN-1** or 310/277-2000), the much-anticipated 35,000-square-foot **Spa Mystique**—the largest in L.A.—in now open for business. This gorgeous Asian-inspired pamper palace features 27 indoor treatment rooms, outdoor cabanas, and even a meditation garden. Book an appointment even if you're not staying at the hotel.

Also on the Zen luxury bandwagon is **Le Meridien,** 465 S. La Cienega Blvd. (© **800/645-5687** or 310/247-0400), with its new "Organic Pacific Rim" suites made from all-organic textiles and sporting Shoji screens instead of curtains. But what we really dig is the lobby Caviar Bar and those bedside remotes that operate all things electrical (lights, TV, climate control).

And if you know when to hold or fold 'em, we've also included the new **Commerce Casino & Hotel,** 6121 East Telegraph Rd. (© **888/676-3000** or 323/728-7800), located just 6 miles (10km) south of downtown L.A. right off I-5. Even if you've never played cards at a casino, there's little to lose—a mere $40 buys you hours of thrills at one of the low-stakes tables.

See chapter 5 for complete details.

DINING Here's something new—Peranakan cuisine. Pasadena's new **Nonya** restaurant, 61 N. Raymond St. (© **626/583-8398**), combines Chinese and Malaysian styles for a truly unique dining experience. The designer dining room is a must-see as well.

Westwood newcomer **Tanino Ristorante and Bar,** 1043 Westwood Blvd. (© **310/208-0444**), is worth checking out just to marvel at the 1929 Italianate Renaissance–style building designed by renowned Southern California architect Paul Revere Williams. Chef/owner Tanino Drago's *cartoccio*-style Mediterranean cuisine is reviving Westwood's dining scene.

If you're young, pretty, hip, and hungry, head to **El Coyote** 7312 Beverly Blvd. (© **323/939-2255**), where the rowdy bar scene is filled with slick showbiz player-types, rockers, and wannabe movie stars swilling cheap margaritas. Great fajita platters as well.

At **Crustacean,** 9646 Little Santa Monica Blvd. (© **310/205-8990**), a real Vietnamese princess runs the show at this see-and-be-seen Beverly Hills hotspot. If you love Dungeness crab and juicy prawns you'll want what's in the An Family's Secret Kitchen.

See chapter 6 for complete details.

WHAT TO SEE & DO   Shame on us for forgetting to include the **Bergamot Arts Station** & **Santa Monica Museum of Art,** 2525 Michigan Ave. (© 310/829-5854), a campuslike complex housing unique installations ranging from photography and sculpture to interactive pieces that are both eclectic and cutting edge. Many pieces are even available for purchase.

And if you've brought the kids along, do everyone a huge favor and bring them to the new **Winnick Family Children's Zoo,** 5333 Zoo Dr. (© 323/644-6400), within the L.A. Zoo in Griffith Park. Loaded with kid-hip exhibits such as petting areas, exhibition animal care center, and a storytelling theater, it's both educational and artistically designed.

On a final note, cancel those plans to visit the **Griffith Observatory.** The entire area is closed for a major renovation and expansion and won't reopen until May 2005.

See chapter 7 for complete details.

SHOPPING   Hollywood Boulevard got a much-needed shot in the arm with the recent opening of the long-awaited **Hollywood & Highland** shopping and entertainment complex, 6834 Hollywood Blvd. (© 323/460-6003), the centerpiece of the once-seedy (okay, still a little seedy) historic boulevard's ongoing rejuvenation. Sound familiar? That's where they hosted the 2002 Academy Awards. Named for the prime street corner that it dominates, the project includes shops and restaurants and the luxurious new Radisson high-rise hotel (see above).

Also spanking new is Pasadena's **Paseo Colorado** shopping mall, 280 E. Colorado Blvd. (© 626/795-8891). Anchored by Macy's, the two-level monolith houses about 140 retailers and restaurants, a fitness center, a 14-screen multiplex theater, and even condos on the top floor.

See chapter 9 for complete details.

AFTER DARK   The downtown arts triumvirate of the Dorothy Chandler Pavilion, Ahmanson Theater, and Mark Taper Forum—long referred to as the Music Center—has a new name: **The Performing Arts Center of Los Angeles County,** 135 N. Grand Ave. (© 213/972-7200). It's a mouthful, but reflects the diversity of these powerhouse venues, which it's hoped will increase several-fold when they're joined by the under-construction **Walt Disney Concert Hall,** designed by Frank Gehry.

Across town, in the fast-improving Hollywood nightlife district, serious rock/pop aficionados are flocking to the brand-new **Knitting Factory,** 7021 Hollywood Blvd. (© 323/463-0204), which brings the wired-for-the-21st-century New York club into the heart of historic Hollywood. And West Hollywood's LunaPark is no more, but that club/restaurant's well-located multilevel space has been transformed into another West Coast branch of a New York hotspot, **Moomba,** 665 N. Robertson Blvd. (© 310/652-6364). Boasting excellent food in a sophisticated party atmosphere, the club is also environmentally and socially conscious, a welcome trend indeed.

See chapter 10 for complete details.

SIDE TRIPS   Hey, is that an island out there? Ditch smoggy L.A. for a day and head for the party on **Catalina Island.** An hour-long boat ride (or 15 min. by helicopter) from Long Beach lands you in little ol' Avalon, where the weekend summer scene is an orgy of shorts, tank tops, and an endless sup-ply of tropical cocktails. Check out the whole new section we've added that fills you in on the best of Catalina Island.

Other new side trip additions include: the **St. Regis Monarch Beach Resort & Spa,** 1 Monarch Beach Rd. (© **800/325-3589** or 949/234-3200), in Dana Point, the finest new luxury hotel we've ever reviewed; **Hotel Oceana,** 202 West Cabrillo Blvd.

(© **800/956-9776** or 805/965-4577), Santa Barbara's newest oceanfront hotel consisting of 122 "beach chic" guest rooms housed in Spanish Mis-sion-style setting; and the **Yard House** restaurant, 401 Shoreline Village Dr. (© **562/628-0455**), in Long Beach, featuring one of the *world's* largest selection of draft beers, great food, and sunny deck seating overlooking the marina.

See chapter 11 for complete details.

1

The Best of Los Angeles

The entire world knows what Los Angeles looks like. It's a real-life version of one of those souvenir postcard folders that spill out images accordion-style: tall palm trees sweeping an azure sky; the "Hollywood" sign gleaming huge and white against a shrub-blanketed hillside; freeways flowing like concrete rivers across the landscape; a lone surfer, silhouetted against the sunset's glow, riding the day's last wave. These seductive images are just a few of many that bring to mind the city that just about everyone loves to hate—and should experience, at least once.

Los Angelenos know their city will never have the sophisticated style of Paris or the historical riches of London—but they cheerfully lay claim to living in the most fun city in the United States, maybe the world. Home to the planet's first amusement park, L.A. regularly feels like one, as the line between fantasy and reality is often obscured. From the unattainable, anachronistic glamour of Beverly Hills to the earthy, often-scary street energy of Venice, each of the city's diverse neighborhoods is like a mini–theme park, offering its own kind of adventure. The colors of this city seem a little bit brighter—and more surreal—than they do in other cities, the angles just a little sharper. Drive down Sunset Boulevard, and you'll see what we mean. The billboards are racier, the fashions sexier, the cars fancier, the sun brighter, and the energy higher than anyplace you've ever been. Darlin', you're not in Kansas anymore—you're in LA-LA Land now.

1 Frommer's Favorite L.A. Experiences

- **Driving Along the Coast:** Driving along the coast with the top down is the quintessential Southern California activity—one that never loses its appeal, even for the natives. The ocean has a spirit all its own in every season of the year: August's respite from the glaring inland heat; January's surprise warmth under wide blue skies; March's gray, bleary, almost New England–like chill; and the first warm breezes of summer in June. Stop wherever catches your fancy—a Malibu cantina, a Santa Monica boutique, or a South Bay beach; your day along the shore is an exercise in free will. BYO Mustang convertible.

- **Watching One of Your Favorite TV Sitcoms Being Taped:** Alternately boring and fascinating (the old hurry-up-and-wait syndrome), being in the audience is your chance to wander the soundstage, marvel at the cheesy three-wall sets that look so real on TV, and get an inside look at the bloopers that never make it to broadcast—and are often far more entertaining than the scripted dialogue. See chapter 7.

- **Dining at Spago (or The Ivy, or Patina, or Matsuhisa):** Less expensive than admission to Universal or Disneyland, dining at one of L.A.'s übertrendy A-list celebrity watering holes is an experience to be filed under "only in L.A." Hear dialogue straight out of *The Player* while eating fine food prepared for some of the world's pickiest eaters ("I can't eat *that!* Take it away."). See chapter 6.

- **Going to the Getty Center:** See the result of unlimited funds and very expensive taste at this multi-faceted cultural center looming large over the city. The ultramodern facility, more airy and inviting than it looks from below, features a museum housing the impressive art collection of deep-pocketed industrialist J. Paul Getty, a postmodern garden, and breathtaking views of L.A. A sleekly high-tech funicular whisks you from freeway level to this city in the clouds. Best of all, it's free (J. Paul don't need yo' money). See p. 162.

- **Paying Your Respects at the Cemetery of the Stars:** Get down and dirty with Humphrey Bogart, Clark Gable, Karen Carpenter, and all their famous pals at Forest Lawn in Glendale. This palatial and often-garish "memorial park" was satirized by expatriate Brit Evelyn Waugh in his classic novel *The Loved One.* See p. 201.

- **Going Gidget:** This is, after all, L.A.—so get thee buttocks to a beach. Watch a volleyball tournament in Manhattan Beach, a bikini contest in Marina del Rey, or the world's vainest weight lifters pumping themselves up at Venice Beach. Surfers carve waves at Malibu, and families pitch umbrellas at Zuma. See chapter 7.

- **Visiting the Happiest Place on Earth—The Disneyland Resort:** Go on a weekday to avoid the crowds, or during the off-season, between January and April. And fer gawd's sake use that new Fast Pass system unless you enjoy standing in line. The resort's

worldwide appeal is evident in the virtual United Nations of revelers traipsing between Adventureland, Fantasyland, Tomorrowland, and the new Disney's California Adventure park; you'll hear lots of international voices without even having to endure "it's a small world," a song that is now stuck in your head. See p. 213.

- **Spending a Day Downtown:** If you're looking for ethnic culture, you'll find it in downtown L.A. Visit the cutting edge Museum of Contemporary Art, stop in for a snack at the bustling Grand Central Market, pick up some inexpensive Mexican handcrafts along colorful and historic Olvera Street, and have dim sum in Chinatown. See chapter 7.

- **Taking a Specialty Tour of the City:** You might think that guided tours are for the imagination-impaired, but consider the following: an L.A. Conservancy walking tour of Downtown's extravagant abandoned movie houses, their ornate glory intact; an LA Bike Tours ride through the flat, landscaped streets of Beverly Hills, viewing the homes of the rich and famous (or just plain rich); and even an only-in-California jogging tour. If you're a do-it-yourselfer type, see the Homes of the Stars driving tour in chapter 7.

- **Shopping 'til You Drop:** You'll see "I'd Rather Be Shopping at Nordstrom" license-plate frames on Lexuses all over L.A., evidence that spending money is a major pastime here. Whether it's $5 vintage bowling shirts, $10,000 Beverly Hills baubles, or anything in between, you're sure to find it in L.A.'s cornucopia of consumerism. Even window-shopping is an L.A. pastime on kooky Melrose Avenue and tony Rodeo Drive. See chapter 9.

- **Strolling Wilshire Boulevard's Museum Row:** Natural history meets pop culture meets modern art with the La Brea Tar Pits, the Petersen Automobile Museum, the Craft and Folk Art Museum, and the Los Angeles County Museum of Art all shoulder to shoulder in the heart of L.A. The only problem is that it's too much to see in a day. Pick your favorite for an in-depth visit, and just browse the bookstore/gift shops at the others. See chapter 7.

- **Visiting Venice's Oceanfront Walk:** You haven't visited L.A. properly until you've rented some skates in Venice and embarrassed yourself in front of thousands while taking in the human carnival around you. Nosh on a Jody Maroni's haute dog; buy some cheap sunglasses, silver jewelry, or ethnic garb; realize how pathetically out of shape you are compared to all the tan and trim locals—all while enjoying the wide beach, blue sea, and assorted performers along the boardwalk. Can't skate? Sissies can rent a bicycle and pedal along the bike path. See p. 208.

- **Taking a Gourmet Picnic to the Hollywood Bowl:** What better way to spend a typically warm L.A. evening than under the stars with a picnic basket, bottle of wine, and some naturally amplified entertainment? In addition to being the summer home of the Los Angeles Philharmonic, the Bowl hosts visiting performers ranging from chamber music quartets to jazz greats to folk humorists. The imposing white Frank Lloyd Wright–designed band shell always elicits appreciative gasps from first time Bowl-goers. See chapter 10.

- **Cruising Mulholland Drive:** Ogle the homes with million-dollar views, then pull over to catch the view yourself, particularly at night, when the lights of the city twinkle below. Canine lovers should stop by the dog park just west of Laurel Canyon Boulevard; ever since city parks tightened leash laws, many owners have been bringing their pooches to this doggie free-for-all nestled in the hills.

2 Best Bets for Accommodations

- **Best Luxury Hotel:** The **Hotel Bel-Air,** 701 Stone Canyon Rd., Bel Air (© 800/648-4097), wins our vote hands down. Spread over 11½ luxuriant acres of gardens and parkland, this opulent castle-away-from-home is a magical oasis in the middle of the urban jungle, the place to live out your golden age of Hollywood fantasies. See p. 85.

- **Best Historic Hotel:** Since 1923, the imposing, architecturally magnificent **Millennium Biltmore Hotel Los Angeles,** 506 S. Grand Ave., Downtown (© 800/245-8673), has been hosting globetrotting royalty, U.S. presidents, and international celebs. Now under the guiding hand of the Millennium Hotels group, Downtown's crown jewel shines brighter than ever. See p. 100.

- **Best New Hotel:** The former tower annex of Century City's Century Plaza has been transformed into the serene and elegant **St. Regis Los Angeles,** 2055 Ave. of the Stars (© 800/325-3589), easily L.A.'s finest new hotel among a large group of newbies. Everything is just right, from the graceful neomasculine lobby to the extralarge, extragorgeous guest rooms boasting a classic-goes-contemporary style, plus ultra-luxe, state-of-the-art everything. See p. 87.

- **Best for Business Travelers:** With an oversized work desk, fax machine, two-line phones, a terrific business/copy center, extensive recreational facilities, plus 24-hour room service and a wet bar for late-night, report-due-in-the-morning munchies, the guest office suites at the **Westin Bonaventure,** 404 S. Figueroa St. (© **800/WESTIN-1**), are Downtown's best accommodations for business travelers See p. 102. The top Westside choice is **Raffles L'Ermitage,** 9291 Burton Way, Beverly Hills (© **800/323-7500**), where the technology is incomparable, extending well beyond the standard fax/printer/copier and extralarge executive work desk to include a 40-inch TV with CD/DVD player, and a state-of-the-art direct-dial, three-line phone system (including a cellphone you can take with you around town). Flexible check-in/check-out plus free printed stationery, business cards, and fax cover sheets with your direct-dial numbers are part of the package. See p. 87.

- **Best for Beachfront Romance:** If a luxurious oceanfront room at **Shutters on the Beach,** 1 Pico Blvd., Santa Monica (© **800/334-9000**), or sister hotel **Casa del Mar,** 1910 Ocean Way, Santa Monica (© **800/898-6999**), doesn't put a spring in your relationship, it's hard to imagine what will. Which one is best for you depends on your taste: Shutters is dressed up like a really rich friend's contemporary-chic beach house, while the glamorous Casa del Mar is an impeccably restored Deco-era delight. See p. 71 and 70.

- **Best-Kept Secret:** Romance-seeking couples who want oceanfront luxury for less should skip Santa Monica's on-the-beach hotels for the **Beach House at Hermosa Beach,** 1300 The Strand, Hermosa Beach (© **888/895-4559**), a beautiful boutique resort comprised of plush, luxury-laden studio suites that go for roughly half the price of an average room at Shutters or Casa del Mar. Book one overlooking the sand for the ultimate beach getaway. See p. 74.

- **Best for Families:** With a great location close to both beach and boardwalk, a terrific ocean-view pool, and a kids-stay-free policy, plus welcome goodies and special menus for young ones, the **Loews Santa Monica Beach Hotel,** 1700 Ocean Ave., Santa Monica (© **800/23-LOEWS**), tops our list as L.A.'s best family hotel. See p. 71. If you're heading to Universal Studios, stay at the **Sheraton Universal Hotel,** 333 Universal Terrace Pkwy. (© **800/325-3535**), which offers free shuttle service to the theme park and adjacent Universal CityWalk, both just a minute away. Families on a budget might prefer Westwood's **Hotel Del Capri,** 10587 Wilshire Blvd. (© **800/444-6835**), a great buy in a centrally located West L.A. neighborhood. See p. 106 and 96.

- **Best Moderately Priced Hotel:** The well-maintained, ultracharming **Casa Malibu,** 22752 Pacific Coast Hwy., Malibu (© **800/831-0858**), has a terrific beachfront location and rates left over from more carefree days. Innkeepers don't come any friendlier, and oceanfront accommodations don't get more affordable. See p. 76. For a more central location, stay at the **Carlyle Inn,** 1119 S. Robertson Blvd. (© **800/332-7595**), another hidden gem cleverly tucked away in the heart of West L.A. A pleasing courtyard setting, a dash of Deco-inspired style in the guest rooms, and abundant freebies—including a generous breakfast spread and weekday wine and hors d'oeuvres—make the Carlyle a real find for those in search of value-priced comforts. See p. 93.

- **Best Budget Hotel:** The bargain of the beach is the friendly, family run **Sea Shore Motel,** 2637 Main St. (© **310/392-2787**), whose motel-basic but beautifully kept rooms couldn't be better located, in the heart of stylish Main Street shopping and dining and just a stone's throw from Santa Monica's pier and sand. See p. 81. Downtown boasts the **Hotel Figueroa,** 939 S. Figueroa St. (© **800/421-9092**), a 1925 building recreated as a stunning Spanish Colonial–Gothic palace with an eye for detail and commitment to the needs of budget travelers. Rooms have tons more style than your average budget hotel; what's more, this spit-shined corner of Downtown also offers easy, car-free Metro Line access to Hollywood and Universal Studios. See p. 104.

- **Best Inn:** If you crave the slower pace and personal attention that only a bed-and-breakfast can offer, book a room at the **Inn at Playa del Rey,** 435 Culver Blvd., Playa del Rey (© **310/574-1920**), which merges easy airport access with a one-of-a-kind natural setting, thoughtful service, and luxury comforts. The spacious View Suites, which boast a two-sided fireplace that casts a romantic glow on both the beautifully dressed king bed and the Jacuzzi for two, are the ideal choice for celebrating couples. See p. 75.

- **Best Suite Deals:** Suites aren't just for big spenders anymore—regular folks who crave comforts above and beyond what a standard hotel

room can offer have options, too. The best-value suites in town are found at the **Wyndham Bel Age Hotel,** 1020 N. San Vicente Blvd., West Hollywood (© **800/WYNDHAM**), where you can have a mammoth, stylish suite and a prime, just-off-the–Sunset Strip location for the same price—often less—than the price of a standard room at most neighboring hotels. See p. 92.

- **Best for Travelers with Disabilities:** With a total of 25 accessible rooms, the **Sheraton Universal Hotel,** 333 Universal Terrace Pkwy., Universal City (© **800/325-3535**), offers the most extensive facilities for wheelchair-using and vision-impaired visitors. Two bathrooms have roll-in showers; the rest have tubs with available benches, lowered closet rods and peepholes, and raised vanities and toilets. There are also Strobe kits for door and phone, and Braille symbols on the restaurant menus and on all public facilities. See p. 106. Downtown, the **Westin Bonaventure Hotel & Suites,** 404 S. Figueroa St. (© **800/WESTIN-1**), boasts 39 rooms with similarly extensive auxiliary aids, 15 with roll-in showers. For more information on resources for travelers with disabilities, see "Tips for Travelers with Special Needs," in chapter 2.

- **Best Spa:** The new Spa Mystique at the **Century Plaza Hotel & Spa,** 2025 Ave. of the Stars, Century City (© **800/WESTIN-1**) dominates L.A.'s spa scene. With a record-setting 35,000 square feet of space, features include an epic menu of traditional and Asian treatments, hydrotherapy features that include two Japanese *furo* pools, complete salon services, and a 21st-century fitness center with cardio machines that let you surf the Web as you pump, a meditation garden, and alfresco cafe.

Book your treatments now—relaxation doesn't get better than this.

3 Best Bets for Dining

- **Best Spot for a Romantic Dinner:** While it's lovely during day for brunch with the in-laws or tea with friends, you'd be unwise to bring anyone but a lover to **The Raymond,** 1250 S. Fair Oaks Ave., Pasadena (② **626/441-3136**), after dark. This restaurant is tucked away in an enchanting, candle-lit cottage with lush English gardens. Charming restaurateur Suzanne Bourg works magic with both setting and cuisine. Though pricey, the Raymond always offers a prix fixe meal and multicourse deals that soften the blow. See p. 152.

- **Best Places for a Power Lunch:** Between 12:30 and 2pm, industry honchos swarm like locusts to a handful of watering holes du jour. Actors, agents, lawyers, and producers flock to perennial favorites **The Ivy,** 133 N. Robertson Blvd., West Hollywood (② **310/274-8303**), and **Maple Drive,** 345 N. Maple Dr., Beverly Hills (② **310/274-9800**). The music industry's darling is the L.A. branch of New York's venerable **The Palm,** 9001 Santa Monica Blvd., West Hollywood (② **310/550-8811**), a steakhouse where the food is impeccable and the conversations read like dialogue from *The Player.* Lucky for us, the acoustics of this sawdust-strewn room are such that patrons in roomy booths can be clearly overheard across the restaurant. See chapter 6.

- **Best Place to Relive Old Hollywood: Musso & Frank Grill,** 6667 Hollywood Blvd., Hollywood (② **323/467-7788**), is haunted by the ghosts of Faulkner, Fitzgerald, and Hemingway, who

drank here during their screenwriting days. This comfortable, dark-paneled room, virtually unchanged since 1919, begs you to order up one of L.A.'s best martinis and some chops or the legendary chicken pot pie, and listen to the longtime wait staff wax nostalgic about the days when Hollywood Boulevard was still fashionable and Orson Welles held court at Musso's. See p. 142.

- **Best Spot for People-Watching:** Nowhere in L.A. is better for people-watching than Venice's Ocean Front Walk, and no restaurant offers a better seat for the action than the **Sidewalk Café,** 1401 Ocean Front Walk, Venice (② **310/399-5547**). Unobstructed views of parading skaters, bikers, skateboarders, musclemen, break dancers, street performers, sword swallowers, and other participants in the daily carnival overshadow the food, which is a whole lot better than it needs to be. See p. 128.

- **Best Spots for Celebrity Sighting:** You'll always find well-known faces frequenting Sunset Strip hot spots, the most sizzling of which is the Mondrian hotel and its chic Chino-Latin restaurant, **Asia de Cuba,** 8440 Sunset Blvd., West Hollywood (② **323/848-6000**) (this restaurant is included in the Mondrian's listing in chapter 5); celebrity dieters can be glimpsed bypassing the eats for the A-list-only Skybar on the other side of the pool. And the perennial power-spot **The Ivy,** 133 N. Robertson Blvd., West Hollywood (② **310/274-8303**) is *still* jam-packed with L.A.'s more conservative celebrities. See p. 86 and 130.

- **Best Alfresco Dining:** You'll find that more and more Los Angeles restaurants are eager to create appealing outdoor seating, even if it means placing bistro tables along a busy sidewalk. Taking advantage of the climate? Trying to compensate for the new no-smoking ordinances? Both, really. At the high end of L.A. alfresco is **Four Oaks,** 2181 N. Beverly Glen Blvd., Los Angeles (© **310/470-2265**), nestled under romantically lit trees in the canyon of Beverly Glen. See p. 130. A more affordable way to enjoy a meal outdoors is by strolling **Sunset Boulevard around Sunset Plaza Drive.** There are at least a half-dozen pleasant sidewalk cafes—and the people-watching is extra good.

- **Best View:** Look for art-world bigwigs and Getty higher-ups at the **Restaurant at the Getty Center,** 1200 Getty Center Dr., West L.A. (© **310/440-7300**), whose in-the-clouds locale makes for breathtaking views when the L.A. sky is smogless (read: winter). Reservations are a must, even for lunch (served Tues–Sun); dinner is served only Friday and Saturday when the museum is open late. Make reservations online at www.getty.edu. See p. 162.

- **Best Wine List:** Year after year, plenty of other restaurants offer thoughtfully chosen vintages, but no one comes close to toppling **Valentino,** 3115 Pico Blvd., Santa Monica (© **310/829-4313**), which still boasts L.A.'s best cellar and is continually honored with *Wine Spectator*'s highest ratings. See p. 122.

- **Best California Cuisine:** At chef/owner Michael McCarty's eponymous Santa Monica restaurant **Michael's,** 1147 3rd St., Santa Monica (© **310/451-0843**), the

cuisine at this perennial makes it clear why McCarty is considered an originator of California cuisine. See p. 121.

- **Best Chinese Cuisine:** While Chinatown is the place to go for traditional wonton and chow mein, **Joss,** 9255 Sunset Blvd., West Hollywood (© **310/276-1886**), is our pick for some provocative twists on Chinese essentials. The sophisticated minimalist decor combined with excellent and personable service make this great for a group or a romantic dinner for two—and the food is always superbly presented and heavenly. See p. 135.

- **Best Continental Cuisine: Chaya Brasserie,** 8741 Alden Dr., Los Angeles (© **310/859-8833**), best known for superb grilled fish and meats, takes Continental staples and raises them to a new art form using local flavorings and some Asian techniques. Chef Shigefumi Tachibe is far from traditional, but then again, this is Los Angeles. See p. 134.

- **Best French Cuisine:** While the elegant Lavande may be the critics' darling, our vote goes to **Mimosa,** 8009 Beverly Blvd., Los Angeles (© **323/655-8895**), the Provençal bistro that has everyone drinking pastis and speaking with a fake French accent. See p. 133.

- **Best Italian Cuisine:** Former *New York Times* food critic Ruth Reichl called **Valentino,** 3115 Pico Blvd., Santa Monica (© **310/829-4313**), the best Italian restaurant in America. This restaurant is very traditional and unusually formal—for L.A.—but the dining experience is worth dressing up for. See p. 122.

- **Best Mexican Cuisine:** They aren't called the "Two Hot Tamales" for nothing: One taste of

Mary Sue Milliken and Susan Feniger's groundbreaking **Border Grill,** 1445 Fourth St., Santa Monica (℡ **310/451-1655**), and you'll be instantly transported to Central America. The pair has spent countless hours traveling through Mexico, absorbing regional tastes and aromas, and returning with secret ingredients and kitchen savvy to pass onto their lucky patrons. See p. 122.

- **Best Seafood: Water Grill,** 544 S. Grand Ave., Downtown (℡ **213/ 891-0900**), is a beautiful contemporary fish house that serves imaginative dishes influenced by America's regional cuisines. An absolutely huge raw bar features the best clams, crabs, shrimp, and oysters available, and the fish is so fresh it practically jumps onto the plate. See p. 144.

- **Best Burgers:** They do just one thing at **The Apple Pan,** 10801 Pico Blvd., Los Angeles (℡ **310/ 475-3585**), and they do it well. Choose from the "steakburger" or the saucy "hickory burger"— though regulars know to get hickory sauce on the side instead (for french fry dipping). You'll feel that the 1940s live again in the decor and atmosphere of this family run cottage on the busy Westside. I actually suspect the wallpaper dates from opening day in 1947. See p. 138.

- **Best Desserts:** A fancy treatment for a childhood fave is at **Tahiti,** 7910 W. 3rd St., Los Angeles (℡ **323/651-1213**), where the menu describes every nuance of "Hot Vahlrona chocolate pudding with Tahitian vanilla sauce." See p. 142.

- **Best Afternoon Tea:** Surrounded by botanical gardens, the tearoom at the **Huntington Library,** 1151 Oxford Rd., San Marino (℡ **818/683-8131**), is truly an oasis. The Huntington, located in a wealthy residential area of Pasadena, has the added appeal of pre- and post-tea activities, such as strolling the theme gardens, viewing the art gallery or library, and visiting the bookstore/gift shop. The moderately priced tea ($13) is buffet style, so you can stuff yourself with fresh-baked scones, finger sandwiches, and strawberries with thick Devonshire cream. Admission to the Huntington is another $8.50. See chapter 7 for details. See p. 188.

- **Best Value:** Feeding teenage boys or a football team? Or just famished after a day of sightseeing? Former mayor Richard Riordan's **The Original Pantry,** 877 S. Figueroa St., Downtown (℡ **213/ 972-9279**), stays open 24 hours a day, serving up large plates of traditional American comfort food (meat loaf, coleslaw, ham 'n' eggs) that won't win any culinary awards but offers some of the best values in town. *Tip:* They've got the best chocolate layer cake in town. See p. 148.

- **Best Picnic Fare:** Open since 1917, **Grand Central Market,** 317 S. Broadway, Downtown (℡ **213/ 624-2378**), is L.A.'s largest and oldest food hall, selling everything from fresh bread to local and exotic produce, fresh fruit juice, smoked meats, Chinese noodles, and chili. And the cultural experience of a visit here is a terrific precursor to any picnic. See chapter 9.

- **Best Newcomer:** Yet another reason to make the drive to Pasadena is **Nonya,** 61 N. Raymond Ave. (℡ **626/583-8398**), a gorgeous new restaurant that serves a cuisine you've probably never even heard of: Peranakan, a blend of Chinese and Malaysian culinary styles.

Chili-marinated chicken grilled in banana leaves? A mango-halibut salad? Bring it on. See p. 154.

• **Best for Late-Night Dining:** On the theory that later is better, our vote goes to **Toi on Sunset,** 75051/2 Sunset Blvd., Los Angeles (© **323/874-8062**), and its sister

Toi on Wilshire, 1120 Wilshire Blvd., Santa Monica (© **310/394-7804**). You'll never feel like the last patron at these places—they're open till 4am and 3am, respectively—and the terrific Thai food will give your wee hours a spicy kick. See p. 144.

2

Planning Your Trip
to Los Angeles

We want you to have a great vacation in Southern California—and it all begins in the planning stage. This chapter contains practical information to help you make your travel arrangements, pick a time to visit, find local resources for specialized needs, and access megabytes of useful information on the Internet.

1 Visitor Information

If you'd like information before you go, contact the **Los Angeles Convention and Visitors Bureau** (© **800/366-6116;** Events Hotline 213/689-8822; www.lacvb.com). They will send you a free visitor's kit, provide a schedule of upcoming events, and answer questions over the phone. A walk-in visitor center is located downtown at 685 S. Figueroa St.

In addition, almost every municipality and district in Los Angeles has a dedicated tourist bureau or chamber of commerce that will be happy to send you information on a particular area; see Chapter 4 (p. 52) for a complete list.

2 Money

If you're visiting from outside the United States, you can find more information on American currency and money exchange in chapter 3, "For International Visitors."

ATMS

One of California's most popular banks is Wells Fargo, linked with the Star, Pulse, Cirrus, and GlobalAccess systems. It has hundreds of ATMs at branches and in-store locations (including most Vons supermarkets) throughout Los Angeles and Southern California. To find the one nearest you, call © **800/869-3557** or visit **www.wellsfargo.com/findus**. Other statewide banks include Bank of America (which accepts PLUS, Star, and Interlink cards) and First Interstate Bank (Cirrus). To locate other

ATMs in the Cirrus system, call © **800/424-7787** or search **www.mastercard.com**; to find a **Plus** ATM, call © **800/843-7587** or visit **www.visa.com**. Be sure to check your bank's daily withdrawal limit before you depart. Also, a Santa Monica city ordinance prohibiting banks from charging ATM fees has led some banks to limit access to their machines to bank customers only.

TRAVELER'S CHECKS

Once the only safe method of guaranteeing ready cash, traveler's checks now seem anachronistic. Most cities (including Los Angeles) have plenty of 24-hour ATMs that allow you to withdraw small amounts of cash as needed.

But if you want to avoid the fees associated with ATM withdrawals, or

What Things Cost in Los Angeles	U.S. $
Taxi from the airport to downtown	35.00
SuperShuttle from LAX to West Hollywood area	22.00
Fine for expired parking meter	25.00 up to 60.00
Double room at the Beverly Hills Hotel (very expensive)	385.00
Double room at the Universal City Hilton (expensive)	220.00
Double room at the Hollywood Roosevelt Hotel (moderate)	129.00
Double room at the Sea Shore Motel (inexpensive)	85.00
Lunch for one at Cafe Pinot (moderate)	14.00
Chili Double-Bacon Burrito Dog at Pink's	3.60
Dinner for one, without wine, at Jozu (expensive)	40.00
Dinner for one, without wine, at Border Grill (moderate)	21.00
Dinner for one, without wine, at Good Stuff (inexpensive)	12.00
Cup of coffee at Philippe The Original	0.90
Cup of coffee at the Peninsula Hotel	3.25
2½-hour Gray Line Tour of Hollywood	40.00
Admission to the Hollywood Wax Museum	10.95
Admission to the J. Paul Getty Museum (parking is $5.00)	Free
Full-price movie ticket	9.00

feel more comfortable with checks that can be replaced if lost or stolen, you can get traveler's checks at almost any bank. Be prepared to pay a 1% to 4% fee. You can get **American Express** traveler's checks over the phone by calling ✆ **800/221-7282;** by using this number, Amex gold and platinum cardholders avoid the 1% fee. **AAA** members can obtain checks without a fee at most AAA offices. Visit **www.aaa-calif.com** on the Web for more information

Visa offers traveler's checks at Citibank nationwide, as well as several other banks. **MasterCard** also offers

traveler's checks. Call ✆ **800/223-9920** for a location near you.

If you opt to carry traveler's checks, keep a record of their serial numbers separate from the checks so that you're ensured a refund in an emergency.

CREDIT CARDS

Most major credit cards are accepted for payment at L.A.'s hotels, restaurants, shops, and attractions; the most popular are Visa, MasterCard, American Express, and Discover. A handful of stores and restaurants accept only cash, so ask if you're unsure. Each hotel and restaurant listing in chapters 5 and

Tips **Expecting the Unexpected**

Before you leave home, make photocopies—two sets—of every traveler's ID (including passports for international travelers), credit cards (front and back), and plane tickets or itinerary confirmation. Leave one at home or with a friend, and carry one with you separately from your wallet and/or purse (your cosmetic case or shaving kit is a safe bet). In case of unexpected loss, you'll have proof of your identity, everything necessary to cancel and replace your credit cards, and a receipt for your plane trip home.

6 lists the credit cards they accept. Almost every credit-card company has an emergency 800-number you can call if your wallet or purse is stolen. The company can usually deliver an emergency credit card in a day or two and may be able to wire you a cash advance off your card immediately.

Los Angeles can be fairly expensive; however, you should find it less expensive than both San Francisco and New York.

3 When to Go

Many visitors don't realize that Los Angeles—despite its blue ocean, swaying palm trees, green lawns, and forested foothills—is actually the high desert. But with the desert climes tempered by sea breezes (which make air-conditioning largely unnecessary even 20 miles/32km inland), and the landscape kept green with water carried by aqueduct from all around the West, L.A. might be the most accommodating desert you've ever visited. No matter how hot it gets, low humidity keeps things dry and comfortable.

Tourism peaks during **summer,** when coastal hotels fill to capacity, restaurant reservations can be hard to get, and top attractions are packed with visitors and locals off from work or school. Summer can be miserable in the inland valleys, where daytime temperatures—and that L.A. smog—can be stifling, but the beach communities almost always remain comfortable. Moderate temperatures, fewer crowds, and lower hotel rates make travel to L.A. most pleasurable during the **winter.** The city is at its best from early autumn to late spring, when the skies are less smoggy. Rain is rare in Los Angeles, but it can cause flooding when it does sneak up on the unsuspecting city; precipitation is most likely from February to April, and virtually unheard of between May and November. Even in January, daytime temperatures reach into the 60s and higher—sometimes up to the 80s.

Pundits claim L.A. has no seasons; it might be more accurate to say the city has its own unique seasons. Two of them are "June Gloom" and "the Santa Anas." The first refers to the ocean fog that keeps the beach cities (and often all of L.A.) overcast into early afternoon; it's most common in June but can occur anytime between late April and mid-August. Mid-autumn (Oct and Nov) often brings the "Santa Anas"—strong, hot winds from across the desert that increase brush-fire danger and cause Indian summer giddiness in animals and people alike (but surfers love the offshore conditions they usually cause).

Los Angeles remains relatively temperate year-round. It's possible to sunbathe throughout the year, but only die-hard enthusiasts and wet-suited surfers venture into the ocean in winter when water temps hover around 50° to 55°F. The water is warmest in summer and fall, usually about 65° to 70°F, but, even then, the Pacific can be too chilly for many.

Los Angeles's Average Temperatures (°F/°C)

	Jan	Feb	Mar	Apr	May	June	July	Aug	Sept	Oct	Nov	Dec
Avg. High	66/19	68/20	69/21	71/22	73/23	77/25	82/28	84/29	82/28	78/26	73/23	68/20
Avg. Low	48/9	50/10	51/11	54/12	57/14	60/16	63/17	64/18	63/17	59/15	53/12	50/10

LOS ANGELES–AREA CALENDAR OF EVENTS

January

Tournament of Roses, Pasadena. A spectacular parade down Colorado Boulevard, with lavish floats, music, and extraordinary equestrian entries, followed by the Rose Bowl football game. Call ☎ **626/449-4100** (www.tournamentofroses.com) for details, or watch it on TV (you'll have a better view). January 1.

Native American Film Festival, Los Angeles. Cinematic works by or about Native Americans express their visions, diversity, and ideas. Call the Southwest Museum at ☎ **323/221-2164** for schedule and details. Mid-January.

Martin Luther King Parade, Long Beach. This annual parade down Alameda and 7th streets ends with a festival in Martin Luther King Park. For more information, contact the city manager, Kathy Parsons, at (☎ **562/570-6711**). Third Monday in January.

Bob Hope Chrysler Classic, Palm Springs area. Celebrating the 44th year of this PGA golf tournament in 2002, this golfing classic raises money for charity and includes a celebrity-studded Pro-Am. For spectator information and tickets, call ☎ **760/346-8184.** Mid- to late January.

February

National Date Festival, Indio (Palm Springs area). Crowds gather for 2 weeks to celebrate the Coachella Valley desert's most beloved cash crop with events like camel and ostrich races, the Blessing of the Date Garden, and festive Arabian Nights pageants. Plenty of date-sampling booths are set up, along with rides, food vendors, and other county-fair trappings. Call ☎ **800/811-3247** or 760/863-8247; www.datefest.org. Two weeks in February.

Nissan L.A. Open Golf Tournament, Pacific Palisades. The PGA Tour makes its only Tinseltown appearance at the Riviera Country Club overlooking the ocean. Expect to see stars in attendance, watching defending champion Len Mattiace going for another L.A. win. For information, call the Los Angeles Junior Chamber of Commerce at ☎ **213/482-1311.** Mid-February.

Chinese New Year, Los Angeles. Dragon dancers parade through the streets of downtown's Chinatown. Chinese opera and other events are scheduled. For this year's schedule, contact the Chinese Chamber of Commerce at ☎ **213/617-0396.** Late January or early February.

Mardi Gras, West Hollywood. The festivities—including live jazz and lots of food—take place along Santa Monica Boulevard, from Doheny Drive to La Brea Avenue, and in the alley behind Santa Monica Boulevard. Contact the West Hollywood Convention & Visitors Bureau at ☎ **800/368-6020** for details. Late February or early March.

March

Los Angeles Marathon. This 26.2-mile/42km run attracts thousands of participants, from world champions to the guy next door; the big day also features a 5K run/walk and a bike marathon on the same route. The run starts in downtown Los Angeles. Call ☎ **310/444-5544** or visit **www.lamarathon.com** for registration or spectator information. Early March.

Santa Barbara International Film Festival. For 10 days each March, Santa Barbara does its best impression of Cannes. There's a flurry of foreign and independent film premieres, appearances by actors and directors, and symposia on cinematic topics. For a rundown of events, call ☎ **805/963-0023.** Early- to mid-March.

California Poppy Blooming Season, Antelope Valley. Less than an hour's drive north of Los Angeles lies the California Poppy Reserve, part of the state park system. In spring, miles of hillside blaze with brilliant hues of red and orange, dazzling the senses of motorists who flock to witness the display. For information and directions call ☎ **661-723-6077.** Mid-March to mid-May. For information on the annual **California Poppy Festival,** held at full bloom (usually in late April), call ☎ **661-723-6077** or visit **www.cityoflancasterca.org/Parks/poppy_festival.htm.**

Nabisco Dinah Shore, Rancho Mirage (Palm Springs area). This 33-year-old LPGA golf tournament takes place during the last week of March near Palm Springs. After the celebrity Pro-Am early in the week, the best female pros get down to business. For further information, call ☎ **760/324-4546.** Other special-interest events for women usually take place around the Dinah Shore, including "The White Party," the country's largest annual lesbian gathering.

American Indian Festival and Market, Los Angeles Natural History Museum. A showcase of Native American arts and culture; the fun includes traditional dances, storytelling, and arts and crafts, as well as a chance to sample Native American foods. Admission to the museum includes festival tickets. For further details, call ☎ **213/744-DINO.** Late March.

April

Toyota Grand Prix, Long Beach. An exciting weekend of Indy-class auto racing and entertainment in and around downtown Long Beach, drawing world-class drivers from the United States and Europe, plus many celebrity contestants and spectators. Contact the Grand Prix Association at ☎ **888/82-SPEED** or 562/981-2600; www.longbeachgp.com. Mid-April.

Renaissance Pleasure Faire, San Bernardino. This annual event in the relatively remote Glen Helen Regional Park is one of America's largest Renaissance festivals. It features an Elizabethan marketplace with costumed performers. The fair provides an entire day's activities, including shows, food, and crafts. You're encouraged to come in period costume. For ticket information, call ☎ **800/52-FAIRE,** or log onto the national website **http://renaissance-faire.com.** Weekends from late April to Memorial Day.

May

Cinco de Mayo, Los Angeles. A weeklong celebration of Mexico's Independence Day takes place throughout the city. There's a carnival atmosphere with large crowds, live music, dancing, and food. The main festivities are held at El Pueblo de Los Angeles State Historic Park, downtown; call ✆ **213/628-1274** for information. Other events are held around the city. The week surrounding May 5.

National Orange Show, San Bernardino. An Inland Empire tradition since 1911—when there were more orange groves than houses in Southern California—this weeklong county fair includes stadium events, celebrity entertainment, livestock shows, craft and food booths, and carnival rides. Call ✆ **909/888-6788.** Second half of May.

Venice Art Walk, Venice Beach. Celebrating 24 years in 2003, this annual weekend event gives visitors a chance to take docent-guided tours of galleries and studios, plus a Sunday self-guided art walk through the private home studios of more than 50 emerging and well-known artists. For details, call the Venice Family Clinic, which coordinates the event (✆ **310/392-8630,** ext. 1), or visit its website at www.venicefamilyclinic.org. Second half of May.

Long Beach Lesbian & Gay Pride Parade and Festival, Shoreline Park, Long Beach. There are health-awareness booths, rock and country music, dancing, food, and more than 100 decorated floats. Call ✆ **562/987-9191.** Second half of May.

Doheny Blues Festival, Doheny State Beach, Dana Point. Features great live music (past acts have included the likes of Little Richard, Bo Diddley, and Chuck Berry) on three stages—blues, rock, and soul—at a waterfront grass park with two stages at opposite ends of the venue. Arts and crafts vendors, memorabilia, and unique displays surround an International Food Court with various restaurants and beverages of all types. Proceeds benefit the Surfrider Foundation, San Clemente Chapter. Call ✆ **949/262-2662,** or log onto www.omega events.com. Mid- to late May.

June

Playboy Jazz Festival, Los Angeles. Bill Cosby is the traditional master of ceremonies, presiding over the top artists at the Hollywood Bowl. Call ✆ **310/449-4070.** Mid-June.

Gay & Lesbian Pride Celebration, West Hollywood. In its 32nd year, this West Hollywood gathering promises to be larger than ever. Outdoor stages, disco- and Western-dance tents, food, and revelry culminate in Sunday's parade down Santa Monica Boulevard. Call ✆ **323/658-8700.** Last weekend in June.

Mariachi USA Festival, Los Angeles. A 2-day family oriented celebration of Mexican culture and tradition at the Hollywood Bowl, where festival goers pack their picnic baskets and enjoy music, folkloric ballet, and related performances by special guests. Call ✆ **323/848-7717.** Late June.

July

Lotus Festival, Echo Park. Celebrants gather to witness the spectacular blooms of Echo Lake's floating lotus grove. In keeping with an Asian and South Pacific islands theme, the festivities include tropical music and entertainment, ethnic foods, exotic birds, and plenty of lotus-inspired arts and crafts for sale. Admission is free. Call ✆ **213/485-1310** for information, or log onto www.la parks.org/grifmet/lotus.htm. Second weekend of July.

Festival of Arts & Pageant of the Masters, Laguna Beach. A 60-plus-year tradition in artsy Laguna, this festival centers on a fantastic performance-art production in which actors re-create famous Old Masters paintings. Other festivities include live music, crafts sales, art demonstrations and workshops, and the grassroots Sawdust Festival across the street. Grounds admission is $3 to $5; pageant tickets range from $15 to $65. Call ✆ **800/487-FEST** or 949/494-1145; there's online info at www.foapom.com. July through August.

August

Beach Festival, Huntington Beach. Two weeks of fun in the sun, featuring two surfing competitions—the US Open of Surfing and the world-class Pro of Surfing—plus extreme sports like BMX biking, skateboarding, and more. Includes entertainment, food, tons of product booths and giveaways—and plenty of tanned, swimsuit-clad bodies of both sexes. For more information, call ✆ **714/969-3492,** or log onto www.hbvisit.com. End of July.

Nisei Week Japanese Festival, Los Angeles. This weeklong celebration of Japanese culture and heritage is held in the Japanese American Cultural and Community Center Plaza in Little Tokyo. Festivities include parades, food, music, arts, and crafts. Call ✆ **213/687-7193.** Mid-August.

African Marketplace and Cultural Fair. African arts, crafts, food, and music are featured at this cultural-awareness event. Call ✆ **323/734-1164.** Held at Rancho La Cienega Park, 5001 Rodeo Rd. Weekends, from mid-August to Labor Day.

Long Beach Blues Festival. Great performances by blues legends such as Etta James, Dr. John, the Allman Brothers, and Ike Turner make this an event you won't want to miss if you love the blues. Located in the

middle of the Athletic field at Long Beach State, cold beer, wine, and food are served throughout the event. Call ✆ **562/985-5566,** or log onto www.klon.org. Held at Long Beach State University, Labor Day weekend.

September

Los Angeles County Fair, Pomona. Horse racing, arts, agricultural displays, celebrity entertainment, and carnival rides are among the attractions at one of the largest county fairs in the world. At the Los Angeles County Fair and Exposition Center; call ✆ **909/623-3111,** or visit **www.fairplex.com** for information. Throughout September.

Watts Towers Day of the Drum Festival, Los Angeles. This event celebrates the historic role of drums and drummers throughout the world. Performers range from Afro-Cuban musicians to East Indian tabla players. Call ✆ **213/847-4646.** Late September.

October

Catalina Island Jazz Trax Festival. Contemporary jazz greats play at Avalon's legendary Casino Ballroom. This enormously popular festival takes place over two consecutive 3-day weekends. Call ✆ **888/330-5252** (www.jazztrax.com) for advance ticket sales and a schedule of performers. Early October.

American Film Institute's Los Angeles International Film Festival. Some of the biggest names in the international film community gather to see new movies from around the world. Ray Lawrence's *Lantana* and Marc Forster's *Monster's Ball* starring Billy Bob Thornton, Halle Berry, and Heath Ledger had an early screening at AFI's 2001 fest. Call ✆ **323/856-7707** (www.afifest.com) for info and tickets. Late October or early November.

November

Catalina Island Triathlon. This is one of the top triathlons in the world. Participants run on unpaved roads, swim in the cleanest bay on the west coast, and bike on challenging trails. There's also a "kid's tri." Call Pacific Sports at ☎ **714/978-1528.** Early November.

Doo Dah Parade, Pasadena. An outrageous spoof of the Rose Parade, featuring such participants as the Briefcase Precision Drill Team and a kazoo-playing marching band. Call ☎ **626/440-7379.** Near Thanksgiving.

Hollywood Christmas Parade. This spectacular, star-studded parade marches through the heart of Hollywood. For information call ☎ **323/469-2337.** Sunday after Thanksgiving.

December

Christmas Boat Parade of Lights. Sailors decorate their crafts with colorful lights. Several Southern California harbors hold nighttime parades. Participants range from tiny dinghies with a single strand of lights to showy yachts with Nativity scenes twinkling on deck. Bundle up, hold hands, sip a hot toddy, and enjoy Christmas, So Cal style. Call the following for information: Ventura Harbor, ☎ **805/382-3001;** Marina Del Rey (Los Angeles), ☎ **310/821-0555;** Long Beach, ☎ **562/435-4093;** Huntington Harbour, ☎ **714/840-7542.**

4 Insurance, Health & Safety

WHAT TO DO IF YOU GET SICK AWAY FROM HOME

If you worry about getting sick away from home, you may want to consider **medical travel insurance** (see below). In most cases, however, your existing health plan will provide all the coverage you need. Be sure to carry your identification card in your wallet.

If you suffer from a chronic illness, consult your doctor before your departure. For conditions like epilepsy, diabetes, or heart problems, wear a **Medic Alert Identification Tag** (☎ **800/825-3785;** www.medicalert.org), which will immediately alert doctors to your condition and give them access to your records through Medic Alert's 24-hour hot line.

Pack prescription medications in your carry-on luggage. Carry written prescriptions in generic, not brand name, form, and dispense all prescription medications from their original labeled vials. Also bring along copies of your prescriptions in case you lose your pills or run out.

INSURANCE

There are three kinds of travel insurance: trip cancellation, medical, and lost luggage coverage. (For information on car renter's insurance, see "Getting Around," in chapter 4.)

Trip cancellation insurance may be a good idea if you have paid a large portion of your vacation expenses up front. The other two types of insurance, however, don't make sense for most. Some

Tips Sun Safety

If you plan to spend time outdoors or at the beach, use a sunscreen with a high protection factor and apply it liberally. Children usually need more protection than adults do. Try Bull Frog or Aloe Gator—SPF 30—for a complete block that applies clearly and is nongreasy.

Destination: Los Angeles—Red Alert Checklist

- Do any theater, restaurant, or travel reservations need to be booked in advance?
- Did you make sure your favorite attraction is open? Some attractions are often closed for security or maintenance reasons. Many scheduled tours, festivals, and special events may have also been canceled. Call ahead for opening and closing hours. (Please see the Los Angeles–Area Calendar of Events, earlier in this chapter, for specific phone numbers.)
- If you purchased traveler's checks, have you recorded the check numbers, and stored the documentation separately from the checks?
- Did you pack your camera and an extra set of camera batteries, and purchase enough film? If you packed film in your checked baggage, did you invest in protective pouches to shield film from airport X-rays?
- Do you have a safe, accessible place to store money?
- Did you bring your ID cards that could entitle you to discounts such as AAA and AARP cards, student IDs, and so on?
- Did you bring emergency drug prescriptions and extra glasses and/or contact lenses?
- Do you have your credit card PIN numbers?
- If you have an E-ticket, do you have documentation?

insurers provide coverage for events like jury duty; natural disasters close to home, like floods or fire; even the loss of a job. A few have added provisions for cancellations due to terrorist activities. Always check the fine print before signing on, and don't buy trip-cancellation insurance from the tour operator that may be responsible for the cancellation; buy it only from a reputable travel insurance agency. Don't overbuy. You won't be reimbursed for more than the cost of your trip.

Medical travel insurance is usually unnecessary; your existing health insurance should cover you if you get sick while on vacation (although if you belong to an HMO, you should check to see whether you are fully covered when away from home). It's the same with **lost luggage insurance;** airlines are responsible for $2,500 on domestic flights if they lose your luggage (if you have homeowner's insurance, that usually covers stolen luggage). If you plan to bring anything valuable, keep it in your carry-on bag.

Some credit card companies may insure you against **travel accidents** if you buy plane, train, or bus tickets with their cards. Before purchasing additional insurance, read your policies and agreements carefully. Call your insurers or credit/charge card companies if you have any questions.

Check your existing policies before you buy any additional coverage. If you do require additional insurance, try one of these reputable companies: **Access America** (© **800/284-8300;** www.accessamerica.com); **Travel Guard International** (© **800-826-4919;** www.travel-guard.com); **Travelex Insurance Services** (© **888/457-4602;** www.travelexinsurance.com); or **Travel Insured International** (© 800/243-3174; www.travelinsured.com).

> **Tips** **What to Do if Your Wallet Gets Stolen**
>
> Be sure to block charges against your account the minute you discover a credit card has been lost or stolen. Then be sure to file a police report. Odds are that if your wallet is gone, the police won't be able to recover it for you. However, it's still worth informing the authorities. Your credit card company or insurer may require a police report number or record of the theft.
>
> Almost every credit card company has an emergency 800-number to call if your card is stolen. They may be able to wire you a cash advance off your credit card immediately, and in many places, they can deliver an emergency credit card in a day or two. The issuing bank's 800-number is usually on the back of your credit card—though of course, if your card has been stolen, that won't help you unless you recorded the number elsewhere.
>
> Citicorp Visa's U.S. emergency number is ☏ **800/336-8472.** American Express cardholders and traveler's check holders should call ☏ **800/ 221-7282.** MasterCard holders should call ☏ **800/307-7309.** Otherwise, call the toll-free number directory at ☏ **800/555-1212.**

5 Tips for Travelers with Special Needs

FOR TRAVELERS WITH DISABILITIES

Los Angeles's spirit of tolerance and diversity has made it a welcoming place for travelers with disabilities. Strict building codes make most public facilities and attractions extremely accessible (though some historic sites and older buildings simply can't accommodate drastic remodeling), and the city provides many services for those with disabilities.

Some advance planning is always useful. There are more resources out there than ever before: *A World of Options,* a 658-page book for travelers with disabilities, covers everything from biking trips to scuba outfitters. It costs $45 (less for members) and is available from **Mobility International USA,** P.O. Box 10767, Eugene, OR, 97440 (☏ **541/343-1284,** voice and TDD; www.miusa.org). Annual membership for Mobility International is $35, which includes their quarterly newsletter, *Over the Rainbow.*

You can join **The Society for the Advancement of Travel for the Handicapped** (SATH), 347 Fifth Ave., Suite 610, New York, NY 10016 (☏ **212/447-7284;** www.sath.org), for $45 annually, $30 for seniors and students, to gain access to a vast network of travel industry connections. The Society provides information on travel destinations and referrals to tour operators that specialize in travelers with disabilities. Its quarterly magazine, *Open World,* is full of information and resources. A year's subscription is included with membership, or costs $18 ($35 outside the U.S.).

Access-Able Travel Source is a home-grown online tip sheet that's grown to offer a comprehensive online index of accessible hotels, restaurants, attractions, and disabled-service providers around the country; log onto www.access-able.com (or call ☏ **303/232-2979**).

The **Los Angeles County Commission on Disabilities** (☏ **213/974-1053**) provides telephone referrals and information about L.A. for the physically challenged. The **Junior League of Los Angeles,** Farmers Market, 3rd and Fairfax streets, Gate 12, Los Angeles, CA 90036 (✆ **323/957-4280**), distributes *Around the Town with Ease,* a free brochure detailing the accessibility of various Los Angeles sites. There's a $2 handling fee for mail orders.

CAR RENTALS   Many major car-rental companies now offer hand-controlled cars for drivers with disabilities. **Avis** can provide such a vehicle at any of its locations in the United States with 48-hour advance notice; **Hertz** requires between 24 and 72 hours of advance reservation at most locations. **Wheelchair Getaways** (✆ **800/642-2042;** www.wheelchair-getaways.com) rents specialized vans with wheelchair lifts and other features in more than 100 cities across the United States.

FOR GAY & LESBIAN TRAVELERS

When **West Hollywood** was incorporated in 1984, it elected a lesbian mayor and a predominantly gay city council. West Hollywood, also known as WeHo, has been waving the rainbow flag ever since. While L.A.'s large gay community is too vast to be contained in this 2-square-mile city, West Hollywood has the largest concentration of gay- and lesbian-oriented businesses and services. Santa Monica, Venice, Silver Lake, and Studio City are other lesbian and gay enclaves.

GUIDES & PUBLICATIONS   There are many gay-oriented publications with information and up-to-date listings, including *Frontiers,* a Southern California–based biweekly; and *Nightlife,* a local weekly with comprehensive entertainment listings, complete with maps. *Out and About* (✆ **800/929-2268;** www.outandabout.com), hailed for its "straight" and savvy reporting on gay travel, offers guidebooks and a monthly newsletter packed with good information on the gay and lesbian scene. Publications from *Travel & Leisure* to the *New York Times* have praised the newsletter; a year's subscription costs $49.

The periodicals above are available at most newsstands citywide, and at **A Different Light Bookstore** (8853 Santa Monica Blvd., West Hollywood; ✆ **310/854-6601;** www.adlbooks.com), L.A.'s largest and best gay-oriented bookshop. Their website is also enormously helpful.

ORGANIZATIONS   The **International Gay & Lesbian Travel Association** (IGLTA; ✆ **800/448-8550** or 954/776-2626; www.iglta.org) links travelers with the appropriate gay-friendly service organization or tour specialist. With around 1,200 members, it offers quarterly newsletters, marketing mailings, and a membership directory that's updated quarterly.

For more information on L.A.'s gay and lesbian neighborhoods and nightlife, see "Out & About" in chapter 10.

FOR SENIORS

Nearly every attraction in Los Angeles offers a senior discount; age requirements vary, and we list specific prices in chapter 7. Public transportation and movie theaters also have reduced rates. Don't be shy about asking for discounts, but always carry some kind of identification, such as a driver's license, that shows your date of birth. Also, mention the fact that you're a senior citizen when you first make your travel reservations. For example, both **Amtrak** (✆ **800/USA-RAIL;** www.amtrak.com) and **Greyhound** (✆ **800/752-4841;** www. greyhound.com) offer discounts to persons over 62. **Southwest Airlines (800/435-9792;** www.southwest.com) offers discounts to persons over 65.

Members of the **American Association of Retired Persons (AARP),** 601 E St. NW, Washington, DC

Kids   Bringing Baby Along

Babyland rents strollers, cribs, car seats, and the like from two Los Angeles–area locations, at 1782 S. La Cienega Blvd. (north of I-10), Los Angeles (© **310/836-2222**); and 7134 Topanga Canyon Blvd., Woodland Hills (© **818/704-7848**). Rates vary; expect to spend around $35 per week for strollers and $65 per week plus deposit for a crib. If you need a baby sitter in L.A., contact the **Baby-Sitters Guild** (© **323/658-8792** or 818/552-2229), recently named the city's best by *Los Angeles* magazine. The concierge at larger hotels can also often recommend a reliable sitter.

20049 (© **800/424-3410** or 202/434-2277; www.aarp.org), get discounts not only on hotels but on airfares and car rentals too. AARP also offers members a wide range of other benefits, including *Modern Maturity* magazine and a monthly newsletter; membership is only $10 per year.

The Mature Traveler, a monthly newsletter on senior citizen travel, is a valuable resource. It is available by subscription ($30 a year) from GEM Publishing Group, Box 50400, Reno, NV 89513-0400. GEM also publishes *The Book of Deals,* a collection of more than 1,000 senior discounts on airlines, lodging, tours, and attractions around the country; it's available for $7.95 by calling © **800/460-6676.** Another helpful publication is *101 Tips for the Mature Traveler,* free from Grand Circle Travel, 347 Congress St., Suite 3A, Boston, MA 02210 (© **800/221-2610** or 617/350-7500; www.gct.com). Also check your newsstand for the quarterly magazine *Travel 50 & Beyond.*

FOR FAMILIES

Several books offer tips on traveling with kids. *Family Travel* (Lanier Publishing International) and *How to Take Great Trips with Your Kids* (The Harvard Common Press) are full of good general advice. *The Unofficial Guide to California with Kids* (Hungry Minds, Inc.) is an excellent resource that covers the entire state. It rates and ranks attractions for each age group, lists dozens of family-friendly

accommodations and restaurants, and suggests lots of beaches and activities that are fun for the whole clan.

Family Travel Times is published six times a year (© **888/822-4388** or 212/477-5524; www.familytravel times.com), and includes a weekly call-in service for subscribers. Subscriptions are $39 a year.

FOR STUDENTS

The best resource for students is the **Council on International Educational Exchange,** or CIEE. Its travel branch, **Council Travel Service** (© **800/226-8624;** www.council travel.com), is the biggest student travel agency in the world, with branches in many major cities. It can get discounts on plane tickets, rail passes, and the like. Council Travel's L.A. office is in Westwood at 931 Westwood Blvd., Los Angeles, CA 90024 (© **310/208-3551;** fax 310/208-4407).

TRAVELING WITH PETS

If you're thinking of taking Fido along with you to romp on a California beach, make sure you do a little research. For one thing, dogs are restricted from most public beaches in the L.A. area. To find out where you can bring man's best friend, check out the online **Pets Welcome** service (www.petswelcome.com), which has lists of accommodations that allow pets. The site also lists pet-related publications, medical travel tips, and links to other pet-related websites.

A good book to carry along is *The California Dog Lover's Companion: The Insider's Scoop on Where to Take Your Dog* (Publisher's Group West, 1998), a 900-page source for complete statewide listings of fenced dog parks, dog-friendly beaches, and other indispensable information.

Los Angeles has strict leash laws (including stiff penalties for failing to pick up waste), prompting the formation of a dog owner/supporter group called **Freeplay** (© **310/301-1550;** www.freeplay.org). Contact them for the latest developments on dog-related issues, including information on off-leash parks around town.

In the event your pet requires medical care while you're visiting, call or visit the **California Animal Hospital,** 1736 S. Sepulveda Blvd., Suite D (south of Santa Monica Blvd.), Los Angeles (© **310/478-0248**). The **Animal Emergency Facility** (© **310/473-1561**), located in adjoining suite A, is open 24 hours a day.

6 Getting There

ARRIVING BY PLANE

Los Angeles, an international travel hub, is served by virtually every major commercial airline. For a list of airlines' toll-free numbers and websites, see the appendix in the back of this book.

LAX & THE OTHER LOS ANGELES–AREA AIRPORTS

There are five airports in the Los Angeles area. Most visitors fly into **Los Angeles International Airport** (© **310/646-5252;** www.lawa.org/lax/laxframe.html), better known as LAX. This behemoth is situated ocean side, between Marina del Rey and Manhattan Beach. LAX is a convenient place to land; it's located within minutes of Santa Monica and the beaches, and not more than a half hour from Downtown, Hollywood, and the Westside. Despite its size, the eight-terminal airport has a straightforward,

---

Tips   What You Can Carry On—And What You Can't

The Transportation Security Administration (TSA), the government agency that now handles all aspects of airport security, has devised new restrictions for carry-on baggage, not only to expedite the screening process but to prevent potential weapons from passing through airport security. Passengers are now limited to bringing just one carry-on bag and one personal item onto the aircraft (previous regulations allowed two carry-on bags and one personal item, like a briefcase or a purse). For more information, go to the TSA's website www.tsa.gov. The agency has released an updated list of items passengers are not allowed to carry onto an aircraft:

Not permitted: knives and box cutters, corkscrews, straight razors, metal scissors, golf clubs, baseball bats, pool cues, hockey sticks, ski poles, ice picks.

Permitted: nail clippers, nail files, tweezers, eyelash curlers, safety razors (including disposable razors), syringes (with documented proof of medical need), walking canes and umbrellas (must be inspected first).

The airline you fly may have **additional restrictions** on items you can and cannot carry on board. Call ahead to avoid problems.

L.A. Freeways

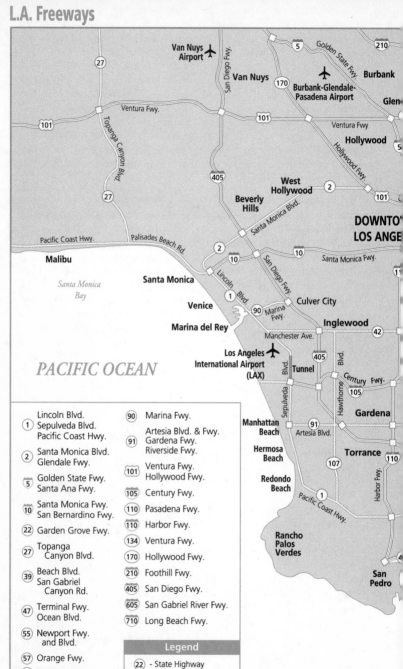

Lincoln Blvd.
(1) Sepulveda Blvd.
     Pacific Coast Hwy.

(2) Santa Monica Blvd.
     Glendale Fwy.

(5) Golden State Fwy.
     Santa Ana Fwy.

(10) Santa Monica Fwy.
     San Bernardino Fwy.

(22) Garden Grove Fwy.

(27) Topanga
     Canyon Blvd.

(39) Beach Blvd.
     San Gabriel
     Canyon Rd.

(47) Terminal Fwy.
     Ocean Blvd.

(55) Newport Fwy.
     and Blvd.

(57) Orange Fwy.

(60) Pomona Fwy.

(90) Marina Fwy.

(91) Artesia Blvd. & Fwy.
     Gardena Fwy.
     Riverside Fwy.

(101) Ventura Fwy.
      Hollywood Fwy.

(105) Century Fwy.

(110) Pasadena Fwy.

(110) Harbor Fwy.

(134) Ventura Fwy.

(170) Hollywood Fwy.

(210) Foothill Fwy.

(405) San Diego Fwy.

(605) San Gabriel River Fwy.

(710) Long Beach Fwy.

Legend

(22) - State Highway

(101) - U.S. Highway

(210) - Interstate Highway

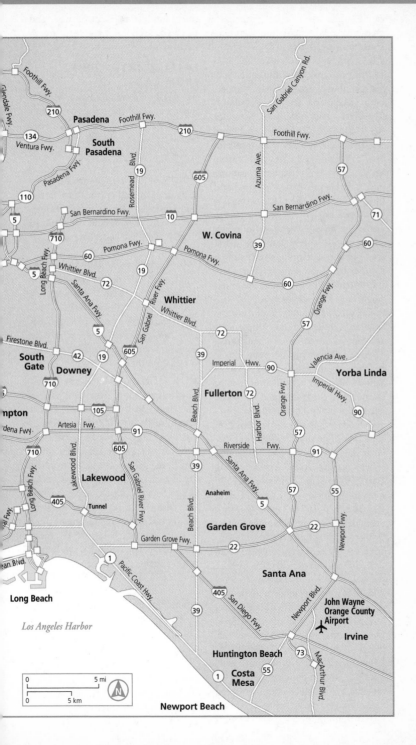

easy-to-understand design. Free blue, green, and white **Airline Connections shuttle buses** (© 310/646-2911) connect the terminals and stop in front of each ticket building. Special minibuses accessible to travelers with disabilities are also available. **Travelers Aid of Los Angeles** (© 310/646-2270; www.travelersaid. org) operates booths in each terminal. You can find extensive information about LAX—including maps, parking and shuttle-van information, and links to weather forecasts—online at **www.lawa.org**. All car-rental agencies are in the neighborhood surrounding LAX, within a few minutes' drive; each provides a complimentary shuttle to and from the airport. For more information on car rentals, see "Getting Around," in chapter 4.

For some travelers, one of the area's smaller airports might be more convenient than LAX. **Burbank-Glendale-Pasadena Airport** (2627 N. Hollywood Way, Burbank; © 818/840-8840; www.burbankairport.com) is the best place to land if you're headed for Hollywood or the valleys—and it's even closer to downtown L.A. than LAX. The small airport has especially good links to Las Vegas and other southwestern cities. **Long Beach Municipal Airport** (4100 Donald Douglas Dr., Long Beach; © 562/570-2678; www.lgb.org), south of LAX, is the best place to land if you're visiting Long Beach or northern Orange County and want to avoid L.A. **John Wayne Airport** (19051 Airport Way N., Anaheim; © 949/252-5200; www.ocair.com) is closest to Disneyland, Knott's Berry Farm, and other Orange County attractions. **Ontario International Airport** (Terminal Way, Ontario; © 909/975-5360; www.lawa.org/ont/ontframe. html) is not a popular airport for tourists; businesspeople use it to head to San Bernardino, Riverside, and other inland communities. It's convenient if

you're heading to Palm Springs, and also a viable choice if you're staying in Pasadena.

GETTING INTO TOWN FROM LAX

BY CAR   To reach Santa Monica and other northern beach communities, exit the airport, take Sepulveda Boulevard north, and follow the signs to Calif. 1 (Pacific Coast Hwy., or PCH) north.

To reach Redondo, Hermosa, Newport, and the other southern beach communities, take Sepulveda Boulevard south, then follow the signs to Calif. 1 (Pacific Coast Hwy., or PCH) south.

To reach Beverly Hills or Hollywood, exit the airport via Century Boulevard, then take I-405 north to Santa Monica Boulevard east.

To reach downtown or Pasadena, exit the airport, take Sepulveda Boulevard south, then take I-105 east to I-110 north.

BY SHUTTLE   Many city hotels provide free shuttles for their guests; ask when you make reservations. **SuperShuttle** (© 800/554-3146 or 310/782-6600; www.supershuttle. com) offers regularly scheduled minivans from LAX to any location in the city. The fare can range from about $15 to $35 per person, depending on your destination. It's cheaper to cab it to most places if you're a group of three or more, but the vans are far more comfortable; you might have to stop at other passengers' destinations before you reach your own. Reservations aren't needed for your arrival, but required for a return to the airport.

BY TAXI   Taxis line up outside each terminal. Rides are metered. Expect to pay about $35 to Hollywood and downtown, $25 to Beverly Hills, $20 to Santa Monica, and $45 to $60 to the Valley and Pasadena, *including* a $2.50 service charge for rides originating at LAX.

Finds **A Shortcut to LAX**

One of the city's busiest interchanges is from the Santa Monica Freeway (I-10) to the San Diego Freeway (I-405) on the way to Los Angeles International Airport. Therefore, when you're heading to LAX for your flight home, the scenic route may prove to be the fastest. From the Santa Monica Freeway (I-10) westbound, exit south to La Brea Avenue. Go right on Stocker Street, then left on La Cienega Boulevard. Veer right on La Tijera Boulevard and left on Airport Boulevard, then follow the signs. You can use this trick from West Hollywood and Beverly Hills as well—simply take La Cienega south, continuing as above.

BY RAIL Budget-minded travelers heading to downtown, Universal City, or Long Beach can take L.A.'s Metro Rail service from LAX. An airport shuttle can take you to the Green Line light rail station; from there, connections on the Blue and Red Lines can get you where you're headed; it's a good idea to contact your hotel for advice on the closest station. The service operates from 5am to midnight and the combined fare is under $2—but you should be prepared to spend 1 to 2 hours in transit. Call the **Los Angeles County Metropolitan Transit Authority (MTA)** at © **213/626-4455** (www.mta.net) for information.

BY PUBLIC BUS The city's MTA buses also go between LAX and many parts of the city. Phone **MTA Airport Information** (© **213/626-4455;** www.mta.net) for the schedules and fares.

ARRIVING BY CAR

Los Angeles is well connected to the rest of the United States by several major highways. Among them are Interstate 5, which enters the state from the north; Interstate 10, which originates in Jacksonville, Florida, and terminates in Los Angeles; and U.S. 101, a scenic route that follows the western seaboard from Los Angeles north to the Oregon state line. If you're planning to take smaller roads, call the **California Highway Patrol** (© **323/906-3400**) to check road conditions before heading out.

If you're driving **from the north,** you have two choices: the quick route, along I-5 through the middle of the state, or the scenic route along the coast. Heading south along I-5, you'll pass a small town called Grapevine. This marks the start of the mountain pass with the same name. Once you've reached the southern end of the pass, you'll be in the San Fernando Valley, which is the start of Los Angeles County. To reach the beach communities and L.A.'s Westside, take I-405 south; to get to Hollywood, take Calif. 170 south to U.S. 101 south (this route is called the Hollywood Freeway the entire way); I-5 will take you along the eastern edge of downtown and into Orange County.

If you're taking the **scenic coastal route** from the north, take U.S. 101 to I-405 or I-5, or stay on U.S. 101, following the instructions above to your destination.

If you're approaching **from the east,** you'll be coming in on I-10. For Orange County, take Calif. 57 south. I-10 continues through downtown and terminates at the beach. If you're heading to the Westside, take I-405 north. To get to the beaches, take Calif. 1 (PCH) north or south, depending on your destination.

From the south, head north on I-5. At the southern end of Orange County, I-405 splits off to the west; take this road to the Westside and beach communities. Stay on I-5 to reach downtown and Hollywood.

Tips **Flying for Less: Getting the Best Airfares**

Passengers in the same airplane cabin rarely pay the same fare for their seats, and almost no one ever pays full fare. Here are a few ways to save.

1. Keep checking your newspaper for **sales.** You'll almost never see a sale during the peak summer vacation months of July and August, or during the Thanksgiving or Christmas holidays, but during slower times, airlines may slash their fares dramatically.

2. If your schedule is flexible, ask if you can secure a cheaper fare by staying an extra day, by staying over Saturday night, or by flying midweek. Many airlines won't volunteer this information, so ask them lots of questions.

3. Formerly known as "bucket shops," **consolidators** (wholesalers who buy tickets in bulk at a discount) today are legitimate and offer some of the best deals around. You can get virtually any flight, on any airline, from them; sometimes their fare is identical to the airline's, but often it's discounted 15% to 50%. The tickets carry the same restrictions the airline imposes on advance and discount fares. There are lots of fly-by-night consolidators, though, and problems can range from disputing never-received tickets to finding you have no seat booked when you get to the airport. Play it safe by going with a reputable business. Here are some suggestions: **1-800-FLY-CHEAP** (www.flycheap.com); **Cheap Seats** (☎ **1-800-675-7482;** www.cheapseatstravel.com); or my favorite, **Cheap Tickets** (☎ **1.888.922.8849;** www.cheaptickets.com). **Council Travel** (☎ **800/226-8624;** www.counciltravel.com) and **STA Travel** (☎ **800/781-4040;** www.statravel.com) cater especially to young travelers, but their bargain-basement prices are available to people of all ages; **Travel Hub** www.travelhub.com) offers the deep discounts on many major airlines.

4. **Surf the Net** for bargains. Subscribe to the "specials" newsletters offered by the major airlines; among the best sites for finding great deals are Microsoft Expedia (**www.expedia.com**) and Travelocity (**www.travelocity.com**). The Internet Travel Network (**www.itn.net**) provides one-stop shopping for air, car, and hotel bookings; its "Fare Mail" keeps you informed of low-cost deals to any of six locations you request. Smarter Living (**www.smarter living.com**) also offers a customized e-mail summarizing the discount fares available from your departure city.

5. Are you a **frequent flyer?** Are you close to awards travel? You may be able to purchase the miles you need from the airline to make up the difference for a free round trip. Call the airline, or visit their website.

Here are some **driving times** if you're on one of those see-the-USA car trips: From Phoenix, it's about 350 miles (564km), or 6 hours (okay, 7, if you drive the speed limit) to Los Angeles via I-10. Las Vegas is

265 miles (427km) northeast of Los Angeles (about a 4- or 5-hr. drive). San Francisco is 390 miles (628km) north of Los Angeles on I-5 (6–7 hr.), and San Diego is 115 miles (185km) south (about 2 hr.).

ARRIVING BY TRAIN

Amtrak (© **800/USA-RAIL;** www. amtrak.com) connects Los Angeles with about 500 American cities. As with plane travel along popular routes, fares fluctuate depending on season and special promotions. As a general rule, heavily restricted advance tickets are competitive with similar airfares. Remember, however, those low fares are for coach travel in reclining seats; private sleeping accommodations cost substantially more. The *Sunset Limited* is Amtrak's regularly scheduled transcontinental service, originating in Florida and making 52 stops along the way as it passes through Alabama, Mississippi, Louisiana, Texas, New Mexico, and Arizona before arriving in Los Angeles 2 days later. Amtrak's *Coast Starlight* travels along the Pacific Coast between Seattle and Los Angeles. This stylish train (with its wonderfully scenic route) has been steadily growing in popularity (see the box above for more information).

Amtrak also runs trains along the California coast, connecting San Diego, Los Angeles, San Francisco, and all points in between. There are multiple trains each day. One-way fares for popular segments can range from $20 (Los Angeles–Santa Barbara) to $23 (Los Angeles–San Diego) to $85 (San Francisco–Los Angeles) but, again, fares fluctuate.

Ask about special family plans, tours, and other money-saving promotions. You can call for a brochure outlining routes and prices for the entire system; up-to-date schedules and fares are also available on Amtrak's comprehensive, but often unwieldy, website (**www.amtrak.com**).

The L.A. train terminus is **Union Station,** 800 N. Alameda (© **213/ 624-0171**), on downtown's northern edge. Completed in 1939, this was the last of America's great train depots—a unique blend of Spanish Revival and Streamline Moderne architecture (see "Architectural Highlights," in chapter 7). From the station, you can take one of the taxis that line up outside, board the Metro Red Line to Hollywood or Universal City, or the Metro Blue Line to Long Beach. If you're headed to the San Fernando Valley or Anaheim, Metrolink commuter trains leave from Union Station; call © 800/371-LINK (www.metrolinktrains.com).

ARRIVING BY BUS

Bus travel is an inexpensive and often-flexible option. **Greyhound** (© **800/ 231-2222;** www.greyhound.com) can get you to L.A. from anywhere and offers several money-saving multiday passes. The main station for arriving buses is downtown at 1716 E. Seventh St., east of Alameda. For additional area terminal locations, use the phone number or website above.

Tips If You're Driving

If you're planning a road trip, it's a good idea to join the **American Automobile Association** (AAA). Members who carry their cards receive free roadside assistance as well as access to a wealth of free travel information (detailed maps and guidebooks). Also, many hotels and attractions offer discounts to AAA members—always inquire. Call © **800/922-8228** or your local branch for membership information.

Moments The *Coast Starlight:* All Aboard for Nostalgia

If you're traveling by rail along the west coast between Seattle and Los Angeles, treat yourself to a ride aboard Amtrak's luxurious *Coast Starlight.* In an effort to recapture the glory days of 1940s Streamline luxury liners, Amtrak is pulling out all the stops on these double-decker Superliners, which come complete with gourmet dining car, first-class and coach lounge cars, standard and deluxe sleeping compartments, and enough diversions (including feature-length films, live entertainment, games for kids and adults, and a full bar) to make the overnight, 2-day trip a pleasure. All sleeping-car fares include three meals daily, prepared fresh on board with an emphasis on regional and seasonal flavor, with wines from vintners in Washington, Oregon, and California.

This excursion is perfect for those who believe the journey is as important as the destination. The highlight of the trip is the exceptional scenery you'll enjoy from the upper-level, panoramic windows of the coach and observation cars. Sweeping views of lushly green Washington state, California's rugged coastline, farmland, rolling hills, sparkling beaches, and charming railroad stations all provide a memorable travelogue.

Fares on the *Coast Starlight* fluctuate, though not as wildly as airline fares. Kids 2 to 15 travel half price, and seniors 62 and over receive a 15% discount. Coach fare buys assigned seating in comfortable upper-level reclining chairs. Between San Francisco and Los Angeles, one-way adult coach ranges from $49 to $75; between Seattle and L.A. it's $106 to $176. Sleeping-car passengers are guaranteed the lowest coach rate for travel (even if it's "sold out" for coach passengers) but pay extra for their compartments. For travel between Seattle and L.A., a standard sleeper for two adds $228; a deluxe with private bathroom adds $536. A family sleeper for two adults/two kids (no bathroom) adds $455. The sleeper charge is per compartment, not per passenger, and includes all meals. Passengers who haven't paid for a compartment must purchase their meals a la carte. For coach passengers, blankets and pillows are offered in the evening and fold-up leg rests help make sleeping more comfortable than you might imagine. Full bathrooms are available.

It's advisable to book several months ahead for peak periods (summer, weekends, and holidays). Since the splendid views depend on daylight, also consider carefully before traveling during the short days of winter. For information and tickets, call Amtrak at ⓒ 800/USA-RAIL, or visit its *Coast Starlight* website at www.coaststarlight.com.

7 Planning Your Trip Online

With a mouse, a modem, and a certain do-it-yourself determination, Internet users can tap into the same travel-planning databases that were once accessible only to travel agents.

Sites such as **Travelocity, Expedia,** and **Orbitz** allow consumers to comparison shop for airfares, book flights, find last-minute bargains, and reserve hotel rooms and rental cars.

But don't fire your travel agent yet. Although online booking sites offer tips and data to help you shop, they cannot endow you with the experience that makes a seasoned, reliable travel agent an invaluable resource, even in the Internet age. And for consumers with a complex itinerary, a trusty travel agent is still the best way to arrange the most direct flights to and from the best airports.

Still, there's no denying the Internet's emergence as a powerful tool in researching and plotting travel time. The benefits of researching your trip online can be well worth the effort:

- **Last-minute specials,** known as "E-savers," such as weekend deals or Internet-only fares, are offered by airlines to fill empty seats. Most of these are announced on Tuesday or Wednesday and must be purchased online. They are only valid for travel that weekend, but some can be booked weeks or months in advance. Sign up for weekly e-mail alerts at airline websites (see p. 320) or check megasites that compile comprehensive lists of E-savers, such as Smarter Living (www.smarterliving.com) or WebFlyer (www.webflyer.com).
- Some sites will send you **e-mail notification** when a cheap fare becomes available to your favorite destination. Some will also tell you when fares to a particular destination are lowest.
- The best of the travel planning sites are now **highly personalized;** they track your frequent-flier miles, and store your seating and meal preferences, tentative itineraries, and credit-card information, letting you plan trips or check agendas quickly.
- All major airlines offer **incentives**—bonus frequent-flier miles, Internet-only discounts, sometimes even free cellphone rentals—when you purchase online or buy an E-ticket.
- Some airlines allow you to **purchase frequent-flier miles** on the Internet, by phone or by mail. It's worth investigating this option if you're within a couple of thousand miles of award travel.
- Advances in mobile technology provide business travelers and

---

Tips **All About E-Ticketing**

Only yesterday **electronic tickets (E-tickets)** were the fast and easy ticket-free alternative to paper tickets. E-tickets allowed passengers to avoid long lines at airport check-in, all the while saving the airlines money on postage and labor. With the increased security measures in airports, however, an E-ticket no longer guarantees an accelerated check-in. You often can't go straight to the boarding gate, even if you have no bags to check. You'll probably need to show your printed E-ticket receipt or confirmation of purchase, as well as a photo ID, and sometimes even the credit card with which you purchased your E-ticket. That said, buying an E-ticket is still a fast, convenient way to book a flight; instead of having to wait for a paper ticket to come through the mail, you can book your fare by phone or on the computer, and the airline will immediately confirm by fax or e-mail. In addition, airlines often offer frequent-flier miles as incentive for electronic bookings.

other frequent travelers with **the ability to check flight status, change plans, or get specific directions** from hand-held computing devices, mobile phones, and pagers. Some sites will e-mail or page a passenger if a flight is delayed.

TRAVEL PLANNING & BOOKING SITES

The best travel planning and booking sites cast a wide net, offering domestic and international flights, hotel and rental-car bookings, plus news, destination information, and deals on cruises and vacation packages. Keep in mind that free (one-time) registration is often required for booking. Because several airlines are no longer willing to pay commissions on tickets sold by online travel agencies, be aware that these online agencies will either charge a $10 surcharge if you book a ticket on that carrier—or neglect to offer those air carriers' offerings.

Value **Package Tours**

Independent fly/drive packages (not escorted tours, but bulk rates on your airfare, hotel, and possibly rental car) are offered by **American Airlines Vacations** (© 800/321-2121; www.aavacations.com), **Continental Airlines Vacations** (© 800/634-5555; www.coolvacations.com), **Delta Vacations** (© 800/872-7786; www.deltavacations.com), **Southwest Airlines Vacations** (© 800/423-5683; www.swavacations.com), or **United Vacations** (© 800/328-6877; www.unitedvacations.com).

In addition to these airline agencies, travel package services are offered to Amex customers at **American Express Travel** (© 800/AXP-6898; www.americanexpress.com/travel), which books packages through various vendors, including Continental Vacations and Delta Vacations. Or contact **Liberty Travel** (© 888/271-1584; www.liberty-travel.com), one of the oldest and biggest packagers; they offer great deals—with or without air—to the many popular California destinations, including San Diego and Disneyland.

Try not to be too picky about your hotel. That's not to say packages book you in dumps—quite the contrary, they often include premier hostelries—but you might have a limited selection. Pinpoint roughly where you'd like to stay within the city, and ask if there's a participating hotel there. The biggest hotel chains and resorts also offer package deals. If you know where you want to stay, call the hotel and ask if it can offer land/air packages.

If you can schedule your departure and arrival so you're not flying on the weekend, airfares will usually be at least $25 to $50 lower per person. And it goes without saying that summer is the most restrictive season, though package deals can still save you some money over booking separately.

Engage the reservationist in conversation, mentioning all the activities you're considering for your visit. All of the companies have access to various goodies they can hitch to your package for far less than you'd pay separately. Examples include tickets to Universal Studios or Disneyland; passes for city tours, studio tours, and other excursions; tickets for theater events; car-rental upgrades; and more.

The sites in this section are not intended to be a comprehensive list, but rather a discriminating selection to help you get started. Recognition is given to sites based on their content value and ease of use and is not paid for—unlike some website rankings, which are based on payment. Remember: This is a press-time snapshot of leading websites—some undoubtedly will have evolved or moved by the time you read this.

- **Travelocity** (www.travelocity.com or www.frommers.travelocity.com) and **Expedia** (www.expedia.com) are the most long-standing and reputable sites, each offering excellent selections and searches for complete vacation packages. Travelers search by destination and dates coupled with how much they are willing to spend.
- The latest buzz in the online travel world is about **Orbitz** (www.orbitz.com), a site launched by United, Delta, Northwest, American, and Continental airlines. It shows all possible fares for your desired trip, offering fares lower than those available through travel agent.
- **Qixo** (www.qixo.com) is another powerful search engine that allows you to search for flights and hotel rooms on 20 other travel-planning sites (such as Travelocity) at once. Qixo sorts results by price, after which you can book your travel directly through the site.

SMART E-SHOPPING

The savvy traveler is one who arms himself with good information. Here are a few tips to help you navigate the Internet successfully and safely.

- **Know when sales start.** Last-minute deals may vanish in minutes. If you have a favorite booking site or airline, find out when last-minute deals are released to the public. (For example, Southwest's specials are posted every Tuesday at 12:01am central time.)
- **Shop around.** Compare results from different sites and airlines—and against a travel agent's best fare, if you can. If possible, try a range of times and alternate airports before purchasing.
- **Follow the rules of the trade.** Book in advance, and choose an off-peak time and date if possible. Some sites tell you when fares to a destination tend to be cheapest.
- **Stay secure.** Book only through secure sites (some airline sites are not secure). Look for a key icon (Netscape) or a padlock (Internet Explorer) at the bottom of your Web browser before you enter credit card information or other personal data.
- **Avoid online auctions.** Sites that auction airline tickets and frequent-flier miles are the number-one perpetrators of Internet fraud, according to the National Consumers League.
- **Maintain a paper trail.** If you book an E-ticket, print out a confirmation, or write down your confirmation number, and keep it safe and accessible—or your trip could be a virtual one!

ONLINE TRAVELER'S TOOLBOX

Veteran travelers usually carry some essential items to make their trips easier. Following is a selection of online tools to bookmark and use.

- **Visa ATM Locator** (www.visa.com/pd/atm) or **MasterCard ATM Locator** (www.mastercard.com/atm). Find ATMs in hundreds of cities in the United States and around the world.
- **Foreign Languages for Travelers** (www.travlang.com). Learn basic terms in more than 70 languages and click on any underlined phrase to hear what it sounds like.

Ⓒ Site Seeing: The Best of L.A. Online

Although the best vacations are the ones that allow for spontaneity, there's no substitute for a little pretrip research when it comes to planning a great vacation. And even though you're reading the best darn guidebook to Los Angeles, we can't even come close to listing everything there is to see and do in L.A.—only the Internet can pull that hat trick. Ergo, we scoured the Web and came up with the following list: These are the mother lodes of L.A.'s best entertainment, dining, lodging, and nightlife websites, crammed with enough timely information to plan your dream L.A. vacation a dozen times over.

Please keep in mind that this is not a comprehensive list, but rather a discriminating selection to get you started. Finally, remember this is a press-time snapshot of leading websites—some undoubtedly will have evolved, changed, or moved by the time you read this.

- **calendarlive.com** Hosted by the *L.A. Times*, **Calendar Live** is loaded with entertainment and nightlife reviews and listings in greater Los Angeles. Other topics include restaurants, museums, outdoor recreation, and Orange County.

- **www.at-la.com** The home page of **@LA,** whose exceptional search engine provides links to close to 60,000 sites in thousands of categories relating to all of Southern California.

- **Lamag.com** The online edition of **Los Angeles Magazine** offers "The Guide," an oft-updated listing of LA's theater, music scene, museums, and more, as well as an excellent "Dining Out" guide listing hundreds of restaurants organized geographically. Very groovy.

- **www.lacvb.com** The **L.A. Convention & Visitors Bureau** lets you browse its site by region or category, view sample itineraries keyed to selected neighborhoods, activities, ethnic themes, or type of visitor. The African American and/or Latino **"Heritage and Culture Guides"** provide comprehensive listings in categories like dining, attractions, cultural resources, heritage and history, entertainment, and worship.

- **www.santamonica.com** Everything you could possibly want to know about travel and tourist information in Santa Monica is covered in this vibrant website hosted by the Convention & Visitors Bureau.

- **www.bhvb.org** This official site of the Beverly Hills Visitors Bureau is as perfectly manicured as Beverly Hills itself, offering tons of practical information (including an indispensable map of parking lots, complete with rates), plus extras like a short historical walking tour, and a list of spas and salons as long as Cher's hair.

- **www.TheatreLA.org** Theatre LA is an association of live theaters and producers in Los Angeles (and the organization that puts on the yearly Ovation Awards, L.A.'s answer to Broadway's Tonys). The website is a great place to look for small and midsize productions, plus information on what's currently on sale at their half-price ticket booth (Times Tix) in West Hollywood.

- **www.visitwesthollywood.com** The West Hollywood Convention & Visitors Bureau hosts this frequently updated guide to everything to see/do/eat/buy in WeHo, as it's come to be known. Learn about the Avenues of Art & Design (a district of L.A.'s best galleries and showrooms), plus browse extensive activity and service guides for WeHo's prominent gay and lesbian community.

- **www.tvtickets.com** Your online source for free tickets to dozens of sitcoms and talk shows. The site, hosted by Audiences Unlimited, Inc., includes a taping schedule, studio information, news about shows, updates on specials, and just about everything else you need to help you figure out what show you'd like to catch.
- **www.digitalcity.com/losangeles** is the local outpost of the nationally popular Digital City series, offering up-to-date articles on life in L.A., including dining, shopping, and entertainment info.
- **losangeles.citysearch.com** The local City Search site features movie/sports/entertainment listings, specialty guides like "Destination: Disney" and "Weekend Planner," online drawings for tickets and prizes, and an interactive match engine for singles.
- **www.disneyland.com** Check out the resorts, dining facilities, travel-package options, and activities and rides in the Magic Kingdom at Disneyland's official website. Get specific hours and ride closures in advance by selecting the day of your visit; this site is guaranteed to rev up your enthusiasm level. Also visit **Disneyland Inside & Out (www.intercotwest.com)**, an independent guide to Disneyland with updates on activities, rides, entertainment, and the ever-expanding Disneyland resort; consult tips on what to bring, best times of year to visit, and more.
- **www.universalstudios.com** Almost as fun as visiting the Universal Studios Hollywood theme park. Take a virtual tour of the attractions, view current show schedules, check out special ticket offers (and purchase tickets online), or play games based on Universal's most popular rides: "Jurassic Park" and "Back to the Future."
- **www.laweekly.com** Straight from the pages of the alternative *L.A. Weekly* paper, this site combines listings with social commentary, with an events calendar, arts listings and critiques, and restaurant reviews.
- **www.pasadenavisitor.org** A colorful website hosted by the Pasadena Convention & Visitors Bureau that's crammed with months worth of things to do in pretty Pasadena, plus links to everything from CalTech to Tournament of Roses FAQ.
- **www.losangeles.com** is the L.A. feature of Boulevards, whose national alternative websites emphasize travel, arts, entertainment, contemporary culture, and politics.
- **www.musictoday.com** is a great source of information for local music, including venues, artists, and the ability to purchase tickets.
- **www.festivalfinder.com OR www.festivalusa.com** is a site that can locate music festivals in and around Los Angeles.

Note: Free audio software and speakers are required.

- **Intellicast** (www.intellicast.com). Weather forecasts for all 50 states and cities around the world. *Note:* Temperatures are in Celsius for many international destinations.

- **Mapquest** (www.mapquest.com). This best of the mapping sites lets you choose a specific address or destination, and in seconds, it returns a map and detailed directions.

- **Cybercafes.com** (www.cybercafes. com). Locate Internet cafes at hundreds of locations around the globe. Catch up on your e-mail and log onto the Web for a few dollars per hour.

- **Universal Currency Converter** (www.xe.net/currency). See what your dollar or pound is worth in more than 100 other countries.

- **U.S. State Department Travel Warnings** (www.travel.state.gov/ travel_warnings.html). Reports on places where health concerns or unrest might threaten U.S. travelers. It also lists the locations of U.S. embassies around the world.

3

For International Visitors

The pervasiveness of American culture around the world may make you feel you know the United States pretty well, but leaving your own country requires an additional degree of planning. This chapter can help prepare you for the more common problems that visitors may encounter.

1 Preparing for Your Trip

ENTRY REQUIREMENTS

Immigration laws are a hot issue in the United States these days, and the following requirements may have changed somewhat by the time you plan your trip. Check at any U.S. embassy or consulate for current information and requirements. You can also plug into the **U.S. State Department's** Internet site (**www.state.gov**).

VISAS The U.S. State Department has a **Visa Waiver Pilot Program** allowing citizens of certain countries to enter the United States without a visa for stays of up to 90 days. At press time these included Andorra, Australia, Austria, Belgium, Brunei, Denmark, Finland, France, Germany, Iceland, Ireland, Italy, Japan, Liechtenstein, Luxembourg, Monaco, the Netherlands, New Zealand, Norway, Portugal, San Marino, Singapore, Slovenia, Spain, Sweden, Switzerland, the United Kingdom, and Uruguay. Citizens of these countries need a valid passport, proof of financial solvency, and a round-trip air or cruise ticket in their possession upon arrival. If they first enter the United States, they may also visit Mexico, Canada, Bermuda, and/or the Caribbean islands and return to the United States without a visa. Further information is available from any U.S. embassy or consulate. Canadian citizens may enter the United States without visas; they need only proof of residence.

Citizens of all other countries must have (1) a valid passport that expires at least 6 months later than the scheduled end of their visit to the United States, and (2) a visitor visa, which may be obtained with a nonrefundable US$45 application fee from any U.S. consulate.

OBTAINING A VISA To obtain a visa, the traveler must submit a completed application form (either in person or by mail) with a 1½-inch-square photo, and must demonstrate binding ties to a residence abroad. Usually you can get a visa at once or within 24 hours, but it may take longer during the summer rush from June through August. If you cannot go in person, contact the nearest U.S. embassy or consulate for directions on applying by mail. Your travel agent or airline office may also be able to provide you with visa applications and instructions. The U.S. consulate or embassy that issues your visa will determine whether you will be issued a multiple- or single-entry visa and any restrictions regarding the length of your stay.

British subjects can obtain up-to-date passport and visa information by calling the **U.S. Embassy Visa Information Line** (© **0891/200-290**) or the **London Passport Office**

Travel Tip

If you have questions about U.S. Immigration policies or laws, call the **Immigration and Naturalization Service's "Ask Immigration System"** at ℂ **800/375-5283** or visit the INS website at www.ins.us.doj.gov. Representatives are available from 9am to 3pm, Monday through Friday; a 24-hour automated information option also addresses common questions.

(ℂ **0990/210-410** for recorded information).

MEDICAL REQUIREMENTS Unless you're arriving from an area known to be suffering from an epidemic (particularly cholera or yellow fever), inoculations or vaccinations are not required for entry into the United States. If you have a disease that requires treatment with narcotics or syringe-administered medications, carry a valid signed prescription from your physician to allay any suspicions that you may be smuggling narcotics (a serious offense that carries severe penalties in the United States). See "Insurance," below, for information on health insurance for your trip.

For **HIV-positive visitors**, requirements for entering the United States are somewhat vague and change frequently. According to the publication *HIV and Immigrants: A Manual for AIDS Service Providers*, although INS doesn't require a medical exam for everyone trying to come into the United States, INS officials may keep out people who they suspect are HIV positive. INS may stop people because they look sick or because they are carrying AIDS/HIV medicine.

If an HIV-positive noncitizen applying for a nonimmigrant visa knows that HIV is a communicable disease of public health significance but checks "No" on the question about communicable diseases, INS may deny the visa because it thinks the applicant committed fraud. If a nonimmigrant visa applicant checks "Yes," or if INS suspects the person is HIV positive, it will deny the visa unless the applicant asks for a special waiver for visitors. This waiver is for people visiting the United States for a short time, to attend a conference, for instance, to visit close relatives, or to receive medical treatment. It can be a confusing situation, so for up-to-the-minute information concerning HIV-positive travelers, contact the Center for Disease Control's **National AIDS Hotline** (ℂ **800/342-AIDS**, in Spanish 800/344-7432, or a TGY line for the hearing impaired 800/243-7889) or the **Gay Men's Health Crisis** (ℂ **212/367-1000**; www.gmhc.org).

PASSPORT INFORMATION

Safeguard your passport in a secure place like a money belt. If you lose it, visit the nearest consulate of your native country as soon as possible for a replacement. You can download passport applications from the Internet sites listed below.

FOR RESIDENTS OF CANADA

You can pick up a passport application at one of 28 regional passport offices or most travel agencies. As of December 11, 2001, Canadian children who travel will need their own passport. However, if you hold a valid Canadian passport issued before December 11, 2001, that bears the name of your child, the passport remains valid for you and your child until it expires. Passports cost C$85 for those 16 years and older (valid 5 years), C$35 children 3 to 15 (valid 5 years), and C$20, children under 3 (valid for 3 years). Applications, which must be accompanied by two identical passport-sized photographs and proof of Canadian citizenship, are available at travel agencies throughout Canada or from the central **Passport Office, Department of Foreign Affairs and International Trade,** Ottawa, Ont. K1A 0G3 (**℃ 800/567-6868;** www.dfait-maeci.gc.ca/passport). Processing takes 5 to 10 days if you apply in person, or about 3 weeks by mail.

FOR RESIDENTS OF THE UNITED KINGDOM

As a member of the European Union, you need only an identity card, not a passport, to travel to other EU countries. However, if you already possess a passport, it's always useful to carry it. To pick up an application for a regular 10-year passport (the Visitor's Passport has been abolished), visit your nearest passport office, major post office, or travel agency. You can also contact the **United Kingdom Passport Service** at **℃ 0870/571-0410** or search its website at www.ukpa.gov.uk. Passports are £30 for adults and £16 for children under 16.

FOR RESIDENTS OF IRELAND

You can apply for a 10-year passport, costing 57€ at the **Passport Office,** Setanta Centre, Molesworth Street, Dublin 2 (**℃ 01/671-1633;** www.irlgov.ie/iveagh). Those under age 18 and over 65 must apply for a 3-year passport, costing 12€. You can also apply at 1A South Mall, Cork (**℃ 021/272-525**) or over the counter at most main post offices.

FOR RESIDENTS OF AUSTRALIA

Apply at your local post office or passport office or search the government website at www.passports.gov.au. Passports cost A$136 for adults and A$68 for those under 18. The **Australia State Passport Office** can be reached at **℃ 131232;** travelers must schedule an interview to submit their passport application materials.

FOR RESIDENTS OF NEW ZEALAND

You can pick up a passport application at any travel agency or Link Centre. For more info, contact the **Passport Office,** Dept. of Internal Affairs, P.O. Box 10-526, Wellington (**℃ 0800/225-050;** www.passports.govt.nz). Passports are NZ$80 for adults and NZ$40 for those under 16.

CUSTOMS
WHAT YOU CAN BRING IN

Every visitor over 21 years of age may bring in, free of duty, the following: (1) 1 liter of wine or hard liquor; (2) 200 cigarettes, 50 cigars (but not from Cuba), or 2 kilograms (4.4 lb.) of smoking tobacco; and (3) $100 worth of gifts. These exemptions are offered to travelers who spend at least 72 hours in the United States and who have not claimed them within the preceding 6 months. It is altogether forbidden to bring into the country foodstuffs (particularly fruit, cooked meats, and canned goods) and plants (vegetables, seeds, tropical plants, and the like). Foreign tourists may bring in or take out up to $10,000 in U.S. or foreign currency with no formalities; larger sums must be declared to U.S. Customs on entering or leaving, which includes filing form CM 4790. For more specific information regarding U.S. Customs, call your nearest U.S. embassy or consulate, call **U.S. Customs (℃ 202/ 927-1770**), or see the website at www.customs.ustreas.gov.

WHAT YOU CAN BRING HOME

U.K. citizens have a customs allowance of 200 cigarettes; 50 cigars; 250g of smoking tobacco; 2 liters of still table wine; 1 liter of spirits or strong liqueurs (over 22% volume); 2 liters of fortified wine, sparkling wine or other liqueurs; 60cc (ml) perfume; 250cc (ml) of toilet water; and £145 worth of all other goods, including gifts and souvenirs. People under 17 cannot have the tobacco or alcohol allowance. For more information, contact **HM Customs & Excise,** Passenger Enquiry Point, 2nd Floor Wayfarer House, Great South West Road, Feltham, Middlesex, TW14 8NP (✆ **0181/910-3744;** from outside the U.K. 44/181-910-3744), or consult their website at www.open.gov.uk.

For a clear summary of **Canadian** rules, write for the booklet *I Declare,* issued by the **Canada Customs and Revenue Agency** (✆ **800/461-9999** in Canada, or 204/983-3500; www.ccra-adrc.gc.ca). Canada allows its citizens a Can$750 exemption, and you're allowed to bring back duty-free one carton of cigarettes, 1 can of tobacco, 40 imperial ounces of liquor, and 50 cigars. In addition, you're allowed to mail gifts to Canada valued at less than Can$60 a day, provided they're unsolicited and don't contain alcohol or tobacco (write on the package "Unsolicited gift, under $60 value"). All valuables should be declared on the Y-38 form before departure from Canada, including serial numbers of valuables you already own, such as expensive foreign cameras. *Note:* The $750 exemption can only be used once a year and only after an absence of 7 days.

The duty-free allowance in **Australia** is A$400 or, for those under 18, A$200. Personal property mailed back from England should be marked "Australian goods returned" to avoid payment of duty. Upon returning to Australia, citizens can bring in 250 cigarettes or 250g of loose tobacco, and 1,125ml of alcohol. If you're returning with valuable goods you already own, such as foreign-made cameras, you should file form B263. A helpful brochure, available from Australian consulates or Customs offices, is *Know Before You Go.* For more information, contact **Australian Customs Services,** GPO Box 8, Sydney NSW 2001 (✆ **02/9213-2000**).

The duty-free allowance for **New Zealand** is NZ$700. Citizens over 17 can bring in 200 cigarettes, or 50 cigars, or 250g of tobacco (or a mixture of all three if their combined weight doesn't exceed 250g); plus 4.5 liters of wine and beer, or 1.125 liters of liquor. New Zealand currency does not carry import or export restrictions. Fill out a certificate of export, listing the valuables you are taking out of the country; that way, you can bring them back without paying duty. Most questions are answered in a free pamphlet available at New Zealand consulates and Customs offices: *New Zealand Customs Guide for Travellers, Notice no. 4.* For more information, contact **New Zealand Customs,** 50 Anzac Ave., P.O. Box 29, Auckland (✆ **09/359-6655**).

INSURANCE

Though lack of health insurance may prevent you from being admitted to a hospital in nonemergencies, don't worry about being left on a street corner to die: The American way is to fix you now and bill the living daylights out of you later. Health insurance is not required of travelers, but it's highly recommended. Unlike many European countries, the United States does not usually offer free or low-cost medical care to its citizens or visitors. Doctors and hospitals are expensive, and in most cases will require advance payment or proof of coverage before they render their services. Policies can cover everything from the loss or theft of your baggage and trip cancellation to the guarantee of bail in case you're arrested. Good policies will also cover the costs of an accident, repatriation, or death. Packages such as **Europ Assistance** in Europe are sold by automobile clubs and travel agencies at attractive rates. **Worldwide Assistance Services, Inc.** (✆ **800/ 821-2828**), is the agent for Europ Assistance in the United States. See

"Insurance, Health & Safety," in chapter 2, for more information.

British travelers will notice that most big travel agents offer their own insurance, which they'll probably try to sell you when you book a holiday. Think before you sign. Britain's Consumers' Association recommends that you insist on seeing the policy and reading the fine print before buying travel insurance. The **Association of British Insurers** (① 0171/600-3333) gives advice by phone and publishes the free *Holiday Insurance,* a guide to policy provisions and prices. You might also shop around for better deals: Try **Columbus Travel Insurance Ltd.** (① 0171/375-0011) or, for students, **Campus Travel** (① 0171/730-2101).

Canadians should check with their provincial health plan offices or call **HealthCanada** (① 613/957-2991) to find out the extent of their coverage and what documentation and receipts they must take home in case they are treated in the United States.

MONEY

CURRENCY The U.S. monetary system is painfully simple: The most common bills (all ugly, all green) are the $1 (colloquially, a "buck"), $5, $10, and $20 denominations. There are also $2 bills (seldom encountered), $50 bills, and $100 bills (the last two are usually not welcome as payment for small purchases). Note that newly designed bills are now in circulation. Despite rumors to the contrary, the old-style bills are still legal tender.

There are six denominations of coins: 1¢ (1 cent, or a penny), 5¢ (5 cents, or a nickel), 10¢ (10 cents, or a dime), 25¢ (25 cents, or a quarter), 50¢ (50 cents, or a half dollar), and the $1 piece (the older, large silver dollar and the newer, small Susan B. Anthony coin and the newest Sacajawea coin).

Note: The "foreign-exchange bureaus" so common in Europe are rare even at airports in the United States, and nonexistent outside major cities. It's best not to change foreign money (or traveler's checks denominated in a currency other than U.S. dollars) at a small-town bank, or even a branch in a big city; in fact, leave any currency other than U.S. dollars at home—it may prove a greater nuisance to you than it's worth.

TRAVELER'S CHECKS Though traveler's checks are widely accepted, make sure that they're denominated in U.S. dollars, as foreign-currency checks are often difficult to exchange. The three traveler's checks that are most widely recognized—and least likely to be denied—are **Visa, American Express,** and **Thomas Cook.** Be sure to record the numbers of the checks, and keep that information separately in case they get lost or stolen. Most L.A. businesses are pretty good about taking traveler's checks, but you're better off cashing them in at a bank (in small amounts, of course) and paying in cash. *Remember:* You'll need identification, such as a driver's license or passport, to change a traveler's check.

CREDIT CARDS & ATMS Credit cards are the most widely used form of payment in the United States: **Visa** (BarclayCard in Britain), **MasterCard** (EuroCard in Europe, Access in Britain, Chargex in Canada), **American Express, Diners Club, Discover,** and **Carte Blanche.** You must have a credit or charge card to rent a car. There are a handful of stores and restaurants in Los Angeles that may not take credit cards, however, so be sure to ask in advance. Most businesses display a sticker near their entrances to let you know which cards they accept. (*Note:* Often businesses require a minimum purchase price, usually around $10, for use of a credit card.)

It is strongly recommended that you bring at least one major credit card. Hotels, car-rental companies, and airlines usually require a credit-card imprint as a deposit against expenses, and in an emergency a credit card can be priceless.

You'll find automated-teller machines (ATMs) on just about every block in L.A.'s business districts. Some ATMs will allow you to draw U.S. currency against your bank and credit cards. Check with your bank before leaving home, and remember that you will need your personal identification number (PIN) to do so. Most accept Visa, MasterCard, and American Express, as well as ATM cards from other U.S. banks. Expect to be charged up to $3 per transaction, however, if you're not using your own bank's ATM. *Tip:* One way around these fees is to ask for cash back at grocery stores that accept ATM cards and don't charge usage fees. Of course, you'll have to purchase something first. For detailed information on Los Angeles's ATMs, see "Money" (p. 13), in chapter 2.

MONEYGRAMS   If the proverbial poop hits the fan, you can also have someone wire money to you very quickly via Western Union. Call ℭ **800/325-6000** for the office nearest you.

SAFETY
GENERAL SAFETY SUGGESTIONS   While tourist areas are generally safe, crime is still a problem, and U.S. urban areas tend to be less safe than those in Europe or Japan. Always stay alert. Ask your hotel front-desk staff or the city or area's tourist office if you're in doubt about which neighborhoods are safe.

Avoid deserted areas, especially at night, and don't go into public parks at night unless there's a concert or similar event that will attract a crowd. It's perfectly okay to drive into Griffith Park after dark to visit the observatory or see a show at the Greek Theater, but save any exploration beyond the parking lot for daylight hours. If you are near the Coliseum or Sports Arena in South Central L.A. try not to venture far from the venues.

Avoid carrying valuables with you on the street, and don't display expensive cameras or electronic equipment. Hold onto your pocketbook, and place your billfold in an inside pocket. In theaters, restaurants, and other public places, keep your possessions in sight.

Remember also that hotels are open to the public, and in a large hotel, security may not be able to screen everyone entering. Always lock your room door—don't assume that inside your hotel you are automatically safe.

Driving safety is important, too. Ask your rental agency about personal safety, and ask for a traveler-safety brochure when you pick up your car. Ask for written directions to your destination or a map with the route clearly marked. (Many agencies offer the option of renting a cellular phone for the duration of your car rental; check with the rental agent when you pick up the car.) Try to arrive and depart during daylight hours.

Recently, more crime has involved cars and drivers. If you drive off a highway into a doubtful neighborhood, leave the area as quickly as possible. If you have an accident, even on the highway, stay in your car with the doors locked until you assess the situation or until the police arrive. If you're bumped from behind on the street or are involved in a minor accident with no injuries, and the situation appears to be suspicious, motion to the other driver to follow you. Never get out of your car in such situations. Go directly to the nearest police precinct, well-lit service station, or 24-hour store.

Always try to park in well-lit and well-traveled areas. Never leave any packages or valuables in sight. If someone attempts to rob you or steal your car, don't try to resist the thief or carjacker. Report the incident to the police department immediately by calling ✆ **911.** This is a free call, even from pay phones.

2 Getting to the United States

AIRLINES In addition to the domestic U.S. airlines listed in chapter 2 and the appendix, many international carriers serve LAX and other U.S. gateways. These include, among others: **Aer Lingus** (✆ **01/886-8888** in Dublin; www.aerlingus.ie), **Air Canada** (✆ **800/776-3000;** www.air canada.ca), **British Airways** (✆ **0845/ 77 33-377** in the U.K.; www.british-airways.com), **Canadian Airlines** (✆ **800/426-7000**), **Japan Airlines** (✆ **0354/89-1111** in Tokyo; www.jal. co.jp), **Qantas** (✆ **13-13-13** in Australia; www.qantas.com.au), and **Virgin Atlantic** (✆ **01293/747-747** in the U.K.; www.fly.virgin.com). British Airways and Virgin Atlantic offer direct flights to Los Angeles from London. **Air New Zealand** (✆ **73-7000** in New Zealand; www.airnewzealand. co.nz) also flies direct to Los Angeles.

Overseas visitors can take advantage of the APEX (Advance Purchase Excursion) reductions offered by all major U.S. and European carriers. For more money-saving airline advice, see "Getting There," in chapter 2.

NEW AIR TRAVEL SECURITY MEASURES

In the wake of the terrorist attacks of September 11, 2001, the airline industry began implementing sweeping security measures in airports. Expect a lengthy check-in process and extensive delays. Although regulations vary from airline to airline, you can expedite the process by taking the following steps:

- **Arrive early.** Arrive at the airport at least 2 hours before your scheduled flight.
- **Try not to drive your car to the airport.** Parking and curbside access to the terminal may be limited. Call ahead and check.

- **Don't count on curbside check-in.** Some airlines and airports have stopped curbside check-in altogether, whereas others offer it on a limited basis. For up-to-date information on specific regulations and implementations, check with the individual airline.
- **Be sure to carry plenty of documentation.** A government-issued photo ID (federal, state, or local) is now required. You may need to show this at various checkpoints. With an E-ticket, you may be required to have with you printed confirmation of purchase, and perhaps even the credit card with which you bought your ticket (see "All About E-Ticketing," in chapter 2). This varies from airline to airline, so call ahead to make sure you have the proper documentation. And be sure that your ID is **up-to-date:** An expired driver's license, for example, may keep you from boarding the plane altogether.
- **Know what you can carry on— and what you can't.** Travelers in the United States are now limited to one carry-on bag, plus one personal bag (such as a purse or a briefcase). The FAA has also issued a list of newly restricted carry-on items; see the box "What You Can Carry On—And What You Can't," in chapter 2.
- **Prepare to be searched.** Expect spot-checks. Electronic items, such as a laptop or cellphone, should be readied for additional screening. Limit the metal items you wear on your person.
- **It's no joke.** When a check-in agent asks if someone other than you packed your bag, don't decide that this is the time to be funny.

The agents will not hesitate to call an alarm.

• **No ticket, no gate access.** Only ticketed passengers will be allowed beyond the screener checkpoints, except for those people with specific medical or parental needs.

IMMIGRATION & CUSTOMS CLEARANCE Visitors arriving by air, no matter what the port of entry, should cultivate patience and resignation. Getting through immigration control may take as long as 3 hours, especially on summer weekends, so have this guidebook or something else to read. Add the time it takes to clear Customs, and you'll see that you should make a 2- to 3-hour allowance for delays when you plan your connections between international and domestic flights.

In contrast, for the traveler arriving by car or rail from Canada, the border-crossing formalities have been streamlined to the vanishing point. People traveling by air from Canada, Bermuda, and some places in the Caribbean can sometimes clear Customs and Immigration at the point of departure, which is much quicker.

3 Getting Around the United States

BY PLANE Some major American carriers—including Delta and Continental—offer travelers on their transatlantic or transpacific flights special low-price tickets on U.S. continental flights under the **Discover America** program (sometimes called **Visit USA,** depending on the airline). Offering one-way travel between U.S. destinations at significantly reduced prices, this coupon-based airfare program is the best and easiest way to tour the United States at low cost. You must purchase these discounted fare coupons abroad in conjunction with your international ticket. Ask your travel agent or the airline reservations agent about this program well in advance of your departure date—preferably when you buy your international ticket—since the regulations may affect your trip planning, and conditions can change without notice.

BY TRAIN International visitors can buy a **USA Rail Pass,** good for 15 or 30 days of unlimited travel on **Amtrak** (© 800/USA-RAIL; www.amtrak. com). The pass is available through many foreign travel agents. Prices (in U.S. dollars) in 2001 for a 15-day pass were $295 off-peak, $440 peak; a 30-day pass was $385 off-peak, $550 peak. (With a foreign passport, you can also buy passes at some Amtrak offices in the U.S., including Los Angeles, San Francisco, Chicago, New York, Miami, Boston, and Washington, D.C.) Reservations are generally required and should be made for each part of your trip as early as possible.

BY BUS Although bus travel is often the most economical form of public transit for short hops between U.S. cities, it can also be slow and uncomfortable—certainly not an option for everyone (particularly when Amtrak, which is far more luxurious, offers reasonable rates). **Greyhound/Trailways** (© 800/231-2222), the sole nationwide bus line, offers an **Ameripass** (© 888/454-7277) for unlimited travel for 7 days at $185, 15 days at $285, 30 days at $385, and 60 days at $509. Passes must be purchased at a Greyhound terminal. Special rates are available for seniors and students.

BY CAR The most cost-effective, convenient, and comfortable way to travel around the United States—especially California and Los Angeles—is by car. The Interstate highway system connects cities and towns all over the country; in addition to these high-speed, limited-access roadways, there's an extensive network of federal, state, and local highways and roads. California has no toll roads, but it does charge a toll fee at many major bridges. Some of the national car-rental companies that have offices in Los Angeles include **Alamo** (© 800/327-9633), **Avis** (© 800/831-2847), **Budget** (© 800/527-0700), **Dollar** (© 800/800-4000), **Hertz** (© 800/654-3131), **National** (© 800/227-7368), and **Thrifty** (© 800/847-4389).

If you plan on renting a car in the United States, you probably won't need the services of an additional automobile organization. If you plan to buy or borrow a car, automobile-association membership is recommended. **AAA**, the **American Automobile Association** (© 800/922-8228 from Northern California, or 800/924-6141 from Southern California; www.aaa.com), is the country's largest auto club and supplies its members with maps, insurance, and, most important, emergency road service. The cost of joining runs from $66 for singles to $93 for two members, but if you're a member of a foreign auto club with reciprocal arrangements, you can enjoy free AAA service in America.

For detailed information on car rentals in Los Angeles, see "Getting Around" (p. 61), in chapter 4. A comprehensive list of agencies, complete with websites and toll-free U.S. phone numbers, can be found in the appendix at the end of this book.

Ⓒ FAST FACTS: For the International Visitor

Business Hours Banks and offices are usually open weekdays from 9am to 5pm. Stores, especially in shopping complexes, tend to stay open until about 9pm on weekdays and 6pm on weekends.

Climate See "When to Go," in chapter 2.

Currency & Currency Exchange See "Entry Requirements" and "Money," under "Preparing for Your Trip," earlier in this chapter.

Drinking Laws The legal age for purchase and consumption of alcoholic beverages is 21. Proof of age is required and often requested at bars, nightclubs, and restaurants, so bring an ID when you go out. Supermarkets and convenience stores in California sell beer, wine, and liquor.

Do not carry open containers of alcohol in your car or any public area that isn't zoned for alcohol consumption. The police can, and probably will, fine you on the spot. And nothing will ruin your trip faster than getting a citation for DUI ("driving under the influence"), so don't even think about driving while intoxicated.

Electricity Like Canada, the United States uses 110 to 120 volts AC (60 cycles), compared to 220 to 240 volts AC (50 cycles) in most of Europe, Australia, and New Zealand. If your small appliances use 220 to 240 volts, you'll need a 110-volt transformer and a plug adapter with two flat parallel pins to operate them here. Converters that change 220–240 volts to 110–120 volts are difficult to find in the United States, so bring one with you.

Embassies & Consulates All embassies are in Washington, D.C. Some consulates are in major U.S. cities, and most nations have a mission to the United Nations in New York. If your country isn't listed below, call Washington, D.C., directory assistance (© 202/555-1212) for the number of your national embassy.

The embassy of **Australia** is at 1601 Massachusetts Ave. NW, Washington, DC 20036 (✆ **202/797-3000**; www.austemb.org). The nearest consulate is at 2049 Century Park E., 19th Floor, Los Angeles, CA 90067 (✆ **310/229-4800**).

The embassy of **Canada** is at 501 Pennsylvania Ave. NW, Washington, DC 20001 (✆ **202/682-1740**; www.canadianembassy.org). The nearest consulate is at 300 S. Grand Ave., 10th Floor, Los Angeles, CA 90071 (✆ **213/346-2700**).

The embassy of **Ireland** is at 2234 Massachusetts Ave. NW, Washington, DC 20008 (✆ **202/462-3939**; www.irelandemb.org). The nearest consulate is at 44 Montgomery St., Suite 3830, San Francisco, CA 94104 (✆ **415/392-4214**).

The embassy of **Japan** is at 2520 Massachusetts Ave. NW, Washington, DC 20008 (✆ **202/238-6700**; www.embjapan.org). The nearest consulate is at 50 Fremont St., San Francisco, CA 94105 (✆ **415/777-3533**).

The embassy of **New Zealand** is at 37 Observatory Circle, Washington, DC 20008 (✆ **202/328-4800**; www.nzemb.org). The nearest consulate is at 12400 Wilshire Blvd., Suite 1150, Los Angeles, CA 90025 (✆ **310/207-1605**).

The embassy of the **United Kingdom** is at 3100 Massachusetts Ave. NW, Washington, DC 20008 (✆ **202/462-1340**; www.britainusa.com/consular/embassy). The nearest consulate is at 11766 Wilshire Blvd., Suite 400, Los Angeles, CA 90025 (✆ **310/481-0031**).

Emergencies Call ✆ **911** to report a fire, call the police, or get an ambulance anywhere in the United States. This is a toll-free call (no coins are required at public telephones). If that doesn't work, another useful way of reporting an emergency is to call the telephone company operator by dialing 0 (zero, not the letter *O*).

If you encounter traveler's problems, call the Los Angeles chapter of the **Traveler's Aid Society** (✆ **310/646-2270**), a nationwide, nonprofit, social-service organization that helps travelers in difficult straits. Its services might include reuniting families separated while traveling, providing food and/or shelter to people stranded without cash, or even emotional counseling.

Gasoline (Petrol) Petrol is known as gasoline (or simply "gas") in the United States, and petrol stations are known as both gas stations and service stations. Gasoline costs about half as much as it does in Europe (about $1.30 per gallon at press time), and taxes are already included in the printed price. One U.S. gallon equals 3.8 liters or 0.85 Imperial gallons.

Holidays Banks, government offices, post offices, and many stores, restaurants, and museums are closed on the following legal national holidays: January 1 (New Year's Day), the third Monday in January (Martin Luther King Jr. Day), the third Monday in February (Presidents' Day, Washington's Birthday), the last Monday in May (Memorial Day), July 4 (Independence Day), the first Monday in September (Labor Day), the second Monday in October (Columbus Day), November 11 (Veterans' Day/Armistice Day), the fourth Thursday in November (Thanksgiving Day), and December 25 (Christmas).

Legal Aid The foreign tourist will probably never become involved with the American legal system. If you are "pulled over" for a minor infraction (for example, of the highway code, such as speeding), never attempt to pay the fine directly to a police officer; this could be construed as attempted bribery, a much more serious crime. Pay fines by mail, or directly into the hands of the clerk of the court. If accused of a more serious offense, say and do nothing before consulting a lawyer. Everyone has the right to remain silent, whether he or she is suspected of a crime or actually arrested. Once arrested, a person can make one telephone call to a party of his or her choice. Call your embassy or consulate.

Mail If you aren't sure what your address will be in the United States, mail can be sent to you, in your name c/o General Delivery, at the main post office of the city or region where you expect to be. Call ✆ **800/ASK-USPS** (275-8777), or log onto **www.usps.com** for more information. The addressee must pick mail up in person and must produce proof of identity (driver's license or passport, for example). Most post offices will hold your mail for up to 1 month, and are open Monday through Friday from 8am to 5pm, and Saturday from 9am to 3pm. See also "Post Office" under "Fast Facts: Los Angeles," in chapter 4.

Generally found at intersections, mailboxes are blue with an eagle logo and carry the inscription U.S. MAIL. Domestic postage rates are 23¢ for a postcard and 37¢ for a letter. International rates vary; visit a post office for precise postage information and stamps.

Medical Emergencies To call an ambulance, dial ✆ **911** from any phone—no coins are needed in pay phones. For hospitals and other emergency information, see chapter 4.

Newspapers & Magazines The **Los Angeles Times** (www.latimes.com) is a high-quality daily with strong local and national coverage. Its Sunday "Calendar" section (www.calendarlive.com) is an excellent guide to entertainment in and around L.A., and includes listings of what's doing and where to do it. The **L.A. Weekly** (www.laweekly.com), a free weekly listings magazine, is packed with information on current events around town. **Los Angeles** magazine (www.lamag.com) is a city-based monthly full of news, information, and previews of L.A.'s art, music, and food scenes.

Smoking Heavy smokers are in for a tough time in Los Angeles. There is no smoking in public buildings, sports arenas, elevators, theaters, banks, lobbies, restaurants, offices, stores, bed-and-breakfasts, most small hotels, and bars. That's right—as of January 1, 1998, you can't even smoke in a bar in California. The only exception is a bar where drinks are served solely by the owner. You will find, however, that many neighborhood bars turn a blind eye and pass you an ashtray.

Taxes In the United States there is no value-added tax (VAT) or other indirect tax at the national level. Sales tax is levied on goods and services by state and local governments, however, and is not included in the price tags you'll see on merchandise. This tax is not refundable. Sales tax in Los Angeles is 8%. Hotel tax is charged on the room tariff only (which is not subject to sales tax) and is set by the city, ranging from 12% to 17% around Southern California.

Telephone & Fax The telephone system in the United States is run by private corporations, so rates, especially for long-distance service and operator-assisted calls, can vary widely. Generally, hotel surcharges on long-distance calls are astronomical, so you're usually better off charging the call to a telephone charge card or a credit card—or using a **public pay telephone,** which you'll find clearly marked in most public buildings and private establishments as well as on the street. Convenience stores and gas stations often have them. Many convenience groceries and other stores sell **prepaid calling cards** in denominations up to $50; these can be the least expensive way to call home. Many public phones at airports now accept American Express, MasterCard, and Visa credit cards. **Local calls** made from public pay phones cost either 25¢ or 35¢. Pay phones do not accept pennies, and few will take anything larger than a quarter.

Most long-distance and international calls can be dialed directly from any phone. For **direct overseas calls,** dial 011 (the international access code), then the country code (Australia, 61; Republic of Ireland, 353; New Zealand, 64; United Kingdom, 44), followed by the city code, then the local number. To place a call to Canada or the Caribbean, just dial 1, the area code, and the local number.

Calls to area codes **800, 888,** and **877** are toll-free. However, calls to numbers in area codes **700** and **900** (chat lines, bulletin boards, "dating" services, and so on) can be very expensive—usually a charge of 95¢ to $3 or more per minute, and they sometimes have minimum charges that can run as high as $15 or more.

For **reversed-charge or collect calls,** and for **person-to-person calls,** dial 0 (zero) followed by the area code and number you want; an operator comes on the line to assist you.

For **directory assistance** ("information"), dial ☎ **411.** 411 operators can also provide long-distance information; or you can dial 1, then the appropriate area code and **555-1212.**

Before calling from a hotel room, always ask the hotel phone operator if there are any telephone surcharges. They can sometimes be reduced by calling collect or by using a telephone charge card. Hotel charges, which can be exorbitant, can be avoided altogether by using a pay phone in the lobby.

Most hotels have **fax machines** available for guest use (be sure to ask about the charges), and many places even have in-room fax machines. A less expensive way to send and receive faxes is to visit **Mail Boxes Etc.,** a national chain of office service stores. Locations in the L.A. area include 8391 Beverly Blvd., Los Angeles (☎ **323/655-9980**), and 1158 26th St., Santa Monica (☎ **310/453-4111**). You can also search for convenient locations online at www.mbe.com.

Telephone Directory There are two kinds of telephone directories in the United States. The general directory is the so-called **White Pages,** which lists private and business subscribers in alphabetical order. The inside front cover lists the emergency number for police, fire, and ambulance, and other vital numbers (like the Coast Guard, poison-control center, crime-victims hot line, and so on). The first few pages are devoted to community-service numbers, including a guide to long-distance and international calling, complete with country codes and area codes.

The second directory, printed on yellow paper (hence its name, the **Yellow Pages**), lists local services, businesses, and industries by type of activity, with an index at the back. The listings cover not only such obvious items as automobile repairs by make of car and drugstores (pharmacies), often by geographical location, but also restaurants by type of cuisine and geographical location, bookstores by special subject or language, places of worship by religious denomination, and other information that the tourist might otherwise not readily find. The Yellow Pages also include city plans or detailed maps, often showing postal ZIP codes and public-transportation routes.

Time   The continental United States is divided into **four time zones:** eastern standard time (EST), central standard time (CST), mountain standard time (MST), and Pacific standard time (PST). When it is 9am in Los Angeles (PST), it is noon in New York (EST), 5pm in London (GMT), and 2am the next day in Sydney.

Daylight saving time is in effect from 1am on the first Sunday in April to 1am on the last Sunday in October, except in Arizona, Hawaii, part of Indiana, and Puerto Rico. Daylight saving time moves the clock 1 hour ahead of standard time.

For the correct time, call ✆ **853-1212** (in any L.A. area code).

Tipping   Tipping is so ingrained in the American way of life that the annual income tax of tip-earning service personnel is based on how much they should have received in light of their employers' gross revenues. Accordingly, they may have to pay tax on a tip you didn't actually give them.

Here are some rules to follow:

In hotels, tip **bellhops** at least $1 per bag ($2–$3 if you have a lot of luggage), and tip the **maid or chamber staff** $1 per day. Tip the **doorman** or **concierge** only if he or she has provided you with some specific service (for example, calling a cab for you or obtaining difficult-to-get theater tickets). Tip the **valet parking attendant** $1 every time you get your car.

In restaurants, bars, and nightclubs, tip **service staff** 15% to 20% of the check, tip **bartenders** 10% to 15%, tip **checkroom attendants** $1 per garment, and tip **valet-parking attendants** $1 per vehicle. Tip the **doorman** if he has provided you with some specific service (such as calling a cab). Tipping is not expected in cafeterias and fast-food restaurants, but is expected at buffet-style restaurants and steakhouses where servers may bring food you've ordered, clear your table, and refill your drinks.

Tip **cab drivers** 15% of the fare.

As for other service personnel, tip **skycaps** at airports at least $1 per bag ($2–$3 if you have a lot of luggage), and tip **hairdressers** and **barbers** 15% to 20%.

Tipping ushers at movies and theaters, and gas-station attendants, is not expected.

4

Getting to Know Los Angeles

The freeways crisscrossing the Los Angeles metropolitan area are your lifelines to the sights, but it takes time to master the maze. Even locals sometimes have trouble getting around this sprawling city. This chapter can help you get familiar with the setup of the city and start you on the road to negotiating it like a native.

1 Orientation

VISITOR INFORMATION CENTERS

The **Los Angeles Convention and Visitors Bureau** (© 800/366-6116; Events Hotline 213/689-8822; www.lacvb.com) is the city's main source for information. In addition to maintaining an informative Internet site and answering telephone inquiries, the bureau provides a **walk-in visitor center** at 685 S. Figueroa St., downtown (open Mon–Fri from 8am–5pm, and Sat 8:30am–5pm).

Many Los Angeles–area communities also have their own information centers, and often maintain detailed and colorful websites. **Beverly Hills Visitors Bureau,** 239 S. Beverly Dr. (© 800/345-2210 or 310/248-1015; www.bhvb. org), is open Monday through Friday from 9am to 5pm.

West Hollywood Convention and Visitors Bureau, 8687 Melrose Ave., M-26, West Hollywood, CA 90096 (© 800/368-6020 or 310/289-2525; www. visitwesthollywood.com), is open Monday through Friday from 8am to 6pm.

Hollywood Arts Council, P.O. Box 931056, Dept. 1995, Hollywood, CA 90093 (© 323/462-2355; www.discoverhollywood.com), distributes the magazine *Discover Hollywood* for a $2 postage-and-handling fee. This publication contains listings and schedules for the area's many theaters, galleries, music venues, and comedy clubs; the current issue is always available online.

Santa Monica Convention and Visitors Bureau (© 310/393-7593; www.santamonica.com), is the best source for information about Santa Monica. Their Palisades Park walk-up center is located near the Santa Monica Pier, at 1400 Ocean Ave. (between Santa Monica Blvd. and Broadway), and is open daily from 10am to 5pm.

Pasadena Convention and Visitors Bureau, 171 S. Los Robles Ave. (© 626/795-9311; www.pasadenavisitor.org), is open Monday through Friday from 8am to 5pm and Saturday from 10am to 4pm.

OTHER INFORMATION SOURCES

Local tourist boards are great for information regarding attractions and special events, but they often fail to keep a finger on the pulse of what's really happening, especially with regard to dining, culture, and nightlife. Several city-oriented newspapers and magazines offer more up-to-date info. *L.A. Weekly* (www.la weekly.com), a free listings magazine, is packed with information on current events around town. It's available from sidewalk news racks and in many stores and restaurants around the city; it also has a lively website.

Tips L.A.'s California Welcome Center

If you're the type that likes to load up on tourist information before you start exploring a city, you'll want to make a beeline for the **California Welcome Center**. Located at the Beverly Center (a massive shopping mall) on Beverly Boulevard between La Cienega and San Vicente boulevards near the Hard Rock Cafe, the center offers a wealth of useful tourist information as well as direct and same-day ticket purchases to L.A.'s main attractions, museums, and entertainment venues. But wait, there's more: the "travel counselors" staffing the center also provide answers just about any question you have regarding the city, as well as foreign language assistance and translations, a hotel reservations service, and maps of L.A. and California. Open daily from 10am to 6pm; ② **310/854-7616**.

The *Los Angeles Times* **"Calendar"** section of the Sunday paper, an excellent guide to the world of entertainment in and around L.A., includes listings of what's doing and where to do it. The *Times* also maintains a comprehensive website at **www.calendarlive.com**; once there you can find departments with names like "Southland Scenes," "Tourist Tips," "Family & Kids," and "Recreation & Fitness." Information is culled from the newspaper's many departments and is always up to date. If you want to check out L.A.'s most immediate news, the *Times*'s main website is **www.latimes.com**.

Los Angeles Magazine (www.lamag.com) is a glossy city-based monthly full of real news and pure gossip, plus guides to L.A.'s art, music, and food scenes. Its calendar of events, which has been getting better lately, gives an excellent overview of goings-on at museums, art galleries, musical venues, and other places. The magazine is available at newsstands around town and in other major U.S. cities; you can also access stories and listings from the current issue on the Internet. Cybersurfers should visit **At L.A.'s** website at **www.at-la.com**; its exceptional search engine (one of our favorite tools) provides links to more than 23,000 sites relating to the L.A. area, including many destinations covered in chapter 10. For more Internet research options, see "Site Seeing: The Best of L.A. Online," in chapter 2.

CITY LAYOUT

Los Angeles is not a single compact city, but a sprawling suburbia comprising dozens of disparate communities. Most of the communities are located between mountains and ocean, on the flatlands of a huge basin. Even if you've never visited L.A. before, you'll recognize the names of many: Hollywood, Beverly Hills, Santa Monica, and Malibu. Ocean breezes push the city's infamous smog inland, toward dozens of less well-known residential communities, and through mountain passes into the sprawl of the San Fernando and San Gabriel valleys.

Downtown Los Angeles—which, by the way, isn't where most tourists go—is in the center of the basin, about 12 miles (19km) east of the Pacific Ocean. Most visitors spend the bulk of their time either on the coast or on the city's Westside (see "Neighborhoods in Brief," below, for complete details on all of the city's sectors). For a detailed map of L.A.'s freeway system, see p. 26.

MAIN ARTERIES & STREETS

L.A.'s extensive system of toll-free, high-speed freeways connects the city's patchwork of communities. The system works well to get you where you need

L.A. Neighborhoods in Brief

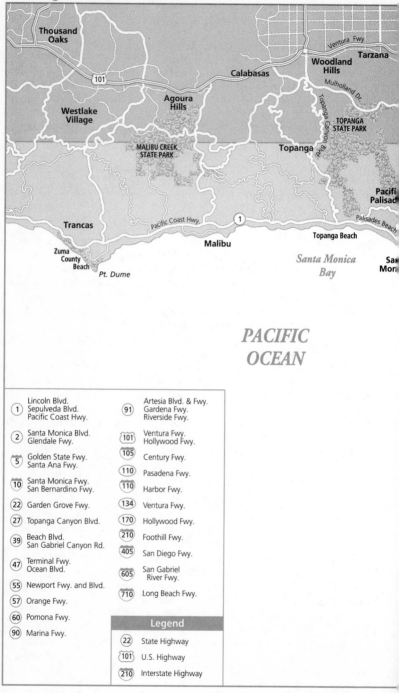

(1)	Lincoln Blvd. Sepulveda Blvd. Pacific Coast Hwy.	(91)	Artesia Blvd. & Fwy. Gardena Fwy. Riverside Fwy.
(2)	Santa Monica Blvd. Glendale Fwy.	(101)	Ventura Fwy. Hollywood Fwy.
(5)	Golden State Fwy. Santa Ana Fwy.	(105)	Century Fwy.
(10)	Santa Monica Fwy. San Bernardino Fwy.	(110)	Pasadena Fwy.
(22)	Garden Grove Fwy.	(110)	Harbor Fwy.
(27)	Topanga Canyon Blvd.	(134)	Ventura Fwy.
(39)	Beach Blvd. San Gabriel Canyon Rd.	(170)	Hollywood Fwy.
(47)	Terminal Fwy. Ocean Blvd.	(210)	Foothill Fwy.
(55)	Newport Fwy. and Blvd.	(405)	San Diego Fwy.
(57)	Orange Fwy.	(605)	San Gabriel River Fwy.
(60)	Pomona Fwy.	(710)	Long Beach Fwy.
(90)	Marina Fwy.		

Legend

(22)	State Highway
(101)	U.S. Highway
(210)	Interstate Highway

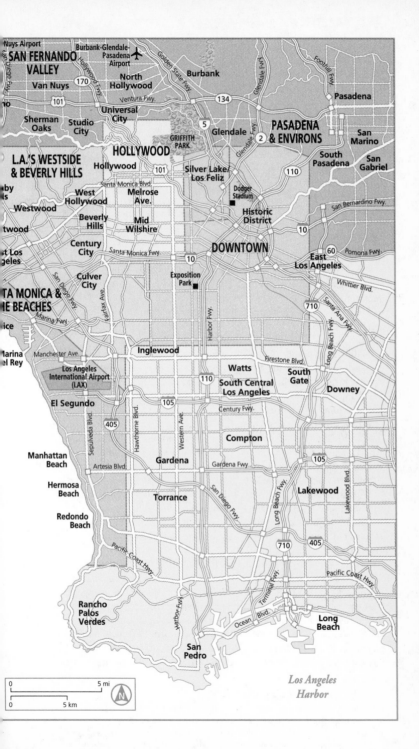

to be, although rush-hour (roughly 7am–9am and 4–6pm) traffic can be bumper-to-bumper. Here's an overview (best read with an L.A. map in hand):

U.S. 101, called the "Ventura Freeway" in the San Fernando Valley and the "Hollywood Freeway" in the city, runs across L.A. in a roughly northwest-southeast direction, from the San Fernando Valley to the center of downtown.

Calif. 134 continues as the "Ventura Freeway" after U.S. 101 turns into the city and becomes the Hollywood Freeway. This branch of the Ventura Freeway continues directly east, through the valley towns of Burbank and Glendale, to I-210 (the "Foothill Freeway"), which takes you through Pasadena and out toward the eastern edge of Los Angeles County.

I-5, otherwise known as the "Golden State Freeway" north of I-10 and the "Santa Ana Freeway" south of I-10, bisects downtown on its way from Sacramento to San Diego.

I-10, labeled the "Santa Monica Freeway" west of I-5 and the "San Bernardino Freeway" east of I-5, is the city's major east-west freeway, connecting the San Gabriel Valley with downtown and Santa Monica.

I-405, known as the "San Diego Freeway," runs north-south through L.A.'s Westside, connecting the San Fernando Valley with LAX and southern beach areas. This is one of the areas busiest freeways.

I-105, Los Angeles's newest freeway—called the "Century Freeway"—extends from LAX east to I-605.

I-110, commonly known as the "Harbor Freeway," starts in Pasadena as Calif. 110 (the "Pasadena Freeway"); it becomes an interstate in downtown Los Angeles and runs directly south, where it dead-ends in San Pedro. The section that is now the Pasadena Freeway was Los Angeles's first freeway, known as the Arroyo Seco when it opened in 1940.

I-710, aka the "Long Beach Freeway," runs in a north-south direction through East Los Angeles and dead-ends at Long Beach.

I-605, the "San Gabriel River Freeway," runs roughly parallel to the I-710 farther east, through the cities of Hawthorne and Lynwood and into the San Gabriel Valley.

Calif. 1—called "Highway 1," the "Pacific Coast Highway," or simply "PCH"—is really more of a scenic parkway than a freeway. It skirts the ocean, linking all of L.A.'s beach communities, from Malibu to the Orange Coast.

A complex web of surface streets complements the freeways. From north to south, the major east-west thoroughfares connecting downtown to the beaches are **Sunset Boulevard, Santa Monica Boulevard, Wilshire Boulevard,** and **Olympic, Pico,** and **Venice boulevards.** The section of Sunset Boulevard from Crescent Heights Boulevard to Doheny Drive is the famed **Sunset Strip.**

NEIGHBORHOODS IN BRIEF

Los Angeles is a very confusing city, with fluid neighborhood lines and labels. The best way to grasp the city is to break it into six regions: Santa Monica and the beaches; L.A.'s Westside and Beverly Hills; Hollywood; Downtown; the San Fernando Valley; and Pasadena and environs. Each encompasses a more-or-less distinctive patchwork of city neighborhoods and independently incorporated communities.

Throughout the book, we discuss the regions in the order of their natural geographical progression from west to east (except for the San Fernando Valley, which is roughly north of the city's other major regions, separated by the Hollywood Hills). Most visitors arrive at Los Angeles International Airport (LAX), located on the coast just south of L.A.'s primary beach communities. Unless you're coming to L.A. on business, you're likely to concentrate your visit in the city's western districts, since that's where the majority of attractions, restaurants, and shops are; many visitors never make it as far east as Downtown.

Santa Monica & the Beaches

These are nearly everyone's favorite L.A. communities. The 60-mile (97km) beachfront stretching from Malibu to the Palos Verdes Peninsula has milder weather and less smog than the inland communities, and traffic is nominally lighter, except on summer weekends. The towns along the coast all have a distinct mood and charm. They're listed below from north to south.

Malibu, at the northern border of Los Angeles County, 25 miles (40km) from downtown, was once a privately owned ranch—purchased in 1857 for 10¢ an acre. Today its wide beaches, sparsely populated hills, and relative remoteness from the inner city make it popular with rich recluses. Indeed, the resident lists of Malibu Colony and nearby Broad Beach—oceanfront strips of closely packed mansions—read like a who's who in Hollywood. With plenty of green space and dramatic rocky outcroppings, Malibu's rural beauty is unsurpassed in L.A. and surfers flock to "The 'Bu" for great, if crowded, waves.

Pretty **Santa Monica,** Los Angeles's premier beach community, is known for its long ocean pier, artsy atmosphere, and somewhat wacky residents. It's also noted for its acute homeless problem. The city has taken great pains to alleviate the situation and the Third Street Promenade, a pedestrian-only outdoor mall lined with great shops and restaurants, is one of the country's most successful revitalization projects.

Venice, a planned community in the spirit of its Italian forebear, was constructed with a series of narrow canals connected by quaint one-lane bridges. It had become infested with grime and crime, but regentrification is now in full swing, bringing scores of great restaurants and boutiques and rising property values for the quaint canal-side homes and apartment duplexes. Some of L.A.'s most innovative and interesting architecture lines funky Main Street. But without question, Venice is best known for its Ocean Front Walk, a nonstop circus of skaters, vendors, and poseurs of all ages, colors, types, and sizes.

Marina del Rey, just south of Venice, is a somewhat-quieter, more upscale community best known for its small-craft harbor, one of the largest of its kind in the world.

Manhattan, Hermosa, and **Redondo beaches** are laid-back, mainly residential neighborhoods with modest homes (except for oceanfront real estate), mild weather, and residents happy to have fled the L.A. hubbub. There are excellent beaches for volleyball players, surfers, and sun worshippers here, but when it comes to cultural activities, pickings can be slim. The restaurant scene, while limited, has been improving steadily and some great new bars and clubs have opened near their respective piers.

L.A.'s Westside & Beverly Hills

The Westside, an imprecise, misshapen L, sandwiched between Hollywood and the city's coastal communities, includes some of Los

Angeles's most prestigious neighborhoods, virtually all with names you're sure to recognize:

Beverly Hills is bounded roughly by Olympic Boulevard on the south, Robertson Boulevard on the east, and the districts of Westwood and Century City on the west; it extends into the hills to the north. Politically distinct from the rest of Los Angeles, this famous enclave is best known for its palm tree-lined streets of palatial homes and high-priced shops. But it's not all glitz and glamour; the healthy mix of filthy rich, wannabes, and tourists that peoples downtown Beverly Hills creates a unique—and sometimes snobby-surreal—atmosphere.

West Hollywood is a key-shaped community whose epicenter is the intersection of Santa Monica and La Cienega boulevards. It's bounded on the west by Doheny Drive and on the south roughly by Melrose Avenue. The tip of the key extends east for several blocks north and south of Santa Monica Boulevard as far as La Brea Avenue, but West Hollywood is primarily located to the west of Fairfax Avenue. Nestled between Beverly Hills and Hollywood, this politically independent town can feel either tony or tawdry, depending on which end of the city you're in. In addition to being home to some of the area's best restaurants, shops, and art galleries, West Hollywood, or WeHo as it's come to be known, is the center of L.A.'s gay community.

Bel Air and **Holmby Hills,** located in the hills north of Westwood and west of Beverly Hills, are wealthy residential areas featured prominently on most maps to the stars' homes.

Brentwood is best known as the famous backdrop to the O. J. Simpson melodrama. If Starbucks ever designed a neighborhood, this is what it would look like—a quiet, relatively upscale mix of homes, restaurants, and strip malls. It's west of I-405 and north of Santa Monica and West Los Angeles. The Getty Center looms over Brentwood from its hilltop perch next to I-405.

Westwood, an urban village that is home to the University of California at Los Angeles (UCLA), is bounded by I-405, Santa Monica Boulevard, Sunset Boulevard, and Beverly Hills. It used to be a hot destination for a night on the town, but has lost much of its appeal due to overcrowding, general rudeness, and even some minor street violence. There's still a high concentration of movie theaters here, but we're waiting for Westwood to regain its old charm.

Century City is a compact, busy, rather bland high-rise area sandwiched between West Los Angeles and Beverly Hills. It was once the back lot of 20th Century Fox studios. The primary draws here are the Shubert Theatre and the Century City Marketplace, a pleasant (though ugly) open-air mall. Century City's three main thoroughfares are Century Park East, Avenue of the Stars, and Century Park West; the area is bounded on the north by Santa Monica Boulevard and on the south by Pico Boulevard.

West Los Angeles is a label that generally applies to everything that isn't one of the other Westside neighborhoods. It's basically the area south of Santa Monica Boulevard, north of Venice Boulevard, east of Santa Monica and Venice, and west and south of Century City.

Hollywood

Yes, they still come. Young hopefuls with stars in their eyes are attracted to this town like moths fluttering to the glare of neon lights. But Hollywood is much more a state of mind than a glamour center. Many of the neighborhood's former movie studios have moved to more spacious venues in Burbank, on the Westside, and in other parts of the city.

For our purposes, the label "Hollywood" extends beyond the worn central area of Hollywood itself to the surrounding neighborhoods. It encompasses everything between Western Avenue to the east and Fairfax Avenue to the west and from the Hollywood Hills south.

Hollywood itself, which centers on Hollywood and Sunset boulevards (between La Brea and Vine), is the historic heart of L.A.'s movie industry. Visitors have always flocked to see landmark attractions like the star-studded Walk of Fame and Mann's Chinese Theatre. The Boulevard is, for the first time in decades, showing signs of rising out of a seedy slump, with refurbished movie houses and stylish restaurants and clubs making a fierce comeback. The centerpiece "Hollywood & Highland" complex anchors the neighborhood, with shopping, entertainment, and a luxury hotel built around the beautiful new Kodak Theater designed to host the Academy Awards (really, you'll want to poke your head into this theater).

Melrose Avenue, scruffy but fun, is the city's funkiest shopping district, catering to often-raucous youth with second-hand and avant-garde clothing shops—there are also several appealing restaurants in between.

The stretch of Wilshire Boulevard running through the southern part of Hollywood is known as the **Mid-Wilshire** district, or Miracle Mile. It's lined with contemporary apartment houses and office buildings. The section just east of Fairfax

Avenue, known as Museum Row, is home to almost a dozen museums, including the Los Angeles County Museum of Art, the La Brea Tar Pits, and that shrine to L.A. car culture, the Petersen Automotive Museum.

Griffith Park, up Western Avenue in the northernmost part of Hollywood, is one of the country's largest urban parks, home to the Los Angeles Zoo, the famous Griffith Observatory, and the outdoor Greek Theater.

Downtown

Roughly bounded by the U.S. 101, I-110, I-10, and I-5 freeways, L.A.'s downtown is home to a tight cluster of high-rise offices, the El Pueblo de Los Angeles Historic District, and the neighborhoods of Koreatown, Chinatown, and Little Tokyo. The construction of skyscrapers—bolstered by earthquake-proof technology—transformed Downtown into the business center of the city. Despite the relatively recent construction of numerous cultural centers (such as the Music Center and the Museum of Contemporary Art) and a few hip restaurants, it isn't the hub that it would be in most cities. The Westside, Hollywood, and the beach communities are all far more popular.

For our purposes, the residential neighborhoods of Silver Lake and Los Feliz, Exposition Park (home to Los Angeles Memorial Coliseum, the L.A. Sports Arena, and several downtown museums), and East and South-Central L.A., the city's famous barrios, all fall under the Downtown umbrella.

El Pueblo de Los Angeles Historic District, a 44-acre ode to the city's early years, is worth a visit. Chinatown is small and touristy, but can be plenty of fun for souvenir-hunting or traditional dim sum.

Little Tokyo, on the other hand, is a genuine gathering place for the Southland's Japanese population, with a wide array of shops and restaurants with an authentic flair.

Silver Lake, a residential neighborhood just north of downtown, and adjacent **Los Feliz,** just to the west, has arty areas with unique cafes, theaters, graffiti, and art galleries—all in equally plentiful proportions. The local music scene has been burgeoning of late.

Exposition Park, south and west of downtown, is home to the Los Angeles Memorial Coliseum and the L.A. Sports Arena, as well as the Natural History Museum, African-American Museum, and the California Science Center. The University of Southern California (USC) is next door.

East and **South-Central L.A.,** just east and south of downtown, are home to the city's large barrios. This is where the 1992 L.A. Riots were centered; it was here, at Florence and Normandie avenues, that a news station's reporter, hovering above in a helicopter, videotaped Reginald Denny being pulled from the cab of his truck and beaten. These neighborhoods are, without question, quite unique, though they contain few tourist sites (the Watts Towers being a notable exception). This can be a rough part of town, so be smart and alert if you decide to visit, particularly at night.

The San Fernando Valley

The San Fernando Valley, known locally as "The Valley," was nationally popularized in the 1980s by the notorious mall-loving "Valley Girl" stereotype. Snuggled between the Santa Monica and the San Gabriel mountain ranges, most of the Valley is residential and commercial and off the beaten track for tourists. But some of its attractions are

bound to draw you over the hill. **Universal City,** located west of Griffith Park between U.S. 101 and Calif. 134, is home to Universal Studios Hollywood and the trippy shopping and entertainment complex CityWalk. And you may make a trip to **Burbank,** west of these other suburbs and north of Universal City, to see one of your favorite TV shows being filmed at NBC or Warner Brothers Studios. There are also a few good restaurants and shops along Ventura Boulevard, in and around Studio City.

Glendale is a largely residential community north of downtown between the Valley and Pasadena. Here you'll find Forest Lawn, the city's best cemetery for sightseeing.

Pasadena & Environs

Best known as the site of the Tournament of Roses Parade each New Year's Day, **Pasadena** was spared from the tear-down epidemic that swept L.A., so it has a refreshing old-time feel. Once upon a time, Pasadena was every Angeleno's best-kept secret—a quiet community whose slow and careful regentrification meant excellent, unique restaurants and boutique shopping without the crowds, in a revitalized downtown respectful of its old brick and stone commercial buildings. Although the area's natural and architectural beauty still shines through—so much so that Pasadena remains Hollywood's favorite backyard location for countless movies and TV shows— Old Town has become a pedestrian mall similar to Santa Monica's Third Street Promenade, complete with huge crowds, midrange chain eateries, and standard-issue mall stores. It still gets our vote as a scenic alternative to the congestion of central L.A., but it has lost much of its small-town charm.

Pasadena is also home to the famous California Institute of Technology (Caltech), which boasts 22 Nobel Prize winners among its alumni. The Caltech-operated Jet Propulsion Laboratory was the birthplace of America's space program, and Caltech scientists were the first to report earthquake activity worldwide.

The residential neighborhoods in Pasadena and its adjacent communities—**Arcadia, La Cañada–Flintridge, San Marino,** and **South Pasadena**—are renowned for well-preserved historic homes, from humble bungalows to lavish mansions. These areas feature public gardens, historic neighborhoods, house museums, and bed-and-breakfast inns.

2 Getting Around

BY CAR

Need we tell you that Los Angeles is a car city? You're really going to need one to easily get around. An elaborate network of well-maintained freeways connects this urban sprawl, but you have to learn how to make sense of the system and cultivate some patience for dealing with the traffic. The golden rule of driving in Los Angeles is this: Always allow more time to get to your destination than you think you might need, especially during morning and evening rush hours. For an explanation of the city layout and details on the freeway system, see "Orientation," earlier in this chapter.

RENTALS

Los Angeles is one of the cheaper places in America to rent a car. Major national car-rental companies usually rent economy- and compact-class cars for about $35 per day and $120 per week with unlimited mileage.

All the major car-rental agencies have offices at the airport and in the larger hotels. See the Appendix at the back of this book for a comprehensive list of toll-free phone numbers and websites. If you're thinking of splurging, the place to call is **Budget Beverly Hills Car Collection,** 9815 Wilshire Blvd. (© **800/227-7117** or 310/274-9173), which rents SUVs, exotics, and luxury cars for $130 to $600 a day (a cute Audi TT roadster will set you back $250, for example).

SAVING MONEY ON A RENTAL CAR   Car-rental rates vary even more than airline fares. The price you pay will depend on the size of the car, where and when you pick it up and drop it off, the length of the rental period, where and how far you drive it, whether you purchase insurance, and a host of other factors. A few key questions could save you hundreds of dollars:

- Are weekend rates lower than weekday rates? Ask if the rate is the same for pickup Friday morning, for instance, as it is for Thursday night.
- Does the agency assess a drop-off charge if you don't return the car to the location where you picked it up?
- Are special promotional rates available? If you see an advertised price in your local newspaper, be sure to ask for that specific rate; otherwise, you may be charged the standard cost. Terms change constantly.
- Are discounts available for members of AARP, AAA, frequent-flyer programs, or trade unions? If you belong to any of these organizations, you may be entitled to discounts of up to 30%.
- How much tax will be added to the rental bill? Local tax? State use tax?
- How much does the company charge for gas if you return with the tank less than full? Though most companies claim these prices are "competitive," you

> ⸜ *Tips* **Traveling in Style**
>
> If you're looking to rub elbows with the stars but don't want to roll up in your '93 Ford Hooptee, why not rent a limo and do it up right? **Limo 4 Less** (© 562/592-5377; Limo4Less@aol.com), guarantees both a grand entrance and a great way to see the city in style (plus you can drink Champagne in the back seat). Whether you hire a stretch limousine or Lincoln Town Car, they both provide luxury transportation for any and all occasions, cover the entire Southern California region 24-7, and can pick you up at your hotel. Prices start at $40 per hour and vary according to type of vehicle and number of passengers.

will almost always save money if you refill the car yourself before you return it. Some offer "refueling packages," in which you pay for an entire tank of gas up front. The price is usually fairly competitive with local prices, but you don't get credit for any gas remaining in the tank. If a stop at a gas station on the way to the airport will make you miss your plane, then take advantage of the fuel purchase option; otherwise, skip it.

DEMYSTIFYING RENTER'S INSURANCE Before you drive off in a rental car, be sure you're insured. Assumptions about your personal auto insurance or a rental agency's additional coverage could end up costing you a lot—even if you are involved in an accident that was not your fault.

If you already hold a **private auto insurance** policy in the United States, you are most likely covered for loss of or damage to a rental car and liability in case of injury to any other party involved in an accident. Be sure to find out whether you are covered in the area you are visiting, whether your policy extends to all persons who will be driving the rental car, how much liability is covered in case an outside party is injured in an accident, and whether the type of vehicle you are renting is included under your contract. (Rental trucks, sport-utility vehicles, and luxury vehicles or sports cars may not be covered.)

Most **major credit cards** provide some degree of coverage as well—provided they were used to pay for the rental. Terms vary widely, so call your credit-card company before you rent. The credit card will usually cover damage or theft of a rental car for the full cost of the vehicle, minus a deductible. (In a few states, however, theft is not covered; ask specifically about state law where you will be renting and driving.) If you already have auto insurance, your credit card will provide secondary coverage—which basically covers your deductible.

Credit cards will not cover liability, or the cost of injury to an outside party and/or damage to an outside party's vehicle. If you do not hold an insurance policy, you may want to consider purchasing additional liability insurance from your rental company. Be sure to check the terms, however: Some rental agencies cover liability only if the renter is not at fault; even then, the rental company's obligation varies from state to state.

The basic insurance coverage offered by most car-rental companies, known as the **Loss/Damage Waiver (LDW)** or **Collision Damage Waiver (CDW),** can cost as much as $20 per day. It usually covers the full value of the vehicle with no deductible if an outside party causes an accident or other damage to the rental car. In all states but California, you will probably be covered in case of theft as well. Liability coverage varies according to the company policy and state law, but the minimum is usually at least $15,000. If you are at fault in an accident, however, you will be covered for the full replacement value of the car but not for liability. Some states allow you to buy additional liability coverage for such cases. Most rental companies will require a police report in order to process any claims you file, but your private insurer will not be notified of the accident.

Be sure to communicate any special needs in advance to the reservations agent. Most companies offer infant/child seats and vehicles equipped for drivers with disabilities. Many now offer portable cell phones with their cars—it's a good idea to consider this option. In addition to being invaluable for summoning help in case of an accident, they're also useful for calling for directions when you're lost and for getting roadside assistance in the event of mechanical difficulties.

PARKING

Explaining the parking situation in Los Angeles is like explaining the English language—there are more exceptions than rules. In some areas, every establishment has a convenient free lot or ample street parking; other areas are pretty manageable, as long as you have a quick eye and are willing to take a few turns around the block; but there are some frustrating parts of town (particularly around restaurants after 7:30pm) where you might have to give in and use valet parking. Whether there's valet parking depends more on the congestion of the area than on the elegance of the establishment these days; the size of an establishment's lot often simply won't allow for self-parking.

Restaurants and nightclubs sometimes provide a complimentary valet service, but more often they charge between $3 and $6. Some areas, like Santa Monica and Beverly Hills, offer self-park lots and garages near the neighborhood action; costs range from $2 to $10. Most of the hotels that we list in this book offer off-street parking, which ranges from free all the way up to $27 per day.

Here are a few parking tips to remember:

- **Be prepared for anything.** Always have a pocketful of quarters and a few $1 bills in case you need them. Downtown and Santa Monica are two of the worst areas for free parking.
- **Be creative.** "Case" the immediate area by taking a turn around the block. In many parts of the city you can find an unrestricted street space less than a block away from eager valets.
- **Read posted restrictions carefully.** You can avoid a ticket if you pay attention to the signs, which warn of street-cleaning schedules, rush hour "no parking," and resident "permit only" zones.

DRIVING

You may turn right at a red light after stopping unless a sign says otherwise. Likewise, you can turn left on a red light from a one-way street onto another

---

Tips **One-Stop Transportation Shopping**

Have to get somewhere? You can get your bearings by calling © 800/COMMUTE, an automated system that connects you to information on bus and rail transit schedules, freeway/highway information, bicycle and ride-share agencies, and more. Online, point your browser to **http://caltrans511.dot.ca.gov**, which provides links to the above information. Both systems were designed primarily to help L.A.'s commuters navigate the city and environs, but they have plenty to offer visitors as well.

one-way street after coming to a full stop. Keep in mind that pedestrians in Los Angeles have the right-of-way at all times, so stop for people who have stepped off the curb. Also, California has a seat-belt law for both drivers and passengers, so buckle up before you venture out.

Many Southern California freeways have designated **carpool lanes,** also known as High Occupancy Vehicle (HOV) lanes or "white diamond" lanes (after the large diamonds painted on the blacktop along the lane). Some require two passengers, others three. Most on-ramps are metered during even light congestion to regulate the flow of traffic onto the freeway; cars in HOV lanes can pass the signal without stopping. Although there are tales of drivers sitting life-sized mannequins next to them in order to beat the system, don't use the HOV lane unless you have the right numbers—fines begin at $271.

BY PUBLIC TRANSPORTATION

There are visitors who successfully tour Los Angeles entirely by public transportation, but we can't honestly recommend that plan for most readers. L.A. is a metropolis that's grown up around—and is best traversed by—the automobile, and many areas are inaccessible without one. As a result, an overwhelming number of visitors rent a car for their stay. Still, if you're in the city for only a short time, are on a very tight budget, or don't expect to be moving around a lot, public transport might be for you.

The city's trains and buses are operated by the **Los Angeles County Metropolitan Transit Authority** (MTA; ✆ 213-922-2000; www.mta.net), and MTA brochures and schedules are available at every area visitor center.

BY BUS

Spread-out sights, sluggish service, and frequent transfers make extensive touring by bus impractical. For short hops and occasional jaunts, however, buses are economical and environmentally correct. However, we don't recommend riding buses late at night.

The basic bus fare is $1.35 for all local lines, with transfers costing 25¢. Express buses, which travel along the freeways, and buses on intercounty routes charge higher fares; phone for information.

The **Downtown Area Short Hop (DASH)** shuttle system operates buses throughout Downtown and the Westside of L.A. Service runs every 5 to 20 minutes, depending on the time of day, and costs just 25¢. Contact the Dept. of Transportation (✆ 213/808-2273; www.ladottransit.com) for schedules and route information.

BY RAIL & SUBWAY

The **MetroRail** system is a sore subject around town. For years the MTA has been digging up the city's streets, sucking huge amounts of tax money, and pushing exhaust vents up through peaceful parkland—and for what? Let's face it, L.A. will never have New York's subway or San Francisco's BART. Today, the system is

---

Tips **Public Transport Tip**

The L.A. County Metropolitan Transit Authority (MTA) website, www.mta.net, provides all the practical information you need—hours, routes, fares—for using L.A.'s nearly invisible network of public transportation (buses, subways, light rail).

still in its infancy, mainly popular with commuters from outlying suburbs. Here's an overview of what's currently in place:

The **Metro Blue Line,** an aboveground rail line, connects downtown Los Angeles with Long Beach. Trains operate daily from 6am to 9pm; the fare is $1.35.

The **Metro Red Line,** L.A.'s first subway, has been growing since 1993 and opened a highly publicized Hollywood–Universal City extension in 2000. The line begins at Union Station, the city's main train depot, and travels west underneath Wilshire Boulevard, looping north into Hollywood and the San Fernando Valley. The fare is $1.35; discount tokens are available at Metro service centers and many area convenience stores.

The **Metro Green Line,** opened in 1995, runs for 20 miles (32km) along the center of the new I-105, the Glenn Anderson (Century) Freeway, and connects Norwalk in eastern Los Angeles County to LAX. A connection with the Blue Line offers visitors access from LAX to downtown L.A. or Long Beach. The fare is $1.35.

Call the **MTA** (✆ **213-922-2000;** www.mta.net) for information on the Metro, including construction updates and details on purchasing tokens or passes.

BY TAXI

Distances are long in Los Angeles, and cab fares are high; even a short trip can cost $10 or more. Taxis charge $1.90 at the flag drop, plus $1.60 per mile. A service charge is added to fares originating at LAX.

Except in the heart of downtown, cabs will usually not pull over when hailed. Cabstands are located at airports, at downtown's Union Station, and major hotels. To ensure a ride, order a taxi in advance from **Checker Cab** (✆ **323/654-8400**), **L.A. Taxi** (✆ **213/627-7000**), or **United Taxi** (✆ **213/483-7604**).

✆ *FAST FACTS:* **Los Angeles**

American Express In addition to those at 327 N. Beverly Dr., Beverly Hills (✆ **310/274-8277**), and at the Beverly Connection, 8493 W. 3rd St., Los Angeles (✆310/659-1682), offices are located throughout the city. To locate one nearest you, call ✆ **800/221-7282.**

Area Codes Within the past 20 years, L.A. has gone from having a single (213) area code to a whopping seven—with more promised by 2003. Even residents can't keep up. As of press time, here's the basic layout: Those areas west of La Cienega Boulevard, including Beverly Hills and the city's beach communities, use the **310** area code. Portions of Los Angeles county east and south of the city, including Long Beach, are in the **562** area. The San Fernando Valley has the **818** area code, while points east—including parts of Burbank, Glendale, and Pasadena—use the newly created **626** code. What happened to 213, you ask? The downtown business area still uses **213.** All other numbers, including Griffith Park, Hollywood, and parts of West Hollywood (east of La Cienega Blvd.) now use the new area code **323.** If it's all too much to remember, just call directory assistance at ✆ **411.**

Babysitters If you're staying at one of the larger hotels, the concierge can usually recommend a reliable babysitter. If not, contact the **Baby-Sitters**

Guild in Glendale (© **323/658-8792** or 818/552-2229), L.A.'s oldest and largest babysitting service.

Camera Repair On-site repairs are the specialty at family owned **General Camera Repair,** 2218 E. Colorado Blvd., Pasadena (© **626/449-4533**); they opened in 1964 at this spot on the Rose Parade route.

Dentists For a recommendation in the area, call the **Dental Referral Service** (© **800/422-8338**).

Doctors Contact the **Uni-Health Information and Referral Hotline** (© **800/922-0000**) for a free, confidential physician referral.

Emergencies For police, fire, or highway patrol, or in case of life-threatening medical emergencies, dial © **911.**

Hospital The centrally located (and world-famous) **Cedars-Sinai Medical Center,** 8700 Beverly Blvd., Los Angeles (© **310/855-5000**), has a 24-hour emergency room staffed by some of the country's finest MDs.

Hot Lines Alcoholics Anonymous © **323/936-4343;** Poison Hotline © **800/876-4766;** National AIDS Hotline © **800/342-AIDS;** Rape/Domestic Violence Hotline (L.A. Commission on Assault Against Women) © **213/626-3393;** Suicide Crisis Line © **310/391-1253.**

Liquor Laws Liquor and grocery stores can sell packaged alcoholic beverages between 6am and 2am. Most restaurants, nightclubs, and bars are licensed to serve alcoholic drinks during the same hours. The legal age for purchase and consumption is 21; proof of age is required.

Newspapers & Magazines See "Other Information Sources" earlier in this chapter. **World Book & News Co.,** at 1652 N. Cahuenga Blvd., near Hollywood and Vine and Mann's Chinese Theater, stocks lots of out-of-town and foreign papers and magazines. No one minds if you browse through the magazines, but you'll be reprimanded for thumbing through the newspapers. It's open 24 hours.

Pharmacies **Horton & Converse** has locations around L.A., including 2001 Santa Monica Blvd., Santa Monica (© **310/829-3401**); 9201 Sunset Blvd., Beverly Hills (© **323/272-0488**); and 11600 Wilshire Blvd., West Los Angeles (© **310/478-0801**). Hours vary, but the West L.A. location is open until 2am.

Police In an emergency, dial © **911.** For nonemergency police matters, call © **213/485-2121;** in Beverly Hills, dial © **310/550-4951.**

Post Office Call © **800/ASK-USPS** to find the one closest to you.

Taxes The combined Los Angeles County and California state sales taxes amount to 8.25%; hotel taxes add 12% to 17% to room tariffs.

Taxis See "Getting Around,"earlier in this chapter.

Time Zone Los Angeles is in the Pacific time zone, which is 8 hours behind Greenwich mean time and 3 hours behind eastern time. Call © **853-1212** for the correct time (operates in all local area codes).

Weather Call **Los Angeles Weather Information** (© **213/554-1212**) for the daily forecast. For beach conditions, call the **Zuma Beach Lifeguard** recorded information (© **310/457-9701**).

5

Where to Stay

In sprawling Los Angeles, location is everything. The neighborhood you choose as a base can make or break your vacation. If you plan to spend your days at the beach but stay Downtown, for example, you're going to lose a lot of valuable relaxation time on the freeway. For business travelers, choosing a location is easy: Pick a hotel near your work—don't commute if you don't have to. For vacationers, though, the decision about where to stay is more difficult. Consider where you want to spend your time before you commit yourself to a base. But wherever you stay, count on doing a good deal of driving—no hotel in Los Angeles is convenient to everything.

The relatively smog-free **beach communities** are understandably popular with visitors—just about everybody loves to stay at the beach. Book ahead, because hotels fill up quickly, especially in summer.

Most visitors stay on the city's **Westside,** a short drive from the beach and close to most of L.A.'s most colorful sights. The city's most elegant and expensive accommodations are in **Beverly Hills** and **Bel Air;** a few of the hotels in these neighborhoods, such as the Beverly Hills Hotel, have become visitor attractions unto themselves. The focal point of L.A. nightlife, **West Hollywood** is home to the greatest range and breadth of hotels, from $300-plus-per-night boutiques to affordably priced motels.

There are fewer hotels in **Hollywood** than you might expect. Accommodations are generally moderately priced and well maintained but unspectacular. Centrally located between Downtown and Beverly Hills, just a stone's throw from Universal Studios, Hollywood makes a convenient base if you're planning to do a lot of exploring, but it has more tourists and is less attractive than some other neighborhoods.

Downtown hotels are generally business-oriented, but thanks to direct Metro (L.A.'s subway) connections to Hollywood and Universal Studios, the demographic has begun to shift. The top hotels offer excellent-value weekend packages. But chances are good that Downtown doesn't embody the picture of L.A. you've been dreaming of; you need a coastal or Westside base for that.

Families might want to head to the **San Fernando Valley** to be near Universal Studios, or straight to Anaheim and Disneyland (see chapter 8). **Pasadena** boasts historic charm, small-town ambience, and picture-postcard beauty, but driving to the beach can take forever.

RACK RATES The **rates** quoted in the listings that follow are the rack rates—the maximum rates that a hotel charges for rooms. But rack rates are only guidelines, and there are often ways around them; see "Tips for Saving on Your Hotel Room," below.

The hotels that we list in this chapter have provided us with their best estimates for 2003, and all rates were correct at press time. **Be aware that rates can change at any time,** and are subject to availability, seasonal fluctuations, and plain old increases.

Value Tips for Saving on Your Hotel Room

In the listings in this chapter, we try to give you an idea of the kind of deals that may be available at particular hotels: which ones have the best discounted packages, which ones offer AAA and other discounts, which ones allow kids to stay with Mom and Dad for free, and so on. But there's no way of knowing what the offers will be when you're booking, so also consider these general tips:

- **Don't be afraid to bargain.** Always ask for a lower price than the first one quoted. Most rack rates include commissions of 10% to 25% for travel agents, which many hotels might cut if you haggle. Ask politely whether a less-expensive room is available or whether any special rates apply to you, such as corporate, student, military, senior citizen, or other discounts. Always mention membership in AAA, AARP, frequent-flyer programs, corporate or military organizations, or trade unions, which might entitle you to deals. The big chains tend to be good about trying to save you money, but reservation agents often won't volunteer the information; you have to dig for it.

- **Remember the law of supply and demand.** Coastal and resort hotels are most crowded and therefore most expensive on weekends, so discounts are often available for midweek stays. On the other hand, downtown and business hotels are busiest during the week, while discounts tend to be abundant on weekends. Planning your vacation just before or after the peak summer season can mean big savings. For more on L.A.'s travel seasons, see "When to Go" in chapter 2.

- **Book early.** As hotels fill up and the number of available rooms goes down, rates go up—so book as far in advance as possible. You can even get burned at those hotels that don't jack up their rates according to demand, because hotels often have only a limited number of rooms in a particular price category, and the most affordable ones usually go first.

- **Dial direct.** When booking a room in a chain hotel, call the hotel's local line, as well as the toll-free number, and see where you get the best deal. The clerk who runs the place is more likely to know vacancies and will often grant discounts in order to fill up.

- **Rely on a qualified professional.** Certain hotels give travel agents discounts in exchange for steering business their way, so an agent may be better equipped to negotiate discounts for you.

- **Buy a package deal.** A travel package that includes your plane tickets and hotel stay for one price might be the best bargain of all. In some cases, you can get airfare, accommodations, transportation to and from the airport, plus extras—maybe even discounts on theme-park admission—for less than the price of the hotel if you booked it yourself. See the box called "Package Tours" in chapter 2.

- **Investigate reservation services.** These services usually work as consolidators, buying up or reserving rooms in bulk and then dealing them out to customers. They sometimes garner special rates that range from 10% to 50% off rack rates. If you don't like bargaining, this is certainly a viable option. Among the more reputable reservations services, offering both telephone and online bookings, are: **Accommodations Express** (© 800/950-4685; www.accommodation sexpress.com); **Hotel Reservations Network** (© 800/715-7666; www.hoteldiscounts.com or www.180096HOTEL.com); **Quikbook** (© 800/789-9887, includes fax on demand service; www.quik book.com). Online, try booking your hotel through **Arthur Frommer's Budget Travel** (www.frommers.com). **Microsoft Expedia** (www.expedia.com) features a "Travel Agent" that will also direct you to affordable lodgings.

    Important tips: Never just rely on a reservations service. Do a little homework; compare the rack rates to the discounted rates being offered by the service. And always check the rate a reservations service offers you with the rate you can get directly from the hotel, which can be better. If you're being offered a stay in a hotel we haven't recommended, do more research to learn about it, especially if it isn't a known brand. *It's not a deal if you end up at a dump.* And make sure the hotel is really based in L.A.; many of these reservations services try to pass off properties as being in the city while they're actually in the boonies. Santa Clarita is *not* "L.A. proper," or anything resembling Vacationland.

- **Consider a suite.** If you are traveling with your family or another couple, a suite can be a terrific bargain, as they're almost always cheaper than two hotel rooms, and usually feature sofa beds in the living room. Some places charge for extra guests beyond two, some don't, so check.

- **Book a room with kitchen facilities.** A room with a kitchenette allows you to grocery shop and eat some meals in. Even if you only use it to prepare breakfast, you're bound to save money on food.

- **Use the Web.** A lot of hotel rate specials are only offered on the Web, particularly for the less expensive hotels. See the **"Site Seeing: The Best of L.A. Online"** sidebar on p. 36 for links to a wide range of L.A. hotel websites. Happy hunting.

- **If you're traveling with the kids, choose a hotel that lets them stay for free.** Most hotels add a surcharge—from $10 to $30 per night—for each person beyond two sharing a hotel room. If you're traveling with kids, look for a hotel where they stay for free. Age limits for free kid stays can range from 10 to 18. Even if the hotel usually charges for kids, it might be willing to drop this extra charge to draw you in, so always ask.

PET POLICIES   We indicate in the listings below those hotels that generally accept pets. However, these policies may have limitations, such as weight and breed restrictions; may require a deposit and/or a signed waiver against damages; and may be revoked at any time. Always inquire when booking if you're bringing Bowser or Fluffy along—*never* just show up with pet in tow.

1 Santa Monica & the Beaches

Southern California means one thing to many people—the beach. If surf and sand comprise the So Cal image in your mind's eye, don't consider staying anywhere but here. Not only will you avoid the traffic crush as everyone from the rest of the city flocks to the seaside on clear, sunny days, but also you can soak up the laid-back vibe that only beach communities have.

With its wide beach, amusement pier, abundant dining and shopping, and easy freeway access, Santa Monica is the glittering jewel of the L.A. coast. A Venice location puts you at the heart of the wild, colorful human carnival that is Venice Beach, while Marina del Rey is the destination for those who want a sparkling, serene marina scene. World-famous Malibu is the ultimate symbol of the star-studded, sun-soaked coastal L.A. lifestyle, and offers good surf to boot—but be prepared to spend lots of time in the car, as this high-rent enclave is at least a half-hour drive from everything.

LAX is also near the coast, so airport-area accommodations are found in this section as well.

VERY EXPENSIVE

Casa del Mar ★★★   Housed in a former 1920s Renaissance Revival beach club, this Art Deco stunner is a real dream of a resort hotel, equal in every respect to big sister Shutters just down the beach (see below). Which one you prefer depends on your personal sense of style. While Shutters is outfitted like a chic contemporary beach house, this impeccable, U-shaped villalike structure radiates period glamour. The building's shape awards ocean views to most of the guest rooms; unfortunately, windows don't open more than an inch or two (which gives Shutters, whose rooms have floor-to-ceiling windows and balconies, a slight advantage). You're unlikely to be too disappointed thanks to the gorgeous summery European inspired decor in golds and sea grass hues, plus abundant luxuries that include sumptuously dressed beds, big Italian marble bathrooms with extra-large whirlpool tubs and separate showers; rubber duckies and turndown teddies are playful treats. Rooms are laid out for relaxation, not business, so travelers with work on their minds should stay elsewhere.

Downstairs you'll find a big, elegant living room with ocean views, a stylish lounge, and the **Oceanfront** restaurant, which has earned justifiable kudos (and more than a few celebrity fans) for its lovely setting, great service, and seafood-heavy California cuisine. Outdoors, the Mediterranean-evocative Palm Terrace boasts a gorgeous Roman-style pool and Jacuzzi with spectacular ocean views.

1910 Ocean Way (next to the Santa Monica Pier), Santa Monica, CA 90405. © **800/898-6999** or 310/581-5533. Fax 310/581-5503. www.hotelcasadelmar.com. 129 units. $345–$625 double; from $875 suite. AE, DC, DISC, MC, V. Valet parking $21. **Amenities:** Oceanfront restaurant; Lobby Lounge for cocktails and light fare; alfresco cafe for daytime dining; heated outdoor Roman-style pool; plunge pool; and Jacuzzi overlooking Santa Monica Beach; state-of-the-art health club with spa services; 24-hour concierge; business center; 24-hour room service; dry-cleaning/laundry service. *In room:* A/C, TV/VCR, CD, dataport, minibar, hair dryer, iron, laptop-size safe.

Hotel Oceana ★★ *Kids*   Located right across the street from the ocean, this all-suite hotel sits alongside low-rise, high-rent condos on a gorgeous stretch of Ocean Avenue, several blocks north of the Santa Monica hubbub. With their bright Matisse-style interiors and cushy IKEA-ish furniture, the wonderful apartment-like suites are colorful, modern, and amenity laden: Goodies run the gamut from comfy robes, multiple TVs, and CD players to full gourmet kitchens stocked with Wolfgang Puck microwavable pizzas, Häagen-Dazs pints, and bottles of California Merlot. The enormous size of the suites—even the studios are huge—makes the Oceana terrific for families or shares. Ocean-view suites feature balconies and two-person whirlpool tubs in the mammoth bathrooms, but don't feel the need to stretch your budget for a view, as all units sit garden style around the darling courtyard, with its cushiony chaises and cute boomerang-shaped pool. Everything is fresh, welcoming, and noninstitutional—the primary colors and playful modern style suits the beach location perfectly, and service is excellent—so it's no wonder advertising execs and others who could stay anywhere make the Oceana their choice for long-term stays.

849 Ocean Ave. (south of Montana Ave.), Santa Monica, CA 90403. © **800/777-0758** or 310/393-0486. Fax 310/309-2762 (reservations) or 310/458-1182. www.hoteloceana.com. 63 units. $380 studio suite; $390–$500 1-bedroom suite; $750–$800 2-bedroom suite. AE, DC, DISC, MC, V. Valet parking $21. **Amenities:** Outdoor heated pool; 24-hour room service; exercise room; access to nearby health club; watersports equipment; concierge; business center; room service from Wolfgang Puck Cafe (7am–10pm); in-room massage; babysitting; dry-cleaning/laundry service. *In room:* A/C, TV/VCR w/pay movies, video games, and Internet access; CD player; dataport; kitchen with minibar, fridge, coffeemaker, and microwave; hair dryer; iron; safe.

Loews Santa Monica Beach Hotel ★ *Kids*   L.A.'s finest family friendly hotel is also a great choice for anybody looking for comfortable accommodations, an A-1 Santa Monica location, outstanding service, and a wealth of first-rate facilities. Loews isn't exactly beachfront; it's on a hill less than a block away, but the unobstructed ocean views are fabulous. The hotel emerged from a massive $15 million renovation that erased its greatest disadvantage—dour rooms that didn't live up to the luxury price tag. Those who've been here before will notice the differences immediately upon entering the dramatic atrium lobby, whose nondescript fittings have been replaced with a playful So Cal style (include dual rows of huge palm trees) that puts greater emphasis on the spectacular ocean views. The formerly dowdy guest rooms have been redone in an inviting, clean-lined contemporary style in light, earthy colors. But the best news is still the top-rate facilities, which include an excellent heated pool, plus the Fitness Center & Spa with a state-of-the-art gym, yoga and Pilates classes, health and fitness counseling, and full slate of spa and salon services.

1700 Ocean Ave. (south of Colorado Blvd.), Santa Monica, CA 90401. © **800/235-6397** or 310/458-6700. Fax 310/458-6761. www.loewshotels.com. 340 units. $305–$460 double; from $675 suite. Ask about corporate rates, Internet offers, and other discounts. Children under 18 stay free in parents' room. AE, DC, DISC, MC, V. Valet parking $18. Pets under 50 pounds accepted with $500 refundable deposit, plus $5-per-day cleaning fee. **Amenities:** Elegant Cal-Mediterranean dining at Lavande; Papillon Lobby Bar and Fireside Lounge (for afternoon tea, light dining, Visiting Artists Series); poolside lunch service; ocean-view outdoor heated pool and whirlpool; Pritikin Longevity Center & Spa with full spa services, state-of-the-art workout room, steam, and sauna; bike and skate rentals; welcome kit for kids under 10; concierge; Hertz car-rental desk; executive business center; salon; 24-hour room service; dry-cleaning/laundry service. *In room:* A/C, TV, CD, dataport, minibar, daily newspaper, hair dryer, iron.

Shutters on the Beach ★★★   This Cape Cod–style luxury hotel enjoys one of the city's most prized locations: directly on the beach, a block from Santa Monica Pier. Only relative newcomer Casa del Mar (above) can compete, but

Accommodations in Santa Monica & the Beaches

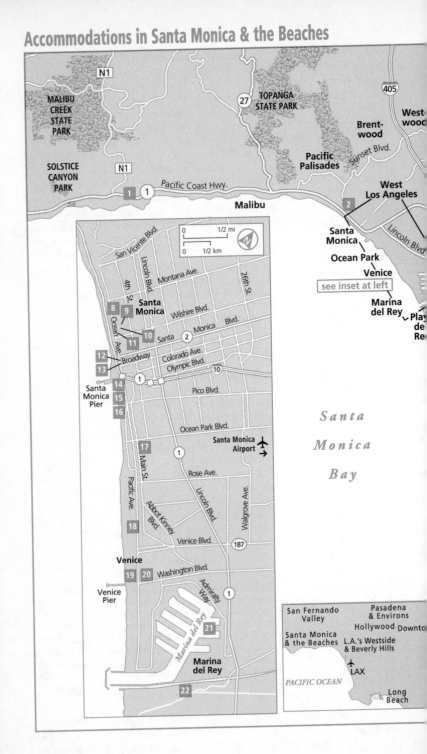

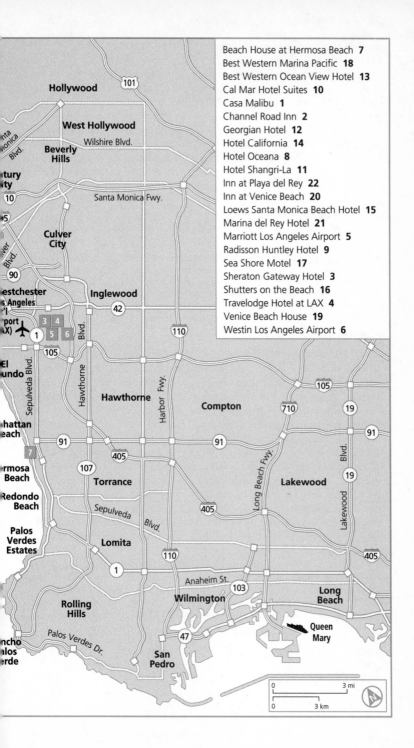

Beach House at Hermosa Beach **7**
Best Western Marina Pacific **18**
Best Western Ocean View Hotel **13**
Cal Mar Hotel Suites **10**
Casa Malibu **1**
Channel Road Inn **2**
Georgian Hotel **12**
Hotel California **14**
Hotel Oceana **8**
Hotel Shangri-La **11**
Inn at Playa del Rey **22**
Inn at Venice Beach **20**
Loews Santa Monica Beach Hotel **15**
Marina del Rey Hotel **21**
Marriott Los Angeles Airport **5**
Radisson Huntley Hotel **9**
Sea Shore Motel **17**
Sheraton Gateway Hotel **3**
Shutters on the Beach **16**
Travelodge Hotel at LAX **4**
Venice Beach House **19**
Westin Los Angeles Airport **6**

Shutters bests the Casa by attaching alfresco balconies to every guest room. The beach-cottage rooms overlooking the sand are more desirable and no more expensive than those in the towers. The views and sounds of the ocean are the most outstanding qualities of the spacious, luxuriously outfitted, Cape Cod–inspired rooms, some of which have fireplaces and/or whirlpool tubs; all have floor-to-ceiling windows that open. The elegant marble bathrooms come with generous counter space and welcome whimsies that include waterproof radios and toy whales. A relaxed and elegant ambience pervades the contemporary art-filled public spaces, which feel like the common areas of a deluxe Montauk beach house. The small swimming pool and the sunny lobby lounge overlooking the sand are two great perches for spotting the celebrities who swear by Shutters as an alternative hangout to smoggy Hollywood. **One Pico,** the hotel's premier restaurant, serves Modern American Cuisine in a seaside setting; the best meals at the more casual **Pedals Cafe** come from the wood-burning grill.

1 Pico Blvd., Santa Monica, CA 90405. ℭ **800/334-9000** or 310/458-0030. Fax 310/458-4589. www. shuttersonthebeach.com. 198 units. $380–$615 double; from $895 suite. AE, DC, DISC, MC, V. Valet parking $22. **Amenities:** Restaurant; cafe; lobby lounge; outdoor heated pool and Jacuzzi; health club with spa services; sauna; extensive beach equipment rentals; concierge; activities desk; courtesy car; business center with secretarial services; 24-hour room service; babysitting; dry-cleaning/laundry service; video library. *In room:* A/C, TV/VCR, CD, dataport, private mini wine cellar, hair dryer, iron, laptop-size safe.

EXPENSIVE

Beach House at Hermosa Beach ★★ *(Finds)*　Sporting a Cape Cod style that suits the on-the-sand location, this luxurious, romantic inn is comprised of beautifully designed and outfitted split-level studio suites. Every unit boasts a plush, furnished living room, with wood-burning fireplace (Duraflame logs provided) and entertainment center; a micro-kitchen with china and flatware for four; an elevated sleeping niche with a down-dressed king bed, a second TV, and a generous work area; an extra-large bathroom with extra-deep soaking tub, a separate shower, cotton robes, and Aveda products; and a furnished balcony, many of which overlook the beach. (While sofas convert into second beds, the unit configuration is best suited to couples rather than families; more than three is too many.) Despite the summertime carnival atmosphere of the Strand, the Beach House keeps serene with double-paned windows and noise-insulated walls. The attentive staff has an easygoing attitude that suits the property perfectly. While L.A.'s city center is an easy half-hour's drive away, charming Hermosa is airport-convenient and ideal for a beach getaway.

1300 The Strand, Hermosa Beach, CA 90254. ℭ **888/895-4559** or 310/374-3001. Fax 310/372-2115. www.beach-house.com. 96 units. $209–$349 double. Rates include continental breakfast. AE, DC, DISC, MC, V. Valet parking $17. **Amenities:** Room service from nearby restaurant; concierge; dry-cleaning/laundry service. *In room:* Menu of spa services, A/C, 2 TVs; stereo with 5-disk CD changer; dataport; stocked kitchenette with microwave, coffee-maker, stovetop, fridge; hair dryer; iron.

Channel Road Inn ★　The innkeeper has used her eye for design to outfit this beautiful Colonial revival house in gracious period style. The individually appointed rooms boast pine furnishings, carefully selected antiques, top-quality textiles and linens, VCRs, and spacious, nicely renovated baths. Some have four-poster beds covered with hand-sewn Amish quilts; others have fireplaces, and others feature whirlpool tubs. Don't expect much from the promise of an ocean view, however; you'll overlook a busy street, wires, and rooftops for your sliver of blue. Another quirk is the lot on which the house sits, which boasts no greenery or garden space other than a hillside hot tub. Dominated by an impressive Batch elder tile fireplace, the impeccably decorated living room makes an ideal place to curl up with a book. If you'd rather head outside, the staff will provide bicycles, beach chairs, and towels for your use. We prefer Channel Road's sister property, the Inn at Playa del Rey (see below), which doesn't have the quirks that this property does; still, this is a lovely, comfortable, and well-run B&B in a terrific location for beach lovers.

219 W. Channel Rd., Santa Monica, CA 90402. ⓒ 310/459-1920. Fax 310/454-9920. www.channelroad inn.com. 14 units. $145–$285 double; from $295 suite. AE, MC, V. All rates include full breakfast and afternoon tea, wine, and hors d'oeuvres. Free parking. **Amenities:** Outdoor Jacuzzi; access to nearby health club; business center; video library. *In room:* A/C, TV/VCR, dataport, hair dryer, iron.

Georgian Hotel ★ *Finds*   This eight-story Art Deco beauty boasts luxury comforts, loads of historic charm, and a terrific ocean-view location, just across the street from Santa Monica's beach and pier, with prime Ocean Avenue dining just steps away. Established in 1933, the former Lady Windermere was popular among Hollywood's golden-age elite; it even had its own speakeasy, rumored to have been established by Bugsy Siegel (guests now enjoy breakfast in the historic room). Today, the elegant classic-revival architecture is beautifully accented with a well-chosen palette of bold pastels (à la Miami Beach's hotels of the same era). A wonderful veranda with cushy wicker chaises and unobstructed ocean views opens onto a light and airy lobby with comfortable seating nooks. An attended elevator leads to beautifully designed guest rooms that are an ideal blend of nostalgic style and modern-day amenities. Fittings include furnishings upholstered in gorgeous nubby textiles, mattresses dressed in goose-down comforters, ceiling fans, and terry robes; suites have sleeper sofas and CD players as well. The hotel has an unobstructed coastal vista, so most rooms have at least a partial or full ocean view; the best views are above the third floor. Front rooms can be a bit noisy, so ask for a Malibu view for the best of both worlds. Back-facing rooms have city views that are more attractive than you'd expect, so nobody loses; these rooms are best for light sleepers.

1415 Ocean Ave. (between Santa Monica Blvd. and Broadway), Santa Monica, CA 90401. ⓒ 800/ 538-8147 or 310/395-9945. Fax 310/656-0904. www.georgianhotel.com. 84 units. $235–$310 double; from $350 suite. Inquire about packages. AE, DC, DISC, MC, V. Valet parking $18. **Amenities:** Speakeasy Restaurant for breakfast; lobby bar; exercise room; concierge; activities desk; room service (6:30am–10:30pm); dry-cleaning/laundry service. *In room:* TV w/pay movies and Nintendo, fax, dataport, minibar, coffeemaker, hair dryer, iron, laptop-size safe.

Inn at Playa del Rey ★★ *Finds*   A half-hour drive from L.A. proper, our favorite L.A. B&B is less than ideal for sightseers with packed itineraries, but great for those looking for romance, a relaxed small-town vibe, or airport convenience. Only 5 minutes from LAX, the pampering inn is as much a sanctuary from the city as the protected wetlands outside the back door. From the street, the contemporary structure looks like a set of condos; inside, it glows with its true character. Fresh salty breezes and the soft chirps of waterfowl fill a spacious yet cozy fireplace lounge, whose long veranda overlooks peaceful marshland. Hiking trails wind through the wildlife preserve; a wooden observation platform 50 yards out is ideal for contemplation, bird-watching, or spying on sailboats that pass through the channel. A beach suitable for swimming is a short walk away, and bicycles are on hand for cruising a coastal path.

The impeccably decorated, amenity-laden guest rooms are outfitted in a classy-yet-casual, sophisticated style that evokes the best of Nantucket or Santa Barbara. Country-chic furnishings, snuggly comforters, and plush bathrobes and towels are on hand. Luxuries include DirecTV hidden in handsome armoires and all-new bathrooms, many with whirlpool tubs; most rooms have balconies as well. The ultimate in romance are the spacious View Suites, whose two-sided fireplaces cast a heavenly glow on both the luxuriously made bed and the inviting double Jacuzzi. A garden hot tub is available for those booking simpler accommodations.

435 Culver Blvd., Playa del Rey, CA 90293. (C) **310/574-1920.** Fax 310/574-9920. www.innatplaya delrey.com. 21 units. $185–$265 double; $350 suite. Midweek discounts available. Rates include full breakfast and afternoon wine and cheese. AE, MC, V. Free parking. From LAX, take Sepulveda Blvd. north, veering left onto Lincoln Blvd.; turn left at Jefferson Blvd., which turns into Culver Blvd. **Amenities:** Outdoor Jacuzzi; access to nearby health club; small gym; business center; massage; complimentary bicycles; video library. *In room:* A/C, TV/VCR w/ free movies, dataport, hair dryer, iron, safe.

MODERATE

Best Western Ocean View Hotel   This ocean-facing chain hotel, located just across the street from Santa Monica Beach and amusement pier, offers welcome price relief in high-rent Santa Monica. The clean and modern property offers terrific bargains to those willing to forego an ocean view from their room. But even the deluxe view rooms, which all have private balconies looking out across Ocean Avenue to beach and pier, are a steal for this area. Rooms are decently and comfortably outfitted in chain-hotel style; all have coffeemakers, while ocean-view rooms have fridges, too (microwaves are available upon request). Don't pay extra for a balcony, though, unless you know it's ocean view, or you may end up overlooking the subterranean parking lot. The staff is courteous and professional, and many fine restaurants are within walking distance. Heck, they even offer complimentary continental breakfast.

1447 Ocean Ave., Santa Monica, CA 90401. (C) **800/452-4888** or 310/458-4888. Fax 310/458-0848. www.bestwestern.com/oceanviewhotel. 66 units. Summer $149–$229 double; winter $99–$179. Rates include continental breakfast. AAA, AARP, midweek, and other discounts available. AE, DC, DISC, MC, V. Parking $10. **Amenities:** Activities desk; fax and copy services; dry-cleaning/laundry service. *In room:* A/C, TV, dataport, coffeemaker, hair dryer, iron.

Casa Malibu ★★ *Finds*   Sitting right on its very own beach, this leftover jewel from Malibu's golden age doesn't try to play the sleek resort game (and what a refreshing exception). Instead, the modest, low-rise inn sports a traditional California-beach-cottage look that's cozy and timeless.

Tips More Important Advice on Accommodations

The prices given in this book do not include state and city **hotel taxes,** which run from 12% to 17%, depending upon which municipality the hotel is based in. Most hotels in densely populated parts of the city make additional charges for **parking** (with in-and-out privileges), which we include in their listings. Also, some provide a **free airport shuttle;** if you're not renting a car, check to see what your hotel offers before you hop in a cab.

For an easy-to-scan introduction to the best of what the city has to offer, check out **"Best Bets for Accommodations"** in chapter 1. For help in choosing a location, take a look at **"Neighborhoods in Brief"** in chapter 4.

Wrapped around a palm-studded inner courtyard brightened with well-tended flower beds and climbing *cuppa d'oro* vines, the 21 rooms are comfortable, charming, and thoughtfully outfitted. Many have been upgraded with Mexican-tile bathrooms, air-conditioning (almost never needed on the coast), and VCRs, but even the older ones are in great shape and boast top-quality bedding and bathrobes. Depending on which you choose, you might also find a fireplace, a kitchenette (in a half-dozen or so), a CD player (in suites), a tub (instead of shower only), and/or a private deck over the sand. The upstairs Catalina Suite (Lana Turner's old hideout) has the best view, while the gorgeous Malibu Suite—the best room in the house, and, like the Beachfront rooms, located right on the beach—offers state-of-the-art pampering. More than half have ocean views, but even those facing the courtyard are quiet and offer easy beach access via wooden stairs to the private stretch of beach, which is raked smooth each morning. There's also a handsome, wind-shielded brick sun deck, which extends directly over the sand, allowing everyone to enjoy the blue Pacific even in cool months. Book well ahead for summer—this one's a favorite of locals and visitors alike.

22752 Pacific Coast Hwy. (about ¼ mile south of Malibu Pier), Malibu, CA 90265. ℂ 800/831-0858 or 310/456-2119. Fax 310/456-5418. www.casamalibu.com. 21 units. $99–$169 garden- or ocean-view double; $199–$229 beachfront double; $229–$349 suite. Rates include continental breakfast. Extra person $15. AE, MC, V. Free parking. **Amenities:** Private beach; room service for lunch and dinner; access to nearby private health club; in-room massage; dry-cleaning/laundry service. *In room:* TV, 2-line telephone with dataport, fridge, coffeemaker, hair dryer, iron.

The Hotel California ⭐ *Finds*   New management has remade this former backpackers' flophouse into a clean, welcoming hacienda-style beachfront motel that reflects the owner's love of surfing and California beach nostalgia. Boasting an enviable location on Ocean Avenue—right next door to the behemoth Loews—this place embodies the ocean ambience we all want from Santa Monica. The well-tended complex sits above and across an alley from the beach, but offers excellent views and direct access to the sand via a 5-minute walk along a pretty stepped path. Fully renovated in 2000, the inn offers small, comfortable rooms with brand-new furnishings, including beds with down comforters; freshly refinished woodwork on doors, floors, and decks; retiled bathrooms with new fixtures; and lovingly tended landscaping. Five one-bedroom suites also have kitchenettes and pullout sofas that make them great for families or longer stays; all rooms have minifridges and ceiling fans. The suites and some rooms have a partially obstructed ocean view. A handful of rooms have showers only in the bathrooms, so be sure to request a room with a tub from the friendly front-desk staff if it matters to you. *Tip:* Pay a few bucks extra for a courtyard view, as the cheapest rooms face the parking lot and noisy Ocean Avenue.

1670 Ocean Ave. (south of Colorado Ave.), Santa Monica, CA 90401. ℂ 866/571-0000 or 310/393-2363. Fax 310/393-1063. www.hotelca.com. 26 units. $169–$279 double or suite. AE, DISC, MC, V. Self-parking $9. **Amenities:** Jacuzzi; activities desk; discount car-rental desk; high-speed Internet access, fax/copier, and coffeemaker in front office. *In room:* TV/VCR, dataport, fridge, hair dryer, iron.

Hotel Shangri-La   Perched on Ocean Avenue overlooking the Pacific, in a high-rent residential neighborhood just 2 blocks from Third Street Promenade shopping and dining, the seven-story Shangri-La has a great location. Built in 1939, the hotel sports an ultramodern exterior and Art Deco interiors to match. The laminated furnishings are ugly and the hotel is decidedly low-tech, but considering the location, size, and comfort of these rooms—not to mention the free parking—the Shangri-La is a very good deal and the management is constantly making improvements. Guest rooms, which are mostly studio suites (most with kitchenettes, all with fridges), are extremely spacious, and most offer unencumbered ocean views. Bathrooms are small and simple but clean. The two-bedroom/two-bathroom suites are spectacular bargains for large families. Just across the street is a gorgeous stretch of Palisades Park, which overlooks the beach and offers the coast's finest sunset views.

1301 Ocean Ave. (at Arizona Ave.), Santa Monica, CA 90401. 📞 **800/345-STAY** or 310/394-2791. Fax 310/451-3351. www.shangrila-hotel.com. 54 units. From $170 studio; from $215 1-bedroom suite, from $330 2-bedroom suite. Rates include continental breakfast and afternoon tea. Inquire about 10% discount for AAA members. AE, DC, DISC, MC, V. Free parking. **Amenities:** Small ocean-view exercise room; coin-op laundry; dry-cleaning/laundry service. *In room:* A/C, TV, dataport, fridge, hair dryer, laptop-size safe.

Marina del Rey Hotel   Beautifully situated on a pier jutting into the harbor, this modest low-rise hotel is bounded on three sides by the world's largest man-made marina; in fact, location is its best feature. The property is peaceful and quiet—the only noise you're likely to hear is the soothing metallic clang of sail-boat rigging. Guest rooms are motel-basic but perfectly fine, with contemporary furnishings and a nautical nods here and there. Most units have balconies or patios as well as harbor views; ask for one overlooking the main channel for the best view of the constant parade of boats. As long as you snare a rate below $170 or so, you're in good-value territory; otherwise, book elsewhere.

13534 Bali Way (west of Lincoln Blvd.), Marina del Rey, CA 90292. 📞 **800/882-4000** or 310/301-1000. Fax 310/301-8167. www.marinadelreyhotel.com. 157 units. $130–$220 double; from $300 suite. Check for seasonal specials and packages (as low as $119 at press time). AE, DC, MC, V. Free parking. **Amenities:** Bar and grill with marina views and alfresco seating; small heated outdoor pool; access to nearby health club; water-sports equipment rentals; concierge; activities desk; car-rental desk; room service (6am–10:30pm); coin-op laundry. *In room:* A/C, TV w/pay movies and video games, dataport, hair dryer, iron.

Radisson Huntley Hotel   Housed in one of Santa Monica's tallest buildings (18 floors), this business-minded hotel offers reliable, quality accommodations with a style and attitude a notch above your average midrange chain hotel—plus a great location, close to Third Street Promenade dining and shopping and just a stone's throw from the beach. The guest rooms boast either ocean or mountain views, a good work desk, and bathrooms with Italian marble tile; executive suites also feature terry robes and minibars. **Toppers,** the rooftop Mexican restaurant, has a great view, serves very good margaritas, and hosts live entertainment nightly. *Fun tip:* Take a thrilling ride in the ocean-side glass elevator (acrophobes will prefer the interior lobby elevators).

1111 2nd St. (north of Wilshire Blvd.), Santa Monica, CA 90403. 📞 **800/333-3333** or 310/394-5454. Fax 310/458-9776. www.radisson.com/santamonicaca. 213 units. $189–$259 double. Ask about "Supersaver" and Internet-only rates, bed-and-breakfast packages, AAA and senior rates, and other discounts (from $159 at press time). AE, DC, DISC, MC, V. Valet parking $12. **Amenities:** Restaurant and bar; fitness center; concierge; room service (6am–11pm); dry-cleaning/laundry. *In room:* A/C, TV w/pay movies and video games, dataport, coffeemaker, hair dryer, iron.

Venice Beach House *Finds*   Listed on the National Register of Historic Places, this 1911 craftsman bungalow is now a homey bed-and-breakfast on one of funky Venice's unique sidewalk streets, just a block from the beach. The interiors bear witness to years of family life—well-worn furnishings and hardwood floors, faded Oriental rugs, shelves of vintage books—that add charm for romantics, but won't live up to the expectations of travelers who like their B&Bs to be antique-filled and pristine. What's more, the inn hums noisily with activity when there's a full house—seekers of absolute quiet and designer appointments will *not* be comfortable here (nor will folks who don't care for cats). Still, the huge repeat clientele base doesn't seem to mind the little imperfections. Our favorite room is the upstairs Venice Pier Suite—light and airy, with a wood-burning fireplace, king-sized bed, private bathroom, and sunny sitting room. An expanded continental breakfast with homemade baked goods is served in the sunroom overlooking a splendid garden. Bicycles are available for borrowing.

15 30th Ave. (at Speedway, 1 block west of Pacific Ave.), Venice, CA 90291. ⓒ **310/823-1966.** Fax 310/823-1842. www.venicebeachhouse.com. 9 units (5 with private bathroom). $95 double with shared bathroom; $130–$165 double with private bathroom. Extra person $20. Rates include expanded continental breakfast. AE, MC, V. Free parking. *In room:* TV.

INEXPENSIVE

Best Western Marina Pacific Hotel & Suites 🌟 *Kids*   This bright, newly renovated four-story hotel is a haven of smart value just off the newly renovated Venice Boardwalk. A simple, contemporary lobby and new elevator leads to spacious rooms brightened with beachy colors and brand-new everything, including chain-standard furnishings, fridges, and two-line phones. The one-bedroom suites are terrific for families, boasting master bedrooms with king-size beds, fully outfitted kitchens with microwave and dishwasher, dining areas, queen-size sofa sleepers, balconies and fireplaces, plus (if needed) a connecting door that can form a well-priced two-bedroom, two-bathroom suite. Photos of local scenes and rock-and-roll legends, plus works by local artists lend the public spaces a wonderful vibe, and many rooms have at least partial ocean views. Additional incentives include complimentary upscale continental breakfast, free local shuttle service, and secured indoor parking. Stay elsewhere if you need a lot in the way of service or if you won't relish the party-hearty human carnival of Venice Beach (Santa Monica is generally quieter and more refined).

1697 Pacific Ave. (at 17th Ave.), Venice, CA 90291. ⓒ **800/780-7234** (Best Western reservations), 800/421-8151 (direct), or 310/452-1111. Fax 310/452-5479. www.mphotel.com or www.bestwestern.com. 88 units. $109–$159 double; $169–$269 suite. Rates include continental breakfast. Extra person $10. Children 12 and under stay free in parents' room. Ask about AAA, senior, and other discounts; weekly and monthly rates also available. AE, DC, DISC, MC, V. Self-parking $9. **Amenities:** Dry-cleaning/laundry service; coin laundry; free shuttle to Santa Monica and Marina del Rey. *In room:* A/C, cable TV w/ HBO, high-speed dataport, fridge, coffeemaker, hair dryer, iron and ironing board.

Cal Mar Hotel Suites 🌟 *Value*   Tucked away in a beautiful residential neighborhood just 2 blocks from the ocean, this garden apartment complex is lovingly cared for and delivers a lot of bang for your vacation buck. Each unit is an apartment-style suite with a living room with a pullout sofa, a full-size kitchen, and a separate bedroom; most are spacious enough to accommodate four in comfort. The building was constructed in the 1950s with an eye for quality (attractive tile work, large closets). While the furnishings aren't luxurious and fixtures are from a couple of decades past, everything is well kept and every need is provided for. It's easy to be comfortable here for stays of a week or more. The staff is attentive and courteous, which helps account for the high rate of repeat guests. The garden courtyard boasts a nice swimming pool and plenty of chaises for lounging.

220 California Ave., Santa Monica, CA 90403. ⓒ **800/776-6007** or 310/395-5555. Fax 310/451-1111. www.calmarhotel.com. 36 units. $109–$169 suite. Extra person $10. Children under 10 stay free in parents' room. AE, DC, DISC, MC, V. Free parking. **Amenities:** Heated outdoor pool; coin-op laundry. *In room:* TV, full kitchen with fridge and coffeemaker, hair dryer, iron.

Inn at Venice Beach *Kids*   This cheery motel at the (relatively) quiet residential south end of Venice is a good choice for travelers who want a near-the-beach,

C A Little Las Vegas in L.A.

OK, so California-style casinos aren't for everyone, but if you enjoy playing poker with the guys every once in a while, you really should consider a visit or overnight stay at the **Commerce Casino.** Located only 6 miles (10km) south of downtown L.A. right off I-5, the huge 250-table casino looks intimidating at first (most of the patrons here are die-hard gamblers), but when you sit down at one of the low-stakes tables, you'll soon find out that it's just like playing at home. There's a wide variety of games offered—Hold 'em, "No Bust" blackjack, baccarat, pai gow, and so on—but if you're a beginner we recommend you start with a friendly game of 7-Card Stud.

The stakes are so low—it's only 50¢ to be in, the max raise is a few dollars, and you can fold at any time—that you can afford to make a few mistakes until you get the hang of it (the same game is played at the same table all day and night long). Even if you don't know how to play, one of the friendly tuxedoed floor managers will show you how, and most players will give you free advice all night long. There's a full-time dealer at each table so you don't need to shuffle, deal, or even cut the cards. Just like Vegas-style gambling, you buy $1 chips at the table and cash them in for real money when you're finished. Essentially the casino just acts as a host, dealer, and banker—whom you play against depends on who shows up (usually some real characters). You can even drink alcohol and dine at the gaming table; smoking isn't allowed, but you can leave the table between hands to light up outside or in one of the designated smoking rooms.

To lure visitors and tourists, the casino recently added a 200-room Crowne Plaza Hotel complete with retail shops, health spa, fitness room, sports bar, and (but of course) a Las Vegas–style buffet. Sure, it's all a bit Vegas-tacky, but you'll be surprised at how fun and thrilling it is to win a big hand. Bottom line: If you like playing poker or blackjack, you're going to enjoy a night at the Commerce Casino.

It's at 6121 East Telegraph Rd. (take the Washington Blvd. exit off I-5), Commerce, CA 90040. (*C* hotel/casino: **888/676-3000** or 323/728-7800; www.commercecasino.com or www.crowneplazacommerce.com).

near-the-boardwalk location without being at the center of the fray. Rooms are simple yet comely, with colorful bedspreads; and open-beam ceilings add to the spacious feel. All rooms overlook a cobblestone courtyard, where complimentary continental breakfast is served on warm, clear days. It all adds up to a reasonable value for budget-minded travelers (the bi-level loft suites are an extragood value if there's more than two of you). Since the hotel is just 3 blocks from the ocean on the border between Venice and Marina del Rey, there's an endless parade of people exploring the marina, the beach, or the nearby canals on foot, bike, or in-line skates (rentals are 2 blocks away). About the only thing missing is a pool, but the staff will lend you beach towels for an ocean dip.

327 Washington Blvd., Venice, CA 90291. *C* **800/828-0688** or 310/821-2557. Fax 310/827-0289. www. innatvenicebeach.com. 43 units. $99–$149 double; $159 suite. Extra person $10. Rates include continental

breakfast. Ask for AAA, AARP, corporate, and other available discounts. AE, DC, DISC, MC, V. Parking $4. **Amenities:** Activities desk; dry-cleaning/laundry service. *In room:* A/C, TV, dataport, fridge, coffeemaker, hair dryer, iron, safe, daily paper.

Sea Shore Motel ★★ *Value* *Finds*   Located in the heart of Santa Monica's best dining and shopping action, this small, friendly, family run motel is the bargain of the beach. The Sea Shore is such a well-kept secret that most denizens of stylish Main Street are unaware of the incredible value in their midst. A recent total upgrade of the property—furnishings, fixtures, and exterior—has made the entire place feel fresh and new. Arranged around a parking courtyard, rooms are small and unremarkable, but the conscientious management has done a nice job with them, installing attractive terra-cotta floor tiles, granite countertops, and conveniences like voice mail and data-jack phones. Boasting a sitting room and microwave, the suite is a phenomenal deal; book it as far in advance as possible. With a full slate of restaurants out the front door and the Santa Monica Pier and beach just a couple of blocks away, the a terrific bargain base for exploring the sandy side of the city. A cute deli is attached, selling morning muffins and sandwiches and homemade soup at lunchtime, and a Laundromat is next door. A real find!

2637 Main St. (south of Ocean Park Blvd.), Santa Monica, CA 90405. ☎ 310/392-2787. Fax 310/392-5167. www.seashoremotel.com. 20 units. $75–$95 double; $100–$120 suite. Extra person $5. Children under 12 stay free in parents' room. Midweek discounts available. AE, DISC, MC, V. Free parking. Pets accepted for $10-per-night fee. **Amenities:** Deli; coin-op laundry, sun deck. *In room:* TV, coffeemaker, dataport, fridge, iron.

ACCOMMODATIONS NEAR LAX
EXPENSIVE

Westin Los Angeles Airport ★   This newly renovated 12-story hotel stands a cut above the rest thanks to an invention that borders on miracle status: Westin's own Heavenly Bed. Touted as "10 layers of heaven"—from custom pillow-top mattress to the fluffy down comforter and family of pillows—the Heavenly Bed is the best hotel bed in the business. The like-new rooms are nicely outfitted in chain-standard style, and some have balconies (don't expect anything resembling a view). All of the conveniences are on hand, including a free airport shuttle and a very nice pool and fitness center.

5400 W. Century Blvd., Los Angeles, CA 90045. ☎ 800/937-8461 or 310/216-5858. Fax 310/417-4545. www.westin.com. 740 units. $189–$299 double; from $349 suite. Discounted rates can go as low as $139. AE, DC, DISC, MC, V. Parking $21. Small pets allowed. **Amenities:** California-style restaurant; lobby court for cocktails; heated outdoor pool and whirlpool; exercise room; billiards room; Westin Kids Club; 24-hour concierge; car-rental desk; free airport shuttle; business center; secretarial services; 24-hour room service; dry-cleaning/laundry service. *In room:* A/C, TV w/pay movies, dataport, minibar, coffeemaker, hair dryer, iron.

MODERATE

Marriott Los Angeles Airport   This huge 18-story Marriott is a good airport choice, designed for travelers on the fly. Rooms are decorated in standard chain-hotel style; some have balconies, and a select few are designed expressly for business travelers.

5855 W. Century Blvd. (at Airport Blvd.), Los Angeles, CA 90045. ☎ 800/228-9290 or 310/641-5700. Fax 310/337-5358. www.marriott.com. 1,026 units. $109–$248 double. AE, DC, DISC, MC, V. Ask about discounted AAA and AARP rates, as well as bed-and-breakfast packages. Valet parking $14; self-parking $11. **Amenities:** 2 restaurants; coffee shop; sports bar; outdoor heated pool; exercise room; whirlpool; sauna; business center; secretarial services; concierge; Hertz car-rental desk; free airport shuttle; 24-hour room service; coin-op laundry; dry-cleaning/laundry service. *In room:* A/C, TV w/pay movies, dataport, minibar, coffeemaker, hair dryer, iron.

Sheraton Gateway Hotel Los Angeles Airport This 15-story hotel is so close to the Los Angeles Airport that it literally overlooks the runway. Rooms have a California look, with comfortable furnishings and triple-pane windows that block out even the loudest takeoffs.

6101 W. Century Blvd. (near Sepulveda Blvd.), Los Angeles, CA 90045. ℂ 800/325-3535 or 310/642-1111. Fax 310/645-1414. www.sheraton.com. 727 units. $119–$209 double. AE, DC, DISC, MC, V. Valet parking $14; self-parking $11. **Amenities:** 2 restaurants; sushi bar; 2 cocktail lounges; heated outdoor pool; exercise room; whirlpool; concierge; car-rental desk; free airport shuttle; business center; 24-hour room service; dry-cleaning/laundry service; executive-level rooms. *In room:* A/C, TV w/pay movies, dataport, minibar, coffeemaker, hair dryer, iron, safe.

INEXPENSIVE

Travelodge Hotel at LAX *Value* The lobby is nondescript and the rooms are standard, but there's a beautiful tropical garden surrounding the pool area, and amenities extend beyond the budget-motel standard such as courtesy airport/car-rental shuttle service and a free morning paper. Some units have terraces; about two-thirds of the rooms have showers only, request a tub if you require one. A 24-hour Denny's adjoins the hotel. If you've brought the kids along, request the "Sleepy Bear Den," a separate sleeping room designed for children.

5547 W. Century Blvd., Los Angeles, CA 90045. ℂ 800/421-3939 or 310/649-4000. Fax 310/649-0311. www.travelodgelax.com. 147 units. $69–$99 double. Rates include continental breakfast. Extra person $8; children under 18 stay free in parents' room. AE, DC, DISC, MC, V. Free parking. Pet fee is $10. **Amenities:** 24-hour Denny's on site; outdoor heated pool; exercise room; activities desk; car-rental desk; free 24-hour airport shuttle; business center; babysitting; room service (6am–10pm); coin-op laundry; dry-cleaning/laundry service. *In room:* A/C, TV w/pay movies and Nintendo, dataport, coffeemaker, hair dryer, iron.

2 L.A.'s Westside & Beverly Hills

These are the city's most centrally located, star-studded, and dining-, shopping-, and nightlife-rich communities. As such, hotels tend toward the pricey end of the scale—this is where you can find L.A.'s largest concentration of luxury hotels, many of which you've no doubt heard of. There aren't many bargains to be found, so travelers in search of the best values shouldn't set their hearts on a Westside location. That said, a few good midpriced and budget options are at hand.

VERY EXPENSIVE

Beverly Hills Hotel & Bungalows ★★★ Behind the famous facade (pictured on the Eagles' *Hotel California*) lies this star-studded haven where legends were, and still are, made: The "Pink Palace" was center stage for both deal- and star making in Hollywood's golden days. Today, stars and industry hotshots can still be found around the Olympic-size pool, into which Katharine Hepburn once dove fully clothed, and digging into Dutch apple pancakes in the iconic **Polo Lounge,** where Hunter S. Thompson kicked off his adventure to Las Vegas. Following a $100 million restoration a few years ago, the hotel's grand lobby and impeccably landscaped grounds retain their over-the-top glory, while the lavish guest rooms boast every state-of-the-art luxury, including extralarge bathrooms with double Grecian marble sinks and TVs. The best original touches have been retained, like butler service at the touch of a button. Many rooms feature private patios, Jacuzzi tubs, kitchens, and/or dining rooms. The bungalows are more luxurious than ever—and who knows who your neighbor might be?

Accommodations in L.A.'s Westside & Beverly Hills

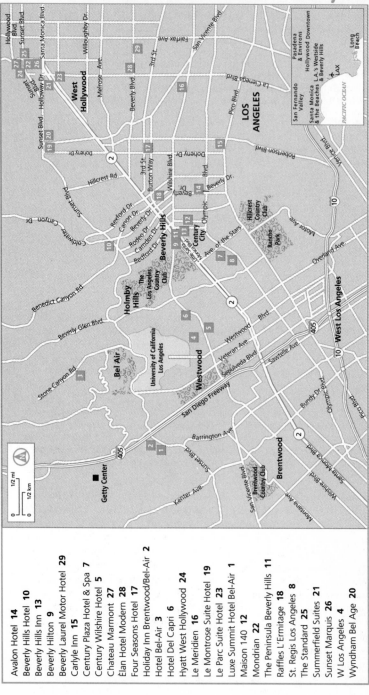

Avalon Hotel **14**
Beverly Hills Hotel **10**
Beverly Hills Inn **13**
Beverly Hilton **9**
Beverly Laurel Motor Hotel **29**
Carlyle Inn **15**
Century Plaza Hotel & Spa **7**
Century Wilshire Hotel **5**
Chateau Marmont **27**
Elan Hotel Modern **28**
Four Seasons Hotel **17**
Holiday Inn Brentwood/Bel-Air **2**
Hotel Bel-Air **3**
Hotel Del Capri **6**
Hyatt West Hollywood **24**
Le Meridien **16**
Le Montrose Suite Hotel **19**
Le Parc Suite Hotel **23**
Luxe Summit Hotel Bel-Air **1**
Maison 140 **12**
Mondrian **22**
The Peninsula Beverly Hills **11**
Raffles L'Ermitage **18**
St. Regis Los Angeles **8**
The Standard **25**
Summerfield Suites **21**
Sunset Marquis **26**
W Los Angeles **4**
Wyndham Bel Age **20**

9641 Sunset Blvd. (at Rodeo Dr.), Beverly Hills, CA 90210. ℂ 800/283-8885 or 310/276-2251. Fax
310/281-2905. www.beverlyhillshotel.com. 203 units. $345–$375 double; from $745 suite or bungalow. AE,
DC, MC, V. Parking $23. Pets accepted in bungalows only. **Amenities:** 3 restaurants (Polo Lounge, Fountain
Coffee Shop, alfresco Cabana Club Cafe); 2 lounges (Sunset Lounge for high tea and cocktails, bar in Polo
Lounge); Olympic-size outdoor heated pool; whirlpool; fitness center; 2 outdoor tennis courts (lit for night
play); concierge; car-rental desk; courtesy limo; business center with computers; salon services; 24-hour room
service; in-room or poolside massage; babysitting; dry-cleaning/laundry service; video rentals. *In room:* A/C,
TV/VCR, CD, DSL dataport, fax/copier/scanner, minibar, hair dryer, safe.

Century Plaza Hotel & Spa ★★   Despite the almost-foreboding scale, we
love this place. The recently renovated guest rooms are more beautiful than
you'd expect, with designer furnishings, gorgeous warm-hued textiles, attractive
contemporary prints, big closets with terry robes, and almost universally impressive views from the small deck. The beautiful Italian-tile-and-glass bathrooms
are some of L.A.'s best. Westin's celestial Heavenly Bed—touted as "10 layers of
heaven"—is a treat, and the cushioned headboards are a nice finishing touch.
Guest office rooms add a fax/printer/copier, an ergonomic desk chair, glare-free
task lighting, a coffeemaker, late checkout, and continental breakfast for a few
extra dollars.

Now open for business is the much-anticipated 35,000-square-foot, Asian-
inspired **Spa Mystique,** the largest in L.A. Its features include an epic menu of
traditional and Eastern treatments, 27 indoor treatment rooms and four outdoor
cabanas, impressive hydrotherapy features (including two Japanese *furo* pools),
salon services, and a fitness center with cardio machines that let you surf the Web
as you pump, plus a meditation garden and alfresco spa cafe. Even if you're not
staying at the hotel, it's worth a splurge to pamper yourself at this amazing spa.
Recently opened **Breeze,** the hotel's brand-new 250-seat restaurant and raw bar
designed by architect-of-the-moment Stephen Jacobs, is worth a look.

2025 Ave. of the Stars (south of Santa Monica Blvd.), Century City, CA 90067. ℂ 800/WESTIN-1 or
310/277-2000. Fax 310/551-3355. www.centuryplazala.com or www.westin.com. 724 units. $350–$415 double; from $500 suite. Weekend, off-season, and other discounts available (from $279 at press time). AE, DC,
DISC, MC, V. Valet parking $23; self-parking $15. Pets accepted with $50 deposit. **Amenities:** Restaurant and
lounge; spa cafe; lobby bar; outdoor heated pool and Jacuzzi; Spa Mystique health club and sauna; Westin
Kids Club; concierge; Hertz car-rental desk; business center; salon; 24-hour room service; in-room massage;
dry-cleaning/laundry service. *In room:* A/C, TV w/pay movies, dataport, minibar, coffeemaker, hair dryer, iron,
laptop-size safe.

Chateau Marmont ★★ *Finds*   Perched secretively in a curve above the Sunset
Strip, the Norman-style château is a landmark from 1920s-era Hollywood; step
inside and you expect to find John Barrymore or Errol Flynn holding inebriated
court in the baronial living room. Greta Garbo regularly checked in as "Harriet
Brown"; Jim Morrison was only one of many to call this home in later years.
This historical landmark built its reputation on exclusivity and privacy, which
was shattered when John Belushi overdosed in Bungalow No. 2. Now under the
guiding hand of boutique hotelier Andre Balazs (also lord of the Standard
[below] and New York's temple of SoHo style, the Mercer Hotel), the funky luxury oasis revels in its lore-filled past, yet it's hipper and more exclusive than ever.
No two of the antique-filled accommodations—standard rooms, suites, cottages, and bungalows—are alike: The poolside Spanish-style garden cottages are
outfitted in Arts and Crafts style, while suites and bungalows may get a '50s look
or a Gothic style. Many units have fireplaces and CD stereos, and all but 11 have
kitchenettes or full kitchens.

The Chateau Marmont is beautifully kept, eternally chic, faultlessly service oriented, and overflowing with Hollywood and rock-and-roll lore (not to mention a megawatt regular clientele), but it's not for everybody. This is a place where quirkiness rules, so don't expect traditional luxuries (in fact, some say it's actually haunted!). It's best for those with left-of-center attitudes and a real penchant for Hollywood romanticism. If that's you, don't stay anywhere else—you'll adore this legendary place.

8221 Sunset Blvd. (between La Cienega and Crescent Heights blvds.), West Hollywood, CA 90046. (C) **800/CHATEAU** or 323/656-1010. Fax 323/655-5311. www.chateaumarmont.com. 63 units. $250–$325 double; from $375 suite; from $400 cottage; from $875 bungalow. AE, DC, MC, V. Valet parking $21. Pets accepted with $100-per-pet fee. **Amenities:** Restaurant (serves in lobby, garden, and dining room); Bar Marmont; outdoor heated pool with brick sun deck; exercise room; access to nearby health club; 24-hour concierge; business center; secretarial services; 24-hour room service; in-room massage; babysitting; same-day laundry and dry-cleaning; CD library. *In room:* A/C, TV/VCR, CD, dataport, minibar, fridge, coffeemaker, hair dryer, iron, laptop-size safe.

Four Seasons Hotel Los Angeles at Beverly Hills ★★   This intimate-feeling 16-story hotel attracts a mix of A-list jet-setters loyal to the Four Seasons brand and an L.A. showbiz crowd who cherish the hotel as an après-event gathering place. The small marbled lobby is anchored by an always-stunning floral extravaganza, and lovely gardens will help you forget you're in the heart of the city. Four Seasons operates terrific hotels, with a concierge that's famously well connected and service that goes the distance. Guest rooms are sumptuously furnished in traditional style and pastel hues. Luxuries include custom extrastuffed Sealy mattresses with heavenly linens and pillows, marble bathrooms with vanity TV, and French doors leading to private balconies. Room rates rise with the elevator, so bargain hunters sacrifice the view; ask for a corner room to get extra space at no additional cost.

New as of 2000 is a petite but first-rate full-service spa. The view-endowed fourth-floor deck features a lap pool, poolside grill, and glass-walled fitness center. **Gardens** is a refined and excellent California-French restaurant often overlooked by locals.

300 S. Doheny Dr. (at Burton Way), Los Angeles, CA 90048. (C) **800/819-5053**, 800/332-3442, or 310/273-2222. Fax 310/859-3824. www.fourseasons.com. 285 units. $370–$470 double; from $600 suite. AE, DC, DISC, MC, V. Valet parking $21; free self-parking. Pets under 15 lb. welcomed (no charge). **Amenities:** Restaurant and lounge; poolside grill; rooftop heated pool; exercise room; full-service spa; Jacuzzi; children's program; concierge; courtesy limo within 5-mile radius; business center; 24-hour room service; in-room massage; dry-cleaning/laundry service. *In room:* A/C, TV/VCR w/pay movies (suites have DVD), CD, dataport, minibar, hair dryer, iron, safe.

Hotel Bel-Air ★★★   Spread over 12 luxuriant garden acres, this stunning Mission-style hotel is one of the most beautiful, romantic, exclusive, and all-around impressive hotels not just in L.A., but in all of California. This opulent early-20th-century castle wins a never-ending stream of praise for its faultless service, luxurious accommodations, and magical ambience. The parklike grounds—rich with ancient trees, fragrant flowers, bubbling fountains, playful statuary, and swan-dotted ponds—are enchanting, and the welcoming, richly traditional public rooms are filled with fine antiques. Rooms, villas, and garden suites are individually decorated but equally stunning; some have Jacuzzis, many have private patios and wood-burning fireplaces, but all feature romantic country French décor. A $14 million renovation in 2000 merely upped the ante on the impeccable detail and overall luxury.

The hotel is a natural for honeymooners and other celebrants, but families might be put off by the Bel-Air's relative formality, which is geared to the jet set, CEO types, and ladies who lunch. Even if you don't stay here, you might consider brunch, lunch, or dinner at the highly regarded and ultraromantic restaurant or on the woodsy outdoor terrace, or drinks at the cozy bar.

701 Stone Canyon Rd. (north of Sunset Blvd.), Los Angeles, CA 90077. © **800/648-4097** or 310/472-1211. Fax 310/476-5890. www.hotelbelair.com. 92 units. $465–$555 double; from $700–$3,500 suite. AE, DC, DISC, MC, V. Parking $20. **Amenities:** Indoor/outdoor restaurant; lounge with pianist nightly; outdoor heated pool; exercise room; concierge; business center; 24-hour room service; in-room massage; babysitting; dry-cleaning /laundry service; video library. *In room:* A/C, digital TV/VCR w/pay movies, CD, dataport and high-speed connection, fax, minibar, hair dryer, laptop-size safe.

Mondrian ★★ Theatrical, enchanted, sophisticated—this is the kind of place superhotelier Ian Schrager has created from a once-drab apartment building. Working with his regular partner, enfant terrible French designer Philippe Starck (as he successfully did at Miami's Delano and Manhattan properties like the Royalton and Hudson), Schrager used the Mondrian's breathtaking views (from every room) as the starting point for his vision of a "hotel in the clouds." Purposely underlit hallways lead to bright, clean rooms done in shades of white, beige, and pale gray and outfitted with simple furniture casually slipcovered in white; about three-quarters of the rooms and suites have fully outfitted kitchenettes. Truthfully, the accommodations themselves are only secondary—stay here if you want to be part of a superhip, star-studded scene. Set poolside and in a magical treehouse, **Skybar** is still one of L.A.'s hottest watering holes, and booking a room guarantees admission. (Soundproof windows on the entire south side of the building have already dealt with a troublesome noise problem in rooms overlooking the raucous late-night scene.) In addition to its terrific— and ultrahip—Asian-Latin fusion restaurant **Asia de Cuba,** light meals and sushi are served at a quirky communal table in the lobby. The beautiful-people staff isn't strong on service, but so what? They look great.

8440 Sunset Blvd., West Hollywood, CA 90069. © **800/525-8029** or 323/650-8999. Fax 323/650-5215. www.mondrianhotel.com and www.ianschragerhotels.com. 238 units. $310–$560 double; from $385 suite. Weekend rates available. AE, DC, DISC, MC, V. Valet parking $23. **Amenities:** Asia de Cuba restaurant; Seabar for sushi in lobby; Skybar alfresco bar; outdoor pool; exercise room with sauna and Jacuzzi; concierge; business center; 24-hour room service; in-room massage; dry-cleaning/laundry service; video, DVD, and CD libraries. *In room:* A/C, TV/VCR, CD, dataport, minibar, coffeemaker, hair dryer, iron, safe.

Peninsula Beverly Hills ★★★ The Peninsula is one of L.A.'s two or three finest hotels (a group that includes the Hotel Bel-Air and *maybe* the new St. Regis, although the latter needs a little age before a proper declaration). This stellar hotel—like its sister Peninsula properties in exotic locales like Hong Kong, Beijing, and Bangkok—has risen above the rest by making ultra service its hallmark. Set at Beverly Hills's main crossroads, this gardenlike oasis is impeccable in every respect (although laid-back types will surely consider it too formal).

The refined air begins the moment you enter the marbled lobby, and continues through the gardenlike grounds. Special features in the large, lavish, European-styled guest rooms include controls for everything—lighting, climate, DO NOT DISTURB—beside the luxurious Frette-made bed, an extra-large work desk, an oversize marble bath with soaking tub and separate shower, and round-the-clock personal valets; the 16 private villa suites, ensconced within lush gardens, also boast gas fireplaces, kitchens, CD players, and individual security systems. Sure, rooms are ultra-expensive, but a unique 24-hour check-in/check-out policy—which allows you to keep your room for a full 24 hours, no matter what time you check in—means you get your money's worth.

Belvedere is L.A.'s premier hotel dining room; breakfast is a tradition among CAA agents (whose office is across the street) and their look-at-me-don't-look-at-me clients (insiders order the nowhere-on-the-menu banana-stuffed Brioche French Toast), and Sunday brunch is the best in town. The mahogany-paneled bar is also popular among the power suits, while the English Garden-style **Living Room** pours L.A.'s best high tea. The cutting-edge Peninsula Heath Spa is day-spa worthy even if you don't stay.

9882 S. Santa Monica Blvd. (at Wilshire Blvd.), Beverly Hills, CA 90212. © **800/462-7899** or 310/551-2888. Fax 310/788-2319. www.peninsula.com. 196 units. $415–$500 double; from $725 suite. AE, DC, DISC, MC, V. Parking $23. **Amenities:** Restaurant; The Roof Garden cafe for casual dining; The Club Bar lounge; rooftop heated lap pool and Jacuzzi; state-of-the-art fitness center; terrific full-service spa with hydrotherapy features; concierge; courtesy Rolls Royce within 5-mile radius; business center; salon; 24-hour room service; in-room massage; dry-cleaning/laundry service; 24-hour check-in/check-out. *In room:* A/C, TV/VCR w/pay movies and WebTV, dataport and high speed connection, fax/copier/scanner, minibar, hair dryer, safe.

Raffles L'Ermitage ★★★

If the Beverly Hills Hotel symbolizes Hollywood opulence as it once was, L'Ermitage epitomizes what it is today. Each enormous (around 700 sq. ft.), superbly decorated room is done in a contemporary Asian-meets-Scandinavian style that screams "understatement!" The real treat is the in-room technology, which includes a CD/DVD player, Bose tuner and speakers, a three-line phone system with a whopping five phones throughout the room (including a cellphone you can take with you around town), and "smart" bedside control panels that remember your lighting and climate preferences. The work desk is large, seating is copious and comfortable, carpeting is Berber, fabrics tend to tailored silk, and lighting is soft and on dimmers. The bathrooms feature soaking tub, shower for two, and cotton *and* terry robes. The faultless service includes flexible check-in/check out and a wealth of freebies that include local and 800 calls, all nonalcoholic beverages in your minibar, customized stationery and business cards with your name and direct-dial phone and fax numbers, and CD and DVD lending. Room service is reasonable and carries no automatic service charges. Some of the luxe textiles don't wear well, and traditionalists may find the decor too austere. Still, millennial luxury doesn't get better.

9291 Burton Way, Beverly Hills, CA 90210. © **800/800-2113** or 310/278-3344. Fax 310/278-8247. www. lermitagehotel.com. 124 units. $418 double; from $850 suite. Ask about corporate rates, specials, and packages. AE, DC, MC, V. Valet parking $21. Pets up to 40 lb. accepted. **Amenities:** Jaan Restaurant with outdoor patio; Living Room for afternoon tea and light meals; Writer's Bar; heated rooftop pool; Amrita spa and health club; 24-hour concierge; courtesy car; 24-hour room service; in-room massage; dry-cleaning/laundry service. *In room:* A/C, 40-in. TV with DVD (WebTV upon request), CD, dataport, fax/printer/copier, minibar, hair dryer, safe.

St. Regis Los Angeles ★★★

The former tower of the Century Plaza (above) has been transformed (for a mere $43 million) into L.A.'s finest new hotel, and easily a competitor for best overall in a very competitive luxury market. Everything is right on target here, from the richly paneled, Oriental-carpeted lobby to the oversize guest rooms boasting classic-goes-contemporary decor in creamy mustard, chocolate, and tobacco hues. The cutting-edge luxury includes extra-long California king beds dressed in 300-count Frette; bedside controls for everything—climate, lighting, the DO NOT DISTURB sign—plus a 21st-century system that lets you reach almost anybody in one touch; a sitting area with sofa and ultraplush wool throw; an executive leather-top worktable with desk-level inputs; floor-to-ceiling windows with balconies; and gorgeous mahogany-and-marble bathrooms with deep soaking tubs and separate showers. State-of-the-art services include coffee or tea delivered with your wake-up call, plus "day before" check-in for red-eye flyers; Grand Luxe rooms also benefit from 24-hour butler service.

The tone is sedate and effortlessly elegant, the crowd more Hugo Boss than Gap. Indoor/outdoor **Encore** is a stunning botanically inspired setting for sophisticated Provençal dining. High tea, light meals, and cocktails are served in the **St. Regis Lounge,** but the best spot for martinis is the richly paneled **St. Regis Bar,** presided over by a stunning Goya-inspired mural (a la New York's landmark King Cole Bar). The European-style spa stars an extensive treatment menu and a view-endowed, cutting-edge fitness center.

2055 Ave. of the Stars, Los Angeles, CA 90067. (C) **800/325-3589** or 310/277-6111. Fax 310/277-3711. www.stregis.com. 297 units. $460–$575 double; from $1,000 suite. AE, DC, DISC, MC, V. Valet parking $23; self-parking $15. **Amenities:** Restaurant; St. Regis Lounge for high tea and light meals; St. Regis Bar; outdoor heated pool and Jacuzzi; state-of-the-art exercise room with personal trainers; full-service spa with steam and sauna; 24-hour concierge; courtesy car within 5-mile/8km radius; salon; 24-hour room service; 6 outdoor tennis courts; in-room massage; dry-cleaning/laundry service; executive-level rooms; butler-assisted unpacking/packing; babysitting; early "day before" check-in. *In room:* A/C, TV/VCR w/ DVD, VCR, CD, fax/copier/printer, dataport and high-speed connection, minibar, hair dryer, iron, laptop-recharging safe.

EXPENSIVE

Avalon Hotel ★★ *Finds* The first style-conscious boutique hotel on the L.A. scene, this marvelous mid-century-inspired gem in the heart of Beverly Hills still leads the pack. Boasting a soothing sherbet-hued palette and classic atomic age furnishings—Eames cabinets, Heywood-Wakefield chairs, Nelson bubble lamps—mixed with smart custom designs, every room looks as if it could star in a *Metropolitan Home* photo spread. But fashion doesn't forsake function at this beautifully designed hotel, which boasts enough luxury comforts and amenities to please design-blind travelers, too.

The property is comprised of the former Beverly-Carlton (seen on *I Love Lucy* and once home to Marilyn Monroe and Mae West) as well as two neighboring 1950s-era apartment houses. The main building is the hub of a chic but low-key scene, but I prefer the quieter Canon building, where many of the units have kitchenettes and/or furnished terraces. No matter which one you end up in, you'll find a gorgeous, restful cocoon with terry bathrobes, and top-of-the-line bedding that includes a cozy, nubby throw. You'll also have easy access to the sunny courtyard with its retrohip amoeba-shaped pool, the fitness room, and the groovy *Jetsons*-style restaurant and bar, which shakes a terrific green apple martini. Service is friendlier than you'll find in other style-minded hotels.

9400 W. Olympic Blvd. (at Beverly Dr.), Beverly Hills, CA 90212. (C) **800/535-4715** or 310/277-5221. Fax 310/277-4928. www.avalon-hotel.com. 88 units. $199–$289 double; from $249 junior or 1-bedroom suite. Extra person $25. AE, DC, MC, V. Valet parking $17. **Amenities:** Restaurant and lounge; courtyard pool; concierge; 24-hour room service; in-room massage; dry-cleaning/laundry service. *In room:* A/C, TV/VCR w/pay movies and video games, CD, fax, dataport, minibar, coffeemaker, hair dryer, iron, safe.

Beverly Hilton ★ If you're a fan of awards shows, you'll probably recognize this Merv Griffin–owned hotel, at the crossroads of Wilshire and Santa Monica in the heart of Beverly Hills, as the annual home to the star-studded Golden Globe Awards. This boxlike eight-story hotel has been attracting movie city business travelers, movie stars, U.S. presidents, royalty, and tourists alike since 1955. The recently refurbished rooms are similar but not all alike—only about half have balconies, and some are decidedly larger than others. During the summer, the ground-level poolside rooms are a good choice, thanks to French doors that open directly onto the sun deck. For city views request one of the tower rooms. Among the Beverly Hilton's best advantages are its food and cocktail outlets: It's hard to beat a pupu platter and a rum-spiked "Navy Grog" at the supergroovy Polynesian-style **Trader Vic's,** often favored by celebs looking for a quiet hangout (we've spotted David Spade with a leggy model on a quiet Tuesday night); you can also dine poolside at **Griff's** on nice days. The lavish buffets offered for breakfast, lunch, and dinner are a good deal for big eaters. All in all, a nice, well-located, and relatively affordable slice of Hollywood glamour.

9876 Wilshire Blvd. (at Santa Monica Blvd.), Beverly Hills, CA 90210. ℂ 310/274-7777. Fax 310/285-1313. www.merv.com or www.hilton.com. 581 units. $169–$350 double; from $375 suite. Ask about discounts, packages, and weekend rates. AE, DC, DISC, MC, V. Valet parking $24; self-parking $21. Pets under 20 lb. accepted. **Amenities:** 2 restaurants and 3 lounges; heated Olympic-size outdoor pool; poolside exercise facility; 24-hour concierge; courtesy car within 5-mile/8km radius; business center; gift shop; salon; 24-hour room service; dry-cleaning/laundry service. *In room:* A/C, TV/VCR w/pay movies, dataport connection, minibar, coffeemaker, hair dryer, iron.

Hyatt West Hollywood ★   An extensive renovation of this legendary 13-story Sunset Strip hotel erased any last remnants of its former debauched life as the rock-and-roll "Riot Hyatt." It doesn't even look like other Hyatt's, since the management eschewed the standard corporate decor and contracted locally; the end result is a stylish cross between the clean black-and-white geometrics of a 1930s movie set and a Scandinavian birch-and-ebony aesthetic. While not as fancy as the Mondrian across the street, neither is it as expensive or snobbish. Rooms have beautiful city or hillside views (about half have balconies), but stay away from front-facing rooms on the lower floors—too close to noisy Sunset Boulevard. Beyond the smart decor, the standard rooms bear generic but justfine comforts. Suites have VCRs, CD players, wet bars, plus a groovy tropical aquarium built into the wall stocked with colorful temporary pets, who make the suites worth the extra bucks all by themselves. The rooftop pool is a real plus, offering cushy lounge chairs and a killer perch for peeping into the luxury homes that dot the hill behind the hotel; other features include a well-equipped exercise room and a restaurant and bar.

8401 Sunset Blvd. (at Kings Rd., 2 blocks east of La Cienega Blvd.), West Hollywood, CA 90069. ℂ 800/ 233-1234 or 323/656-1234. Fax 323/650-7024. www.hyatt.com. 262 units. $129–$245 double; from $325 suite. Check for discounted weekend, AAA, and senior rates. Extra person $25; children stay free in parents' room. AE, DC, DISC, MC, V. Valet parking $20; self-parking $15. **Amenities:** Indoor/outdoor restaurant; bar; coffee/pastry kiosk in lobby; rooftop heated pool with chaises and terrific views; state-of-the-art exercise room; concierge; business center; room service (6am–midnight); dry-cleaning/laundry service; executive-level rooms. *In room:* A/C, TV w/pay movies, dataport, hair dryer, iron, safe.

Le Meridien ★★   Finally—a hotel designed for business travelers where the primary goal isn't mimicking every other business hotel. Le Meridien refers to its interior decor as "Pacific Rim" ("Organic Pacific Rim" for the suites, which use all-organic textiles), but "Zen luxury" seems just as appropriate. Thanks to amenities such as in-room fax machines, three two-line phones, and large counter/desk space, the rooms function equally well as sleeping quarters and work spaces. All things electrical (lights, TV, climate control) are operated by a bedside remote, and the subdued black marble bathrooms hold elegant Hermès products; after a long day on the job, the huge Japanese soaking tubs are perfect for unwinding. Shoji screens replace curtains, allowing light to filter through or blocking it out entirely. Even if you're not staying here you might want to drop by for the Sunday big-band brunch, which always draws a crowd. Another perk: a caviar bar off the lobby.

465 S. La Cienega Blvd., Los Angeles, CA 90048. © 800/645-5687 or 310/247-0400. Fax 310/247-0315. www.lemeridienbh.com. 300 units. $315–$440 double; from $600 suite. AE, DC, DISC, MC, V. Valet parking $18; free self-parking. Pets accepted with $100 fee (covers 4-night stay). **Amenities:** 1 restaurant; 1 bar; heated pool; 24-hour health club; massage; sauna; concierge; 24-hour room service; same-day dry-cleaning and laundry; business center. *In room:* A/C, TV/VCR w/pay movies, CD, dataport, minibar, hair dryer, iron.

Le Montrose Suite Hotel ★ *Value*   Nobody pays rack at this terrific all-suite hotel, which offers money-saving specials of every stripe for travelers who want more than a standard room for their accommodations dollars. Nestled on a quiet street just 2 blocks from the red-hot Sunset Strip, cozy Le Montrose features large split-level studio and one-bedroom apartments that feel more like comfortable, upscale condos than hotel rooms. Each contemporary-styled suite has a sizable living room with gas fireplace, a dining area, a comfortable sleeping nook (or dedicated bedroom), and a very nice bathroom. Executive and one-bedroom suites have kitchenettes (which can be stocked upon request). The two-bedrooms are a great deal for families or sharing friends. You have to go up to the roof for anything resembling a view, but once you're up there, you can swim in the pool, soak in the Jacuzzi, or brush up on your tennis game. This place is a favorite for long-term stays among the music and film crowd, so don't be surprised if you spot a famous face in the pleasant **Library** restaurant during the breakfast hour.

900 Hammond St., West Hollywood, CA 90069. © 800/776-0666 or 310/855-1115. Fax 310/657-9192. www.lemontrose.com. 132 units. $295–$575 suite. Money-saving deals abound; AAA, AARP, seasonal, and weekend rates as low as $159 at press time; breakfast (from $199), car, and Disneyland and Universal Studios inclusive packages also available. AE, DC, DISC, MC, V. Valet and self-parking $18. Pets accepted with a $100-per-pet nonrefundable fee. **Amenities:** Continental restaurant; outdoor heated pool with whirlpool and sun deck; lighted tennis court; exercise room with sauna; complimentary bicycles; concierge; car-rental desk; business center; secretarial services; 24-hour room service; coin-op laundry; dry-cleaning/laundry service; executive-level rooms; DVD and CD libraries. *In room:* A/C, TV/VCR w/pay movies, Nintendo, Internet access, and DVD; CD; fax/copier/scanner; dataport and high speed connection; minibar; coffeemaker; hair dryer; iron; safe.

Le Parc Suite Hotel ★   Situated on a quiet, tree-lined residential street, Le Parc is a high-quality, all-suite hotel with a pleasantly mixed clientele: Designers stay here because it's a few minutes' walk to the Pacific Design Center, patients and medical consultants check in because it's close to Cedars-Sinai, and tourists enjoy being near the Farmers Market, the Beverly Center and Museum Row. The nicely furnished, apartment-like units are extralarge—studios are 650 square feet, one-bedrooms 875 square feet—and each has a well-outfitted kitchenette, dining area, a living room with fireplace, and a balcony. What this hotel lacks in cachet, it makes up for in value; if you can't snare a good rate at Le Montrose (above), this makes a good alternative.

733 N. West Knoll Dr., West Hollywood, CA 90069. © 800/578-4837 or 310/855-8888. Fax 310/659-7812. www.leparcsuites.com. 154 units. $165–$400 junior or 1-bedroom suite. Check for theater and bed-and-breakfast packages. AE, DC, DISC, MC, V. Parking $18. Pets accepted for $75 fee. **Amenities:** Cafe Le Parc with full bar; outdoor heated pool and Jacuzzi; rooftop night-lit tennis court; well-equipped exercise room with sauna; access to nearby health club; courtesy car; concierge; 24-hour room service; massage; babysitting; coin-op laundry; dry-cleaning/laundry service. *In room:* A/C, TV/VCR w/pay movies, video games, and on-screen Internet access; CD; dataport; kitchenette with minibar, microwave, coffeemaker; hair dryer; iron.

Luxe Summit Hotel Bel-Air ★   Hidden away on 7 garden acres just a stone's throw from the Getty Center and busy Interstate 405, this hotel is composed of two levels: The lobby and public areas—plus some rooms—are in the main building, while the most secluded guest rooms—and the Romanesque swimming pool—are uphill on the Garden level. Guest rooms are huge and sport stylish Gap-inspired fabrics in a sand-and-khaki color scheme; most have a large balcony or patio. The new-in-2000 furnishings give a clean, modern feel to this low-rise property. This is a place that appeals equally to business clientele, who appreciate the extensive amenities, and to leisure travelers, who can relax in the open, green setting. A free shuttle lets guests avoid the parking hassles at the Getty Center. The hotel is popular for wedding receptions on weekends, and the full-service spa attracts a sizable local clienteles, so be prepared for lots of lobby traffic; still, the overall ambience is relaxing.

11461 Sunset Blvd. (just east of I-405), Los Angeles, CA 90049. © **800/HOTEL-41** or 310/476-6571. Fax 310/476-4982. www.luxehotels.com. 161 units. $239–$289 double; $325–$495 suite. Ask about corporate rates as well as bed-and-breakfast and spa packages. Extra person $25. AE, DC, DISC, MC, V. Valet parking $15. **Amenities:** Indoor/outdoor restaurant; cocktail and piano lounge; pool; 1 outdoor tennis (lit for night play) court; full-service day spa; concierge; hourly shuttle to the Getty Center; secretarial services; room service (6:30am–10:30pm); dry-cleaning/laundry service. *In room:* A/C, TV w/pay movies, fax, minibar, coffeemaker, hair dryer.

Summerfield Suites Hotel—West Hollywood ★   This four-story all-suite property in a residential West Hollywood neighborhood looks and feels much like a high-quality apartment building. An unassuming interior and quiet public areas are hallmarks of value—less flash for less cash. Likewise, accommodations are nicely outfitted without being excessive in either size or style. All of the pastel-colored suites have kitchenettes, contemporary furnishings, dedicated living areas, pretty good original art, and petite balconies overlooking Hollywood or Beverly Hills; some larger units feature sunken living rooms, gas fireplaces, and full kitchens. A complimentary full breakfast buffet is offered daily.

1000 Westmount Dr. (1 block west of La Cienega Blvd.), West Hollywood, CA 90069. © **800/833-4353** or 310/657-7400. Fax 310/854-6744. www.wyndham.com/Summerfield/WestHollywood. 109 units. $150–$315 junior or 1-bedroom suite. Rates include full breakfast. Check for specials and packages. AE, DC, DISC, MC, V. Parking $16. Pets accepted with $75 deposit and $10 daily charge. **Amenities:** Heated rooftop pool and Jacuzzi; exercise room; sauna; room service (11am–midnight); coin-op laundry; dry-cleaning/laundry service; video library; grocery shopping service. *In room:* A/C; TV/VCR; fax; dataport and high speed connection; kitchenette with fridge, microwave, and coffeemaker; hair dryer; iron.

Sunset Marquis Hotel & Villas ★★ *Finds*   This sprawling Mediterranean-style all-suite hotel is the ultimate music-industry hostelry, regularly hosting the biggest names in rock (The Rolling Stones, Aerosmith, U2 and even Eminem are all repeat customers). In fact, to lure in the megastars the hotel even installed a state-of-the-art recording studio in the basement. After their recording session, the musicians can then retire to the dark and sexy **Whiskey Bar** (a favorite refuge of celebs) where their newly recorded session can be piped in directly. Of course, unless you're staying at the hotel, you'll never get in (which, in itself, is reason enough to stay). The hotel is located a short walk from rowdy Sunset Strip, but it feels a world away, with its lush gardens, koi ponds, exotic birds, brick paths, and tropical foliage. The only shortcoming used to be the standard suites, outfitted in traditional motel style—until now, that is. They were remade in 2001 in a practical but attractive and comfortable modern style, with clean-lined furnishings in mahogany, metal, and nubby textiles, earth-toned fabrics, Noguchi Akari rice-paper lamps, and marble counters. The villas take hospitality to a totally new level—they have private alarm systems and butlers, plus select features like baby grand pianos and Jacuzzi tubs.

1200 N. Alta Loma Rd. (just south of Sunset Blvd.), West Hollywood, CA 90069. © **800/858-9758** or 310/657-1333. Fax 310/657-1330. www.srs-worldhotels.com. 114 units. $275–$350 junior or 1-bedroom suite; from $850 1- or 2-bedroom villa. Ask about corporate rates. AE, DC, DISC, MC, V. Valet parking $18. Small pets accepted with partially nonrefundable deposit. **Amenities:** Restaurant; bar; 2 outdoor heated pools; exercise room; Jacuzzi; sauna; excellent 24-hour concierge service; business center; 24-hour room service; in-room massage; babysitting; dry-cleaning/laundry service; 48-track/112-channel automated recording studio. *In room:* A/C, TV w/pay movies, CD, minibar, fridge, iron, laptop-size safe.

W Los Angeles ★★   Design-savvy hipsters looking for cutting-edge style and familiar comforts will enjoy this 15-story, all-suite hotel near UCLA. The former Westwood Marquis underwent a transformation in 2000 under new owners, W Hotels, the "boutique" hotel brand backed by corporate giant Starwood Hotels. Hidden behind a severe concrete exterior, this oasis-like property has always had advantages: an all-suite configuration, 2 lush acres of greenery, and eye-catching '60s architectural detailing that's been newly liberated from its long-standing Sheetrock prison. Each large two-room suite features bold, angular furnishings in dark African *wenge* wood, accented with gray carpeting and soft plum textiles. Luxuries include divinely dressed beds, two 27-inch TVs, and two CD players. The bathrooms are spacious but unremarkable, save for inviting waffle-weave robes.

Like the all-black-clad staff (which run around with silly Secret Service–style headsets), the public spaces are dressed to impress. **Mojo** restaurant serves Latin-inspired cuisine and colorful cocktails to überstylish industry types, but ends up being more flash than substance. Nightlife impresario Rande Gerber runs the bar, **Whiskey Sky,** which pretty much guarantees a hipster scene on weekend nights. The well-furnished gardenlike pool area has its own outdoor cafe. The full-service spa will even schedule massages in the boldly striped poolside cabanas.

930 Hilgard Ave., Los Angeles, CA 90024-3033. ✆ 877/W-HOTELS or 310/208-8765. Fax 310/824-0355. 258 units. From $299 1- or 2-bedroom suite. Check for AAA, AARP, and weekend discounts, plus Internet-only rates (usually 10%–20% less) and packages ($269 at press time). AE, DC, DISC, MC, V. Valet parking $21. Pets accepted. **Amenities:** Restaurant; cocktail lounge; 2 outdoor heated pools; full-service spa and exercise room; concierge; car-rental desk; courtesy car; business center; 24-hour room service; in-room massage; babysitting; dry-cleaning/laundry service; video and CD libraries. *In room:* A/C, TV/VCR w/pay movies and onscreen Internet access, CD, dataport, minibar, coffeemaker, hair dryer, iron, laptop-size safe.

Wyndham Bel Age Hotel ★★ *Kids* *Value*   This high-rise all-suite hotel is one of West Hollywood's best. The Bel Age has it all: huge, amenity-laden suites, excellent service, terrific rooftop sun deck with pool and Jacuzzi, and A-1 location just half a block off the Sunset Strip, but removed from the congestion and noise. What's more, thanks to an excellent art collection (assembled by the hotel's original owners) that fills the public spaces and guest rooms, the hotel has far more personality than your average chain hotel.

Accommodations hardly get better for the money. The monster-size suites boast brand-new contemporary decor with a few classic touches and a serious, soothing palette of navy, burgundy, and gray. Selected to suit every need—including those of families and business travelers—luxuries include brand-new pillow-top mattresses with cushioned headboards and plush bedding, a sleeper sofa in the living area that opens into a queen bed, plus an excellent work desk with an ergonomically correct Herman Miller desk chair. The bathrooms boast generous counter space and robes. The best rooms face south; on a clear day, you can see all the way to the Pacific. Be sure to make reservations before you leave home for a special meal at the Franco-Russian **Diaghilev** restaurant (see p. 130). The pretty **Brasserie** offers good Cal-Tuscan cuisine and top-flight jazz on Friday and Saturday nights.

1020 N. San Vicente Blvd. (between Sunset and Santa Monica blvds.), West Hollywood, CA 90069. ☏ **800-WYNDHAM** or 310/854-1111. Fax 310/854-0926. www.wyndham.com. 200 units. $199–$339 suite (accommodates up to 4 at no extra charge). Ask about weekend rates, holiday specials, and discounts on longer stays. AE, DC, DISC, MC, V. Valet parking $18. **Amenities:** Restaurant; bar and grill with live entertainment; rooftop outdoor heated pool and Jacuzzi; exercise room; concierge; salon; room service (6am–2am); dry-cleaning/laundry service. *In room:* A/C, TV/VCR w/pay movies, Sony Playstation, and onscreen Internet access; CD; dataport and high-speed connection; minibar; coffeemaker; hair dryer; iron.

MODERATE

Beverly Hills Inn ★ *Value*   This hotel is a real coup for those who want a gold-plated address at a moderate price. The A-1 location—just south of prime Beverly Hills shopping territory—premium comforts, and across-the-board quality add up to one of Beverly Hills's best values. The 50-room hotel is attractively done in a rich European style and boasts extras that usually cost more, like a fitness room with dry sauna, an eager-to-please staff, and a small but well-tended pool. All add up to a very good deal in a high-rent neighborhood. A 2002 renovation should be complete by the time you arrive, and will increase the good value even more.

125 S. Spalding Dr., Beverly Hills, CA 90212. ☏ **800/463-4466** or 310/278-0303. Fax 310/278-1728. www.innatbeverlyhills.com. 50 units. $189–$259 double; from $269 suite. AE, DC, MC, V. Free parking. **Amenities:** Garden Hideaway Restaurant; full room service menu until 10pm; full bar in the Garden Hideaway Room; heated tropical outdoor pool; exercise room with sauna; tour desk; dry-cleaning/laundry service. *In room:* A/C, TV, dataport, fridge, hair dryer, iron.

Carlyle Inn ★★ *Value*   Tucked away on an uneventful stretch of Robertson Boulevard just south of Beverly Hills, this four-story inn is one of L.A.'s best midpriced finds. Making the most of a small lot, architects have created an attractive interior courtyard, which almost every room faces, that gives the property a feeling of openness and serenity that most others in this price range lack—not to mention good outdoor space for enjoying the free breakfast or afternoon munchies at umbrella-covered cafe tables on nice days. The well-planned, contemporary guest rooms are fitted with recessed lighting, Art Deco–inspired furnishings, new firm bedding, well-framed architectural monoprints, plus nice extras like VCRs and bathrobes. Suites have a pullout sofa but are only slightly larger than standard rooms, so families may be better off in a double/double or connecting rooms. The conscientious manager keeps everything in racing form. The hotel's primary drawback is that it lacks views; curtains must remain drawn at all times to maintain any sense of privacy. Still, it doesn't seem to bother the 90% repeat visitors, who know good value when they find it.

1119 S. Robertson Blvd. (between Pico and Olympic blvds.), Los Angeles, CA 90035. ☏ **800/322-7595** or 310/275-4445. Fax 310/859-0496. www.carlyle-inn.com. 32 units. $129–$139 double; from $149 suite. Rates include full buffet breakfast and weekday afternoon hors d'oeuvres. Management will deal, so ask for discounts. AE, DC, DISC, MC, V. Parking $10. **Amenities:** Jacuzzi; sun deck; fitness room; dry-cleaning/laundry service. *In room:* A/C, TV/VCR, minibar, coffeemaker, hair dryer, dataport, daily newspaper, iron, safe.

Century Wilshire Hotel *Value*   This amiable and pretty hotel, located just south of UCLA in the same pleasing Westwood neighborhood of chic high-rise condos as the Hotel Del Capri (below), is a good choice for discerning travelers without a lot of money to spend. The older building boasts a European flair, and a lovely English country-style lobby that leads to a pleasant courtyard, around which 99 guest rooms sit garden style. The individually decorated rooms are simple yet attractively furnished. Units are large, with good closet space; the double/doubles are spacious enough to house four who don't mind sharing to save a few dollars. Junior-, one-, and two-bedroom suites boast fully equipped kitchens. Rooms open either onto the courtyard with pretty wrought-iron cafe tables, or onto a very nice pool. The conscientious management has been at work improving the property, replacing furniture and concentrating on the public spaces in 2001. A complementary continental breakfast (served alfresco on nice days) and parking add to the wallet-friendliness, and discounts on longer stays make a good value even better.

10776 Wilshire Blvd. (between Malcolm and Selby aves.), Los Angeles, CA 90024. ✆ **800/421-7223** or 310/474-4500. Fax 310/474-2535. www.centurywilshirehotel.com. 99 units. $115–$145 double; from $195 suite. Complimentary continental breakfast. Discounted weekly and monthly rates available. AE, DC, DISC, MC, V. Free parking. Pets accepted (subject to management approval) for $200 nonrefundable fee. **Amenities:** Outdoor pool; access to nearby health club; concierge; activities desk; dry-cleaning/laundry service. *In room:* A/C, TV, dataport, voice mail.

Èlan Hotel Modern ★★ *Value*   Silly name aside, this is one of L.A.'s best boutique-style hotels—and one of the city's best values. Rebuilt from the bones of a 1969 retirement home, the ultramodern structure uses design elements from the original 1969 facade to set the stage for 21st-century style. Inside, a mod, loungey lobby leads to mid-century-inspired guest rooms done in serene celadon and natural hues. The design merges form and function beautifully, resulting in amenity-laden, and surprisingly luxurious accommodations, considering the price. The standard rooms aren't huge, but extrahigh ceilings and thoughtfully designed custom blond-wood furnishings create the luxury of space, while plush textured fabrics (mohair, chenille), beautifully made beds—with cushioned headboards, goose-down comforters, 250-thread-count Egyptian cotton linens, and turndown service—VCRs, and bathrooms with cotton robes and the thickest, plushest bath sheets in town elevate comforts well beyond the moderate price point. Double/doubles are roomy enough to accommodate shares, and suites have a separate seating area with pullout sofa. On the downside, there's no view and no pool, and this stretch of Beverly Boulevard isn't exactly the hippest strip in town, but double-paned glass insures that even Beverly-facing rooms are quiet, and the location is central to everything (shoppers will love the walking-distance proximity to the Beverly Center).

8435 Beverly Blvd. (between La Cienega Blvd. and Fairfax Ave.), Los Angeles, CA 90048. ✆ **888/611-0398** or 323/658-6663. Fax 323/658-6640. www.elanhotel.com. 50 units. $140–$195 double; from $215 suite. Rates include continental breakfast. Extra person $15. AE, DC, DISC, MC, V. Valet parking $12. **Amenities:** Exercise room; business center; room service from coffee shop across street (6am–2am); dry-cleaning/laundry service. *In room:* A/C, TV/VCR, dataport and high-speed connection, coffeemaker with coffee, minibar with nonalcoholic beverages, hair dryer, iron, safe.

Holiday Inn Brentwood/Bel-Air   This L.A. landmark is the last of a vanishing breed of circular hotels from the 1960s and 1970s. It's perched beside the city's busiest freeway a short hop from the popular Getty Center and centrally located between the beaches, Beverly Hills, and the San Fernando Valley. Completely refurbished in 2000, each pie-shaped room boasts a private balcony and double-paned glass to keep the noise out; little extras like Nintendo games, in-room bottled water, and great views add panache to otherwise-unremarkable chain-style accommodations. You'll also enjoy a million-dollar 360° view from the hotel's top-floor **Brentwood Terrace** restaurant, which serves a casual, please-all cuisine; the adjoining cocktail lounge features live piano nightly. Popular with older travelers and museum groups, the hotel provides complimentary pickup and drop-off service to the Getty Center and Westwood.

170 N. Church Lane (at intersection of Sunset Blvd. and I-405), Los Angeles, CA 90049. (✆ **800/HOLIDAY** or 310/476-6411. Fax 310/472-1157. www.holiday-inn.com/brentwood-bel. 211 units. $149–$189 double; from $275 suite. Inquire about AAA and AARP discounts, breakfast packages, and "Great Rates," often as low as $119. AE, DC, DISC, MC, V. Valet parking $10; self-parking $8. Small pets accepted for $50-per-pet nonrefundable fee. **Amenities:** Rooftop restaurant and lounge; heated outdoor pool and Jacuzzi; exercise room; concierge; activities desk; free shuttle to Getty Center and within a 3-mile/5km radius; room service (6am–10pm); coin-op laundry; dry-cleaning/laundry service. *In room:* A/C, TV w/pay movies and Nintendo, dataport, coffeemaker, hair dryer, iron.

Maison 140   Tucked away on an unassuming block just behind the Peninsula, Maison 140 is the place to stay for *Wallpaper*-reading style hounds with edgy tastes and midrange budgets. By breaking just about every design rule in the book, designer Kelly Wearstler has created an East-meets-West-meets-mod pied-à-terre that's so audacious it overwhelms the senses (read: it's not for everyone). Narrow black-on-black hallways and a tiny mirrored elevator with a zebra-print rug lead to the guest rooms, which come in a your choice of rule-busting palettes. Autumn ochers and soothing grays is the most sedate choice, the pinks and oranges the wildest. The decor is a striking blend of Franco-Chinese-patterned textiles and wallpapers, original 1930s details juxtaposed with 1960s-modern touches (including Lucite), and individual accent pieces that are likely to be from Wearstler's fabulous collection of silk-shaded Asian figure lamps. Luxuries that surpass the price category include Frette linens, two-line phones, VCRs, CD players, and cotton robes. Be forewarned: Many of the rooms are frighteningly small, and although the space is designed for maximum advantage—platform beds have drawers below, TVs are wall-mounted—those who like to spread out will not be comfortable. Some bathrooms are tiny and have showers only. If you want the high style without the squeeze, book a roomy Grande King, which even has space for a good-size worktable.

140 S Lasky Dr. (just south of Wilshire Blvd.), Beverly Hills, CA 90212. (✆ **800/432-5444** or 310/281-4000. Fax 310/281-4001. www.maison140.com. 45 units. $140–$215 double. Rates include continental breakfast. AE, DC, MC, V. Parking $15. **Amenities:** Cocktail lounge; pool and fitness privileges at Avalon Hotel; concierge; in-room massage; dry-cleaning/laundry service. *In room:* A/C, TV/VCR, CD, dataport and high-speed connection, minibar, hair dryer, iron, safe.

The Standard ★★   If Andy Warhol had gone into the hotel business (which he no doubt would have, if he had arrived on the scene a few decades later), the Standard would've been the end result. Designed to appeal to the under-35 It-crowd, Andre Balazs's swank West Hollywood neomotel is sometimes silly, sometimes brilliant, and always provocative (not to mention crowded!). It's a scene worthy of its Sunset Strip location: Shag carpeting on the lobby ceiling, blue Astroturf around the swimming pool, a DJ spinning ambient sounds while a performance artist showing more skin than talent poses in a display case behind the check-in desk—this place is definitely left of center.

The good news is that the Standard is more than just a pretty (wild) face. Look past the retro clutter and often-raucous party scene, and you'll find a level of service more often associated with hotels costing twice as much. Constructed from the bones of a vintage 1962 motel, it boasts comfortably size rooms outfitted with cobalt-blue indoor-outdoor carpeting, silver beanbag chairs, safety-orange tiles in the bathrooms, and Warhol's Poppy-print curtains, plus private balconies, and minibars whose contents include goodies like sake, condoms, and animal crackers. On the downside, the cheapest rooms face noisy Sunset Boulevard, and the relentless scene can get tiring if you're not into it.

Note: A **Downtown Standar,** 550 S. Flower St. (© 213/892-8080), opened in mid-2002, brings a similar dose of Generation Y–targeted cheap-cool style and tattooed attitude to suit-jacketed downtown L.A.

8300 Sunset Blvd. (at Sweetzer Ave.), West Hollywood, CA 90069. © 323/650-9090. Fax 323/650-2820. www.standardhotel.com. 139 units. $99–$225 double; from $450 suite. AE, DC, DISC, MC, V. Valet parking $18. Pets under 30 lb. accepted for $100-per-pet fee. **Amenities:** 24-hour coffee shop; poolside cafe; bar/lounge; business center; outdoor heated pool; access to nearby health club; concierge; barbershop; 24-hour room service; in-room massage; babysitting; dry-cleaning/laundry service. *In room:* A/C, TV/VCR w/pay movies, CD, dataport and high-speed connection, minibar.

INEXPENSIVE

Beverly Laurel Motor Hotel *Value*   Touted by the *New York Times* for its Gen-X appeal and value, the Beverly Laurel is a great choice for wallet-watching travelers who want a central location and a room with more style than your average motel. Overlooking the parking lot, the budget-basic but well-kept rooms are smartened up with diamond-print spreads and eye-catching artwork; other features include a minifridge, microwave, and ample closet space, and a large kitchenette for an extra 10-spot. The postage-stamp-size outdoor pool is a little public for carefree sunbathing, but does the job on hot summer days. Best of all is the motel's own excellent coffee shop, **Swingers** (see the review on p. 144)— nobody serves burgers and malts better, and you may even spot your favorite alt-rocker tucking into a 3pm breakfast in the vinyl booth next to yours.

8018 Beverly Blvd. (between La Cienega Blvd. and Fairfax Ave.), Los Angeles, CA 90048. © 800/962-3824 or 323/651-2441. Fax 323/651-5225. 52 units. $79–$84 double; $89 double with kitchen. AAA and senior discounts may be available. AE, DC, MC, V. Free parking. **Amenities:** Heated outdoor pool; access to nearby health club; car-rental desk; laundry service. *In room:* A/C, TV, dataport, minifridge, microwave, hair dryer.

Hotel Del Capri *★ Kids*   This well-located and well-kept Westwood hotel/ motel is hugely popular with returning guests, thanks to spacious rooms, a helpful staff, and retro pricing. There are two parts to the Eisenhower-era property: a four-story tower and a charming two-story motel with white louver shutters and flowering vines, whose units surround a pleasant pool that open 24 hours. All guest rooms are clean and well cared for, but the decidedly discount decor won't be winning any style awards, and the basic bathrooms could use some upgrading (not to mention quieter fans). Still, every one is comfortable and well worth the money; free continental breakfast (delivered to your room) and free parking make a good value even better. The most notable room feature is electrically adjustable beds, a novel touch; you'll have to request hair dryers and irons if you want them. More than half of the units are 1- or 2-bedroom suites with kitchenettes, some of which have whirlpool tubs. Nothing is within walking distance of the ritzy high-rise neighborhood, but it's hard to be more freeway-convenient or centrally located. No room service, but nearly 50 restaurants will deliver.

10587 Wilshire Blvd. (at Westholme Ave.), Los Angeles, CA 90024. © 800/44-HOTEL or 310/474-3511. Fax 310/470-9999. www.hoteldelcapri.com. 79 units. $110–$125 double; from $135 suite. Extra person $10. Rates include continental breakfast ($1 gratuity). Price breaks for almost everybody—AAA members, seniors, UCLA grads, military members, and more—so be sure to ask. AE, DC, MC, V. Free parking. **Amenities:** Pool with deck chairs; tour desk; free shuttle service to UCLA, Westwood, Beverly Hills, and Century City with advance notice; coin-op laundry; dry-cleaning/laundry service; VCR rental. *In room:* A/C, TV, adjustable beds.

3 Hollywood

The geographical area called Hollywood is actually smaller and less glamorous than you might expect. In fact, throughout most of the 1980s and '90s,

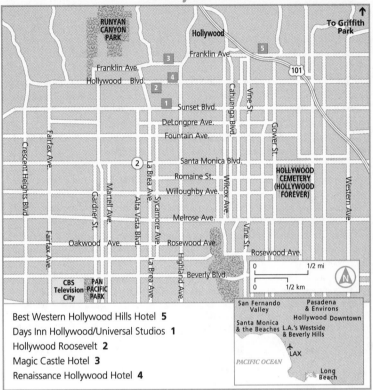

Best Western Hollywood Hills Hotel **5**

Days Inn Hollywood/Universal Studios **1**

Hollywood Roosevelt **2**

Magic Castle Hotel **3**

Renaissance Hollywood Hotel **4**

Hollywood was downright skanky. But the neighborhood has undergone a major overhaul of late—along the lines of the reinvention of New York City's Times Square—that has turned the seedy area into tourism central. The regentrification is ongoing, and we still don't recommend heading down dark alleys on moonless nights; that said, Hollywood is definitely cleaner and safer than it has been in decades. What's more, the hotels below are great for travelers looking for good midpriced and budget lodging, and families will like the easy freeway access to Universal Studios. Still, those with an aversion for tourist traps should book elsewhere.

EXPENSIVE

Renaissance Hollywood Hotel Part of the $615 million Hollywood & Highland project to restore Hollywood to the glory of its heyday, the Renaissance Hollywood opened in late 2001. The hotel now serves as Oscar-night headquarters for the frenzy of participants and paparazzi attending the Academy Awards in the Kodak Theater next door. Despite its high profile, the hotel is principally a convention property and not quite as elite or elegant as the media hype might have you believe. Nonetheless, its commitment to the history of the area infuse it with far more personality than most chain hotels. The hip, retro design draws on Hollywood's glamorous past, and more than 70 works by Los Angeles artists lend it an avant-garde atmosphere.

Wood-paneled headboards and Technicolor furniture (think: *The Jetsons* meets Ikea) paint guest rooms as swinging '50s bachelor pads. Bathrooms are lined with sparkling white tile, and separate dressing rooms display thoughtful touches of humor, such as a bull's eye at the bottom of your trash can. Rooms on the seventh floor and up offer truly impressive views. One-third look toward the Pacific Ocean, one-third face the skyline of downtown L.A., and one-third take in the lush Hollywood Hills (yes, you can see the sign). If your dream is to have all of Hollywood at your feet, the hotel's ultra-swank (and ultra-expensive) rooftop Panorama Suite comes with stunning 270° views of the city.

The hotel's location makes getting around on foot unusually easy in a town where most destinations require navigating L.A.'s notorious freeway system. Site seeing is virtually unavoidable since the hotel shares the same block as two of the city's most famous landmarks—the Hollywood Walk of Fame and Mann's Chinese Theater. The Hollywood Bowl is less than a mile away (check with the concierge about shuttle service), and the new subway stops under the hotel complex, offering access to Universal Studios and destinations farther afield.

Twist, the hotel's restaurant, features a California-eclectic menu that falls into the expensive category, but food here rivals or tops the fare at many Los Angeles restaurants in the same price range.

1775 North Highland Avenue, Hollywood, CA 90028. ℂ Marriott, **800/HOTELS-1** or 323/856-1200. Fax 323/856-1205. www.renaissancehollywood.com. 637 units. $249 double; $279 executive bedroom; one-bedroom suite $299; other suites from $300 and way up. Discount rates and packages available. AE, DC, DISC, MC, V. Valet parking $22. Amenities: Restaurant , 2 bars (lobby and poolside); outdoor pool; small fitness room; concierge; business center; shopping complex; 24-hour room service; dry cleaning. *In room:* A/C, TV w/pay movies, CD, dataport, high-speed internet access, 2-line cordless phone, minibar, coffeemaker, hair dryer, iron, safe, robes.

MODERATE

Hollywood Roosevelt Hotel ℛ *(Kids)*　This 12-story movie-city landmark is located on an unabashedly touristy but no longer seedy section of Hollywood Boulevard, across from Mann's Chinese Theatre and just down the street from the Walk of Fame. This Tinseltown legend—host to the first Academy Awards, not to mention a few famous-name ghosts—is a great value, since you get an A-1 location and buckets of Hollywood history, plus comforts and services that usually cost twice the price. A complete renovation in 2002—down to the plumbing and electrical—has jacked up the rates about 20%, but the stylish new Pan-Asian design is worlds better than the old, unappealing guest rooms. Those on the upper floors have unbeatable skyline views, while cabana rooms have a balcony or patio overlooking the Olympic-size pool, whose mural was painted by David Hockney, and poolside bar. The specialty suites are named after stars who stayed in them during the glory days; some have grand verandas. The **Cinegrill** supper club draws locals with live jazz and top-notch cabaret entertainment. A new, trendy bar lounge and spa should be completed by the fall of 2002.

7000 Hollywood Blvd., Hollywood, CA 90028. ℂ **800/950-7667** or 323/466-7000. Fax 323/462-8056. www.hollywoodroosevelt.com. 330 units. $199–$269 double; from $289 suite. Ask about AAA, senior, business, government, and other discounted rates (as low as $149 at press time). Children under 18 stay free in parents' room. AE, DC, DISC, MC, V. Valet parking $18. **Amenities:** California/Continental restaurant; cocktail lounge; Cinegrill cabaret and nightclub; coffee bar; poolside bar; outdoor pool and Jacuzzi; exercise room; concierge; activities desk; Thrifty car-rental desk; business center; room service (6am–11pm); babysitting; dry-cleaning/laundry service; executive-level rooms. *In room:* A/C; TV w/pay movies, video games, and wireless Internet access; dataport; minibar; coffeemaker; hair dryer; iron; laptop-size safe.

INEXPENSIVE

Best Western Hollywood Hills Hotel ★ Location is a big selling point for this family owned (since 1948) member of the reliable Best Western chain: It's just off U.S. 101 (the Hollywood Freeway), a Metro Line stop just 3 blocks away means easy car-free access to Universal Studios, and the famed Hollywood and Vine intersection is just a walk away. The walls showcase images from the golden age of movies, and the front desk offers an endless variety of arranged tours. Rooms are plain and clean but lack warmth—outer walls are painted cinder block, and closets are hidden behind institutional metal accordion doors. Still, management is constantly striving to improve the hotel, and all rooms have a refrigerator, coffeemaker, microwave, and free movies. Rooms in the back building are our favorites, as they sit well back from busy Franklin Avenue, face the gleaming blue-tiled, heated outdoor pool, and have an attractive view of the neighboring hillside. The new bathrooms are jazzier in the front building, though. A major convenience is the **101 Hills Coffee Shop** located off the lower lobby.

6141 Franklin Ave. (between Vine and Gower sts.), Hollywood, CA 90028. ℂ **800/287-1700** in California only, or 323/464-5181. Fax 323/962-0536. www.bestwestern.com/hollywoodhillshotel. 86 units. $79–$129 double. AAA and AARP discounts available. AE, DISC, MC, V. Free covered parking. Small pets accepted with $25-per-night fee. **Amenities:** Coffee shop; heated outdoor pool; access to nearby health club; tour desk; coin-op laundry. *In room:* A/C, TV, fridge, coffeemaker, microwave, hair dryer, dataport, iron.

Days Inn Hollywood/Universal Studios While it's east of the prime Sunset Strip action, this freshly renovated motel is safe and convenient, and extras like free underground parking and continental breakfast make it an especially good value. Double/doubles are large enough for families. Some rooms have microwaves, fridges, and coffeemakers; if yours doesn't have a hair dryer or an iron, they're available at the front desk. It's usually easy to snare an under-$100 rate; for maximum bang for your buck, ask for a room overlooking the pool.

7023 Sunset Blvd. (between Highland and La Brea aves.), Hollywood, CA 90028. ℂ **800/544-8313,** 800/346-7723, or 323/464-8344. Fax 323/962-9748. www.daysinn.com. 72 units. $82–$160 double; $125–$200 Jacuzzi suite. Rates include continental breakfast. Ask about AAA, AARP, and other discounted rates (as low as $73 at press time). AE, DC, DISC, MC, V. Free secured parking. **Amenities:** Heated outdoor pool; dry-cleaning/laundry service. *In room:* A/C, TV.

Magic Castle Hotel ★ *Kids* *Value* Located a stone's throw Hollywood Boulevard's attractions, this garden-style hotel/motel at the base of the Hollywood Hills offers L.A.'s best cheap sleeps. You won't see the Magic Castle Hotel in a shelter mag spread—the rooms are done in high Levitz style—but the newly refurbished units are spacious, comfortable, and well kept. Named for the Magic Castle, the illusionist club just uphill, the hotel was once an apartment building; it still feels private and insulated from Franklin Avenue's constant stream of traffic. The units are situated around a swimming-pool courtyard ensconced with trees. Most are full, extralarge apartments, with fully equipped kitchens with microwave and coffeemaker (grocery shopping service is available as well). Several units have balconies overlooking the large heated pool. Ideal for wallet-watching families or long-term stays.

7025 Franklin Ave. (between La Brea and Highland), Hollywood, CA 90028. ℂ **800/741-4915** or 323/851-0800. Fax 323/851-4926. www.magiccastlehotel.com. 49 units. $79 double; $89–$169 suite. Extra person $10. Off-season and other discounts available. AE, DC, DISC, MC, V. Free secured parking. **Amenities:** Outdoor heated pool; full-service or coin-op laundry. *In room:* A/C, TV, dataport, coffeemaker, hair dryer, iron, safe.

4 Downtown

Traditionally the domain of business folk and convention attendees, downtown L.A. is becoming increasingly attractive to leisure travelers, thanks to a late-1990s cleanup; a growing number of cultural attractions and destination dining; excellent-value weekend packages at luxury hotels that empty out once the workweek ends; and easy car-free access via the Metro Line to Hollywood and Universal Studios. Every freeway passes through Downtown, so it's a breeze to hop in the car and head off to other precincts, too (except during weekday rush hour, that is). Be forewarned, though: Despite the low, low weekend rates, some travelers detest the relative ghost town scene.

EXPENSIVE/MODERATE

How much you pay at any of the following hotels largely depends on when you come. All become quite affordable once the business travelers go home; more often than not, rooms go for a relative song over holidays and weekends. Some even offer good-value weekday rates to leisure travelers during periods when rooms would otherwise sit open.

Millennium Biltmore Hotel Los Angeles ★★ Built in 1923 and encompassing an entire square block, this Italian-Spanish Renaissance landmark is the grande dame of L.A.'s hotels. You've seen the Biltmore in many movies, including *The Fabulous Baker Boys, Beverly Hills Cop,* and Barbra Streisand's *A Star Is Born;* the hotel lobby appeared upside-down in *The Poseidon Adventure.* Always in fine shape and host to world leaders and luminaries, the former Regal Biltmore is now under the guiding hand of the Millennium Hotels and Resorts group, and the sense of refinement and graciousness endures. The large guest rooms aren't quite as eye-popping, but they've recently undergone a sumptuous redecorating that suits the hotel's vibe beautifully; bathrooms are on the small side, but peach-toned marble and plush robes add a luxurious edge.

A range of dining and cocktail outlets includes **Sai Sai** for Japanese cuisine. Pretty, casual **Smeraldi's** serves homemade pastas and lighter California fare. Off the lobby is the stunning **Gallery Bar,** named by *Los Angeles* magazine as one of the sexiest cocktail lounges in L.A. Afternoon tea and cocktails are served in the **Rendezvous Court** (the hotel's original lobby). Spend the few bucks to appreciate the Art Deco health club, with its gorgeous Roman-style pool.

506 S. Grand Ave. (between Fifth and Sixth sts.), Los Angeles, CA 90071. © **800/245-8673** or 213/624-1011. Fax 213/612-1545. www.millennium-hotels.com. 683 units. $174–$319 double; from $459 suite. Weekend discount packages available. AE, DC, DISC, MC, V. Parking $22. **Amenities:** 3 restaurants and 2 lounges; health club with original 1923 inlaid pool, Jacuzzi, steam, sauna; concierge; Enterprise car-rental desk; courtesy car; business center; salon; 24-hour room service; in-room massage; babysitting; dry-cleaning/laundry service; executive-level rooms. *In room:* A/C, TV w/pay movies, dataport, minibar, hair dryer, laptop-size safe.

New Otani Hotel and Garden ★ Most of the guest rooms in this anonymous 21-story concrete tower are nothing special—fine if you score a low weekend rate, not good enough for the money if your rate starts inching to close to $200. The best reason to stay here is to experience one of the handful of wonderfully unique Japanese-style suites, which recreate an elegant Far East hotel room in every detail: futon beds elegantly dressed and laid out on tatami floors, sliding rice-paper shoji screens, *ofuro* bathrooms with separate showers and soaking tubs, and a prime view of the half-acre rooftop classical tea garden. One- and two-night Japanese Experience cultural packages include suite accommodations, welcome sake, shiatsu massages, dinner, and in-suite breakfast.

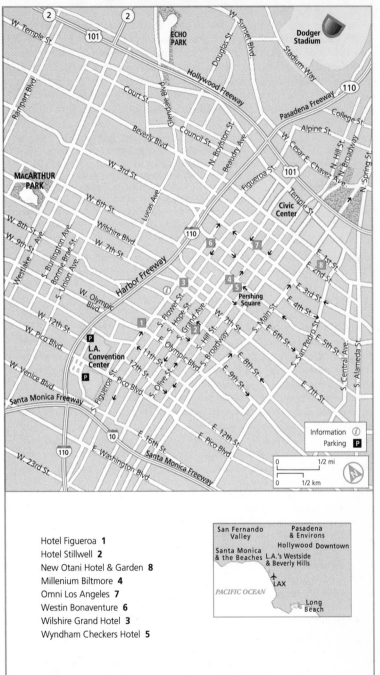

Hotel Figueroa **1**
Hotel Stillwell **2**
New Otani Hotel & Garden **8**
Millenium Biltmore **4**
Omni Los Angeles **7**
Westin Bonaventure **6**
Wilshire Grand Hotel **3**
Wyndham Checkers Hotel **5**

Even if you opt for a more mundane Western-style room, you can enjoy the beautifully sculpted garden; the five restaurants and bars, including **Senbazuru (A Thousand Cranes)** for Japanese cuisine elegantly presented by kimono-clad servers (go for breakfast for the ultimate culinary adventure), and the terrific Japanese-style **Sanwa Spa** for shiatsu massages. The location is close enough to the prime business district to be convenient, far enough to be peaceful. Little Tokyo dining options are nearby, and Downtown shuttles and free taxi vouchers make exploring easy. Expect a clientele that's split between Japanese and Westerners.

120 S. Los Angeles St. (at 1st St.), Los Angeles, CA 90012. © **800/421-8795,** 800/273-2294 in California, or 213/629-1200. Fax 213/622-0980. www.newotani.com. 434 units. $209–$260 double; from $500 suite. Cultural, weekend, bed-and-breakfast, and other packages regularly available, starting as low as $128. AE, DC, DISC, MC, V. Valet parking $22; self-parking $18. **Amenities:** 2 Japanese restaurants (including a Tokyo-style *teppanyaki* grill); California-style bar and grill; 2 cocktail lounges; full-service Japanese-style spa (www.sanwahealth.com) with saunas, baths, and shiatsu massages; fitness center; concierge; tour desk; car-rental desk; courtesy shuttle; business center; shopping arcade; salon; room service (6am–11pm); in-room massage; dry-cleaning/laundry service; executive-level rooms; Japanese garden. *In room:* A/C, TV w/pay movies, dataport, minibar, coffeemaker, hair dryer, iron, laptop-size safe.

Omni Los Angeles ★★   The Omni chain forsook its old location (now the Wilshire Grand, below) to assume this elegant tower (the former Inter-Continental Los Angeles). Its lovely, view-endowed situation as the centerpiece of California Plaza elevates the hotel above the noise and traffic of Downtown. And now that it's adjacent to the Museum of Contemporary Art and within walking distance of the L.A. Music Center, Walt Disney Concert Hall, and the Cathedral of our Lady of the Angles, the Omni is Downtown's best base for culture buffs. Recognizing the geographical appeal, the hotel caters to theatergoers more than any of its peers with complimentary car service until 11:30pm (great for dinner/show evenings) and good-value theater packages.

An eager-to-please staff runs the property beautifully, and public areas enjoy a graceful air thanks to elegant accents and artworks from the likes of Jim Dine and David Hockney (on loan from the Museum of Contemporary Art). Conservatively styled, amenity-packed rooms boast floor-to-ceiling views and oversize bathrooms with separate dressing areas; larger rooms also have a chaise, and business rooms feature an extralarge work desk with halogen task lighting and desk-level inputs (most also have a fax/copier/printer). Soft goods upgrade (bedding, towels, curtains) was in the works at press time, so comforts will only improve. At $35 extra for two, club-level rooms are a great value considering the accompanying freebies: continental breakfast, all-day beverages and pastries, evening cocktails and appetizers. **The Grand Cafe** specializes in sumptuous buffets, while the gorgeous **Angel's Flight** is one of Downtown's best lounges, with stellar views and a pianist tickling the ivories nightly.

251 S. Olive St., Los Angeles, CA 90012. © **213/617-3300.** Fax 213/617-3399. www.omnihotels.com. 453 units. $260–$280 double; from $475 suite. Inquire about weekend rates and packages (as low as $129 at press time), which may include breakfast. AE, DC, DISC, MC, V. Valet parking $24. **Amenities:** Restaurant; lounge; outdoor heated lap pool; exercise room with sauna; access to nearby health club; Omni Kids program; concierge; courtesy car within 3-mile/5km radius; business center with secretarial services; 24-hour room service; babysitting; dry-cleaning/laundry service; executive-level rooms; 24-hour on-call physician. *In room:* A/C, TV w/pay movies, Nintendo, and Internet access; dataport; minibar; hair dryer; iron.

Westin Bonaventure Hotel & Suites ★★   This 35-story, 1,354-room monolith is the hotel that locals love to hate. The truth is that the Bonaventure is a terrific hotel. It's certainly not for travelers who want intimacy or personality in their accommodations—but with more than 20 restaurants and bars, a full-service spa, a monster health club, a Kinko's-size business center, and much more on hand, you'll be hard-pressed to want for anything here (except maybe some individualized attention). And with a $35 million renovation recently completed, this convention favorite has never looked better or felt fresher.

The hotel's five gleaming glass silos encompass an entire square block and form one of Downtown's most distinctive landmarks. The six-story lobby houses fountains and trees (and, surprise, a Starbucks). A tangle of concrete ramps and 12 high-speed glass elevators lead to the extensive array of shops and services. Among the highlights is the rooftop L.A. Prime steakhouse and revolving **BonaVista lounge,** both offering unparalleled views; the **Bonaventure Chowder Bar** for live entertainment; and even a **Krispy Kreme Donut Stand** (Well that settles it!).

The pie-shaped guest rooms are on the small side, but a wall of windows offering great views, nice contemporary furnishings, and Westin's unparalleled Heavenly Bed—the ultimate in hotel-bed comfort—make for a very comfortable cocoon. With an executive workstation, fax, and wet bar, guest office suites are great for business travelers, while tower suites—with a living room, an extra half-bathroom, minifridge, microwave, and two TVs—are ideal for families.

404 S. Figueroa St. (between Fourth and Fifth sts.), Los Angeles, CA 90071. © **800/WESTIN-1** or 213/624-1000. Fax 213/612-4800. 1,354 units. $227–$279 double; from $287 suite. Ask about theater packages. AE, DC, DISC, MC, V. Valet parking $19. **Amenities:** 17 restaurants and fast-food outlets; 5 bars and lounges; outdoor heated lap pool; 15,000-sq.-ft. full-service spa with exercise room, running track, and access to adjacent 85,000-sq.-ft. health club; Westin Kids Club; concierge; tour desk; Dollar Rent-a-Car desk; full-service business and copy center; shops; salon; 24-hour room service; babysitting; dry-cleaning/laundry service; executive club level. *In room:* A/C, TV w/pay movies and video games, dataport, coffeemaker, hair dryer, iron, laptop-size safe.

Wilshire Grand Los Angeles   This former Omni hotel is now independently operated and dedicated to business travelers, but weekend rates can be stellar for bargain-hunting vacationers. The taupe-toned rooms are business hotel average; the best ones have city views or overlook the swimming pool. The executive-level rooms and suites feature extras like a fax machine, plus bathrobes, extra towels, and top-floor views, plus access to the Executive Lounge, which offers free continental breakfast, all-day beverages, and hors d'oeuvres at cocktail hour. The 16-story hotel is centrally located in the heart of downtown shopping, theater, and dining. Five restaurants and bars on site include an American grill, an upscale Korean barbecue, Japanese, an Italian trattoria, a tropical lounge in the Trader Vic's vein, and a coffee bar featuring Starbucks brew. We prefer the Omni (above), but this is a fine choice if you can snare a good rate.

930 Wilshire Blvd. (at Figueroa St.), Los Angeles, CA 90071. © **888/773-2888** or 213/688-7777. Fax 213/612-3989. www.wilshiregrand.com. 900 units. $209–$249 double; from $450 suite. Leisure and weekend rates as low as $148 at press time. AE, DC, DISC, MC, V. Valet parking $24. **Amenities:** 4 restaurants; 1 bar; large outdoor heated pool and hydrotherapy pool; 24-hour fitness room; concierge; Enterprise car-rental desk; courtesy car; business center with secretarial services; salon; 24-hour room service; in-room massage; dry-cleaning/laundry service; executive-level rooms. *In room:* A/C, TV w/pay movies and video games, dataport, minibar, coffeemaker, hair dryer, iron.

Wyndham Checkers Hotel ★★   The atmosphere at this boutique version of the Biltmore is as removed from "Hollywood" as a top L.A. hotel can get. Built in 1927, the 12-story hotel is a Historic Cultural Monument. Plenty of polished brass complements the neutral sand-colored decor; both conspire to accentuate the splendid architectural features that remain intact, despite a complete update over the past couple of years (which included a total guest room overhaul in 2001). Your room is a pristine temple, warmly radiant and immaculately outfitted. Checkers is a European-styled hotel, without a lot of flashy amenities—but first class all the way. Spacious marble bathrooms feature plush terry-cloth bathrobes. Public areas include a wood-paneled library, a bar stocked with fine cigars and an impressive collection of single-malt scotches and cognacs, and serene corridors punctuated with Asian antiques. **Checkers Restaurant** is one of Downtown's finest dining rooms, with a weekend brunch worth planning for in advance. *Tip:* Be sure to check their website for terrific "E-Specials" such as $99 Romantic Weekends rates.

535 S. Grand Ave. (between 5th and 6th sts.), Los Angeles, CA 90071. ✆ 800/423-5798 or 213/624-0000. Fax 213/626-9906. 188 units. $199–$289 double; from $500 suite. www.checkershotel.com or www.wyndham.com. Weekend specials, often as low as $109. AE, DC, DISC, MC, V. Valet parking $23; self-parking (off-site) $20. **Amenities:** Restaurant and lounge; rooftop heated lap pool and whirlpool; exercise room with men's and women's saunas and massage services; concierge; courtesy car; secretarial services; 24-hour room service; in-room massage; babysitting; complimentary shoe shine; dry-cleaning/laundry service. *In room:* A/C, TV w/pay movies, dataport and high-speed connection, minibar, coffeemaker, hair dryer, iron.

INEXPENSIVE

Hotel Figueroa ★★ *Finds* With an artistic eye and a heartfelt commitment to budget travelers, owner Uno Thimansson has transformed a 1925-vintage former YWCA residence into L.A.'s best budget hotel. This enchanting 12-story property sits in a nicely gentrified corner of Downtown, within shouting distance of the STAPLES Center and a block from the Original Pantry Cafe, the landmark 24-hour breakfast house.

The big, airy lobby exudes a romantic Spanish Colonial–Gothic vibe with beamed ceilings and soaring columns, Moroccan chandeliers, and medievalist furnishings. Elevators lead to equally artistic guest rooms. Even the smallest ones are good size and comfortable. Each boasts terra-cotta-sponged walls, a firm, well-made bed with a wrought-iron headboard or canopy and a Georgia O'Keeffe–reminiscent spread, a Mexican-tiled bathroom, and Indian fabrics that double as blackout drapes. Our favorite is no. 1130; a large double-queen with a Spanish terra cotta-print chaise, but you can't go wrong with any room. The Casablanca Suite is a Moroccan pleasure den, ideal for romance. Out back you'll find a gorgeous desert-garden deck with mosaic-tiled pool and Jacuzzi.

939 S Figueroa St. (at Olympic Blvd.), Los Angeles, CA 90015. ✆ 800/421-9092 or 213/627-8971. Fax 213/689-0305. 285 units. $94–$124 double; $195 Casablanca suite. www.figueroahotel.com. AE, DC, MC, V. Parking $8. **Amenities:** Restaurant; bar; outdoor pool area with lounge chairs and Jacuzzi; dry-cleaning/laundry service. *In room:* A/C, TV, dataport, minifridge.

Hotel Stillwell The Stillwell is far from fancy, but its modestly priced rooms are a good option in a generally pricey neighborhood. Built in 1906, this once-elegant 250-room hotel is conveniently located, close to STAPLES Center, the Civic Center, and the Museum of Contemporary Art. Rooms are clean, basic, and simply decorated with decent furnishings; much-needed new paint and carpeting were installed in 2000, but the ancient TVs still look like something from great-uncle Horace's rumpus room. The hotel is quiet, though, and hallways feature East Indian artwork. That said, we much prefer the Hotel Figueroa, but this is a less eccentric and perfectly reasonable choice. The lobby-level Indian restaurant is a popular lunch spot for downtown office workers; other options include a casual Mexican restaurant and so-old-it's-retro **Hank's Bar** for cocktails.

838 S. Grand Ave. (between 8th and 9th sts.), Los Angeles, CA 90017. ✆ 800/553-4774 or 213/627-1151. Fax 213/622-8940. www.stillwell-la.com. 250 units. $59 double; $75–$95 suite. AE, DC, DISC, MC, V. Parking $4. **Amenities:** 2 restaurants; lounge; activities desk; business center; coin-op laundry; dry-cleaning/laundry service. *In room:* A/C, TV, fridge, fax, iron.

5 The San Fernando Valley

Proximity to Universal Studios and the adjacent CityWalk dining and shopping complex means that most hotels on this side of the hill do a booming business with families and theme-park-minded travelers. The Valley is generally more peaceful and affordable than other L.A.-area locales, and freeways put the rest of the city within easy reach; the movie and TV studios are close by for those interested in studio tours and TV-show tapings. On the downside, this side of the hill is more suburban than Hollywood sexy, and late-summer days can get brutally hot. Still, you can often find great deals here.

EXPENSIVE

Hilton Universal City & Towers   Although this shiny 24-story hotel sits right outside Universal Studios, there's more of a conservative business traveler feel here than the raucous family-with-young-children vibe you might expect. Still, free tram service to the theme park and adjacent Universal CityWalk for shopping and dining means that it's hard for families to be better situated. The polished brass and upscale attitude set the businesslike tone, and a light-filled glass lobby leads to a seemingly endless series of conference and banquet rooms, the hotel's bread and butter. The oversize guest rooms are tastefully decorated and constantly refurbished, and have exceptional views (even if the modern, mirror-surfaced windows don't actually open). We prefer the adjacent Sheraton (below) for leisure stays, but go for the best rate.

555 Universal Terrace Pkwy., Universal City, CA 91608. © 800/HILTONS or 818/506-2500. Fax 818/509-2031. www.universalcity.hilton.com. 483 units. $225–$260 double; from $350 suite. Weekend and other discounts often available. AE, DC, DISC, MC, V. Valet parking $16; self-parking $11. **Amenities:** Cafe-style restaurant; outdoor heated pool and whirlpool; exercise room; concierge; activities desk; car-rental desk; business center; 24-hour room service; babysitting; dry-cleaning/laundry service; executive-level rooms. *In room:* A/C, TV w/pay movies and video games, dataport, minibar, coffeemaker, hair dryer, iron, safe.

MODERATE

Beverly Garland's Holiday Inn *Kids*   The "Beverly Garland" in this 258-room hotel's name is the actress who played Fred MacMurray's wife on *My Three Sons*. Grassy areas and greenery abound at this North Hollywood Holiday Inn, a virtual oasis in the concrete jungle. The Mission-influenced buildings are a bit dated, but if you grew up with *Brady Bunch* reruns, this only adds to the charm—the spread looks like something Mike Brady would have designed. Southwestern-themed fabrics complement the natural-pine furnishings in the spacious guest rooms, attracting your attention away from the somewhat unfortunate painted cinder-block walls. On the upside, all of the well-outfitted rooms have balconies overlooking the pleasant grounds, and a nice pool and two lighted tennis courts are on hand. With Universal Studios just down the street and a free shuttle to the park, the location can't be beat for families. Since proximity to the 101 and 134 freeways also means the constant buzz of traffic, ask for a room facing Vineland Avenue for maximum quiet.

4222 Vineland Ave., North Hollywood, CA 91602. © 800/BEVERLY or 818/980-8000. Fax 818/766-0112. www.beverlygarland.com. 255 units. $149–$179 double; from $209 suite. Ask about AAA, AARP, corporate, military, Great Rates, weekend, and other discounted rates (from $109 at press time). Kids 12 and under stay free in parents' room, eat free. AE, DC, DISC, MC, V. Free parking. **Amenities:** Restaurant; heated outdoor pool; lighted tennis courts; sauna; car-rental desk; complimentary shuttle to Universal Studios. *In room:* A/C, TV, coffeemaker, hair dryer, iron.

Radisson Valley Center If you're happy with an affordable, convention-style chain hotel, this may be the choice for you. The Radisson is conveniently located at the crossroads of two major freeways, the San Diego (I-405) and Ventura (U.S. 101). Universal Studios, NBC Studios, Magic Mountain, Griffith Park, Hollywood, and Beverly Hills are all just a short freeway ride away. The spacious, attractive rooms have private balconies, two-line phones, and a work desk; the bathrooms and furnishings are just beginning to show their age, but 42 suites are large (550 sq. ft.) are relatively new. Refrigerators, coffeemakers, and cribs are available upon request. *Money-saving tip:* Ask for discount coupons to Universal Studios at the front desk, and be sure to check their website for special lodging rates.

15433 Ventura Blvd., Sherman Oaks, CA 91403. ⓒ 800/333-3333 or 818/981-5400. Fax 818/981-3175. www.radisson.com/shermanoaksca. 178 units. $119–$195 double; from $179 suite. Special discount packages available. AE, DC, DISC, MC, V. Self-parking $5.50. **Amenities:** Cafe; cocktail lounge; outdoor heated pool and Jacuzzi; exercise room; concierge; tour desk; Avis car-rental desk; salon; room service (7am–10pm); coin-op laundry; dry-cleaning/laundry service; executive-level rooms. *In room:* A/C, TV w/pay movies, dataport, coffeemaker, hair dryer, iron.

Sheraton Universal Hotel ⭐ (Kids) Despite the addition of the sleekly modern Hilton just uphill, the 21-story Sheraton is still considered "the" Universal City hotel of choice for tourists, businesspeople, and industry folks visiting the studios' production offices. Located on the back lot of Universal Studios, it has a spacious 1960s feel, with updated styling and amenities. Although the Sheraton does its share of convention/event business, the hotel feels more leisure-oriented than the Hilton next door (an outdoor elevator connects the two properties). Choose a Lanai room for balconies that overlook the lushly planted pool area, or a Tower room for stunning views and solitude. The hotel is very close to the Hollywood Bowl, and you can practically roll out of bed and into the theme park (via a continuous complementary shuttle). An extra $35 per night buys a Club Level room—worth the money for the extra in-room amenities, plus free continental breakfast and afternoon hors d'oeuvres; business rooms also feature a movable workstation and a fax/copier/printer.

333 Universal Hollywood Dr., Universal City, CA 91608. ⓒ 800/325-3535 or 818/980-1212. Fax 818/985-4980. www.sheraton.com. 436 units. $149–$219 double; from $350 suite. Children stay free in parents' room. Ask about AAA, AARP, and corporate discounts; also inquire about packages that include theme-park admission. AE, DC, DISC, MC, V. Valet parking $16; self-parking $11. **Amenities:** Casual indoor/outdoor restaurant; lobby lounge with pianist; Starbucks coffee cart in lobby; outdoor pool and whirlpool; health club; game room; concierge; free shuttle to Universal Studios every 15 minutes; business center; room service (6am–midnight); babysitting; dry-cleaning/laundry service; executive-level rooms. *In room:* A/C, TV w/pay movies and video games, dataport, minibar, safe (hair dryer and iron in club-level rooms).

Sportsmen's Lodge It's been a long time since this part of Studio City was wilderness enough to justify the lodge's name. This sprawling hotel has been enlarged and upgraded since, but the lovely gardenlike grounds still conjure up images of those days. Done in country style, guest rooms are large and comfortable, not luxurious; all have balconies or patios. L-shaped studio suites can sleep a maximum of five, and new executive business king rooms include features such as two-line phones, work desks, refrigerators, and comfortable club chairs. You might take advantage of the heated Olympic-sized pool and patio cafe/bar, which will let you forget all about busy Ventura Boulevard just out the front door; don't miss the beautiful black-and-white swans frolicking out back in the koi-filled ponds. The neighborhood is pleasant and offers easy canyon and freeway access to L.A., but those of you heading to Universal Studios can usually hop a free shuttle. *Money-saving tip:* Ask about discount tickets to Universal, which are usually available at the front desk.

Accommodations in the San Fernando Valley

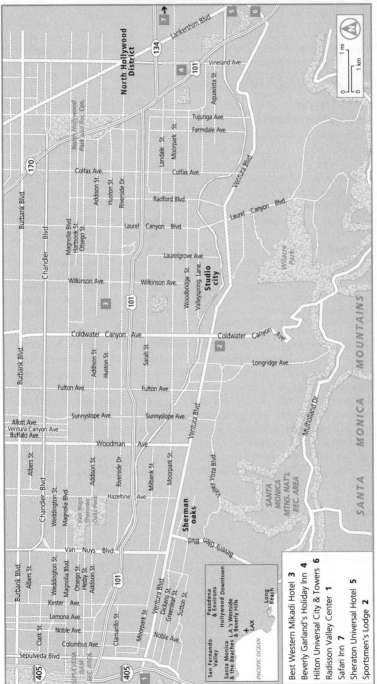

Best Western Mikadi Hotel **3**
Beverly Garland's Holiday Inn **4**
Hilton Universal City & Towers **6**
Radisson Valley Center **1**
Safari Inn **7**
Sheraton Universal Hotel **5**
Sportsmen's Lodge **2**

12825 Ventura Blvd. (east of Coldwater Canyon), Studio City, CA 91604. © **800/821-8511** or 818/769-4700. Fax 818/769-4798. www.slhotel.com. 191 units. $122–$172 double; from $180 suite. Ask about discounted AAA and AARP rates; Internet specials as low as $99 at press time. AE, DC, DISC, MC, V. Free parking. **Amenities:** Cafe-style restaurant; bar and grill; publike bar; outdoor heated Olympic-size pool and Jacuzzi; seasonal pool bar; exercise room; Avis car-rental desk; activities desk; courtesy shuttle to Burbank Airport and Universal Studios; salon; room service (6:45am–8:45pm); coin-op laundry; dry-cleaning/laundry service. *In room:* A/C, TV, coffee makers, iron/ironing board, fax machine, dataport.

INEXPENSIVE

Best Western Mikado Hotel   This nice Asian-flavored garden hotel has been a Valley fixture for 40-plus years. A 1999 renovation muted but didn't obliterate the kitsch value, which extends from the pagoda-style exterior to the sushi bar (the Valley's oldest) across the driveway. Two-story motel buildings face two well-maintained courtyards, one with a koi pond and wooden footbridge, the other with a shimmering blue-tiled pool and hot tub. The facelift stripped most of the Asian vibe from guest rooms, which are fresh feeling, comfortable, and well outfitted. Furnished in 1970s-era chic (leather sofas, earth tones), the one-bedroom apartment is a steal, with enormous rooms and a full-size kitchen.

12600 Riverside Dr. (between Whitsett and Coldwater Canyon), North Hollywood, CA 91607. © **800/ 826-2759** or 800/433-2239 in California, or 818/763-9141. Fax 818/752-1045. www.bestwestern. com/mikadohotel. 58 units. $129–$139 double; $175 1-bedroom apartment. Rates include full breakfast. Ask about AAA, senior, and other discounted rates (as low as $98 at press time). Extra person $10. Children under 12 stay free in parents' room. Rates include full American breakfast. AE, DC, DISC, MC, V. Free parking. **Amenities:** Japanese restaurant and sushi bar; cocktail lounge; outdoor pool and Jacuzzi; fax and copying services at front desk. *In room:* A/C, TV, dataport, coffeemaker, hair dryer, iron.

Safari Inn ⭐ *Finds*   This 1957-vintage motel is so retro that it—and its land-mark neon sign—have starred in such films as *Apollo 13* and *True Romance.* The exterior is still gloriously intact (note the groovy wrought-iron railings and the floating stone fireplace in the lobby), while the interiors have been upgraded with a smart, colorful So Cal look and all the modern comforts. Everything within is 21st-century new, including the attractive IKEA-style furniture, the bright contemporary textiles and wall prints, and the modern bathrooms; about 10 rooms also have microkitchens (basically wet bars) with a microwave. Everything is clean, fresh, and pleasing. Attention families: Book now to snare one of the two suites, which have pullout sofas, huge closets, full kitchens, and a second TV.

Located just down the street from the movie studios, the neighborhood is modest but quiet and nice, convenient for those interested in studio tours, TV-show tapings, and easy freeway access to Universal Studios. In classic motor lodge style, a petite pool sits in a gated corner of the parking lot, but it's attractive and inviting on hot Valley days. Other amenities that elevate the Safari above the motel standard include an exercise room, room service from the modest but surprisingly good restaurant at the Anabelle Hotel (the Safari's sister property) next door, and valet service as well as self-serve laundry.

1911 W Olive Ave., Burbank, CA 91506. © **818/845-8586.** Fax 818/845-0054. 55 units. $109–$119 double; $168 suite. AAA and corporate rate $95. Extra person $10. AE, DC, DISC, MC, V. Free parking. Pets accepted with $100 deposit. **Amenities:** Restaurant and martini bar (in hotel next door); heated outdoor pool; exercise room; sun deck; limited room service; coin-op laundry; dry-cleaning/laundry service. *In room:* TV w/pay movies, dataport, coffeemaker, fridge, iron, hair dryer.

Kids   Family-Friendly Hotels

Best Western Marina Pacific Hotel & Suites (p. 79) now gives families a place to stay just off the carnival-like Venice Boardwalk. The suites are a terrific choice for the brood, since each features a full kitchen, a dining area, a pullout sofa, and a connecting door to an adjoining room that lets you form an affordable two-bedroom, two-bathroom suite.

Beverly Garland's Holiday Inn (p. 105) is a terrific choice for wallet-watching families: rates are low, the North Hollywood location is close to Universal Studios (a free shuttle ride away), and kids stay and eat free.

Loews Santa Monica Beach Hotel (p. 71) welcomes kids under 10 with open arms, gifts, and special menus. And with a great location near the beach and Santa Monica amusement pier, the hotel couldn't be better situated for families in search of surf and sun.

Hollywood Roosevelt Hotel (p. 98) allows kids under 18 to stay free with their parents in this landmark hotel, home to lots of old Hollywood lore (plus a few benevolent ghosts). The heart-of-gentrified Hollywood location makes an excellent base for families who want easy access to the touristy but fun Walk of Fame.

Hotel Del Capri (p. 96) offers spacious, retropriced rooms and suites to families with kids—and anybody who wants a big bang for their buck. You can even hop a free shuttle to Westwood to stroll, shop, and maybe even watch a few celebs walk the red carpet into their latest movie premiere.

Hotel Oceana (p. 71) offers big apartment-style suites outfitted with all the conveniences of home. Kids will love the bright colors, the cushy furniture, the video games on the TV, and the location—across the street from the beach.

Inn at Venice Beach (p. 79) is ideal for ocean-loving families thanks to near-the-beach location. The 3-block walk is lined with snack bars, surf shops, and bike and skate rentals. The under-12 set is welcomed free of charge, and everyone starts the day with complimentary breakfast.

Magic Castle Hotel (p. 99) is a good budget choice, with roomy apartment-style suites and close to Hollywood Boulevard's family friendly attractions.

Sheraton Universal Hotel (p. 106) enjoys a terrifically kid-friendly location, adjacent to Universal Studios and the fun CityWalk mall. Babysitting services are available, and there's a game room on the premises.

Wyndham Bel Age Hotel (p. 92) is a terrific all-suite hotel whose mega-size suites feature everything a family requires, including a sleeper sofa in the living area that opens into a second king bed, VCR and Sony Playstation on the TV, and a wet bar with fridge that allows for easy prep of morning cereal. There's no extra-person charge for kids (rates include up to four per unit), which improves the value-for-dollar ratio even more.

6 Pasadena & Environs

East of Downtown, pretty Pasadena is well preserved and architecturally rich. It's close via freeway to both Hollywood and Valley attractions, but forget about basing yourself here if you plan to spend your days at the beach and your nights trolling West Hollywood nightclubs. Those who like a quieter scene will enjoy Pasadena's charming range of accommodations, and the dining and shopping scene stands on its own.

VERY EXPENSIVE

The Ritz-Carlton, Huntington Hotel & Spa ★★★   Originally built in 1906, the opulent Huntington Hotel was one of America's grandest hotels, but not the most earthquake-proof. No matter—the hotel was rebuilt and opened on the same spot in 1991, and the astonishing authenticity (including reinstallation of many decorative features) even fools patrons from the resort's early days. This Spanish-Mediterranean beauty sits on 23 spectacularly landscaped acres that seem a world apart from L.A., though Downtown is only 20 minutes away. Each oversized guest room is dressed in conservatively elegant Ritz-Carlton style, softened by ultrapretty English garden textiles and a beautiful palette of celadon, cream, and butter yellow. Luxuries include beds dressed in Frette, marble bathrooms, thick carpets, and terry robes. You might consider spending a few extra dollars on a club-level room, which also features featherbeds, down comforters, CD players, morning coffee delivered with your wake-up call, and access to the club lounge with dedicated concierge and complimentary gourmet spreads all day (including breakfast).

The 12,000-square-foot full-service Ritz-Carlton Spa makes the Huntington an ideal place for a pampering getaway. Both guests and locals enjoy dining in the casual elegance of **The Grill,** but we prefer the more casual California-style **Terrace** Restaurant, which also serves at umbrella-covered tables by the Olympic-size pool (Southern California's first). High tea is served in the Lobby Lounge.

1401 S. Oak Knoll Ave., Pasadena, CA 91106. (✆ **800/241-3333** or 626/568-3900. Fax 626/568-3700. www.ritzcarlton.com. 392 units. $310–$420 double; from $415 suite. Discount packages always available. AE, DC, MC, V. Valet parking $21. Pets accepted. **Amenities:** 2 restaurants; 2 lounges (bar, Lobby Lounge for high tea); Olympic-size heated outdoor pool and Jacuzzi; 3 lighted tennis courts; full-service spa with whirlpool, sauna, and steam room; fitness center, concierge; business center; 24-hour room service; salon; in-room massage; babysitting; dry-cleaning/laundry service. *In room:* A/C, TV w/pay movies, CD, dataport and high-speed connection, minibar, hair dryer, iron, laptop-size safe.

MODERATE

Artists' Inn & Cottage Bed & Breakfast   Pleasantly unpretentious and furnished with wicker throughout, this yellow-shingled Victorian-style inn was built in 1895 as a farmhouse and expanded to include a neighboring 1909 home. Each of the ten rooms is decorated to reflect the style of a particular artist or period. Among the artistically inspired choices are the country-cozy New England–style Grandma Moses room; the soft, pastel-hued Degas suite; and the bold-lined, primary-hued Expressionist suite, a nod to such artists as Picasso and Dufy. Every room is thoughtfully arranged and features a private bathroom (many with period fixtures, three with Jacuzzi tubs), phone, fresh roses from the front garden, port wine, and chocolates. Most rooms have TVs; if yours doesn't, friendly innkeeper Janet Marangi will provide one if you want it. She's constantly improving the home—a 30-foot Seurat-inspired mural was added in

Pasadena Area Accommodations

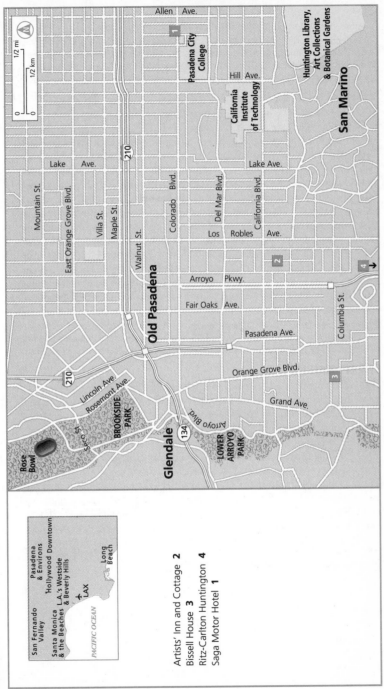

Artists' Inn and Cottage **2**
Bissell House **3**
Ritz-Carlton Huntington **4**
Saga Motor Hotel **1**

2000—so you can expect everything to be in tiptop shape. The quiet residential location is just 5 minutes from the heart of Old Town Pasadena.

1038 Magnolia St., South Pasadena, CA 91030. 📞 **888/799-5668** or 626/799-5668. Fax 626/799-3678. www.artistsinns.com. 10 units. $115–$205 double. Rates include full breakfast and afternoon tea. Check for midweek specials. Extra person $20. AE, MC, V. Free parking. *In room:* A/C, TV (upon request), dataport, hair dryer.

Bissell House Bed & Breakfast ⭐   If you enjoy the true B&B experience, you'll love the Bissell House. Hidden behind hedges that carefully isolate it from busy Orange Grove Avenue, this antique-filled 1887 gingerbread Victorian—the former home of the vacuum heiress and now owned by hosts Russell and Leonore Butcher—offers a unique taste of life on what was once Pasadena's "Millionaire's Row." Outfitted in a traditional chintz-and-cabbage roses style, all individually decorated rooms have private bathrooms (one with an antique claw-foot, one with a whirlpool tub, two with shower only), individual heating and air-conditioning (a B&B rarity), Internet access, and very comfortable beds. If you don't mind stairs, request one of the more spacious top-floor rooms. The modern world doesn't interfere with the mood in these romantic sanctuaries, but the downstairs library features a TV with VCR and a telephone/fax machine for guests' use. The beautifully landscaped grounds boast an inviting pool, Jacuzzi, and deck with lounge chairs. Included in the room rate is an elaborately pre-pared breakfast served in the large dining room, as well as an afternoon tea, cookie, and wine service.

201 Orange Grove Ave. (at Columbia St.), South Pasadena, CA 91030. 📞 **800/441-3530** or 626/441-3535. Fax 626/441-3671. www.bissellhouse.com. 6 units. $125–$185 double. Rates include full breakfast. AE, MC, V. Free parking. **Amenities:** Outdoor pool and Jacuzzi; CD and video libraries. *In room:* A/C, hair dryer, iron.

INEXPENSIVE

Saga Motor Hotel *(Value)*   This 1950s relic of old Route 66 has far more char-acter than most other motels in its price range. The rooms are small, clean, and simply furnished with the basics. The double/doubles are spacious enough for shares, but budget-minded families will prefer the extralarge configuration ded-icated to them, which has a king and two doubles. The best rooms are in the front building surrounding the gated swimming pool, shielded from the street and inviting in warm weather. The grounds are attractive and well kept, if you don't count the Astroturf "lawn" on the pool deck. The location is very quiet and very good, just off the Foothill (210) Freeway about a mile from the Hunting-ton Library and within 10 minutes of both the Rose Bowl and Old Pasadena.

1633 E. Colorado Blvd. (between Allen and Sierra Bonita aves.), Pasadena, CA 91106. 📞 **800/793-7242** or 626/795-0431. Fax 626/792-0559. www.thesagamotorhotel.com. 70 units. $65–$89 double; $99 family suite. Rates include continental breakfast. AE, DC, DISC, MC, V. Free parking. **Amenities:** Outdoor heated pool; free self-serve Laundromat; dry-cleaning/laundry service. *In room:* A/C, TV, dataport.

6

Where to Dine

What a roller coaster ride Los Angeles gastronomy has been. A mere 30 years ago, Southland gourmands, frustrated by their limited choices, could be spotted flying up to San Francisco for a "decent" meal (well, the wealthier ones, that is). All that changed with Wolfgang Puck and the age of culinary enlightenment—but L.A. got a bad reputation in the heady '80s for ultra-trendy restaurants serving bird-size portions of the newly named "California cuisine" complete with a side order of snooty indifference.

Luckily, the economy and social atmosphere leveled out, and restaurants began catering to "real" people again. The California cuisine that was so groundbreaking eventually became a staple across the country, and superstar chef Puck made diversification a veritable art form. His name graces not only several fine restaurants throughout the Southwest, but also a line of frozen foods based on his recipes, as well as a chain of casual Wolfgang Puck Cafés—we've even started spotting him on TV's Food Network.

California cuisine's successor was "fusion," a term describing the blending of Asian, European, and American ingredients and techniques. But that trend led to dishes whose ingredient lists were so long diners were getting tennis elbow just lifting their menus. Drew Nieporent, the Bill Gates of restaurateurs, summed it up when he said, "Fusion food is getting out of control; they should call it confusion food."

As a result, today's chefs believe "less is more." The hottest trend in L.A. dining is New American fare, a rubric that manages to incorporate generous helpings of international flavor adorning the dishes you thought you knew, and diners are busy developing a taste for flavors-of-the-moment squab, kabocha squash, and foie gras. Meat and potatoes has come a long way from the artery-clogging infamy of recent decades, and is now a badge of honor for any gourmet menu. The meats appear both haute (veal cheeks, venison, or dry-aged Midwest beef) and humble (lamb shanks, meatloaf, and skirt steak), while L.A.'s chefs seem to be in a contest for creative potato presentation. We've seen the humble spud mashed with wasabi, curry, and parsnips (not all together, thankfully), held in a deep-fried potato nest, and even shaped to resemble another vegetable entirely; formerly rare varieties like fingerlings or Yukon golds have also become commonplace.

But jazzed-up comfort food is only part of the story. The 2000 census painted a multiethnic portrait of a Los Angeles with more minorities than majorities, and that diversity is represented in the vast array of cuisines Angelenos are happy to consider commonplace. Asian food and Asian hybrids are enormously popular, and join a rainbow of Argentinean, Armenian, Cajun/Creole, Caribbean, Cuban, Ethiopian, Indian, Korean Lebanese, Oaxacan, Peruvian, Spanish, Thai, and Vietnamese choices, so chances are whatever you're in the mood for, L.A.'s serving it.

The city's restaurants are categorized below first by area, then by price (*$$$* is expensive, *$$* is moderate, and *$* is inexpensive). Keep in mind that many of the restaurants listed as "expensive" are usually moderately priced at lunch.

1 Restaurants by Cuisine

AMERICAN/TRADITIONAL

Blueberry ✸ (Santa Monica, $, p. 127)

Crocodile Cafe (Pasadena, $, p. 155)

Du-par's Restaurant & Bakery ✸ (San Fernando Valley, $, p. 150)

Fred 62 (Hollywood, $, p. 143)

Good Stuff (Manhattan Beach, $, p. 127)

Kate Mantilini (Westside, $$, p. 136)

Musso & Frank Grill ✸ (Hollywood, $$, p. 142)

The Original Pantry (Downtown, $, p. 148)

Sidewalk Café (Venice, $, p. 128)

Swingers ✸ (Hollywood, $, p. 144)

NEW AMERICAN/ AMERICAN ECLECTIC

The Ivy ✸✸ (Westside, $$$, p. 130)

JiRaffe ✸✸ (Santa Monica, $$$, p. 120)

Joe's ✸✸ (Venice, $$, p. 126)

Maple Drive ✸✸ (Beverly Hills, $$$, p. 132)

The Raymond ✸✸ (Pasadena, $$$, p. 152)

BREAKFAST

Blueberry ✸ (Santa Monica, $, p. 127)

Bread & Porridge ✸ (Santa Monica, $, p. 126)

Campanile ✸✸ (Hollywood, $$$, p. 139)

Cava (Westside, $$, p. 134)

Cha Cha Cha ✸✸ (Downtown, $$, p. 146)

Chez Melange ✸✸ (Redondo Beach, $$, p. 123)

Du-par's ✸ (San Fernando Valley, $, p. 150)

Fred 62 (Hollywood, $, p. 143)

Jerry's Famous Deli ✸ (San Fernando Valley, $$, p. 150)

Kate Mantilini ✸ (Westside, $$, p. 136)

Kay 'n Dave's Cantina (Santa Monica, $, p. 127)

Langer's ✸ (Downtown, $, p. 148)

Nate & Al ✸ (Beverly Hills, $, p. 138)

The Original Pantry (Downtown, $, p. 148)

Philippe the Original (Downtown, $, p. 148)

Roscoe's House of Chicken 'n' Waffles ✸ (Hollywood, $, p. 143)

Sidewalk Café (Venice, $, p. 128)

Swingers ✸ (Hollywood, $, p. 144)

CALIFORNIA

Chez Melange ✸✸ (Redondo Beach, $$, p. 123)

Encounter at LAX ✸✸ (Airport, $$$, p. 117)

Four Oaks ✸✸✸ (Westside, $$$, p. 130)

Jozu ✸✸ (Westside, $$$, p. 131)

Michael's ✸✸ (Santa Monica, $$$, p. 121)

Parkway Grill ✸ (Pasadena, $$$, p. 152)

Röckenwagner ✸✸ (Santa Monica, $$$, p. 121)

Spago ✸✸✸ (Beverly Hills, $$$, p. 133)

Tahiti ✸ (Hollywood, $$, p. 142)

Traxx ✸ (Downtown, $$, p. 147)

CALIFORNIA-FRENCH

Bistro 45 ★★ (Pasadena, $$$, p. 149)

Cafe Pinot ★ (Downtown, $$, p. 147)

Patina ★★★ (Hollywood, $$$, p. 139)

Paul's Café ★ (San Fernando Valley, $$, p. 150)

Pinot Bistro ★★ (San Fernando Valley, $$$, p. 150)

CALIFORNIA-MEDITERRANEAN

Campanile ★★ (Hollywood, $$$, p. 139)

Granita ★★★ (Malibu, $$$, p. 120)

CARIBBEAN/CUBAN

Cha Cha Cha ★★ (Downtown, $$, p. 146)

Versailles ★ (Westside, $, p. 138)

CHINESE

Joss ★ (Westside, $$, p. 135)

Nonya ★★ (Pasadena, $$, p. 154)

Yang Chow Restaurant ★★ (Downtown, $$, p. 147)

Yujean Kang's Gourmet Chinese Cuisine ★★ (Pasadena, $$, p. 155)

CONTINENTAL

Musso & Frank Grill ★ (Hollywood, $$, p. 142)

The Raymond ★★ (Pasadena, $$$, p. 152)

DELICATESSEN

Jerry's Famous Deli ★ (San Fernando Valley, $$, p. 150)

Langer's ★ (Downtown, $, p. 148)

Nate & Al ★ (Beverly Hills, $, p. 138)

ETHIOPIAN

Nyala ★ (Westside, $$, p. 137)

FRANCO-CHINESE

Chinois on Main ★ (Santa Monica, $$$, p. 117)

FRANCO-JAPANESE

Chaya Brasserie ★★ (Westside, $$, p. 134)

FRANCO-MEDITERRANEAN

Lucques ★★ (West Hollywood, $$$, p. 132)

FRANCO-RUSSIAN

Diaghilev ★★★ (West Hollywood, $$$, p. 130)

FRENCH (PROVENÇAL)

Mimosa ★ (Westside, $$$, p. 133)

Pastis ★ (Westside, $$, p. 137)

GREEK

Café Santorini ★ (Pasadena, $$, p. 154)

Sofi ★ (Hollywood, $$, p. 142)

HEALTH FOOD/VEGETARIAN

Inn of the Seventh Ray (Topanga Canyon, $$, p. 123)

INDIAN

Bombay Café ★★ (Westside, $$, p. 134)

INTERNATIONAL

Bread & Porridge ★ (Santa Monica, $, p. 126)

Crocodile Cafe (Pasadena, $, p. 155)

Good Stuff (Manhattan Beach, $, p. 127)

ITALIAN, NORTHERN

Ca' Brea ★★ (Hollywood, $$, p. 140)

Chianti Cucina ★ (Hollywood, $$, p. 140)

Il Pastaio ★ (Westside, $$, p. 135)

Locanda Veneta ★ (Westside, $$, p. 136)

Valentino ★★ (Santa Monica, $$$, p. 122)

Vincenti Ristorante ★ (Santa Monica, $$$, p. 122)

ITALIAN, SOUTHERN

Tanino Ristorante and Bar ★ (Westwood, $$, p. 137)

ITALIAN, TRADITIONAL
Miceli's (San Fernando Valley, $$, p. 150)

JAPANESE/SUSHI
Matsuhisa ★★★ (Westside, $$$, p. 133)

R23 ★★ (Downtown, $$, p. 147)

LATIN
Ciudad ★★ (Downtown, $$, p. 146)

MALAYSIAN
Nonya ★★ (Pasadena, $$, p. 154)

MEXICAN
Border Grill ★★★ (Santa Monica, $$, p. 122)

Casa Vega ★ (San Fernando Valley, $$, p. 149)

El Cholo ★ (Hollywood, $, p. 143)

El Coyote ★ (Westside, $$, p. 135)

Kay 'n Dave's Cantina (Santa Monica, $, p. 127)

La Serenata Gourmet ★★ (Westside, $$, p. 136)

MIDDLE EASTERN
Skewers' (West Hollywood, $, p. 138)

MOROCCAN
Dar Maghreb ★ (Hollywood, $$$, p. 139)

PACIFIC RIM
Cafe Del Rey ★★ (Marina del Rey, $$$, p. 117)

Jozu ★★ (West Hollywood, $$$, p. 131)

Tahiti ★ (Hollywood, $$, p. 142)

PERANAKAN
Nonya ★★ (Pasadena, $$, p. 154)

SANDWICHES/BURGERS/ HOT DOGS
The Apple Pan ★★ (Westside, $, p. 138)

Jody Maroni's Sausage Kingdom ★ (Venice, $, p. 127)

Philippe the Original (Downtown, $, p. 148)

Pink's Hot Dogs ★ (Hollywood, $, p. 144)

SEAFOOD
Crustacean ★★ (Beverly Hills, $$$, p. 128)

Granita ★★★ (Malibu, $$$, p. 120)

Kincaid's Bay House ★ (Redondo Beach, $$$, p. 120)

Lawry's The Prime Rib ★ (Beverly Hills, $$$, p. 132)

The Lobster ★ (Santa Monica, $$$, p. 121)

Water Grill ★★★ (Downtown, $$$, p. 144)

SOUTHERN
Roscoe's House of Chicken 'n' Waffles ★ (Hollywood, $, p. 143)

SOUTHWESTERN
Authentic Café ★ (Hollywood, $$, p. 140)

SPANISH
Cava (Westside, $$, p. 134)

STEAKS
Kincaid's Bay House ★ (Redondo Beach, $$$, p. 120)

Lawry's The Prime Rib ★ (Beverly Hills, $$$, p. 132)

The Palm ★ (West Hollywood, $$$, p. 133)

THAI
Talesai ★ (San Fernando Valley, $$$, p. 149)

Toi on Sunset ★ (Hollywood, $, p. 144)

VIETNAMESE
Crustacean ★★ (Beverly Hills, $$$, p. 128)

2 Santa Monica & the Beaches

EXPENSIVE

Cafe Del Rey ★★ PACIFIC RIM   Cafe Del Rey is a lively, open, high-tech space that makes a meal feel like an event. The huge menu filled with unusual (and often fusion) choices makes ordering fun, and there's a terrific view of the Marina's bobbing sailboats. In the summer the windows are opened to turn the room in to an indoor-outdoor dining area, or you can opt for a patio table over-looking the harbor. The exhibition kitchen focuses on creative preparations of fresh, seasonal foods. While most dishes are very good, some are a bit too cre-ative or contrived. Cuban black-bean soup, Angus New York steak, and the honey-cured crispy Peking duck are all winners, as is the huge scallop appetizer wrapped with boar bacon. But the menu changes so frequently that it's impos-sible to accurately categorize the cafe's cuisine. What's continually stellar is the *Wine Spectator* award-winning wine list, offering more than 340 selections. Our advice: Request a table by the window, ask your server what's good today, pair it with a nice bottle of wine, and enjoy a long, leisurely cellphone-free meal.

4451 Admiralty Way (between Lincoln and Washington blvds.), Marina del Rey. ✆ 310/823-6395. www.cafedelrey.com. Reservations recommended. Dinner main courses $15–$29; lunch $9–$15. AE, DC, DISC, MC, V. Mon–Sat 11:30am–2:30pm; Mon–Thurs 5:30–10pm; Fri–Sat 5:30–10:30pm; Sun 5–9:30pm; Sun brunch 9:30am–2:30pm. Valet parking free for lunch, dinner $3.50.

Chinois on Main ★ FRANCO-CHINESE   Wolfgang Puck's Franco-Chinese eatery bustles nightly with locals and visitors wowed by the eatery's reputation and rarely disappointed by the food. Groundbreaking in its time, the restaurant still relies on the quirky East-meets-West mélange of ingredients and technique. The menu is about equally split between Chinois's signature dishes and seasonal creations. The most famous of the former are Cantonese duck in a sweet-tangy plum sauce, and farm-raised whole catfish that's perfectly deep fried and dra-matically presented. Terrific newer dishes include lobster and sea bass sautéed together and flavored with porcini oil and ponzu sauce, and rare roasted loin of venison served in a ginger-spiced port and sun-dried cherries sauce. The dining room, designed by Puck's wife, Barbara Lazaroff, is as visually colorful as it is acoustically loud.

2709 Main St. (south of Pico Blvd.), Santa Monica. ✆ 310/392-9025. Reservations required. Main courses $23–$29. AE, DC, MC, V. Wed–Fri 11:30am–2pm; daily 6–10:30pm. Valet parking $5.

Encounter at LAX ★★ CALIFORNIA   There's always been a restaurant in the spacey Theme Building (ca. 1961) perched in LAX's midst, but these days it draws as many Angelenos as fly-by travelers (including John Travolta, who had his star-studded birthday party here). The reason? A recent makeover trans-forming the staid Continental dining room (whose best feature was a panoramic view over the runways) into a 1960s *Star Trek* set gone Technicolor. Outer-space lounge music dominates the entire place, and waitresses endure silver satin minidress costumes complete with go-go boots. The menu features art-food, that L.A. specialty that combines too many ingredients and focuses more on cre-ating sculptural arrangements on the plate than culinary delights for the taste buds; that said, the food is entertaining and adequately satisfying. If you're stop-ping at LAX with kids in tow, not to worry—Encounter's party atmosphere ensures they'll enjoy themselves without disrupting the ambience a bit. Short on time? We suggest at least coming up and having a blue cocktail at the lava lamp–festooned bar, because quirky Encounter is worth an encounter.

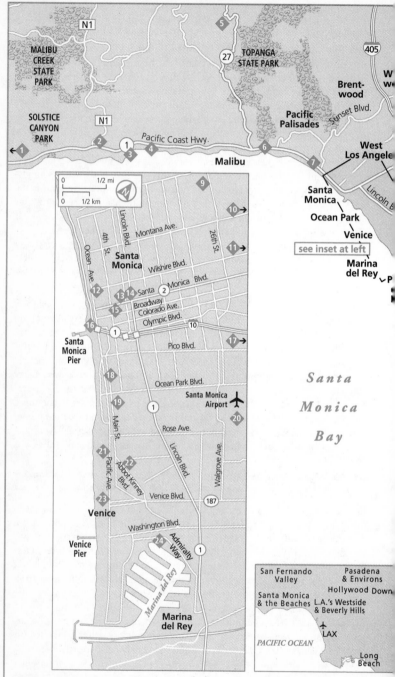

Book your air, hotel, and transportation all in one place.

Hotel or hostel? Cruise or canoe? Car?
Plane? Camel? Wherever you're going,
visit Yahoo! Travel and get total control
over your arrangements. Even choose
your seat assignment. So. One hump
or two? travel.yahoo.com

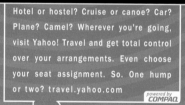

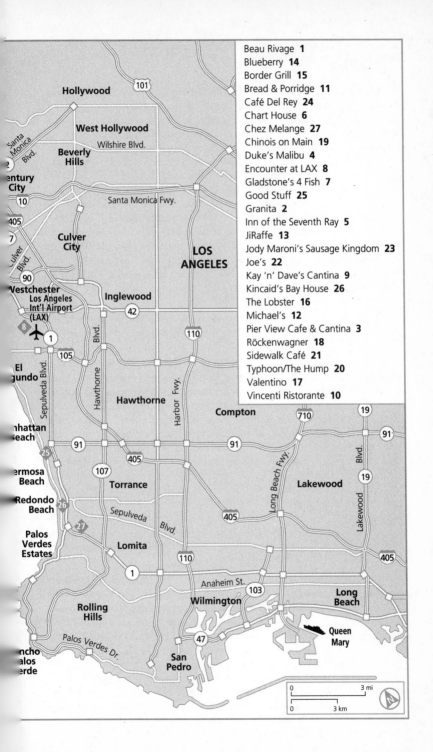

Beau Rivage **1**
Blueberry **14**
Border Grill **15**
Bread & Porridge **11**
Café Del Rey **24**
Chart House **6**
Chez Melange **27**
Chinois on Main **19**
Duke's Malibu **4**
Encounter at LAX **8**
Gladstone's 4 Fish **7**
Good Stuff **25**
Granita **2**
Inn of the Seventh Ray **5**
JiRaffe **13**
Jody Maroni's Sausage Kingdom **23**
Joe's **22**
Kay 'n' Dave's Cantina **9**
Kincaid's Bay House **26**
The Lobster **16**
Michael's **12**
Pier View Cafe & Cantina **3**
Röckenwagner **18**
Sidewalk Café **21**
Typhoon/The Hump **20**
Valentino **17**
Vincenti Ristorante **10**

209 World Way (Theme Building, Los Angeles International Airport). ℂ **310/215-5151.** Reservations recommended for dinner. Dinner main courses $15–$29; lunch $7–$14. AE, DC, DISC, MC, V. Daily 10:30am–9pm. Valet parking $7.

Granita ★★★ CALIFORNIA/MEDITERRANEAN/SEAFOOD   Longtime Granita/Spago staffer Jennifer Naylor now wears the toque at this, one of Wolfgang Puck's earlier Spago cousins, situated in Malibu just blocks from the star-studded "Colony." Although the restaurant's over-the-top decor—a surreal eruption of oceanic kaleidoscopic art augmented by equally colorful fish swimming in lighted aquariums—is a bit dated, lovers of seafood don't seem to mind, judging by the ringing phones, crowded bar, and satisfied diners. Naylor's strength is interpreting the ever-changing selection of fresh seafood at her disposal; the preparations are both Puckish (eclectic California blendings) and reflective of Naylor's Italian training. Look for seared scallops and prawns served over an orzo-mascarpone-porcini mix, or black bass grilled with fennel, citrus reduction, and premium olive oil. Besides fish, the menu always features duck (choice of confit with celery-root gnocchi, or the splendid Cantonese style with blood orange/ginger glaze) and other inventive meat and poultry dishes. Gourmet pizzas are here, too—perfect for light meals or sharing. The appetizers are delectable, expensive, and richly filling.

In the Malibu Colony Plaza, 23725 W. Malibu Rd. (at Webb Way), Malibu. ℂ **310/456-0488.** www.wolfgang puck.com. Reservations required. Main courses $19–$32. AE, DC, DISC, MC, V. Tues–Sun 6–10pm; Sat–Sun 11am–2pm. Free parking.

JiRaffe ★★ NEW AMERICAN/FRENCH   "JiRaffe"—no, it's not named after the long-necked creature, but a blending of names from the two chefs responsible for this overnight sensation. Josiah Citrin has since left partner Raphael Lunetta to carry on alone at this crowded, upscale bistro in restaurant-hungry Santa Monica. The deafening din of conversation here is usually praise for JiRaffe's artistic treatment of whitefish (spiced and served with sugar snap peas, glazed carrots, and ginger-carrot sauce), roasted rabbit, crispy salmon, or pork chop (grilled with wild rice, smoked bacon, apple chutney, and cider sauce). JiRaffe also wins culinary points for highlighting oft-ignored vegetables like salsify, Swiss chard, and fennel, as well as complex appetizers that are more like miniature main dishes. *Tip:* Visit JiRaffe's website for Chef Lunetta's "Recipe of the Month."

502 Santa Monica Blvd. (corner of Fifth St.), Santa Monica. ℂ **310/917-6671.** www.jirafferestaurant.com. Reservations recommended. Main courses $19–$26. AE, DC, MC, V. Mon 6–10pm; Tues–Thurs noon–2pm and 6–10pm; Fri–Sat 6–11pm; Sun 5:30–9pm. Valet parking $4.50.

Kincaid's Bay House ★ SEAFOOD/STEAKS   This branch of the venerable San Francisco/Hawaii surf-and-turf specialists is the classiest joint on the reborn Redondo Beach pier. Sporting a sleek, clubby decor, the restaurant boasts panoramic ocean views, a relaxed bar with outdoor seating, and an open kitchen starring a huge hardwood spit-roaster redolent with the aroma of sweet, smoky Nebraska-bred beef. The menu, composed by Kincaid's Hawaiian executive chef, offers island-influenced dishes, such as char-sui pork skewers grilled over apple wood to caramelize the sweet-tart honey/soy/hoisin marinade. Fresh fish from the Pacific Northwest and Hawaii are featured each day; other seafood specialties include wood-smoked prawns flavored with chipotle-ancho rub and Kincaid's signature barbecue hollandaise, plus crab-and-shrimp hash served with sherry-cream sauce. If the signature spit-roasted prime rib doesn't entice you meat lovers, consider seasoned and buttered sirloin, or pan-seared venison flavored with blackberry and sage. For dessert, there's Key lime pie—the pale yellow color lets you know it's authentic—or pear bread pudding baked in individual ramekins and served with bourbon-custard sauce.

500 Fisherman's Wharf (at Harbor Dr., on the north end of the pier), Redondo Beach. ℂ 310/318-6080. www.kincaidsredondobeach.com. Reservations recommended. Dinner main courses $15–$26; lunch $9–$16. AE, DC, DISC, MC, V. Mon–Thurs 11:30am–10pm; Fri–Sat 11:30am–11pm; Sun 11am–9pm. Self-parking $3–$5.

The Lobster ⭐ SEAFOOD   There's been a seafood shack called The Lobster on the Santa Monica Pier since 1923—almost as long as the pier's been standing—but 2000's revival brings a new sophistication to the old favorite. The interior is completely rebuilt, but still accentuates a seaside ambience and a million-dollar ocean view; the menu has been revamped by chef Allyson Thurber, who brings an impressive culinary pedigree (including Downtown's Water Grill) to the kitchen. Although the namesake crustacean is a great choice, the menu consistently presents a multitude of ultrafresh fish with thoughtful and creative preparation. Specialties range from spicy Louisiana prawns, Jumbo Lump Crab Cakes, to an excellent sautéed North Carolina black bass luxuriating in white truffle sauce accompanied by lobster salad. Creative appetizers include ahi carpaccio with tangy tobiko wasabi, steamed mussels and Manila clams with applewood bacon, and oysters plain or fancy. For something truly decadent, try the Kasu Marinated Seabass and pick a bottle of dry chardonnay from the well-stocked cellar. The menu offers a couple of fine steaks for landlubbers, and there's a practiced bar for dedicated locals.

1602 Ocean Ave. (at Colorado) ℂ 310/458-9294. www.thelobster.com. Reservations recommended. Main courses $15–$32. AE, MC, V. Daily 11:30am–3pm and 5–10pm. Self-parking $3–$6.

Michael's ⭐⭐ CALIFORNIA   Owner Michael McCarty, L.A.'s answer to Alice Waters, is considered by many to be the father of California cuisine. Since Michael's opened in 1979 (when McCarty was only 25), several top L.A. restaurants have caught up to it, but this fetching Santa Monica venue remains one of the city's best. The dining room is filled with contemporary art by Michael's wife, Kim McCarty, and the restaurant's beloved garden is a relaxed setting for always-inventive menu choices like Baqueta sea bass with a chanterelle mushroom ragout and fresh Provençal herbs, seared Hawaiian ahi accented with braised enoki mushrooms and earthy-tangy sesame wasabi ponzu sauce, or grilled pork chop sweetened with sweet potato purée and anise–pinot noir sauce. Don't miss Michael's famous warm mushroom salad, tossed with crumbled goat cheese, watercress, caramelized onion, and mustard-sage vinaigrette. *Note:* Michael's automatically adds a 15% service charge to the check.

1147 Third St. (north of Wilshire Blvd.), Santa Monica. ℂ 310/451-0843. Reservations recommended. Dinner main courses $13–$23; lunch $27–$34. AE, DC, DISC, MC, V. Mon–Fri 11:30am–2:30pm and 6–10:30pm; Sat 6–10:30pm. Valet parking $4.50.

Röckenwagner ⭐⭐ CALIFORNIA   Set in Frank Gehry's starkly modern Edgemar complex (itself a work of art), chef Hans Röckenwagner's eponymous restaurant continues the motif by presenting edible sculpture amid a gallery-like decor. Although it sits in the midst of a popular shopping area, the space manages to be refreshingly quiet. Röckenwagner takes his art—and his food—very seriously, once orchestrating an entire menu around German white asparagus at the height of its short season. The unpretentious staff serves deliciously pretentious dishes fusing Pacific Rim ingredients with traditional European preparations; a good example is the langoustine ravioli with mangoes in port-wine reduction and curry oil. The menu tastes as good as it reads—seared foie gras on raisin toast with tangerines, panko-crusted petrale sole with haricot vert (green bean) tempura—and desserts are to die for. Don't overlook the lunch bargains, the unique European-style breakfast of bread and cheese, or the informal WunderBAR Wine and Snack Bar for a quick drop-in bite.

2435 Main St. (north of Ocean Park Blvd.), Santa Monica. ☎ **310/399-6504**. www.rockenwagner.com. Reservations recommended. Main courses $22–$31. AE, DC, MC, V. Mon–Fri 6–10pm; Sat 5:30–11pm; Sun 10am–2:30pm and 5:30–10pm. Valet parking $4.

Valentino ★★ NORTHERN ITALIAN   Valentino is a good choice if you're splurging on just one special dinner. Charming owner Piero Selvaggio oversees two other restaurants, but his distinctive touch still pervades this 26-year-old flagship. This elegant spot continues to maintain its position as *Wine Spectator* magazine's top wine cellar, and former *New York Times* food critic Ruth Reichl calls this the best Italian restaurant in the United States. The creations of Selvaggio and his brilliant Italian-born chef, Angelo Auriana, make dinners here lengthy multicourse affairs (often involving several bottles of wine). You might begin with a crisp pinot grigio paired with caviar-filled cannoli, or *crespelle*—thin little pancakes with fresh porcini mushrooms and a rich melt of Fontina cheese. A rich *barolo* is the perfect accompaniment to rosemary-infused roasted rabbit; the fantastically fragrant risotto with white truffles is one of the most magnificent dishes we've ever had. Jackets are all but required in the elegant dining room.

3115 Pico Blvd. (west of Bundy Dr.), Santa Monica. ☎ **310/829-4313**. www.welovewine.com. Reservations required. Main courses $22–$32. AE, DC, MC, V. Mon–Thurs 5:30–10:30pm; Fri 11:30am–2:30pm and 5:30–11pm; Sat 5:30–11pm. Valet parking $4.

Vincenti Ristorante ★ NORTHERN ITALIAN   Despite newer trends sweeping L.A., finely executed northern Italian cuisine is still going strong, as evidenced by this Westside standout. Opened by Maureen Vincenti, widow of Mauro (whose Downtown Rex ruled the scene for years), Vincenti lives up to its promising pedigree. The menu, praised as "authentically Italian," offers such unusual fare as homemade pasta with lobster and a touch of red pepper, pumpkin-squash ravioli sauced with asparagus and sage, plus rotisserie-cooked whole fish, game birds, and meat. Economy-minded diners with upwardly mobile palates can easily stick with hearty appetizers and pastas ($9–$18) and still have some left for one of Vincenti's tempting *dolci* (sweets).

11930 San Vicente Blvd. (west of Montana Ave.), Brentwood. ☎ **310/207-0127**. Reservations recommended. Main courses $18–$32. AE, MC, V. Tues–Thurs, Sat 6–10pm; Fri noon–2pm and 6–10pm; Sun 6–9pm. Valet parking $4.50.

MODERATE

Border Grill ★★★ MEXICAN   Before Mary Sue Milliken and Susan Feniger spiced up cable TV as "Too Hot Tamales," they started this restaurant in West Hollywood. Now Border Grill has moved to a boldly painted, cavernous (read: loud) space in Santa Monica, and the gals aren't in the kitchen very much at all (though cookbooks and paraphernalia from their Food Network show are displayed prominently for sale). But their influence on the inspired menu is enough to maintain the cantina's popularity with folks who swear by the authentic flavor of Yucatán fish tacos, rock shrimp with ancho chilies, and meaty *ropa vieja*,

> **Finds   Come Fly with Me . . . Two Great Meals with a View**
>
> Pilot-turned-restaurateur Brian Vidor must have endured too many snack-bar egg-salad sandwiches in his flying days, because he works hard to make his two dinner-only restaurants (alongside Santa Monica Airport's runway) culinary masterpieces. First came **Typhoon,** 3221 Donald Douglas Loop S. (② **310/390-6565;** www.typhoon-restaurant.com), a Pan-Asian spot where Taiwanese spicy crickets punctuate a menu filled with less exotic fare from throughout southeast Asia; the well-stocked bar even offers a Chinese herb-infused vodka reputed to have aphrodisiac qualities. Upstairs is **The Hump** (② **310/313-0977**), bearing the nickname pilots have for the Himalayas. Feeling like an outpost at some airfield in the tropics, this small Japanese restaurant boasts pedigreed sushi master Hiro Nishimura, who presents ultrafresh fish artistically prepared. Despite the odd location, word-of-mouth guarantees a wait any night of the week.

the traditional Latin stew. The best meatless dish is *mulitas de hongos,* a layering of portobello mushrooms, poblano chilies, black beans, cheese, and guacamole, spiced up with roasted garlic and seared red chard. Distracting desserts are displayed prominently near the entrance, so you may spend the meal fantasizing about the yummy coconut flan or Key lime pie.

1445 Fourth St. (between Broadway and Santa Monica Blvd.), Santa Monica. ② **310/451-1655.** www.bordergrill.com. Reservations recommended. Main courses $10–$21. AE, DC, DISC, MC, V. Mon 5–10pm; Tues–Thurs 11:30am–10pm; Fri–Sat 11:30am–11pm; Sun 11:30am–10pm. Metered parking lots; valet parking $4.

Chez Melange ★★ BREAKFAST/CALIFORNIA   Located inside the modest Palos Verdes Inn, this well-regarded brasserie has been presenting artful California cuisine so long it's become a South Bay institution. Though the menu is no longer cutting-edge, it does seem to get more and more eclectic, moving seamlessly from Japanese to Cajun, Italian to Chinese, and keeping up-to-date with premium vodkas and a mouthwatering oyster-and-seafood bar. The decor has a dated, late 1980s feel, but the conservative, moneyed crowd here doesn't mind. Each meal begins with a basket of irresistible breads before moving on to international dishes like shrimp and chicken in orange vindaloo curry over basmati rice with sweet, chunky chutney; rosemary laced pork tenderloin and shallot-sherry cream sauce; Parmesan-crusted albacore with Greek feta salad and tabbouleh; or spicy blackened halibut sauced with horseradish and served with seafood gumbo. Spa cuisine selections are available at every meal.

1716 Pacific Coast Hwy. (between Palos Verdes Blvd. and Prospect Ave.), Redondo Beach. ② **310/540-1222.** www.chezmelange.com. Reservations recommended. Dinner main courses $13–$19; lunch $8–$13. AE, DISC, MC, V. Mon–Thurs 8am–10pm; Fri–Sat 8am–11pm; Sun 8am–10pm. Free parking.

Inn of the Seventh Ray HEALTH FOOD/VEGETARIAN   Topanga Canyon has long been the home of leftover hippies and L.A.'s New Agers; it's a mountainous, sparsely populated area that's undeniably beautiful, even spiritual. This restaurant, a former church, oozes "aura." No one comes here for the food; they come for a romantic dining experience, far from the bright lights of the city. About half of the seating is outdoors, at tables overlooking a creek and endless tangles of untamed vines and shrubs. Inside, the dining room is rustic, with a

Sea Breezes & Sunsets: Ocean-View Dining in Malibu

Despite fires, mudslides, and high rents, Malibu residents remain enamored of their precious parcel of beachfront paradise. There really is a beautifully calm, on-vacation vibe to this upscale stretch of coast. One of the best ways to sample a slice of this happiness pie is to (literally) turn your back on the frenzy of L.A. and gaze upon the sparkling Pacific—at least for the duration of a meal.

From south to north, numerous restaurants dot the coastline, all exploiting as much ocean view as their property line allows. Here are some of our favorites:

Gladstone's 4 Fish, 17300 Pacific Coast Hwy., at Sunset Boulevard (ⓒ 310/454-3474). A local tradition, Gladstone's is totally immersed in the Malibu scene. It shares a parking lot with a public beach, so the restaurant's wood deck has a constant view of surfers, bikini-clad sunbathers, and other frolicking beachgoers. At busy times, Gladstone's even sets up picnic-style tables on the sand. Prices are moderate, and the atmosphere is casual. The menu offers several pages of fresh fish and seafood, augmented by a few salads and other meals for landlubbers—it's mostly fried tourist food, but it gets the job done. Gladstone's is popular for afternoon/evening drinking and offers nearly 20 seafood appetizer platters; it's also known for decadent chocolate desserts large enough for the whole table. Open Monday through Thursday from 11am to 11pm, Friday from 11am to midnight, Saturday from 7am to midnight, Sunday from 7am to 11pm. Parking is $3.50.

The Chart House, 18412 Pacific Coast Hwy., south of Topanga Canyon (ⓒ 310/454-9321). Most branches of this surf-and-turf chain are noted for unique architecture, but the Malibu branch lets its dramatic location steal the show. Built on a rocky point, suspended over the sand, and often perilously close to the breaking surf, the Chart House's dining room is terraced so every table has a great view. The interior is dark and woody, with a cozy bar and the glimmer of copper hoods from the exposed kitchen. There are some outdoor tables, but most seating is inside. The menu, though predictable (prime rib, steaks, lobsters, seafood), is first class. Prices are moderate to expensive but include a generous meal's worth of food. Lunch portions provide a more affordable option. Open Monday and Tuesday from 5 to 9:30pm, Wednesday and Thursday from 11:30am to 9:30pm, Friday and Saturday from 11:30am to 10:30pm, Sunday from 11am to 9:30pm. Complimentary valet parking.

Duke's Malibu , 21150 Pacific Coast Hwy., at Las Flores Canyon (ⓒ 310/317-0777). Lovers of Hawaii and all things Polynesian will thrive

sloped roof and a glass wall offering mountain views. Everything is prepared from scratch, and foods are organic and chemical- and preservative-free with a large vegan menu. The fish are caught in deep water far offshore and served the same day; you can even order unpasteurized wines that are quite good. Ten main in this outpost of the Hawaiian chain. Imagine a South Pacific T.G.I. Fridays where the food is secondary to the decor, then add a rocky perch atop breaking waves, and you have this surfing-themed crowd-pleaser. It's worth a visit for the memorabilia alone—the place is named for Hawaiian surf legend "Duke" Kahanamoku. Duke's offers up pretty good food at inflated, but not outrageous, prices. You'll find plenty of good-quality fresh fish prepared in the Hawaiian regional style, hearty surf and turf, a smattering of chicken and pasta dishes, and plenty of finger-lickin' appetizers to accompany Duke's Day-Glo tropical cocktails. Open Monday through Thursday from 11:30am to 10pm, Friday and Saturday from 11:30am to 10:30pm, Sunday from 10am to 10pm. Valet parking $2 (dinner and weekends only, otherwise free self-parking).

Pier View Cafe & Cantina, 22718 Pacific Coast Hwy. (© 310/456-6962). This appropriately named restaurant sits on the beach about a half mile south of the pier, and it offers huge portions of inexpensive food in an ultracasual ("shirts and shoes required") setting. Inside there's sawdust on the floor and surfboards in the rafters; sun lovers get the wind in their hair at tables along Pier View's clunky wooden deck. The comprehensive menu has something for everyone, including giant farm-style breakfasts, Baja-style fish tacos, burgers served with a mound of curly fries, a terrifically meaty chili, and fresh seafood and enormous main-course salads. For the lingering cocktail crowd, there's a long list of appetizer platters. An added bonus is patrons-only direct beach access from the outdoor deck. Open Sunday through Thursday from 7am to midnight, Friday and Saturday from 7am to 1am. Valet parking $3 (Fri–Sun only, otherwise free self-parking).

Beau Rivage, 26025 Pacific Coast Hwy., at Corral Canyon (© 310/456-5733). Though it's our only pick located on the *other* side of PCH from the beach, this romantic Mediterranean restaurant (whose name means "beautiful shore") has nearly unobstructed ocean views. The baby-pink villa and its flagstone dining patio are overgrown with flowering vines. The place is loveliest at sunset; romantic lighting takes over after dark. The menu is composed of country French and Italian dishes with plenty of moderately priced pastas, many with seafood. Other main courses are more expensive; they include chicken, duck, rabbit, and lamb, all traditionally prepared. An older, nicely dressed crowd dines at this special-occasion place. Open Monday through Saturday from 5 to 11pm, Sunday from 11am to 11pm. Valet parking $4 (Fri–Sat only, otherwise free self-parking). *Tip:* Sunday's brunch menu, which isn't limited to breakfast dishes, is a less pricey alternative to dinner.

dishes from the seasonally changing menu are available daily, and all are served with hors d'oeuvres, soup or salad, and vegetables. There are light dishes, like Five Secret Rays, consisting of lightly steamed vegetables served with lemon-tahini and caraway cheese sauces, but you'll also find a New York steak cut from naturally fed beef. Other dishes range from Vegan Duck with roasted chestnuts to grilled salmon served with French lentils and artichoke hearts. They also have a varied and tasty "raw food" menu.

128 Old Topanga Canyon Rd. (on Calif. 27), Topanga Canyon. ℂ 310/455-1311. Reservations required. Main courses $16–$25. AE, DC, DISC, MC, V. Mon–Fri 11:30am–3pm; Sat 10:30am–3pm; Sun 9:30am–3pm; daily 5:30–10pm. Free parking.

Joe's ★★ *Finds* *Value* AMERICAN ECLECTIC   This is one of L.A.'s best dining bargains. Chef/owner Joeseph Miller excels in simple New American cuisine, particularly grilled fish and roasted meats accented with piquant herbs. Formerly a tiny, quirky storefront with humble elbow room, Joe gutted and completely remodeled the entire restaurant, adding a far more spacious dining room and display wine room (though the best tables are still tucked away on the trellised outdoor patio complete with a gurgling waterfall). But don't let the upscale additions dissuade your budgeted appetite—Joe's remains a hidden treasure for those with a champagne palate but a seltzer pocketbook. Case in point: For lunch an autumn vegetable platter of butternut squash purée, braised greens, grilled Portobello mushrooms, and Brussels sprout leaves wilted with truffle oil and wild mushrooms goes for a mere $11. And this *includes* a fresh mixed green salad or one of Miller's exquisite soups. Dinner entrees are equally sophisticated: fallow deer wrapped in bacon (served in a black currant sauce with a side of roasted root vegetables), monkfish in a saffron broth, wild striped bass with curried cauliflower coulis. A double whammy is Joe's grilled ahi tuna *and* Hudson Valley foie gras appetizer served with rösti potatoes and a red wine herb sauce, and the desserts are equally fantastic. Two four-course prix-fixe menus are offered as well—a real bargain for under $40.

1023 Abbot Kinney Blvd., Venice. ℂ 310/399-5811. www.joesrestaurant.com. Reservations required. Dinner main courses $18–$25; lunch $8–$15. AE, MC, V. Tues–Fri 11:30am–2:30pm and 6–10pm; Sat–Sun 11am–2:30pm and 6–11pm. Free street parking.

INEXPENSIVE

Blueberry ★ AMERICAN/BREAKFAST   This Santa Monica cafe is popular among shoppers and locals from the surrounding laid-back beach community. It serves only breakfast and lunch—Blueberry's owner devotes the dinner hour to the übertrendy Rix around the corner. The setting is 1930s American farmhouse. From the blue bandanna seat cushions to vintage music and print ads, from picket-fence railings to overalls-clad wait staff, this place truly does evoke a Depression-era small-town diner. The food is a "square deal" too, starting with a basket of crispy-edged minimuffins (blueberry, of course) when you're seated, and including hearty egg dishes, waffles, and pancakes, plus generous lunch salads and sandwiches. But we'll bet Ma Kettle never used goat cheese or pancetta in *her* omelets. The menu is up-to-date and served with plenty of fresh-brewed gourmet-roasted coffee. Blueberry is tiny, with just a few tables on the main floor and cozy loft, so expect a wait during peak times.

510 Santa Monica Blvd. (at Fifth St.), Santa Monica. ℂ 310/394-7766. Main courses $4.50–$8. AE, MC, V. Daily 8am–3pm. Metered street parking.

Bread & Porridge ★ INTERNATIONAL/BREAKFAST   A dozen tables are all that compose this neighborhood cafe, but steady streams of locals mill outside, reading their newspapers and waiting for a vacant seat. Once inside, surrounded by the vintage fruit-crate labels adorning the walls and tabletops, you can sample the delicious breakfasts, fresh salads and sandwiches, and superaffordable entrees. There's a vaguely international twist to the menu, which leaps

from breakfast quesadillas and omelets—all served with black beans and salsa—
to the Southern comfort of Cajun crab cakes and coleslaw to typical Italian pastas adorned with Roma tomatoes and plenty of garlic. All menu items are
cheap—truck stop cheap—but with an inventive elegance that truly makes this
a best-kept secret. Get a short stack of one of five varieties of pancakes with any
meal; this place thoughtfully serves breakfast all day.

2315 Wilshire Blvd. (3 blocks west of 26th St.), Santa Monica. ✆ 310/453-4941. Main courses $6–$9. AE,
MC, V. Mon–Fri 7am–2pm; Sat–Sun 7am–3pm. Metered street parking.

Good Stuff *Value* AMERICAN/INTERNATIONAL   A mainstay of local
casual dining, this popular crowd-pleaser suits beachgoers, lunch-breakers, families, couples, and more—there's something for everyone. Inside the gray clapboard corner restaurant you can find brightly painted marine-themed murals,
lifeguard memorabilia, and picture windows to let in the sunshine. On nice days
the outdoor patio fills first; its glass railings ensure a good view of bustling
downtown Manhattan Beach's human parade. Cheerful servers positively
bounce through the restaurant, clad in casual sport togs and ferrying generous
platters of food that's fresh, carefully prepared, and very affordable. The mile-
long menu runs the gamut, featuring standouts like Santa Fe chicken omelet,
cinnamon swirl French toast, a superb homemade veggie burger, burritos and
Mexican favorites, enormous main-course salads, steaming hot pastas, and a
selection of dinner-only entrees. Nightly bargain "get stuffed" dinners are sized
for satisfaction—the seafood stew, for example, is guaranteed to be filling or
your second bowl's on the house.

Other South Bay locations include Hermosa Beach, 1286 The Strand
(✆ 310/374-2334), and Redondo Beach's Riviera Village, 1617 Pacific Coast
Hwy. (✆ 310/316-0262).

1300 Highland Ave. (at 13th St.), Manhattan Beach. ✆ 310/545-4775. www.eatgoodstuff.com. Reservations accepted only for parties of 5 or more. Most menu items under $10. AE, DC, DISC, MC, V. Daily
7am–10pm. Free parking.

Jody Maroni's Sausage Kingdom ★ *Finds* SANDWICHES   Your cardiolo-
gist might not approve, but Jody Maroni's all-natural, preservative-free "haut
dogs" are some of the best wieners served anywhere. The grungy walk-up (or in-
line skate-up) counter looks fairly foreboding—you wouldn't know there was
gourmet fare behind that aging hot dog stand facade, from which at least 14 different grilled-sausage sandwiches are served up. Bypass the traditional hot Italian and try the Toulouse garlic, Bombay curried lamb, all-chicken apple, or
orange-garlic-cumin. Each is served on a freshly baked onion roll and smothered
with onions and peppers. Burgers, BLTs, and rotisserie chicken are also served,
but why bother?

Other locations include the Valley's Universal CityWalk (✆ 818/622-5639),
and inside LAX Terminals 3, 4, and 6, where you can pick up some last-minute
vacuum-packed sausages for home. Having elevated sausage-worship to an art
form, Jody's now boasts a helpful and humorous cookbook, plus its own website
offering franchising opportunities.

2011 Ocean Front Walk (north of Venice Blvd.), Venice. ✆ 310/822-5639. www.maroni.com. Sandwiches
$4–$6. No credit cards. Daily 10am–sunset.

Kay 'n Dave's Cantina *Kids* BREAKFAST/MEXICAN   A beach community favorite for "really big portions of really good food at really low prices,"
Kay 'n Dave's cooks with no lard and has a vegetarian-friendly menu with plenty

of meat items too. Come early (and be prepared to wait) for breakfast, as local devotees line up for five kinds of fluffy pancakes, zesty omelets, or one of the best breakfast burritos in town. Grilled tuna Veracruz, spinach and chicken enchiladas in tomatillo salsa, seafood fajitas tostada, vegetable-filled corn tamales, and other Mexican specialties are served in huge portions, making this mostly locals minichain a great choice to energize for (or reenergize after) an action-packed day of sightseeing. Bring the family—there's a kids' menu and crayons on every table.

262 26th St. (south of San Vicente Blvd.), Santa Monica. © 310/260-1355. Reservations not accepted. Main courses $5–$10. AE, MC, V. Mon–Thurs 11am–9:30pm; Fri 11am–10pm; Sat 8:30am–10pm; Sun 8:30am–9:30pm. Metered street parking.

Sidewalk Café AMERICAN/BREAKFAST   Nowhere in L.A. is the people watching better than along Ocean Front Walk. The constantly bustling Sidewalk Café is ensconced in one of Venice's few remaining early-20th-century buildings. The best seats, of course, are out front, around overcrowded open-air tables, all with a perfect view of the crowd, which provides nonstop entertainment. The menu is extensive, and the food is a whole lot better than it has to be at a location like this. Choose from the seriously overstuffed sandwiches or other oversized American favorites: omelets, salads, and burgers.

1401 Ocean Front Walk (between Horizon Ave. and Market St.), Venice. © 310/399-5547. Main courses $6–$13. MC, V. Sun–Thurs 8am–11pm; Fri–Sat 8am–midnight. Free parking with validation.

3 L.A.'s Westside & Beverly Hills

In addition to the choices that we list in this section, consider dining at the **Daily Grill** (11677 San Vicente Blvd.; © 310/442-0044), which offers terrific American cuisine in a clubby setting. Other locations include Los Angeles (100 N. La Cienega Blvd.; © 310/659-3100), and Studio City (12050 Ventura Blvd.; © 818/769-6336).

EXPENSIVE

Crustacean ★★ SEAFOOD/VIETNAMESE   It's an amazing story how this Beverly Hills restaurant came to be. Helene An, matriarch and executive chef of the An family restaurants, is by title a Vietnamese princess, great-granddaughter of the vice-king of Vietnam. When she and her family fled from Saigon penniless in 1975, they relocated in San Francisco, purchased a small deli, and introduced the city to their now-legendary recipe: An Family's Famous Roast Crab and Garlic Noodles. From this single dish spawned a Horatio Alger story and a family restaurant dynasty. The Beverly Hills location is pure drama from the moment you walk in: You're immediately scrutinized by the patrons to see 1) if you're a somebody and 2) what you're wearing, but you're too busy admiring the Indochina-themed decor—curvaceous copper bar, balcony seating, bamboo garden, waterfall, and an 80-foot-long "stream" topped with glass and filled with exotic koi—to notice. What you won't see is the Secret Kitchen (literally, it's off-limits to most of the staff), where the An family's signature dishes such as tiger prawns with garlic noodles, roasted lobster in tamarind sauce, and roast Dungeness crab are prepared. Although all these dishes are quite good, they're also heavy on the butter—we prefer the lighter sea bass dish with ginger and garlic–black bean sauce. On weekend nights Helene (a real sweetheart and timeless beauty) is often holding court, making sure your dining experience is faultless.

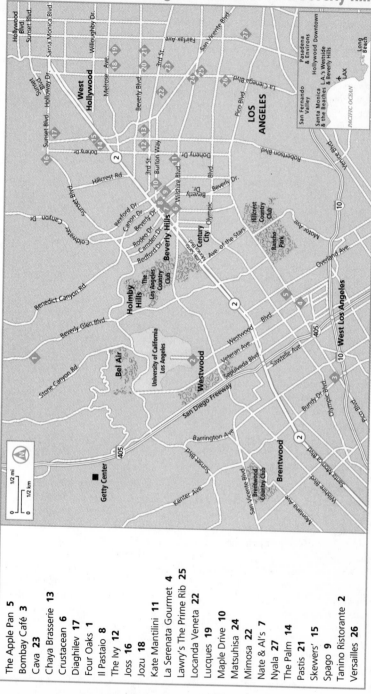

Dining in L.A.'s Westside & Beverly Hills

The Apple Pan **5**
Bombay Café **3**
Cava **23**
Chaya Brasserie **13**
Crustacean **6**
Diaghilev **17**
Four Oaks **1**
Il Pastaio **8**
The Ivy **12**
Joss **16**
Jozu **18**
Kate Mantilini **11**
La Serenata Gourmet **4**
Lawry's The Prime Rib **25**
Locanda Veneta **22**
Lucques **19**
Maple Drive **10**
Matsuhisa **24**
Mimosa **22**
Nate & Al's **7**
Nyala **27**
The Palm **14**
Pastis **21**
Skewers' **15**
Spago **9**
Tanino Ristorante **2**
Versailles **26**

9646 Little Santa Monica Blvd. (at Bedford St.), Beverly Hills. (© **310/205-8990**. Reservations recommended. Main courses $19–$26. AE, DC, DISC, MC, V. Mon–Tues 11:30am–2:30pm and 5:30–10:30pm; Wed 11:30am–2:30pm and 5:30–11:30pm; Thurs–Fri 11:30am–2:30pm and 5:30–10:30pm; Sat 5:30–11:30pm. Valet parking $4.50.

Diaghilev ★★★ FRANCO-RUSSIAN   Sergei Diaghilev, 1920s ballet impresario, would approve of the theatrical ambience that evokes the Parisian dining salons frequented by exiled Russian aristocracy after that nasty little revolution. In this high-ceilinged room, flickering candles play off the rich upholstery and decor. Every table features plush banquette seating and formal tableware that's constantly refreshed by a subtly attentive staff. Your meal begins with a choice of house-infused vodkas (imaginative flavors include coffee, peppercorn, or tea), and proceeds with *six* different (and expensive) caviars—but still includes *borscht* and marinated herring. "Ouefs a la Maxims" are whipped eggs and caviar as served at the famous Paris eatery; fragrant Baltic smoked salmon is sliced paper-thin; foie gras arrives atop a tangy endive salad; and Maine lobster is richly presented with apple-beet slaw and Calvados sauce. Despite its location, Diaghilev attracts very few hotel guests, and is usually filled with Beverly Hills types from the surrounding hills.

In the Wyndham Bel Age Hotel, 1020 N. San Vicente Blvd. (at Sunset Blvd.), West Hollywood. (© **310/854-1111**. Reservations recommended. Main courses $28–$46. AE, DC, DISC, MC, V. Tues–Sat 6:30–11:30pm. Valet parking $7–$10.

Four Oaks ★★★ CALIFORNIA   Just looking at the menu here makes us swoon. The country-cottage ambience and chef Peter Roelant's superlative blend of fresh ingredients with luxurious continental flourishes make a meal at the Four Oaks one of our favorite luxuries. Dinner is served beneath trees festooned with twinkling lights. Appetizers like lavender-smoked salmon with crisp potatoes and horseradish crème fraîche complement mouth-watering dishes like roasted chicken with sage, Oregon forest mushrooms, artichoke hearts, and port-balsamic sauce. If you're looking for someplace special, head to this canyon hideaway.

2181 N. Beverly Glen Blvd., Los Angeles. (© **310/470-2265**. www.fouroaksrestaurant.com. Reservations required. Main courses $22–$29. AE, DISC, MC, V. Tues–Sat 11:30am–2pm and 6–10pm; Sun 10:30am–2pm and 6–10pm. Valet parking $4.

The Ivy ★★ NEW AMERICAN   If you're willing to pay lots for a perfect meal, and willing to endure the cold shoulder to ogle L.A.'s celebrities, the Ivy can be enjoyable. This snobby place attracts one of the most industry-heavy crowds in the city, and treats celebrities and nobodies as differently as Brahmans and untouchables. Just past the cool reception lie two disarmingly countrified dining rooms filled with rustic antiques, comfortably worn chintz, and hanging baskets of fragrant flowers. Huge roses bloom everywhere, including out on the charming brick patio (where the highest-profile patrons are seated). The food is excellent. The Ivy's Caesar salad is perfect, as are the plump and crispy crab cakes. Recommended dishes include spinach linguine with a peppery tomato-basil sauce, prime rib dusted with Cajun spices, and tender lime-marinated grilled chicken. There's even a great burger. The wine list is notable, and there's always a terrific variety of desserts (pink boxes are on hand for chocolate-chip cookies to go).

113 N. Robertson Blvd. (between 3rd St. and Beverly Blvd.), West Hollywood. (© **310/274-8303**. Reservations recommended on weekends. Dinner main courses $22–$38; lunch $10–$25. AE, DC, DISC, MC, V. Mon–Sat 11:30am–3pm; Sun 11am–3pm; Mon–Thurs 6–11pm; Fri–Sat 6–11:30pm; Sun 5:30–10:30pm. Valet parking $4.50.

Ⓚⁱᵈˢ Family-Friendly Restaurants

Cafe Pinot (see p. 147) and **Pinot Bistro** (p. 150)—these upscale off-shoots of chic Patina don't often come to mind when you're searching for family eats, and many kids are certainly too antsy to behave during an entire bistro meal. But the Pinot dynasty welcomes little ones with a special child-friendly menu, and kids under 14 can order anything from the menu, free of charge. It's a great way to enjoy L.A.'s finest and stay close to your budget, too.

On the other end of the scale is **Pink's Hot Dogs** (see p. 144) in Hollywood, an institution that has been serving politically incorrect franks for what seems like forever. Everyone loves Pink's chili dogs, but you may never get the orange grease stains out of your kids' clothes.

Miceli's (see p. 152) in Universal City is a cavernous Italian restaurant that the whole family is sure to love. The gimmick? The wait staff sings show tunes or opera favorites while serving (and sometimes instead of). Kids will love the boisterous atmosphere, which might even drown them out.

Jerry's Famous Deli (see p. 152) in Studio City is frequented mostly by industry types who populate this Valley community; their kids often sport baseball caps or production T-shirts from Mom or Dad's latest project. Jerry's has the most extensive deli menu in town and a casual, coffee-shop atmosphere. Families flock here for lunch, early dinner, and (crowded) weekend breakfast.

Hard Rock Cafe—Sure, it's loud and obnoxious and filled with tourists, but it's a sure bet that the kids will love it, and they make a pretty darn good chicken sandwich. The city has two locations: the Beverly Center, 8600 Beverly Blvd. (at San Vicente Blvd.), Los Angeles (© 310/276-7605); and Universal CityWalk, Universal Center Drive exit off U.S. 101 (© 818/622-7625).

Jozu ★★ PACIFIC RIM/CALIFORNIA   *Jozu* means "excellent" in Japanese, and the word describes everything about this tranquil restaurant. All meals begin with complimentary sake from Jozu's premium sake list. Chef Hisashi Yoshiara's menu presents Asian flavors interpreted with an international inventiveness. Outstanding dishes include delicately roasted sea bass on a bed of crunchy cabbage, accented with tangy ponzu sauce; albacore tuna wrapped in a crispy potato nest and bathed in soy butter; and rack of lamb perfectly char-broiled and presented over a warm bell-pepper and arugula ragout. Appetizers range from shrimp sui-mai in rich lobster sauce to spicy halibut sashimi. The dessert of choice is Asian pear tart, lightly caramelized fruit laid in a buttery crust. The restaurant's interior is warmly comfortable and subtly lit; plenty of beautiful Hollywood types dine here, but it's quiet enough for real dinner conversation.

8360 Melrose Ave. (at Kings Rd.), West Hollywood. © 323/655-5600. www.jozu.com. Reservations recommended. Main courses $16–$25. AE, MC, V. Mon–Fri 6–10:30pm; Sat–Sun 5:30–10:30pm. Valet parking $3.50.

Lawry's The Prime Rib ★ STEAKS/SEAFOOD Most Americans know Lawry's only as a brand of seasoned salt (which was invented here). Going to this family run institution is an old-world event, where the main menu offerings are four cuts of prime rib that vary in thickness from two fingers to an entire hand. Every standing rib roast is dry-aged for 2 to 3 weeks, sprinkled with Lawry's famous seasoning, and then roasted on a bed of rock salt. A carver wheels the cooked beef table side, then slices it properly, rare to well done. All dinners come with creamy whipped horseradish, Yorkshire pudding, and the Original Spinning Bowl Salad (drenched in Lawry's signature sherry French dressing). Lawry's moved across the street from its original location a few years ago but retained its throwback-to-the-1930s clubroom atmosphere, complete with Persian-carpeted oak floors, high-backed chairs, and European oil paintings.

100 N. La Cienega Blvd. (north of Wilshire Blvd.), Beverly Hills. ✆ 310/652-2827. Reservations recommended. Main courses $20–$30. AE, DC, DISC, MC, V. Mon–Thurs 5–10pm; Fri 5–11pm; Sat 4:30–11pm; Sun 4–10pm. Valet parking $3.50.

Lucques ★★ FRANCO-MEDITERRANEAN Once Los Angeles became accustomed to this restaurant's unusual name—"Lucques" is a variety of French olive, pronounced "Luke"—local foodies fell hard for this quietly and comfortably sophisticated home of former Campanile chef Suzanne Goin. The old brick building, once silent star Harold Lloyd's carriage house, is decorated in mute, clubby colors with subdued lighting that extends to the handsome enclosed patio. Goin cooks with bold flavors, fresh-from-the-farm produce, and an instinctive feel for the food of the Mediterranean. The short and oft-changed menu makes the most of unusual ingredients like salt cod and oxtails. Standout dishes include Tuscan bean soup with tangy greens and pistou, grilled chicken served alongside spinach sautéed with pancetta and shallots, rustic mascarpone polenta topped with wild mushroom ragout and wilted greens, and perfect vanilla *pòt de crème* for dessert. Lucques's bar menu, featuring steak frites béarnaise, omelets, and tantalizing hors d'oeuvres (olives, warm almonds, sea salt, chewy bread), is a godsend for late-night diners. *Insider Tip:* On Sundays Lucques offers a bargain $30 prix fixe three-course dinner from a weekly changing menu.

8474 Melrose Ave. (east of La Cienega), West Hollywood. ✆ 323/655-6277. Reservations recommended. Main courses $18–$30. AE, DC, MC, V. Tues–Sat noon–2:30pm and 6pm–1:30am; Sun 5:30pm–midnight. Closed the last 2 weeks of Aug. Metered street parking or valet ($3.50).

Maple Drive ★★ NEW AMERICAN Opened by a partnership of celebrities and industry players, Maple Drive is one of the best traditional American restaurants in, well, America. It's a classy place with great food, high prices, and live dinnertime jazz. Chef Leonard Schwartz cooks great meat loaf, terrific "Bowl of Kick Ass" chili, a $20 plate of Southern fried chicken with mashed potatoes and gravy, and out-of-this-world veal chops (which regulars ask for Milanese style—lightly breaded and served with a squeeze of lemon). The restaurant attracts the biggest celebrities—Barbra, Elton, Arnold, and others who have enjoyed fame for so long they often seem tired of the attention; they enter through a second, more discreet, door and sit in secluded booths in back of the multilevel dining room. That's a bonus for us nobodies—on warm nights, the best seats are out on the patio. Even if Clint isn't at the next table, it's worth lingering for the extraordinary desserts. *Insider Tip:* You can have your Rolls washed while you lunch.

345 N. Maple Dr. (at Alden Dr.), Beverly Hills. ✆ 310/274-9800. Reservations recommended. Dinner main courses $16–$36; lunch $12–$22. AE, DC, MC, V. Mon–Fri 11:30am–2:30pm; Mon–Sat 6–10pm. Limited street parking; valet $4.

Matsuhisa ✿✿✿ JAPANESE/PERUVIAN   Japanese chef/owner Nobuyuki Matsuhisa arrived in Los Angeles via Peru and opened what may be the most creative restaurant in the city. A true master of fish cookery, Matsuhisa creates fantastic dishes by combining Japanese flavors with South American spices and salsas. Broiled sea bass with black truffles, sautéed squid with garlic and soy, and Dungeness crab tossed with chilies and cream are examples of the masterfully prepared delicacies that are available in addition to thickly sliced nigiri and creative sushi rolls. Matsuhisa is perennially popular with celebrities and hard-core foodies, so reserve early for those hard-to-get tables. The small crowded main dining room suffers from poor lighting and precious lack of privacy; many big names are ushered through to private dining rooms. If you dare, ask for *omakase*, and the chef will personally compose a selection of eccentric dishes.

129 N. La Cienega Blvd. (north of Wilshire Blvd.), Beverly Hills. ✆ 310/659-9639. Reservations recommended. Main courses $14–$26; sushi $4–$13 per order; full omakase dinner from $65. AE, DC, MC, V. Mon–Fri 11:45am–2:15pm; daily 5:45–10:15pm. Valet parking $3.50.

Mimosa ✿ FRENCH PROVENÇAL   Decked out in traditional bistro garb (butter-yellow walls, artistic photos, French posters), Mimosa attracts plenty of French expatriates and Euro-style denizens with a truly authentic menu. You won't get the classic French of caviar and truffles, but rather regional peasant specialties like rich veal *daube*, tripe sausage (*andouillette*), perfect steak fries, and a slow-cooked pork roast with horseradish lentils. The appetizer list usually includes a splendid terrine, and bowls of house-cured cornichons (gherkins) and spicy Dijon mustard accompany bread to every table. Despite the occasional tinge of trendy attitude—usually precipitated by the presence of habitués like Tom Cruise, Jennifer Aniston, and Brad Pitt—Mimosa should be appreciated for its casual, comforting bistro fare.

8009 Beverly Blvd. (west of Fairfax), Los Angeles. ✆ 323/655-8895. Reservations recommended. Main courses $13–$24. AE, MC, V. Mon–Fri 11:30am–3pm; daily 5:30pm–midnight. Metered street parking.

The Palm ✿ STEAKS/LOBSTER   Every great American city has a great steak house; in Los Angeles it's The Palm. The child of the famous New York restaurant of the same name, The Palm is widely regarded by local foodies as one of the best traditional American eateries in the city. The glitterati seem to agree, as stars and their handlers are regularly in attendance. In both food and ambience, this West Coast apple hasn't fallen far from the proverbial tree. The restaurant is brightly lit, extremely noisy, and casually decorated, with caricatures on the walls and sawdust on the floor. Live Nova Scotia lobsters are flown in almost daily, then broiled over charcoal and served with big bowls of melted butter. Most are an enormous: 3 to 7 pounds and, although they're obscenely expensive, can be shared. Steaks are similarly sized, perfectly grilled to order, and served a la carte. Diners also swear by the celebrated Gigi Salad, a mixture of lettuce, shrimp, bacon, green beans, pimento, and avocado. For dessert, stick with the Palm's perfect New York cheesecake; they might as well take the rest off the menu.

9001 Santa Monica Blvd. (between Doheny Dr. and Robertson Blvd.), West Hollywood. ✆ 310/550-8811. Reservations required. Dinner main courses $16–$28; lobsters $18 per pound; lunch $8–$15. AE, DC, MC, V. Mon–Fri noon–3pm; Mon–Sat 5–10pm; Sun 5–9:30pm. Valet parking $4.

Spago ✿✿✿ CALIFORNIA   Wolfgang Puck is more than a great chef, he's also a masterful businessman and publicist who has made Spago one of the best-known restaurants in the United States. Despite all the hoopla—and almost 20 years of service—Spago remains one of L.A.'s top-rated restaurants. Talented

Puck henchman Lee Hefter presides over the kitchen, delivering the culinary sophistication demanded by an upscale Beverly Hills crowd. This high-style indoor/outdoor space glows with the aura of big bucks, celebrity, and the perfectly honed California cuisine that can honestly take credit for setting the standard. Spago is also one of the last places in L.A. where men will feel most comfortable in jacket and tie (suggested, but not required). All eyes may be on the romantically twinkle-lit outdoor patio (the most coveted tables), but the food takes center stage. You simply can't choose wrong—highlights include the appetizer of foie gras "three ways"; savory duck either honey-lacquered and topped with foie gras, or Cantonese-style with a citrus tang; and rich Austrian dishes from "Wolfie's" childhood, like spicy beef goulash or perfect veal schnitzel.

176 N. Canon Dr. (north of Wilshire). © 310/385-0880. www.wolfgangpuck.com. Reservations required. Jacket and tie advised for men. Main courses $18–$34; tasting menu $85. AE, DC, DISC, MC, V. Mon–Fri 11:30am–2:30pm and 5:30–10:30pm; Sat noon–2:30pm and 5:30–10:30pm; Sun 5:30–10:30pm. Valet parking $4.50.

MODERATE

Bombay Café ★★ INDIAN   This friendly sleeper may be L.A.'s best Indian spot, serving excellent curries and kurmas typical of South Indian street food. Once seated, immediately order *sev puri* for the table; these crispy little chips topped with chopped potatoes, onions, cilantro, and chutneys are the perfect accompaniment to what's sure to be an extended menu-reading session. Also recommended are the burrito-like "frankies," juicy little bread rolls stuffed with lamb, chicken, or cauliflower. The best dishes come from the tandoor and include spicy yogurt-marinated swordfish, lamb, and chicken. While some dishes are authentically spicy, plenty of others have a mellow flavor for less incendiary palates. This restaurant is phenomenally popular and gets its share of celebrities.

12021 W. Pico Blvd. (at Bundy Dr.). © 310/473-3388. Reservations recommended for dinner. Main courses $9–$17. AE, MC, V. Mon–Thurs 11:30am–3pm and 5–10pm; Fri 11:30am–3pm and 5–11pm; Sat 5–11pm; Sun 5–10pm. Metered street parking (lunch); valet parking $3.50 (dinner).

Cava BREAKFAST/SPANISH   Trendy types in the mood for some fun are attracted to Cava's great mambo atmosphere; the tapas bar is made festive with flamboyant colors, and the Upstairs Supper Club—picture velvet drapes and tassels adorning the walls and comfortable booths—booms with loud, lively Latin jazz, salsa, and flamenco. The cuisine is contemporary Spanish livened up with Latin American touches, an influence reflected in dishes like black-bean tamales with tomatillo salsa and golden caviar; thick, dark tortilla soup; jerk chicken with sweet yams; and pan-seared shrimp in spicy peppercorn sauce. Spanish paella is stewed up three ways—with seafood, chicken and sausage, or just vegetables. If you have room for dessert, try the ruby-colored pears poached in port, the rice pudding, or the flan.

8384 W. Third St. (at Orlando Ave., in the Beverly Plaza Hotel). © 323/658-8898. Reservations recommended on weekends. Dinner main courses $8–$17; lunch $4–$14; breakfast $3–$9. AE, DC, DISC, MC, V. Daily 7am–midnight. Metered street parking or hotel parking.

Chaya Brasserie ★★ FRANCO-JAPANESE   Open for 2 decades, Chaya has become ensconced as one of Los Angeles's finest restaurants. This Continental bistro with Asian overtones is popular with film agents during lunch and a particularly beautiful assembly of stars at night (spotted recently: George Clooney, Mark Walberg, the Baldwin brothers). The place is loved for its exceptionally good food and unpretentious atmosphere. Despite a high noise level, the stage-lit dining room feels sensuous and swoony. On warm afternoons and evenings, the best tables are on the outside terrace, overlooking the busy street. Chaya is best known for superb grilled fish and meats, like seared soy-marinated Hawaiian tuna and Long Island duckling. Chef Shigefumi Tachibe's lobster ravioli with pesto-cream sauce is both stylish and delicious, as is tangy grilled chicken Dijon, a house specialty. Chaya is also a hot late-night rendezvous, with a short but choice late-dinner menu served from Tuesday through Saturday (see below for hours).

8741 Alden Dr. (east of Robertson Blvd.). ℂ **310/859-8833.** Reservations recommended on weekends. Dinner main courses $15–$27; lunch $10–$16. AE, DC, MC, V. Mon–Fri 11am–2:30pm; Mon–Thurs 6–10:30pm; Fri–Sat 6–11pm; Sun 6–10pm. Late-night dinner (bar menu) Tues–Thurs 10:30–11:30pm; Fri–Sat 10:30–12am; Valet parking $3.50.

El Coyote ✩ *Value* MEXICAN   Everyone from 20-something hipsters to slick showbiz player-types, rockers, movie stars and families can be found at this local cantina. The rowdy bar scene alone is a great reason to hang out at this highly popular (yet eminently affordable) Mexican restaurant. During prime dining hours the restaurant's bustling atmosphere spills over into the bar, which is frequently crowded to capacity. Settle in by sampling from the *grande*-sized menu of appetizers such as taquitos, quesadillas, and nachos, and be sure to wash them down with a couple of cheap and tasty margaritas. The fare is traditional Mexican and well prepared, with a wide array of taco, enchilada, and burrito combinations and sizzling fajita platters.

7312 Beverly Blvd. (at La Brea Ave.), Los Angeles. ℂ **323/939-2255.** Main courses $8–$10. AE, MC, V. Mon–Thurs 11am–10pm; Fri–Sat 11am–11pm.

Il Pastaio ✩ NORTHERN ITALIAN   Sicilian-born Celestino Drago is a terrific chef who has been at the helm at high-profile L.A. restaurants for years. Branching out on his own, Chef Drago hit the jackpot with this hugely successful, value-priced eatery. The restaurant is a simple pasta place with white walls, a long bar, and a pasta-making area; it's as narrow as a bowling alley and almost as loud. Only starters, pastas, and desserts are served, but the selections are vast and great for grazing. Swordfish carpaccio with shaved fennel and blood oranges, and seafood and spaghetti in a flaky phyllo envelope, are Drago's signature dishes. Drago offered a sautéed foie gras appetizer with a buttery balsamic vinegar glaze at Chianti, and continues to serve it here—to those who know enough to ask for it. Pastas include lobster-stuffed ravioli in a silky lobster reduction, and *garganelli:* wheat pasta curls in *amatriciana* sauce (puréed tomato, pancetta, pecorino, and onion). Two risotti are offered nightly, both usually hit the proverbial bull's-eye. Unfortunately, Il Pastaio is too small. There's almost always a wait, and an uncomfortable one at that. But by meal's end, it always seems worth it.

400 N. Canon Dr. (at Brighton Way), Beverly Hills. ℂ **310/205-5444.** Dinner main courses $12–$23; lunch $7–$12. AE, DC, MC, V. Mon–Sat 11am–11pm.

Joss ✩ CHINESE   Located on the fringe between Beverly Hills and the Sunset Strip, Joss has a minimalist yet welcoming decor of beige linen chairs, white tablecloths, and tiny halogen lights suspended over each table. The entryway's ever-present sherry decanter hints at the surprisingly well-chosen and affordable wine list, compiled by owner Cecile Tang Shu Shuen, whose inventive menu takes Chinese essentials beyond your expectations—not by creating fussy "fusion" dishes, but by subtly manipulating ingredients and preparations according to her superb artist's palate. Fried rice is spiked with the tang of dried black beans and ginger; velvety curry sauce is creamed with coconut milk and tossed with chicken; and tender beef is marinated with spicy red chilis but mellowed with tangerine liqueur. You could make a meal of the dozen dim sum varieties, which include delicately steamed dumplings served in stacked bamboo steaming trays, crisp-bottom pot stickers filled with Peking duck or lamb and leeks, and crispy wonton or spring rolls. Desserts, never overly sweet, complement Joss's sublime meals perfectly. The restaurant's location draws many celebrities and industry honchos—but gawking is definitely uncool.

9255 Sunset Blvd. (west of Doheny Dr.), West Hollywood. (✆ **310/276-1886.** Reservations suggested. Main courses $13–$20; dim sum $4 per order. AE, DC, MC, V. Mon–Fri noon–3pm; daily 6–10:30pm (until midnight Fri–Sat). Parking $2.50–$3.50.

Kate Mantilini ✿ AMERICAN/TRADITIONAL/BREAKFAST   It's rare to find a restaurant that feels comfortably familiar yet cutting-edge trendy at the same time—and also happens to be one of L.A.'s few late-night eateries. Kate Mantilini fits the bill perfectly. One of the first to bring meat loaf back into fashion, Kate's offers a huge menu of upscale truck-stop favorites like "white" chili (made with chicken, white beans, and Jack cheese), grilled steaks and fish, a few token pastas, and just about anything you might crave. At 2am, nothing quite beats a steaming bowl of lentil-vegetable soup and some garlic-cheese toast, unless your taste runs to fresh oysters and a dry martini—Kate has it all. The huge mural of the Hagler-Hearns boxing match that dominates the stark, open interior provides the only clue to the namesake's identity: Mantilini was an early female boxing promoter, around 1947.

9101 Wilshire Blvd. (at Doheny Dr.), Beverly Hills. (✆ **310/278-3699.** Reservations accepted only for parties of 6 or more. Main courses $7–$16. AE, MC, V. Mon–Thurs 7:30am–1am; Fri 7:30am–2am; Sat 11am–2am; Sun 10am–midnight. Validated valet parking.

La Serenata Gourmet ✿✿ MEXICAN   Westsiders rejoiced when this branch of Boyle Heights's award-winning La Serenata de Girabaldi began serving its authentic, but innovative, Mexican cuisine just a block away from the Westside Pavilion shopping center. This place is casual, fun, and intensely delicious. Specialties like shrimp enchiladas, fish tacos, and pork *gorditas* are all accented with hand-patted corn tortillas, fresh chips dusted with *añejo* cheese, and flavorful fresh salsas. Always packed to capacity, the restaurant finally expanded in 1998, but try to avoid the prime lunch and dinner hours nevertheless.

10924 W. Pico Blvd., West L.A. (✆ **310/441-9667.** Main courses $8–$13. AE, MC, V. Daily 11am–3:30pm and 5–10pm (Fri–Sat until 10:30pm). Metered street parking.

Locanda Veneta ✿ NORTHERN ITALIAN   Locanda Veneta's citywide renown belies its tiny size and unpretentious setting. Its location, across from the unsightly monolith that is Cedars-Sinai Hospital, is a far cry from Venice's Grand Canal, and the single, loud, tightly packed dining room can sometimes feel like Piazza San Marco at the height of tourist season. But the sensible prices reflect the restaurant's efficient decor. While the dining room is decidedly unfancy, the kitchen is dead serious, making this restaurant a kind of temple for knowledgeable foodies. The soups are excellent, seafood dishes extraordinary, and pastas as good as they get. Signature dishes include pasta-and-bean soup, veal chops, lobster ravioli, shrimp risotto, and perfectly grilled vegetables. Though the dessert menu is long and tempting, we usually go for the *crema de vaniglia,* a dense, silky custard topped with caramel and chocolate sauces.

8638 W. Third St. (between San Vicente and Robertson blvd.). © **310/274-1893**. www.locandaveneta.com. Reservations required. Main courses $10–$26. AE, MC, V. Mon–Fri 11:30am–2:30pm and 5:30–11pm; Sat 5:30–11pm. Valet parking $3.50.

Nyala ⋆ ETHIOPIAN   There are no fewer than four Ethiopian eateries along 2 compact blocks of Fairfax, but our favorite is Nyala; it's one of the larger ones, and probably the most popular. In a mellow setting—all earthen colors, tribal prints, and African music—an ethnically mixed crowd finds common ground in the expertly-spiced (smoldering, rather than fiery) cuisine. For the uninitiated, Ethiopian food is a mosaic of chopped salads, chunky stews, and saucy vegetables, all served on a colorful enamel platter for communal enjoyment. There are no utensils, merely a basket of *injera*, the thick, tangy crepe used to scoop up the other food. Choices range from hearty chicken or lamb chunks stewed with tomatoes and onions to a parade of vegetarian choices (lentils, chickpeas, greens), each with a distinctive marinade. African beers and honey wine are perfect accompaniments.

1076 S. Fairfax Ave. (south of Olympic). © **323/936-5918**. Reservations suggested. Main courses $8–$15. AE, DISC, MC, V. Daily 11:30am–11pm. Street parking.

Pastis ⋆ FRENCH PROVENÇAL   Of the country French bistros in town, Pastis usually takes a back seat to the ultrahip, celebrity-frequented Mimosa, which happens to be just a block away. But locals and regulars often prefer this rustic yet civilized spot, named for the licorice-flavored liqueur. Intimate and friendly, with sidewalk tables and a warmly ocher-toned dining room, Pastis manages to be both elegant and the kind of place you can scrape your chair, raise your voice, or drink a little too much wine. Distinctive menu selections include curly endive salad with bacon and poached-egg garnish, wine-braised rabbit, and Marseilles-style seafood bouillabaisse. For chocolate lovers: Dessert is *chocolat pòt au crème*, a beautiful thick custard served in rustic glazed pots.

8114 Beverly Blvd. (west of Crescent Heights), Los Angeles. © **323/655-8822**. Reservations recommended. Main courses $15–$20. AE, MC, V. Mon–Fri 11am–2pm; daily 6–10pm. Metered street parking or valet parking ($3.50).

Tanino Ristorante and Bar ⋆ SOUTHERN ITALIAN   It's worth visiting Tanino just to marvel at the 1929 Italianate Renaissance–style building, one of only 12 remaining since Westwood's founding days. Designed by renowned Southern California architect Paul Revere Williams, the decor consists of magnificent original ceiling frescos, carvings, murals, and artisan plaster that blends well with the checkerboard terrazzo marble flooring, dark hardwoods, sumptuous booths, wrought-iron chandeliers, and candlelit tables—an ideal setting for a romantic evening. Chef/owner Tanino Drago (scion of L.A.'s well-known Drago restaurateur family) has created a menu based on regional dishes from his native home of Sicily; most dishes are cooked *cartoccio*-style (in their own juices), such as lamb shank osso buco atop soft polenta, roasted rabbit in green Mediterranean olive sauce, and striped bass baked in papillote with white wine. Be sure to start with the *tortellini in brodo*, house-made tortellini in a pheasant broth with black truffles. A wide array of pasta and risotti are available as well. The charming Italian-accented serves add to the faux-Mediterranean atmosphere. Be sure to arrive a little early to enjoy a glass of grappa by the fireplace.

1043 Westwood Blvd. (between Kinross and Weyburn sts.), Westwood. © **310/208-0444**. www.tanino.com. Reservations recommended. Main courses $11–$29. AE, DC, MC, V. Mon–Fri 11:30am–3pm and 5:30–11:30pm; Sat 5:30–11:30pm; Sun 5:30–10pm. Valet parking $4.

INEXPENSIVE

The Apple Pan ★★ SANDWICHES/AMERICAN   There are no tables, just a U-shaped counter, at this classic American burger shack and L.A. landmark. Open since 1947, the Apple Pan is a diner that looks—and acts—the part. It's famous for juicy burgers, speedy service, and an authentic frills-free atmosphere. The hickory burger is best, though the tuna sandwich also has its share of fans. Ham, egg-salad, and Swiss-cheese sandwiches round out the menu. Definitely order fries and, if you're in the mood, the home-baked apple pie too.

10801 Pico Blvd. (east of Westwood Blvd.). ✆ 310/475-3585. Most menu items under $6. No credit cards. Tues–Thurs and Sun 11am–midnight; Fri–Sat 11am–1am. Free parking.

Nate & Al ★ DELICATESSEN/BREAKFAST   If you want to know where old-money rich-and-famous types go for comfort food, look no further. Despite its location in the center of Beverly Hills's "Golden Triangle," Nate & Al has remained unchanged since 1945, from the Naugahyde booths to the motherly waitresses, who treat you the same whether you're a house-account celebrity regular or just a visitor stopping in for an overstuffed pastrami on rye. Their too-salty chicken soup keeps Nate & Al from being the best L.A. deli (actually, we'd be hard-pressed to choose any one deli as the city's best), but staples like chopped liver, dense potato pancakes, blintzes, borscht, and well-dilled pickles more than make up for it.

414 N. Beverly Dr. (at Brighton Way), Beverly Hills. ✆ 310/274-0101. Main courses $8–$13. AE, DISC, MC, V. Daily 7:30am–9pm. Free parking with validation.

Skewers' MIDDLE EASTERN   Santa Monica Boulevard is the heart of West Hollywood's commercial strip, and Skewers' sidewalk tables are a great place to see all kinds of neighborhood activity (and audacity). Inside is a New York–like narrow space with changing artwork adorning bare brick walls. From the zesty marinated carrot sticks you get the moment you're seated, to sweet, sticky squares of baklava for dessert, this Mediterranean grill is sure to please. You'll get baskets of warm pita bread for scooping up traditional salads like *baba ghanoush* (grilled eggplant with tahini and lemon) and *tabbouleh* (cracked wheat, parsley, and tomatoes). Try marinated chicken and lamb off the grill, or *dolmades* (rice-and meat-stuffed grape leaves) seared with a tangy tomato glaze.

8939 Santa Monica Blvd. (between Robertson and San Vicente blvd.), West Hollywood. ✆ 310/271-0555. Main courses $7–$9; salads and pita $4–$7. AE, MC, V. Daily 11am–midnight.

Versailles ★ *Value* CARIBBEAN/CUBAN   Outfitted with Formica tabletops and looking something like an ethnic IHOP, Versailles feels much like any number of Miami restaurants that cater to the Cuban community. The menu reads like a veritable survey of Havana-style cookery and includes specialties like "Moors and Christians" (flavorful black beans with white rice), *ropa vieja* (a stringy beef stew), *eastin lechón* (suckling pig with sliced onions), and fried whole fish (usually sea bass). Shredded roast pork is particularly recommendable, especially when tossed with the restaurant's trademark garlic-citrus sauce. But what everyone comes for is the chicken—succulent, slow roasted, smothered in onions and either garlic-citrus sauce or barbecue sauce. Almost everything is served with black beans and rice; wine and beer are available. Because meals are good, bountiful, and cheap, there's often a wait.

Another Versailles restaurant is located in Culver City at 10319 Venice Blvd. (✆ 310/558-3168).

1415 S. La Cienega Blvd. (south of Pico Blvd.). ✆ 310/289-0392. Main courses $5–$11. AE, MC, V. Daily 11am–10pm. Free parking.

4 Hollywood

EXPENSIVE

Campanile ★★ BREAKFAST/CALIFORNIA-MEDITERRANEAN   Built as Charlie Chaplin's private offices in 1928, this lovely building has a multilevel layout with flower-bedecked interior balconies, a bubbling fountain, and a skylight through which diners can see the campanile (bell tower). The kitchen, headed by Spago alumnus chef/co-owner Mark Peel, gets a giant leg up from pastry chef/co-owner (and wife) Nancy Silverton, who also runs the now-legendary La Brea Bakery next door. Meals here might begin with fried zucchini flowers drizzled with melted mozzarella or lamb carpaccio surrounded by artichoke leaves—a dish that arrives looking like one of van Gogh's sunflowers. Chef Peel is particularly known for his grills and roasts; try the grilled prime rib smeared with black-olive tapenade or pappardelle with braised rabbit, roasted tomato, and collard greens. And don't skip dessert—the restaurant's many sweets fans have turned Nancy's dessert book into a bestseller. The weekend brunch is a surprising crowd-pleaser and a terrific way to appreciate this beautiful space on a budget.

624 S. La Brea Ave. (north of Wilshire Blvd.). ℂ 323/938-1447. www.campanilerestaurant.com. Reservations required. Main courses $26–$38. AE, DC, DISC, MC, V. Mon–Thurs 11:30am–2:30pm and 6–10pm; Fri 11:30am–2:30pm and 5:30–11pm; Sat 9:30am–1:30pm and 5:30–11pm; Sun 9:30am–1:30pm. Valet parking $3.50.

Dar Maghreb ★ MOROCCAN   If you're a lone diner in search of a quick bite, this isn't the place for you. Dinner at Dar Maghreb is an entertaining dining experience that improves exponentially the larger your party and the longer you linger. Enter an exotic Arab world of genie waitresses who wash your hands with warm water and belly dancers who shimmy around an exquisite fountain in the center of a patio. You'll feel like a guest in an ornately tiled palace as you dine at traditional tables on either low sofas or goatskin cushions.

Nothing is available a la carte here. The fixed-price meal is a multicourse feast, starting with bread and traditional Moroccan salads, followed by *b'stilla,* an appetizer of shredded chicken, eggs, almonds, and spices wrapped in a flaky pastry shell and topped with powdered sugar and cinnamon. The main courses— your choice of lamb, quail, chicken, and more—are each sublimely seasoned and delectable. Perhaps it's the atmosphere that makes everyone eat more than they expected, but you'll be thankful that dessert is a simple fruit-and-nut basket, accompanied by warm mint tea poured into traditional glasses. All is eaten with your hands—a sensual experience that grows on you as the night progresses. *Note:* If you have high-speed Internet access, be sure to check out the restaurant's most entertaining belly dancer/waitress video.

7651 Sunset Blvd. (corner of Stanley Ave.). ℂ 323/876-7651. www.darmaghrebrestaurant.com. Reservations recommended. Fixed-price dinner $38. DC, MC, V. Mon–Fri 6–11pm; Sat 5:30–11pm; Sun 5:30–10:30pm. Valet parking $4.50.

Patina ★★★ CALIFORNIA-FRENCH   Joachim Splichal, arguably L.A.'s very best chef, is also a genius at choosing and training top chefs to cook in his kitchens while he jets around the world. Patina routinely wins the highest praise from demanding gourmands, who are happy to empty their bank accounts for unbeatable meals. The dining room is straightforwardly attractive, low key, well lit, and professional, without a hint of stuffiness. The menu is equally disarming: "Mallard Duck with Portobello Mushrooms" gives little hint of the brilliant colors and flavors that appear on the plate. The seasonal menu features partridge, pheasant, venison, and other game in winter and spotlights exotic local vegetables in warmer months. Seafood is always available; if Maine lobster cannelloni or asparagus-wrapped John Dory is on the menu, order it. Patina is justifiably famous for its mashed potatoes and potato-truffle chips; be sure to include one (or both) with your meal.

5955 Melrose Ave. (west of Cahuenga Blvd.). ℂ 323/467-1108. www.patinagroup.com. Reservations required. Main courses $18–$30. AE, DC, DISC, MC, V. Mon–Thurs 6–10pm; Fri noon–2pm and 6–10pm; Sat 5:30–10:30pm. Valet parking $4.

MODERATE

Authentic Café ⭐ SOUTHWESTERN   True to its name, this restaurant serves authentic Southwestern food in a casual atmosphere. It's a winning combination that made this place an L.A. favorite, although popularity has dropped off recently due to the rush for the next big thing. But Authentic Café still has a loyal following of locals who appreciate generous portions and lively flavor combinations. You can sometimes find an Asian flair to chef Roger Hayot's dishes. Look for brie, papaya, and chili quesadillas; other worthwhile dishes are the chicken casserole with a corn-bread crust, fresh corn and red peppers in chili-cream sauce, and meat loaf with caramelized onions.

7605 Beverly Blvd. (at Curson Ave.). ℂ 323/939-4626. Reservations accepted only for parties of 8 or more. Main courses $9–$19. AE, MC, V. Mon–Thurs 11:30am–11pm; Fri 11:30am–midnight; Sat 10:30am–midnight; Sun 10:30am–11pm. Metered street parking or evening valet parking $3.50.

Ca' Brea ⭐⭐ NORTHERN ITALIAN   When Ca' Brea opened in 1991, its talented chef/owner, Antonio Tommasi, was catapulted into a public spotlight shared by only a handful of L.A. chefs—Wolfgang Puck, Michel Richard, and Joachim Splichal. Since then, Tommasi has opened two other celebrated restaurants, **Locanda Veneta** in Hollywood and **Ca' Del Sole** in the Valley, but, for many, Ca' Brea remains tops. The restaurant's refreshingly bright two-story dining room is a happy place, hung with colorful, oversized contemporary paintings and backed by an open prep-kitchen where you can watch as your seafood cakes are sautéed and your Napa cabbage braised. Booths are the most coveted seats; but with only 20 tables in all, be thankful you're sitting anywhere. Detractors might complain that Ca' Brea isn't what it used to be since Tommasi began splitting his time between three restaurants, but Tommasi stops in daily and keeps a very close watch over his handpicked staff. Consistently excellent dishes include the roasted pork sausage, the butter squash–stuffed ravioli, and a different risotto each day—always rich, creamy, and delightfully indulgent.

346 S. La Brea Ave. (north of Wilshire Blvd.). ℂ 323/938-2863. Reservations recommended. Dinner main courses $9–$21; lunch $7–$20. AE, DC, MC, V. Mon–Fri 11:30am–2:30pm; Mon–Thurs 5:30–10:30pm; Fri–Sat 5:30–11pm; Sun 5:30–10pm. Valet parking $3.50.

Chianti Cucina ⭐ NORTHERN ITALIAN   Innocent passersby and locals in search of a secret hideaway go to the dimly lit, crimson-colored Ristorante Chianti, where waiters whip out flashlights so customers can read the menu. Cognoscenti, on the other hand, bypass this 60-year-old standby and head straight for Chianti Cucina, the bright, bustling eat-in "kitchen" next door, which features excellent meals at fair prices. The menu, which changes frequently, is always interesting and often exceptional. Hot and cold appetizers range from fresh handmade mozzarella and prosciutto to lamb carpaccio with asparagus and marinated grilled eggplant filled with goat cheese, arugula, and sun-dried tomatoes. As for main dishes, the homemade pasta is superior and

Authentic Café **9**

Ca'Brea **13**

Campanile **14**

Chianti Cucina **5**

Dar Maghreb **1**

El Cholo **15**

El Coyote **10**

Musso & Frank Grill **3**

Patina **7**

Pink's Hot Dogs **6**

Roscoe's House of
  Chicken 'n' Waffles **4**

Sofi **11**

Swingers **8**

Tahiti **12**

Toi on Sunset **2**

deliciously inventive. Try the black tortellini filled with fresh salmon, or the giant ravioli filled with spinach and ricotta.

7383 Melrose Ave. (between Fairfax and La Brea aves.). ℂ **323/653-8333.** Reservations recommended. Main courses $10–$25. AE, DC, DISC, MC, V. Chianti Cucina Mon–Thurs 11:30am–10:30pm; Fri–Sat 11:30am–11:30pm; Sun 4:30–10:30pm. Ristorante Chianti Sun–Thurs 5:30–10:30pm; Fri–Sat 5:30pm–11pm. Valet parking $3.75 (dinner), free for lunch.

Musso & Frank Grill ✮ AMERICAN/CONTINENTAL   A survey of Hollywood restaurants that leaves out Musso & Frank is like a study of Las Vegas singers that fails to mention Wayne Newton. As L.A.'s oldest eatery (since 1919), Musso & Frank is the paragon of Old Hollywood grillrooms. This is where Faulkner and Hemingway drank during their screenwriting days and where Orson Welles used to hold court. The restaurant is still known for its bone-dry martinis and perfectly seasoned Bloody Marys. The setting is what you'd expect: oak-beamed ceilings, red-leather booths and banquettes, mahogany room dividers, and chandeliers with tiny shades. The extensive menu is a veritable survey of American/Continental cookery. Hearty dinners include veal scaloppini Marsala, roast spring lamb with mint jelly, and broiled lobster. Grilled meats are a specialty, as is the Thursday-only chicken potpie. Regulars also flock in for Musso's trademark "flannel cakes," crepe-thin pancakes flipped to order.

6667 Hollywood Blvd. (at Cherokee Ave.). ℂ **323/467-7788.** Reservations recommended. Main courses $13–$32. AE, DC, MC, V. Tues–Sat 11am–11pm. Self-parking $2.25 with validation.

Sofi ✮ *Finds* GREEK   Look for the simple black awning over the narrow passageway that leads from the street to this hidden Aegean treasure. Be sure to ask for a table on the romantic patio amid twinkling lights, and immediately order a plate of their thick, satisfying *tsatziki* (yogurt-cucumber-garlic spread) accompanied by a basket of warm pita for dipping. Other specialties (recipes courtesy of Sofi's old-world grandmother) include herbed rack of lamb with rice, fried calamari salad, *saganaki* (kasseri cheese flamed with ouzo), and other hearty taverna favorites. Sofi's odd, off-street setting, near the Farmers Market in a popular part of town, has made it an insiders' secret.

8030¾ W. Third St. (between Fairfax Ave. and Crescent Heights Blvd.). ℂ **323/651-0346.** Reservations recommended. Main courses $7–$14. AE, DC, MC, V. Mon–Sat noon–3pm; daily 5:30–11pm. Metered street parking or valet parking $3.

Tahiti ✮ CALIFORNIA/PACIFIC RIM   Tahiti has a rapidly growing fan base of showbiz types and artists who inhabit the eclectic surrounding neighborhood. Chef/owner Tony DiLembo's distinctive "world cuisine" is a provocative mix of influences that produces diverse specialties like rare ahi tuna drizzled with lime-ginger butter, sprinkled with toasted sesame seeds, and served with wasabi horseradish and papaya garnish; Argentinean-style T-bone with chimichurri dipping sauce; sherry-sautéed chicken and spinach pot stickers accented with mint; and perennial standout rosemary chicken strips with fettuccine in sun-dried tomato/ cream sauce. The relaxing decor is sophisticated South Seas with a modern twist, incorporating thatch, batik, rattan, and palm fronds. In the adjacent Tiki Lounge (daily 6pm–2am; happy hour 6–8pm), tropical concoctions contribute to the island ambience. If the weather is nice, try to get a table on the patio. And don't forget to save room for Tahiti's tropical-tinged desserts.

7910 W. Third St. (at Fairfax), Los Angeles. ℂ **323/651-1213.** Reservations recommended. Main courses $11–$17. AE, MC, V. Mon–Fri 11:30am–2:30pm; Mon–Thurs 6–10pm; Fri–Sat 6–11pm; Sun 5–9pm. Valet parking $3.50.

INEXPENSIVE

El Cholo ⭐ MEXICAN   There's authentic Mexican and then there's traditional Mexican—El Cholo is comfort food of the latter variety, south-of-the-border cuisine regularly craved by Angelenos. They've been serving it up in this pink adobe hacienda since 1927, even though the once-outlying mid-Wilshire neighborhood around them has turned into Koreatown. El Cholo's expertly blended margaritas, invitingly messy nachos, and classic combination dinners don't break new culinary ground, but the kitchen has perfected these standards over 70 years. We wish they bottled their rich enchilada sauce! Other specialties include seasonally available green-corn tamales and creative sizzling vegetarian fajitas that go way beyond just eliminating the meat. The atmosphere is festive, as people from all parts of town dine happily in the many rambling rooms that compose the restaurant. There's valet parking as well as a free self-park lot directly across the street.

Westsiders head to El Cholo's Santa Monica branch at 1025 Wilshire Blvd. (© **310/899-1106**).

1121 S. Western Ave. (south of Olympic Blvd.). © **323/734-2773**. www.elcholo.com. Reservations suggested. Main courses $8–$14. AE, DC, DISC, MC, V. Mon–Thurs 11am–10pm; Fri–Sat 11am–11pm; Sun 11am–9pm. Free self-parking or valet parking $3.

Fred 62 AMERICAN/BREAKFAST   Opened in the heart of trendy Los Feliz by chef Fred Eric—whose overly contrived Vida restaurant is just a couple of blocks away—this slightly skewed coffee shop comes by its retro kitsch honestly. Eric remodeled the tiny corner diner with spiffy 1950s car-culture icons, including hood-ornament sconces and blue service-station smocks for the wait staff. He then named it after himself (and his birth year, 1962) and peppered the menu with puns and inside jokes. There's a daily "cream of what Fred wants" soup, plus sandwiches, burgers, salads, and a handful of Asian noodle bowls, including "SEOUL-FULL NOO*DEL +I," a cryptic name for Korean potato noodles, vegetables, and sesame dressing in hot broth. You might feel like you've stepped into a "Route 66" beatnik diner in TV land, but the clientele is very real, the food comforting yet stylish. Don't miss the homemade potato chips and the fresh lemonade dispensed from a churning tank on the counter.

1850 N. Vermont Ave., Los Feliz. © **323/667-0062**. Main courses $3.15–$9.65. MC, V. Daily 24 hr. Metered street parking.

Pink's Hot Dogs ⭐ *Kids* SANDWICHES/BURGERS/HOT DOGS   Pink's isn't your usual guidebook recommendation, but then again, this crusty corner stand isn't your usual dog cart either. The heartburn-inducing chili dogs ("World's Best!") are craved by even the most upstanding, health-conscious Angelenos. Bruce Willis reportedly proposed to Demi Moore at the 63-year-old shack that grew around the late Paul Pink's 10¢ wiener cart. Pray the bulldozers stay away from this little nugget of a place. Cool website, too.

709 N. La Brea Ave. (at Melrose Ave.). © **323/931-4223**. www.pinkshollywood.com. Hot dogs $2.10. No credit cards. Sun–Thurs 9:30am–2am; Fri–Sat 9:30am–3am.

Roscoe's House of Chicken 'n' Waffles ⭐ BREAKFAST/SOUTHERN   It sounds like a bad joke: Only chicken and waffle dishes are served here, a rubric that also encompasses eggs and chicken livers. Its close proximity to CBS Television City has turned this simple restaurant into a kind of de facto commissary for the network. A chicken-and-cheese omelet isn't everyone's ideal way to begin the day, but it's de rigueur at Roscoe's. At lunch, few calorie-unconscious diners can resist the chicken smothered in gravy and onions, a house specialty that's served with waffles or grits and biscuits. Large chicken-salad bowls and chicken sandwiches also provide plenty of cluck for the buck. Homemade corn bread, sweet-potato pie, homemade potato salad, and corn on the cob are available as side orders, and wine and beer are sold.

Roscoe's can also be found at 106 W. Manchester St. (at Main St.; ℂ **323/ 752-6211**), and 5006 W. Pico Blvd. (at La Brea Ave.; ℂ **323/934-4405**).

1514 N. Gower St. (at Sunset Blvd.). ℂ **323/466-7453**. www.chickenandwaffles.com. Main courses $4–$11. No credit cards. Sun–Thurs 9am–midnight; Fri–Sat 9am–4am. Metered street parking.

Swingers ⊛ AMERICAN/TRADITIONAL/BREAKFAST Resurrected from a motel coffee shop, Swingers was transformed by a couple of L.A. hipster nightclub owners into a 1990s version of comfy Americana. The interior seems like a slice of the 1950s until you notice the plaid upholstery and Warhol-esque graphics, which contrast nicely with the retro red-white-and-blue "Swingers" logo adorning *everything*. Guests at the attached Beverly Laurel Motor Hotel chow down alongside body-pierced industry hounds from nearby record companies, while a soundtrack that runs the gamut from punk rock to "Schoolhouse Rock" plays in the background. It's not all attitude, though—you'll enjoy a menu of high-quality diner favorites with trendy crowd-pleasers: Steel-cut Irish oatmeal, challah French toast, grilled Jamaican jerk chicken, and a selection of tofu-enhanced vegetarian dishes are just a few of the eclectic offerings. Sometimes we just "swing" by for a malt or milkshake to go—they're among the best in town.

8020 Beverly Blvd. (west of Fairfax Ave.). ℂ **323/653-5858**. Most items less than $8. AE, DISC, MC, V. Sun–Thurs 6am–2am; Fri–Sat 9am–4am. Metered street parking.

Toi on Sunset ⊛ *Value* THAI Because they're open *really* late, Toi has become an instant fave of Hollywood hipsters like Sean Penn and Woody Harrelson, who make postclubbing excursions to this rock-and-roll eatery a few blocks from the Sunset Strip. After all the hype, we were surprised to find possibly L.A.'s best bargain Thai food, authentically prepared and served in portions so generous the word *enormous* seems inadequate. Menu highlights include hot-and-sour chicken, coconut soup, and the house specialty: chicken curry *somen,* a spicy dish with green curry and mint sauce spooned over thin Japanese rice noodles. Vegetarians will be pleased with the vast selection of meat-free items like *pad kee mao,* rice noodles served spicy with tofu, mint, onions, peppers, and chili. The interior is a noisy amalgam of cultish movie posters, rock-and-roll memorabilia, and haphazardly placed industrial-issue dinette sets; and the plates, flatware, and drinking glasses are cheap coffee-shop issue. In other words, it's all about the food and the scene—neither will disappoint.

Westsiders can opt for **Toi on Wilshire,** 1120 Wilshire Blvd., Santa Monica (ℂ **310/394-7804**), open daily from 11am to 3am.

7505½ Sunset Blvd. (at Gardner). ℂ **323/874-8062**. Reservations accepted only for parties of 6 or more. Main courses $6–$11. AE, DISC, MC, V. Daily 11am–4am.

5 Downtown

EXPENSIVE

Water Grill ⭑⭑⭑ SEAFOOD This restaurant is popular with the suit-and-tie crowd at lunch and with concertgoers en route to the Music Center at night. The dining room is a stylish and sophisticated fusion of wood, leather, and brass, but gets a lighthearted lift from cavorting papier-mâché fish that play against an

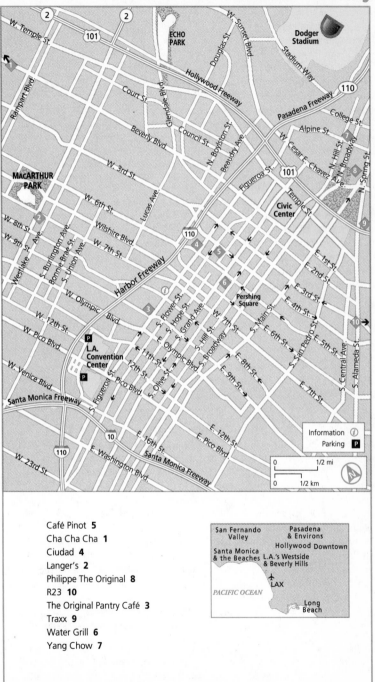

Café Pinot **5**
Cha Cha Cha **1**
Ciudad **4**
Langer's **2**
Philippe The Original **8**
R23 **10**
The Original Pantry Café **3**
Traxx **9**
Water Grill **6**
Yang Chow **7**

San Fernando Valley
Pasadena & Environs
Hollywood Downtown
Santa Monica & the Beaches
L.A.'s Westside & Beverly Hills
LAX
PACIFIC OCEAN
Long Beach

aquamarine ceiling painted with bubbles. Water Grill, considered by many to be L.A.'s best seafood house, is known for its shellfish; among the appetizers are a dozen different oysters. Main courses are imaginative dishes influenced by the cuisines of Hawaii, the Pacific Northwest, New Orleans, and New England. Try the appetizer seafood platter, a mouthwatering assortment served with well-made aioli; bluefin tuna tartare; Santa Barbara spot prawns paired with fingerling potato salad; Maine lobster stuffed with Dungeness crab; perfectly pan-roasted Alaskan halibut; and simple desserts like mascarpone with figs and cherries.

544 S. Grand Ave. (between 5th and 6th sts.). 📞 **213/891-0900.** Reservations recommended. Main courses $19–$31. AE, DC, DISC, MC, V. Mon–Tues 11:30am–9pm; Wed–Fri 11:30am–10pm; Sat 5–10pm; Sun 4:30–9pm. Valet parking $4.

MODERATE

Cafe Pinot ☆ *Kids* CALIFORNIA-FRENCH   A member of superstar-chef Joachim Splichal's L.A. restaurant empire, Cafe Pinot is modeled after the top-ranked Patina, but designed to be less formal and lighter on the palate—and the pocketbook. The restaurant's location, in the front garden of the L.A. Public Library, makes it a natural for downtown business folk; at night there's a free shuttle to the Music Center. Cafe Pinot's tables are mostly on the patio, shaded by umbrellas and the well-landscaped library courtyard.

Splichal has installed a giant rotisserie in the kitchen, and this is where the best meals come from. The moist, tender, mustard-crusted roast chicken is your best bet—unless it's Friday night, when you can order the roast suckling pig with its crackling skin. Other recommended dishes include duck-leg confit, grilled calf's liver, and seared peppered tuna.

700 W. Fifth St. (between Grand and Flower sts., next to the L.A. Public Library) 📞 **213/239-6500.** www. patinagroup.com. Reservations recommended. Main courses $15–$25. AE, DC, DISC, MC, V. Mon–Fri 2:30am–5pm and 5–9:30pm; Sat 5–9:30pm; Sun 5–9pm. Express window open Mon–Fri 11:30–2:30am. Self-parking free–$3.

Cha Cha Cha ☆☆ BREAKFAST/CARIBBEAN/CUBAN   Cha Cha Cha serves the West Coast's best Caribbean food in a fun and funky space on the seedy fringe of Downtown. The restaurant is a festival of flavors and colors both upbeat and offbeat. It's impossible to feel down when you're part of this eclectic hodgepodge of pulsating Caribbean music, wild decor, and kaleidoscopic clutter; still, the intimate dining rooms cater to lively romantics, not the obnoxious types. Claustrophobes should choose seats in the airy covered courtyard. The very spicy black-pepper jumbo shrimp gets top marks, as does the paella, a generous mixture of chicken, sausage, and seafood blended with saffron rice. Other Jamaican-, Haitian-, Cuban-, and Puerto Rican–inspired recommendations include jerk pork and mambo gumbo, a zesty soup of okra, shredded chicken, and spices. Hard-core Caribbeanites might visit for breakfast, when the fare ranges from plantain, yucca, onion, and herb omelets to scrambled eggs with fresh tomatillos served on hot grilled tortillas.

656 N. Virgil Ave. (at Melrose Ave.), Silver Lake. 📞 **323/664-7723.** Reservations recommended. Main courses $8–$15. AE, DC, DISC, MC, V. Sun–Thurs 8am–10:30pm; Fri–Sat 8am–11:30pm. Valet parking $3.50.

Ciudad ☆☆ LATIN   The latest venture of TV's *Too Hot Tamales*—Susan Feniger and Mary Sue Milliken—is this intriguing restaurant in the heart of Downtown. Ciudad means "city" in Spanish, and is a nod to the partners' long-ago venture City Restaurant. Here, amid juicy sherbet pastel walls and 1950s geometric abstract designs, exuberant crowds gather to revel in a menu that brings together cuisines from the world's great Latin urban centers: Havana, Rio de Janeiro, Barcelona, and so on. Standout dishes include Honduran ceviche presented in a martini glass and accented with tropical coconut and pineapple, Argentine rib-eye stuffed with jalapeño chilis and whole garlic cloves, and citrus-roasted Cuban-style chicken served with Puerto Rican rice and fried plantains. Between 3 and 7pm on weekdays, Ciudad presents *cuchifrito,* traditional Latin snacks served at the bar; it's easy to make a meal of several, choosing from sweet-savory pork-stuffed green tamales, *papas rellenos* (mashed potato fritters stuffed with oxtail stew), plantain gnocchi in tomatillo sauce, and more. As with the pair's Border Grill, desserts are worth saving room for, and large enough to share.

445 S. Figueroa St. ✆ **213/486-5171.** www.cuidad-la.com. Reservations recommended. Main courses $12–$23; *cuchifrito* $5–$8. AE, MC, V. Mon–Fri 11:30am–10pm; Sat–Sun 5–10pm. Free parking days; valet parking (after 5pm) $3.50.

R23 ★★ JAPANESE/SUSHI   This gallerylike space in Downtown's out-of-the-way warehouse/artist loft district has been the secret of sushi connoisseurs since 1991. At the back of R23's single, large dining room, the 12-seat sushi bar shines like a beacon; what appear at first to be ceramic wall ornaments are really stylish sushi platters hanging in wait for large orders. More functional art reveals itself in the corrugated cardboard chairs—they're funky, yet far more comfortable than wood! Genial sushi wizards stand in wait, cases of the finest fish before them. Salmon, yellowtail, shrimp, tuna, and scallops are among the always-fresh selections; an excellent and unusual offering is seared *toro,* where the rich belly tuna absorbs a faint and delectable smoky flavor from the grill. Though R23's sublimely perfect sushi is the star, the short but inventive menu also includes pungent red miso soup, creamy baked scallops, finely sliced beef "sashimi," and several other choices. Their latest addition is a wide selection of premium wines and sakes (try the addictively sweet nigori).

923 E. Second St. (between Alameda St. and Santa Fe Ave.). ✆ **213/687-7178.** Reservations recommended. Main courses $12–$20; sushi $4–$8. AE, DC, DISC, MC, V. Mon–Fri 11:45–2pm and 5:45–10pm; Sat 5:45–10pm. Free parking.

Traxx ★ *Finds* CALIFORNIA   There's always been a restaurant—of some sort—inside the Union Station passenger concourse, but Traxx is the first to do justice to its grand, historic setting. Boasting the right mix of retro-evocative Art Deco character with sleek contemporary touches, the interior blends seamlessly with the station's architecture, a unique fusion of Spanish Colonial Revival and streamline moderne. Elegant enough for a romantic dinner, yet welcoming to the casual commuter in search of a stylish lunch or sit-down snack, Traxx features a menu with the same cosmopolitan flavor as the station itself. Samples range from "small plates" of ahi tuna napoleon with crispy wonton or "Really Good" (and they are) crab cakes with a chipotle kick, to main dishes like grilled salmon with a Mediterranean flair or the much-talked-about Gorgonzola-crusted beef tenderloin presented atop crispy and mashed potatoes surrounded by a pool of demi-glace/herb reduction.

In Union Station, 800 N. Alameda St. (at Cesar E. Chavez Ave.). ✆ **213/625-1999.** Reservations suggested for dinner. Dinner main courses $10–$25; lunch $10–$15 . AE, MC, V. Mon–Fri 11am–10pm; Sat 6–10pm. Free valet parking with validation.

Yang Chow Restaurant ★★ CHINESE   Open for more than 30 years, family operated Yang Chow is one of Downtown's more popular Chinese restaurants. It's not the dining room's bland and functional decor that accrues accolades; what makes Yang Chow so popular is an interesting menu of seafood specialties complementing well-done Chinese standards. After covering the Mandarin and Szechwan basics—sweet-and-sour pork, shrimp with broccoli, moo shu chicken—the kitchen leaps into high gear, concocting dishes like spicy Dungeness crab, a tangy and hot sautéed squid, and sautéed shellfish with a pungent hoisin-based dipping sauce. The key to having a terrific meal is to first order the house specialty—plump steamed pork dumplings presented on a bed of fresh spinach—then respectfully ask for recommendations from your server.

819 N. Broadway (at Alpine St.), Chinatown. ℂ **213/625-0811.** Reservations recommended on weekends. Main courses $8–$14. AE, MC, V. Daily 11:30am–2:30pm; Sun–Thurs 5–9:30pm; Fri–Sat 5–10:30pm. Free parking.

INEXPENSIVE

Langer's ⭐ BREAKFAST/DELICATESSEN A leader in L.A.'s long-running deli war, Langer's makes some of the best kishka and matzo-ball soup this side of the Hudson. For many, however, it's the fresh chopped liver and lean and spicy hot pastrami sandwiches that make Langer's L.A.'s best deli. It's been serving the business community and displaced New Yorkers for almost 50 years. After the riots, when things got dicey around this neighborhood, the restaurant began a curbside pickup service: Phone in your order with an ETA, and they'll wait for you at the curb—with change.

704 S. Alvarado St. (at 7th St.). ℂ **213/483-8050.** Main courses $6–$14. MC, V. Mon–Sat 8am–4pm. Free parking with validation.

The Original Pantry *Value* AMERICAN/BREAKFAST An L.A. institution if there ever were one, this place has been serving huge portions of comfort food around the clock for more than 60 years. In fact, there isn't even a key to the front door. Owned by former L.A. mayor and botched governor contender Richard Riordan, the Pantry is popular with politicos, who come here for weekday lunches, and with conference-goers en route to the nearby L.A. Convention Center. The well-worn restaurant is also a welcoming beacon to clubbers after hours, when Downtown becomes a virtual ghost town. A bowl of celery stalks, carrot sticks, and whole radishes greets you at your Formica table, and creamy coleslaw and sourdough bread come free with every meal. Famous for quantity rather than quality, the Pantry serves huge T-bone steaks, densely packed meat loaf, macaroni and cheese, and other American favorites. A typical breakfast (served all day) might consist of a huge stack of hotcakes, a big slab of sweet cured ham, home fries, and coffee.

877 S. Figueroa St. (at 9th St.). ℂ **213/972-9279.** Main courses $6–$11. No credit cards. Daily 24 hr. Free parking with validation.

Philippe the Original BREAKFAST/SANDWICHES Good old-fashioned value is what this legendary landmark cafeteria is all about. Popular with both South Central project residents and Beverly Hills elite, Philippe's unspectacular dining room is one of the few places in L.A. where everyone can get along. Philippe's claims to have invented the French-dipped sandwich at this location in 1908; it remains the most popular menu item. Patrons push trays along the counter and watch while their choice of beef, pork, ham, turkey, or lamb is sliced and layered onto crusty French bread that's been dipped in meat juices. Other menu items include homemade beef stew, chili, and pickled pigs' feet. A hearty breakfast, served daily until 10:30am, is worthwhile if only for Philippe's uncommonly good cinnamon-dipped French toast. Beer and wine are available.

Insider Tip: For added entertainment, request a booth in the new Train Room, which houses the nifty Model Train Museum.

1001 N. Alameda St. (at Ord St.). © **213/628-3781**. www.philippes.com. Most menu items under $7. No credit cards. Daily 6am–10pm. Free parking.

6 The San Fernando Valley

EXPENSIVE

Pinot Bistro ★★ *Kids* CALIFORNIA/FRENCH   When the Valley crowd doesn't want to make the drive to Patina, they pack into Pinot Bistro, one of Joachim Splichal's other successful restaurants. The Valley's only great bistro is designed with dark woods, etched glass, and cream-colored walls that scream "trendy French" almost as loudly as the rich, straightforward cooking. The menu, a symphony of California and Continental elements, includes a beautiful warm potato tart with smoked whitefish, and baby lobster tails with creamy polenta—both studies in culinary perfection. The most popular dish here is the French-ified Tuscan bean soup, infused with oven-dried tomatoes and roasted garlic and served over crusty ciabatta bread. The generously portioned main dishes continue the gourmet theme: baby lobster risotto, braised oxtail with parsley gnocchi, and puff pastry stuffed with bay scallops, Manila clams, and roast duck. The service is good, attentive, and unobtrusive. Many regulars prefer Pinot Bistro at lunch, when a less expensive menu is served to a more easy-going crowd.

12969 Ventura Blvd. (west of Coldwater Canyon Ave.), Studio City. © **818/990-0500**. www.patinagroup. com. Reservations required. Dinner main courses $16–$22; lunch $7–$13. AE, DC, DISC, MC, V. Mon–Fri noon–2pm; Mon–Thurs 6–10pm; Fri 6–10:30pm; Sat 5:30–10:30pm; Sun 5:30–9:30pm. Valet parking $3.50.

Talesai ★ THAI   Thai food fans will either love or hate this "haute Thai" sibling of a Sunset Strip institution. Talesai's minimalist decor punctuated by crisp white tablecloths complements a sophisticated and innovative Thai cuisine that elevates the usual takeout favorites. Prices reflect this aesthetic, but if you're sick of gummy *pad Thai* and tough satay, Talesai will be a welcome change. Meat dishes accented with curry, coconut milk, and mint can be prepared as spicy or mild as you wish. Two Talesai specialties are "Hidden Treasures," in which chili- and coconut-soaked shrimp and crabmeat are baked in tiny clay pots; and "Heavenly BBQ Chicken," marinated in spices and coconut milk and then grilled to "heavenly" perfection.

You can find Talesai's Sunset Strip outpost at 9043 Sunset Blvd. (at Doheny Dr.), West Hollywood (© **310/275-9724**).

11744 Ventura Blvd. (between Colfax Ave. and Laurel Canyon Blvd.), Studio City. © **818/753-1001**. Reservations recommended. Main courses $9–$18. AE, DC, MC, V. Mon–Fri 11:30am–2:30pm; daily 5:30–10:30pm. Valet parking $3.50.

MODERATE

Casa Vega ★ MEXICAN   We believe that everyone loves a friendly dive, and Casa Vega has been a local favorite for nearly half a century. A faux-weathered adobe exterior conceals red Naugahyde booths lurking among fake potted plants and 1960s amateur oil paintings of dark-eyed Mexican children and cape-waving bullfighters. (The decor achieves critical mass at Christmas, when everything drips with tinsel.) Locals and celebs love this family owned and operated place for its good, cheap margaritas (order on the rocks), bottomless baskets of hot and salty chips, and traditional combination dinners, which all come with

Casa Vega's patented tostada-style dinner salad. Street parking is so plentiful here you should use the valet only as a last resort. An outdoor patio was added in the summer of 2002.

13371 Ventura Blvd. (at Fulton Ave.), Sherman Oaks. ✆ 818/788-4868. Main courses $5–$11. AE, DC, DISC, MC, V. Mon–Fri 11am–2am; Sat 4:30pm–2am; Sun noon–2am. Metered street parking or $2.50 valet.

Jerry's Famous Deli ★ *Kids* BREAKFAST/DELICATESSEN   Here's a simple yet sizable deli where all the Valley's hipsters go to relieve their late-night munchies. This place probably has one of the largest menus in America—a tome that spans cultures and continents, from Central America to China to New York. From salads to sandwiches to steak-and-seafood platters, everything—including breakfast—is served all day. Jerry's is consistently good at lox and eggs, pastrami sandwiches, potato pancakes, and all the deli staples. It's also an integral part of L.A.'s cultural landscape and a favorite of the show-business types who populate the adjacent foothill neighborhoods. It even has a full bar.

12655 Ventura Blvd. (just east of Coldwater Canyon Ave.), Studio City. ✆ 818/980-4245. Dinner main courses $9–$14; breakfast $2–$11; sandwiches and salads $4–$12. AE, MC, V. Daily 24 hr. Free parking.

Miceli's *Kids* TRADITIONAL ITALIAN   Mostaccioli marinara, lasagna, thin-crust pizza, and eggplant parmigiana are indicative of the Sicilian-style fare at this cavernous, stained-glass windowed Italian restaurant adjacent to Universal City. The wait staff sings show tunes or opera favorites in between serving dinner (and sometimes instead of); make sure you have enough Chianti to get into the spirit of it all. This is a great place for kids, but too rollicking for romance.

If you're near Hollywood Boulevard, visit the original (since 1949) Miceli's at 1646 N. Las Palmas (✆ 323/466-3438).

3655 Cahuenga Blvd. (east of Lankershim), Los Angeles. ✆ 818/508-1221. Main courses $7–$12; pizza $9–$15. AE, DC, MC, V. Mon–Thurs 5pm–midnight; Fri 5pm–1am; Sat 4pm–1am; Sun 4–11pm. Parking $2.50.

Paul's Café ★ CALIFORNIA/FRENCH   One of the Valley's hardest reservations (hint: call early, dine early, or both) is at this midsize neighborhood bistro, where a quietly elegant setting belies the friendly prices that have made Paul's a big success. Expect Chef Ricardo Macchi's seasonal menu to include plenty of seafood (roasted sea bass laid atop spinach with a mushroom vinaigrette, sautéed sea scallops with saffron risotto and lobster sauce), hearty meats (filet mignon with port sauce accompanied by a creamy sweet potato–Gorgonzola gratin, garlic-rubbed rack of lamb sweetened with mint), and appetizers that ought to be main courses (pepper crusted seared ahi drizzled with scallion vinaigrette, crab cakes with lobster aioli). Soup or a small salad is only $1 with any dinner, and locals love the mere $2 corkage fee. Paul's manages to be intimate enough for lovers (though we've received complaints about the "dark as a coal mine" dining room) yet also welcoming for families—its success is no surprise.

13456 Ventura Blvd. (between Dixie Canyon and Woodman Ave.), Sherman Oaks. ✆ 818/789-3575. Dinner main courses $12–$17; lunch $8–$11. AE, MC, V. Mon–Thurs 11:30am–2:30pm and 5:30–10pm; Fri 11:30am–2:30pm and 5:30–11pm; Sat 5–11pm; Sun 5–9:30pm. Metered street parking or valet parking $4.

INEXPENSIVE

Du-par's Restaurant & Bakery ★ AMERICAN/TRADITIONAL/BREAKFAST   It's been called a "culinary wax museum," the last of a dying breed, the kind of coffee shop Donna Reed took the family to for blue-plate specials. This isn't a trendy new theme place, it's the real deal—and that motherly waitress who calls everyone under 60 "hon" has probably been slinging hash here for 20 or

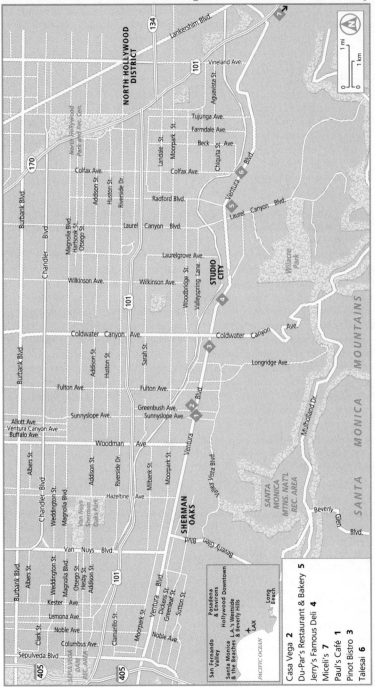

Casa Vega 2
Du-Par's Restaurant & Bakery 5
Jerry's Famous Deli 4
Miceli's 7
Paul's Café 1
Pinot Bistro 3
Talesai 6

30 years. Du-par's is popular among old-timers who made it part of their daily routine decades ago, show business denizens who eschew the industry watering holes, a new generation that appreciates a tasty, cheap meal . . . well, everyone, really. It's common knowledge that Du-par's makes the best buttermilk pancakes in town, though some prefer the eggy, perfect French toast (extra crispy around the edges, please). Mouth-watering pies (blueberry cream cheese, coconut cream, and more) line the front display case and can be had for a song.

West Hollywood denizens can visit the branch of Du-par's in the Ramada Hotel, 8571 Santa Monica Blvd., west of La Cienega (© 310/659-7009); they're open until 3am on weekends *and* have a full bar. There's another Du-par's in Los Angeles at the Farmers Market, 6333 W. 3rd St., at Fairfax St. (© 323/933-8446), but it doesn't stay open as late.

12036 Ventura Blvd. (1 block east of Laurel Canyon Blvd.), Studio City. © 818/766-4437. www.Dupars.com. All items under $11. AE, DC, DISC, MC, V. Sun–Thurs 6am–1am; Fri–Sat 6am–4am. Free parking.

7 Pasadena & Environs

EXPENSIVE

Bistro 45 ★★ CALIFORNIA-FRENCH   All class, yet never stuffy, Bistro 45 is a favorite among Pasadena's old guard and nouvelle riche. The restaurant's warm, light ambience and gallerylike decor are an unexpected surprise after the ornately historic Art Deco exterior (the building is a former bank), but provide a perfect backdrop for owner Robert Simon's refreshing cuisine. The seasonally inspired menu changes frequently; dishes might include salmon and tuna tartares flavored with cilantro, rock shrimp risotto with saffron, pan-roasted monkfish with garlic polenta, roasted veal loin filled with Roquefort, Fanny Bay oyster salad, and Nebraska pork with figs. For dessert, try the "chocolate soup," a creamy soufflé served with chocolate-kirsch sauce and vanilla ice cream. The knowledgeable wait staff can answer questions about the excellent wine list; Bistro 45 appears regularly on *Wine Spectator's* "Best of" lists, and hosts special-event wine dinners.

45 S. Mentor Ave. (between Colorado and Green), Pasadena. © 626/795-2478. Reservations recommended. Dinner main courses $17–$27; lunch $11–$16. AE, MC, V. Tues–Thurs 11:30am–2:30pm and 6–10pm; Fri 11:30am–2:30pm and 6–11pm; Sat 6–11pm; Sun 5–9pm. Valet parking $4.

Parkway Grill ★ CALIFORNIA   This vibrant, quintessentially Southern California restaurant has been one of the L.A. area's top-rated spots since 1985, quickly gaining a reputation for avant-garde flavor combinations and gourmet pizzas to rival Spago's. Although some critics find many dishes too fussy, others thrill to appetizer innovations like lobster-stuffed cocoa crepes or Dungeness crab cakes with ginger cream and two salsas. The stars of the menu are meat and game from the iron mesquite grill, followed by richly sweet (and substantial) desserts. Located where the old Arroyo Seco Parkway glides into an ordinary city street, the Parkway Grill is within a couple of minutes' drive from Old Pasadena and thoughtfully offers free valet parking.

510 S. Arroyo Pkwy. (at California Blvd.), Pasadena. © 626/795-1001. Reservations recommended. Main courses $8–$27. AE, DC, MC, V. Mon–Thurs 11:30am–2:30pm and 5:30–11pm; Fri 11:30am–2:30pm and 5pm–midnight; Sat 5pm–midnight; Sun 5–11pm. Free valet parking.

The Raymond ★★ NEW AMERICAN/CONTINENTAL   With its easy-to-miss setting in a sleepy part of Pasadena, the Raymond is a jewel few locals even know about. This Craftsman cottage was once the caretaker's house for a grand

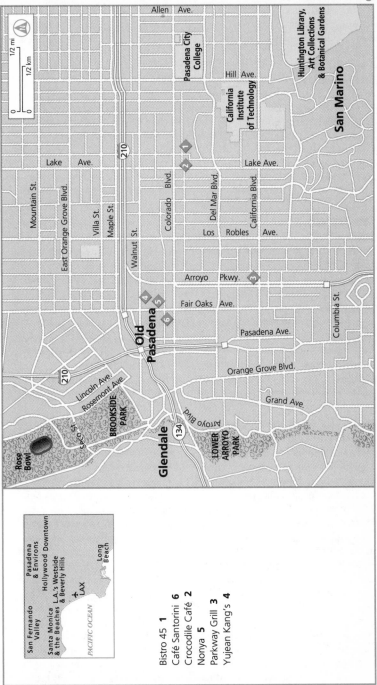

Pasadena Area Dining

Pasadena City College

California Institute of Technology

Huntington Library, Art Collections & Botanical Gardens

San Marino

Allen Ave.
Hill Ave.
Lake Ave.
Lake Ave.
Del Mar Blvd.
California Blvd.
Los Robles Ave.
Colorado Blvd.
Maple St.
Villa St.
Mountain St.
East Orange Grove Blvd.
Walnut St.
Arroyo Pkwy.
Fair Oaks Ave.
Columbia St.
Pasadena Ave.
Orange Grove Blvd.
Grand Ave.
Arroyo Blvd.
Lincoln Ave
Rosemont Ave.
Seco St.
210
134

Old Pasadena

BROOKSIDE PARK
Rose Bowl
Glendale
LOWER ARROYO PARK

1/2 mi
1/2 km

San Fernando Valley
Pasadena & Environs
Hollywood Downtown
Santa Monica & the Beaches
L.A.'s Westside & Beverly Hills
LAX
Long Beach
PACIFIC OCEAN

Bistro 45 **1**
Café Santorini **6**
Crocodile Café **2**
Nonya **5**
Parkway Grill **3**
Yujean Kang's **4**

Victorian hotel called The Raymond. Though the city has grown to surround it, the place maintains an enchanting air of seclusion and serenity. Chef/owner Suzanne Bourg brings a romantic sensibility and impeccable culinary instincts to dishes that are mostly haute American—with an occasional European flair. The menu changes weekly. One night a grilled rack of lamb is sauced with orange, Grand Marnier, and peppercorns; another night it comes with a creamy white wine and chèvre sauce with dried cherries. Bourg's soups are always heavenly (the restaurant gladly gives out the recipes), and desserts are inspired. Tables are scattered throughout the house and in the lush English garden, and there's plenty of free, nonvalet parking. (You wouldn't find *that* on the Westside!)

1250 S. Fair Oaks Ave. (at Columbia St.), Pasadena. ℂ 626/441-3136. www.theraymond.com. Reservations required. Dinner main courses $30–$34; 4-course dinner $45–$49; prix fixe 3-course dinner $36 (including wine); lunch $13–$20. AE, DC, DISC, MC, V. Tues–Thurs 11:30am–2:30pm and 6–9:30pm; Fri 11:30am–2:30pm and 5:45–10pm; Sat 11am–2:30pm and 5:45–10pm; Sun 10am–2:30pm and 4:30–8pm; afternoon tea Tues–Fri noon–4pm and Sat–Sun noon–3pm. Free parking.

MODERATE

Café Santorini ⭐ GREEK   Located at ground zero of Pasadena's crowded Old Town shopping mecca, this second-story gem has a secluded Mediterranean ambience, due in part to its historic brick building with splendid patio tables overlooking, but insulated from, the plaza below. In the evening, lighting is subdued and romantic, but ambience is casual; many diners are coming from or going to an adjacent movie-theater complex. The food is outstanding and affordable, featuring grilled meats and kebabs, pizzas, fresh and tangy hummus, plenty of warm pita, and other staples of Greek cuisine. The menu includes regional flavors like lamb, feta cheese, spinach, or Armenian sausage; the vegetarian baked butternut squash is filled with fluffy rice and smoky roast vegetables.

64 W. Union St. (main entrance at the shopping plaza at the corner of Fair Oaks and Colorado), Pasadena. ℂ 626/564-4200. www.cafesantorini.com. Reservations recommended on weekends. Main courses $9–$22. AE, DC, DISC, MC, V. Daily 11am–11pm (until midnight Fri–Sat). Valet or self-parking $4.

Nonya ⭐⭐ *Finds* CHINESE/MALAYSIAN/PERANAKAN   It's a rare day in a travel writer's career when he enjoys a cuisine he's never even heard of. Peranakan cuisine (aka Nonya) was developed in the 15th century by Peranakans, a people whose heritage stems from the intermarriage between Chinese settlers of Singapore and the local Malaysians. It's a complex and sophisticated style of cooking, involving exotic ingredients and a layering of flavors, and there's only a few chefs in the Western world—including Nonya's executive chef Tony Pat, a Hong Kong native—who know the authentic techniques to make it. Pungent roots such as ginger, turmeric, and galangal are used liberally along with aromatic and often spicy seasonings to an eclectic and wondrous effect. Case it point: It's a sure bet you haven't had a *mangga ikan* salad—a light yet flavorful dish made with fresh mango, tender halibut, thinly sliced red onions and a lemongrass-lime vinaigrette. Nor are you familiar with *khaj panggang*, thin slices of chicken breast marinated in chili and grilled in banana leaves. The seafood dishes are equally enticing: red snapper spiced with turmeric and tamarind, cooked in banana leaves and served with house-pickled vegetables; whole Dungeness crab sautéed with curry leaves and black pepper. Owner Simon Tong, who owned Asian restaurants in London for 25 years until recently settling in Pasadena, hired designer Dodd Mitchell to create a gorgeous dining room, replete with glimmering hardwoods, metals, and lush foliage that surround a tranquil elevated pond (it's both sexy and soothing, the perfect date place).

61 N. Raymond St. (at Union St.), Pasadena. ✆ **626/583-8398.** Reservations recommended. Main courses $9–$42. AE, MC, V. Sun–Thurs 11am–2:30pm and 5–10pm; Fri–Sat 11am–2:30pm and 5–11pm. Valet parking $4.

Yujean Kang's Gourmet Chinese Cuisine ★★ CHINESE   Many Chinese restaurants put the word *gourmet* in their name, but few really mean it—or deserve it. Not so at Yujean Kang's, where Chinese cuisine is taken to an entirely new level. A master of "fusion" cuisine, the eponymous chef/owner snatches bits of techniques and flavors from both China and the West, commingling them in an entirely fresh way. Can you resist such provocative dishes as "Ants on Tree" (beef sautéed with glass noodles in chili and black sesame seeds), or lobster with caviar and fava beans, or Chilean sea bass in passion-fruit sauce? Kang is also a wine aficionado and has assembled a magnificent cellar of California, French, and particularly German wines. Try pairing a German Spätlese with tea-smoked duck salad. The red-wrapped dining room is less subtle than the food, but just as elegant.

67 N. Raymond Ave. (between Walnut St. and Colorado Blvd.), Pasadena. ✆ **626/585-0855.** Reservations recommended. Main courses $8–$19. AE, MC, V. Daily 11:30am–2:30pm and 5–10pm. Street parking.

INEXPENSIVE

Crocodile Cafe AMERICAN/TRADITIONAL/INTERNATIONAL   Casual and colorful, this offshoot of Pasadena's groundbreaking Parkway Grill builds a menu around simple crowd-pleasers (pizza, pasta, burgers, salads) prepared with fresh ingredients and jazzed up with creative marinades, vinaigrettes, and salsas. It's a formula that works; this Lake Avenue branch is the original location, but siblings have sprung up throughout the San Fernando and San Gabriel Valleys— even as far away as Santa Monica. Favorite selections include the oakwood-grilled burger with curly french fries, the Croc's signature blue corn chicken tostada with warm black beans and fresh guacamole, wood-grilled gourmet pizzas in the California Pizza Kitchen style, zesty tortilla soup, and ooey-gooey desserts.

Other branches include Old Town Pasadena, 88 W. Colorado Blvd. (✆ **626/ 568-9310**); Glendale, 626 N. Central Ave (✆ **818/241-1114**); and Santa Monica, 101 Santa Monica Blvd. (✆ **310/394-4783**)

140 S. Lake Ave., Pasadena. ✆ **626/449-9900.** www.crocodilecafe.com. Main courses $8–$18. AE, MC, V. Daily 11am–10pm (till midnight Fri–Sat). Free self-parking.

7

What to See & Do in Los Angeles

There's plenty for the visitor to see and do in L.A.—traditional tourist draws such as Hollywood Boulevard, Farmers Market, and the Santa Monica Pier are being spruced up at considerable expense, and newer ones like Universal CityWalk and the spectacular Getty Center are continually being added to the city's repertoire. The problem is you have to drive everywhere, so to get the most out of the city's attractions, advance planning is necessary, as is a good map.

Your best bet is to plan your days geographically to avoid freeway rush hours (unless sitting in traffic is your idea of a holiday in L.A.). The itineraries below contain suggestions for maximizing a whole day—exploring beach cities one day, the heart of Hollywood the next, and so on—and the chapter's filled with insider tips to make your L.A. adventure all the more interesting.

To find out what's going on while you're in town, pick up a copy of the free tabloid *L.A. Weekly*, the monthly magazine *Los Angeles*, or the Sunday *Los Angeles Times* "Calendar" section; each has detailed listings covering what's going on around town, often accompanied by entertaining and helpful commentary on which activities might be worth your while. Better yet, plan ahead via the Web (see "Site Seeing: The Best of L.A. Online" in chapter 2) and buy those hard-to-get show tickets in advance.

SUGGESTED ITINERARIES

Note: These itineraries represent just a sampling of what's available and are definitely doable in a short time span. But often more is less, so don't try to cram too much stuff into 1 day if you don't have the energy. If you really want to enjoy even a fraction of what L.A. has to offer you really need at least 3 days.

If You Have 1 Day

Forget the culture/museum stuff—it's time to see for yourself all those famous Hollywood sites you've watched on TV since you were a toddler. Start by spending the morning on **Hollywood Boulevard:** See the stars on the **Walk of Fame,** compare your hands and feet with the famous prints outside **Mann's Chinese Theatre,** and pick up some silly memorabilia (the tackier the better) or some cool rock posters at one of the souvenir shops.

Next, hop in your rented convertible Mustang (red, of course) and cruise the world-renowned **Sunset Boulevard** to the sea. This 45-minute drive takes you through an entertaining cross section of all that is L.A.: from seedy **Hollywood** to flamboyant **West Hollywood** (hello, fellahs!), past glittering **Beverly Hills** and the practical **Westside,** through **Brentwood** (O.J.'s old neighborhood), into the secluded enclave of **Pacific Palisades,** and finally to the sea. It's a fun drive, often curvy and always scenic.

Next, head south on Palisades Beach Road into the big-city beach town of **Santa Monica.** Park at the **Santa Monica Pier** and head south on foot toward **Venice Beach** along the carnival-like **Ocean Front Walk.** Be sure to stop at **Jody Maroni's Sausage Kingdom** for a "haut dog" and situate yourself ocean-side at dusk to take in a spectacular L.A. sunset (good smog equals great sunsets). In the even-ing, after dinner (restaurant choices abound, but we highly recommend **Joe's** in Venice), you can check out the club and music scene in Hollywood and West Hollywood (pick up an *L.A. Weekly* to see what's on). Or, with a little advance planning, you could take in a play at one of the many smaller theaters in Hollywood or a concert at downtown's music center. Be sure to hit up a late-night bar or after-hours club (**Three Clubs** is a good bet) to stretch the day to its fullest.

If You Have 2 Days

Spend your first day in **Hollywood** and the **Westside,** saving the beach for Day 2. On Day 1, check out the **Walk of Fame, Mann's Chinese,** and one of the showbiz museums along **Hollywood Boulevard**—a schmaltzy one like the **Hollywood Wax Museum,** or a serious one like the **Hollywood Entertainment Museum.** If that's not your style, take a guided tour of one of the actual studios in Hollywood or in the Valley (great star-sighting opportunities). Then do a little window-shopping along trendy **Melrose Avenue** or in **Beverly Hills's "Golden Triangle."** Both have great lunch options where you can rest your feet, recharge your body, and restore your spirit.

If you have some more energy, take in one of the attractions of

Museum Row; perhaps an exhibit at the **Los Angeles County Museum of Art,** or the main floor of the **Petersen Automotive Museum.** True culture vultures might want to enjoy the **Getty Center**—just remember to make weekday-parking reservations in advance. In the evening, if you don't have theater tickets, have a special dinner at one of L.A.'s premier restaurants—perhaps **Spago, Jozu,** or **Patina** (be sure to reserve at least a few days in advance). Perhaps end your evening with some libations at **Daddy's** or **The Whiskey Bar** in **Hollywood** and see what kind of trouble you can get into.

On Day 2, head down to **Topanga State Beach** early and enjoy an invigorating swim or surf session before a leisurely breakfast at **Bread & Porridge** in Santa Monica. Next, you might want to visit one of Santa Monica's art gallery complexes like the **Bergamot Station** or outdoor shopping venues along Third Street. Have lunch overlooking the ocean at the **Sidewalk Café** in Venice, and then work it off by renting bikes or skates and joining the human carnival along **Venice Beach.** Cap off the day with sunset cocktails and appetizers at **The Lobster** before heading back to your hotel. Wrap up your evening with some late-night cocktails at Santa Monica's **Circle Bar** or **World Café.**

If You Have 3 Days

Three days is just enough to see L.A. proper. After you've spent your first 2 days in Hollywood and at the beach (see above), it's time to go to the **Disneyland Resort.** Arrive early to beat the crowds; you can party all day with Mickey and pals and still be back in L.A. by dinnertime. Be sure to check out the new **Downtown Disney,** especially if a

L.A.'s Attractions at a Glance

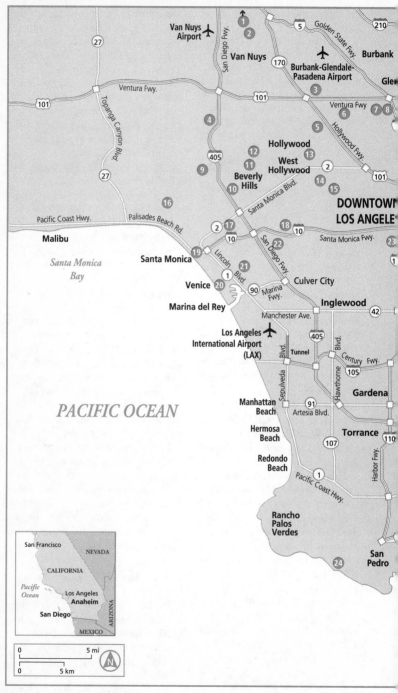

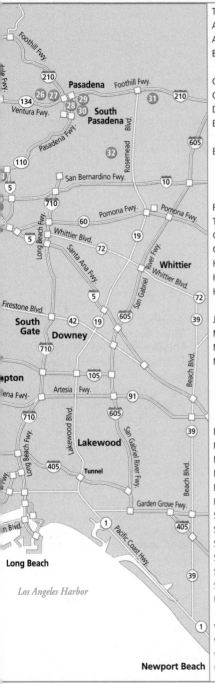

Value CityPass Money Saver

If you're the type who loves to cram in as many tourist attractions as possible in one trip, then you need a **CityPass** (© 707/256-0490; www.city pass.com). This money-saving booklet includes tickets to six popular attractions, a 2-hour bus tour of Beverly Hills and celebrity homes from **Starline Tours,** and savings coupons for Beverly Center shopping. The main draw, and the primary reason to purchase CityPass, is **Universal Studios Hollywood;** the rest are the **Hollywood Entertainment Museum, American Cinematheque at the Egyptian Theatre, Museum of Television and Radio, Petersen Automotive Museum,** and **Autry Museum of Western Heritage.** Purchase the pass at any of the seven attractions, or visit the website to buy advance passes online, find links to the attraction websites, and peruse hotel packages that include CityPass. The pass costs $59 for adults ($39 for kids 3–11) and will expire 30 days from the first use. Is it a good deal? If you use all the tickets, you end up saving 45% over individual, full-price admissions.

---

good band is playing at the **House of Blues.**

If Disneyland's not your thing, try putting on your hiking boots, grabbing some sandwiches, and exploring L.A.'s parks: rural **Will Rogers** and **Temescal** overlooking the ocean, or central **Griffith Park,** which straddles the city and Valley. Or you may prefer to stimulate the economy—there's more shopping here than can be appreciated in a month. Be creative: Head to L.A.'s **3rd Street Promenade** or **La Brea Avenue,** or to **Studio City** in the **San Fernando Valley.** All have a warm, neighborly feel, and goods won't be priced out of reach.

If You Have 4 or 5 Days

With 4 or 5 days in LA-LA Land, you should spend one at **Disneyland** or **Universal Studios;** both perhaps if you love amusement parks. Or use the extra time to explore **downtown L.A.,** an area

usually ignored by tourists but one rich in culture and historical adventures. Plan to arrive hungry, and choose authentic Mexican food on **Olvera Street,** Chinese dim sum in **Chinatown,** a variety of fresh ethnic offerings in the **Grand Central Market,** or an old-fashioned roast-beef dip sandwich at **Philippe the Original,** a downtown institution.

If you're a museum buff, revisit **Museum Row,** since you have a little extra time to appreciate it. The whole family will enjoy the **La Brea Tar Pits** and adjoining **George C. Page Museum,** as well as the **Petersen Automotive Museum** across the street. Speaking of cars, you could take advantage of L.A.'s great location and consider heading south, taking a leisurely drive along the **Orange Coast** or a day trip to **Long Beach** to see the **Queen Mary** and the **Aquarium of the Pacific** and have lunch on the water at the **Yard House.**

1 L.A.'s Top Attractions

Universal Studios Hollywood ★★★ *Kids* Believing that filmmaking itself is a bona fide attraction, Universal Studios began offering tours to the public in

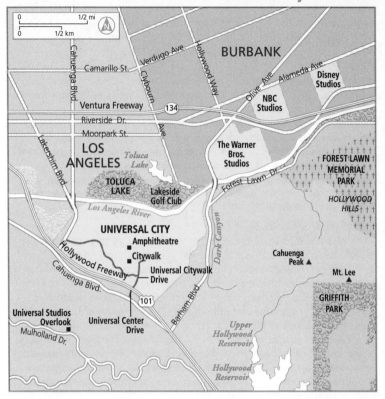

1964. The concept worked. Today Universal is more than just one of the largest movie studios in the world—it's one of the biggest amusement parks.

The main attraction continues to be the **Studio Tour,** a 1-hour guided tram ride around the company's 420 acres. En route you pass stars' dressing rooms and production offices before visiting famous back-lot sets that include an eerily familiar Old West town, a clean New York City street, the famous town square from the *Back to the Future* films, and newer sets such as Curse of the Mummy's Tomb, Jurassic Park III, and The Grinch. Along the way the tram encounters several staged "disasters," which we won't divulge here lest we ruin the surprise.

Other attractions are more typical of high-tech theme-park fare, but all have a film-oriented slant. On **Back to the Future—The Ride,** you're seated in a mock time-traveling DeLorean and thrust into a fantastic multimedia roller-coasting extravaganza—it's far and away Universal's best ride. The **Waterworld** live action stunt show is thrilling to watch (and probably more successful than the film that inspired it), while the special effects showcase, **Jurassic Park—The Ride,** is short in duration but long on dinosaur illusions and computer magic lifted from the Universal blockbuster. The latest thrills are **Mummy Returns Chamber of Doom** ride (scarrrrrrryyyy) and **Terminator 2 3-D,** a virtual adventure using triple-screen technology to impact all the senses. **Totally Nickelodeon** is an interactive live show from the kids' TV network, providing adventure and gallons of green slime, and the new **Animal Planet Live!** stars trained monkeys and other animals doing various entertaining tricks.

Located just outside the gate of Universal Studios Hollywood is the shiny new **Universal CityWalk** (© 818/622-4455), Universal Studio's version of Downtown Disney. If you have any money left from the amusement park, you can spend it here among the 30 stores selling brand-name everything, 25 restaurants (Hard Rock Café, Daily Grill, Jerry's Famous Deli, and so on), 8 nightclubs (Blues at B. B. King's, Howl at the Moon dueling piano bar, Rumba Room Latin dance club), a six-story 3-D IMAX theater, NASCAR virtual racing, and even a bowling alley (Take *that,* Disney!).

Universal Studios is a really fun place, but just as in any theme park, lines can be brutally long; the wait for a 5-minute ride can sometimes last more than an hour. In summer, the stifling Valley heat can dog you all day. To avoid the crowds, skip weekends, school vacations, and Japanese holidays.

Hollywood Fwy. (Universal Center Dr. or Lankershim Blvd. exits), Universal City. © 818/662-3801. www. universalstudios.com. Admission $45 adults, $35 children ages 3–9, free for kids under age 3. Parking $7. Weekdays 10am–6pm, weekends 9am–7pm.

J. Paul Getty Museum at the Getty Center ★★ *Kids*   Since opening in 1997, the Richard Meier–designed Getty Center has quickly assumed its place in the L.A. landscape (literally and figuratively) as a cultural cornerstone and international mecca. Headquarters for the Getty Trust's research, education, and conservation concerns, the complex is most frequently visited for the museum galleries displaying collector J. Paul Getty's enormous collection of art. Always known for antiquities, expanded galleries now allow the display of Impressionist paintings, truckloads of glimmering French furniture and decorative arts, fine illuminated manuscripts, contemporary photography, and previously overlooked graphic arts. The area that's open to the public consists of five two-story pavilions set around an open courtyard, and each gallery within is specially designed to complement the works on display. A sophisticated system of programmable window louvers allows many outstanding works (particularly paintings) to be displayed in the natural light they were created in for the first time in the modern era. One of these is van Gogh's *Irises,* one of the museum's finest holdings. Trivia buffs will enjoy knowing that the museum spent $53.9 million to acquire this painting; it's displayed in a complex that cost roughly $1 *billion* to construct.

Visitors to the center park at the base of the hill and ascend via a cable-driven electric tram. On clear days, the sensation is of being in the clouds, gazing across Los Angeles and the Pacific Ocean (and into a few chic Brentwood backyards). If you're like us and don't remember a thing from your college art appreciation class, plunk down $3 for a self-guided audio tour that gives a brief overview of the 250-plus works in the collection. The 45-minute architectural tours, offered throughout the day, are also worth looking into. Dining options include several espresso/snack carts, a cafeteria, a self-service cafe, and the elegant (though informal) "Restaurant" offering table service for lunch (Tues–Sun) and dinner (Fri–Sat) with breathtaking views overlooking of the ocean and mountains (reservations are recommended, though walk-ins are accepted; call © **310/ 440-7300** or make reservations online at www.getty.edu).

Realizing that fine-art museums are usually dreadfully boring for kids, the center provides several clever programs for kids, including: exploratory games such as *Perplexing Paintings* and *The Getty Art Detective;* a Family Room filled with puzzles, computers, picture books, and games; mythical storytelling sessions on weekends at 11am, noon, and 1pm; weekend family workshops; and self-guided audio tours made specifically for families.

Entrance to the Getty Center is free—they don't need your money—but parking reservations are required weekdays (though we've heard of people getting in without one on slow days). College students with current ID and those arriving by public transportation, motorcycle, or bicycle do not require reservations. Reservations are not required after 4pm, or all day Saturday and Sunday. Cameras and video cams are permitted but only if you use existing light (flash units are verboten). *Tip:* Avoid the crowds by visiting in the late afternoon or evening; the center is open until 9pm Friday and Saturday, the nighttime view is breathtaking, and you can finish with a late dinner on the Westside.

1200 Getty Center Dr., Los Angeles. © **310/440-7300.** www.getty.edu. Free admission. Tues–Thurs and Sun 10am–6pm; Fri–Sat 10am–9pm. Closed major holidays. Parking $5; reservations required weekdays (see above).

Santa Monica Pier ★★   Piers have been a tradition in Southern California since the area's 19th-century seaside resort days. Many have long since disappeared (like Pacific Ocean Park, an entire amusement park perched on offshore pilings), and others have been shortened by battering storms and are now mere shadows (or stumps) of their former selves, but you can still get a chance to experience those halcyon days of yesteryear at world-famous Santa Monica Pier.

Built in 1909 for passenger and cargo ships, the Santa Monica Pier does a pretty good job of recapturing the glory days of Southern California. The wooden wharf is now home to seafood restaurants and snack shacks, a touristy Mexican cantina, and a gaily colored turn-of-the-20th-century indoor wooden carousel (which Paul Newman operated in *The Sting*). Summer evening concerts, which are free and range from big band to Miami-style Latin, draw crowds, as does the small amusement area perched halfway down. Its name, **Pacific Park** (© **310/260-8744;** www.pacpark.com), hearkens back to the granddaddy pier amusement park in California, Pacific Ocean Park; this updated version has a roller coaster and other rides, plus a high-tech arcade shoot-out. But anglers still head to the end to fish, and nostalgia buffs to view the photographic display of the pier's history. This is the last of the great pleasure piers, offering rides, romance, and perfect panoramic views of the bay and mountains.

The pier is about a mile up Ocean Front Walk from Venice; it's a great round-trip stroll. Parking is available for $6 to $8 on both the Pier Deck and the Beachfront nearby. Limited short term parking is also available. For information on twilight concerts (generally held Thurs between mid-June and the end of Aug), call © **310/458-8900** or visit www.santamonicapier.org.

Ocean Ave. at the end of Colorado Blvd., Santa Monica.

Six Flags California (Magic Mountain and Hurricane Harbor) ★★   What started as a countrified little amusement park with a couple of relatively tame roller coasters in 1971 has been transformed by Six Flags into a thrill-a-minute daredevil's paradise . . . now called "The Xtreme Park." Located about 20 to 30 minutes north of Universal Studios, Six Flags Magic Mountain is one of the only ones out of the 38 Six Flags parks that is open year-round. The world-class roller coasters make it enormously popular with teenagers and young adults and a recently renovated children's playland—Bugs Bunny World—creates excitement for the pint-sized set (kids that are under 48 in. tall.) Bring an iron constitution; rides with names like Goliath, Déjà Vu, Ninja, Viper, Colossus, and Psyclone will have your cheeks flapping with the G-force and queasy expressions are common at the exit. But, where else can you experience zero gravity weightlessness, careen down vertical tracks into relentless hairpin turns, or "race" another train on a side-by-side wooden roller coaster. Some rides are themed to action-film characters like (Superman The Escape and The Riddler's Revenge); others are loosely tied to their themed surroundings, like a Far East pagoda or gold rush mining town. Arcade games and summer only entertainment (stunt shows, animal shows, and parades) round out the park's attractions.

Hurricane Harbor is Six Flags's tropical paradise, which is located right next door to Magic Mountain. You really can't see both in one day—combo tickets allow you to return sometime before the end of the season. Bring your own swimsuit; the park has changing rooms with showers and lockers. Like Magic Mountain, areas have themes like a tropical lagoon or an African river (complete with ancient temple ruins). The primary activities are swimming, water slides, rafting, volleyball, and lounging; many areas are designed especially for the little "buccaneer."

Magic Mountain Pkwy. (off Golden State Fwy. [I-5] north), Valencia. © **661/255-4100** or 818/367-5965. www.sixflags.com. Magic Mountain $43 adults, $27 seniors 55 and older and children age 2 to 48 inches high, free for kids under 2; Hurricane Harbor $22 adults $15 seniors and children; combo ticket $53. Magic Mountain: daily Apr to Labor Day and weekends and holidays the rest of the year. Hurricane Harbor: daily Memorial Day to Labor Day; weekends May and Sept; closed Oct–Apr. Both parks open 10am, closing hours vary between 6pm–midnight. Parking $7. All prices and hours are subject to change without notice so please call before you arrive.

Venice Ocean Front Walk ★★ *Kids*   This has long been one of L.A.'s most colorful areas. Founded at the turn of the last century, Venice was a development inspired by its Italian namesake. Authentic gondolas plied miles of inland waterways lined with rococo palaces. In the 1950s, Venice became the stomping grounds of Jack Kerouac, Allen Ginsberg, William S. Burroughs, and other beats. In the 1960s, this was the epicenter of L.A.'s hippie scene.

Today, Venice is still one of the world's most engaging bohemian locales. It's not an exaggeration to say that no visit to L.A. would be complete without a stroll along the famous beach path, an almost surreal assemblage of every L.A. stereotype—and then some. Among stalls and stands selling cheap sunglasses, Mexican blankets, and "herbal ecstasy" pills, swirls a carnival of humanity that includes bikini-clad in-line skaters, tattooed bikers, muscle-bound pretty boys, panhandling vets, beautiful wannabes, and plenty of tourists and gawkers. On any given day, you're bound to come across all kinds of performers: mimes, break-dancers, buskers, chain-saw jugglers, talking parrots, or an occasional apocalyptic evangelist.

On the beach, between Venice Blvd. and Rose Ave, Venice. www.venicebeach.com.

Farmers Market ★ *Kids*   The original market was little more than a field with stands set up by farmers during the Depression so they could sell directly to city dwellers. Eventually, permanent buildings grew up, including the trademark shingled 10-story clock tower. Today the place has evolved into a sprawling marketplace with a carnival atmosphere, a kind of "turf" version of San Francisco's Fisherman's Wharf. About 100 restaurants, shops, and grocers cater to a mix of workers from the CBS Television City complex, locals, and tourists, brought here by the busload. Retailers sell greeting cards, kitchen implements, candles, and souvenirs; but everyone comes for the food stands, which offer oysters, Cajun gumbo, fresh-squeezed orange juice, roast-beef sandwiches, fresh-pressed peanut butter, and all kinds of international fast foods. You can still buy produce here—it's no longer a farm-fresh bargain, but the selection's better than at the grocery store. Don't miss **Kokomo** (© 323 /933-0773), a "gourmet" outdoor coffee shop that has become a power breakfast spot for showbiz types. Red turkey hash and sweet-potato fries are the dishes that keep them coming back.

6333 W. 3rd St. (at Fairfax Ave.), Hollywood. © 323/933-9211. www.farmersmarketla.com. Mon–Fri 9am–9pm; Sat 9am–8pm; Sun 10am–7pm.

The "Hollywood" Sign ✯   These 50-foot-high white sheet-metal letters have come to symbolize the movie industry and the city itself. The sign was erected in 1923 as an advertisement for a real-estate development. The full text originally read HOLLYWOODLAND. The sign gained dubious notoriety when actress Peg Entwistle leapt to her death from the "H" in 1932. The installation of motion detectors around the sign made this graffiti tagger's coup a target even more worth boasting about. A thorny hiking trail leads toward the sign from Durand Drive near Beachwood Drive, but the best view is from down below, at the corner of Sunset Boulevard and Bronson Avenue.

At the top of Beachwood Dr., Hollywood.

Hollywood Walk of Fame ✯ *Kids*   More than 2,500 celebrities are honored along the world's most famous sidewalk. Each bronze medallion, set into the center of a granite star, pays homage to a famous television, film, radio, theater, or recording personality. Although about a third of them are just about as obscure as Andromeda—their fame simply hasn't withstood the test of time—millions of visitors are thrilled by the sight of famous names like **James Dean** (1719 Vine St.), **John Lennon** (1750 Vine St.), **Marlon Brando** (1765 Vine St.), **Rudolph Valentino** (6164 Hollywood Blvd.), **Marilyn Monroe** (6744 Hollywood Blvd.), **Elvis Presley** (6777 Hollywood Blvd.), **Greta Garbo** (6901 Hollywood Blvd.), **Louis Armstrong** (7000 Hollywood Blvd.), and **Barbra Streisand** (6925 Hollywood Blvd). **Gene Autry's** all over the place: The singing cowboy earned five different stars (a sidewalk record), one in each category.

The sight of bikers, metalheads, druggies, hookers, and hordes of disoriented tourists all treading on memorials to Hollywood's greats makes for quite a bizarre tribute. But the Hollywood Chamber of Commerce has been doing a terrific job sprucing up the pedestrian experience with filmstrip crosswalks, swaying palms, and more. And at least one weekend a month, a group of fans calling themselves Star Polishers busy themselves scrubbing tarnished medallions.

The legendary sidewalk is continually adding new names. The public is invited to attend dedication ceremonies; the honoree—who pays a whopping $15,000 for the eternal upkeep—is usually in attendance. Contact the **Hollywood Chamber of Commerce,** 6255 Sunset Blvd., Suite 911, Hollywood, CA 90028 (© 323/469-8311), for information on who's being honored this week.

Hollywood Blvd., between Gower St. and La Brea Ave.; and Vine St., between Yucca St. and Sunset Blvd. © 323/469-8311.

The Lakers at STAPLES Center ✯   Nine professional sports teams call Los Angeles home. Don't be fooled; L.A. is Laker town. With 14 franchise championships, including five during the '80s Showtime era of Magic Johnson, Kareem Abdul-Jabbar, and James Worthy, the Lakers are the second most winning team in NBA history. And sadly for the rest of the league, more championships may be on the way. In Shaquille O'Neal and Kobe Bryant, the current squad boasts the NBA's most dominant big man as well as its best all-around perimeter player. With help from their gutsy role players, the two Laker supernovas led Los Angeles to its third consecutive NBA Championship in 2002, frustrating Laker-haters everywhere, and establishing this team as a budding dynasty in the process.

The Lakers play at the $300 million **STAPLES Center,** which bares a greater resemblance to an outlet mall than a sports arena, and their somnambulant fans often seem more interested in the luster of courtside celebs than regular season games. Still, Lakers games are quintessential L.A. and on those terms alone, the Lake Show is worth a look—if you can get the tickets. Tickets range from $22 (nose bleed) to $165, and prices for anything remotely near the floor increase exponentially the closer you get to courtside. Tickets can be obtained at local **Ticketmaster** outlets (www.ticketmaster.com), or contact the STAPLES Center box office, 1111 S. Figueroa St. (**213/742-7304;** www.staplescenter.com).

S. Figueroa St., on the corner of 11th St., 1 block south of Olympic Blvd., downtown.

Mann's Chinese Theatre ★ This is one of the world's great movie palaces and one of Hollywood's finest landmarks. The theater was opened in 1927 by impresario Sid Grauman, a brilliant promoter who's credited with originating the idea of the paparazzi-packed movie "premiere." Outrageously conceived, with both authentic and simulated Chinese embellishments, Grauman's theater was designed to impress. Original Chinese heavenly doves top the facade, and two of the theater's columns once propped up a Ming dynasty temple.

Visitors by the millions flock to the theater for its famous entry court, where stars like Elizabeth Taylor, Paul Newman, Ginger Rogers, Humphrey Bogart, Frank Sinatra, Marilyn Monroe, and about 160 others set their signatures and hand-/footprints in concrete. It's not always hands and feet: Betty Grable made an impression with her shapely leg; Gene Autry with the hoof prints of his horse, Champion; and Jimmy Durante and Bob Hope with their trademark noses.

6925 Hollywood Blvd. (1 block west of Highland Ave.). © **323/464-MANN** or 323/461-3331. www.mann theaters.com. Movie tickets $9. Call for show times.

Rancho La Brea Tar Pits ★ *Kids* An odorous swamp of congealed oil oozes to the earth's surface in the middle of Los Angeles. No, it's not a low-budget horror-movie set—it's the La Brea Tar Pits, an awesome, primal pool on Museum Row, where hot tar has been bubbling from the earth for more than 40,000 years. The glistening pools, which look like murky water, have enticed thirsty animals throughout history. Thousands of mammals, birds, amphibians, and insects—many of which are now extinct—crawled into the sticky sludge, got stuck in the worst way, and stayed forever. In 1906 scientists began a systematic removal and classification of entombed specimens, including ground sloths, giant vultures, mastodons, camels, bears, lizards, a Starbucks, and even prehistoric relatives of today's superrats. The best finds are on display in the adjacent **George C. Page Museum of La Brea Discoveries,** where an entertaining 15-minute film documenting the recoveries is also shown. Archaeological work is ongoing; you can watch as scientists clean, identify, and catalog new finds in the Paleontology Laboratory.

5801 Wilshire Blvd. (east of Fairfax Ave.), Los Angeles. © **323/934-PAGE.** www.tarpits.org. Admission $6 adults, $3.50 seniors 62 and older and students with ID, $2 children ages 5–12, free for kids age 4 and under; free for everyone the 1st Tues of every month. Mon–Fri 9:30am–5pm; Sat–Sun 10am–5pm (museum).

Griffith Observatory Made world-famous in the film *Rebel Without a Cause,* Griffith Observatory's bronze domes have been Hollywood Hills landmarks since 1935. Most visitors don't actually go inside; they come to this spot on the south slope of Mount Hollywood for unparalleled city views. On warm nights, with the lights twinkling below, this is one of the most romantic places in L.A.

Overrated L.A.'s Top Tourist Traps

You've heard of the following attractions, of course—but you should know exactly what you're in for before you part with your dollars. Not surprisingly, they're all located in the heart of Hollywood on Hollywood Boulevard.

Hollywood Guinness World Records Museum Scale models, photographs, and push-button displays of the world's fattest man, biggest plant, smallest woman, fastest animal, and other superlatives don't make for a superlative experience. 6764 Hollywood Blvd., Hollywood. ✆ **323/463-6433.** Admission $10.95 adults, $8.50 seniors, $6.95 children ages 6–11. Sun–Thurs 10am–midnight; Fri–Sat 10am–1am.

The Hollywood Wax Museum Cast in the Madame Tussaud mold, the Hollywood Wax Museum features dozens of lifelike figures of famous movie stars and events. This "museum" is pretty cheesy, but it can be good for a cheeky laugh or two. A "Chamber of Horrors" exhibit includes the coffin used in *The Raven*, as well as a diorama from the Vincent Price classic *The House of Wax*. The "Movie Awards Theatre" exhibit is a short film highlighting Academy Award presentations from the past 4 decades. 6767 Hollywood Blvd., Hollywood. ✆ **323/462-8860.** Admission $10.95 adults, $8.50 seniors, $6.95 children ages 6–12, free for kids age 5 and under. Sun–Thurs 10am–midnight; Fri–Sat 10am–1am.

Ripley's "Believe It Or Not!" Museum Believe it or not, this amazing and silly "museum" is still open. Its bizarre collection of wax figures, photos, and models depicts unnatural oddities from Robert Leroy Ripley's infamous arsenal. Our favorites include the skeleton of a two-headed baby, a statue of Marilyn Monroe sculpted with shredded money, and a portrait of John Wayne made from laundry lint. 6780 Hollywood Blvd. ✆ **323/466-6335.** www.ripleys.com. Admission $10.95 adults, $9.95 students and seniors, $7.95 children ages 6–12, free to children age 5 and under. Mon–Thurs 10am–10pm; Fri–Sat 10am–11:30pm.

The main dome houses a **planetarium,** where narrated projection shows reveal the stars and planets that are hidden from the naked eye by the city's lights and smog. Other shows take you on excursions into space to search for extraterrestrial life, or examine the causes of earthquakes and moonquakes.

The adjacent **Hall of Science** holds exhibits on galaxies, meteorites, and other cosmic objects, including a telescope trained on the sun, a Foucault pendulum, and earth and moon globes 6 feet in diameter. On clear nights you can gaze at the heavens through the powerful 12-inch telescope.

Please note: The entire Griffith Observatory area is closed for a major renovation and expansion and will not reopen until May 2005. An "Observatory Satellite Temporary Facility" with public access will open in the fall of 2002, near the Los Angeles Zoo. Call ✆ **323/664-1191** for more information.

2800 E. Observatory Rd. (in Griffith Park, at the end of Vermont Ave.). ✆ **323/664-1191,** or 323/663-8171 for the Sky Report, a recorded message on current planet positions and celestial events. www.griffithobservatory. org.

2 Museums & Galleries

See "The Top Attractions," earlier in this chapter, for **J. Paul Getty Museum** information.

L.A.'S WESTSIDE & BEVERLY HILLS

Museum of Television and Radio   Want to see the Beatles on *The Ed Sulli-van Show* (1964), or Edward R. Murrow's examination of Joseph McCarthy (1954), or Arnold Palmer's victory in the 1958 Masters Tournament, or listen to radio excerpts like FDR's first "Fireside Chat" (1933) and Orson Welles's famous *War of the Worlds* UFO hoax (1938)? All these, plus a gazillion episodes of *The Twilight Zone, I Love Lucy,* and other beloved series, can be viewed within the starkly white walls of architect Richard Meier's neutral, contemporary museum building. Like the ritzy Beverly Hills shopping district that surrounds it, the museum is more flash than substance. Once you gawk at the celebrity and indus-try-honcho names adorning every hall, room, and miscellaneous area, it becomes quickly apparent that "library" would be a more fitting name for this collection, since the main attractions are requested via sophisticated computer catalogs and viewed in private consoles. Although no one sets out to spend a vacation watch-ing TV, it can be tempting once you start browsing the archives. This West Coast branch of the venerable New York facility succeeds in treating our favorite pas-time as a legitimate art form, with the respect history will prove it deserves.

465 N. Beverly Dr. (at Santa Monica Blvd.), Beverly Hills. ✆ 310/786-1025. www.mtr.org. Suggested con-tribution $6 adults, $4 students and seniors, $3 kids age 12 and under. Wed and Fri–Sun noon–5pm; Thurs noon–9pm. Closed New Year's Day, July 4, Thanksgiving Day, and Christmas Day. Parking free for 2 hours with validation.

Museum of Tolerance ✦   The Museum of Tolerance is designed to expose prejudices and to teach racial and cultural tolerance. It's located in the Simon Wiesenthal Center, an institute founded by the legendary Nazi-hunter. While the Holocaust figures prominently here, this is not just a Jewish museum—it's an academy that broadly campaigns for a live-and-let-live world. Tolerance is an abstract idea that's hard to display, so most of this $50 million museum's exhibits are high-tech and conceptual in nature. Fast-paced interactive displays are designed to touch the heart as well as the mind, and engage both serious inves-tigators and the MTV crowd. One of two major museums in America that deal with the Holocaust, the Museum of Tolerance is considered by many to be infe-rior to its Washington, D.C., counterpart. *Note:* Visitors might be frustrated by the museum's policy of insisting that you follow a prescribed 2½-hour route through the exhibits.

9786 W. Pico Blvd. (at Roxbury Dr.). ✆ 310/553-8403. www.wiesenthal.com/mot. Admission $9 adults, $7 seniors 62 and above, $5.50 students w/ID, $5.50 children ages 3–10, free for children age 2 and under. Advance purchase recommended; photo ID required for admission. Mon–Thurs 11:30am–4pm; Fri 11:30am–3pm (to 1pm Nov–Mar); Sun 11am–5pm. Closed many Jewish and secular holidays; call for schedule.

Skirball Cultural Center ✦   This strikingly modern museum/cultural center is quick to remind us that Jewish history is about more than the Holocaust. Nes-tled in the Sepulveda Pass uphill from the Getty Center, the Skirball explores American Jewish life, American democratic values, and the pursuit of the Amer-ican Dream—a theme shared by many immigrant groups. The Skirball's core exhibits chronicle the journey of the Jewish people through the ages, with emphasis on American Jewry. Related events are held here throughout the year;

one recent highlight was a rollicking festival of klezmer music (a traditional Jewish folk style). Call for free docent-led tour times.

2701 No. Sepulveda Blvd. (at Mulholland Dr.). ℂ 310/440-4500. www.skirball.org. Admission $8 adults, $6 students and seniors 65 and over, free for kids under 12. Tues–Sat noon–5pm; Sun 11am–5pm. Free parking. From I-405, exit at Skirball Center Dr./Mulholland Dr.

UCLA Hammer Museum   Created by the former chairman and CEO of Occidental Petroleum, the Hammer Museum has had a hard time winning the respect of critics and the public. Barbs are aimed at both the museum's relatively flat collection and its patron's tremendous ego. The Hammer is ensconced in a two-story Carrara marble building attached to the oil company's offices. It's better known for its high profile and often provocative visiting exhibits, such as the opulent prerevolution treasures of Russian ruler Catherine the Great. In conjunction with UCLA's Wight Gallery, a feisty gallery with a reputation for championing contemporary political and experimental art, the Hammer continues to present often daring and usually popular special exhibits, and it's definitely worth calling ahead to find out what will be there during your visit to L.A. The permanent collection (Armand Hammer's personal collection) consists mostly of traditional Western European and Anglo-American art, and contains noteworthy paintings by Toulouse-Lautrec, Degas, and van Gogh.

10899 Wilshire Blvd. (at Westwood Blvd.). ℂ 310/443-7000. www.hammer.ucla.edu. Admission $4.50 adults, $3 students and seniors 55 and over, free for kids age 17 and under; free for everyone Thurs. Tues–Wed and Fri–Sat 11am–7pm; Thurs 11am–9pm; Sun 11am–5pm. Parking $2.75 for first 3 hours.

HOLLYWOOD

Autry Museum of Western Heritage ★★   If you're under the age of 45, you might not be familiar with Gene Autry, a Texas-born actor who starred in 82 Westerns and became known as the "Singing Cowboy." Located north of Downtown in Griffith Park, his eponymous museum is one of California's best, a collection of art and artifacts of the European conquest of the West, remarkably comprehensive and intelligently displayed. Evocative exhibits illustrate the everyday lives of early pioneers, not only with antique firearms, tools, saddles, and the like, but with many hands-on displays that successfully stir the imagination and the heart. You'll find footage from Buffalo Bill's Wild West Show, movie clips from the silent days, contemporary films, the works of Wild West artists, and plenty of memorabilia from Autry's own film and TV projects. The "Hall of Merchandising" displays Roy Rogers bedspreads, Hopalong Cassidy radios, and other items from the collective consciousness—and material collections—of baby boomers. Provocative visiting exhibits (whose banners are visible from Interstate 5) usually focus on cultural or domestic regional history.

4700 Western Heritage Way (in Griffith Park). ℂ 323/667-2000. www.autry-museum.org. Admission $7.50 adults, $5 seniors 60 and over and students ages 13–18, $3 children ages 2–12, free for kids under age 2. Tues–Sun 10am–5pm (Thurs until 8pm). Free to all 2nd Tues each month.

Craft & Folk Art Museum   This gallery, housed in a prominent Museum Row building, has grown into one of the city's largest. "Craft and folk art" encompasses everything from clothing, tools, religious artifacts, and other everyday objects to wood carvings, papier-mâché, weaving, and metalwork. The museum displays folk objects from around the world, but its strongest collection is masks from India, America, Mexico, Japan, and China. The museum is also known for its annual International Festival of Masks, held each October in Hancock Park, across the street. Be sure to stop in the funky, eclectic Museum Shop to peruse the wearable art, folk art books, and various crafts.

5814 Wilshire Blvd. (at Curson Ave.). ✆ 323/937-4230. Admission $3.50 adults, $2.50 seniors and students, free for children under age 12, free to all the first Wed each month. Museum exhibits: Wed–Sun 11am–5pm; Museum Shop Tues–Sun 11am–5pm.

Frederick's of Hollywood Lingerie Museum   God bless Frederick Mellinger, inventor of the push-up bra (originally known as the "Rising Star"). Frederick's of Hollywood opened this world-famous purple-and-pink Art Deco panty shop in 1947, and dutifully installed a small exhibition saluting all the stars of stage, screen, and television who glamorized lingerie. The collection now includes Madonna's pointy-breasted corset, a pair of Tony Curtis's skivvies, and a Cher-autographed underwire bra (size 32B). Some exhibits were lost during the 1992 L.A. riots, when looters ransacked the place. Mercifully, the bra worn by Milton Berle on his 1950s TV show was saved.

6608 Hollywood Blvd. ✆ 323/466-8506. www.fredericks.com. Free admission. Mon–Sat 10am–6pm; Sun noon–5pm.

Hollywood Entertainment Museum   Initially intended to be a cornerstone of Hollywood Boulevard renewal, this facility was plagued by internal politicking and faulty architecture long before it opened in 1996. Once you find its awkward subterranean entrance, you'll enter a seriously unkitschy museum devoted to the entertainment arts. On display are selections from a sizable collection of original sets and props from film, TV, and radio, including the complete *Cheers* bar and the Starship *Enterprise* bridge from the original *Star Trek* series. The best part is a series of interactive demonstration rooms that teach various tricks of filmmaking; visitors can create Foley soundtracks for a movie segment, test their skills at digital editing, and try out other fun, educational procedures. Fans of the defunct Max Factor Museum of Beauty will be happy to learn that the collection from Hollywood's premier motion-picture cosmetic designer is shown here—antique makeup pots, glamour photos, and superstar toupees intact.

7021 Hollywood Blvd. (at Sycamore Ave.). ✆ 323/465-7900. www.hollywoodmuseum.com. Admission $8.75 adults, $5.50 seniors, students $4.50, $4 kids 5–12, free to children under 5. Thurs–Tues 11am–6pm. Parking $2 w/validation.

Los Angeles County Museum of Art ★★   This is one of the finest art museums around, housing works by Degas, Rembrandt, Hockney, and Monet. The huge complex was designed by three very different architects over a span of 30 years. The architectural fusion can be migraine inducing, but this city landmark is well worth delving into.

The newest wing is the **Japanese Pavilion,** which has exterior walls made of Kalwall, a translucent material that, like shoji screens, permits the entry of soft natural light. Inside is a collection of Japanese Edo paintings that's rivaled only by the holdings of the emperor of Japan. The **Anderson Building,** the museum's contemporary wing, is home to 20th-century painting and sculpture. Here you'll find works by Matisse, Magritte, and a good number of Dada artists. The **Ahmanson Building** houses the rest of the museum's permanent collections. You'll find everything from 2,000-year-old pre-Columbian Mexican ceramics to 19th-century portraiture to a unique glass collection spanning the centuries. Other displays include one of the nation's largest holdings of costumes and textiles, and an important Indian and Southeast Asian art collection. The **Hammer Building** is primarily used for major special-loan exhibitions. Free guided tours covering the museum's highlights depart on a regular basis from here.

Hollywood Area Attractions

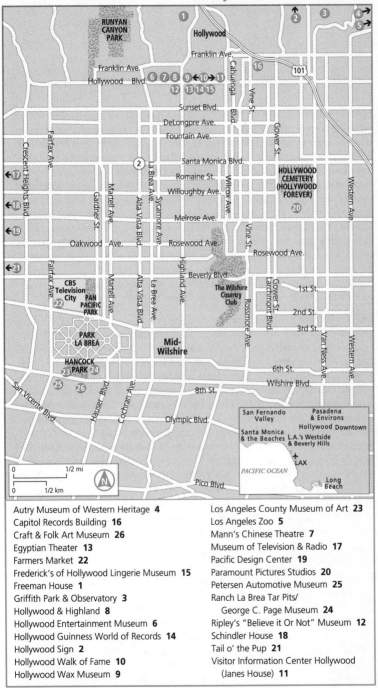

Autry Museum of Western Heritage **4**
Capitol Records Building **16**
Craft & Folk Art Museum **26**
Egyptian Theater **13**
Farmers Market **22**
Frederick's of Hollywood Lingerie Museum **15**
Freeman House **1**
Griffith Park & Observatory **3**
Hollywood & Highland **8**
Hollywood Entertainment Museum **6**
Hollywood Guinness World of Records **14**
Hollywood Sign **2**
Hollywood Walk of Fame **10**
Hollywood Wax Museum **9**

Los Angeles County Museum of Art **23**
Los Angeles Zoo **5**
Mann's Chinese Theatre **7**
Museum of Television & Radio **17**
Pacific Design Center **19**
Paramount Pictures Studios **20**
Petersen Automotive Museum **25**
Ranch La Brea Tar Pits/
    George C. Page Museum **24**
Ripley's "Believe it Or Not" Museum **12**
Schindler House **18**
Tail o' the Pup **21**
Visitor Information Center Hollywood
    (Janes House) **11**

The museum recently took over the former May Company department store 1 block away, converting the historic Art Deco building into gallery space. For information on film programs at the museum's **Leo S. Bing Theater,** see "Movies: Play It Again, Sam," p. 264, in chapter 10.

5905 Wilshire Blvd. ℂ 323/857-6000. www.lacma.org. Admission $7 adults, $5 students and seniors age 62 and over, $1 children ages 6–17, free for kids age 5 and under; regular exhibitions free for everyone the 2nd Tues of each month. Mon–Tues and Thurs noon–8pm; Fri noon–9pm; Sat–Sun 11am–8pm. Parking $5

Petersen Automotive Museum ★ When the Petersen opened in 1994, many locals were surprised that it had taken this long for the city of freeways to salute its most important shaper. Indeed, this museum says more about the city than probably any other in L.A. Named for Robert Petersen, the publisher responsible for *Hot Rod* and *Motor Trend* magazines, the four-story museum displays more than 200 cars and motorcycles, from the historic to the futuristic. Cars on the first floor are exhibited chronologically, in period settings. Other floors are devoted to frequently changing shows of race cars, early motorcycles, and famous movie vehicles. Past shows have included a comprehensive exhibit of "woodies" and surf culture, and displays of the Flintstones' fiberglass-and-cotton movie car and of a three-wheeled scooter that folds into a Samsonite briefcase (created in a competition by a Mazda engineer).

6060 Wilshire Blvd. (at Fairfax Ave.). ℂ 323/930-CARS. www.petersen.org. Admission $7 adults, $6 seniors and students, $5 children ages 5–12, free for kids age 4 and under. Tues–Sun 10am–6pm. Parking $6.

DOWNTOWN

California African American Museum This small museum is both a celebration of individual African Americans and a living showplace of contemporary culture. The best exhibits are temporary, and touch on themes as varied as the human experience. Recent shows have included a sculpture exhibit examining interpretations of home, a survey of African puppetry, and a look at black music in Los Angeles in the 1960s. Multimedia biographical retrospectives are also commonplace: An exhibit honoring jazz genius Duke Ellington included his instruments and handwritten music. In the gift shop you'll find sub-Saharan wooden masks and woven baskets, as well as hand-embroidered Ethiopian pillows. There are also posters, children's books, and calendars. The museum offers a full calendar of lectures, concerts, and special events; call for the latest. *Note:* The museum was undergoing renovation at press time and is scheduled to reopen in the fall of 2002; call ahead to confirm.

600 State Dr., Exposition Park. ℂ 213/744-7432. www.caam.ca.gov. Free admission; donation requested. Tues–Sun 10am–5pm. Closed Thanksgiving, Christmas, New Year's Day. Parking $5.

California Science Center ★★ *Kids* A $130 million renovation—reinvention, actually—has turned the former Museum of Science and Industry into Exposition Park's newest attraction. Using high-tech sleight-of-hand, the center stimulates kids of all ages with questions, answers, and lessons about the world. One of the museum's highlights is Tess, a 50-foot animatronic woman whose muscles, bones, organs, and blood vessels are revealed, demonstrating how the body reacts to a variety of external conditions and activities. (Appropriate for children of all ages, Tess doesn't possess reproductive organs.)

There are nominal fees, ranging from $2 to $5, to enjoy the science center's more thrilling attractions. You can pedal a bicycle across a high-wire suspended 43 feet above the ground (demonstrating the principle of gravity and counterweights) or get strapped into the Space Docking Simulator for a virtual-reality

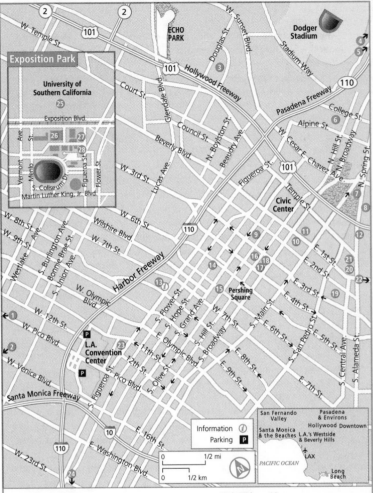

Angel's Flight **16**
Angelino Heights **3**
Boyle Heights **12**
Bradbury Building **8**
California African American Museum **28**
California Science Center **27**
Central Library **14**
Chinatown **6**
City Hall **11**
El Alisal **4**
El Pueblo de Los Angeles
   Historic District **7**
Geffen Contemporary at MOCA **21**
Grand Central Market **17**
Japanese American National Museum **20**
Leimert Park Village **2**

Little Tokyo **19**
Mariachi Plaza **22**
Museum of Contemporary Art **9**
Museum of Tolerance **1**
Natural History Museum
   of Los Angeles County **26**
Pershing Square **15**
The Los Angeles Times Building **10**
The Southwest Museum **5**
Staples Center **23**
Union Station **8**
University of
   Southern California (USC) **25**
Visitors Information Center **13**
Watts Towers **24**

taste of zero gravity. There's plenty more, and plans for expansion in the works. The IMAX theater boasts a screen seven stories high and 90 feet wide, with state-of-the-art surround sound and 3-D technology. Films are screened throughout the day until 9pm and are nearly always breathtaking, even the two-dimensional ones.

700 State Dr., Exposition Park. ✆ **213/SCIENCE** or 213/744-7400; IMAX theater ✆ **213/744-2014.** www.cascilencectr.org. Free admission to the museum; IMAX theater $7 adults, $4.25 ages 4–12, $5.25 seniors over 60 and children ages 13–17. Multishow discounts available. Parking $6. Daily 10am–5pm. Closed Thanksgiving, Christmas, and New Year's Day.

Japanese American National Museum 🌟 Located in an architecturally acclaimed modern building in Little Tokyo, this museum is a private nonprofit institute created to document and celebrate the history of the Japanese in America. Its fantastic permanent exhibition chronicles Japanese life in the United States, while temporary exhibits highlight distinctive aspects of Japanese-American culture, from the internment camp experience to the lives of Japanese-Americans in Hawaii. Don't miss the museum store, which carries everything from hand-fired sake sets to mini-Zen gardening kits.

369 E. First St. (at Central Ave.). ✆ 213/625-0414. www.janm.org. Admission $6 adults, $5 seniors, $3 students and kids 6–17, free for kids age 5 and under; free to all the 3rd Thurs of each month, and every Thurs after 5pm. Tues–Sun 10am–5pm (Thurs till 8pm).

Museum of Contemporary Art/Geffen Contemporary at MOCA ⭐⭐ MOCA is Los Angeles's only institution devoted to art from 1940 to the present. Displaying works in a variety of media, it's strong in works by Cy Twombly, Jasper Johns, and Mark Rothko, and shows are often superb. For many experts, MOCA's collections are too spotty to be considered world class, and the conservative museum board blushes when offered controversial shows (they passed on a Whitney exhibit that included photographs by Robert Mapplethorpe). Nevertheless, we've seen some excellent exhibitions here.

MOCA is housed in three buildings: The Grand Avenue main building (250 S. Grand Ave., Los Angeles) is a contemporary red sandstone structure by renowned Japanese architect Arata Isozaki. The museum restaurant, **Patinette** (daily 11am–4pm; ✆ **213/626-1178**), located here, is the casual-dining creation of celebrity chef Joachim Splichal (see Patina, in chapter 6). The museum's second space, on Central Avenue in Little Tokyo (152 North Central Ave., Los Angeles), was the "temporary" Contemporary while the Grand structure was being built, and now houses a superior permanent collection in a warehouse-type space recently renamed for entertainment mogul and art collector David Geffen. An added feature is a detailed timeline corresponding to the progression of works. Unless there's a visiting exhibit of great interest at the main museum, we recommend that you start at the Geffen building—where it's also easier to park. The third gallery, which opened in January 2001, is at the Pacific Design Center (8687 Melrose Ave., West Hollywood)—it's the compact building next to the Pacific Design Center. Unlike the other two, admission to this galley is only $3, and emphasis is on contemporary architecture and design, as well as new work by emerging and established artists.

Main MOCA information line: ✆ 213/626-6222. www.moca-la.org. Admission $8 adults, $5 seniors 65 and over and students, free for children age 11 and under. Tues–Wed and Fri–Sun 11am–5pm; Thurs 11am–8pm.

Natural History Museum of Los Angeles County *Kids* The "Fighting Dinosaurs" are not a high school football team but the trademark symbol of this massive museum: *Tyrannosaurus rex* and triceratops skeletons poised in a stance so realistic that every kid feels inspired to imitate their *Jurassic Park* bellows. Opened in 1913 in a beautiful domed Spanish renaissance building, this museum is a 35-hall warehouse of Earth's history, chronicling the planet and its inhabitants from 600 million years ago to the present day. There's a mind-numbing number of exhibits of prehistoric fossils, bird and marine life, rocks and minerals, and North American mammals. The best permanent displays include the world's rarest shark, a walk-through vault of priceless gems, and an Insect Zoo.

The Dinosaur Shop sells ant farms and exploding volcano and model kits. The Ethnic Arts Shop has one-of-a-kind folk art and jewelry from around the world. The bookstore has an extensive selection of scientific titles and hobbyists' field guides.

900 Exposition Blvd., Exposition Park. ✆ 213/763-DINO. www.nhm.org. Admission $8 adults; $5.50 children ages 13–17, seniors, and students with ID; $2 children ages 5–12; free for kids under 5; free for everyone the 1st Tues of each month. Daily 10am–5pm.

The Southwest Museum ★ *Finds*   This is the city's oldest museum, considered by some a "best-kept secret" that suffers from lack of recognition and space for its superlative collection. However, an expansion and renovation is underway that will enable the museum to display much more of the Native American art that is currently in storage. The museum will be open during the renovation. Originally opened in 1907 by amateur historian and Native American expert Charles F. Lummis (who also designed Downtown's landmark "castle," El Alisal; see later in this chapter), this privately funded anthropological museum contains the finest examples of Native American art and artifacts found anywhere, including rare paintings, weapons, and a Cheyenne summer teepee. The largest exhibition chronicles 10,000 years of history of the people of the American Southwest. The California Hall focuses on the lifestyles of the first Californians; a separate two-level hall is dedicated to the culture of cold-climate tribes. The museum has a particularly active events calendar that includes a Native American Film Festival, regular lectures, and special children's programs. Phone for the latest. In the shop you'll find authentic Native American drums, kachina dolls, pottery, and sterling-silver jewelry by Native American artist Vernon Begaye.

234 Museum Dr., in the Highland Park District (northeast of downtown). ✆ 323/221-2164. www.southwestmuseum.org. Admission $6 adults, $4 seniors (over age 62) and students, $3 children ages 7–18, free for children age 6 and under. Tues–Sun 10am–5pm. Free parking. From the Pasadena Fwy. (Calif. 110), exit onto Ave. 43 and follow the signs zigzagging up the hill to the museum at Museum Dr.

SANTA MONICA & THE BEACHES

Bergamot Arts Station & Santa Monica Museum of Art ★★   One of L.A.'s primary cultural destinations is the Bergamot Arts Station. Home to the **Santa Monica Museum of Art,** this campuslike complex is a hugely popular destination for visitors from around the world. The location dates from 1875 when it was a stop for the Red Line trolley and retains its industrial, rustic look. Filled with varied spaces, the unique installations range from photography to sculpture to interactive pieces that are both eclectic and cutting edge. Its central location allows visitors to park and spend the day seeing art rather than driving from one gallery to the next, and many pieces are available for purchase. A must for the arts lover.

2525 Michigan Ave., Santa Monica. ✆ 310/829-5854. www.bergamotstation.com. Most galleries open Tues–Sat 10am–6pm.

(Kids) Kid-Cool Attractions in L.A.

Much of larger-than-life L.A. is as appealing to kids as it is to adults. Many of the city's best attractions, like the **Venice Ocean Front Walk,** Hollywood's **Farmers Market,** and downtown's **Olvera Street** (part of the El Pueblo de Los Angeles Historic District) have a kid-friendly, carnival-like atmosphere. The novelty of sights such as the **Walk of Fame** and **Mann's Chinese Theatre** appeals to TV-brainwashed kids as well. Kids who are into dinosaurs will love the Rancho **La Brea Tar Pits.** Older kids in particular also love to go on **studio tours** and to **TV tapings.**

The **California ScienCenter** will entertain, stimulate, and even teach (sshhhh) kids about science, technology, biology, and the world around them.

The **Natural History Museum,** the Science Center's neighbor in Exposition Park, has giant dinosaur skeletons, an insect zoo, and a museum shop packed with terrifically fun model kits and other irresistible toys.

Thanks to the new **Winnick Family Children's Zoo,** the Los Angeles Zoo is an all-day adventure for the kids. This excellent children's zoo has a top-notch petting zoo, exhibition animal care center, "Adventure Theater," and other kid-cool attractions.

Here's one you haven't thought of: **The Getty Museum.** Deceptively educational programs for kids include exploratory games such as *The Getty Art Detective* and *Perplexing Paintings.* There's also a Family Room filled with picture books and games, storytelling sessions, weekend family workshops, and self-guided audio tours made specifically for families.

In addition to these kid-specific attractions, young tourists will also love the wacky **Universal CityWalk,** the carousel at **Santa Monica Pier,** and the **Travel Town Transportation Museum** in Griffith Park. And if all this isn't enough, there's always **Universal Studios Hollywood, Disneyland, Knott's Berry Farm** and **Six Flags** amusement parks, and **Santa Monica State Beach.**

Museum of Flying ⭐ (Kids)   Once headquarters of the McDonnell Douglas corporation, the Santa Monica Airport is the birthplace of the DC-3 and other pioneers of commercial aviation. The museum celebrates this bit of local history with 24 authentic aircraft displays and some interactive exhibits. In addition to antique Spitfires and Sopwith Camels, there's a kid-oriented learning area, where hands-on exhibits detail airplane parts, pilot procedures, and the properties of air and aircraft design. The museum shop is full of scale models of World War II birds; the coffee-table book *The Best of the Past* beautifully illustrates 50 years of aviation history.

At Santa Monica Airport, 2772 Donald Douglas Loop N., Santa Monica. ℭ 310/392-8822. www.museumof flying.com. Suggested contribution $8 adults, $6 seniors, $4 children 3–17, free for children under 3. Wed–Sun 10am–5pm.

PASADENA & ENVIRONS

Norton Simon Museum of Art ⭐⭐ (Finds)   Named for a food-packing king and financier who reorganized the failing Pasadena Museum of Modern Art, this has become one of California's most important museums. Comprehensive collections of masterpieces by Degas, Picasso, Rembrandt, and Goya are augmented by sculptures by Henry Moore and Auguste Rodin, including *The Burghers of Calais,* which greets you at the gates. The "Blue Four" collection of works by Kandinsky, Jawlensky, Klee, and Feininger is impressive, as is a superb collection of Southeast Asian sculpture. *Still Life with Lemons, Oranges, and a Rose* (1633), an oil by Francisco de Zurbarán, is one of the museum's most important holdings. One of the most popular pieces is *The Flower Vendor/Girl with Lilies* by Diego Rivera. Architect Frank Gehry recently helped remodel the galleries.

411 W. Colorado Blvd., Pasadena. (C) 626/449-6840. www.nortonsimon.org. Admission $6 adults, $3 seniors, free for students and kids 12 and under. Wed–Mon noon–6pm (Fri till 9pm). Free parking.

Pacific Asia Museum   The most striking aspect of this museum is the building itself. Designed in the 1920s in Chinese Imperial Palace style, it's rivaled in flamboyance only by Mann's Chinese Theatre in Hollywood (see "L.A.'s Top Attractions," earlier in this chapter). Rotating exhibits of Asian art span the

L.A.'s Outdoor Art Galleries

L.A. boasts an astonishing collection of public art, from nationally acclaimed pieces requiring an endowment for their installation to an ever-increasing panorama of murals, some little more than inspired graffiti. Local freeway corridors are blessed with new works every day; see how many you can spot in your travels. The **Mural Conservancy of Los Angeles** ((C) 818/487-0416; www.lamurals.org) enthusiastically promotes these public works, and it offers monthly $25 tours of mural sights and muralists' studios. Visit their website for tour monthly tour schedules.

Downtown Los Angeles in particular is a treasure trove of outdoor art. During the past decade, a concerted effort has been made to rattle the "skyscrapers or skid row" blinders that most residents and visitors cling to. Check out **Pershing Square** (bounded by 5th, 6th, Olive, and Hill sts.), which was transformed from an overgrown, crime- and drug-ridden eyesore into a modern art park.

L.A.'s own **"Spanish Steps,"** across 5th Street from the Central Library, wind sensuously alongside a flowing stream. Meanwhile, the **Central Library's** front courtyard (on Flower St.) was filled with commissioned art for the 1993 grand reopening. Each bench, fountain, and wall bears an inscription, representing the passions of a varied collection of artists. The centerpiece is Judd Fine's "Spine," a cascading series of pools leading up to the library's entrance. From the bottom upward, the components of each level (stair risers, carved inscriptions, pool sculptures, and water spouts) work together to represent evolution in terms of language and intellect. You don't need a degree in art to enjoy this work.

For more information on downtown's public art, contact the **Los Angeles Conservancy** ((C) 213/623-2489; www.laconservancy.org) or the **Museum of Contemporary Art** ((C) 213/626-6222; www.moca-la.org).

centuries, from 100 B.C. to the current day. This manageably-sized museum is worth a visit.

46 N. Los Robles Ave., Pasadena. ✆ **626/449-2742**, ext. 10. www.pacificasiamuseum.org. Admission $5 adults, $3 students and seniors, free for children under 12; free for everyone the 3rd Sat of each month. Wed–Thurs and Sat–Sun 10am–5pm; Fri 10am–8pm. Free parking.

3 L.A.'s Ethnic Neighborhoods

Los Angeles has the highest concentration of Mexicans outside Mexico, Koreans outside Korea, even Samoans outside Samoa. Tiny Russian, Ethiopian, Armenian, and even British enclaves also coexist throughout L.A. But to call the city a "melting pot" wouldn't be quite accurate; to paraphrase Alex Haley, it's really more of a tossed salad, composed of distinct, albeit overlapping, cultures.

The following neighborhoods all fall under the "Downtown" label, as we've defined it in "Orientation," in chapter 4.

Boyle Heights In the first decades of the 20th century, Boyle Heights was inhabited by Jewish immigrants, who have since migrated west to the Fairfax district and beyond. They left behind the oldest orthodox synagogue in Los Angeles, and Brooklyn Avenue, which has since been renamed Cesar E. Chavez Avenue. Boyle Heights is now the heart of the Latino barrio.

Westsiders come here for cheap Mexican food, but many miss our favorite Boyle Heights sight: Near the corner of Boyle Avenue and First Street is **Mariachi Plaza,** a colorful street corner where three-, four-, and five-man mariachi bands stand ready to entertain each afternoon and evening. Resplendent in matching ruffled shirts and tailored bolero jackets with a rainbow of embroidery, the mariachis loiter beneath three-story murals of their forebears with guitars at the ready. It's not unusual to see someone drive up in a minivan, offer a price for a night's entertainment, and carry off an ensemble to play a private party or other gathering.

East of downtown; bounded by U.S. 101, I-10, Calif. 60, and Indiana St.

Chinatown Many Chinese settled in this once-rural area during the second half of the 19th century. Today, most Angelenos of Chinese descent are well integrated into the city's suburbs; few can be found living in this rough pocket of downtown. But though the neighborhood hardly compares in quality or size to the Chinese quarters of London, San Francisco, or New York, Chinatown's bustling little mom-and-pop shops and profusion of ethnic restaurants provide an interesting downtown diversion.

Chinatown centers on a mall, **Mandarin Plaza,** 970 N. Broadway, reconstructed in 1938 a few blocks from its original site just south of Dodger Stadium. Go on a Sunday morning for dim sum at **Empress Pavilion,** 988 N. Hill St. (✆ **213/617-9898**), then browse through the collection of shops jammed with Chinese slippers, cheap jewelry, and china. You'll also find some upscale stores specializing in inlaid furniture, Asian art, fine silks, and other imports.

Chinatown is especially worth going out of your way for during **Chinese New Year,** a month-long celebration that usually begins in late January. The neighborhood explodes into a colorful fantasy of sights and sounds with the Golden Dragon Parade, a beauty pageant, and a 5K/10K run. There are plenty of firecrackers and all the Lin Go New Year's cakes you can eat.

Downtown; bounded by N. Broadway, N. Hill St., Bernard St., and Sunset Blvd.

El Pueblo de Los Angeles Historic Monument ★   This historic district was built in the 1930s, on the site where the city was founded, as an alternative to the razing of a particularly unsightly slum. The result is a contrived nostalgic fantasy of the city's beginnings, a kitschy theme park portraying Latino culture in a Disney-esque fashion. Nevertheless, El Pueblo has proven wildly successful, as L.A.'s Latinos have adopted it as an important cultural monument.

El Pueblo is not without authenticity. Some of L.A.'s oldest buildings are here, and the area really does exude the ambience of Old Mexico. At its core is a Mexican-style marketplace on old Olvera Street. The carnival of sights and sounds is heightened by mariachis, piñatas, and more-than-occasional folkloric dancing. Olvera Street, the district's primary pedestrian street, and adjacent Main Street are home to about two dozen 19th-century buildings; one houses a Mexican restaurant, **La Golondrina.** A self-guided tour brochure describing the historic buildings is available at the information desk in the Plaza, or at the El Pueblo Visitors Center (© **213/628-1274;** open Mon–Sat 10am–3pm) located in the Sepulveda house midway down Olvera Street on the west side. Don't miss the **Avila Adobe,** at E-10 Olvera St. (open Mon–Sat 10am–5pm; free admission); built in 1818, it's the oldest building in the city. Enter on Alameda St. across from Union Station (© **213/628-3562;** www.cityofla.org/elp).

Leimert Park Village   The neighborhood around tiny Leimert Park is becoming a center of African-American artistic life and historical focus. It features galleries, restaurants, and shops filled with local crafts and African imports. Folks flock here to jazz clubs that evoke the heyday of L.A.'s Central Avenue jazz scene, when greats like Ella Fitzgerald mesmerized audiences. In December, Kwanzaa celebrations enliven Leimert Park further.

Southwest of downtown; bounded by Crenshaw Blvd., Vernon Ave., Leimert Blvd., and 43rd Place.

Little Tokyo   Like nearby Chinatown, this redeveloped ethnic neighborhood isn't home to the majority of Angelenos of Japanese ancestry; suburban Gardena has that distinction. But Little Tokyo functions as the community's cultural focal point and is home to several malls filled with bakeries, bookshops, restaurants, and boutiques, as well as the occasional Buddhist temple. The **Japanese American National Museum** (see p. 174) is here, as is the **Japanese American Cultural and Community Center,** 244 S. San Pedro St. (© **213/628-2725;** www. jaccc.org), which regularly offers traditional Kabuki dramas and modern music concerts.

Little Tokyo is shabbier than almost any district in the Japanese capital, and it has difficulty holding a visitor's attention for much longer than the time it takes to eat lunch. Exceptions to this rule come twice yearly, during the **Cherry Blossom Festival** in spring, and **Nisei Week** in late summer. Both heritage festivals celebrate Japanese culture with parades, traditional Ondo street dancing, a carnival, and an arts fair. The Japanese American Network provides a community calendar, map of Little Tokyo points of interest, and useful Web links online at http://janet.org/janet_little_tokyo/ja_little_tokyo.html. Downtown, southeast of the Civic Center; bounded by 1st, 2nd, San Pedro, and Los Angeles streets.

4 Architectural Highlights

Los Angeles is a veritable Disneyland of architecture. The city is home to an amalgam of distinctive styles, from Art Deco to Spanish revival to coffee-shop kitsch to suburban ranch to postmodern—and much more.

L.A.'s Top Architectural Tours

The **L.A. Conservancy** (© **213/623-2489;** www.laconservancy.org) conducts a dozen information-packed walking tours of historic **Downtown L.A.,** seed of today's sprawling metropolis. The most popular is "Broadway Theaters," a look at movie palaces. Other intriguing tours include "Marble Masterpieces," "Art Deco," "Little Tokyo," and tours of the Biltmore Hotel and City Hall. They cost $8 and are usually held Saturday mornings. Call Monday through Friday between 9am and 5pm for information or, better yet, click on the "Walking Tours" link on their website.

In **Pasadena,** various tours spotlighting architecture or neighborhoods are intriguing, given this area's history of wealthy estates and ardent preservation. Call **Pasadena Heritage** (© **626/441-6333;** www. pasadenaheritage.org) for a schedule of guided tours, or pick up one of the self-guided walking or driving maps available at the **Pasadena Convention and Visitors Bureau,** 171 S. Los Robles Ave. (© **626/795-9311**).

For a unique and entertaining tour of Southern California's "vernacular architecture"—what we laypeople might call "kitsch"—sign up for a **Googie Tour** of L.A. and environs. Named for the defunct mid-century coffee shop chain whose style was best captured in the cartoon chic of *The Jetsons,* the grass-roots safari takes you to an "Aztec/Egyptian/atomic bowling center," a Polynesian-themed cocktail lounge, and various other exuberant expressions of the Atomic Age. Reservations are required, and prices start at $40 per person for a 3- to 5-hour tour. For a current schedule, call John English at © **323/980-3480.**

The movie industry, more than anything else, has defined Los Angeles. The process of moviemaking has never has been confined to studio offices and back lots; it spills into the city's streets and other public spaces. The city itself is an extension of the movie set, and Angelenos have always seen it that way. All of Los Angeles has an air of Hollywood surreality (or disposability), even in its architecture. The whole city seems a bit larger than life. Cutting-edge, over-the-top styles that would be out of place in other cities, from Tail o' the Pup to the mansions lining the streets of Beverly Hills, are perfectly at home in L.A. The world's top architects, from Frank Lloyd Wright to Frank Gehry, have flocked to L.A., reveling in the artistic freedom here. Between 1945 and 1966, *Arts & Architecture* magazine focused the design world's attention on L.A. with its series of "Case Study Houses," prototypes for postwar living, many of which were designed by prominent émigrés like Pierre Koenig, Richard Neutra, and Eero Saarinen. Los Angeles has taken some criticism for not being a "serious" architectural center, but in terms of innovation and style, the city gets high marks.

Although much of it is gone, you can still find some prime examples of the kitschy roadside art that defined L.A. in earlier days. The famous Brown Derby is no more, but you can still find an oversized hot dog (the aforementioned **Tail o' the Pup;** see below) and a neon-lit **1950s gas station/spaceship** (at the corner of Little Santa Monica Boulevard and Crescent Drive in Beverly Hills), in addition to some new structures carrying on the tradition, such as the **Chiat/Day offices** in Venice (see below).

SANTA MONICA & THE BEACHES

When you're strolling the historic canals and streets of Venice, be sure to check out the **Chiat/Day** offices at 340 Main St. What would otherwise be an unspectacular contemporary office building is made fantastic by a **three-story pair of binoculars** that frames the entrance. The sculpture is modeled after a design created by Claes Oldenburg and Coosje van Bruggen.

When you're on your way in or out of LAX, be sure to stop for a moment to admire the **Control Tower** and **Theme Building.** The spacey *Jetsons*-style Theme Building, which has always loomed over LAX, has been joined by a more recent silhouette. The main control tower, designed by local architect Kate Diamond to evoke a stylized palm tree, is tailored to present Southern California in its best light. You can go inside to enjoy the view from the Theme Building's observation deck, or have a space-age cocktail at the Technicolor bachelor pad that is the **Encounter at LAX** restaurant (see chapter 6 for a complete listing).

Constructed on a broad cliff with a steep face, the **Wayfarers Chapel** in Rancho Palos Verdes enjoys a fantastic spot overlooking the waves of the Pacific. It was designed by Lloyd Wright, son of celebrated architect Frank Lloyd Wright. Known locally as the "glass church," Wayfarers is a memorial to Emanuel Swedenborg, an 18th-century Swedish philosopher who claimed to have visions of spirits and heavenly hosts. The church is constructed of glass, redwood, and native stone. Rare plants, some of which are native to Israel, surround the building. The church is open daily from 9am to 5pm and is located at 5755 Palos Verdes Dr. S. Call *C* **310/377-1650** (www.wayfarerschapel.org) in advance to arrange a free escorted tour.

L.A.'S WESTSIDE & BEVERLY HILLS

In addition to the sights below, don't miss the **Beverly Hills Hotel** (see chapter 5), and be sure to wind your way through the streets of Beverly Hills off Sunset Boulevard (see "Hollywood at Home: A Beverly Hills Driving Tour," p. 194).

Church of the Good Shepherd   Built in 1924, this is Beverly Hills's oldest house of worship. In 1950, Elizabeth Taylor and her first husband, Nicky Hilton, were married here. The funerals of Alfred Hitchcock, Gary Cooper, Eva Gabor, and Frank Sinatra were all held here as well.

505 N. Bedford Dr., Beverly Hills. *C* **310/276-3139.**

Pacific Design Center   The bold architecture and overwhelming scale of the Pacific Design Center, designed by Argentinean architect Cesar Pelli, aroused controversy when it was erected in 1975. Sheathed in gently curving cobalt-blue glass, the seven-story building houses more than 750,000 square feet of wholesale interior-design showrooms and is known to locals as "the blue whale." When the property for the design center was acquired in the 1970s, almost all of the small businesses that lined this stretch of Melrose Avenue were demolished. Only Hugo's Plating, which still stands in front of the center, successfully resisted the wrecking ball. In 1988, a second boxlike structure, dressed in equally dramatic Kelly green, was added to the design center and surrounded by a protected outdoor plaza.

8687 Melrose Ave., West Hollywood. *C* **310/657-0800.**

Schindler House ★ A protégé of Frank Lloyd Wright and contemporary of Richard Neutra, Austrian architect Rudolph Schindler designed this innovative modern house for himself in 1921–22. It's now home to the Los Angeles arm of Austria's Museum of Applied Arts (MAK). The house is noted for its complicated interlocking spaces; the interpenetration of indoors and out; simple, unadorned materials; and technological innovations. Docent-guided tours are conducted at no additional charge on weekends only.

The MAK Center offers guides to L.A.-area buildings by Schindler and other Austrian architects, and presents visiting related exhibitions and creative arts programming. Call for schedules.

835 N. Kings Rd. (north of Melrose Ave.), West Hollywood. © 323/651-1510. www.makcenter.com. Admission $5 adults, free to children age 12 and under. Free to all on Sept 10 (Schindler's birthday), May 24 (International Museum Day), Dec 1, and every Fri after 4pm. Daily 11am–6pm.

Tail o' the Pup At first glance, you might not think twice about this hot dog–shaped bit of kitsch just across from the Beverly Center. But locals adored this closet-sized wiener dispensary so much that when it was threatened by the developer's bulldozer, they spoke out en masse to save it. One of the last remaining examples of 1950s representational architecture, the "little dog that could" serves up an "only in L.A." experience to go with its great Baseball Special.

329 N. San Vicente Blvd. (between Beverly Blvd. and Melrose Ave.), West Hollywood. © 310/652-4517.

HOLLYWOOD

In addition to the buildings listed below, don't miss the **Griffith Observatory** and **Mann's Chinese Theatre** (see "L.A.'s Top Attractions," earlier in this chapter), the **Hollywood Roosevelt hotel** (see chapter 5), and the **Egyptian Theatre,** 6712 Hollywood Blvd (© **323/466-FILM;** www.egyptiantheatre.com). Conceived by grandiose Sid Grauman, the Egyptian Theatre is just down the street from the better-known Chinese Theatre, but it remains less altered from its 1922 design, which was based on the then-headline-news discovery of hidden treasures in Pharaohs' tombs. The building recently underwent a sensitive restoration by American Cinematheque, which now screens rare, classic, and independent films (see chapter 10 for details).

Capitol Records Building Opened in 1956, this 12-story tower, just north of the legendary intersection of Hollywood and Vine, is one of the city's most recognizable buildings. This circular tower is often, but incorrectly, said to have been made to resemble a stack of 45s under a turntable stylus (it kinda does, though). Nat "King" Cole, songwriter Johnny Mercer, and other 1950s Capitol artists populate a giant exterior mural.

1750 Vine St. © 323/462-6252.

Freeman House Frank Lloyd Wright's Freeman House, built in 1924, was designed as an experimental prototype of mass-produced affordable housing. The home's richly patterned "textile-block" exterior was Wright's invention and is the most famous aspect of the home's design. Situated on a dramatic site overlooking Hollywood, Freeman House is built with the world's first glass-to-glass corner windows. Dancer Martha Graham, bandleader Xavier Cugat, art collector Galka Sheye, photographer Edward Weston, and architects Philip Johnson and Richard Neutra all lived or spent significant time at this house, which became known as an avant-garde salon. The house currently closed for restoration; call ahead to see if it's open.

1962 Glencoe Way (off Hillcrest, near Highland and Franklin aves.). © 323/851-0671.

DOWNTOWN

For a taste of what downtown's Bunker Hill was like before the bulldozers, visit the residential neighborhood of **Angelino Heights,** near Echo Park. Entire streets are still filled with stately gingerbread Victorian homes; most still enjoy the splendid views which led early L.A.'s elite to build here. The 1300 block of Carroll Avenue is the best preserved. Don't be surprised if a film crew is scouting locations while you're there—these blocks appear often on the silver screen.

The Bradbury Building　This National Historic Landmark, built in 1893, is Los Angeles's oldest commercial building and one of the city's most revered architectural achievements. Capped by a magical five-story skylight, Bradbury's courtyard combines glazed brick, Mexican tile, rich Belgian marble, handsome oak paneling, and lacelike wrought-iron railings. The glass-topped atrium is often used as a movie and TV set; you've seen it in *Chinatown* and *Blade Runner.*

304 S. Broadway (at 3rd St.). © **213/626-1893.** Mon–Fri 9am–6pm; Sat–Sun 9am–5pm.

Central Library ★★　This is one of L.A.'s early architectural achievements. The city rallied to save the library when arson nearly destroyed it in 1986; the triumphant restoration has returned much of its original splendor. Working in the early 1920s, architect Bertram G. Goodhue employed the Egyptian motifs and materials popularized by the recent discovery of King Tut's tomb, and combined them with a more modern use of concrete block to great effect. *Warning:* Parking in this area can involve a heroic effort. Try visiting on the weekend and using the Flower Street parking entrance; the library will validate your ticket and you can escape for only $2.

630 W. 5th St. (between Flower St. and Grand Ave.). © **213/228-7000.** www.lapl.org.

City Hall　Built in 1928, the 27-story triangular Los Angeles City Hall was the tallest building in the city for more than 30 years. The structure's distinctive ziggurat roof was featured in the film *War of the Worlds,* but it is probably best known as the headquarters of the *Daily Planet* in the *Superman* TV series. When it was built, City Hall was the sole exception to an ordinance outlawing buildings taller than 150 feet. On a clear day (yeah, right), the top-floor observation deck offers views to Mount Wilson, 15 miles (24km) away.

200 N. Spring St. © **213/485-2121.** www.lacityhall.org. Observation deck open Mon–Fri 10am–4pm.

El Alisal ★　El Alisal is a small, rugged, two-story "castle," built between 1889 and 1910 from large rocks and telephone poles purchased from the Santa Fe Railroad. The architect and creator was Charles F. Lummis, a Harvard graduate, archaeologist, and writer, who walked from Ohio to California and coined the slogan "See America First." A fan of Native American culture, Lummis is credited with popularizing the concept of the "Southwest," referring to New Mexico and Arizona. He often lived the lifestyle of the Indians, and he founded the nearby Southwest Museum (see p. 175 for a full listing), a repository of Indian artifacts. Lummis held fabulous parties for the theatrical, political, and artistic elite; his guest list often included Will Rogers and Theodore Roosevelt. The outstanding feature of his house is the fireplace, which was carved by Mount Rushmore creator Gutzon Borglum. The lawn has been turned into an experimental garden of water-conserving plants.

200 E. Ave. 43, Highland Park. © **323/222-0546.** www.socalhistory.org. Free. Fri–Sun noon–4pm.

Union Station ★　Union Station, completed in 1939, is one of the finest examples of California Mission-style architecture. It was built with the opulence and attention to detail that characterize 1930s WPA projects. The cathedral-size, richly paneled ticket lobby and waiting area of this fantastic cream-colored structure stand sadly empty most of the time, but the MTA does use Union Station for Blue Line commuter trains. When you're strolling through these grand historic halls, it's easy to imagine the glamorous movie stars who once boarded *The City of Los Angeles* and *The Super Chief* to journey back east during the glory days of rail travel; I also like to picture the many joyous reunions between returning soldiers and loved ones following the victorious end to World War II, in the station's heyday. There's always been a restaurant in the station; the latest to occupy this unusually beautiful setting is **Traxx** (see p. 147 in chapter 6, "Dining," for a full listing).

Alameda St. (at Cesar E. Chavez Ave.).

Watts Towers & Art Center   Watts became notorious as the site of riots in the summer of 1965, during which 34 people were killed and more than 1,000 injured. Today, a visit to Watts is a lesson in inner-city life. It's a high-density land of gray strip malls, well-guarded check-cashing shops, and fast-food restaurants; but it's also a neighborhood of hardworking families struggling to survive in the midst of gangland. Although there's not much for the casual tourist here, the Watts Towers are truly a unique attraction, and the adjoining art gallery illustrates the fierce determination of area residents to maintain cultural integrity.

The Towers are colorful, 99-foot-tall cement and steel sculptures ornamented with mosaics of bottles, seashells, cups, plates, pottery, and ceramic tiles. They were completed in 1954 by folk artist Simon Rodia, an immigrant Italian tile-setter who worked on them for 33 years in his spare time. True fans of decorative ceramics will enjoy the fact that Rodia's day job was at the legendary Malibu Potteries (are those fragments of valuable Malibu tile encrusting the Towers?). Closed since 1994 due to earthquake damage, the towers were triumphantly reopened in 2001. At press time, tour schedules were limited due to restoration projects; we suggest calling for the latest information.

Note: Next to these designated Cultural Landmarks is the Art Center, which has a fascinating collection of ethnic musical instruments as well as several visiting art exhibits throughout the year.

1765 E. 107th St., Los Angeles. ☎ 213/847-4646. www.culturela.org. Gallery open Tues–Sat 10am–4pm and Sun noon–4pm; call for tower tour schedule and directions.

PASADENA & ENVIRONS
See "Sightseeing Tours" under "Studio & Sightseeing Tours," later in this chapter, for more information on touring the many well-preserved historic neighborhoods in Pasadena. For a quick but profound architectural fix, stroll past Pasadena's grandiose and baroque **City Hall,** 100 N. Garfield Ave., 2 blocks north of Colorado Boulevard; closer inspection will reveal its classical colonnaded courtyard, formal gardens, and spectacular tiled dome.

The Gamble House 🌟🌟   The huge two-story Gamble House, built in 1908 as a California vacation home for the wealthy family of Procter and Gamble fame, is a sublime example of Arts and Crafts architecture. The interior, designed by the famous Pasadena-based Greene and Greene architectural team, abounds with handcraftsmanship, including intricately carved teak cornices, custom-designed furnishings, elaborate carpets, and a fantastic Tiffany glass door. No detail was overlooked. Every oak wedge, downspout, air vent, and switch plate contributes to the unified design. Admission is by 1-hour guided tour only, which departs every 15 minutes. No reservations are necessary.

If you can't fit the tour into your schedule but have a love of Craftsman design, visit the well-stocked bookstore and museum shop located in the former garage (you can also see the exterior and grounds of the house this way). The bookstore is open Tuesday through Saturday 10am to 5pm, Sunday 11:30am to 5pm

Additional elegant Greene & Greene creations (still privately owned) abound 2 blocks away along **Arroyo Terrace,** including nos. **368, 370, 400, 408, 424,** and **440.** The Gamble House bookstore can give you a walking-tour map and also conducts guided neighborhood tours by appointment.

4 Westmoreland Place (in the 300 block of North Orange Grove Blvd.), Pasadena. ℭ 626/793-3334. www.gamblehouse.usc.edu. Admission $8 adults, $5 students and seniors 65 and over, free for children under 12. Thurs–Sun noon–3pm. Closed holidays.

Mission San Fernando   In the late 18th century, Franciscan missionaries established 21 missions up the California coast, from San Diego to Sonoma. Each uniquely beautiful Mission was built 1 day's trek from the next, along a path known as *El Camino Real* (the Royal Road), remnants of which still exist today. The Missions' construction marked the beginning of European settlement of California and the displacement of the Native American population. The two L.A.-area Missions are located in the valleys that took their names: the San Fernando Valley and the San Gabriel Valley (see below). A third Mission, San Juan Capistrano, is located in Orange County (see chapter 11).

Established in 1797, Mission San Fernando once controlled more than 1½ million acres, employed 1,500 Native Americans, and boasted more than 22,000 head of cattle and extensive orchards. The fragile adobe Mission complex was destroyed several times, but was always faithfully rebuilt with low buildings surrounding grassy courtyards. The aging church was replaced in the 1940s, and again in the 1970s after an earthquake. **The Convento,** a 250-foot-long colonnaded structure dating from 1810, is the compound's oldest remaining building. Some of the Mission's rooms, including the old library and the private salon of the first bishop of California, have been restored to their late-18th-century appearance. A half-dozen padres and many hundreds of Shoshone Indians are buried in the adjacent cemetery.

15151 San Fernando Mission Blvd., Mission Hills. ℭ 818/361-0186. Admission $4 adults, $3 seniors and children 7–15, free for kids under 7. Daily 9am–5pm. From I-5, exit at San Fernando Mission Blvd. east and drive 5 blocks to the Mission.

Mission San Gabriel Arcangel   Founded in 1771, Mission San Gabriel Arcangel retains its original facade, notable for its high oblong windows and large capped buttresses said to have been influenced by the cathedral in Cordova, Spain. The Mission's self-contained compound encompasses an aqueduct, a cemetery, a tannery, and a working winery. Within the church stands a copper font with the dubious distinction of being the first one used to baptize a Native Californian. The most notable contents of the Mission's museum are Native American paintings depicting the Stations of the Cross, done on sailcloth, with colors made from crushed desert flower petals.

428 S. Mission Dr., San Gabriel (15 min. south of Pasadena). ℭ 626/457-3048. www.sangabrielmission.org. Admission $5 adults, $4 seniors and students, $2 children ages 6–12, free for kids age 5 and under. Daily 9am–4:30pm. Closed holidays.

5 L.A. Parks, Gardens, Views & Zoos

PARKS

In addition to the two excellent examples of urban parkland below, check out **Pan Pacific Park,** a hilly retreat near Farmers Market and CBS Studios, named for the Art Deco auditorium that unfortunately no longer stands at its edge.

Griffith Park ★★ *Kids*   Mining tycoon Griffith J. Griffith donated these 4,000 acres to the city in 1896. Today, Griffith Park is the largest city park in America. There's a lot to do here, including hiking, horseback riding, golfing, swimming, biking, and picnicking (see "Golf, Hiking & Other Fun in the Warm California Sun," later in this chapter). For a general overview of the park, drive the mountainous loop road that winds from the top of Western Avenue, past Griffith Observatory, and down to Vermont Avenue. For a more extensive foray, turn north at the loop road's midsection, onto Mt. Hollywood Drive. To reach the golf courses, the **Autry Museum** (see p. 169 for a full listing), or **Los Angeles Zoo** (see p. 188 for a full listing), take Los Feliz Boulevard to Riverside Drive, which runs along the park's western edge.

Near the zoo, in a particularly dusty corner of the park, you can find the **Travel Town Transportation Museum,** 5200 Zoo Dr. (© **323/662-5874;** www.cityofla.org/RAP/grifmet/tt), a little-known outdoor museum with a small collection of vintage locomotives and old airplanes. Kids love it. The museum is open Monday through Friday from 10am to 4pm, Saturday and Sunday from 10am to 5pm; admission is free. Griffith Park entrances are along Los Feliz Blvd., at Riverside Dr., Vermont Ave., and Western Ave. (Hollywood; © **323/ 913-4688;** www.cityofla.org/rap/grifmet/gp). Park admission is free.

Will Rogers State Historic Park   Will Rogers State Historic Park was once Will Rogers's private ranch and grounds. Willed to the state of California in 1944, the 168-acre estate is now both a park and a historic site, supervised by the Department of Parks and Recreation. Visitors may explore the grounds, the former stables, and the 31-room house filled with the original furnishings, including a porch swing in the living room and many Native American rugs and baskets. Charles Lindbergh and his wife, Anne Morrow Lindbergh, hid out here in the 1930s during part of the craze that followed the kidnap and murder of their first son. There are picnic tables, but no food is sold.

Will Rogers (1879–1935) was born in Oklahoma and became a cowboy in the Texas Panhandle before drifting into a Wild West show as a folksy, speechifying roper. The "cracker-barrel philosopher" performed lariat tricks while carrying on a humorous deadpan monologue on current events. The showman moved to Los Angeles in 1919, where he become a movie actor as well as the author of numerous books detailing his down-home "cowboy philosophy."

1501 Will Rogers State Park Rd., Pacific Palisades (between Santa Monica and Malibu). © 310/454-8212. Park entrance $6 per vehicle. Daily 8am–sunset. House opens daily from 10am–5pm; guided tours can be arranged for groups of 10 or more. From Santa Monica, take the Pacific Coast Hwy. (Calif. 1) north, turn right onto Sunset Blvd., and continue to the park entrance.

BOTANICAL GARDENS

The Arboretum of Los Angeles County   This horticultural and botanical center was formerly the estate of silver magnate "Lucky" Baldwin—the man responsible for bringing horse racing to Southern California—who lived until 1909 on these lushly planted 127 acres overlooking Santa Anita racetrack. You might recognize Baldwin's red-and-white Queen Anne cottage from the opening sequence of *Fantasy Island* ("de plane, de plane"); the gardens are also a favorite location for movie filming and local weddings. In addition to spectacular flora, the Arboretum boasts a bevy of resident peafowl who seem unafraid of humans—one of the best treats here is being up close when the peacocks, attempting to impress passing hens, unfold their brilliant rainbow plumage. Avid gardeners will want to visit the nurserylike gift shop on the way out.

301 N. Baldwin Ave., Arcadia. (C) 626/821-3222. www.arboretum.com. Admission $5 adults, $3 students and seniors 62 and over, $1 children ages 5–12, free for kids age 4 and under. Daily 9am–4:30pm. Closed Christmas Day.

Descanso Gardens ★ Camellias—evergreen flowering shrubs from China and Japan—were the passion of amateur gardener E. Manchester Boddy, who began planting them here in 1941. Today his 160-acre Descanso Gardens contain more than 100,000 camellias in more than 600 varieties, blooming under a canopy of California oak trees. The shrubs now share the limelight with a 9-acre International Rosarium, home to hundreds of varieties. This is a really magical place, with paths and streams that wind through the towering forest, bordering a lake, bird sanctuary, Japanese Garden & Tea House, and Boddy House art museum. Each season features different plants: daffodils, azaleas, tulips, and lilacs in the spring; chrysanthemums in the fall; and so on. Monthly art exhibits are held in the garden's hospitality house, and Courtyard Café offers light meals daily from 10am to 3pm.

Free docent-guided walking tours are offered every Sunday at 1pm; guided tram tours, which cost $1.50, run Tuesday through Friday at 1, 2, and 3pm, and Saturday and Sunday at 11am and 1, 2, and 3pm. Picnicking is allowed in specified areas.

1418 Descanso Dr., La Cañada (about 20 min. from downtown L.A.). (C) 818/952-4400. www.descanso gardens.org. Admission $5 adults, $3 students and seniors 62 and over, $1 children ages 5–12, free for kids age 4 and under. Daily 9am–4:30pm. Closed Christmas Day. Free parking.

Huntington Library, Art Collections & Botanical Gardens ★★ The Huntington Library is the jewel in Pasadena's crown. The 207-acre hilltop estate was once home to industrialist and railroad magnate Henry E. Huntington (1850–1927), who bought books on the same massive scale on which he acquired businesses. The continually expanding collection includes dozens of Shakespeare's first editions, Benjamin Franklin's handwritten autobiography, a Gutenberg Bible from the 1450s, and the earliest known manuscript of Chaucer's *Canterbury Tales*. Although some rare works are available only to visiting scholars, the library has a regularly changing (and always excellent) exhibit showcasing different items in the collection.

If you prefer canvas to parchment, Huntington also put together a terrific 18th-century British and French art collection. The most celebrated paintings are Gainsborough's *The Blue Boy*, and *Pinkie*, a companion piece by Sir Thomas Lawrence depicting the youthful aunt of Elizabeth Barrett Browning. These and other works are displayed in the stately Italianate mansion on the crest of this hillside estate, so you can also get a glimpse of its splendid furnishings. American art and Renaissance paintings are exhibited in two additional galleries.

But it's the **botanical gardens** that draw most locals to the Huntington. The Japanese Garden comes complete with a traditional open-air Japanese house, koi-filled stream, and serene Zen garden. The cactus garden is exotic, the jungle garden is intriguing, the lily ponds are soothing—and there are many benches scattered about so you can sit and enjoy the surroundings.

Because the Huntington surprises many with its size and wealth of activities to choose from, first-timers might want to start with a tour. One-hour garden tours are offered daily; no reservations or additional fees required. Times vary, so check at the information desk on arrival. We also recommend that you tailor your visit to include the popular English high tea served Tuesday through Friday from noon to 4:30pm, and Saturday and Sunday from 10:45am to 4:30pm (last seating at 3:30pm). The charming **tearoom** overlooks the Rose Garden (home to 1,000 varieties displayed in chronological order of their breeding), and since the finger sandwiches and desserts are served buffet style, it's a genteel bargain even for hearty appetites at $12.95 per person (please note that museum admission is a separate required cost). Phone © **626/683-8131** for tearoom reservations.

1151 Oxford Rd., San Marino. © 626/405-2100. www.huntington.org. Admission $10 adults, $8.50 seniors 65 and over, $7 students and children age 12 and over, free to children under age 12; free to all the 1st Thurs of each month. Sept–May Tues–Fri noon–4:30pm, Sat–Sun 10:30am–4:30pm; June–Aug Tues–Sun 10:30am–4:30pm. Closed major holidays.

VIEWS

It's not always easy to get a good city view. Even if you find the right vantage, the smog may keep you from having any kind of panorama. But, as they say, on a clear day you can see forever. One of the best views of the city can be had from **Griffith Observatory** (see "L.A.'s Top Attractions," earlier in this chapter); unfortunately, it's closed for renovation until May 2005. The view of Santa Monica Bay from the end of **Santa Monica Pier** is also great.

Angel's Flight A once-popular downtown landmark constructed in 1901, Angel's Flight was a tiny, open-car cable railway, or funicular, that transported passengers up the steep eastern slope of Bunker Hill, from Hill Street (in the business sector) to Olive Street (then a neighborhood of Victorian homes). Residents agreed to see it torn down in 1969, with the promise that the pieces would be stored and someday reassembled. They got their wish in 1996, as the world's shortest railroad reopened and began offering rides for 25¢. The station atop Bunker Hill offers a great overview of downtown; however, operation of the funicular has been suspended due to an accident on February 1, 2001, that killed one person and injured seven.

Hill St., between 3rd and 4th sts., downtown. No phone. www.westworld.com/~elson/larail/angelsflight.html.

Mulholland Drive ★ Mulholland Drive travels 21 miles (34km) along the peaks and canyons of Hollywood Hills and the Santa Monica mountains, straddling Hollywood and the San Fernando Valley. The winding road provides some amazing views of the city (particularly at night) and offers many opportunities to pull over and simply enjoy.

Between Coldwater Canyon Dr. and U.S. 101.

ZOOS

Los Angeles Zoo ★ *Kids* The L.A. Zoo, which shares its parking lot with the Autry Museum, has been welcoming visitors and busloads of school kids since 1966. In 1982, the zoo inaugurated a display of cuddly koalas, still one of its biggest attractions. Although it's quite smaller than the world famous San Diego Zoo, the L.A. Zoo is surprisingly enjoyable and easy to fully explore. As much an arboretum as a zoo, the grounds are thick with mature shade trees from around the world that help cool the once-barren grounds, and new habitats are

Stargazing in L.A.: Top Spots for Sighting Celebrities

Celebrities pop up everywhere in L.A. If you spend enough time here, you'll surely bump into a few of them. If you're in the city for only a short time, however, it's best to go on the offensive.

Restaurants are your surest bet. Dining out is such a popular recreation among Hollywood's elite that you sometimes wonder whether frequently sighted folks like Johnny Depp, Nicole Kidman, Bridget Fonda, Nicolas Cage, Brad Pitt, or Cindy Crawford ever actually eat at home. **Matsuhisa, Locanda Veneta, Mimosa, Jozu, Maple Drive,** and **Lola's** can almost guarantee sightings any night of the week. The city's stylish hotels can also be good bets—the **Mondrian** draws stars galore to its dining room **Asia de Cuba,** as well as the elite Sky Bar; and **Shutters'** lobby lounge is the rendezvous of choice for famous faces heading to dinner at the hotel's **One Pico** restaurant. The trendiest clubs and bars—**Whiskey Bar, House of Blues, Viper Room,** and **Sky Bar**—are all good for star sighting, but cover charges can be astronomical and the velvet rope gauntlet oppressive. And it's not always Mick and Quentin and Madonna; a recent night on the town turned up only Yanni, Ralph Macchio, and Dr. Ruth.

Often, the best places to see members of the A-list aren't as obvious as a back-alley stage door or the front room of Spago. Shops along Sunset Boulevard, like **Tower Records** and the **Virgin Megastore,** are often star-heavy, as are chichi shops within the **Beverly Center** mall. **Book Soup,** that browser's paradise across the street from Tower, is usually good for a star or two. A midafternoon stroll along **Melrose Avenue** might also produce a familiar face; likewise the chic European-style shops of **Sunset Plaza.**

Or you can seek out the celebrities on the job. It's not uncommon for star-studded movie productions to use L.A.'s diverse cultural landscape for **location shots;** in fact, it's such a regular occurrence that locals are usually less impressed with an A-list presence than perturbed about the precious parking spaces lost to all those equipment trucks and dressing-room trailers. On-the-street movie shoots are part of what makes L.A. unique, and onlookers gather wherever hastily scrawled production signs point to a hot site. For the inside track on where the action is, check the **"Daily Shoot Sheet"** at www.eidc.com. This isn't some word-of-mouth groupie posting. This is a strictly legit online listing of every filming permit applied for within the city limits. Entries are classified by type (commercial advertisement, feature film, student film, TV program) and working title, and the site lists production hours and exact street addresses.

Keep your eyes peeled for celebrities—everyone does in L.A.—and you'll more than likely be rewarded. And don't forget to peer through the windows of any Land Rover or Mercedes driving by; even movie stars have errands to run.

light-years ahead of the cruel concrete roundhouses originally used to exhibit animals (though you can't help feeling that, despite the fancy digs, all the creatures would rather be in their natural habitat). Highlights include the **Chimpanzees of the Mahale Mountains** habitat, where visitors can see plenty of primate activity; **the Red Ape Rain Forest,** a natural orangutan habitat; the entertaining **World of Birds** show; and the silverback gorilla exhibit. The gargantuan Andean condor had us enthralled as well (the facility is renowned in zoological circles for the successful breeding and releasing of California condors, and occasionally it has some of these majestic and endangered birds on exhibit).

The zoo's latest attraction (and one they're rightfully proud of) is the **Winnick Family Children's Zoo,** a fantastic and forward-thinking children's zoo that contains a petting area, exhibition animal care center, "Adventure Theater" storytelling and puppet show, and other kid-hip exhibits and activities. *Tip:* To avoid the busloads of rambunctious school kids, arrive after noon.

5333 Zoo Dr., Griffith Park. ✆ 323/644-6400. www.lazoo.org. Admission $8.25 adults, $3.25 kids ages 2–12, $5.25 seniors 65 and over, free to children under age 2. Daily 10am–5pm. Closed Christmas Day. Free parking.

6 Studio & Sightseeing Tours

STUDIO TOURS

NBC Studios 🉑   According to a security guard, John Wayne and Redd Foxx once got into a fight here after Wayne refused to ride in the same limo as Foxx, who called the movie star a "redneck." Well, your NBC tour will probably be a bit more docile than that. The guided 70-minute tour includes a behind-the-scenes unstaged look at *The Tonight Show with Jay Leno* set; wardrobe, makeup, and set-building departments; and several sound studios. The tour also includes some cool video demonstrations of high-tech special effects. *Note:* Tours are sold on a first-come, first-serve basis and sell out early during peak vacation season.

3000 W. Alameda Ave., Burbank. ✆ 818/840-3537. Tours $7.50 adults, $6.75 seniors 60 and over, $4 children ages 5–12, under 5 free. Mon–Fri 9am–3pm (open weekends and extended hours during summer and holiday season—call for current schedule).

Paramount Pictures 🉑   Paramount's 2-hour walking tour around its Hollywood headquarters is both a historical ode to filmmaking and a real-life look at a working studio—it's the only major movie studio still located in Hollywood. Tours depart hourly; the itinerary varies, depending on what productions are in progress. Visits might include a walk through the soundstages of TV shows or feature films, though you can't enter while taping is taking place. Cameras, recording equipment, and children under 10 are not allowed.

5555 Melrose Ave. ✆ 323/956-5575. www.paramount.com. Tours $15 per person. Mon–Fri 9am–2pm.

Warner Brothers Studios 🉑🉑   Warner Brothers offers the most comprehensive—and the least theme park–like—of the studio tours. The tour takes visitors on a 2-hour informational drive-and-walk jaunt around the studio's faux streets. After a brief introductory film, you'll pile into glorified golf carts and cruise past parking spaces marked "Clint Eastwood," "Michael Douglas," and "Sharon Stone," then walk through active film and television sets. Whether it's an orchestra scoring a film or a TV show being taped or edited, you'll get a glimpse of how it's done (nothing is staged for the tour). Stops include the wardrobe department or the mills where sets are made. Whenever possible, you can also visit working sets to watch actors filming actual productions. Reservations are required; children under 8 are not admitted.

WB Studio Gate 3, 4301 W. Olive Ave. (at Hollywood Way), Burbank. ℂ 818/972-TOUR; www.wbstudiotour. com. Advance reservations recommended. Tours $32 per person, departing on the half hour Mon–Fri 9am–4pm (9am–3pm winter).

Sony Pictures Studio Tour   Although it doesn't have quite the historical cachet as Warner Brothers or Paramount, a lot of movie history was made at this Culver City lot. The 2-hour walking tour includes stops at classic stage scenes such as the Yellow Brick Road winding through Munchkinland, sets from modern thrillers like *Men in Black,* and an opportunity to drop in on the *Jeopardy!* set to test your trivia prowess. But the main reason for the tour is the chance to catch a glimpse at the stars who work here (it's one of the busiest studio lots in the world).

Sony Picture Studios, 10202 W. Washington Blvd., Culver City. ℂ 323/520-TOUR. Advance reservations highly recommended; children under 12 are not admitted. Tours $20 per person, departing Mon–Fri at 9:30am, 11am, noon, and 2:30pm. Photo ID required.

SIGHTSEEING TOURS

L.A. Tours (ℂ **323/993-0093;** www.la-tours.com) operates regularly scheduled tours of the city. Plush shuttle buses (27 passengers maximum) pick up riders from major hotels for morning or afternoon tours of Sunset Strip, the movie studios, Farmers Market, Hollywood, homes of the stars, and other attractions. Different itineraries are available, if you're interested in downtown and the Music Center, for example, or want to spend your time exploring the beaches and shopping in Santa Monica. Tours vary in length from a half day to a full day and cost $42 to $58 for adults. There are discounts for kids; book online for a $4-per-person discount. Advance reservations are required.

The **L.A. Conservancy** (ℂ **213/623-2489;** www.laconservancy.org) conducts a dozen fascinating walking tours of historic downtown L.A., seed of today's sprawling metropolis. (See "**L.A.'s Top Architectural Tours**" box, earlier in this chapter). In Pasadena, **Pasadena Heritage** (ℂ **626/441-6333;** www. pasadenaheritage.org) offers various tours spotlighting neighborhoods and their wealthy estates. Call for a schedule of guided tours, or pick up one of the self-guided walking or driving maps available at the **Pasadena Convention and Visitors Bureau,** 171 S. Los Robles Ave. (ℂ **626/795-9311**).

For a more aerobic way to see L.A., sign up with **LA Bike Tours** (ℂ **888/ 775-BIKE** or 323/466-5890; www.labiketours.com), which offers guided rides of Hollywood or Beverly Hills, plus longer excursions to the Getty Center, Venice Beach, Griffith Park, and Topanga's Redrock Canyon. Most tours last around 3 hours; prices range from $40 to $50 and include bike rental plus safety gear, snacks, and bottled water.

Off 'N Running Tours (ℂ **800/523-TOUR** or 310/246-1418) combines sporting with sightseeing, taking joggers on guided runs through Los Angeles. One-on-one tours are customized to take in the most beautiful areas around your hotel and can accommodate any skill level for 4 to 12 miles (6.5–19km). It's a fun way to get the most out of your morning jog. Tours cost about $45 and include a T-shirt and runner's breakfast.

7 TV Tapings

Being part of the audience for the taping of a television show might be the quintessential L.A. experience. This is a great way to see Hollywood at work, to find out how your favorite sitcom or talk show is made, and to catch a glimpse of your favorite TV personalities. Timing is important—remember that most series

Confessions of a Game Show Contestant

People are still impressed when they hear that I was a game-show contestant, even though it's been more than 17 years since I won $28,224 on *The $25,000 Pyramid*—a prize that seems paltry these days to anyone "who wants to be a millionaire." But there's definitely a pop-culture cachet to a game-show appearance: shaking hands with Alex Trebek or Regis Philbin . . . pulling out bits of grade-school logic or otherwise-worthless pop trivia from the vast recesses of your brain . . . knowing that your friends and family are watching your winnings tally up.

Perhaps you've been thinking of taking a chance on fame and fortune the next time you're in L.A. Both are more attainable than you might think—actress Markie Post's career began with her audition for a game show; and as far as fortune goes, *someone* has to win the big money!

If you're serious about trying to get on a show, be sure you have some flexibility in your schedule; although most production companies go out of their way to give priority to out-of-town contestants, you should be prepared to return to Los Angeles one or more times for a final audition and/or taping. My own journey from first interview to victory hug from host Dick Clark took 4 months. Here are some tips that might help you prepare:

The Bubblier the Better: Be friendly, cheerful, and bright at your audition and during taping. Be good-natured when you lose or make mistakes, and above all, be exuberant if you win the "big money." When you're onstage, nothing feels quite real; I really did have to remind myself to look thrilled when I suddenly had 25 grand more than I had 60 seconds earlier.

Dress for Success: Contestant coordinators look for players who won't alienate viewers. It's awfully hard for a granny in the heartland to relate

go on hiatus between March and July. And tickets to the top shows, like *Friends* and *Everybody Loves Raymond*, are in greater demand than others, so getting your hands on them takes advance planning—and possibly some waiting in line.

Request tickets as far in advance as possible. Several episodes may be shot on a single day, so you may be required to remain in the theater for up to 4 hours (in addition to the recommended 1-hr. early check-in). If you phone at the last moment, you may luck into tickets for your top choice. More likely, however, you'll be given a list of shows that are currently filming, and you won't recognize many of the titles; studios are always taping pilots, few of which end up on the air. But you never know who may be starring in them—look at all the famous faces that have launched new sitcoms in the past couple of years. Tickets are always free, usually limited to two per person, and are distributed on a first-come, first-served basis. Many shows don't admit children under the age of 10; in some cases no one under the age of 18 is admitted.

Tickets are sometimes given away to the public outside popular tourist sites like Mann's Chinese Theatre in Hollywood and Universal Studios in the Valley; L.A.'s visitor information centers in downtown and Hollywood often have to a trendy big-city type. So dress as conservatively as possible for your auditions, and avoid the fashion no-no's—white, black, stripes, metallics—that would require lighting and camera adjustments.

Most Unglamorous Advice: Remember income taxes. Should you be lucky enough to win big, bear in mind that all cash winnings, as well as the retail value of all your prizes, will be reported to the IRS as earnings.

Some Game Shows Currently in Production:

Jeopardy! (syndicated)   Trivia quiz not for the fainthearted (contestant, that is; watching isn't nearly as difficult!). Call ✆ **310/244-5367.**

Wheel of Fortune (syndicated)   Less about your skill with the "hangman"-style puzzles than your luck spinning the carnival wheel. Call ✆ **213/520-5555.**

Win Ben Stein's Money (cable)   Test your trivia reflexes on this hip, irreverent Comedy Central show. You win by outsmarting the acerbic, intelligent, and sneaker-clad Stein. Call ✆ **213/520-4BEN** or check out www.comedycentral.com.

Rock & Roll Jeopardy (cable)   Call it Jeopardy Lite for the rock-and-roll generation. The questions on this colorful VH1 show are easy, and the contestants say "dude" a lot. Register online at www.rockjeopardy.com or call ✆ **800/482-9840.**

The Price is Right (network)   Contestants are chosen from the studio audience to test their shopping expertise. For ticket information call The Price is Right 24-hour ticket hot line at ✆ **323/575-2449.**

(*Note:* Popular game shows *The Weakest Link* and *Who Wants to be a Millionaire* are taped in New York City.)

tickets as well (see "Orientation" in chapter 4). But if you're determined to see a particular show, contact the following suppliers:

Audiences Unlimited, Inc. (✆ **818/753-3470;** www.tvtickets.com), is a good place to start. It distributes tickets for most of the top sitcoms, including *Friends, That '70s Show, Will & Grace, The Drew Carey Show, Everybody Loves Raymond,* and many more. This service is organized and informative (as is their website), and fully sanctioned by production companies and networks. ABC, for example, no longer handles ticket distribution directly, but refers all inquiries to Audiences Unlimited, Inc. **Television Tickets** (✆ **323/467-4697**) distributes tickets for numerous talk and game shows, including *Jeopardy!,* as does **TVTIX. COM** (✆ **323/653-4105;** www.tvtix.com).

You also may want to contact the networks for information on a specific show, including some whose tickets are not available at the above agencies. At **ABC,** all ticket inquiries are referred to Audiences Unlimited (see above), but you may want to check out ABC's website at **www.abc.com** for a colorful look at their lineup and links to specific shows' sites.

For **CBS Television City,** 7800 Beverly Blvd., Los Angeles, CA 90036, call ✆ **323/575-2458** to see what's being filmed while you're in town. Tickets for

CBS tapings are distributed on a first-come, first-served basis; you can write in advance to reserve them or pick them up at the studio up to an hour before taping. Tickets for many CBS sitcoms, including *Everybody Loves Raymond,* are also available from Audiences Unlimited (see above). For tickets to *The Price Is Right* call the 24-hour ticket hot line at © **323/575-2449.** For a virtual visit to CBS's shows, log onto **www.cbs.com.**

For **NBC,** 3000 W. Alameda Ave., Burbank, CA 91523 (© **818/840-3537**), call to see what's on while you're in L.A. Tickets for NBC tapings, including *The Tonight Show with Jay Leno* (minimum age to attend this show is 16), can be obtained in two ways: either pick them up at the NBC ticket counter on the day of the show (they're distributed on a first-come, first-served basis at the ticket counter off California Avenue), or, at least 6 weeks before your visit, send a self-addressed, stamped envelope with your ticket request to the address above. Be sure to include show name, number of tickets (four per request), and dates desired. All the NBC shows are represented online at www.nbc.com.

8 Hollywood at Home: A Beverly Hills Driving Tour

Ever since the days before talkies, visitors to Los Angeles have wanted to see just where the rich and famous live. Today it's big business—maps of dubious accuracy are sold on Sunset Strip street corners, and at least a dozen tour operators shuttle van loads of voyeurs daily through Beverly Hills.

Well, it's easy to lay out your cash, climb on the bus, and sit back for the ride and the regular spiel. But we think it's much more fun to do it yourself, cruising L.A.'s most chic streets—with a special emphasis on Hollywood's golden age legends and scandals. So we've gathered a very special list of addresses, and mapped out a route especially for you.

DRIVING TOUR   A STAR-STUDDED DRIVE IN L.A.

Start:	Sunset Boulevard at Foothill Road in Beverly Hills.
Finish:	Sunset Boulevard at Beverly Glen in Bel-Air.
Time:	Allow about 3 hours, not including time spent dining.
Best and	
Worst Times:	Anytime during daylight hours is good for the drive itself, but try to avoid the 12:30 to 1:30pm showbiz lunch rush at the restaurants listed.
Related Tip:	Notice the streetlamps all along the way—some of the city's most elaborate fixtures line the route.

Start at:

① 9521 Sunset Blvd

The conservative mansion (at the corner of Foothill Road) is the childhood home of pint-size star **Shirley Temple,** who had her own miniature playhouse on the grounds.

Drive east on Sunset, watching between Palm and Hillcrest on the left side of the street for:

② 9419 Sunset Blvd

Imagine MGM "boy wonder" executive **Irving Thalberg** and his actress wife, **Norma Shearer,** holding court behind these dense shrubbery walls; this was their estate until Thalberg's death at age 37 in 1936.

Turn right on Hillcrest Road to Santa Monica Boulevard, right to Palm Drive, and right once again.

Notice the pleasing symmetry of the landscaping on these streets in the "flats" of Beverly Hills—each north-south drive is planted with a different tree, though clearly not according to name (palm trees line Hillcrest Road, while Palm Drive displays the lavender blooms of jacaranda trees).

On Palm you'll find:

③ 508 Palm Drive

This was home to **Marilyn Monroe** and **Joe DiMaggio** during their short marriage in 1954.

Two houses up is:

④ 512 Palm Drive

This modest Mediterranean-style enclave was blonde bombshell **Jean Harlow's** last home, where she died in 1937—at the age of 26—of sudden uremic poisoning.

Two blocks farther is another former Marilyn Monroe home:

⑤ 718 Palm Drive

She briefly shared this ivy-covered house with William Morris agent Johnny Hyde in 1950, the year she began to make a name for herself with small but pivotal roles in *The Asphalt Jungle* and *All About Eve.*

Turn back toward Elevado Avenue, turn left, and then right on Rexford Avenue. Follow Rexford up past Sunset Boulevard to where it intersects Beverly Drive. Make a right turn and look to the left for:

⑥ 1011 Beverly Drive

This was the opulent estate of **Marion Davies,** the actress and mistress of William Randolph Hearst. Nearly as lavish and excessive as the Santa Monica beach house that Hearst built for her, this mansion is where he died in 1951 (and later she did, in 1961). The driveway is so enormous you might mistake it for a street; stone lions perch atop peach-colored walls guarding the gate, behind which you can see a broad road winding up the hill.

Turn around at Shadow Hill Way and slow down (if traffic allows) on the way back for another look. Turn right at the T-intersection, continuing south on Beverly Drive to Sunset Boulevard, then make a hairpin right turn onto Crescent Drive, where you'll come to:

⑦ 904 Crescent Drive

This was the former home of **Gloria Swanson,** silent film star and *Sunset Boulevard*'s original Norma Desmond.

Across the street are the:

⑧ Beverly Hills Hotel and Bungalows

This was a secluded locale for many legendary trysts, including the rumored **Marilyn Monroe–John F. Kennedy** affair. Howard Hughes virtually lived here during his Hollywood years, keeping several regular bungalows for his family and staff—including his private food-taster. You might want to stop off at the **Fountain Coffee Shop** here for a break (see "Winding Down," below).

Continue to:

⑨ 1001 Crescent Drive

This elegant mansion was formerly occupied by *Dynasty* star **Linda Evans,** and was owned for many years by Blake Edwards and **Julie Andrews.**

Follow Crescent as it curves around, taking Oxford Way past Sunset Boulevard onto Rodeo Drive, which is residential here but becomes Beverly Hills's most extravagant shopping avenue farther south.

⑩ 725 Rodeo Drive

This was the modest residence of the late, multitalented **Gene Kelly.**

Turn right on Carmelita, and right onto Bedford, and look for:

⑪ 620 Bedford Drive

This was the former residence of **Marlene Dietrich.**

One block farther is:

⑫ 730 Bedford Drive

In 1958 in this home, **Lana Turner's** teenage daughter, Cheryl Crane, stabbed to death Turner's abusive boyfriend, gangster Johnny Stompanato.

Turn left onto Lomitas Avenue to Linden Drive, turn right, and proceed to:

⑬ 810 Linden Drive

This home looks exactly as it did the night in 1947 when hoodlum

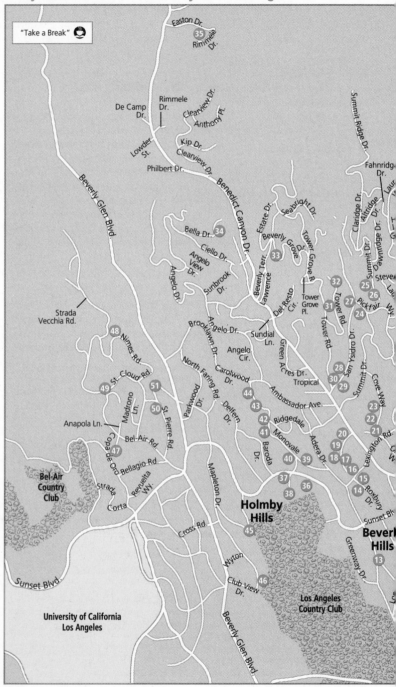

"Take a Break"

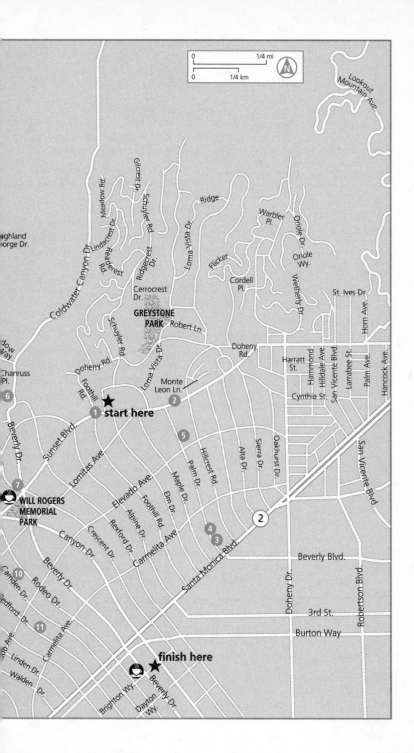

start here

finish here

Benjamin "Bugsy" Siegel was gunned down through the living-room window. A notorious gangster best remembered for creating Las Vegas from a patch of desert, Siegel had been relaxing in the home of his girlfriend, small-time actress Virginia Hill.

Linden will merge into Whittier Drive; make a right onto Sunset Boulevard and take the next left, onto Roxbury Drive, where you'll find several noteworthy homes:

⑭ 911 Roxbury Drive
Bewitched star **Elizabeth Montgomery's** lived here until her death in 1995.

⑮ 918 Roxbury Drive
This was the site of the longtime home of actor **James Stewart** and his beloved wife, **Gloria.** Stewart turned the adjoining corner lot into a walled garden to indulge his favorite hobby, gardening, but found little pleasure in it following Gloria's death. He died in 1997. The house was demolished by its new owner in 1998 to make way for a larger, Italian-style villa.

Down the street is:

⑯ 1000 Roxbury Drive
This was the longtime home of comedienne **Lucille Ball.** Disturbed once too often by huge busloads of tourists pouring onto her front lawn, the famous redhead forced the city of Beverly Hills to create stringent guidelines for tour operators. While Lucy lived here, the house was old-fashioned, with simple white clapboard; following her death, new owners updated the exterior to what you see today.

⑰ 1002 Roxbury Drive
Ball's neighbor for many years at this home was another great comedian, **Jack Benny.**

A few houses down and across the street is:

⑱ 1019 Roxbury Drive
This was the home of **Rosemary Clooney** (whose hunky nephew George rocketed to fame on TV's *ER*).

Next door is:

⑲ 1021 Roxbury Drive
This was the modest home of composer **Ira Gershwin.**

⑳ 1023 Roxbury Drive
Here you'll find a newer house built on the site where **Spencer Tracy,** and later **Agnes Moorhead,** once resided.

Stay on Roxbury, cross over Benedict Canyon Drive, and make the second left onto Cove Way, in front of:

㉑ 1000 Cove Way
This stylish and traditional home was formerly the property of both movie villain **Jack Palance** and funnyman **W. C. Fields.**

Across the street is:

㉒ 1007 Cove Way
This was home to **Sidney Poitier.**

㉓ 1011 Cove Way
The rough-hewn stone exterior suited the moniker of its previous owner **Rock Hudson.**

Make a right turn on Summit Drive and follow it up the hill to:

㉔ 1143 Summit Drive
This is the former site of a Beverly Hills legend. When **Douglas Fairbanks Sr.** and **Mary Pickford**—Hollywood's golden couple in the 1920s—moved here, they lived in the only structure in sight, a small hunting lodge. Later on, they enlarged the dwelling, adding the first residential swimming pool in Beverly Hills; the gracious hilltop manor became known as "Pickfair." Pickford continued to live here until her death in 1979. In 1990 singer **Pia Zadora** leveled the 42-room landmark to make way for the larger—and decidedly tackier—mansion you see today. About the only remnants of the glorious original are the stone cherubs adorning the front gate, a gift to the Fairbankses from Charlie Chaplin.

Veer to the right past no. 1143 and proceed up the street to:

㉕ 1167 Summit Drive

This is the home of actress and Elvis widow, **Priscilla Presley.**

Turn around safely where you can; descending, you'll get a fine view of:

㉖ 1151 Summit Drive

This was the home of **Sammy Davis Jr.** at the time of his death. Sadly, his family was forced to sell the home and auction off its contents to settle the debts he left behind.

Turn right on Pickfair Way (behind Pia Zadora's house). As Pickfair Way dips to meet San Ysidro Drive, glance straight ahead; atop the hill is:

㉗ 1155 San Ysidro Drive

Here's you'll find the former **Fred Astaire** estate.

Make a left at the corner, and you'll see his winding driveway on the right. Farther down the street are a trio of homes:

㉘ 1103 San Ysidro Drive

Here is the last home of **Danny Kaye,** of which only the impressive gateway is visible.

㉙ 1106 San Ysidro Drive

This is the heavily remodeled former home of **Rex Harrison.**

Across the street is:

㉚ 1100 Tower Road

The overly theatrical Romanesque columns, gargoyles, and garden statuary must have suited **Laurence Olivier** and **Vivien Leigh,** who were living here when Leigh won her Best Actress Oscar for *Gone With the Wind.*

Make a right turn around the house and continue up Tower Road to:

㉛ 1151 Tower Road

Jay Leno lives here, and it's a sure bet the house has an extensive garage, for Jay maintains a spectacular collection of vintage automobiles; you might see him motoring about town in one.

Farther up the hill, you'll see the short brick wall that defines:

㉜ 1162 Tower Road

Here's the estate of the late **Michael Landon.** A devoted family man, the star of *Bonanza, Little House on the Prairie,* and *Highway to Heaven* erected a full-size playground here for his many children and grandchildren; it's easy to see the swings, seesaws, and jungle gyms from the street.

You can turn around in the cul-de-sac at the end of Tower Road and gaze out at the extraordinary city view from what was once John Barrymore's vast estate on this hilltop, appropriately named "Bella Vista" (beautiful view). Backtrack down to where Tower Grove Drive heads up the hill to the right, and follow it up to Beverly Grove Drive; turn left. Just as you emerge at the next mini-canyon, look on the left for:

㉝ 9966 Beverly Grove

Cary Grant's last home. Slow down, if you can, and look back through the gates to catch a glimpse of the gracious home (remodeled by Grant in 1982), as well as the spectacular view of L.A. and the ocean.

Follow Beverly Grove down the hill to the T-shaped intersection with Beverly Estate Drive, taking it down to Beverly Glen Boulevard. Turn right on Beverly Glen, then left on Cielo Drive, following the road to where it widens slightly for the intersection with a tiny overgrown spur called Bella Drive. Although technically a public road—and therefore fair game to the curious—there's only one home at the top of this nearly private driveway. But it's worth disturbing the wild rabbits to get to:

㉞ 1436 Bella Drive

This white-walled estate has scarcely changed since 1925, when screen heartthrob **Rudolph Valentino** bought it and named it "Falcon Lair." Valentino's steel pennant emblazoned with the letter *V* still flies atop the house's red-tiled roof. The estate was last owned by heiress **Doris Duke.**

Looking down into the canyon from the summit, you can see 10050 Cielo Dr., the infamous site where in August 1969, members of the Manson family murdered actress **Sharon Tate** and four others. The house itself was torn down in 1994, just after **Nine Inch Nails** recorded their multiplatinum—and

Stargazing in L.A., Part II: The Less-Than-Lively Set

Almost everybody who visits L.A. hopes to see a celebrity—they are, after all, our most common export. But celebrities usually don't cooperate, failing to gather in readily viewable herds. There is, however, an absolutely guaranteed method to approach within 6 feet of many famous stars. Cemeteries are *the* place for star (or at least headstone) gazing: The star is always available, and you're going to get a lot more up close and personal than you probably would to anyone who's actually alive. Here is a guide to the most fruitful cemeteries, listed in order of their friendliness to stargazers.

Weathered Victorian and Art Deco memorials add to the decaying charm of **Hollywood Forever** (formerly Hollywood Memorial Park), 6000 Santa Monica Blvd., Hollywood (© **323/469-1181**). Fittingly, there's a terrific view of the Hollywood sign over the graves, as many of the founders of the community rest here. The most notable tenant is Rudolph Valentino, who rests in an interior crypt. Outside are Tyrone Power Jr.; Douglas Fairbanks Sr.; Cecil B. DeMille (facing Paramount, his old studio); Carl "Alfalfa" Spritzer from *The Little Rascals* (the dog on his grave is not Petey); Hearst mistress Marion Davies; John Huston; and a headstone for Jayne Mansfield (she's really buried in Pennsylvania with her family). In 2000, Douglas Fairbanks Jr. joined his dad at Hollywood Forever.

Catholic **Holy Cross Cemetery,** 5835 W. Slauson Ave., Culver City (© **310/670-7697**), hands out maps to the stars' graves. In one area, within mere feet of each other, lie Bing Crosby, Bela Lugosi (buried in his Dracula cape), and Sharon Tate; not far away are Rita Hayworth and Jimmy Durante. Also here are "Tin Man" Jack Haley and "Scarecrow" Ray Bolger, Mary Astor, John Ford, and Gloria Morgan Vanderbilt. More recent arrivals include John Candy and Audrey Meadows.

The front office at **Hillside Memorial Park,** 6001 Centinela Ave., Baldwin Hills (© **310/641-0707**), can provide a guide to this Jewish cemetery, which has an L.A. landmark: the behemoth tomb of Al Jolson. His rotunda, complete with a bronze reproduction of Jolson and cascading fountain, is visible from I-405. Also on hand are Jack Benny, Eddie Cantor, Vic Morrow, and Michael Landon.

You just know developers get stomachaches looking at **Westwood Memorial Park,** 1218 Glendon Ave., Westwood (© **310/474-1579;** the staff can direct you around), smack-dab in the middle of some of L.A.'s

angst-ridden—album, *The Downward Spiral,* in it.

One unfortunate houseguest and Manson victim was jet-setting hairstylist **Jay Sebring,** visiting from farther up the canyon, where he lived in a secluded house supposedly haunted

by the ghost of movie studio head Paul Bern, who was newly married to starlet Jean Harlow at the time of his death. Bern's death here in 1932 was officially called a suicide, but many speculated about a scandalous murder and cover-up.

priciest real estate. But it's not going anywhere, especially when you consider its most famous resident: Marilyn Monroe. It's also got Truman Capote, John Cassavetes, Armand Hammer, Donna Reed, and Natalie Wood. Walter Matthau was buried here in 2000.

Forest Lawn Glendale, 1712 S. Glendale Ave. (© **323/254-3131**), likes to pretend it has no celebrities. The most prominent of L.A. cemeteries, it's also the most humorless. The place is full of bad art, all part of the continuing vision of founder Huburt Eaton, who thought cemeteries should be happy places. So he banished those gloomy upright tombstones and monuments in favor of flat, pleasant, character-free, flush-to-the-ground slabs. Contrary to urban legend, Walt Disney was *not* frozen and placed under Cinderella's castle at Disneyland. His cremated remains are in a little garden to the left of the Freedom Mausoleum. Turn around, and just behind you are Errol Flynn and Spencer Tracy. In the Freedom Mausoleum itself are Nat "King" Cole, Chico Marx, Gummo Marx, and Gracie Allen—finally joined by George Burns. In a columbarium near the Mystery of Life is Humphrey Bogart. Unfortunately, some of the best celebs—such as Clark Gable, Carole Lombard, and Jean Harlow—are in the Great Mausoleum, which you often can't get into unless you're visiting a relative.

You'd think a place that encourages people to visit for fun would understand what the attraction is. But no—Forest Lawn Glendale won't tell you where any of their illustrious guests are, so don't ask. This place is immense—and, frankly, dull in comparison to the previously listed cemeteries, unless you appreciate the kitsch value of the Forest Lawn approach to art.

Forest Lawn Hollywood Hills, 6300 Forest Lawn Dr. (© **800/204-3131**), is slightly less anal than the Glendale branch, but the same basic attitude prevails. On the right lawn, near the statue of George Washington, is Buster Keaton. In the Courts of Remembrance are Lucille Ball, Charles Laughton, and the not-quite-gaudy-enough tomb of Liberace. Outside, in a vault on the Ascension Road side, is Andy Gibb. Bette Davis's sarcophagus is in front of the wall, to the left of the entrance to the Courts. Gene Autry was also buried here, almost within earshot of the museum that bears his name.

—*Mary Herczog*

You can reach the Bern/Sebring house if you're willing to ascend Easton Drive, a narrow and roughly paved alley.

Return via Cielo Drive to Benedict Canyon, turn left, and proceed to Easton. Turn right to:

③ 9820 Easton Drive
The address isn't really visible from the street, but if you go to the end and turn around, you can see the two-story Bavarian-style house on your left, set back and above the others.

Return via Benedict Canyon to Sunset Boulevard and make a right turn to:

⑯ 10000 Sunset Blvd

Howard Hughes, **Vincente Minelli**, and **Judy Garland** all owned this home, but today it gets the most attention for the whimsical statues adorning the front lawn. The sightseeing couple was the first installed, and tricked many passersby into thinking there was really someone looking over the wall!

Turn left at Carolwood, marked by the bubble-gum-pink Spanish-style structure at:

⑰ 10100 Sunset Blvd

This has been owned by singer **Rudy Vallee** and later by **Engelbert Humperdinck,** but its personality was indelibly stamped in the 1960s by **Jayne Mansfield,** who chose the color scheme and built a heart-shaped pool in the backyard.

The street dead-ends at:

⑱ 141 South Carolwood Drive

An English-style estate named "Owlwood" and owned at various times by **Sonny and Cher, Tony Curtis,** and movie mogul **Joseph Schenck,** at whose invitation Curtis's future *Some Like It Hot* costar **Marilyn Monroe** occupied a guest house during 1949.

Return to Sunset Boulevard and make a right, then a left onto Ladera Drive, and left on Monovale. You'll come to:

⑲ 144 Monovale Drive

This was the L.A. home of **Elvis** and **Priscilla Presley,** who purchased the white cottage in 1972 for a mere $335,000.

Follow Monovale as it merges with Carolwood, and proceed to:

⑳ 245 Carolwood Drive

This was the L.A. home of **Burt Reynolds** and **Loni Anderson** during their marriage; it also once belonged to Beatle **George Harrison.**

Down the street is:

㉑ 325 Carolwood Drive

Up the ivy garland–adorned driveway is **Clark Gable's** former abode.

You can't miss:

㉒ 355 Carolwood Drive

This was **Walt Disney's** former home, with its wrought-iron mouse-ear motif on the gate. Disney's widow, Lillian, lived here alone for years, until her death at age 98 (in 1997).

Next you'll see:

㉓ 375 Carolwood Drive

This is the former home to distinguished actor **Gregory Peck,** who was probably less than thrilled by the loud partying at next door (see below).

㉔ 391 Carolwood Drive

This home was owned by rocker **Rod Stewart** and his model wife, **Rachel Hunter.**

Return via Carolwood to Sunset Boulevard and turn right, then turn left onto Charing Cross. Slow down and smile for the sophisticated surveillance system (including cameras, microphones, and guards) at:

㉕ 10236 Charing Cross Road

This ostentatious stone manor has been known since 1971 as the **"Playboy Mansion,"** a party haven later transformed in the politically correct 1990s into the family homestead of Mr. and Mrs. **Hugh Hefner** and their two children. After Hef's divorce in 1999, the wife and kids moved next door, and the Mansion now once again features a bevy of nubile starlets.

Follow Charing Cross to Mapleton Drive, turn left, and proceed to:

㉖ 594 South Mapleton Drive

The community of Holmby Hills was outraged when **Aaron Spelling,** producer of such successful TV shows as *Charlie's Angels; The Love Boat; Beverly Hills, 90210;* and *Melrose Place*—and **Tori's** dad—razed an estate overlooking the prestigious Los Angeles Country Club and erected this oversize, ostentatious monstrosity.

Pass the Spelling residence, turn right on Club View Drive, and right again on Beverly Glen Boulevard. Take Beverly Glen past Sunset Boulevard, straight through the stately entrance to Bel-Air. Turn left at Bellagio Road, then right at Copa de Oro ("cup of gold"). Straight ahead is:

47 363 Copa De Oro Road

This ornate redbrick mansion was for many years home to heartthrob **Tom Jones,** and it was also occupied at one time by fellow Las Vegas headliner the late **Dean Martin.** See if you can catch a glimpse of **Nicolas Cage,** the current owner.

Veer right past the house to the intersection with Bel Air Road, turn right, and then left on St. Cloud Road to Nimes Road. As you approach:

48 700 Nimes Road

The exotic flowers in varying shades of purple and lavender provide the only clues to the identity of the glamorous owner who dwells behind this imposing gate: **Elizabeth Taylor.**

Follow Nimes around and back down to St. Cloud Road, turning left. On the left side is:

49 668 St. Cloud Road

This has been the home of President and Mrs. **Ronald Reagan** since his departure from the White House. **Nancy** had the original house number, 666, changed to a less demonic one. If the former president is in residence, the gatehouse will be staffed with Secret Service agents.

Continue past Nimes and turn left on St. Pierre. On the right-hand side is:

50 345 St. Pierre Road

Errol Flynn's alleged statutory rape—the scandal out of which the expression "in like Flynn" was born—took place at this peach-colored house with green-patina iron fence work.

Across the street, diagonally to the left is:

51 414 St. Pierre Road

This home which sits abandoned, its carved stone entryway and Mediterranean-tiled patio visible through the overgrowth. As the street curves around the corner, peek into the neglected backyard at the spectacular swimming pool built for original owner **Johnny Weissmuller.** The athletic swimmer and on-screen Tarzan created a junglelike setting for his daily laps when he and this house were in their prime.

Continuing to the end of the block, you'll find yourself back at Beverly Glen Boulevard. A right turn will lead you to Sunset Boulevard.

WINDING DOWN
If all this sightseeing has left your stomach grumbling, stay in the neighborhood and visit one of these local watering holes: Recently reopened after an extensive restoration, the **Beverly Hills Hotel** (no. 8, above) has been the unofficial "clubhouse" of the swank Hollywood crowd since it opened in 1912. Katharine Hepburn played tennis here daily, Marlene Dietrich shocked the staid Polo Lounge by strolling in wearing trousers, and Marilyn Monroe and Yves Montand emerged from their 1959 tryst in one of the secluded bungalows to smooch over a milkshake in the hotel's **Fountain Coffee Shop** (© 310/276-2251). Stopping in yourself for a sandwich and fountain treat at the shop's counter provides a perfect excuse to stroll these legendary grounds.

Or try **Nate & Al** delicatessen, at 414 North Beverly Dr. (© 310/274-0101), a regular Beverly Hills fixture for ages. Despite its location among the boutiques of the "Golden Triangle," Nate & Al remains comfortably homey and unchanged, from the sweet condescension of the motherly waitresses to the best pastrami, pickles, and chopped liver in town. And you won't believe the famous faces lining the brown Naugahyde booths—many have had house accounts for decades (p. 138).

9 Beaches

Los Angeles County's 72-mile (116km) coastline sports more than 30 miles (48km) of beaches, most of which are operated by the **Department of Beaches & Harbors,** 13837 Fiji Way, Marina del Rey (© **310/305-9503**).

Los Angeles Beaches & Coastal Attractions

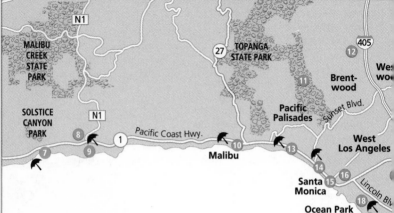

BEACHES

El Pescador, La Piedra,
  & El Matador Beaches **3**
Hermosa City Beach **22**
Leo Carrillo Beach **2**
Malibu Lagoon State Beach **7**
Manhattan State Beach **21**
North County Line Beach **1**
Paradise Cove **6**
Point Dume Beach **5**
Redondo State Beach **23**
Santa Monica State Beach **14**
Surfrider Beach **9**
Topanga State Beach **10**
Venice Beach **19**
Will Rogers State Beach **13**
Zuma Beach County Park **4**

SIGHTS & ATTRACTIONS

Aquarium of the Pacific **24**
Bergamot Arts Station **16**
Chiat/Day Headquarters **18**
Getty Center **12**
Long Beach Museum of Art **26**
Museum of Flying **16**
Pepperdine University **8**
Queen Mary **24**
Venice Ocean Front Walk **20**
Will Rogers State Historic Park **11**
Santa Monica Pier **15**

Beach

0	3 mi
0	3 km

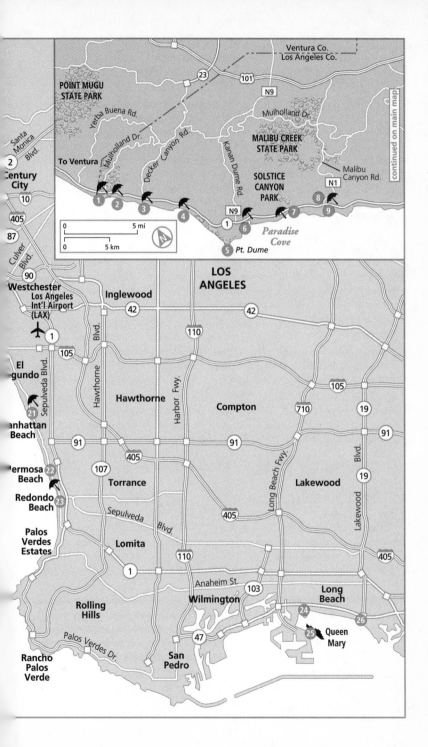

POINT MUGU
STATE PARK

Ventura Co.
Los Angeles Co.

23

101

N9

Mulholland Dr.

MALIBU CREEK
STATE PARK

Yerba Buena Rd.

Mulholland Dr.

Decker Canyon Rd.

Kanan Dume Rd.

SOLSTICE
CANYON
PARK

Malibu
Canyon Rd.

To Ventura

N1

①

②

③

④

N9

①

⑥

⑧

⑦

⑨

0   5 mi

0   5 km

⑤ Pt. Dume

*Paradise
Cove*

continued on main map

Santa
Monica
Blvd.

2

Century
City

10

405

87

Culver
Blvd.

90

Westchester

Los Angeles
Int'l Airport
(LAX)

1

El
Segundo

105

Sepulveda Blvd.

21

Manhattan
Beach

91

107

Hermosa
Beach

22

Redondo
Beach

23

Palos
Verdes
Estates

Sepulveda   Blvd.

1

Rolling
Hills

Palos Verdes Dr.

Rancho
Palos
Verde

LOS
ANGELES

Inglewood

42

110

Hawthorne

Blvd.

Hawthorne

Harbor Fwy.

42

Compton

110

91

405

Torrance

Lomita

Anaheim St.

103

47

San
Pedro

Wilmington

105

710

Long Beach Fwy.

Lakewood

405

Lakewood   Blvd.

19

19

91

405

Long
Beach

24

25   Queen
Mary

26

County-run beaches usually charge for parking ($4–$8). Alcohol, bonfires, and pets are prohibited. For recorded **surf conditions** (and coastal weather forecast), call ℂ **310/457-9701.** The following are the county's best beaches, listed from north to south.

EL PESCADOR, LA PIEDRA & EL MATADOR BEACHES *Finds*   These rugged and isolated beaches front a 2-mile (3km) stretch of the Pacific Coast Highway (Calif. 1) between Broad Beach and Decker Canyon roads, a 10-minute drive from the Malibu Pier. Picturesque coves with unusual rock formations are great for sunbathing and picnicking, but swim with caution as there are no lifeguards. The beaches can be difficult to find; only small signs on the highway mark them. There are a limited number of parking spots atop the bluffs. Descend to the beach via stairs that cling to the cliffs.

ZUMA BEACH COUNTY PARK ⚲   Jam-packed on warm weekends, L.A. County's largest beach park is located off the Pacific Coast Highway (Calif. 1), a mile past Kanan Dume Road. While it can't claim to be the loveliest beach in the Southland, Zuma has the most comprehensive facilities: plenty of restrooms, lifeguards, playgrounds, volleyball courts, and snack bars. The southern stretch, toward Point Dume, is Westward Beach, separated from the noisy highway by sandstone cliffs. A trail leads over the point's headlands to Pirate's Cove, once a popular nude beach.

PARADISE COVE   This private beach in the 28000 block of the Pacific Coast Highway (Calif. 1) charges $15 to park and $5 per person if you walk in. Changing rooms and showers are included in the price. The beach is often full by noon on weekends.

MALIBU LAGOON STATE BEACH ⚲⚲   Not just a pretty white-sand beach but an estuary and wetlands area as well, Malibu Lagoon is the historic home of the Chumash Indians. The entrance is on the Pacific Coast Highway (Calif. 1) south of Cross Creek Road, and there's a small admission charge. Marine life and shorebirds teem where the creek empties into the sea, and the waves are always mild. The historic **Adamson House** is here, a showplace of Malibu tile now operating as a museum.

SURFRIDER BEACH   Without a doubt, L.A.'s best waves roll ashore here. One of the city's most popular surfing spots, this beach is located between the Malibu Pier and the lagoon. In surf lingo, few "locals-only" wave wars are ever fought here—surfing is not as territorial here as it can be in other areas, where out-of-towners can be made to feel unwelcome. Surfrider is surrounded by all of Malibu's hustle and bustle; don't come here for peace and quiet and the surf is always crowded.

TOPANGA STATE BEACH   Highway noise prevents solitude at this short, narrow strip of sand located where Topanga Canyon Boulevard emerges from the mountains. Why go? Ask the surfers who wait in line to catch Topanga's excellent right point breaks. There are rest rooms and lifeguard services here, and across the street you'll find one of the best fresh fish restaurants around.

WILL ROGERS STATE BEACH   Three miles (5km) along the Pacific Coast Highway (Calif. 1), between Sunset Boulevard and the Santa Monica border, are named for the American humorist whose ranch-turned-state-historic-park (see "L.A. Parks, Gardens, Views & Zoos," earlier in this chapter) is nestled above the palisades that provide the backdrop for this popular beach. A pay parking lot extends the entire length of Will Rogers, and facilities include restrooms, lifeguards, and a snack hut in season. While the surfing is not the best, the waves are friendly for swimmers and there are always competitive volleyball games to be found.

SANTA MONICA STATE BEACH *Kids*   The beaches on either side of the Santa Monica Pier (see "L.A.'s Top Attractions," earlier in this chapter) are popular for their white sands and accessibility. There are big parking lots, eateries, and lots of well-maintained restrooms. A paved beach path runs along here, allowing you to walk, bike, or skate to Venice and points south. Colorado Boulevard leads to the pier; turn north on the Pacific Coast Highway (Calif. 1) below the coastline's bluffs, or south along Ocean Avenue; you can find parking in both directions.

VENICE BEACH *★★*   Moving south from the city of Santa Monica, the paved pedestrian Promenade becomes Ocean Front Walk and gets progressively weirder until it reaches an apex at Washington Boulevard and the Venice fishing pier. Although there are people who swim and sunbathe, Venice Beach's character is defined by the sea of humanity on the Ocean Front Walk, plus the bevy of boardwalk vendors and old-fashioned pedestrian streets a block away (see "L.A.'s Top Attractions," earlier in this chapter). Park on the side streets or in the plentiful lots west of Pacific Avenue.

MANHATTAN STATE BEACH   The Beach Boys used to hang out at this wide, friendly beach backed by beautiful ocean view homes. Plenty of parking on 36 blocks of side streets (between Rosecrans Ave. and the Hermosa Beach border) draws weekend crowds from the L.A. area. Manhattan has some of the best surfing around, restrooms, lifeguards, and volleyball courts. Manhattan Beach Boulevard leads west to the fishing pier and adjacent seafood restaurants.

HERMOSA CITY BEACH *★*   A very, very wide, white-sand beach with tons to recommend it, Hermosa extends to either side of the pier and includes "The Strand," a pedestrian lane that runs its entire length. Main access is at the foot of Pier Avenue, which is lined with interesting shops. There is plenty of street parking, as well as restrooms, lifeguards, volleyball courts, a fishing pier, playgrounds, and good surfing.

REDONDO STATE BEACH   Popular with surfers, bicyclists, and joggers, Redondo's white sand and ice-plant-carpeted dunes are just south of tiny King Harbor, along "The Esplanade" (South Esplanade Dr.). Get there via the Pacific Coast Highway (Calif. 1) or Torrance Boulevard. Facilities include restrooms, lifeguards, and volleyball courts.

10 Golf, Hiking & Other Fun in the Warm California Sun

Bisected by the Santa Monica Mountains and fronted by long stretches of beach, Los Angeles is one of the best cities in the world for nature and sports lovers. Where else can you hike in the mountains, in-line skate along the beach, swim in the ocean, enjoy a gourmet meal, and then take in a basketball or ice hockey or baseball game—all in the same day?

BICYCLING   Los Angeles is great for biking. If you're into distance pedaling, you can do no better than the flat 22-mile (35km) paved **Ocean Front Walk** that runs along the sand from Pacific Palisades in the north to Torrance in the south. The path attracts all levels of riders and gets pretty busy on weekends. For information on this and other city bike routes, phone the **Los Angeles Dept. of Transportation** (© 213/485-9957).

The best place to mountain bike is along the trails of **Malibu Creek State Park** (✆ **818/880-0367**), in the Santa Monica Mountains between Malibu and the San Fernando Valley in Calabasas. Fifteen miles (24km) of trails rise to a maximum of 3,000 feet and are appropriate for intermediate to advanced bikers. Pick up a trail map at the park entrance, 4 miles (6km) south of U.S. 101 off Las Virgenes Road, just north of Mulholland Highway. Park admission is $5 per car.

Spokes 'N Stuff Bike Rental has two locations: 4175 Admiralty Way, Marina del Rey (✆ **310/306-3332**), and 1715 Oceanfront Walk, behind Loews Hotel, Santa Monica (✆ **310/458-6700**). They rent 10-speed cruisers for $7 per hour and $16 per day; 15-speed mountain bikes rent for $8 per hour and $20 per day.

FISHING   Del Rey Sport Fishing, 13759 Fiji Way (✆ **310/822-3625;** www. marinadelreysportfishing.com), has four deep-sea boats departing daily on half- and full-day ocean fishing trips. Of course, it depends on what's running when you're out, but bass, barracuda, halibut, and yellowtail are the most common catches on these party boats. Excursions cost from $22 to $30; tackle rental is available. Phone for reservations.

No permit is required to cast from shore or drop a line from a pier. Local anglers will hate me for giving away their secret spot, but the **best saltwater fishing spot** in all of L.A. is at the foot of Torrance Boulevard in Redondo Beach.

GOLF   The greater Los Angeles area has more than 100 golf courses, which vary in quality from abysmal to superb. Most of the city's public courses are administered by the Department of Recreation and Parks, which follows a complicated registration/reservation system for tee times. While visitors cannot reserve start times in advance, you're welcome to play any of the courses by showing up and getting on the call sheet. Expect to wait for the most popular tee times, but try to use your flexible vacationer status to your advantage by avoiding the early morning rush.

Of the city's seven 18-hole and three 9-hole courses, you can't get more central than the **Rancho Park Golf Course,** 10460 W. Pico Blvd. (✆ **310/838-7373**), located smack-dab in the middle of L.A.'s Westside. The par-71 course has lots of tall trees, but not enough to blot out the towering Century City buildings next door. Rancho also has a nine-hole, par-3 course.

For a genuinely woodsy experience, try one of the three courses inside Griffith Park, northeast of Hollywood (see "L.A. Parks, Gardens, Views & Zoos," earlier in this chapter). The courses are extremely well maintained, challenging without being frustrating, and (despite some holes alongside I-5) a great way to leave the city behind. Bucolic pleasures abound, particularly on the nine-hole **Roosevelt,** on Vermont Avenue across from the Greek Theatre; early morning wildlife often includes deer, rabbits, raccoons, and skunks (fore!). **Wilson** and **Harding** are each 18 holes and start from the main clubhouse off Riverside Drive, the park's main entrance.

Greens fees on all city courses are $18 Monday through Friday, and $25 on weekends and holidays; nine-hole courses cost $11 weekdays, $14 on weekends and holidays. For details on other city courses, or to contact the starter directly by phone, call the Department of Recreation and Parks at ✆ **888/527-2757.**

Industry Hills Golf Club, 1 Industry Hills Pkwy. City of Industry (✆ **626/810-4653**), has two 18-hole courses designed by William Bell. Together they encompass eight lakes, 160 bunkers, and many long fairways. The Eisenhower

Course, consistently ranked among *Golf Digest's* top 25 public courses, has extralarge undulating greens and the challenge of thick *Kikuyu* rough. An adjacent driving range is lit for night use. Greens fees are $59 Monday through Thursday and $89 Friday through Sunday, including cart; call in advance for tee times.

HANG GLIDING   Up and down the California coast, it's not uncommon to see people poised on the crests of hills, hanging from enormous colorful kites. You can, too. **Windsports International,** 16145 Victory Blvd., Van Nuys (② **818/988-0111;** www.windsports.com), offers instruction and rentals for both novices and experts. A 1-day lesson in a solo hang glider on a bunny hill costs $99. If it's more of a thrill you're looking for, choose the $149, 3,000-foot-high tandem flight, where you fly with an instructor. Beginner lessons are waterside at Dockweiler State Beach Training Flight Park (near LAX), while tandem flights take off from a San Fernando Valley hilltop. Phone for reservations.

HIKING   The **Santa Monica Mountains,** a small range that runs only 50 miles (81km) from Griffith Park to Point Mugu, on the coast north of Malibu, makes Los Angeles a great place for hiking. The mountains, which peak at 3,111 feet, are part of the Santa Monica Mountains National Recreation Area, a contiguous conglomeration of 350 public parks and 65,000 acres. Many animals live in this area, including deer, coyote, rabbit, skunk, rattlesnake, fox, hawk, and quail. The hills are also home to almost 1,000 drought-resistant plant species, including live oak and coastal sage.

Hiking is best after spring rains, when the hills are green, flowers are in bloom, and the air is clear. Summers can be very hot; hikers should always carry fresh water. Beware of poison oak, a hearty shrub that's common on the west coast. Usually found among oak trees, poison oak has leaves in groups of three, with waxy surfaces and prominent veins. If you come into contact with this itch-producing plant, bathe yourself in calamine lotion, or the ocean.

For trail maps and more information, contact the **National Park Service** (② **818/597-1036**), or stop by its visitor center at 30401 Agoura Rd., Suite 100, in Agoura Hills. It's open Monday through Friday from 8am to 5pm, and Saturday and Sunday from 9am to 5pm. Some areas are administered by the **California Department of Parks** (② **800/275-8777**); the offices are located in Calabasas at 1925 Las Virgenes Rd.

Santa Ynez Canyon, in Pacific Palisades, is a long and difficult climb that rises steadily for about 3 miles (5km). At the top, hikers are rewarded with fantastic views over the Pacific. At the top is **Trippet Ranch,** a public facility providing water, restrooms, and picnic tables. From Santa Monica, take Pacific Coast Highway (Calif. 1) north. Turn right onto Sunset Boulevard, then left onto Palisades Drive. Then continue for 2½ miles (4km), turn left onto Veranda de la Montura, and park at the cul-de-sac at the end of the street, where you can find the trailhead.

Temescal Canyon, in Pacific Palisades, is far easier than the Santa Ynez trail and, far more popular, especially among locals. This is one of the quickest routes into the wilderness. Hikes here are anywhere from 1 to 5 miles (1.5–8km). From Santa Monica, take Pacific Coast Highway (Calif. 1) north; turn right onto Temescal Canyon Road, and follow it to the end. Sign in with the gatekeeper, who can also answer your questions.

Will Rogers State Historic Park, Pacific Palisades, is also a terrific place for hiking. An intermediate-level hike from the park's entrance ends at Inspiration

Point, a plateau from which you can see a good portion of L.A.'s Westside. See "Parks," earlier in this chapter, for complete information.

HORSEBACK RIDING   The **Griffith Park Livery Stable,** 480 Riverside Dr. (in the Los Angeles Equestrian Center), Burbank (© 818/840-8401), rents horses by the hour for Western or English riding through Griffith Park's hills. There's a 200-pound weight limit, and children have to be at least 6 and at least 4 feet tall. Horse rental costs $20 per hour; maximum rental is 2 hours. You can also arrange for private 1-hour lessons by calling © 818/569-3666. The stables are open daily from 8am to 5pm, and cash is required for payment.

SEA KAYAKING   Sea kayaking is all the rage in Southern California; if you've ever tried it, you know why. Unlike river kayaks, in which your legs are actually inside the boat's hull, paddlers sit on top of sea kayaks, which can be maneuvered more easily than canoes.

  Southwind Kayak Center (© 800/768-8494 or 949/261-0200; www. southwindkayaks.com) rents sea kayaks for use in the bay or open ocean at rates of $12 to $16 per hour; instructional classes are available on weekends only. The center also conducts bird-watching kayak expeditions into Upper Newport Bay Ecological Reserve at rates of $50 to $65.

SKATING   The 22-mile-long (35km) Ocean Front Walk that runs from Pacific Palisades to Torrance is one of the premier skating spots in the country. In-line skating is especially popular, but conventional skates are often seen here, too. Skating is allowed just about everywhere bicycling is, but be advised that cyclists have the right of way. **Spokes N' Stuff,** 4175 Admiralty Way, Marina del Rey (© 310/306-3332), is just one of many places to rent wheels near the Venice portion of Ocean Front Walk. In the South Bay, in-line skate rentals are available 1 block from the Strand at **Hermosa Cyclery,** 20 13th St. (© 310/374-7816). Skates cost around $6 per hour ($18 max); kneepads and wrist guards come with every rental.

SURFING   Surfing was invented by the Polynesians; Captain Cook made note of it in Oahu in 1778. George Freeth (1883–1918), who first surfed Redondo Beach in 1907, is widely credited with introducing the sport to California. But surfing didn't catch on until the 1950s, when Cal Tech graduate Bob Simmons invented a more maneuverable lightweight fiberglass board. The Beach Boys and other surf-music groups popularized Southern California in the minds of beach-babes and -dudes everywhere, and the rest, as they say, is history. You'll also find some great surf an hour or two down the coast in the Huntington Beach and Newport areas of Orange County.

  If you're a first-timer eager to learn the sport, contact **Pure Surfing Experience** (© 310/546-4451; www.campsurf.com) in Manhattan Beach. This highly respected school features a team of experienced instructors and will supply all necessary equipment. Single lessons are $80, but subsequent follow-ups are deeply discounted. Call for reservations (also available online).

  Boards are available for rent at shops near all top surfing beaches in the L.A. area. **Zuma Jay Surfboards,** 22775 Pacific Coast Hwy., Malibu (© 310/456-8044), is about a quarter mile south of Malibu Pier. Rentals are $20 per day, plus $8 for wet suits in winter.

TENNIS   While soft-surface courts are more popular on the East Coast, hard surfaces are most common in California. If your hotel doesn't have a court and can't suggest any courts nearby, try the well-maintained, well-lit **Griffith Park**

Tennis Courts, on Commonwealth Road, just east of Vermont Avenue (© 323/ 662-7772). Or call the **City of Los Angeles Department of Recreation and Parks** (© 888/527-2757) to make a reservation at a municipal court near you.

WINDSURFING   Invented and patented by Hoyle Schweitzer of Torrance in 1968, windsurfing, or sail-boarding, is a fun sport that's much more difficult than it looks. The **Long Beach Windsurfing Center,** 3850 E. Ocean Ave., Long Beach (© 562/433-1014), offers lesson and rentals in Alamitos Bay. Twenty-five dollars will get you the use of a board for 4 hours; an $115 learner's package includes instruction from 8am to noon, use of board and wet suit, and a certificate for a free half-day rental once you've gotten the hang of it. Kayak and in-line skate rentals and instruction are also available.

11 Spectator Sports

BASEBALL   The **Los Angeles Dodgers** (© 323/224-1-HIT) play at Dodger Stadium, 1000 Elysian Park, near Sunset Boulevard. The team's slick, interactive website (www.dodgers.mlb.com) offers everything from game schedules to souvenir merchandise online. The Disney-owned **California Angels** (© 888/796-HALO;** www.angels.mlb.com) play at Anaheim Stadium, at 2000 S. State College Blvd. (near Katella Ave.), in Anaheim.

BASKETBALL   Los Angeles has two NBA franchises, the **L.A. Lakers** (www. nba.com/lakers), who won their third consecutive NBA Championship in 2002, and the **L.A. Clippers** (www.nba.com/clippers). Both teams play in **STAPLES Center** in downtown L.A., 1111 S. Figueroa St. (© **213/742-7155;** www. staplescenter.com). Celebrity fans like Jack Nicholson and Dyan Cannon have the best tickets, but this 20,000-seater should have room for you too. (For more information about the L.A. Lakers, see "L.A.'s Top Attractions," earlier in this chapter.)

The **L.A. Sparks** (© **310/330-2434;** www.wnba.com/sparks), who at presstime were making a run at back-to-back WNBA titles, play at the STAPLES Center May through August. The Sparks are especially proud of star center, 2001 MVP and Olympic gold-medalist Lisa Leslie.

FOOTBALL   Los Angeles suffers from an absence of major-league football, but is blessed with two popular college teams and an Arena League team. The college season runs September through November; if you're interested in checking out a game, contact **UCLA Bruins Football** (© **310/825-2101;** www. uclabruins.fansonly.com) or **USC Trojan Football** (© **213/740-2311;** www. usctrojans.com). Described as "fun, fast and furious," many fans find Arena League football to be action-packed and exciting, and it sure costs a lot less than its NFL counterpart. The local team is the **L.A. Avengers** (© **310/788-7744;** www.laavengers.com); games run from April through July and are played downtown at the STAPLES Center (see "Basketball," above).

HORSE RACING   The scenic **Hollywood Park Racetrack,** 1050 S. Prairie Ave., in Inglewood (© **310/419-1500;** www.hollywoodpark.com), with its lakes and flowers, features thoroughbred racing from early April to July, as well as in November and December. The $1 million Hollywood Gold Cup is also run here. Well-placed monitors project views of the backstretch as well as stop-action replays of photo finishes. Races are usually held Wednesday through Sunday. Post times are 1pm in summer (7pm on Fri), and 12:30pm weekends and holidays. General admission is $7; admission to the clubhouse is $10.

One of the most beautiful tracks in the country, **Santa Anita Racetrack,** 285 W. Huntington Dr., Arcadia (© **626/574-RACE;** www.santaanita.com), offers racing from October to mid-November and December to late April. The track was featured in the Marx Brothers' film *A Day at the Races* and in the 1954 version of *A Star Is Born.* On weekdays during the season, the public is invited to watch morning workouts from 7:30 to 9:30am. Post time is 12:30 or 1pm. Admission is $4.

ICE HOCKEY   The NHL's **L.A. Kings** (www.lakings.com) also call the STAPLES Center home (see above) and down the road in Orange County, the **Mighty Ducks** (www.mightyducks.com) play at the Arrowhead Pond in Anaheim (© **714/704-2500;** www.arrowheadpond.com).

8

The Disneyland Resort & Knott's Berry Farm

The sleepy Orange County town of Anaheim grew up around Disneyland, the West's most famous theme park. Now, even beyond the park that bills itself as "The Happiest Place on Earth," the city and its neighboring communities are kid central. Otherwise unspectacular, sprawling suburbs have become a playground of family hotels and restaurants, and unabashedly tourist-oriented attractions. Among the nearby draws is Knott's Berry Farm, another family oriented theme park, in nearby Buena Park. At the other end of the scale are the Richard Nixon Library and Birthplace, a compelling presidential library and museum, just 7 miles (11km) northeast of Disneyland in Yorba Linda (see review later in this chapter).

1 The Disneyland Resort

33 miles (53km) S of Los Angeles

ESSENTIALS

GETTING THERE   From Los Angeles, take I-5 south till you see signs for Disneyland; dedicated offramps from both directions lead to into the attraction's parking lots and surrounding streets. The drive from downtown L.A. takes approximately 45 minutes. If Anaheim is your first—or only—destination, and you want to avoid L.A. altogether, try flying directly into **John Wayne Airport** in Santa Ana (© 949/252-5200; www.ocair.com), Orange County's largest airport. It's about 15 miles (24km) from Disneyland. Check to see if your hotel has a free shuttle to and from either airport (some will pick you up at LAX, 30 min. away), or call one of the following commercial shuttle services (fares are generally $10 one way from John Wayne): **L.A. Xpress** (© 800/I-ARRIVE), **Prime Time** (© 800/262-7433), or **SuperShuttle** (© 714/517-6600). Car-rental agencies located at the John Wayne Airport include **Budget** (© 800/221-1203) and **Hertz** (© 800/654-3131).

VISITOR INFORMATION   The **Anaheim/Orange County Visitor and Convention Bureau,** 800 W. Katella Ave. (© 714/765-8888; www.anaheimoc. org), can fill you in on area activities and shopping shuttles. It's across the street from Disneyland inside the Convention Center, next to the dramatic cantilevered arena. It's open Monday through Friday from 8:30am to 5:30pm. The **Buena Park Convention and Visitors Office,** 6280 Manchester Blvd., Suite 103 (© 800/541-3953 or 714/562-3560; www.buenapark.com/cvo), provides specialized information on the area, including Knott's Berry Farm.

THE DISNEYLAND RESORT (Kids) ✯✯✯   It's not called "The Happiest Place on Earth" for nothing! Disney sister parks have sprung up in Florida,

Tokyo, and even France, but there's still nothing to compare with the original. Smaller than Walt Disney World, Disneyland has always capitalized on being the original—and the world's first family oriented mega-theme park. Nostalgia is a big part of the appeal, and despite many advancements, changes, and expansions over the years, Disneyland remains true to the original vision of founder Walt Disney.

In 2001, Disney unveiled a brand-new theme park (**Disney's California Adventure**), a new shopping/dining/entertainment district (**Downtown Disney**), and a third on-site hotel (**Disney's Grand Californian Hotel**). They also revamped their own name to "The Disneyland Resort," reflecting a greatly expanded array of entertainment options. What does this all mean for you? Well, first of all, you might want to think seriously about budgeting more time (and yes, more money) for your Disney visit—you'll need at least 3 full days to see it all. If you have limited time, plan carefully so you don't skip what's important to you; in the pages ahead we describe what to expect throughout the new resort. And, most of all, get ready to have fun—there's lots of great new stuff to check out!

ADMISSION, HOURS & INFORMATION   Admission to *either* Disneyland or Disney's California Adventure, including unlimited rides and all festivities and entertainment, is $43 for adults and children over 11, $41 for seniors 60 and over, $33 for children 3 to 11, and free for children under 3. Parking is $7. Three- and 4-day passports are available; you can see both parks this way, but you can only enter one park *each* day. Prices for adults/children are $111/$87 (3-day) and $137/$107 (4-day). In addition, some area accommodations offer lodging packages that include admission for 1 or more days.

Disneyland and Disney's California Adventure are open every day of the year, but operating hours vary, so we recommend that you call for information that applies to the specific day(s) of your visit (② **714/781-7290**). The same information, including ride closures and show schedules, can also be found online at **www.disneyland.com**. Generally speaking, the parks are open from 9 or 10am to 6 or 7pm on weekdays, fall to spring; and from 8 or 9am to midnight or 1am on weekends, holidays, and during winter, spring, or summer vacation periods.

WHEN TO GO   Disneyland is busiest from mid-June to mid-September and on weekends and school holidays year-round. Peak hours are from noon to 5pm; visit the most popular rides before and after these hours, and you'll cut your waiting times substantially. If you plan to arrive during a busy time, buy your tickets in advance and get a jump on the crowds at the ticket counters. Advance tickets may be purchased through Disneyland's website (www.disneyland.com), at Disney stores in the United States, or by calling the ticket mail-order line (② **714/781-4043**).

Attendance falls dramatically during the winter, so the park offers discounted (about 25% off) admission to Southern California residents, who may buy up to five tickets per ZIP code verification. If you'll be visiting the park with someone who lives here, be sure to take advantage of this "Resident Salutes" promotion.

Once in the park, many visitors tackle Disneyland (or California Adventure) systematically, beginning at the entrance and working their way clockwise around the park. My advice: Arrive early and run to the most popular rides—the Indiana Jones Adventure, Star Tours, Space Mountain, Big Thunder Mountain Railroad, Splash Mountain, the Haunted Mansion, and Pirates of the Caribbean in Disneyland; and Soarin' Over California, California Screamin', Grizzly River Run, and It's Tough to be a Bug in California Adventure. Waits for

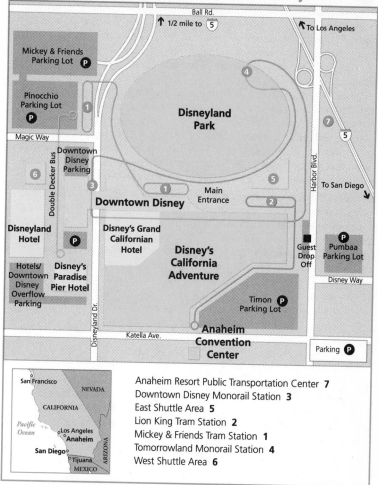

these can last an hour or more in the middle of the day. This time-honored plan of attack may eventually become obsolete, thanks to the new **FastPass** system. Here's how it works: Say you want to ride Space Mountain, but the line is long—*so* long the wait sign indicates a 75-minute standstill! Now you can head to the Automated FastPass ticket dispensers, which allow you to swipe the magnetic strip of your Disneyland entrance ticket, get a FastPass for later that day, and return to use the reduced-wait FastPass entrance (to the envy of everyone in the slowpoke line). At press time, about a dozen Disneyland rides were equipped with FastPass; several more will be added by the time you read this. The hottest features at California Adventure had FastPass built in from the start; for a complete list for each park, check your official map/guide when you enter.

TOURING DISNEYLAND

Disneyland is divided into several theme "lands," each of which has a number of rides and attractions that are, more or less, related to that land's theme.

MAIN STREET U.S.A. At the park's entrance, Main Street U.S.A. is a cinematic version of turn-of-the-20th-century small-town America. The whitewashed Rockwellian fantasy is lined with gift shops, candy stores, a soda fountain, and a silent theater that continuously runs early Mickey Mouse films. Here you can find the practical things you might need, such as stroller rentals and storage lockers.

Because there are no rides, it's best to tour Main Street during the middle of the afternoon, when lines for rides are longest, and in the evening, when you can rest your feet in the theater that features "Great Moments with Mr. Lincoln," a patriotic (and audio-animatronic) look at America's 16th president delivering the Gettysburg Address and other Civil War–related themes. There's always something happening on Main Street; stop in at the information booth to the left of the main entrance for a schedule of the day's events.

ADVENTURELAND Inspired by the most exotic regions of Asia, Africa, India, and the South Pacific, Adventureland is home to several popular rides. Here's where you can cavort inside **Tarzan's Treehouse,** a climb-around attraction based on the animated film. Its African-themed neighbor is the **Jungle Cruise,** where passengers board a large authentic-looking Mississippi River paddleboat and float along an Amazon-like river; a spear's throw away is the **Enchanted Tiki Room,** one of the most sedate attractions in Adventureland. Inside, you can sit down and watch a 20-minute musical comedy featuring electronically animated tropical birds, flowers, and "tiki gods."

Value **The Art of the (Package) Deal**

If you intend to spend 2 or more nights in Disney territory, it pays to investigate the bevy of packaged vacation options. Start by contacting your hotel (even those in Los Angeles or San Diego), to see whether they have Disneyland admission packages. Many vacation packagers include Disneyland and/or California Adventure (and other attractions) with their inclusive packages; see p. 34 in chapter 2 for contact information.

Put a call in to the official Disney agency, **Walt Disney Travel Co.** (© **877/700-DISNEY** or 714/520-5050). You can request a glossy catalog by mail, or log onto www.disneyland.com and click on "Book Your Vacation" to peruse package details, take a virtual tour of participating hotel properties, and get online price quotes for customized, date-specific packages. Their packages are value-packed time-savers with abundant flexibility. Hotel choices range from the official Disney hotels to one of 35 "neighbor hotels" in every price range (economy to superior) and category (from motel to all-suite); a wide range of available extras includes admission to other Southern California attractions and tours (like Universal Studios, or a Tijuana shopping spree), and behind-the-scenes Disneyland tours, all in limitless combinations.

Every time we check, rates are highly competitive, considering each package includes multiday admission, early park entry, free parking (at the Disney hotels), plus keepsake souvenirs, and Southern California coupon books.

The **Indiana Jones Adventure** is Adventureland's star ride. Based on the Steven Spielberg films, this ride takes adventurers into the Temple of the Forbidden Eye, in joltingly realistic all-terrain vehicles. Riders follow Indy and experience the perils of bubbling lava pits, whizzing arrows, fire-breathing serpents, collapsing bridges, and the familiar cinematic tumbling boulder (an effect that's very realistic in the front seats!).

NEW ORLEANS SQUARE   A large, grassy green dotted with gas lamps, New Orleans Square is home to the **Haunted Mansion,** the most high-tech ghost house we've ever seen; the clever events inside are as funny as they are scary.

Even more fanciful is **Pirates of the Caribbean,** one of Disneyland's most popular rides. Visitors float on boats through mock underground caves, entering an enchanting world of swashbuckling, rum-running, and buried treasure. Even in the middle of the afternoon you can dine by the cool moonlight and to the sound of crickets in the **Blue Bayou** restaurant, situated in the middle of the ride itself.

CRITTER COUNTRY   An ode to the backwoods, Critter Country is a sort of Frontierland without those pesky settlers. Older kids and grown-ups head straight for **Splash Mountain,** one of the largest water flume rides in the world. Loosely based on the Disney movie *Song of the South,* the ride is lined with about 100 characters that won't stop singing "Zip-A-Dee-Doo-Dah." Be prepared to get wet, especially if someone sizable is in the front seat of your log-shaped boat.

FRONTIERLAND   Inspired by 19th-century America, Frontierland features a raft to **Tom Sawyer's Island,** a do-it-yourself play area with balancing rocks, caves, and a rope bridge. You'll also find the **Big Thunder Mountain Railroad,** a runaway roller coaster that races through a deserted 1870s gold mine. Children will enjoy the petting zoo and there's an Abe Lincoln–style log cabin; both are great for exploring with the little ones.

On Saturdays, Sundays, and holidays, and during vacation periods, head to Frontierland's **Rivers of America** after dark to see the FANTASMIC! show. It mixes magic, music, live performers, and sensational special effects. Just as he did in *The Sorcerer's Apprentice,* Mickey Mouse appears and uses his magical powers to create giant water fountains, enormous flowers, and fantasy creatures. There's plenty of pyrotechnics, lasers, and fog, as well as a 45-foot-tall dragon that breathes fire and sets the water of the Rivers of America aflame.

MICKEY'S TOONTOWN   This is a colorful, whimsical world inspired by the "Roger Rabbit" films—a wacky, gag-filled land populated by 'toons. There are several rides, including **Roger Rabbit's CarToonSpin,** but they take a back seat to Toontown itself—a smile-inducing world without a straight line or right angle in sight.

FANTASYLAND   With a storybook theme, this is the catchall "land" for stuff that doesn't quite fit anywhere else. Most of the rides are geared to the under-6 set, including the **King Arthur Carousel, Dumbo the Flying Elephant ride,** and the **Casey Jr. Circus Train.** Some, like **Mr. Toad's Wild Ride** and **Peter Pan's Flight,** appeal to grownups as well. You'll also find **Alice in Wonderland, Snow White's Scary Adventures, Pinocchio's Daring Journey,** and more.

The most lauded attraction is **"it's a small world,"** a slow-moving indoor river ride through a saccharine nightmare of all the world's children singing the song everybody loves to hate. For a different kind of thrill, try the **Matterhorn Bobsleds,** a zippy roller coaster through chilled caverns and drifting fog banks. It's one of the park's most popular rides.

TOMORROWLAND   Conceived as an optimistic look at the future, Tomorrowland employs an angular, metallic look popularized by futurists like Jules
Verne. Long-time Tomorrowland favorites include **Space Mountain** (a pitch-
black indoor roller coaster that assaults your equilibrium and ears), and **Star
Tours,** the original Disney–George Lucas joint venture. It's a 40-passenger Star-
Speeder that encounters a space-load of misadventures on the way to the Moon
of Endor, achieved with wired seats and video effects—not for the queasy.

DISNEY'S CALIFORNIA ADVENTURE ★★

With a grand entrance designed to resemble one of those "Wish you were here"
scenic postcards, California Adventure starts out with a bang. Beneath a scale
model of the Golden Gate Bridge (watch carefully, the monorail passes over-
head), handmade tiles of across-the-state scenes glimmer on either side. Just
inside, an enormous gold titanium "sun" shines all day, illuminated by computerized heliostats that follow the real sun's path. From this point, visitors can head
into three distinct themed areas, each containing rides, interactive attractions,
live-action shows, and plenty of dining, snacking, and shopping opportunities.

THE GOLDEN STATE   This multidimensional area represents California's
history, heritage, and physical attributes. Sound boring? Actually, the park's
splashiest attractions are here. "Condor Flats" is a tribute to daring aviators;
inside a weathered corrugated test-pilots' hangar is **Soarin' Over California,** the
ride that immediately rose to the top on everyone's "ride first" list (it's equipped
with FastPass and we highly recommend using it). It uses cool cutting-edge
technology to combine suspended seats with a spectacular IMAX-style sur-
round-movie—so riders literally "soar" over California's scenic wonders.

Nearby, California Adventure's iconic "Grizzly Peak" towers over the **Grizzly
River Run,** a splashy gold-country ride through caverns, mine shafts, and water
slides; it culminates with a wet plunge into a spouting geyser. Kids can cavort
nearby on the **Redwood Creek Challenge Trail,** a forest playground with
smoke-jumper cable slides, net climbing, and swaying bridges.

Pacific Wharf was inspired by Monterey's Cannery Row, and features mouth-
watering demonstration attractions by **Boudin Sourdough Bakery, Mission
Tortillas,** and **Lucky Fortune Cookies.** If you get hungry, each has a food
counter where you can enjoy soup-in-a-sourdough-bowl; tacos, burritos, and
enchiladas; and teriyaki bowls, egg rolls, and wonton soup.

Straight from the imagination of Disney CEO Michael Eisner comes the
"Bountiful Farm," constructed to pay tribute to California's rich agriculture.
The Robert Mondavi **Golden Vine Winery** boasts a demonstration vineyard,
Mission-style "aging room" (with a presentation on the art of winemaking),
wine bars, and the park's most upscale eatery, **Vineyard Room** (see "Where to
Dine," later in this chapter). Next to a demonstration produce garden lies
another California Adventure "E-ticket," the interactive film **"It's Tough To Be
A Bug."** Using next-generation 3-D technology, *A Bug's Life* characters Flik and
Hopper lead the audience on an underground romp with bees, termites,
grasshoppers, stink bugs, spiders, and a few surprises that keep everyone hopping, ducking, and laughing along (we could see how little kids might find the
show rather terrifying, however).

PARADISE PIER   Journey back to the glory days of California's beachfront
amusement piers—remember Santa Monica, Santa Cruz, Belmont Park?—on
this fantasy boardwalk. Highlights include **California Screamin',** a classic roller
coaster that replicates the whitewashed wooden white-knucklers of the past—but

with state-of-the-art steel construction and a smooth, computerized ride. There's also the **Maliboomer,** a trio of towers (giant strongman sledgehammer tests) that catapult riders to the tip-top bell, then lets them down bungee-style with dangling feet; the **Orange Stinger,** a whooshing swing ride inside an enormous orange, complete with orange scent piped in; **Mulholland Madness,** a wacky wild-trip along L.A.'s precarious hilltop street; and the **Sun Wheel Carousel,** featuring unique zigzagging cars that bring new meaning to the familiar ride.

There are all the familiar boardwalk games (complete with stuffed prizes), guilty pleasure fast foods like pizza, corn dogs, and burritos, plus a full-service overwater restaurant by Wolfgang Puck, **Avalon Cove.**

HOLLYWOOD PICTURES BACKLOT   If you've visited Disney in Florida, you might recognize many elements of this trompe l'oeil re-creation of a Hollywood movie studio lot. Pass through a classic studio archway flanked by gigantic golden elephants, and you'll find yourself on a surprisingly realistic "Hollywood Boulevard." In the **Disney Animation** building, visitors can participate in six different interactive galleries—learn how stories become animated features; watch Robin Williams become an animated character; listen to a Disney illustrator invent "Mushu," from *Mulan;* and even take a computerized personality test to see which Disney character *you* resemble most.

At the end of the street, the replica movie palace **Hyperion Theater** presents a live-action tribute to classic Disney films. Across the way, step aboard the **Superstar Limo,** where you're cast as a hot new star being chauffeured around Hollywood to sign a big movie deal; the wacky but tame ride winds through Malibu, Rodeo Drive, Beverly Hills, and the Sunset Strip. The latest attraction is **"Who Wants to Be a Millionaire—Play It!,"** an interactive, high-energy mockup of the popular game show. It's re-created to look and feel as it does on television, complete with the dramatic lighting and high tech set.

The Backlot's main attraction is **Jim Henson's MuppetVision 3D,** an onscreen blast from the past featuring Kermit, Miss Piggy, Gonzo, Fozzie Bear—and even hecklers Waldorf and Statler. Although it's not nearly as entertaining as **"It's Tough To Be A Bug,"** it has its moments and won't scare the bejeezus out of little kids. A bevy of dining options is led by the **ABC Soap Opera Bistro,** where you can dine in replica sets from your favorite soap operas.

DOWNTOWN DISNEY 👀

Borrowing a page from Central Florida's successful Disney compound, **Downtown Disney** is filled with restaurants, shops, and entertainment for all ages. Whether you want to stroll with kids in tow, have an upscale dinner for two, or party into the night, this colorful and sanitized "street scene" fills the bill.

The promenade begins at the amusement park gates and stretches toward the Disneyland Hotel; there are nearly 20 shops and boutiques, and a dozen-plus restaurants, live music venues, and entertainment options.

Highlights include **House of Blues,** the blues-jazz restaurant/club that features Delta-inspired cuisine and big-name music; **Ralph Brennan's Jazz Kitchen,** a spicy mix of New Orleans traditional foods and live jazz; **ESPN Zone,** the ultimate sports dining and entertainment experience, including an interactive game room; **Y Arriba! Y Arriba!,** where Latin cuisine combines with spicy entertainment and dancing; and **World of Disney,** one of the biggest Disney shopping experiences anywhere, with a vast and diverse range of toys, souvenirs, and collectibles. There is also a 12-screen multiplex, LEGO Imagination Center, Sephora cosmetics store, and much more.

Even if you're not staying at a Disney hotel, Downtown Disney is worth a visit. Locals and day-shoppers take advantage of the free entry and validated Downtown Disney parking lots (3 hr. free; 5 with restaurant or theater validation).

WHERE TO STAY
EXPENSIVE

The Disneyland Hotel ★★ *Kids*   The holy grail of Disney-goers has always been this, the "Official Hotel of the Magic Kingdom." A monorail connection via Downtown Disney means you'll be able to return to your room anytime, whether to take a much-needed nap or to change your soaked shorts after your Splash Mountain or Grizzly Peak adventure. The theme hotel is an attraction unto itself, and the best choice for families with small children. The rooms aren't fancy, but they're comfortably and attractively furnished, like a good-quality business hotel, and all have balconies. In-room amenities include movie channels (with free Disney Channel, naturally) and cute-as-a-button Disney-themed toiletries and accessories. This all-inclusive resort offers more than 10 combined restaurants, snack bars, and cocktail lounges; every kind of service desk imaginable; a fantasy swimming lagoon with white-sand beach; and video game center. The complex includes the adjoining Paradise Pier Hotel, which offers a Disney version of Asian tranquility; adults and older kids looking to escape the frenetically colorful Disney atmosphere will appreciate this option.

Best of all, hotel guests get to enter the park early almost every day and enjoy the major rides before the lines form. The amount of time varies from day to day, but usually you can enter 1½ hours early. Call ahead to check the schedule.

When you're planning your trip, inquire about multiday packages that allow you to take on the park at your own pace and usually include free parking.

1150 Magic Way, Anaheim, CA 92802. ⓒ **714/956-MICKEY** (central reservations), 714/778-6600 (Disneyland Hotel), or 714/999-0990 (Paradise Pier Hotel). Reservations fax 714/956-6582. 990 units. $170–$310 double; from $265 suite. AE, MC, V. Parking $10. **Amenities:** 4 restaurants; 3 lounges; 3 outdoor pools; health club; whirlpool; children's programs; game room; concierge; shopping arcade; salon; room service; babysitting; laundry/dry-cleaning service. *In room:* A/C, TV w/ pay movies, dataport, minibar, coffeemaker, hair dryer, safe.

Disney's Grand Californian Hotel ★★ *Kids*   Disney didn't miss the details when constructing this enormous version of an Arts and Crafts–era lodge (think Yosemite's Awhanee, Pasadena's Gamble House), hiring craftspeople throughout the state to contribute one-of-a-kind tiles, furniture, sculptures, and artwork. Taking inspiration from California's redwood forests, Mission pioneers, and plein-air painters, designers managed to create a nostalgic yet state-of-the-art high-rise hotel.

Enter through subtle (where's the door?) stained-glass sliding panels to the hotel's centerpiece, a six-story "living room" with a William Morris–designed marble "carpet," angled skylight seen through exposed support beams, display cases of Craftsman treasures, and a three-story walk-in "hearth" whose fire warms Stickley-style rockers and plush leather armchairs.

Guest rooms are spacious and smartly designed, carrying through the Arts and Crafts theme surprisingly well considering the hotel's grand scale. The best ones overlook the park (but you'll pay for that view). Despite the sophisticated air of the Grand Californian, this is a hotel that truly caters to families, with a bevy of room configurations including one with a double bed plus bunk beds with trundle. Since the hotel provides sleeping bags (rather than rollaways) for kids, this standard-size room will sleep a family of 6—but you have to share the bathroom.

> (*Tips* **For Hotel Guests Only**
>
> When you stay at one of the Disneyland Resort's hotels, you can pur-
> chase—separately, or as part of a lodging package—the **Ultimate Park
> Hopper** ticket. With it, you can "park-hop" between Disneyland and Cal-
> ifornia Adventure as many times as you want each day from the day you
> check in (including the day you check out), and it includes an ESPN Zone
> play credit and extra features like breakfast or special tours. The deal is
> exclusive to the Disney hotels; off-site overnighters should opt for a mul-
> tiday passport, which allows for only one admission—to either park—
> each day. Prices start at $116/$92 (adult/child) for a 3-day Ultimate Park
> Hopper, and the savings get better the more you play; the 6-day ticket
> averages out to a mere $30 per day (adult).

1600 S. Disneyland Dr., Anaheim, CA 92802. ℂ **714/956-MICKEY** (central reservations) or 714/635-2300. Fax 714/956-6099. www.disneyland.com. 751 units. $205–$335 double; from $345 suite. AE, DC, DISC, MC, V. Free self-parking; valet $6. **Amenities:** 3 restaurants; lounge; 2 outdoor pools; health club and spa; whirlpool; children's center; game room/arcade; concierge; business center; 24-hour room service; laundry/dry-cleaning service; concierge-level rooms. *In room:* A/C, TV w/ pay movies, dataport, minibar, coffeemaker, hair dryer, iron, safe, bathrobes, portable crib.

Sheraton Anaheim Hotel ⭐ This hotel rises to the festive theme-park occasion with its fanciful English Tudor architecture; it's a castle that lures business
conventions, Disney-bound families, and local high school proms. The public
areas are quiet and elegant—intimate gardens with fountains and koi ponds,
plush lobby and lounges—which can be a pleasing touch after a frantic day at
the amusement park. The rooms are modern and unusually spacious, but otherwise not distinctive. A large swimming pool sits in the center of the complex,
surrounded by attractive landscaping. Don't be put off by the high rack rates;
rooms commonly go for $100 to $130, even on busy summer weekends.

1015 W. Ball Rd. (at I-5), Anaheim, CA 92802. ℂ **800/325-3535** or 714/778-1700. Fax 714/535-3889. 489 units. $190–$225 double; $290–$360 suite. AE, DC, MC, V. Parking $10; free Disneyland shuttle. **Amenities:** 2 restaurants; lounge; outdoor pool; fitness center; whirlpool; concierge; 24-hour room service; coin-op laundry; laundry/dry-cleaning service. *In room:* A/C, TV w/ pay movies, dataport, minibar, coffeemaker, hair dryer, iron.

WestCoast Anaheim Hotel ⭐ Although this hotel, in the Anaheim Convention Center complex (across the street from Disneyland), draws primarily a
business crowd, it has much to appeal to the leisure traveler. The contemporary,
comfortable rooms in the 12-story tower all have balconies overlooking either
Disneyland or the hotel's luxurious pool area, which includes an attractive sun
deck, and snack and cocktail-bar gazebo. The front desk can provide fax
machines and refrigerators upon request. The Old West frontier-themed restaurant serves steak and seafood along with a few colorful game selections.

1855 S. Harbor Blvd. (south of Katella Ave.), Anaheim, CA 92802. ℂ **800/426-0670** or 714/750-1811. Fax 714/971-2485. www.westcoasthotels.com. 500 units. $195 double. Disneyland package available. AE, DC, DISC, MC, V. Self-parking $10; valet $13. **Amenities:** 2 restaurants; 2 lounges; outdoor pool; fitness center; deluxe whirlpool; activities desk; car-rental desk; 24-hour business center; room service (6am–11pm); laundry/dry-cleaning service. *In room:* AC, TV w/ pay movies and Sony Playstation, dataport, coffeemaker, hair dryer, iron.

MODERATE

Anaheim Vagabond Hotel ⭐ *Value*   You can easily cross the street to Disneyland's main gate, or take the Anaheim Plaza's free shuttle. Once you return, you'll appreciate the way this 32-year-old hotel's clever design shuts out the noisy world. In fact, the seven two-story garden buildings remind me more of 1960s Waikiki than busy Anaheim. The Olympic-size heated outdoor pool and whirlpool are unfortunately surrounded by Astroturf, and the plain motel-style furnishings are beginning to look a little tired. On the plus side, nothing's changed about the light-filled modern lobby, nor the friendly rates, which often drop as low as $49.

1700 S. Harbor Blvd., Anaheim, CA 92802. ✆ 800/228-1357 or 714/772-5900. Fax 714/772-8386. 300 units. $79–$150 double; from $185 suite. Rates include continental breakfast. AE, DC, DISC, MC, V. Free parking and Disneyland shuttle. **Amenities:** Restaurant; lounge; outdoor pool; whirlpool; room service (8am–11pm); coin-op laundry; laundry/dry-cleaning service. *In room:* A/C, TV, coffeemaker.

Candy Cane Inn ⭐⭐ *Value*   Take your standard U-shaped motel court with outdoor corridors, spruce it up with cobblestone drives and walkways, old-time street lamps, and flowering vines engulfing the balconies of attractively painted rooms, and you have the Candy Cane. The facelift worked, making this gem near Disneyland's main gate a treat for the stylish bargain hunter. The rooms are decorated in bright floral motifs with comfortable furnishings, including queen beds and a separate dressing and vanity area. Breakfast is served in the courtyard, where you can also splash around in a heated pool, spa, or kids' wading pool.

1747 S. Harbor Blvd., Anaheim, CA 92802. ✆ 800/345-7057 or 714/774-5284. Fax 714/772-5462. 173 units. $84–$129 double. Rates include expanded continental breakfast. AAA discount available. AE, DC, DISC, MC, V. Free parking and Disneyland shuttle. **Amenities:** Outdoor pool; whirlpool; coin-op laundry; laundry/dry-cleaning service. *In room:* A/C, TV, coffeemaker, hair dryer.

Howard Johnson Hotel ⭐   This hotel occupies an enviable location, directly opposite Disneyland, and a cute San Francisco trolley car runs to and from the park every 30 minutes. Guest rooms were renovated in 1999. They're divided among several low-profile buildings, all with balconies opening onto a central garden with two heated pools for adults and one for children. Garden paths lead under eucalyptus and olive trees to a splashing circular fountain. During the summer you can see the nightly fireworks display at Disneyland from the upper balconies of the park-side rooms. Try to avoid the rooms in the back buildings, which get some freeway noise. Services and facilities include room service from the attached **Coco's Restaurant,** airport shuttle, and family lodging/Disney admission packages. We think it's pretty classy for a HoJo.

1380 S. Harbor Blvd., Anaheim, CA 92802. ✆ 800/422-4228 or 714/776-6120. Fax 714/533-3578. www.hojoanaheim.com. 320 units. $74–$109 double. AE, DC, DISC, MC, V. Free parking and Disneyland trolley. **Amenities:** Restaurant; 2 outdoor pools; whirlpool; concierge; game room; room service (7am–11pm); coin-op laundry; laundry/dry-cleaning service. *In room:* A/C, TV w/ pay movies, dataport, fridge, coffeemaker.

Portofino Inn & Suites ⭐ *Kids*   Emerging from the rubble of the former Jolly Roger Hotel renovation, this brand-spanking new complex of low- and high-rise all-suite buildings sports a cheery yellow exterior and family friendly interior—just in time for the expanded Disneyland Resort. The location couldn't be better—directly across the street from California Adventure's back side, and they'll shuttle you straight to the front gate. Designed to work as well for business travelers from the nearby Convention Center as for Disney-bound families, the Portofino offers contemporary, stylish furnishings as well as vacation-friendly rates and suites for any family configuration. We especially love the "Kid's Suite," which features bunk beds and sofa sleeper, plus TV, fridge, and microwave—and that's just in the kids' room; Mom and Dad have a separate bedroom with grown-up comforts like double vanity, shower massage, and their own TV.

1831 S. Harbor Blvd. (at Katella), Anaheim, CA 92802. 📞 **888/297-7143** or 714/782-7600. Fax 714/782-7619. 190 units. $94–$159 double; $109–$219 suite. Midweek, off-season, and other discounts available. AE, DC, DISC, MC, V. Free parking and Disneyland shuttle. **Amenities:** Restaurant; outdoor pool; fitness center; whirlpool; game room; tour desk; laundry/dry-cleaning service; coin-op laundry. *In room:* A/C, TV w/ pay movies, dataport, coffeemaker, hair dryer, iron.

INEXPENSIVE

Best Western Anaheim Stardust   Located on the back side of Disneyland, this modest hotel appeals to the budget-conscious traveler who isn't willing to sacrifice everything. All rooms have a refrigerator and microwave, breakfast is served in a refurbished train dining car, and you can relax by the large outdoor heated pool and spa while using the laundry room. The extra-large family rooms accommodate virtually any brood, and shuttles run regularly to the park.

1057 W. Ball Rd., Anaheim, CA 92802. 📞 **800/222-3639** or 714/774-7600. Fax 714/535-6953. 121 units. $64–$89 double; $105 family room. Rates include full breakfast. AE, DC, DISC, MC, V. Free parking and Disneyland shuttle. **Amenities:** Restaurant; outdoor pool; whirlpool; self-service laundry. *In room:* A/C, TV, fridge.

WHERE TO DINE

If you're visiting the Disneyland Resort, chances are you'll probably eat at one of the many choices inside the theme parks or at Downtown Disney; there are plenty of restaurants to choose from for all tastes and budgets. At Disneyland, in the Creole-themed **Blue Bayou,** you can sit under the stars inside the Pirates of the Caribbean ride—no matter what time of day it is. California Adventure features two bona fide sit-down options; **Avalon Cove** is a Wolfgang Puck seafood restaurant overlooking a boardwalk amusement zone, and the Robert Mondavi–backed **Vineyard Room** offers upscale prix fixe wine country cuisine matched to Mondavi wines (the more casual Golden Vine Terrace is downstairs). Make reservations early in the day for dinner, as they all fill up pretty quickly.

At Knott's Berry Farm, try the fried-chicken dinners and boysenberry pies at historic **Mrs. Knott's Chicken Dinner Restaurant** (see below for full listing). We also list some of the best bests in the surrounding area, including nearby **Orange,** whose charming historic downtown is home to several of the region's best dining options, if you're willing to drive 10 to 15 minutes.

Anaheim White House ★★ ITALIAN/FRENCH   Once surrounded by orange groves, this stately 1909 Colonial-style mansion now sits on a wide industrial street just 5 minutes from Disneyland. It's set back, though, framed by lawns and gardens, and exudes gentility and nostalgia. The home is nicely restored inside and out; the restaurant opened in 1981, named after its stylistic cousin in Washington—the White House. Owner Bruno Serato maintains this architectural treasure, serving northern Italian cuisine—with a French accent—in elegant white-on-white rooms on the main and second floors. Dinner courses are whimsically named for fashion giants (Versace whitefish, Prada rack of lamb), and sometimes arrive on oddly shaped platters that work better as artwork than dishware. But chef David Libby knows what he's doing, applying just the right amount of sauce to pastas both formal (gnocchi in velvety Gorgonzola sauce) and rustic (linguini with chunky garlic, roasted peppers, and olives).

Prices tend to reflect the expense account and well-heeled retiree crowd, but lunch prices (including a terrific prix fixe) deliver the same bang for fewer bucks.

887 Anaheim Blvd. (north of Ball Rd.), Anaheim. (*) 714/772-1381. www.anaheimwhitehouse.com. Reservations recommended at dinner. Dinner main courses $18–$28; lunch $10–$16. AE, MC, V. Mon–Fri 11:30am–2pm and 5–10pm; Sat–Sun 5–10pm.

Citrus City Grille ★★ CALIFORNIAN   Though housed in Orange's sec-ond-oldest brick building, this sophisticated crowd pleaser is furnished without an antique in sight, paying homage to the town's agricultural (citrus) legacy with a bold industrial chic. World-inspired appetizers range from Hawaiian-style *ahi poke* (raw tuna salad) to Southeast Asian coconut shrimp tempura accented with spiced apricots. Main courses come from the Mediterranean (pasta and risotto), Mexico (carne asada with avocado-corn relish), the American South (authentic Louisiana gumbo), and your Mom's kitchen (meat loaf smothered in gravy and fried onions). Gleaming bar shelves house myriad bottles for the extensive mar-tini menu, and outdoor foyer tables are nicely protected from the street.

122 No. Glassell St. (½ block north of Chapman), Orange. (*) 714/639-9600. Reservations recommended. Main courses $8–$13 lunch, $12–$24 dinner. AE, DC, MC, V. Tues–Sat 11:30am–3pm and 5–10pm.

Felix Continental Cafe ★ CUBAN/SPANISH   If you like the re-created Main Street in the Magic Kingdom, you'll love the historic 1886 town square in the city of Orange, on view from the cozy sidewalk tables outside the Felix Con-tinental Cafe. Dining on traditional Cuban specialties (such as citrus-marinated chicken, black beans and rice, and fried plantains) and watching traffic spin around the magnificent fountain and rose bushes of the plaza evokes old Havana or Madrid rather than the cookie-cutter Orange County communities just blocks away. The food is praised by restaurant reviewers and loyal locals alike.

36 Plaza Sq. (at the corner of Chapman and Glassell), Orange. (*) 714/633-5842. Reservations recom-mended for dinner. Main courses $6–$14. AE, DC, MC, V. Mon–Thurs 7am–9pm; Fri 7am–10pm; Sat 8am–10pm, Sun 8am–9pm.

2 Knott's Berry Farm

30 miles (48km) SE of downtown Los Angeles

Cynics say that Knott's Berry Farm is for people who aren't smart enough to find Disneyland. The reality is that Knott's simply can't compete with the Disney allure, but instead focuses on newer and faster thrill rides that target Southern California youths and families instead.

Like Disneyland, Knott's Berry Farm is not without historical background. Rudolph Boysen crossed a loganberry with a raspberry, calling the resulting hybrid the boysenberry. In 1933, Buena Park farmer Walter Knott planted the boysenberry and launched Knott's berry farm on 10 acres of leased land. When things got tough during the Depression, Mrs. Knott set up a roadside stand, sell-ing pies, preserves, and home-cooked chicken dinners. Within a year she was selling 90 meals a day. Lines became so long that Walter decided to create an Old West Ghost Town as a diversion for waiting customers.

Today the amusement park offers a whopping 165 shows, attractions, and high-tech rides that are far more thrilling than most of rides at the Disney Resort. Granted, it doesn't have nearly the magical appeal of Disneyland, but if you're more into fast-paced amusement rides than swirling tea cups, spend your money here.

Locals flock to Knott's Berry Farm in the second half of October, when the entire park is revamped as "Knott's *Scary* Farm." The ordinary attractions are made spooky and haunted, every grassy area is transformed into a graveyard or gallows, and even the already-scary rides get special surprise extras, like costumed ghouls who grab your arm in the middle of a roller-coaster ride!

GETTING THERE   Knott's Berry Farm is at 8039 Beach Blvd. in Buena Park. It's a 10-minute ride north on I-5 from Disneyland. From I-5 or Calif. 91, exit south onto Beach Boulevard. The park is about half a mile south of Calif. 91.

ADMISSION, HOURS & INFORMATION   Admission to the park, including unlimited access to all rides, shows, and attractions, is $40 for adults and children 12 and over, $30 for seniors over 60, kids 3 to 11, nonambulatory visitors, and expectant mothers; children under 3 are admitted free. Admission is $20 for adults and $15 kids 3 to 11 after 4pm on day's when park is open past 6pm. Parking is $7. Like Disneyland, Knott's offers discounted admission for Southern California residents during the off-season, so if you're bringing local friends or family members along, be sure to take advantage of the bargain. Also like Disneyland, Knott's Berry Farm's hours vary both during the week and week to week, so call ahead. The park is generally open during the summer daily from 9am to midnight. The rest of the year, it opens at 10am and closes at 6 or 8pm, except Saturday, when it stays open till 10pm. Knott's is closed December 25. Special hours and prices are in effect during Knott's Scary Farm in late October (a hugely popular event). Stage shows and special activities are scheduled throughout the day. Pick up a schedule at the ticket booth.

For more information, call ✆ 714/220-5200 or log onto **www.knotts.com**.

TOURING THE PARK

Despite all the new multimillion-dollar rides, Knott's Berry Farm still maintains much of its original Old West motif, and is divided into six themed areas spread across 150 acres. The newest attraction is the **Xcelerator,** which launches you from 0 to 82 mph in 2.3 seconds. Other new attractions include the **California MarketPlace,** the Farm's version of Downtown Disney, and **Knott's Soak City U.S.A.,** a 21-ride water adventure park located right next to Knott's Berry Farm (separate admission required).

GHOST TOWN   The park's original attraction is a collection of refurbished 19th-century buildings relocated from deserted Old West towns. You can pan for gold, ride an authentic stagecoach, take rickety train cars through the Calico Mine, get held up aboard the Denver and Rio Grande Calico Railroad, and hiss at the villain during a melodrama in the Birdcage Theater. If you love wooden roller coasters, don't miss the clackity GhostRider.

FIESTA VILLAGE   Here you'll find a south-of-the-border theme. That means festive markets, strolling mariachis, and wild rides like Montezooma's Revenge and Jaguar, a roller coaster that includes two heart-in-the-mouth drops and a loop that turns you upside down.

WILD WATER WILDERNESS   This 3½-acre attraction is styled like a turn-of-the-20th-century California wilderness park. The top ride is a white-water adventure called Bigfoot Rapids, with a long stretch of artificial rapids; it's the longest ride of its kind in the world. You can also look Mystery Lodge right in the eye—it's a truly amazing high tech, trick-of-the-eye attraction based on the legends of local Native Americans. Don't miss this wonderful theater piece.

The Richard Nixon Library & Birthplace

Although he was the most vilified U.S. president in modern history (yes, more than Clinton), there has always been a warm place in the hearts of Orange County locals for Richard Nixon. This presidential library, located in Nixon's boyhood town, celebrates the roots, life, and legacy of America's 37th president. The 9-acre site contains the modest farmhouse where Nixon was born, manicured flower gardens, a modern museum housing presidential archives, and the final resting place of Mr. Nixon and his wife, Pat.

Displays include videos of the famous Nixon-Kennedy TV debates, an impressive life-size statuary summit of world leaders, state gifts (including a gun from Elvis), and exhibits on China and Russia. There's also a display of Pat Nixon's sparkling First Lady gowns and a 12-foot-high graffiti-covered chunk of the Berlin Wall, symbolizing the defeat of Communism, but hardly a mention is made of Nixon's leading role in the anti-Communist witch hunts of the 1950s. Similarly, there are exhibits on Vietnam, yet no mention of Nixon's illegal expansion of that war into neighboring Cambodia. Only the Watergate Gallery is relatively forthright, allowing visitors to listen to actual White House tapes and view a montage of the president's last day in the White House.

18001 Yorba Linda Blvd., Yorba Linda. © **714/993-5075.** Fax 714/993-3393. www.nixonfoundation.org. Admission $5.95 adults, $3.95 seniors, $2 children 8 to 11, free for children 7 and under. Monday to Saturday 10am to 5pm; Sunday 11am to 5pm.

CAMP SNOOPY   This will probably be the youngsters' favorite area. It's meant to re-create a wilderness camp in the picturesque High Sierra. Its 6 rustic acres are the playgrounds of Charles Schulz's beloved beagle and his pals, Charlie Brown and Lucy, who greet guests and pose for pictures. The rides here, including the new Charlie Brown Speedway and Beary Tales Playhouse, are tailor-made for the 6-and-under set.

INDIAN TRIALS   A nod to Native Americans is this Native American interpretive center on the outskirts Ghost Town. Exhibits include authentic tipis, hogans and big houses. There's also daily educational events such as native craft making, storytelling, music, and dance.

THE BOARDWALK   This theme area is a salute to Southern California's beach culture. The main attractions are the 30-story Supreme Scream, one of the tallest (and scariest) thrill rides in the world, and a white-water adventure called Perilous Plunge, the world's tallest, steepest (think four-story waterfall) and wettest water ride.

WHERE TO STAY

Radisson Resort Knott's Berry Farm 🌟 *Kids*   Within easy walking distance of Knott's Berry Farm, this spit-shined Radisson (the former Buena Park Hotel) also offers a free shuttle to Disneyland, 7 miles (11km) away. The pristine lobby has the look of a business-oriented hotel, and that it is. But vacationers can also benefit from the elevated level of service. Ask about "Super Saver" rates (as low as $99—with breakfast—at press time), plus Knott's or Disneyland package deals. The rooms in the nine-story tower were tastefully redecorated when Radisson took over. Doting parents can even treat their kids to a Peanuts-themed room with Snoopy turndown service.

7675 Crescent Ave. (at Grand), Buena Park, CA 90620. © **800/333-3333** or 714/995-1111. Fax 714/828-8590. www.radisson.com/buenaparkca. 320 units. $129–$139 double; $159–$299 suite. Discounts and packages available. AE, DC, DISC, MC, V. Free parking and Disneyland shuttle. **Amenities:** 2 restaurants; lounge; outdoor pool; 1 outdoor tennis court (lit for night play); fitness center; whirlpool; video arcade; concierge; 24-hour room service; self-service laundry; laundry/dry-cleaning service. *In room:* A/C, TV w/ pay movies, fax, dataport, coffeemaker, hair dryer, iron, safe, bathrobes.

WHERE TO DINE

Mrs. Knott's Chicken Dinner Restaurant ★ *(Kids)* AMERICAN   Knott's Berry Farm got its start as a down-home diner in 1934, and you can still get a hearty all-American meal without even entering the theme park. The restaurant that started it all, descended from Cordelia Knott's Depression-era farmland tea room, stands just outside the park's entrance, with plenty of free parking for patrons. Looking just as you'd expect—country cute, with window shutters and paisley aplenty—the restaurant's featured attraction is the original fried chicken dinner, complete with soup, salad, buttermilk biscuits, mashed potatoes and gravy, and a slice of famous pie. Country fried steak, pot roast, roast turkey, and pork ribs are options, as well as sandwiches, salads, and a terrific chicken potpie. Boysenberries abound (of course!), from breakfast jam to traditional double-crust pies, and there's even an adjacent take-out shop that's always crowded.

8039 Beach Blvd. (near La Palma), Buena Park. © **714/220-5080.** Reservations not accepted. Main courses $5–$7; complete dinners $10.95. AE, DC, DISC, MC, V. Sun–Thurs 7am–8:30pm; Fri 7am–9pm; Sat 7am–9:30pm.

9

Shopping

Whether you're looking for So Cal souvenirs, cutting-edge Melrose Avenue fashions, Hollywood memorabilia, or just some silly tourist schlock to remind you of your trip, Los Angeles has your shopping needs covered like no other place in the world. Heck, Los Angeles practically *invented* the shopping mall.

A note on hours: Street shops are generally open Monday through Saturday from 10 or 11am to 5 or 6pm. Many are open Sunday, particularly those near the beaches, movie theaters, or clusters of other stores. In addition, quite a few choose 1 night a week, often Wednesday or Thursday, to offer extended evening hours. Mall shops take their cue from the anchor department stores; as a rule, they open around 10am and do business until 8 or 9pm. Sundays shave an hour or two off each side, while holiday periods increase mall hours substantially.

Sales tax in Los Angeles is 8%; savvy out-of-state shoppers know to have larger items shipped directly home to save the tax.

1 L.A.'s Top Shopping Streets & Neighborhoods

Here's a rundown of L.A.'s most interesting shopping areas—from the fine and chic to the funky and cheap—along with some highlights of each neighborhood, to give you an idea of what you'll find there. If addresses and phone numbers are *not* given, refer to the store's expanded listing by category in "Shopping A to Z," later in this chapter.

L.A.'S WESTSIDE & BEVERLY HILLS

BEVERLY BOULEVARD (from Robertson Blvd. to La Brea Ave.)   Although these businesses are too far apart to be considered adjacent, they are representative of the variety you can find along this stylish street.

Every Picture Tells a Story, 7525 Beverly Blvd., a gallery devoted to the art of children's literature, displays antique children's books as well as the works of more than 100 illustrators, including lithos of Curious George, Eloise, and Charlotte's Web. Across the street from Cedars-Sinai Medical Center, the **Mysterious Bookshop** carries more than 20,000 used, rare, and out-of-print titles in the field of mystery, espionage, detective stories, and thrillers. Author appearances and other special events are regularly scheduled. If you can name more than three tenors, then pleasantly cluttered **Opera Shop of Los Angeles,** 8384 Beverly Blvd. (3 blocks east of La Cienega Blvd.; © **323/658-5811**), is for you. Everything imaginable with an opera theme is available: musical motif jewelry, stationery, T-shirts, opera glasses, and tapes, videos, and CDs of your favorite productions.

If you complain that they just don't make 'em like they used to . . . well, they do at **Re-Mix,** 7605½ Beverly Blvd. (between Fairfax and La Brea aves.; © **323/936-6210**). This shop sells only vintage (1940s–70s)—but brand-new (as in unworn)—shoes for men and women, such as wingtips, Hush Puppies,

Joan Crawford pumps, and 1970s platforms. It's more like a shoe-store museum. A rack of unworn vintage socks all display their original tags and stickers, and the prices are downright reasonable. Celebrity hipsters and hep cats from Madonna to Roseanne are often spotted here. Other vintage wares are found at **Second Time Around Watch Co.,** 8840 Beverly Blvd. (west of Robertson Blvd.; ✆ **310/271-6615**). The city's best selection of collectible timepieces includes dozens of classic Tiffanys, Cartiers, Piagets, and Rolexes, plus rare pocket watches. Priced for collectors, but a fascinating browse for the Swatch crowd too.

Beverly is also L.A.'s premier boulevard for mid-century furnishings; showrooms line the street, but the one who started it all is **Modernica,** 7366 Beverly Blvd. (✆ **323/933-0383**). You can still find vintage Stickley and Noguchi pieces, but Modernica has become best known for the authentic—and more affordable—replicas they offer (Eames storage units are one popular item).

LA BREA AVENUE (north of Wilshire Blvd.) This is L.A.'s artiest shopping strip. La Brea is anchored by the giant **American Rag, Cie** alterna-complex, and is also home to lots of great urban antiques stores dealing in Art Deco, Arts and Crafts, 1950s modern, and the like. You'll also find vintage clothiers, furniture galleries, and other warehouse-size stores, as well as some of the city's hippest restaurants, such as Campanile (see chapter 6 for a compete listing).

Bargain hunters find flea-market furnishings at **Nick Metropolis,** 100 S. La Brea Ave. (✆ **323/934-3700**), while more upscale seekers of home decor head to **Mortise & Tenon,** 446 S. La Brea Ave. (✆ **323/937-7654**), where handcrafted heavy wood pieces sit next to overstuffed velvet-upholstered sofas and even vintage steel desks. The best place for a snack is Nancy Silverton's **La Brea Bakery,** 624 S. La Brea Ave. (✆ **323/939-6813;** www.labreabakery.com), which foodies know from gourmet markets and the attached Campanile restaurant.

Stuffed to the rafters with hardware and fixtures of the past 100 years, **Liz's Antique Hardware,** 453 S. La Brea Ave. (✆ **323/939-4403;** www.lahardware. com), thoughtfully keeps a canister of wet wipes at the register—believe us, you'll need one after sifting through bags and crates of doorknobs, latches, finials, and any other home hardware you can imagine. Perfect sets of Bakelite drawer pulls and antique ceramic bathroom fixtures are some of the more intriguing items. Be prepared to browse for hours, whether you're redecorating or not. There's also a respectable collection of coordinatingly trendy clothing for men and women. Hipsters also head up the street to **Yellowstone** for vintage duds, and souvenir seekers know to visit **Moletown** for studio merchandise featuring logo graphics from the hottest new movies.

RODEO DRIVE & BEVERLY HILLS' GOLDEN TRIANGLE (between Santa Monica Blvd., Wilshire Blvd., and Crescent Dr., Beverly Hills) Everyone knows about Rodeo Drive, the city's most famous shopping street. Couture shops from high fashion's Old Guard are located along these 3 hallowed blocks, along with plenty of newer high-end labels. And there are two examples of the Beverly Hills version of minimalls, albeit more insular and attractive—the **Rodeo Collection,** 421 N. Rodeo Dr.; and **Two Rodeo,** at Wilshire Boulevard. The 16-square-block area surrounding Rodeo Drive is known as the "Golden Triangle." Shops off Rodeo are generally not as name-conscious as those on the strip (and you might actually be able to afford something), but they're nevertheless plenty upscale. Little Santa Monica Boulevard has a particularly colorful line of specialty stores, and Brighton Way is as young and hip as relatively staid Beverly Hills gets.

The big names to look for here are **Giorgio Beverly Hills,** 327 N. Rodeo Dr. (© **800/GIORGIO**); **Gucci,** 347 N. Rodeo Dr. (© **310/278-3451**); **Hermès,** 434 N. Rodeo Dr. (© **310/278-6440**); **Louis Vuitton,** 295 N. Rodeo Dr. (© **310/859-0457**); **Polo/Ralph Lauren,** 444 N. Rodeo Dr. (© **310/281-7200**); and **Tiffany & Co.,** 210 N. Rodeo Dr. (© **310/273-8880**). The newest arrival is **NikeTown,** corner of Wilshire Boulevard and Rodeo Drive (© **310/275-9998**), a behemoth shrine to the reigning athletic-gear king.

Wilshire Boulevard is also home to New York–style department stores (each in spectacular landmark buildings) like **Saks Fifth Avenue,** 9600 Wilshire Blvd. (© **310/275-4211**), **Barneys New York,** 9570 Wilshire Blvd. (© **310/276-4400**), and **Neiman Marcus,** 9700 Wilshire Blvd. (© **310/550-5900**).

THE SUNSET STRIP (between La Cienega Blvd. and Doheny Dr., West Hollywood)   The monster-size billboards advertising the latest rock god make it clear this is rock-and-roll territory. So it makes sense that you'll find legendary **Tower Records** in the heart of the action. Tower insists that it has L.A.'s largest selection of compact discs (more than 125,000 titles)—despite the Virgin Megastore's contrary claim—and it's open 365 days a year. At the east end of the strip sits the gigantic **Virgin Megastore.** Some 100 CD "listening posts" and an in-store "radio station" make this place a music-lover's paradise. Virgin claims to stock 150,000 titles, including an extensive collection of hard-to-find artists.

The "Strip" is lined with trendy restaurants, industry-oriented hotels, and dozens of shops offering outrageous fashions and stage accessories. One anomaly is Sunset Plaza, an upscale cluster of Georgian-style shops resembling Beverly Hills at its snootiest. You'll find **Billy Martin's,** 8605 Sunset Blvd. (© **310/289-5000**), founded by the legendary Yankees manager in 1978. This chic men's Western shop—complete with fireplace and leather sofa—stocks hand-forged silver and gold belt buckles, Lucchese and Liberty boots, and stable staples like flannel shirts. Next door is our favorite fine-jewelry store, **Philip Press, Inc.,** 8601 Sunset Blvd. (© **310/360-1180**), which specializes in platinum and diamonds, handcrafted to evoke ornate estate jewelry. If you want to commemorate a special occasion or want the best selection, this is the place to go. **Book Soup** has long been one of L.A.'s most celebrated bookshops, selling mainstream and small-press books and hosting book signings and readings.

WEST THIRD STREET (between Fairfax and Robertson blvds.)   You can shop till you drop on this trendy strip, anchored on the east end by the **Farmers Market** (see "L.A.'s Top Attractions," in chapter 7). Many of Melrose Avenue's shops have relocated here, along with terrific up-and-comers, several cafes, and the much-lauded restaurant Locanda Veneta (see chapter 6 for a full listing). *Fun* is more the catchword here than *funky*, and the shops (including the vintage clothing stores) are a bit more refined than those along Melrose. **The Cook's Library** is where the city's top chefs find classic and deliciously offbeat cookbooks and other food-oriented tomes. Browsing is welcomed, even encouraged, with tea, tasty treats, and rocking chairs. **Traveler's Bookcase** is one of the best travel bookshops in the West, stocking a huge selection of guidebooks and travel literature, as well as maps and travel accessories. Nearby **Memory Lane** is filled with 1940s, 1950s, and 1960s collectibles.

There's lots more to see along this always-growing street. Refuel at **Chado Tea Room,** 8422 W. 3rd St. (© **323/655-2056**), a temple for tea lovers. Chado is designed with a nod to Paris's renowned Mariage Frères tea purveyor; one wall is lined with nooks whose recognizable brown tins are filled with more than

250 different varieties of tea from around the world. Among the choices are 15 kinds of Darjeeling, Indian teas blended with rose petals, and ceremonial Chinese and Japanese blends. You can also get tea meals here, featuring delightful sandwiches and individual pots of any loose tea in the store.

HOLLYWOOD

HOLLYWOOD BOULEVARD (between Gower St. and La Brea Ave.)   One of Los Angeles's most famous streets is, for the most part, a cheesy tourist strip. But along the Walk of Fame, between the T-shirt shops and greasy pizza parlors, you'll find some excellent poster shops, souvenir stores, and Hollywood-memorabilia dealers worth getting out of your car for—especially if there's a chance of getting your hands on that long-sought-after Ethel Merman autograph or *200 Motels* poster.

Some long-standing purveyors of memorabilia include **Book City Collectibles,** which has more than 70,000 color prints of past and present stars, along with a good selection of famous autographs. **Hollywood Book and Poster Company** has an excellent collection of posters (from about $15 each), strong in horror and exploitation flicks. Photocopies of about 5,000 movie and television scripts are sold for $10 to $15 each, and the store carries music posters and photos. The **Collector's Book Store** is a movie buff's dream, with enough printed memorabilia for an afternoon of browsing; vintage copies of *Photoplay* and other fan mags cost $2 to $5, and the selection of biographies is outstanding.

LARCHMONT BOULEVARD (between Beverly Blvd. and 2nd St.)   Neighbors congregate on this old-fashioned street just east of busy Vine Avenue. As the surrounding Hancock Park homes become increasingly popular with artists and young Industry types, the shops and cafes lining Larchmont get more stylish. Sure, chains like Jamba Juice and the Coffee Bean are infiltrating this formerly mom-and-pop terrain, but plenty of unique shopping awaits amidst charming elements like diagonal parking, shady trees, and sidewalk bistro tables.

One of L.A.'s landmark independent bookstores is **Chevalier's Books,** 126 N. Larchmont Blvd. (© 323/465-1334), a 60-year Larchmont tradition. If your walking shoes are letting you down, stop into **Village Footwear,** 240 N. Larchmont Blvd. (© 323/461-3619), which specializes in comfort lines like Josef Siebel.

MELROSE AVENUE (between Fairfax and La Brea aves.)   It's showing some wear—some stretches have become downright ugly—but this is still one of the most exciting shopping streets in the country for cutting-edge fashions—and some eye-popping people-watching to boot. There are scores of shops selling the latest in clothes, gifts, jewelry, and accessories. Melrose is a playful stroll, dotted with plenty of hip restaurants and funky shops that are sure to shock. Where else could you find green patent-leather cowboy boots, a working 19th-century pocket watch, an inflatable girlfriend, and glow-in-the-dark condoms in the same shopping spree? From east to west, here are some highlights.

l.a. Eyeworks, 7407 Melrose Ave. (© 323/653-8255), revolutionized eyeglass designs from medical supply to stylish accessory, and now their brand is nationwide. **Retail Slut,** 7308 Melrose Ave. (© 323/934-1339), is a rock-and-roll shop carrying new clothing and accessories for men and women. The unique designs are for a select crowd (the name says it all), so don't expect to find anything for your next PTA meeting here. **Betsey Johnson Boutique** is a favorite among the young and pencil-thin; the New York–based designer has brought to

L.A. her brand of fashion—trendy, cutesy, body-conscious women's wear in colorful prints and faddish fabrics. Across the street, **Off The Wall** is filled with neon-flashing, bells-and-whistles kitsch collectibles, from vintage Wurlitzer jukeboxes to life-size fiberglass cows. The L.A. branch of a Bay Area hipster hangout, **Wasteland** has an enormous steel-sculpted facade. There's a lot of leather and denim, and some classic vintage—but mostly funky 1970s-style garb, both vintage and contemporary. More racks of vintage treasures (and trash) are found at **Aardvark's Odd Ark,** which stocks everything, from suits and dresses to neckties, hats, handbags, and jewelry. This place also manages to anticipate some of the hottest new street fashions.

SANTA MONICA & THE BEACHES

MAIN STREET (between Pacific St. and Rose Ave., Santa Monica and Venice blvds.)   An excellent street for strolling, Main Street boasts a healthy combination of mall standards as well as upscale, left-of-center individual boutiques. You can also find plenty of casually hip cafes and restaurants. The primary strip connecting Santa Monica and Venice, Main Street has a relaxed, beach-community vibe that sets it apart from similar strips. The stores here straddle the fashion fence between upscale trendy and beach bum edgy. Highlights include **C.P. Shades,** 2937 Main St. (between Ashland and Pier sts.; (C) **310/392-0949**), a San Francisco ladies' clothier whose loose and comfy cotton and linen line is carried by many department stores and boutiques. **Horizons West,** 2011 Main St. (south of Pico Blvd.; (C) **310/392-1122**), sells brand-name surfboards, wet suits, leashes, magazines, waxes, lotions, and everything else you need to catch the perfect wave. Stop in and say hi to Randy, and pick up a free tide table. If you're looking for some truly sophisticated, finely crafted eyewear, friendly **Optical Shop of Aspen,** 2904 Main St. (between Ashland and Pier sts.; (C) **310/392-0633**), is for you. Ask for frames by cutting-edge L.A. designers Bada and Koh Sakai. If you're lucky enough to have perfect vision, consider some stylish shades. Outdoors types will get lost in 5,600-square-foot **Patagonia,** 2936 Main St. ((C) **310/314-1776;** www.patagonia.com), where climbers, surfers, skiers, and hikers can gear up in the functional, colorful duds that put this environmentally friendly firm on the map.

MONTANA AVENUE (between 17th and 7th sts., Santa Monica)   This breezy stretch of slow-traffic Montana is one of our favorite regentrified parts of the city. It's gotten a lot more pricey than in the late 1970s when tailors and Laundromats ruled the roost, but the specialty shops still outnumber the chains. Look around and you can see upscale moms with strollers and cellphones shopping for designer fashions, country home decor, and gourmet takeout.

Montana is still original enough for residents from across town to make a special trip here, seeking out distinctive shops like **Shabby Chic,** 1013 Montana Ave. ((C) **310/394-1975**), a much-copied purveyor of slipcovered sofas and fleamarket furnishings, while clotheshorses shop for designer wear at minimalist **Savannah,** 706 Montana Ave. ((C) **310/458-2095**); ultrahip **Jill Roberts,** 920 Montana Ave. ((C) **310/260-1966**); and sleekly professional **Weathervane,** 1209 Montana Ave. ((C) **310/393-5344**). Upscale moms can find tiny fashions at **Real Threads,** 1527 Montana Ave. ((C) **310/393-3175**). For more grown-up style, head to **Ponte Vecchio,** 702 Montana Ave. ((C) **310/394-0989**), which sells Italian hand-painted dishes and urns, or to **Cinzia,** 1129 Montana Ave. ((C) **310/393-7751**), which features a smattering of both Tuscan and English home accessories. If Valentine's Day is approaching, duck into **Only Hearts,** 1407 Montana

Ave. (© **310/393-3088**), for heart-themed gifts and seductively comfortable intimate apparel. The stylish choice for lunch is **Wolfgang Puck Cafe,** 1323 Montana Ave. (© **310/393-0290**).

THIRD STREET PROMENADE (3rd St. from Broadway to Wilshire Blvd., Santa Monica)   Packed with chain stores and boutiques as well as dozens of restaurants and a large movie theater, Santa Monica's pedestrians-only section of 3rd Street is one of the most popular shopping areas in the city. The Promenade (www.downtownsm.com) bustles on into the evening with a seemingly endless assortment of street performers and shoppers. Stores stay open late (often till 1 or 2am on the weekends) for the movie-going crowds. There's plenty of metered parking in structures on the adjacent streets, so bring lots of quarters.

Highlights include **Hennessey & Ingalls,** a bookstore devoted to art and architecture; **Midnight Special Bookstore,** a medium-size general bookshop known for its good small-press selection and regular poetry readings; **Restoration Hardware,** 1221 Third Street Promenade (© **310/458-7992**), the retro-current source for reproduction home furnishings and accessories; and **Puzzle Zoo,** 1413 Third Street Promenade (© **310/393-9201**), where you'll find the double-sided World's Most Difficult Puzzle, the Puzzle in a Bottle, and many other brain-teasing challenges. Puzzle Zoo was voted "Best in L.A." by *Los Angeles* magazine. Music lovers can get CDs and vinyl at **Hear Music** and **Pyramid Music** and can check out the rock-and-roll collectibles at **Mayhem.**

SILVER LAKE & LOS FELIZ
Located at the eastern end of Hollywood, and technically part of Los Angeles, these two communities have been rising steadily on the hipness-meter. Silver Lake, named for the man-made Silver Lake reservoir at its center, is a bohemian community of artists and ethnic families that's popular for nightclubbing and barhopping. Los Feliz is northwest of Silver Lake, centered on Vermont and Hillhurst avenues between Sunset and Los Feliz boulevards; it's slightly tamer, and filled with 1920s and 1930s buildings. You'll find tons of unique businesses of all sorts, including artsy boutiques, music stores, and furniture dealers that have inspired some to compare the area with New York's SoHo.

Because so many alternative bands call Silver Lake home, it's not surprising to find cutting-edge music stores around every corner. A neighborhood mainstay with lots of used CDs, collectible disks, and new releases is **Rockaway Records,** 2395 Glendale Blvd. (south of Silver Lake Blvd.; © **323/664-3232;** www.rockaway.com). **Destroy All Music,** 3818 Sunset Blvd. (south of Santa Monica Blvd.; © **323/663-9300**), covers all punk bases, from hard core to ska, indie, and lo-fi, while platter collectors head to the local branch of Melrose's **Vinyl Fetish,** 1750 N. Vermont Ave. (© **323/660-4500**), for new and used vinyl records (yes, it carries CDs too).

Vintage clothing is another big draw in these parts. The most reliable yet eclectic selections to browse through are at **Ozzie Dots,** 4637 Hollywood Blvd. (west of Hillhurst; © **323/663-2867**); **Pull My Daisy,** 3908 Sunset Blvd. (at Griffith Park Blvd.; © **323/663-0608**); and **Squaresville,** 1800 N. Vermont Ave. (south of Franklin; © **323/669-8464**).

Although the art of millinery often seems to have gone the way of white afternoon gloves for ladies, inventive **Drea Kadilak** bucks the trend with her reasonably priced hat shop called Clover (2756 Rowena Ave (at Glendale Blvd; © **323/661-4142**). Drea designs in straw, cotton duck, wool felt, and a number of more unusual fabrics. She does her own blocking, cheerfully takes

Silver Lake & Los Feliz Shopping

Destroy All Music **4**
Edna Hart **8**
Koma Bookstore **1**
Ozzie Dots **2**
Pull My Daisy **5**
Rockaway Records **7**
Rubbish **6**
Soap Plant/Wacko/
  La Luz de Jesus **3**
Squaresville **1**
Vinyl Fetish **1**
Y-Que **1**

measurements for custom ladies' head wear, and gives away signature hatboxes with your purchase. Handmade furniture and unique gift items are available as well.

Hollywood set designers know to prowl the vintage furniture stores of Silver Lake: The best for mid-century gems are **Edna Hart,** 2945 Rowena Ave. (south of Hyperion; © **323/661-4070**); and **Rubbish,** 1630 Silver Lake Blvd. (north of Sunset; © **323/661-5575**). One not-to-be-missed highlight is the wacky and eclectic **Soap Plant/Wacko/La Luz de Jesus Art Gallery,** 4633 Hollywood Blvd. (west of Hillhurst; © **323/663-0122**), a three-in-one business with candles, art books, erotic toys, soap and bathing items, and a large selection of lava lamps. Local fixture **Y-Que,** 1770 N. Vermont Ave. (© **323/664-0021**), almost defies description, selling a variety of stuff ranging from a knockoff *Austin Powers* penis pump to psychedelic lava lamps. Truly left-of-center bibliophiles head to the R-rated **Koma Bookstore,** 1764 N. Vermont Ave. (© **323/665-0956;** www.komabookstore.com), still called Amok by the faithful legions who come for hard-to-find volumes on Satanic rituals, radical political tracts, and lurid 1940s pulp erotica.

DOWNTOWN

Since the late, lamented department store Bullock's closed in 1993 (its Art Deco masterpiece salons rescued to house the Southwestern Law School's library),

Downtown has become less of a shopping destination than ever. Although many of the once-splendid streets are lined with cut-rate luggage and electronics stores, shopping here can be a rewarding if gritty experience for the adventuresome.

Savvy Angelenos still go for bargains in the garment and fabric districts (see "Discount" under "Fashions," later in this chapter); florists and bargain hunters arrive at the vast Flower Mart before dawn for the city's best selection of fresh blooms; and families of all ethnicities stroll the **Grand Central Market,** 317 S. Broadway (between 3rd and 4th sts.; © **213/624-2378;** www.grandcentral square.com). Opened in 1917, this bustling market has watched the face of downtown L.A. change while changing little. Today, it serves Latino families, enterprising restaurateurs, and cooks in search of unusual ingredients and bargain-priced produce. On weekends you'll be greeted by a mariachi band at the Hill Street entrance, near our favorite market feature—the fruit-juice counter, which dispenses 20 fresh varieties from wall spigots, and blends the tastiest, healthiest "shakes" in town. Farther into the market you'll find produce sellers and prepared-food counters, spice vendors who seem straight out of a Turkish bazaar, and a grain and bean seller who'll scoop out dozens of exotic rices and dried legumes.

THE SAN FERNANDO VALLEY

STUDIO CITY (Ventura Blvd. between Laurel Canyon Blvd. and Fulton Ave.) Long beloved by Valley residents, Studio City is conveniently located, freeway- and canyon-close to Hollywood and the Westside. Ventura Boulevard has a distinct personality in each of Valley communities it passes through; Studio City is where you'll find small boutiques and antiques stores, quirky little businesses (many dating from the 1940s and 1950s), and less congested branches of popular chains like Gap, Pier 1 Imports, and Blockbuster. Antiques hounds check the Cranberry House (Studio City Antique Mall), and camera buffs stop at the full-service Studio City Camera Exchange for everything from film processing to camera repairs. Parking is a cinch on the street except during holiday season, when stores team up to decorate these blocks and often observe extended evening hours. The 4 blocks between Laurel Canyon Boulevard and Whitsett Avenue are the most concentrated. Start with the city's best pancakes at Du-par's Restaurant & Bakery (see chapter 6).

PASADENA & ENVIRONS

Compared to L.A.'s behemoth shopping malls, the streets of pretty, compact Pasadena are a true pleasure to stroll. As a general rule, stores are open daily from about 10am, and while some close at the standard 5 or 6pm, many stay open till 8 or 9pm to accommodate the before- and after-dinner/movie crowd.

OLD PASADENA (centered around the intersection of Colorado Blvd. and Fair Oaks Ave.)   In our opinion, Old Pasadena has some of the best shopping in L.A., but we hope the area retains more of the mom-and-pop businesses currently being pushed out by the likes of Banana Republic and Crate & Barrel. As you move eastward, the mix begins to include more eclectic shops and galleries commingling with dusty, preyuppie relics.

Penny Lane, 12 W. Colorado Blvd. (© **626/564-0161**), carries new and used CDs, plus a great selection of music magazines and kitschy postcards. The stock is less picked-over here than at many record stores in Hollywood. Travelers also seem to find something they need at **Distant Lands Bookstore and Outfitters,** a duo of related stores. The bookstore has a terrific selection of maps, guides, and travel-related literature, while the outfitter two doors away offers everything from luggage and pith helmets to space-saving and convenient travel accessories. An Old Town mainstay is **Rebecca's Dream,** 16 S. Fair Oaks Ave. (© 626/796-1200), where both men and women can find vintage clothing treasures. The store is small and meticulously organized (by color scheme); be sure to look at the vintage hats adorning the walls.

OTHER PASADENA SHOPPING

In addition to Old Town Pasadena, there are numerous good hunting grounds in the surrounding area. Antiques hounds might want to head to the **Green Street Antique Row,** 985–1005 E. Green St., east of Lake Avenue; or the **Pasadena Antique Center,** on South Fair Oaks Boulevard south of Del Mar. Each has a rich concentration of collectibles that can captivate for hours.

You never know what you might find at the **Rose Bowl Flea Market,** at the Rose Bowl, 1001 Rose Bowl Drive, Pasadena (© 323/560-SHOW [7469]; www.rgcshows.com/rosebowl.asp). The horseshoe-shaped Rose Bowl, built in 1922, is one of the world's most famous stadiums, home to UCLA's Bruins, the annual Rose Bowl Game, and an occasional Super Bowl. California's largest monthly swap meet, held here on the second Sunday of every month from 9am to 3pm, is a favorite of Los Angeles antiques hounds (who know to arrive as early as 6am for the best finds). Antique furnishings, clothing, jewelry, and other collectibles are assembled in the parking area to the left of the entrance, while the rest of the flea market surrounds the exterior of the Bowl. Expect everything from used surfboards and car stereos to one-of-a-kind lawn statuary and bargain athletic shoes. Admission is $5 after 9am (early bird admission $10–$15).

Anglophiles will delight in **Rose Tree Cottage,** 828 E. California Blvd., just west of Lake Avenue (© 818/793-3337; www.rosetreecottage.com), and its charming array of all things British. This cluster of historic Tudor cottages surrounded by traditional English gardens holds three gift shops and a tearoom, where a superb $19.50 high tea is served thrice daily among the knickknacks (and supervised by the resident cat, Miss Moffett). In addition to imported teas, linens, and silver trinkets, Rose Tree Cottage sells English delicacies like steak-and-kidney pies, hot cross buns, and shortbread. It's also the local representative of the British Tourist Authority and offers a comprehensive array of travel publications.

2 Shopping Malls

L.A.'S WESTSIDE & BEVERLY HILLS

THE BEVERLY CENTER When the eight-story Beverly Center opened on L.A.'s Westside, there was more than a bit of concern about the impending "mallification" of Los Angeles. Loved for its convenience and disdained for its penitentiary-style architecture (and the "no validations" parking fee), Beverly Center contains about 160 standard mall shops, including a few that are open by advance reservation only (*so* L.A.); it's anchored on opposite sides by Macy's and Bloomingdale's department stores. You can see it blocks away, looking like a gigantic angular boulder with the Hard Rock Cafe's (America's first) roof-mounted Cadillac on one corner. 8500 Beverly Blvd. (at La Cienega Blvd.). © 310/854-0070; www.beverlycenter.com.

CENTURY CITY MARKETPLACE This open-air mall, anchored by **Macy's** and **Bloomingdale's,** is located on what was once a Twentieth-Century Fox back lot, just west of Beverly Hills. Most of the 140 or so retailers here are upscale chain-store fare. Among the offerings are **Pottery Barn, Ann Taylor, Joan & David,** and **Brentano's,** as well as a giant **Crate & Barrel,** a 14-screen multiplex movie theater, and 22 restaurants. If you have to "mall it" in the L.A. area, this is the most pleasant place to do it. 10250 Santa Monica Blvd. (at Ave. of the Stars), Century City. © 310/277-3898; www.centurycityshoppingcenter.com.

PACIFIC DESIGN CENTER   Something of an architectural and cultural landmark, the Pacific Design Center is the West Coast's largest facility for interior design goods and fine furnishings. It houses 200 showrooms filled with furniture, fabrics, flooring, wallcoverings, kitchen and bath fixtures, lighting, art, and accessories. Locals refer to the PDC as the "Blue Whale" in reference to its exterior, composed entirely of brilliant blue glass. Technically, businesses here sell to the trade only, and their wholesale prices reflect that; for a small fee, however, the center will provide a decorator-for-the-day to serve as official broker for your purchase. 8687 Melrose Ave., West Hollywood, CA 90069. © 310/657-0800. www.pacificdesigncenter.com.

HOLLYWOOD

HOLLYWOOD & HIGHLAND   A sure sign that this formerly seedy section of the city is on the fast track to recovery is the massive $615 million complex at the corner of Hollywood Blvd. and Highland St. (hence the name). Surrounded by souvenir shops and tattoo parlors, the gleaming 8.7-acre center contains all the top-end merchants—Ann Taylor, Tommy Hilfiger, Louis Vuitton, bebe—as well as studio broadcast facilities and the gorgeous new **Kodak Theatre,** home of the Academy Awards (really, you'll want to take a peek at this theater). The mall's other centerpiece is Babylon Court; designed after a set from the 1916 film *Intolerance,* the open-air space attempts to re-create an over-the-top golden age movie set complete with giant pillars topped with 13,500-pound elephants and a colossal arch that frames the Hollywood sign in the distance. Parking isn't a problem, as the six-level underground lot can cram in 3,000 cars. 6834 Hollywood Blvd., Hollywood. © 323/460-6003. www.hollywoodandhighland.com

SANTA MONICA & THE BEACHES

SANTA MONICA PLACE   About 140 shops occupy these three bright stories, located a mere 2 blocks from the beach and anchored by Robinson's/May and Macy's department stores. The usual mall shops are augmented by more unusual finds like a branch of Frederick's of Hollywood. The mall's food pavilion sells an array of fast foods, and it includes several health-oriented eateries. Colorado Ave. (at 2nd St.), Santa Monica. © 310/394-5451. www.santamonicaplace.com.

PASADENA

PASEO COLORADO   It seems a new shopping mall sprouts up every year in L.A., and one the newest is this open-air mall in the heart of Pasadena. Anchored by Macy's, the two-level monolith houses about 140 retailers and restaurants (but few men's fashions), a Gelson's market, a fitness center, and a 14-screen multiplex theater. What's unique about the Paseo is the dozens of offices, apartments and studios built atop the mall, which allows residents easy access to just about all the daily necessities a city boy needs to survive. 280 E. Colorado Blvd. (at Marengo Ave.), Pasadena. ℂ 626/795-8891. www.paseocolorado.com.

THE SAN FERNANDO VALLEY
UNIVERSAL CITYWALK *(Kids)*   Designed to resemble an almost-cartoonish depiction of an urban street, Universal CityWalk gets mention here because it's unique. Situated next door to Universal Studios—you must walk through it if you use Universal City's main parking structure—CityWalk is dominated by brightly colored, surreal oversize storefronts. The heavily touristed faux street is home to a number of restaurants, including **B. B. King's Blues Club,** the newest **Hard Rock Cafe,** and a branch of the **Hollywood Athletic Club** featuring a restaurant and pool hall. It's been called the commercial equivalent to the gated community, a place where the fear-driven middle class can shop and dine in sanitized safety. In terms of shopping, CityWalk is not worth a special visit, but kids will love the carnival atmosphere and the **Warner Brothers store.** You can get an online preview at **www.mca.com/citywalk**. Universal Center Dr., Universal City. ℂ 818/622-9841.

3 Shopping A to Z
ANTIQUES
SANTA MONICA & THE BEACHES
The Art of Living Antique Market   Boasting more than 150 cream-of-the-crop dealers, this classy indoor mall features a fine selection of decorative items, jewelry, toys and memorabilia, pottery, vintage glassware and kitchen accessories, and a smattering of smaller furniture pieces. 1607 Lincoln Blvd., Santa Monica. ℂ 310/314-4899.

L.A.'S WESTSIDE & BEVERLY HILLS
The Antique Guild   Billing itself as "the world's largest antique outlet," the Guild is a veritable warehouse of history, with more than 2 acres of antiques displayed in the former Helms Bakery headquarters. Its buyers regularly purchase entire contents of European castles, beer halls, estates, and mansions. Look for everything from old armoires to chandeliers to stained glass, crystal, china, clocks, washstands, tables, mirrors, and much more. 3225–3231 Helms Ave. (at Venice Blvd.), near Culver City. ℂ 310/838-3131. www.theantiqueguild.com.

Del Mano   A contemporary crafts gallery, it's a lot of fun to see the creations—some whimsical, some exquisite—of American artists working with glass, wood, ceramics, or jewelry. 11981 San Vicente Blvd. Los Angeles (Brentwood). ℂ **310-476-8508.**

Memory Lane   This narrow shop filled with 1940s, 1950s, and 1960s collectibles features such treasures as Formica dinette sets, Bakelite radios, cocktail shakers and sets, unusual lamps, and a few well-chosen coats, dresses, and accessories. 8387 W. 3rd St. (at Orlando), Los Angeles. ℂ 323/655-4571.

HOLLYWOOD
Off The Wall   This collection of oversized antiques includes kitschy statues, Art Deco furnishings, carved wall reliefs, Wurlitzer jukeboxes, giant restaurant and gas-station signs, pinball machines, and lots and lots of neon. 7325 Melrose Ave., Los Angeles. ℂ 323/930-1185.

THE SAN FERNANDO VALLEY

Arte de Mexico   Seven warehouses full of carved furniture and wrought iron once sold only to moviemakers and restaurants are now available to the public. This is one of the most fascinating places in North Hollywood. 5356 Riverton Ave., North Hollywood. ✆ 818/769-5090. www.arteshowrooms.com.

The Cranberry House (Studio City Antique Mall)   Several storefront windows under a berry-colored awning hint at the treasures within this antiques and collectibles store featuring more than 100 different sellers. Be sure to haggle: even front-desk staff is often authorized by the dealers to strike a bargain. 22106 Ventura Blvd. (1 block west of Topanga and Ventura blvds.), Woodland Hills. ✆ 818/348-8877.

ART
SANTA MONICA & THE BEACHES

Bergamot Station *(Finds)*   Once a station for the Red Car trolley line, this industrial space is now home to the Santa Monica Museum of Art, plus two dozen art galleries, a cafe, a bookstore, and offices. Most of the galleries are closed Monday. The train yard is located at the terminus of Michigan Avenue, west of Cloverfield Boulevard.

Exhibits change often and vary, ranging from a Julius Shulman black-and-white photo retrospective of L.A.'s Case Study Houses, to a provocative exhibit of Vietnam War propaganda posters from the United States and Vietnam, to whimsical furniture constructed entirely of corrugated cardboard. A sampling of offerings includes the **Gallery of Functional Art** (✆ 310/829-6990), which features one-of-a-kind and limited-edition furniture, lighting, bathroom fixtures, and other functional art pieces, as well as smaller items like jewelry, flatware, ceramics, and glass. **The Rosamund Felson Gallery** (✆ 310/828-8488) is well known for showcasing L.A.-based contemporary artists; this is a good place to get a taste of current trends. **Track 16 Gallery** (✆ 310/264-4678) has exhibitions that range from pop art to avant-garde inventiveness—try to see what's going on here. 2525 Michigan Ave. (east of Cloverfield Blvd.), Santa Monica. ✆ 310/829-5854.

L.A.'S WESTSIDE & BEVERLY HILLS

Every Picture Tells a Story *(Kids)*   This gallery, devoted to the art of children's literature, is frequented by young-at-heart art aficionados as well as parents introducing their kids to the concept of an art gallery. Works by Maurice Sendak (*Where the Wild Things Are*), Tim Burton (*The Nightmare Before Christmas*), and original lithos of Curious George and Charlotte's Web are featured. Call to see what's going on; the store usually combines exhibitions of illustrators with story readings and interactive workshops. 7525 Beverly Blvd. (between Fairfax and La Brea aves.), Los Angeles. ✆ 323/932-6070.

BOOKS
SANTA MONICA & THE BEACHES

Hennessey & Ingalls   This bookstore is devoted to art and architecture, from magnificent coffee-table photography books to graphic arts titles and obscure biographies of artists and histories of art movements. 1254 Third Street Promenade, Santa Monica. ✆ 310/458-9074. www.hennesseyingalls.com.

Midnight Special Bookstore   This medium-size general bookshop, located on the Third Street Promenade, is known for its good small-press selection and regular poetry readings. 1318 Third Street Promenade, Santa Monica. ✆ 310/393-2923. www.msbooks.com.

L.A.'S WESTSIDE & BEVERLY HILLS

Barnes & Noble This national chain is represented throughout the city. B&N offers discounts on bestsellers and also comfy chairs to shoppers who like to read a bit before they buy. The Westwood branch is one of their larger stores and is conveniently attached to the vast Westside Pavilion shopping mall; there's plenty of free parking downstairs. You'll also find branches in Santa Monica (1201 Third Street Promenade; ✆ **310/260-9110**) and Pasadena (111 W. Colorado Blvd.; ✆ **626/585-0362**). 10850 W. Pico Blvd. (Westside Pavilion), Los Angeles. ✆ 310/475-4144. www.bn.com.

Book Soup One of L.A.'s most celebrated bookshops, selling mainstream and small-press books and hosting regular book signings and author nights. Book Soup is a great browsing shop; it has a large selection of showbiz books and an extensive outdoor news and magazine stand. The owners recently annexed an adjacent cafe space so they can better cater to hungry intellectuals. The **Book Soup Bistro** has a bar, a charming outdoor patio, and a classical bistro menu. 8818 Sunset Blvd., West Hollywood. ✆ 310/659-3110. www.booksoup.com.

Borders Borders offers one-stop shopping for books, CDs, greeting cards, and even cappuccino. The La Cienega branch is a block away from the Beverly Center; the Westwood branch is favored by students from nearby UCLA. 1360 Westwood Blvd., Westwood. ✆ 310/475-3444. Also at 330 S. La Cienega Blvd. (at 3rd St.), Los Angeles. ✆ 310/659-4045. www.borders.com.

C.G. Jung Bookstore & Library This bookshop specializes in analytical psychology, folklore, fairy tales, alchemy, dream studies, myths, symbolism, and other related topics. Tapes and videocassettes are also sold. 10349 W. Pico Blvd. (east of Beverly Glen Blvd.), Los Angeles. ✆ 310/556-1196.

The Cook's Library There's a specialty bookshop for everyone in L.A.; this is where the city's top chefs find both classic and deliciously offbeat cookbooks and other food-oriented tomes. Browsing is welcomed, even encouraged, with tea, tasty treats, and rocking chairs. 8373 W. 3rd St. ✆ 323/655-3141.

Dutton's Brentwood Books This huge bookshop is well known not only for an extensive selection of new books, but also for its good children's section and an eclectic collection of used and rare books. There are more than 120,000 titles in stock at any one time. Dutton's hosts regular author readings and signings, and sells cards, stationery, prints, CDs, and select software. 11975 San Vicente Blvd. (west of Montana Ave.), Los Angeles. ✆ 310/476-6263. www.duttonsbrentwood.com.

Los Angeles Audubon Society Bookstore A terrific selection of books on nature, adventure travel, and ecology is augmented by bird-watching equipment and accessories. Phone for information on L.A. nature walks. Closed Monday. 7377 Santa Monica Blvd., West Hollywood. ✆ 323/876-0202. www.LAAudubon.org.

Mysterious Bookshop More than 20,000 used, rare, and out-of-print titles make this the area's best mystery, espionage, detective, and thriller bookshop. Author appearances and other special events are regularly scheduled. 8763 Beverly Blvd. (between Robertson and San Vicente blvd.), West Hollywood. ✆ 310/209-0415. www.mysteriousbookshop.com.

Traveler's Bookcase This store, one of the best travel bookshops in the West, stocks a huge selection of guidebooks and travel literature, as well as maps and travel accessories. A quarterly newsletter chronicles the travel adventures of the genial owners, who know firsthand the most helpful items to carry. Look for regular readings by well-known travel writers. 8375 W. 3rd St. © **323/655-0575.** www.travelbooks.com.

HOLLYWOOD
Samuel French Book Store   This is L.A.'s biggest theater and movie book-store. Plays, screenplays, and film books are all sold here, as well as scripts for Broadway and Hollywood blockbusters. 7623 Sunset Blvd. (between Fairfax and La Brea aves.), Hollywood. © **323/876-0570.** www.samuelfrench.com.

CAMERA EQUIPMENT & REPAIR
SAN FERNANDO VALLEY
Studio City Camera Exchange   There's comfort in the 1940s architecture of this corner photography store. Studio City Camera is there if you need film, developing, batteries, frames or albums, and used cameras (some quite col-lectible). You're also welcome to stop just to talk shop with fellow shutterbugs behind the counter. 12174 Ventura Blvd. (1 block west of Laurel Canyon Blvd.), Studio City. © **818/984-0565.** www.studiocitycamera.com.

CDS & MUSIC
SANTA MONICA & THE BEACHES
Hear Music   At the first L.A. branch of Boston's Hear Music chain, albums are grouped by genre, theme, and mood. Headphones are everywhere, so you can test a brand-new disc before you buy. 1429 Third Street Promenade, Santa Monica. © **310/319-9527.**

Pyramid Music   Seemingly endless bins of used compact discs and cassette tapes line the walls of this long, narrow shop on the Promenade. LPs, posters, cards, buttons, and accessories are also available. 1340 Third Street Promenade, Santa Monica. © **310/393-5877.**

L.A.'S WESTSIDE & BEVERLY HILLS
Rhino Records   This is L.A.'s premier alternative shop, specializing in new artists and independent-label releases. In addition to new releases, there's also a terrific used selection; music-industry types come here to trade in the records they don't want for the records they do, so you'll be able to find never-played promotional copies of brand-new releases at half the retail price. You'll also find the definitive collection of records on the Rhino label. Their recently opened store with all new and the latest used CDs, DVDs, books, and more, is at 2028 Westwood Blvd., Westwood. Their "Blow it" outlet, has everything $5 and under and is at 1720 Westwood Blvd., Westwood. © **310/474-8685.** www.rhino westwood.com.

Tower Records   Tower insists that it has L.A.'s largest selection of compact discs—more than 125,000 titles—despite the Virgin Megastore's contrary claim. Even if Virgin has more, Tower's collection tends to be more interesting and browser friendly. And the enormous shop's blues, jazz, and classical selec-tions are definitely better than the competition's. Open 365 days a year. 8811 W. Sunset Blvd., Hollywood. © **310/657-7300.** www.towerrecords.com.

Virgin Megastore   Some 100 CD "listening posts" and an in-store "radio sta-tion" make this megastore a music lover's paradise. Virgin claims to stock 150,000 titles, including an extensive collection of hard-to-find artists. 8000 Sun-set Blvd., Hollywood. © **323/650-8666.**

HOLLYWOOD

Vinyl Fetish   Back in the day, this Melrose staple catered only to serious punks, goths, and industrial-heads. These days dance, house music, and electronica are just as likely to fill their well-stocked bins, which do—despite the name—include CDs. The store still enjoys an edgy reputation as a serious music source among local musicians and industry professionals. 7305 Melrose Ave., Los Angeles. ✆ 323/935-1300.

FASHIONS

FOR MEN & WOMEN
Santa Monica & the Beaches

Fred Segal   They've become an L.A. institution, these breezy collections of ultrahip boutiques linked like departments of a single-story fashion maze. Shops include the latest apparel for men, women, and toddler, plus lingerie, shoes, hats, luggage, cosmetics, workout/lounge wear, and a cafe. Fred Segal also has major star-spotting potential (Matt Damon, Cameron Diaz, Sandra Bullock, and Kate Hudson are regulars; David Duchovny reportedly met his wife here when he asked her to help him pick out a suit). The original Fred Segal complex (1960) is at 8100 Melrose Ave., Los Angeles (✆ **323/651-4129**), but either is a rewarding shopping foray. 500 Broadway, Santa Monica. ✆ **310/458-9940**.

L.A.'s Westside & Beverly Hills

American Rag, Cie   First to draw shoppers back to industrial La Brea in the early '80s, American Rag has grown from a small vintage clothing store to include trendy new fashions on its own label, as well as adjacent boutiques selling shoes and children's clothes; there's even a kitchen and housewares shop with a small cafe. Once a best-kept secret of hip teenagers, the American Rag dynasty today draws more tourists than trendsetters. 150 S. La Brea Ave., Los Angeles. ✆ 323/935-3157.

Maxfield   Here you'll find some of L.A.'s best-quality avant-garde designs, including men's and women's fashions by Yamamoto, Comme des Garçons, Dolce & Gabbana, Jil Sander, and the like. Furniture and home accessories are also sold. The store's provocative window displays have ranged from sharp political statements to a Jerry Garcia tribute. 8825 Melrose Ave., West Hollywood. ✆ 310/274-8800.

FOR WOMEN & CHILDREN
Santa Monica & the Beaches

CP Shades   CP Shades is a San Francisco ladies' clothier whose line is carried by many department stores and boutiques. Fans will love this store, devoted solely to loose, casual cotton and linen separates. CP Shades's trademark monochromatic neutrals are meticulously arranged within an airy, well-lit interior. There's also a boutique in Pasadena, 20 S. Raymond Ave. (✆ **626/564-9304**). 2937 Main St., Santa Monica. ✆ **310/392-0949**.

L.A.'s Westside & Beverly Hills

Oilily (Kids)   This refreshingly colorful line of kids' play clothes came from the Netherlands like a storm, and now kids around town are all sporting candy-bright colors and retrobold florals. Moms get into the action, too, with a coordinating line of sun wear. 9520 Brighton Way, Beverly Hills. ✆ 310/859-9145. www.oilily.nl.

Polkadots & Moonbeams   This is actually two stores several doors apart, one carrying (slightly overpriced) hip young fashions for women, the other a vintage store with clothing, accessories, and fabrics from the 1920s to the 1960s, all in remarkable condition. Vintage store at 8367 and the modern store at 8381 W. 3rd St. © 323/651-1746.

Hollywood

Betsey Johnson Boutique   The New York–based designer has brought to L.A. her brand of fashion—trendy, cutesy, body-conscious women's wear in colorful prints and faddish fabrics. Also in Santa Monica at 2929 Main St. (© **310/ 452-7911**) and in the Beverly Center at 131 N. La Cienega (© **310/652-8391**. 8050 Melrose Ave., Los Angeles. © **323/852-1534**. www.betseyjohnson.com.

DISCOUNT

Loehmann's   Loehmann's is huge, and packed to the rafters with clothes, shoes, and accessories. Most of its stock is name brand and designer labels, though nothing ultratrendy are represented. The store is popular for business attire, conservative leisure wear, and bargains on fancy dress wear. Known for years as a women's enclave, Loehmann's recently opened a men's department offering the same great deals. Serious shoppers should check out the Back Room, where heavyweight designers like Donna Karan and Calvin Klein are represented alongside beaded and formal evening gowns. 333 S. La Cienega Blvd. (south of 3rd St.), Los Angeles. © **310/659-0674**.

Los Angeles downtown garment district   Reminiscent of the New York garment district, but not quite as frenetic, L.A.'s downtown has dozens of small shops selling designer and name-brand apparel at heavily discounted prices. A concentration of retail women's wear bargains—many by name-brand designers—can be found at the Cooper Building, 860 S. Los Angeles St. at 9th (© **213/622-1139**). Men should have some luck along the upper blocks of Los Angeles Street, where mostly business attire is displayed, with deep discounts on Hugo Boss, Armani, and other current suits (mainly Italian), plus similar savings on sport coats and shirts. Ties and vests are usually less stylish. Los Angeles St. between 7th St. and Washington Blvd.

VINTAGE
Santa Monica & the Beaches

Aardvark's Odd Ark   This large storefront near the Venice Beach Walk is crammed with racks of antique and used clothes from the 1960s, 1970s, and 1980s. It stocks vintage everything, from suits and dresses to neckties, hats, handbags, and jewelry—and it manages to anticipate some of the hottest new street fashions. There's another Aardvark's at 7579 Melrose Ave. (© **323/ 655-6769**). 85 Market St. (corner of Pacific Ave.), Venice. © **310/392-2996**.

L.A.'s Westside & Beverly Hills

Golyester   Before she opened this ladies' boutique, the owner's friends would take one look at her collection of vintage fabrics and clothes and gasp "Golly, Esther!"—Hence the whimsical name. You pay a little extra for the pristine condition of hard-to-find garments like unusual embroidered sweaters from the 1940s and 1950s, Joan Crawford–style suits from the 1940s, and vintage lingerie. 136 S. La Brea Ave., Los Angeles. © **323/931-1339**.

Yellowstone Clothing Co.   This Santa Barbara–based vintage clothing shop provides plaid Pendleton shirts and flowered 1950s sundresses to followers of grunge style, but the best stuff here isn't for sale. The owner's collections of aloha shirts, novelty neckties, and other memorabilia are proudly displayed in cases and on walls; they're the real reason we shop here. 712 N. La Brea Ave. (at Melrose Ave.), Los Angeles. © **323/931-6616**.

Tips **Dressing the Part: Where to Find Hollywood's Hand-Me-Downs**

Admit it: You've dreamed of being a glamorous movie or TV star—everyone has. Well, don't expect to be "discovered" during your L.A. vacation, but you can live out your fantasy by dressing the part. Costumes from famous movies, TV show wardrobes, castoffs from celebrity closets—they're easier to find (and more affordable to own) than you might think.

A good place to start is **Studio Wardrobe/Reel Clothes,** 5525 N. Cahuenga Blvd., North Hollywood (© 818/508-7762; www.reel clothes.com). You may recognize some of the clothes from movies and TV shows; most of the items were worn by stars or extras before being turned over for public sale. Prices range from $10 to $1,000. New shipments arrive every few days, and often include props and accessories from sets. Open daily from noon to 6pm.

At **The Place & Co.,** 8820 S. Sepulveda Blvd., Westchester (© 310/645-1539), the anonymity of the well-heeled clientele (sellers and buyers) is strictly honored. Here you'll find men's and women's haute couture—always the latest fashions, gently worn—at a fraction of the Rodeo Drive prices. All the designers are here: Ungaro, Bill Blass, Krizia, Donna Karan. You may have even seen that Armani suit or Sonia Rykiel gown you found in the racks on an Academy Awards attendee last year. Open Monday through Saturday from 10am to 6pm.

For sheer volume, you can't beat **It's A Wrap,** 3315 W. Magnolia Blvd., Burbank (© 818/567-7366; www.movieclothes.com). Every item here is marked with its place of origin, and the list is staggering: *Beverly Hills, 90210; Melrose Place; Seinfeld; Baywatch; Seventh Heaven; Sabrina the Teenage Witch; American Beauty; The Truman Show;* and so on. Many of these wardrobes (which include shoes and accessories) aren't outstanding but for their Hollywood origins: Jerry Seinfeld's trademark Polo shirts, for instance, are standard mall-issue. Some collectible pieces, like Sylvester Stallone's *Rocky* stars-and-stripes boxers,

Hollywood

Wasteland An enormous steel-sculpted facade fronts this L.A. branch of the Berkeley/Haight-Ashbury hipster hangout, which sells vintage and contemporary clothes for men and women. You'll find leathers and denim as well as some classic vintage, but mostly funky 1970s garb. This trendy store is packed with colorful polyester halters and bell-bottoms from the decade we'd rather forget. 7248 Melrose Ave., Los Angeles. © 323/653-3028.

The San Fernando Valley

Playclothes Men and women alike will thrill to the pristine selection of vintage clothes housed in this boutique, tucked into a burgeoning antiques row west of Coldwater Canyon Avenue. Playclothes approaches its stock with a sense of humor and knows exactly how each item was worn and accessorized in its are framed and on display. Open Monday through Saturday from 11am to 6pm, Sunday from 11am to 4pm.

When you're done at It's A Wrap, stop in across the street at **Junk For Joy,** 3314 W. Magnolia Blvd., Burbank (© **818/569-4903**). A Hollywood wardrobe coordinator or two will probably be hunting through the racks right beside you at this wacky little store. The emphasis here is on funky items more suitable as costumes than everyday wear (the store is mobbed each year around Halloween). When we visited, the shop was loaded with 1970s polyester shirts and tacky slacks, but you never know what you'll find. Open Tuesday through Friday from 10am to 6pm, Saturday from 11am to 6pm.

The grande dame of all wardrobe and costume outlets is **Western Costume,** 11041 Vanowen St., North Hollywood (© **818/760-0900;** www.westerncostume.com). In business since 1912, Western Costume still designs and executes wardrobes for major motion pictures; when filming is finished, the garments are added to their staggering rental inventory. This place is perhaps best known for outfitting Vivien Leigh in *Gone with the Wind.* Several of Scarlett O'Hara's memorable gowns were available for rent until they were recently auctioned off at a charity event. Western also maintains an outlet store, where damaged garments are sold at rock-bottom (nothing over $15) prices. If you're willing to do some rescue work, there are definitely hidden treasures here. Open for rentals Monday through Friday from 8am to 5:30pm, for sales Tuesday through Friday from 10am to 5pm.

Finally, don't miss **Golyester,** 136 S. La Brea Ave. (© **323/931-1339**). This shop is almost a museum of finely preserved (but reasonably priced) vintage clothing and fabrics. The staff will gladly flip through stacks of *Vogue* magazines from the 1930s, 1940s, and 1950s with you, pointing out the lavish, star-studded original advertisements for various outfits in their stock. Open Monday through Saturday from 11am to 6pm.

heyday. 11422 Moorpark St. (1 block west of Laurel Canyon Ave.), Studio City. © **818/755-9559.**

MEMORABILIA
SANTA MONICA & THE BEACHES
Mayhem   This shop sells autographed guitars and other music memorabilia from U2, Nirvana, Springsteen, Bon Jovi, Pearl Jam, and other rockers. The buyers are often collectors, including the owners of the Hard Rock Cafes. 1411 Third Street Promenade, Santa Monica. © **310/451-7600.**

HOLLYWOOD
Collector's Book Store   Recently relocated from cramped quarters nearby, this archive of film-related memorabilia, books, and photographs provides

fascinating browsing for even the most jaded Angeleno. Vintage fan mags like *Photoplay* and *Screen Stars;* reproduction lobby cards; black-and-white 8-by-10s, including the classic Betty Grable pinup shot; and an eclectic array of collector's card series are just the beginning. Books here range from the sublime (a vintage copy of the 1943 John Barrymore bio *Good Night, Sweet Prince*) to the ridiculous (*Jen-X,* the biography of outgoing former Playmate Jenny McCarthy) and beyond (the encyclopedia-style *Full Frontal: Male Nudity Video Guide*). 6225 Hollywood Blvd., Hollywood. © 323/467-3296.

Hollywood Book City   More than 70,000 color prints of past and present stars are available, along with a good selection of autographs from the likes of Lucille Ball ($175), Anthony Hopkins ($35), and Grace Kelly ($750). 6627 Hollywood Blvd., Hollywood. © 323/466-2525.

Moletown *(Kids)*   Every movie and TV buff will find something good in this amusement park of a store, where T-shirts, hats, key chains, mugs, jackets, and posters all carry logos and artwork from productions as diverse as *The Sopranos, Sex & the City, Gladiator, Erin Brockovich,* and *The Simpsons.* More traditional are goods with the logos of studios like MGM and Universal; our favorite is merchandise with artwork from classic TV series (*Bewitched, I Dream of Jeannie, Charlie's Angels,* and more). It's all officially manufactured by the studios, and available at each studio's individual gift shop—but Moletown is one-stop, crowd-free shopping. 900 N. La Brea Ave. (at Willoughby), Los Angeles. © 800/851-7221. www.moletown.com.

TRAVEL GOODS
Also see Traveler's Bookcase under "Books," earlier in this chapter.

SANTA MONICA & THE BEACHES
California Map and Travel Center   This store carries a good selection of domestic and international maps and travel accessories, including guides for hiking, biking, and touring. Globes and atlases are also sold. 3312 Pico Blvd., Santa Monica. © 310/396-6277. www.mapper.com.

PASADENA & ENVIRONS
Distant Lands Bookstore and Outfitters   This duo of stores is a practical treasure trove for everyone from daring adventurers to armchair tourists. The bookstore has a terrific selection of maps, guides, and travel-related literature, while the travel outfitter two doors away offers everything from luggage and pith helmets to convenient, space-saving travel accessories. 54 and 62 S. Raymond Ave., Pasadena. © 626/449-3220 or 800/310-3220. www.distantlands.com.

10

Los Angeles After Dark

by Bryan Lane

Los Angeles has some of the most happening clubs and bars in the world and is the polestar for the best and brightest in the music scene. Whether you are looking to hit the town dressed to the nines ready to rub elbows with the stars, or simply want to throw on some jeans and imbibe at a poorly lit "dive," L.A. has a place for you. Live music of all stripes can be found everywhere (from large stadium-type venues to 50-person clubs) and there is a thriving dance and underground scene for you hipsters. L.A. is the place to see and be seen or if you so desire, simply melt into the crowd.

Your best bet for one stop shop info is the *L.A. Weekly* (www.laweekly.com), a free weekly paper available at sidewalk stands, shops, and restaurants. It has all the most up-to-date news on what's happening in Los Angeles's playhouses, cinemas, museums, and live-music venues. The Sunday "Calendar" and Thursday "Weekend" sections of the *Los Angeles Times* (www.calendar-live.com) are also a good source of information on what's going on after dark. **Ticketmaster (𝄐 213/480-3232;** www.ticketmaster.com) is L.A.'s major charge-by-phone ticket agency, selling tickets to concerts, sporting events, plays, and special events.

1 The Live Music Scene

Los Angeles's music scene is a many-headed hydra, a daunting and dizzying beast. But on any given night, finding something to satisfy any musical fancy is easy, because this city is at the center of the entertainment industry. Every day, countless national and international acts are drawn here. From acoustic rock to jazz-fusion, from Judas Priest cover bands to Latin funk, from the up-and-coming to the already gone, L.A.'s got it all.

But there's a rub. The big events are easy to find, but by the time you get to town, odds are the good tickets will be gone. The best advice is to plan ahead. On the Internet both **Ticketmaster** (see above) and concert business trade publication **Pollstar** (www.pollstar.com) have websites that include tour itineraries of acts that are on—or will be going on—the road. Just start your search in advance. For a listing of smaller shows closer to the date of your arrival, remember that both the *L.A. Weekly* and the *Los Angeles Times* "Calendar" section have websites (see above). We also recommend logging onto **www.localmusic2.com**, which provides 2 weeks worth of schedules organized by neighborhood and/or style. Sometimes tickets may come available at the box office before shows, or when all else fails try "negotiating" with some of the locals in front of the venue.

LARGE CONCERTS

Mostly gone are the days of the behemoth stadium shows, excepting, of course, the occasional U2 or Rolling Stones tour. Still, major national and international acts tend to be attracted to some of the city's larger venues.

Tips A Note on Smoking

In 1998, California enacted legislation that banned smoking in all restaurants and bars. Despite repeated efforts by opponents to repeal the law—and willful disregard by some proprietors—it's more widely enforced every year; if you're looking to light up in clubs, lounges, and other nightspots, better check to see what the locals are doing first.

The crown of Downtown and home to the Lakers and Clippers is the **STAPLES Center,** 1111 S. Figueroa St. (© **877/673-6799**). This combination sports/event stadium is now a primary concert venue with recent acts including Crosby, Stills, Nash and Young, and the Eagles.

Amphitheaters are the staple of national rock and pop concert tours. Los Angeles's two main warriors are the outdoor **Greek Theatre** in Griffith Park, 2700 N. Vermont Ave., Los Angeles (© **323/665-1927;** www.nederlander .com/greek.html), and the indoor **Universal Amphitheatre,** Universal City Drive, Universal City (© **818/777-3931**), each seating about 6,000. Both are among the most accommodating and comfortable facilities for big-name acts. Nearly as beautiful as the Hollywood Bowl, the Greek books a full season of national acts, from Carlos Santana and the Brian Setzer Orchestra to John Tesh and Barry Manilow. Be advised that getting out afterward can be a problem, as cars are stacked in packed lots, often making exiting a slow process.

Universal Amphitheatre has one advantage over the Greek: it has a roof, so it can book year-round. It's not as aesthetically pleasing, but it is quite comfortable and none of its seats are too far from the stage. For some events, the "Party in the Pit" offers a general admission section next to the stage. In addition to pop stars from Celine Dion to Jane's Addiction, the Universal has also booked such theater events as *The Who's Tommy.* While the neon jungle of Universal's City-Walk doesn't appeal to everyone, it does offer plenty of pregig dining options.

Orange County's **Verizon Wireless Amphitheatre** (formerly Irvine Meadows), 8800 Irvine Center Dr., Laguna Hills (© **949/855-8096**), which holds 15,000 (including a general-admission lawn *way* in the back), hosts KROQ's often-spectacular summertime "Weenie Roast" and KIIS's "Summer Jam" each year, as well as a plethora of touring rock acts, including recent shows from Marilyn Manson and Garbage. If you're going from L.A. on a weekday, get an early start, since Irvine is located at one of the most heavily traveled freeway junctions in the country.

Another popular venue is the **Arrowhead Pond of Anaheim,** 2695 E. Katella Ave. (1 mile east of I-5), Anaheim (© **714/704-2400;** www.arrowheadpond. com), a combination sports/event stadium that's gaining momentum as a primary concert venue. Recent highlights at the shiny new site include heavy hitters like Ricky Martin, Bruce Springsteen, and local fave No Doubt. It's about an hour from Los Angeles via the always-crowded I-5 freeway, but convenient to Disneyland-goers (about 8 min. away).

MIDSIZE CONCERTS

House of Blues With three great bars, cutting-edge southern art, and a key Sunset Strip location, there are plenty of reasons music fans and industry types keep coming back to House of Blues. Night after night, audiences are dazzled by performances from nationally and internationally acclaimed acts as diverse as

Duran Duran, Eric Clapton, and the Fugees. The food in the upstairs restaurant can be great (reservations are a must), and the Sunday gospel brunch, though a bit pricey, promises a rollicking time. 8430 Sunset Blvd., West Hollywood. © **323/848-5100**. www.hob.com.

The Mayan Theatre   Perhaps the strangest yet coolest concert venue in town, with an elaborate decor in the mode of a Mayan temple (or something), this former movie house is a fine relic of L.A.'s glorious past. It seats about 1,000 for such performers as PJ Harvey, Ani DiFranco, and Depeche Mode. The place is in a part of downtown L.A. that most people don't usually visit; but there's plenty of parking, and the interior makes it seem like another dimension. 1038 S. Hill St., Downtown. © **213/746-4287**. www.mayan-theatre.com.

The El Ray Theatre   Another restored relic of L.A.'s old Art Deco movie theaters, this small venue holds about 1,500 for such performers as Mick Jagger and Little Feat. It offers upstairs and downstairs views of the stage, but plan on standing all night as there are usually no seats available. 5515 Wilshire Blvd., between La Brea and Fairfax. © **323/936-4790**.

The Palace   A classic vaudeville house, the 1,200-capacity theater—just across Vine from the famed Capitol Records tower—was the site of numerous significant alternative-rock shows in the 1990s, including appearances by Nirvana, the Smashing Pumpkins, and Squirrel Nut Zippers. After-hours dance parties are also a huge draw; rock fans stick around to party and watch the musicians as they leave the venue. 1735 N. Vine St., Hollywood. © **323/462-3000**. www.hollywoodpalace.com.

Wiltern Theatre   Saved from the wrecking ball in the mid-1980s, this WPA-era Art Deco showcase is perhaps the most beautiful theater in town. Countless national and international acts such as Radiohead have played here. In addition, plenty of non-pop music events such as Penn & Teller and top ballet troupes complement the schedule. 3790 Wilshire Blvd., Los Angeles. © **213/388-1400**. www.sites andinsights.com/Wiltern/wiltern1.htm.

THE CLUB SCENE

With more small clubs than you can swing a Stratocaster at, Los Angeles is *the* place for live music. Check the *L.A. Weekly* to see who's in town during your visit. Unless otherwise noted, listed clubs admit only patrons 21 and over.

MOSTLY ROCK

Al's Bar, in the American Hotel   Al's is the last of a dying breed of downtown hellholes that regularly attracts fun underground music. If you can brave the neighborhood, which is sketchy at best, a good time can almost always be had here. 305 S. Hewitt St., Downtown. © **213/625-9703**. www.alsbar.net. Cover none–$5.

Coconut Teaszer   In some ways the Teaszer is a carry-over of the 1980s, with prealternative hard-rockin' dudes mostly trying to impress record-company talent scouts. It's a good place for local acts that you've never heard of and most likely will never hear of again. But who knows—the night you're there may be the night a future superstar is discovered. 8117 Sunset Blvd., West Hollywood. © **323/ 654-4773**.

Dragonfly   Not one to miss a trend, Dragonfly went from being a dance club that offered live music to becoming a live stage that offers dancing. From "surprise" shows by top-notch local acts such as Rage Against the Machine and Porno for Pyros to surprising national acts—Run-D.M.C. at an alternative music club?—Dragonfly is soaring. Overheated guests and smokers also enjoy its cool outdoor patio. 6510 Santa Monica Blvd., Hollywood. ✆ **323/466-6111**. www.dragonfly.com.

The Garage This Silver Lake club sprang up from the underground and remains firmly planted therein. With a coat of well-placed paint and some colorful folk art, this former garage books some of the finest names in local bands, both signed and unsigned. On Wednesdays, there's a hip-hop night with guest DJs. 4519 Santa Monica Blvd., Silver Lake. ✆ **323/662-6166**. Cover none–$5.

The Knitting Factory Straight from the New York City legend, a West Coast branch of the famous Knitting Factory has arrived in the redeveloping Hollywood Boulevard nightlife district. The Main Stage was inaugurated by a Posies performance, and sees such diverse bookings as Kristin Hersh, Pere Ubu, and Jonathan Richman; a secondary AlterKnit stage has sporadic shows. The new Factory is totally wired for digital, including interactive online computer stations throughout the club. 7021 Hollywood Blvd., Hollywood. ✆ **323/463-0204**. www.theknittingfactory.com/KFLA.

Largo There's always an eclectic array of performances going on at this dinner and music venue, ranging from the plugged-in folk set to vibrant trip hoppers. Since 1997, pop-music archaeologist Jon Brion has been putting forth some amazing Friday-night shows, including regular appearances by the Eels and Grant Lee Buffalo—and some not-so-regular appearances by Fiona Apple and Colin Haye (from Men at Work). 432 N. Fairfax Ave., Los Angeles. ✆ **323/852-1073** or 323/852-1851. All ages. Cover $5–$15.

Lava Lounge The interior of this small bar and performance space, located in a *très*-ugly strip mall, is very inventive. The lovely owner, a former set decorator, calls the motif "Vegas in hell." Think ticky tacky coupled with big-city chic. Live music includes mostly surf-a-billy with an occasional polyester disco cover band, and regulars include Quentin Tarantino. 1533 La Brea Ave., Hollywood. ✆ **323/876-6612**. Cover $2–$5.

McCabe's Guitar Shop For 20-plus years, this 40-something store has opened its backroom for some memorable acoustic sets from the likes of Doc Watson, Aimee Mann, Bill Frisell, and Ann Wilson. McCabe's is intimate in the extreme; the gig would have to be in your living room to get any cozier. A guitar shop first and music venue second, McCabe's doesn't serve alcohol. 3101 Pico Blvd., Santa Monica. ✆ **310/828-4403**. www.mccabes.com. All ages. Cover $10–$20.

The Mint Once a shotgun shack serving fried chicken and blues in a beer-only bar, the Mint has reemerged as a gloriously loungey hangout for rock/pop/blues devotees. The clientele—ranging from youthful scenesters to middle-aged moms—packs the place to catch regular performances by such diverse artists as G. Love & Special Sauce, Gwen Stefani, the Rembrandts, and Duke Robillard. 6010 W. Pico Blvd., Los Angeles. ✆ **323/954-9630**. www.theminthollywood.com. Cover $5–$10.

Moomba This branch of New York's hot spot opened in 2001, promising New American cuisine, hip supper club entertainment, and several satellite bars for lounging. The nightclub, in the former LunaPark space in West Hollywood's (WeHo's) club zone, was completely overhauled with "cruelty free" and environmentally chic interiors. Proprietor Jeff Gossett is ensuring that, as in NYC, Moomba will be as much a restaurant destination as nightspot—he's garnered a heavy-hitting San Francisco chef de cuisine and former Spago manager. 665 N. Robertson Blvd., West Hollywood. ✆ **310/652-6364**.

Roxy   Veteran record producer/executive Lou Adler opened this Sunset Strip club in the mid-1970s with concerts by Neil Young and a lengthy run of the pre-movie *Rocky Horror Show.* Since then, it's remained among the top showcase venues in Hollywood—although the revitalized Troubadour and such new entries as the House of Blues challenge its preeminence among cozy clubs. 9009 Sunset Blvd. ✆ 310/276-2222.

Spaceland   The wall-to-wall mirrors and shiny brass posts decorating the interior create the feeling that, in a past life, Spaceland must've been a seedy strip joint, but the club's current personality offers something entirely different. Having hosted countless performances by cutting-edge artists, such as Pavement, Mary Lou Lord, Grant Lee Buffalo, Elliot Smith, and the Eels, this hot spot on the fringe of east Hollywood has become one of the most important clubs on the L.A. circuit. 1717 Silver Lake Blvd., Silver Lake. ✆ 323/661-4380.

The Troubadour   This West Hollywood mainstay radiates rock history—from the 1960s to the 1990s; the Troub really has seen 'em all. Audiences are consistently treated to memorable shows from the already-established or young-and-promising acts that take the Troubadour's stage. But bring your earplugs—this beer- and sweat-soaked club likes it loud. 9081 Santa Monica Blvd., West Hollywood. ✆ 310/276-6168. www.troubadour.com. All ages.

Viper Room   This world-famous club on the Strip has been king of the hill since it was first opened by actor Johnny Depp and co-owner Sal Jenco back in 1993. With an intensely electric and often star-filled scene, the intimate club is also known for unforgettable, late-night, surprise performances from such powerhouses as Johnny Cash, Iggy Pop, Tom Petty, Nancy Sinatra, and Everclear (to name but a few) after headline gigs elsewhere in town. 8852 Sunset Blvd., West Hollywood. ✆ 310/358-1880. www.viperroom.com.

Whisky A Go Go   This legendary bi-level venue personifies L.A. rock and roll, from Jim Morrison to X to Guns N' Roses to Beck. Every trend has passed through this club, and it continues to be the most vital venue of its kind. With the hiring of an in-house booker a few years ago, the Whisky began showcasing local talent on free-admission Monday nights. 8901 Sunset Blvd., West Hollywood. ✆ 310/652-4202. www.whiskyagogo.com. All ages.

BLUES & JAZZ

Aside from the clubs that we list in this section, there are several casual options for evenings of free jazz in interesting settings. The **Los Angeles County Museum of Art,** 5905 Wilshire Blvd., Los Angeles (✆ 323/857-6000; www.lacma.org), hosts free concerts in its open central court every Friday night from 5:30 to 8:30pm, April through December. This is a great way to listen to good music with a glass of wine on a warm Los Angeles evening. June through September, the **Museum of Contemporary Art,** 250 S. Grand Ave., Downtown (✆ 213/626-6222; www.moca-la.org), and its sister annex **Geffen Contemporary at MOCA,** 152 N. Central Ave., Downtown in Little Tokyo (✆ 213/663-5334; www.moca-la.org), take turns offering free jazz concerts from 5 to 8pm every Thursday. Both the MOCA and the Geffen Contemporary pair a new wine and microbrew beer to match the flavor of each week's performer.

The Baked Potato   Like its North Hollywood parent (see below), this restaurant/nightspot offers missile-sized spuds while hosting a steady roster of jazz performances by local and visiting acts. Guitarist Andy Summers, formerly of the Police and later the music director for the short-lived *Dennis Miller Show,* does gigs now and again. The valley location is a few blocks from Universal City at 3787 Cahuenga Blvd., North Hollywood (© **818/980-1615;** www.thebaked potato.com). 6266½ Sunset Blvd., Hollywood. © **323/461-6400.** www.bakedpotatojazz.com.

B. B. King's Blues Club   Nestled away in Universal CityWalk's commercial plaza, this three-level club/restaurant—the ribs alone are worth the trip—hosts plenty of great local and touring national blues acts and is a testament to the establishment's venerable namesake. There's no shortage of good seating, but if you find yourself on the top two levels, it's best to grab a table adjacent to the railing to get an ideal view of the stage. CityWalk, Universal City. © **818/622-5464.**

Catalina Bar & Grill   This clubby old-timer represents the very best of down- town Hollywood's golden era. Though the neighborhood has become rough around the edges, this premier supper club still manages to book some of the biggest names in contemporary jazz for multinight stints. The acoustics are great and there really are no bad seats. 1640 N. Cahuenga Blvd., Hollywood. © **323/466-2210.** www.catalinajazzclub.com. All ages. Cover $10–$20.

Fais Do-Do   Most nights of the week this architecturally unique New Orleans–style nightspot hosts jazz, blues, and the occasional rock combo. It's located in a once-upscale suburb west of Downtown, but the surrounding neighborhood has become somewhat sketchy. Originally built as a bank, the building has gone through several jazz-club incarnations. It's even rumored that Miles Davis once graced the stage. The club offers great music in a memorable atmosphere, as well as tasty Cajun and soul food from the busy kitchen. 5257 W. Adams Blvd., Los Angeles. © **323/954-8080.**

Jazz Bakery   Ruth Price's nonprofit venue is renowned for attracting some of the most important names in jazz—and for the restored Helms bakery factory that houses the club and inspires its name. Hers is a no-frills, all-about-the- music affair, and the place is pretty much BYO in the drinks department. Drummer Jimmy Cobb, the last remaining member of Miles Davis's "Kind of Blue" band, had a 4-night stint at JB recently. 3233 Helms Ave., Culver City. © **310/ 271-9039.** www.jazzbakery.org. All ages. Cover $10–$25.

Lunaria   For a civilized evening of jazz and dining, follow the locals to Lunaria, which offers dining Monday through Saturday and entertainment Tuesday through Sunday. The menu of performers ranges from the up-and-com- ing to renowned masters. If you come for dinner, there's no cover charge. 10351 Santa Monica Blvd., West L.A. © **310/282-8870.** All ages.

Harvelles Blues Club   Open since 1931, this Santa Monica hole in the wall claims to be the oldest blues club in Los Angeles. Many famous musicians have passed through including Albert King and Bonnie Raitt, and although it is nor- mally packed and the cover can be a bit steep, you can always rely on good blues here. 1432 4th Street, Santa Monica. © **310/395-1676.**

2 Dance Clubs

The momentous popularity of Latin dance and swing has resulted in the open- ing of new clubs dedicated to both, taking some of the pressure off the old standbys. DJ club culture is also on the rise locally, featuring noteworthy shows at some enjoyable clubs; such dance clubs, however, can come and go as quickly as you can say "jungle rave." Mere whispers of a happening thing elsewhere can practically relegate a club to a been-there-done-that status. Check the *L.A. Weekly* for updates on specific club information.

The Coconut Club   Master of entertainment Merv Griffin, remembering the legendary Coconut Grove ballroom in the now-abandoned Ambassador Hotel, has lavishly re-created its classy swank with this A-list dine-and-dance club in the Beverly Hilton. It offers some of the city's very best in Latin and swing dance on Fridays and Saturdays. This is a great place to bring your guy or doll to reenact the romantic splendor of Hollywood past. Entrance to Chimps Cigar Club is also included in the cover charge. 9876 Wilshire Blvd., Beverly Hills. ✆ **310/285-1358.** Cover $10.

The Conga Room   Attracting such Latin-music luminaries as Pucho & The Latin Soul Brothers, this one-time health club on the Miracle Mile has quickly become *the* nightspot for live salsa and merengue. Break up the evening of heart-melting, sexy Latin dancing with a trip to the dining room, where the chef serves up savory Cuban fare in a setting that conjures the romance of pre-Castro Cuba, or indulge yourself in the Conga Room's stylish cigar lounge. 5364 Wilshire Blvd., Los Angeles. ✆ **323/938-1696.** www.congaroom.com.

Deep   Recently redone to the tune of $1.5 million, this club oozes divine decadence. Visitors can enjoy the outside patio, dance on the glass-enclosed floor, or ogle the "eye-dancers" who float overhead in glass boxes. A maze of mirrors leads to the dance floor that is near the roped-off VIP rooms that served as walk-in refrigerators in a past life but now hold Hollywood's most famous. 1707 N. Vine Street, Hollywood. ✆ **323/462-1144.**

The Derby   This class-A east-of-Hollywood club has been at ground zero of the swing revival since the very beginning. Located at a former Brown Derby site, the club was restored to its original luster and detailed with a heavy 1940s edge. With Big Bad Voodoo Daddy as the onetime house band and regular visits from Royal Crown Revue, hep guys and dolls knew that the Derby was money even before *Swingers* transformed it into one of the city's most happenin' hangs. But if you come on the weekends, expect a wait to get in, and once you're inside, dance space is at a premium. 4500 Los Feliz Blvd., Los Feliz. ✆ **323/663-8979.** www.the-derby.com. Cover $7–$10.

El Floridita   This tiny Cuban restaurant-and-salsa club is hot, hot, hot. Despite its modest strip-lot locale, it draws the likes of Jennifer Lopez, Sandra Bullock, Jimmy Smits, and Jack Nicholson, in addition to a festive crowd of Latin-dance devotees who groove well into the night. The hippest nights continue to be Mondays, when Johnny Polanco and his swinging New York–flavored salsa band get the dance floor jumpin'. 1253 N. Vine St., Hollywood. ✆ **323/ 871-8612.** Cover $10.

Hollywood Athletic Club   Built in 1924, this pool hall, restaurant, and nightclub is home to some groovin' dance clubs. Saturdays feature a lively mix of progressive house music spun by DJs Drew Down and Dave Audé. On Sundays, the sounds of Latin house, merengue, hip-hop, and salsa fill the air. Hollywood Athletic Club also hosts concerts from internationally known DJs and bands as diverse as Mono and the Wu Tang Clan. 6525 Sunset Blvd., Hollywood. ✆ **323/462-6262** or 323/957-0722. Cover $10–$20.

The Palace   Weekend nights this Hollywood landmark music hall turns the power of its 20,000-watt sound system on the dancing set. Fridays feature DJs upstairs and down, plus a cash-reward dance contest. Hip-hop, house, and pop are the order of the day on Saturdays, when Klub KIIS takes control of the turntables while also broadcasting live from the club. 1735 N. Vine Ave., Hollywood. ✆ **323/462-3000.** www.hollywoodpalace.com. 18 and over. Cover $10–$12.

Sugar   Wednesday through Saturday, club-goers pack this popular Santa Monica spot for its great dance clubs. If you're into funky house or soul lounge, try Lollipop or Chocolate on Wednesday and Thursday, respectively; hip-hop and funk are the musical fare on Friday at In the Raw; or you can escape to the world of progressive house, trance, and Euro electronica at Pure on Saturday. 814 Broadway, Santa Monica. (C) **310/899-1989.** Cover $10.

Viper Room   Every Tuesday night this live music hot spot (see "The Live Music Scene," above) hosts Atmosphere, featuring the sounds of trance, drum and bass, garage, techno, and hip-hop spun by an eclectic assemblage of DJs, MCs, and mix masters. On Mondays, a head-banging tribute to '80s metal/hard rock shakes the walls. 8852 Sunset Blvd., West Hollywood. (C) **310/358-1880.** www.viperroom.com. Cover $10.

16-50   Formerly Vynyl, this big open room, located on a Hollywood side street in the former home of a divey rock 'n' roll club, has theatrical—almost gothic—overtones. A trendy dance club with DJs (including occasional big name guests) spinning house and electronica, they also feature concerts by local and visiting bands that range from jazz to glam to contemporary. There's an elevated stage above the dance floor for people watching or checking out the go-go dancers in action. Though the crowd naturally varies according to what's on the night's schedule, it's a bit more upscale than trashy, with a look-like-you-mean-it dress code. 1650 Schrader Blvd., Hollywood. (C) **323/465-7449.** www.vynyl.com.

3 Bars & Cocktail Lounges

Akbar   On the outside, Akbar isn't much to look at with its brown stucco facade and simple (almost imperceptible) sign. Step inside, though, and you'll find one of the city's more moody and elegant rooms. Friendly barkeeps ply patrons with cocktails from behind the arabesque mirrored bar, and an astonishingly diverse CD jukebox is filled to capacity with tunes old and new. All that, plus plenty of cozy seating in dark nooks, makes this mecca an east Hollywood oasis. 4356 W. Sunset Blvd. (at Fountain), Los Angeles. (C) **323/665-6810.** No cover.

Beauty Bar   It's a proven concept in New York and San Francisco; a cocktail lounge/beauty salon. Decorated with vintage salon gear and sporting a hip-retro vibe, the Beauty Bar is campy, fun, and trendy all at once. Where else can you actually get a manicure while sipping cocktails with names like Blue Rinse (made with blue curaçao) or Prell (their version of a grasshopper)? 1638 N Cahuenga Blvd., Hollywood. (C) **323/464-7676.** www.beautybar.com. No cover.

Bob's Frolic Room I   This classic L.A. dive bar is located next door to the Pantages Theatre on Hollywood and Vine and is a great spot for a strong libation before a gig across the street at the Palace. Pumping to loud music from the best CD jukebox in Los Angeles, Hollywood vampires hang out and get their fill of stiff, cheap drinks. Look for Hedy Lamarr's star out front on the Hollywood Walk of Fame ("That's HEDLEY!"). 6245 Hollywood Blvd. Hollywood (C)**213/462-5890.** No Cover.

The Brig   This ultrahip bar and newly remodeled lounge, located at the end of the Abbot Kinney strip in Venice, attracts an eclectic crowd of young club-goers from all over L.A. The spacious main room pumps house beats, creating an atmosphere where the scantily clad women and well-dressed men vie for attention from the opposite sex. If you are just rolling off the beach however, don't be worried about being underdressed, because at The Brig, less is more. If you are lucky enough to get on the lone pool table, you can show off your skills and perhaps attract some of that sought after attention for yourself. 1515 Abbot Kinney Blvd., Venice. ℭ310/399-7537.

Circle Bar This hip spot is particularly popular with the postcollege crowd. A place to see and be seen, the Circle Bar packs them in nightly. Although it's located in Santa Monica, the scene is often more reminiscent of Hollywood. Its namesake, a large circular bar, gets very crowded on the weekends, but the bartenders pour a stiff drink that normally makes the wait worthwhile. The DJ spins everything from '80s to more progressive beats as the crowd dictates. Students, locals, and struggling actors all dance the night away and get their groove on while looking for that special someone. 2926 Main St., Santa Monica. ℭ310/450-0508. No cover.

Daddy's Bar and Lounge Trendy but not snooty, this comfortably laid out bar is the place to go if you actually want to hear your conversation while listening to a DJ spin soul, house, or hip-hop. 1610 Vine Street, Hollywood. ℭ 323/463-7777. No cover.

The Dresden Room Hugely popular with L.A. hipsters because of its longevity, location, often-overlooked cuisine, and elegant ambience "The Den" has been pushed into the mainstream of L.A. nightlife thanks to its inclusion in the movie *Swingers*. But it's the timeless lounge act of Marty and Elayne (the couple has been performing there up to 5 nights a week since 1982) has proven that fad or no fad, this place is always cool. Sidle up to the bar, where blue glasses are seen before patrons as they sip the house classic, Blood and Sand, a space-age margarita of sorts and of course, the ubiquitous martini and Manhattans. 1760 N. Vermont Avenue, Hollywood, ℭ (323)665-4294. No cover.

El Carmen Opened by L.A. restaurant-and-bar impresario Sean Macpherson, the man with the mescal touch, El Carmen conjures the feel of a back-alley Mexican cantina of a bygone era. Vintage Mexican movie posters, vibrant Latin American colors, and oil paintings of masked Mexican wrestlers decorate the Quonset-hut interior, while an eclectic jukebox offers an array of tunes from Tito Puente to the Foo Fighters. The busy bar boasts a gargantuan list of more than 100 tequilas and a small menu of tacos and light fare. 8138 W. 3rd St., Los Angeles. ℭ 323/852-1552. No cover.

Firefly Opened last year by Jeffery Best, a veteran of the Hollywood club scene, this dream of a bar and restaurant has quickly become a meeting place of choice for Hollywood clubbers and those hipsters who live in Silver Lake and Los Feliz. Flavored by '40s noire (think Bogie in *The Big Sleep*), this is a sexy and simple night spot where visitors can recline on comfy cushions or warm up by the fire pit in the middle of the restaurant area that opens onto a patio with cabana-like tables enclosed by drapes. DJs offer up a pumping mixes of soul and ambient sounds, and who knows what could happen in the coed bathrooms. 11720 Ventura Blvd., Studio City. ℭ 818/762-1833. No cover, 21 and over.

Goldfingers Goldfingers is tucked away on a grungy Hollywood corner, but its interior shines like freshly polished metal. It's a shotgun space glamorously swathed in gold from the upholstered walls to the lamé curtains. The crowd consists of anachronistically roguish and handsome Bond wannabes and sinewy, sexy Emma Peels, who pose seductively and converse around a white baby grand on the spotlit stage. 6423 Yucca St., Hollywood. ℭ 323/962-2913. www.goldfingersla.com. Cover $5.

Out & About: L.A.'s Gay & Lesbian Nightlife Scene

Los Angeles has a vibrant, powerful, and active gay and lesbian community. Some of Tinseltown's most celebrated names share equal prominence as both industry and gay and lesbian community leaders and have helped the city gain an outstanding reputation for its gay and AIDS-related activism. Every year in June, this active community comes out (pardon the pun) in full force for one of the city's most widely beloved events: the Gay Pride parade, which all but takes over West Hollywood in the spirit of activism and fun. If you're in town, this is not to be missed (see "Los Angeles–Area Calendar of Events," in chapter 2).

Although **West Hollywood (WeHo),** often referred to as "Boys Town," is probably the best-known gay neighborhood in Los Angeles, there are several other noteworthy enclaves. **Silver Lake** has a long-standing gay community that's worked hard to preserve the area's beautiful homes that Hollywood names like Charlie Chaplin and Cecil B. DeMille once called their own. To the west of WeHo, **Santa Monica** and **Venice** also enjoy a strong gay and lesbian presence. Venice for first-timers can be something of a shock. With its countless tattoo and piercing joints, coupled with the active parade of joggers, surfers, Muscle Beach beefcakes, and the usual cast of beach-bound freaks, Venice is Los Angeles's equivalent to San Francisco's Haight-Ashbury.

If you're looking for specific info on gay culture in L.A. (beyond what we include), there are several local options, including *4-Front Magazine* (© 323/650-7772), *Edge Magazine* (© 323/962-6994), and *Frontiers* (© 323/848-2222). *Edge* and *Frontiers* are the most prominent free biweekly gay mags and are available in coffeehouses and newsstands citywide. For these and other GLBT magazines, give the good people at **A Different Light Bookstore,** 8853 Santa Monica, West Hollywood (© 310/854-6601), a call or visit. The *L.A. Weekly* and *New Times Los Angeles* also have lesbian and gay articles and listings.

The Abbey This is *the* gay coffee bar. You can sit inside or out, drink a latte, and watch the parade of WeHo boys in muscle shirts. Most of West Hollywood seems to end up here on Saturday nights; k.d. lang occasionally makes an appearance. 692 N. Robertson Blvd., West Hollywood. © 310/289-8410. No cover.

Apache Territory The small dance floor fills on weekends with Valley boys bored by the snootier WeHo scene. This is a major pickup scene. It's especially popular on Thursday nights. 11608 Ventura Blvd., Studio City. © 818/506-0404.

Catch One Open until 3am most nights and 4am on weekends, Catch One pulls in an ethnically diverse gay, lesbian, and straight crowd. Thursday nights see a mostly female crowd. 4067 W. Pico Blvd., Los Angeles. © 323/734-8849.

Good Luck Bar Until they installed a flashing neon sign outside, only locals and hipsters knew about this Kung Fu–themed room in the Los Feliz/Silver Lake area. The dark red windowless interior boasts Oriental ceiling tiles, fringed

Club 7969   Fashionable of late, Club 7969 features male and female strippers baring it all while mingling with the gay, lesbian, and straight crowd. Each night has a different theme, ranging from drag burlesques to techno parties. On Tuesdays, Michelle's CC revue—with its legion of topless female dancers—attracts a largely lesbian crowd. 7969 Santa Monica Blvd., West Hollywood. ✆ 323/654-0280.

Cobalt Cantina   For years, the "Martini Lounge" located in this Silver Lake restaurant has been one of the hottest gay cocktail bars in town. Around the long bar and zinc-colored cocktail tables, gargantuan margaritas, and strong martinis are sipped by the buffed-out locals. The crowd is ethnically mixed and largely gay but definitely straight-friendly. The WeHo location's "Bluebar" is a quiet alternative to the nearby wild-party-oriented clubs. 4326 Sunset Blvd., Silver Lake. ✆ 323/953-9991. Also at 616 N. Robertson Blvd., West Hollywood. ✆ 310/659-8691. No cover.

Cuff's   Sparsely decorated with a few street signs and a hanging toilet seat, this dark one-room hangout attempts to exude a tough blue-collar look. Don't be fooled; the button-down exec-by-day crowd likes to butch it up by night in this denim-and-leather joint. 1941 Hyperion Ave., Silver Lake. ✆ 323/660-2649.

Dragstrip 66   Note the cover disparity: If you ain't in drag, prepare to pay for it (and wait in line a bit longer than the more fashionably hip). This great drag club, located in a Mexican restaurant, switches themes each month ("Chicks with Dicks" was a standout), and it offers up every type of music—except disco and Liza. That's entertainment. The second Saturday of each month at Rudolpho's, 2500 Riverside Dr., Silver Lake. ✆ 323/969-2596. Cover $10–$20.

Micky's   A diverse, outgoing and mostly older crowd cruises back and forth between the front-room bar and the dance floor in back. More women—probably looking to party with the friendly crowd and enjoy the great drink specials—are drawn to Micky's than to some of the neighboring bars. 8857 Santa Monica Blvd., West Hollywood. ✆ 310/657-1176. www.mickys.com.

The Other Side   This amiable place reputedly serves the best martini in Silver Lake. It's a handsome and intimate piano bar with plenty of friendly patrons, and the ideal place to meet people if you're new in town. 2538 Hyperion Ave., Silver Lake. ✆ 323/661-4233. No cover.

Rage   For almost 20 years this high-energy, high-attitude disco has been the preferred mainstay on WeHo's gay dance club circuit. Between turns around the dance floor, shirtless muscle boys self-consciously strut about—like peacocks flashing their plumes—looking to exchange vital statistics. 8911 Santa Monica Blvd., West Hollywood. ✆ 310/652-7055.

Chinese paper lanterns, sweet-but-deadly drinks like the "Yee Mee Loo" (translated as "blue drink"), and a jukebox with selections ranging from Thelonius Monk to Cher's "Half Breed." The spacious sitting room, furnished with mismatched sofas, armchairs, and banquettes provides a great atmosphere for conversation or romance. Arrive early to avoid the throngs of L.A. scenesters. 1514 Hillhurst Ave. (between Hollywood and Sunset blvds.), Los Angeles. © 323/666-3524. No cover.

Kane The classic spirit of American lounge is the mainstay at Kane, where sounds from recent decades—ranging from Bobby Darin to the Jackson 5—are spun by a DJ flanked by a duo of go-go dancers in hot pants. Kitsch notwithstanding, owner Ivan Kane has created a warm, friendly, inviting atmosphere reminiscent of 1960s and 1970s Vegas. 5574 Melrose Ave., Hollywood. © 323/466-6263. No cover.

Lola's The swimming pool–sized martinis are enough of a reason to trek over to Lola's. From the classic gin or vodka martini for the purist to the chocolate- or apple-flavored concoctions for the adventurous, Lola has a little something for everyone. Two bars, a billiard table, and plush couches hidden in dark, romantic corners make for an enjoyable setting and plenty of celeb spotting. 945 N. Fairfax Ave. (south of Santa Monica Blvd.), Los Angeles. © 213/736-5652. No cover.

Lounge 217 A lounge in the true sense of the word, these plush Art Deco surroundings just scream "martini"—and the bartenders stand ready to shake or stir up your favorite. Comfortable seating lends itself well to intimate socializing. On Mondays the Lounge hosts classical guitarists, and Thursday the torch singer and cigar bar set. Come early on the weekends for a more raucous late-night crowd. 217 Broadway (between Second and Third sts.), Santa Monica. © 310/281-6692.

The Mix What at first glance appears to be just another harmless Santa Monica cocktail bar, The Mix sucks you in and gets you moving with the crowd to house and trance beats. A local hot spot, it attracts all types of young hipsters looking to break a sweat on an overly crowded but fun dance floor. Despite the critical mass it's an intimate setting, so be prepared to get up close and personal—because at The Mix, an attitude to party is a crucial ingredient. Arrive early, as the place fills up quickly past midnight. 2810 Main St., Santa Monica. © 310/399-1953. Cover $5 after 11pm on weekends only.

Nicks Martini Lounge A laid-back vibe with an Asian flavor, this bar and restaurant elegantly combines good jazz bands and big-band trios with a huge variety of awesome martinis and appetizers. 453 N. Canon Drive, Beverly Hills. © 310/550-5707. No cover.

O'Brien's Pub O'Brien's offers everything it takes to make a great pub, including more beers on tap than one could possibly attempt to drink at one sitting. The food is far better than pub grub, so come hungry. Three levels and a patio allow for you to either post-up inside listening to live bands 6 nights a week, or grab some sun outside during the day. The clientele is mostly on the young side, but everyone seems to be treated like family. 2941 Main St., Santa Monica © 310/396-4725. No cover.

Red Lion Tavern A hidden veteran of the Silver Lake circuit, this kitschy, over-the-top German tavern—complete with dirndl-clad waitresses—is where neighborhood hipsters mingle with cranky, working-class German expats. The place serves hearty half liters of Warsteiner, Becks, and Bitburger, but braver souls—with bottomless bladders—can take on a 1.5-liter boot. The astonishingly good food offerings include schnitzel, bratwurst, and potato pancakes. 2366 Glendale Blvd., Silver Lake. © 323/662-5337. No cover.

The Room Accessed from an alley set back from the street, this low-key bar is a favorite hide-out for locals (you won't find a sign out front for this one).

Though small and crowded, you can usually find some space in the booths or opt for the dance floor where DJs spin music ranging from reggae to hip-hop and acid jazz. Look for the portrait of "the chairman of the board" placed proudly in the middle of the bar. 1626 N. Cahuenga Blvd., Hollywood. ✆ 323/462-7196. No cover.

Saddle Ranch Chophouse Located on the Sunset Strip next to the Hyatt House, this country-and-western–themed restaurant and nightclub resembles a scene taken right from "Urban Cowboy," right down to the mechanical bull, sawdust on the floor and a major rock 'n' roll attitude. The Chophouse has a 60-foot circular bar where the bartenders do an outstanding job of getting your drinks to you even in the thickest of crowds. After 10pm it gets packed with mostly younger Hollywood hopefuls. Food is good, not great, but the portions are huge, with the standard fare of steaks, chops, and monstrous baked potatoes that are great for a late-night snack. 8371 Sunset Blvd., West Hollywood. ✆ 323/650-601. No cover.

Skybar, at Mondrian Hotel Since its opening in hotelier Ian Schraeger's refurbished Sunset Strip hotel, Skybar has been a favorite among L.A.'s most fashionable of the fashionable set. This place is so hot that even the agents to the stars need agents to get in. (Rumor has it that one agent was so desperate to get in he promised one of the servers a contract.) Nevertheless, a little image consulting—affect the right look, strike the right pose, and look properly disinterested—might get you in to rub elbows with some of the faces that regularly appear on the cover of *People* (but please don't stare). 8440 W. Sunset Blvd., West Hollywood. ✆ 323/848-6025.

Three Clubs In the tradition of Hollywood hipster hangouts trying to maintain a low profile, Three Clubs (like the playing card) is absent of any signage indicating where you are. (Look for the BARGAIN CLOWN MART sign on the facade.) Inside this dark and cavernous lounge, you'll find a youthful, hoping-to-become-a-star-soon set mingling into the night. Even with two rooms, plenty of cushiony sofas, two long bars, and lots of spacious tables, this place is always loud and packed. 1123 N. Vine St., Hollywood. ✆ 323/462-6441. No cover.

Trader Vic's Opened in 1955, this trendy but fun bar and lounge is Polynesian tiki-kitsch deluxe, especially if you are in the mood for strong exotic drinks. A favorite watering hole for some Hollywood heavies, this is part of Victor Bergron's famous chain of Tahitian-themed restaurants where the mai tai originated. Vic's has a huge menu of specialty drinks like the mind-melting Scorpion bowl and "Navy Grog" and features great appetizers (aka "Pupu Platters") like the Beef Cho Cho—do-it-yourself skewers of teriyaki beef roasted over a flaming hibachi. 9876 Wilshire Blvd., Beverly Hills. ✆310/276-6345. No cover.

360 This 19th-story, penthouse-perched restaurant and lounge is a perfect place to romance your special someone. It's all about the view here—all 360° of it. The understated and softly lit sleek interior emphasizes the scene outside the plentiful windows, including a spectacular vista of the famed HOLLYWOOD sign. 6290 Sunset Blvd., Hollywood. ✆ 323/871-2995. www.360hollywood.com. No cover.

Voda Upscale and elegant, Voda uses natural elements such as candlelight and a waterfall that runs along the entire wall behind a huge backlit bar to create an atmosphere that pulses with a vibrant, hip undercurrent. Besides many star sightings such as Robert De Niro and Quentin Tarantino, you'll find excellent food and generous martinis. 1449 Second St., Santa Monica. ✆ 310/394-9774. No cover.

World Café Its excellent restaurant, top-notch appetizer menu, low-key jazz bands, unique artwork, and frequent drink specials make this a perfect place to begin any Santa Monica evening adventure. A refreshing venue with spacious and comfortable seating, warm patios, and a buzz of activity, the World acts as a reflection of the beehive of activity that flows around this part of the city. 2820 Main St., Santa Monica [tel}310/392-1661. No cover.

Yamashiro Enjoy the view of the city from this pagoda-and-garden perch in the Hollywood Hills. Though the place has long been considered a "special-occasion" Japanese restaurant, we prefer to sit in the lounge—mai tai in hand—and watch Hollywood's dancing searchlights dot the night sky. Great sushi and even better specialty drinks. There's no cover, but there's also no way around the $3.50 valet parking fee. 1999 N. Sycamore Ave., Hollywood. ℭ 323/466-5125.

4 Performing Arts

CLASSICAL MUSIC & OPERA

While L.A. is best known for its pop realms (see earlier in this chapter), other types of music here consist of top-flight orchestras and companies, both local and visiting, to fulfill the most demanding classical music appetites; scan the papers to find out who's performing while you're in the city.

The world-class **Los Angeles Philharmonic** (ℭ 323/850-2000; www.laphil.org) is the only major classical music company in Los Angeles. Finnish-born music director Esa-Pekka Salonen concentrates on contemporary compositions; despite complaints from traditionalists, he does an excellent job attracting younger audiences. Tickets can be hard to come by when celebrity players like Itzhak Perlman, Isaac Stern, Emanuel Ax, and Yo Yo Ma are in town. In addition to performances at the **Dorothy Chandler Pavilion** in the all-purpose Music Center, 135 N. Grand Ave., Downtown, the Philharmonic also plays a summer season at the **Hollywood Bowl** (see "Concerts Under the Stars," below), and a chamber music series at the **Skirball Cultural Center** (see chapter 7, p. 168). The philharmonic and the master choral will have a new home starting in 2003, the Walt Disney Concert Hall; designed by world-renown architect Frank O. Gehry, this exciting addition to the Music Center of L.A. includes a 2,273-seat concert hall, outdoor park, restaurant, cafe, bookstore, and gift shop.

Slowly but surely, the **Los Angeles Opera** (ℭ 213/972-8001; www.losangelesopera.com), which performs at the Dorothy Chandler Pavilion, is gaining respect and popularity with inventive stagings of classic pieces, modern operas, visiting divas, and the contributions from high profile artistic director Placido Domingo. The 120-voice **Los Angeles Master Chorale** sings a varied repertoire that includes classical and pop compositions. Concerts are usually held at the **Performing Arts Center** of L.A. County (ℭ 213/972-7200) October through June.

The **UCLA Center for the Performing Arts** (ℭ 310/825-2101; www.performingarts.ucla.edu) has presented music, dance, and theatrical

---

Finds Free Morning Music at Hollywood Bowl

It's not widely known, but the Bowl's morning rehearsals are open to the public (and absolutely free). On Tuesday, Thursday, and Friday from 9:30am to 12:30pm, you can see the program scheduled for that evening. So grab some coffee and doughnuts (the concession stands aren't open) and enjoy the best seats in the house.

performances of unparalleled quality for more than 60 years, and continues to be a major presence in the local and national cultural landscape. Presentations occur at several different theaters around Los Angeles, both on and off campus. UCLA's **Royce Hall** is the Center's pride; it has even been compared to New York's Carnegie Hall. Recent standouts from the Center's busy calendar included the famous Gyuto Monks Tibetan Tantric Choir and the Cinderella story "Cendrillon" with an original score by Sergei Prokofiev.

CONCERTS UNDER THE STARS
Also see "The Live Music Scene," earlier in this chapter.

Hollywood Bowl   Built in the early 1920s, the Hollywood Bowl is an elegant Greek-style natural outdoor amphitheater cradled in a small mountain canyon. This is the summer home of the Los Angeles Philharmonic Orchestra. Internationally known conductors and soloists often sit in on Tuesday and Thursday nights. Friday and Saturday concerts often feature orchestral swing or pops concerts. The summer season also includes a jazz series; past performers have included Natalie Cole, Dionne Warwick, and Chick Corea. Other events, from standard rock-and-roll acts like Radiohead to Garrison Keillor programs, summer fireworks galas, and the annual Mariachi Festival, are often on the season's schedule.

To round out an evening at the Bowl, many concertgoers use the occasion to enjoy a picnic dinner and a bottle of wine—it's one of L.A.'s grandest traditions. You can prepare your own, or order a picnic basket with a choice of hot and cold dishes and a selection of wines and desserts from Patina's on-site catering department, which also provides delivery to box seats. Call © **323/850-1885** by 4pm the day before you go to place your food order. 2301 N. Highland Ave. (at Pat Moore Way), Hollywood. © **323/850-2000.** www.hollywoodbowl.org.

THEATER
MAJOR THEATERS & COMPANIES
Tickets for most plays usually cost $10 to $35, although big-name shows at the major theaters can fetch up to $75 for the best seats. **Theatre League Alliance** (© 213/614-0556; www.TheatreLA.org, an association of live theaters and producers in Los Angeles (they also put on the yearly Ovation Awards, L.A.'s theater awards), offers same-day, half-price tickets via **Web Tix,** an Internet-only service at www.TheatreLA.org. Tickets are available Tuesday through Saturday from 4am to 11pm; purchase them online with a credit card and they'll be waiting for you at the box office. The site features a frequently updated list of shows and availability; you can also sign up for e-mail alerts. If you didn't bring your computer, log on at any public library, Internet cafe, or office service store.

The all-purpose **Music Center–Performing Arts Center of Los Angeles County,** 135 N. Grand Ave., Downtown, houses the **Ahmanson Theater** and **Mark Taper Forum,** as well as the **L.A. Philharmonic,** and **L.A. Opera.** The city's top two playhouses are home to the Center Theater Group (www.taperahmanson.com), and both are part of the **Ahmanson Theater** (© 213/628-2772), an active year-round theater, with shows produced by the in-house Center Theater Group or with traveling productions, often Broadway or London bred. Each season has guaranteed a handful of high-profile shows, such as Andrew Lloyd Webber's *Phantom of the Opera,* the Royal National Theatre's production of Ibsen's *Enemy of the People,* starring Sir Ian McKellan, and ballet impresario Matthew Bourne's *Cinderella.* The Ahmanson is so huge that you'll want seats in the front third or half of the theater.

The **Mark Taper Forum** (© **213/628-2772**) is a more intimate, circular theater staging contemporary works by international and local playwrights. Neil
Simon's humorous and poignant *The Dinner Party* and Tom Stoppard's witty
and eclectic *Arcadia* are two recent productions, each ideally suited to this intimate setting. Ticket prices vary depending on the performance. *Tip:* 2 hours
before curtain time, the Mark Taper Forum offers specially priced $12 tickets,
which must be purchased in person with cash.

Across town, the moderately sized **Geffen Playhouse,** 10886 Le Conte Ave.,
Westwood (© **310/208-5454**; www.geffenplayhouse.com), presents dramatic
and comedic work by prominent and emerging writers. UCLA purchased the
theater—which was originally built as a Masonic temple in 1929, and later
served as the Westwood Playhouse—back in 1995 with a little help from phil-
anthropic entertainment mogul David Geffen. This charming venue is often the
West Coast choice of many acclaimed off-Broadway shows, and also attracts
locally based TV and movie actors eager for the immediacy of stage work. One
recent production featured Annette Bening in Ibsen's *Hedda Gabler.* Always
audience-friendly, the Playhouse prices tickets in the $25 to $38 range.

The recently restored **Pantages Theatre,** 6233 Hollywood Boulevard
between Vine and Argyle (© **323/463-4367**), reflects the full Art Deco glory of
L.A.'s theater scene and features musicals on the level of *Cats* and just finished a
multiyear run of Disney's *The Lion King.*

Located at the foot of the Hollywood Hills, the 1,245-seat outdoor **John
Anson Ford Amphitheatre** (© **213/974-1343**; www.lacountyarts.org/ford.
html) is located in a county regional park and is set against a backdrop of cypress
trees and chaparral. It is an intimate setting with no patron more than 96 feet
away from the stage. Music, dance, film, theater, and family events run from
May through September. The indoor theater space, a cozy 87-seat space, that
was extensively renovated in November 1998 and renamed **[Inside] The Ford**,
features live music and theater year-round.

One of the most highly acclaimed professional theaters in L.A., the **Pasadena
Playhouse,** 39 S. El Molino Ave., near Colorado Boulevard, Pasadena (© **626/
356-7529;** www.pasadenaplayhouse.org), is a registered historic landmark that
has served as the training ground for many theatrical, film, and TV stars, including William Holden and Gene Hackman. Productions are staged on the main
theater's elaborate Spanish Colonial revival.

For a schedule at any of the above theaters, check the listings in *Los Angeles
Magazine,* available at most area newsstands, or the "Calendar" section of the
Sunday *Los Angeles Times,* or call the box offices at the numbers listed above.

SMALLER PLAYHOUSES & COMPANIES

On any given night, there's more live theater to choose from in Los Angeles than
in New York City, due in part to the surfeit of ready actors and writers chomp-
ing at the bit to make it in Tinseltown. Many of today's familiar faces from film
and TV spent plenty of time cutting their teeth on L.A.'s busy theater circuit,
which is home to nearly 200 small- and medium-sized theaters and theater companies, ranging from the 'round-the-corner, neighborhood variety to high-profile, polished troupes of veteran actors. With so many options, navigating the
scene to find the best work can be a monumental task. A good bet is to choose
one of the theaters listed below, which have established excellent reputations for
their consistently high quality productions; otherwise, consult the *L.A. Weekly,*
which advertises most current productions, or call **Theatre LA** (© **213/
688-2787**) for up-to-date performance listings.

The **Colony Studio Theatre,** 555 N. Third Street, Burbank (© **818/558-7000;** www.colonytheatre.org), was formed in 1975 and has developed from a part-time ensemble of TV actors longing for their theatrical roots into a nationally recognized company. Moving in 2000 from their longtime home, a converted silent-movie house, the company now produces plays in all genres at the 276-seat Burbank Center Stage, which is shared with other performing arts groups.

Actors Circle Theater, 7313 Santa Monica Blvd., West Hollywood (© **323/882-8043**), is a 47-seater that's as acclaimed as it's tiny. Look for original contemporary works throughout the year.

The **Actor's Gang Theater,** 6201 Santa Monica Blvd., Hollywood (© **323/465-0566**), is not one to shy from irreverence. Back in 1997 the in-house company, a group of UCLA alums, presented *Bat Boy: The Musical,* based on a story in the bizarre tabloid *Weekly World News.* The theater also lends its stage to outside companies, such as the Namaste Theater Company, which performed Tony Kushner's rendition of *The Illusion* in 1999.

The classical theater company **A Noise Within,** 5151 State University Dr. (© **323/224-6320**), has performed everything from Shakespeare to Coward to Molière. In 1999, the company moved to the Luckman Fine Arts Complex on the campus of Cal State L.A., located northeast of Downtown. Recent highlights included Shakespeare's *Cymbeline* and Williams's *Cat on a Hot Tin Roof.*

Founded in 1965, **East-West Players,** 120 N. Judge John Aiso St., Los Angeles (© **323/625-7000;** www.eastwestplayers.com), is now the oldest Asian American theater company in the United States. It's been so successful that the company moved from a 99-seat venue to the 200-seat David Henry Huang Theater in downtown L.A. in 1998. To commemorate the massacre in Tiananmen square, EWP presented the musical *Beijing Spring* in 1999, and in 2001 revived Frank Chin's Asian American classic, *Year of the Dragon.*

The 25-year-old **L.A. Theatre Works** (© **310/827-0889**) is renowned for its marriage of media and theater and has performed more than 200 plays and logged more than 350 hours of on-air programming. Performances are held at the wonderful Skirball Cultural Center (see "Museums & Galleries," in chapter 7), nestled in the Sepulveda Pass near the Getty Center. In the past, personalities such as Richard Dreyfuss, Julia Louis-Dreyfus, Jason Robards, Annette Bening, and John Lithgow have given award-winning performances of plays by Arthur Miller, Neil Simon, Joyce Carol Oates, and more. For 7 years now, the group has performed simultaneously for viewing and listening audiences in its radio theater series. In 2001, L.A. Theatre Works presented Chekhov's *The Cherry Orchard,* starring veteran actress Marsha Mason. Tickets are usually around $35; a full performance schedule can be found online at **www.skirball.org**.

Founded in 1981, **West Coast Ensemble Theater,** 522 N. La Brea Ave., between Melrose and Beverly, Hollywood (© **323/876.8723;** www.wcensemble.org), is a nonprofit multiethnic assemblage of professional actors, writers, and directors. The ensemble has collected accolades from local critics, as well as many awards for its excellent production quality. Expect to see well-written, well-directed, and socially relevant plays, performed by a talented and professional cast. Ticket prices range from $15 to $22.

5 Comedy & Cabaret

L.A.'s comedy clubs have launched the careers of many comics who are now household names. In addition to the clubs below, check out the alternative-comedy featured Monday nights at **Largo** (see "Mostly Rock," earlier in this chapter), 432 N. Fairfax Ave., Los Angeles (© **323/852-1073**).

Acme Comedy Theater   The Acme players provide a barrage of laughs with their improv and sketch comedy acts—a veritable grab bag of funnies. 135 N. La Brea Ave., Hollywood. © 323/525-0202. www.acmecomedy.com. Cover $8–$15.

The Cinegrill   The Cinegrill, located in one of L.A.'s most historic hotels, draws locals with a zany cabaret show and guest chanteuses ranging from Eartha Kitt to Cybill Shepherd. Some of the country's best cabaret singers pop up here regularly. 7000 Hollywood Blvd., in the Hollywood Roosevelt Hotel, Hollywood. © 323/466-7000. www.cinegrill.com.

Comedy Store   You can't go wrong here: New comics develop their material, and established ones work out their kinks, at this landmark owned by Mitzi Shore (Pauly's mom). The **Best of the Comedy Store Room,** which seats 400, features professional stand-ups continuously on Friday and Saturday nights. Several comedians are always featured, each doing about a 15-minute stint. The talent is always first-rate and includes comics who regularly appear on the *Tonight Show* and other shows. The **Original Room** features a dozen or so comedians back-to-back nightly. Sunday night is amateur night: Anyone with enough guts can take the stage for 3 minutes, so who knows what you'll get. 8433 Sunset Blvd., West Hollywood. © 323/650-6268. www.comedystore.com.

Groundling Theater   L.A.'s answer to Chicago's Second City has been around for more than 25 years, yet it remains the most innovative and funny group in town. The skits change every year or so, but they take new improvisational twists every night and the satire is often savage. The Groundlings were the springboard to fame for Pee-Wee Herman, Elvira, and former *Saturday Night Live* stars Jon Lovitz, Phil Hartman, and Julia "It's Pat" Sweeney. You haven't laughed this hard in ages. Phone for show times and reservations. 7307 Melrose Ave., Los Angeles. © 323/934-9700. www.groundlings.com. Tickets $10–$20.

The Improv   A showcase for top stand-ups since 1975, the Improv offers something different each night. Although it used to have a fairly active music schedule, the place is now mostly doing what it does best—showcasing comedy. Owner Budd Freedman's buddies—like Jay Leno, Billy Crystal, and Robin Williams—hone their skills here more often than you would expect. But even if the comedians on the bill are all unknowns, they won't be for long. Shows are at 8pm Sunday and Thursday, at 8:30 and 10:30pm Friday and Saturday. 8162 Melrose Ave., West Hollywood. © 323/651-2583. www.improvclubs.com/hollywood.

6 Movies: Play It Again, Sam

L.A. has its share of megaplexes catering to high-budget, high-profile flicks, featuring the usual big-ticket cast of Slys, Demis, and Leonardos. But there are times when those polished Hollywood-studio stories just won't do. Below are some nonmainstream options that play movies from bygone eras, or those with an artier bent. Consult the *L.A. Weekly* to see what's playing when you're in town.

Film festivals are another great way to explore the other side of contemporary movies. Aside from AFI's yearly October fete (see the "Los Angeles–Area Calendar of Events," in chapter 2), the **Los Angeles Independent Film Festival** (© **888/ETM-TIXS** or 310/432-1200; www.laiff.com) looks at what's new in American indies, short films, and music videos during a weeklong event in April. Each July since 1982, the **Gay and Lesbian Film Festival** (© **323/960-2394;**

L.A. Coffeehouses

The L.A. coffee scene is nearly as bustling as its cocktail-lounge coun-terpart. So if you're looking for something beyond the usual Starbucks experience, check out one of the places that we list in this section.

Anastasia's Asylum   Stop by for a cup of joe to go or stick around and while away the hours at this top-notch coffee house. Anastasia's boasts an eclectic clientele, diverse live music ranging from jazz and folk to acoustic and plugged-in rock, vintage furniture in a classy decor, con-stantly changing art exhibits, and a great menu, making it a favorite draw for folks from around the city. 1028 Wilshire Blvd., Santa Monica. ℂ 310/394-7113.

Bourgeois Pig   With its positively gothic aversion to natural lighting (the only street-front window is covered with a blood-red tint), this dark cavern has more of a bar atmosphere than the usual coffeehouse. In fact, Bourgeois Pig is to Starbucks what Marilyn Manson is to Celine Dion. This veteran, located on a hot business strip at the Hollywood/Los Feliz border, is a favorite among youths and showbiz drones, who enjoy los-ing themselves on couches tucked into shadowed corners, shooting a game of pool, or perusing something from the terrific newsstand next door. 5931 Franklin Ave., Hollywood. ℂ 323/962-6366.

Equator   Airy and comfy, this brick room, on a busy alleyway in the heart of resurgent Old Town Pasadena, has withstood the challenge of a Starbucks that moved in a block away. The menu—with smoothies, soup, and desserts, in addition to a wide variety of coffee drinks—and the friendly service keep people coming back. The post-Haring art on the walls contributes to the distinctive character of the place, which has been used for scenes in *A Very Brady Sequel* and *Beverly Hills, 90210.* 22 Mills Place, Pasadena. ℂ 626/564-8656.

Highland Grounds   Predating the coffeehouse explosion, this com-fortable, relatively unpretentious place set the L.A. standard with a vast assortment of food and drink—not just coffee—and often first-rate live music, ranging from nationally known locals, such as Victoria Williams to open-mike Wednesdays for all comers. The ample patio is often used for readings and record-release parties. 742 N. Highland Ave., Hollywood. ℂ 323/466-1507.

www.outfest.com), also known as "Outfest," has aimed to bring high-quality gay, lesbian, bi, and transgender films to a wider public awareness. In 1998, the festival became Los Angeles's largest, with 31,000 audience members.

Promoting moving pictures as this country's great art form, **The American Cinematheque** in Hollywood (ℂ 323/466-3456; www.egyptiantheatre.com) presents not-readily-seen videos and films, ranging from the wildly arty to the old classics. Since relocating to the historic and beautifully refurbished 1923 **Egyptian Theatre** (6712 Hollywood Blvd., Hollywood), American Cinema-theque has hosted several film events, including a celebration of contemporary flicks from Spain, a tribute to the femme fatales of film noir, and a retrospective of the films of William Friedkin. Events highlighting a specific individual are usually accompanied by at least one in-theater audience Q&A session with the honoree.

The Leo S. Bing Theater at the **L.A. County Museum of Art** (5905 Wilshire Blvd., Los Angeles; ✆ **323/857-6010**) presents a themed film series each month. Past subjects have ranged from 1930s blonde bombshell films to Cold War propaganda flicks to contemporary British satire (complete with a 3-day Monty Python's Flying Circus marathon).

Laemmle's Sunset 5 (8000 Sunset Blvd., West Hollywood; ✆ **323/848-3500**), despite being a multiplex in a bright outdoor mall, features films that most theaters of its ilk won't even touch. This is the place to come to see interesting independent art films. There's often a selection of gay-themed movies.

The Nuart Theater (11272 Santa Monica Blvd., Los Angeles; ✆ **310/478-6379**) digs deep into its archives for real classics, ranging from campy to cool. They also feature frequent in-person appearances and Q&A sessions from stars and filmmakers, and screen *The Rocky Horror Picture Show* (yes, still!) every Saturday at midnight.

Fans of silent-movie classics might already know about the renowned **Silent Movie Theatre,** 611 N. Fairfax Ave. (½ block south of Melrose), near the Miracle Mile (✆ **323/655-2520** for recorded program information, or 323/655-2510 for main office; www.silentmovietheatre.com). This silent movie shrine for over 60 years was itself silent following the tragic murder, in 1996, of the longtime owner. It reopened in November 1999 to crowds eager to step inside, where Charlie Chaplin's appeal, Clara Bow's sexuality, and Edward G. Robinson's menace are once again bigger than life. Live music accompanies the silents (classic "talkies" are shown Tues nights); the theater is open Tuesday through Sunday, and tickets are $8 ($6 for kids and seniors).

If TV's more your thing, the **Museum of Radio and Television** (465 N. Beverly Dr., Beverly Hills; ✆ **310/786-1000**) celebrates this country's long relationship with the tube. The museum often features a movie of the month, and it also shows selections from past television programs. We're still hoping for a retrospective on the wonderful women of *The Avengers.*

7 Late-Night Bites

Finding places to dine in the wee hours is getting easier in L.A., as each year sees more 24-hour and after-midnight eateries staking a place in the culinary landscape.

The Apple Pan   This classic American burger shack, an L.A. landmark, hasn't changed much since 1947—and its burgers and pies continue to hit the spot. Open until 1am Friday and Saturday, until midnight other nights; closed Monday. See chapter 6 for a full restaurant listing. 10801 W. Pico Blvd., West L.A. ✆ **310/475-3585.**

Canter's Fairfax Restaurant, Delicatessen & Bakery   This 24-hour Jewish deli has been a winner with late-nighters since it opened more than 65 years ago. If you show up after the clubs close, you're sure to spot a bleary-eyed celebrity or two alongside the rest of the after-hours crowd, chowing down on a giant pastrami sandwich, matzo-ball soup, potato pancakes, or other deli favorites. Try a potato knish with a side of brown gravy—trust us, you'll love it. 419 N. Fairfax Ave., West Hollywood ✆ **323/651-2030.**

Dolores's One of L.A.'s oldest surviving coffee shops, Dolores's offers just what you might expect: Naugahyde, laminated counters and linoleum, with a comforting predictability. Expect the usual coffee-shop fare of pancakes, burgers, and eggs at this 24-hour joint. 11407 Santa Monica Blvd., Los Angeles. ✆ **310/477-1061.**

Du-par's Restaurant & Bakery During the week, this popular Valley coffee shop serves up blue-plate specials until 1am; come the weekend, they're slingin' hash until 4am. The new West Hollywood location, in the Ramada Hotel at 8571 Santa Monica Blvd., west of La Cienega (✆ **310/659-7009**), is open till 3am on the weekends. See chapter 6 for a full restaurant listing. 12036 Blvd. (1 block east of Laurel Canyon), Studio City. ✆ **818/766-4437.**

Fred 62 Silver Lake/Los Feliz hipsters hankering for a slightly demented take on classic American comfort grub skulk into Fred around the clock. See chapter 6 for a full restaurant listing. 1850 N. Vermont, Los Angeles. ✆ **323/667-0062.**

Jerry's Famous Deli Valley hipsters head to 24-hour Jerry's to satiate the late-night munchies. See chapter 6 for a full restaurant listing. 12655 Ventura Blvd. (east of Coldwater Canyon Ave.), Studio City. ✆ **818/980-4245.**

Kate Mantilini Kate's serves stylish nouveau comfort food in a striking setting, and it's open to 1am Sunday through Thursday, and 2am Friday through Saturday. See chapter 6 for a full restaurant listing. 9101 Wilshire Blvd. (at Doheny Dr.), Beverly Hills. ✆ **310/278-3699.**

Mel's Drive-in Straight from an episode of *Happy Days,* this 24-hour 1950s diner on the Sunset Strip attracts customers ranging from chic shoppers during the day to rock-and-rollers at night. The fries and shakes here are among the best in town. 8585 Sunset Blvd. (west of La Cienega), West Hollywood. ✆ **310/854-7200.**

Operetta This French bakery and cafe is a welcome sight to L.A. night owls. Although the kitchen stops serving sandwiches and other light fare at midnight, Operetta's mouthwatering pastries and breads are available around the clock. 8223 W. 3rd St. (near Harper St.), Los Angeles. ✆ **213/627-7898.**

Original Pantry Cafe Owned by former Los Angeles mayor Richard Riordan, this downtown diner has been serving huge portions of comfort food around the clock for more than 60 years; in fact, they don't even have a key to the front door. See chapter 6 for a full restaurant listing. 877 S. Figueroa St. (at 9th St.), Downtown. ✆ **213/972-9279.**

Pink's Hot Dogs Many a woozy hipster has awakened with the telltale signs of a postcocktailing trip to this greasy street-side hot-dog stand—the oniony morning-after breath and chili stains on your shirt are dead giveaways. Open Friday and Saturday until 3am, all other nights until 2am. See chapter 6 for a full restaurant listing. 709 N. La Brea Ave., Los Angeles. ✆ **323/931-4223.**

Swingers This hip coffee shop keeps L.A. scene-stealers happy with its retro comfort food. Open Friday and Saturday until 2am, all other nights until 1am. See chapter 6 for a full restaurant listing. 8020 Beverly Blvd. (west of Fairfax Ave.), Los Angeles. ✆ **323/653-5858.**

Toi on Sunset Those requiring a little more *oomph* from their late-night snack should come here. At this colorful and *loud* hangout, garbled pop culture metaphors mingle with the tastes and aromas of "rockin' Thai" cuisine in delicious ways, until 3am nightly. See chapter 6 for a full restaurant listing. 7505 Sunset Blvd. (at Gardner), Hollywood. ✆ **323/874-8062.**

11

Side Trips from Los Angeles

Los Angeles may be one of the world's most stimulating cities, but don't let it monopolize your time to the point of ignoring its scenic side trips—from famous resort communities such as Santa Barbara and Palm Springs to sun-filled So Cal beach towns (Newport Beach, Huntington Beach, Laguna Beach) and the island oasis of Catalina.

From L.A. you can reach any of these points in one to two hours by car or boat, and accommodations and dining are available at all these destinations.

1 Long Beach & the *Queen Mary*

21 miles (34km) S of downtown L.A.

The fifth-largest city in California, Long Beach is best known as the permanent home of the former cruise liner *Queen Mary* and the Long Beach Grand Prix, whose star-studded warm-up race sends the likes of hipster Jason Priestly and perennial racer Paul Newman burning rubber through the streets of the city in mid-April. A sleek new aquarium recently joined Long Beach's many waterfront attractions.

ESSENTIALS
GETTING THERE   See chapter 2 for airport and airline information. Driving from Los Angeles, take either I-5 or I-405 to I-710 south, which leads directly to both downtown Long Beach and the *Queen Mary* Seaport.

ORIENTATION   Downtown Long Beach is at the eastern end of the vast Port of Los Angeles; Pine Avenue is the central restaurant and shopping street, which extends south to Shoreline Park and the Aquarium. The *Queen Mary* is docked just across the waterway, gazing south toward tiny Long Beach marina and Naples Island.

VISITOR INFORMATION   Contact the **Long Beach Area Convention & Visitors Bureau,** One World Trade Center, Suite 300 (© **800/4-LB-STAY** or 562/436-3645; www.golongbeach.org). For information on the **Long Beach Grand Prix,** call © **562/981-2600** or check out www.longbeachgp.com.

THE MAJOR ATTRACTIONS
The *Queen Mary* ⓐ   It's easy to dismiss this old cruise ship/museum as a barnacle-laden tourist trap, but it's the only surviving example of this particular kind of 20th-century elegance and excess. From the staterooms paneled lavishly in now-extinct tropical hardwoods to the perfectly preserved crew quarters and the miles of hallway handrails made of once-pedestrian Bakelite, wonders never cease aboard this 81,237-ton Art Deco luxury liner. Stroll the teakwood decks with just a bit of imagination and you're back in 1936 on the maiden voyage

Long Beach

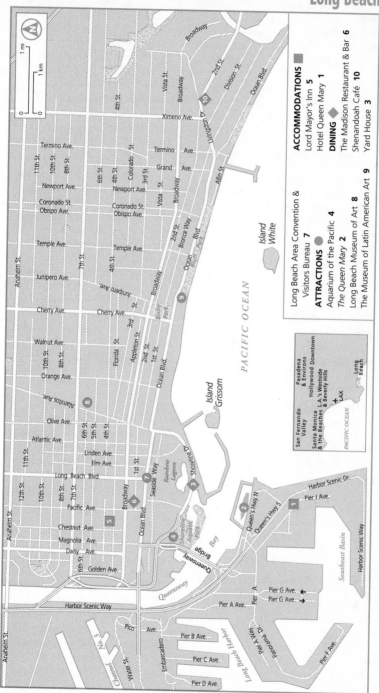

ACCOMMODATIONS ■
Lord Mayor's Inn **5**
Hotel Queen Mary **1**

DINING ◆
The Madison Restaurant & Bar **6**
Shenandoah Cafe **10**
Yard House **3**

Long Beach Area Convention &
Visitors Bureau **7**

ATTRACTIONS ●
Aquarium of the Pacific **4**
The Queen Mary **2**
Long Beach Museum of Art **8**
The Museum of Latin American Art **9**

San Fernando
Valley

Pasadena
& Environs

Hollywood Downtown

Santa Monica
& the Beaches

L.A.'s Westside
& Beverly Hills

PACIFIC OCEAN

LAX

Long
Beach

PACIFIC OCEAN

Island
White

Island
Grissom

from Southampton, England. Don't miss the streamline modern observation lounge, featured often in period motion pictures, and have drinks and listen to some live jazz. Kiosk displays of photographs and memorabilia are everywhere—following the success of the movie *Titanic,* the *Queen Mary* even hosted an exhibit of artifacts from its less fortunate cousin. The Cold War–era Soviet submarine *Scorpion* resides alongside; separate admission is required to tour the sub. Buy both tickets and you'll also get a behind-the-scenes guided tour, peppered with worthwhile anecdotes and details.

1126 Queen's Hwy. (end of I-710), Long Beach. © 562/435-3511. www.queenmary.com. Admission $19 adults, $17 seniors age 55 and over and military, $15 children ages 3–11, free for kids under 3. Daily 10am–6pm (last entry at 5:30pm), with extended summer hours. Parking $8.

Aquarium of the Pacific ★★ *Kids* This enormous aquarium is the cornerstone of Long Beach's new waterfront. Figuring that what stimulated flagging economies in Monterey and Baltimore would work in Long Beach, planners gave their all to this project, creating a crowd-pleasing attraction just across the harbor from Long Beach's other mainstay, the *Queen Mary.* The vast facility—it has enough exhibit space to fill three football fields—re-creates three areas of the Pacific: the warm Baja and Southern California regions, the Bering Sea and chilly northern Pacific, and faraway tropical climes, including stunning re-creations of a lagoon and barrier reef. There are more than 12,000 creatures in all, from sharks and sea lions to delicate sea horses, moon jellies, and gaggles of tropical birds within the Lorikeet Forest. Learn little-known aquatic facts at the many educational exhibits, or come nose-to-nose with sea lions, eels, sharks, and other inhabitants of giant, three-story-high tanks.

100 Aquarium Way, off Shoreline Dr., Long Beach. © 562/590-3100. www.aquariumofpacific.org. Admission $16.95 adults, $13.95 seniors age 60 and over, $9.95 ages 3–11, free for kids under age 3. Daily 9am–6pm. Closed Christmas Day and Toyota Grand Prix weekend (mid-Apr). Parking $7 maximum.

OTHER WATERFRONT DIVERSIONS

A different kind of nautical excursion awaits at the **Tall Ship** *Californian,* the flagship of the Nautical Heritage Society. At 145 feet long, this two-masted wooden cutter class vessel offers barefooters the opportunity to help raise and lower eight sails, steer by compass, and generally experience the "romance of the high seas." Landlubbers might want to choose the 4-hour day sail for $75 ($113 for two), including lunch, while old salts can take 2-, 3-, or 4-day cruises out to Catalina or the Channel Islands at $140 per person per day. The *Californian* sails from Long Beach between late August and mid-April (it's based in northern California in summer). Call © 800/432-2201 for schedule and reservations.

Situated on a prime waterfront knoll, the **Long Beach Museum of Art,** 2300 E. Ocean Ave. (© 562/439-2119; www.lbma.org), was built in 1912 as the summer home of New York philanthropist Elizabeth Milbank Anderson. The mansion functioned as a private social club and World War II officers' club before becoming the museum's home in 1957. In 2000, an ambitious expansion project restored the home to its original state and built a complementary gallery annex on the property. The museum is not only a historic site, but is also notable for its collection of 20th-century European Modernists, postwar art from California, and decorative arts from the past 300 years. Open Tuesday through Sunday from 11am to 7pm. Admission $5 adults, $4 students and seniors, free for kids under 12.

Take to the waterways Italian-style at nearby Naples Island with **Gondola Getaway,** 5437 E. Ocean Blvd. (© 562/433-9595; www.gondolagetawayinc.

com). Since 1982, these authentic Venetian gondolas have been snaking around the man-made canals of Naples Island, under gracefully arched bridges and past the gardens of resort cottages. Perhaps your traditionally clad oarsman will sing an Italian aria or relate the many tales of marriage proposals (some not so successful) made by romance-minded passengers. You'll also get a nice basket of bread, cheese, and salami, plus wineglasses and a full ice bucket; feel free to bring your beverage of choice. Gondola Getaway operates daily between 11am and 11pm; a 1-hour cruise for two is $60.

The Museum of Latin American Art (MoLAA) ☆   Located in the newly developing **East Village Arts District** of Long Beach, and Founded in November 1996, the MoLAA, 628 Alamitos Ave. (© **562/437-1689;** www.mola.com) is the only museum in the western United States that exclusively features contemporary Latin American art. A fine permanent collection, many unique traveling exhibitions, and programs, this museum educates a diverse Southern California audience about contemporary Latin American art. The Museum includes a gift shop featuring unique Latin American pottery, folk art, textiles and glassware as well as a fine restaurant.

628 Alamitos Avenue, Long Beach, © **562/437-1689.** Open Tues–Fri 11:30am–7pm; Sat 11am–7pm; Sun 11am–6pm. Adults $5; seniors and students $3; children under 12 are free. Admission is free Fri.

WHERE TO STAY

Hotel Queen Mary ☆ *Finds*   The *Queen Mary* isn't only a piece of maritime history; it's also a hotel. But although the historic ocean liner is considered the most luxurious vessel ever to sail the Atlantic, with some of the largest rooms built aboard a ship, the quarters aren't exceptional when compared to those on terra firma today, nor are the amenities. The idea is to enjoy the novelty and charm of features like the original bathtub watercocks ("cold salt," "cold fresh," "hot salt," "hot fresh"). The beautifully carved interior is a feast for the eye and fun to explore, and the weekday rates are hard to beat. Three onboard restaurants are overpriced but convenient, and the shopping arcade has a decidedly British feel (one shop sells great *Queen Mary* souvenirs). An elegant Sunday champagne brunch—complete with ice sculpture and harpist—is served in the ship's Grand Salon, and it's always worth having a cocktail in the Art Deco Observation Bar. If you're too young or too poor to have traveled on the old luxury liners, this is the perfect opportunity to experience the romance of an Atlantic crossing—with no seasickness, cabin fever, or week of formal dinners.

1126 Queen's Hwy. (end of I-710), Long Beach, CA 90802-6390. © **800/437-2934** or 562/435-3511. Fax 562/437-4531. www.queenmary.com. 365 units. $109 (inside cabin), $219 (deluxe cabin); from $450 suite. Many packages available. AE, DC, MC, V. Valet parking $12; self-parking $8. **Amenities:** 3 restaurants; spa; shopping arcade. *In room:* A/C, TV.

Lord Mayor's Inn ☆   Situated in a once elite residential neighborhood downtown, this impeccably restored Edwardian home was built in 1904 and belonged to Long Beach's first mayor, Charles H. Windham. The main house offers five charming guest rooms, each furnished with antiques, luxurious high-quality linens, and heirloom bedspreads and accessories (but no phone). All boast private bathrooms cleverly re-created with vintage fixtures and painstakingly matched materials (the original home had only one bathroom). Seven more rooms—four with private bathrooms—are available in two less-formal adjacent cottages, also dating from the early 20th century; they offer a private option for families or those seeking seclusion and independence. Guests gather at their leisure in the main house dining room for innkeeper Laura Brasser's lavish breakfasts, which include specialties like old-world pancakes with fried apples, delicate asparagus eggs, and hearty stuffed French toast.

435 Cedar Ave., Long Beach, CA 90802. ℭ 562/436-0324. www.lordmayors.com. 12 units. $85–$140 double. Rates include full breakfast. AE, DISC, MC, V. **Amenities:** Garden. Garden House has kitchenette with microwave, cable TV, phone; Apple and Cinnamon House have refrigerators.

WHERE TO DINE

The Madison Restaurant & Bar ⋆ STEAKS/SEAFOOD   This elegant 1920s-style supper club offers fine dining reminiscent of majestic ocean-liner dining salons. A beautifully restored historic bank building (and dinner music from the 1940s) provides the backdrop for service that's deferential without being stuffy. The Madison serves exceptional dry aged beef broiled and accompanied by a la carte sides like buttery garlic potatoes or perfectly seasoned creamed spinach. The menu also includes seafood dishes like grilled salmon atop mussels and clams with a creamy ginger-citrus sauce, or oyster-stuffed sole breaded and drizzled with *beurre blanc* and fragrant fresh dill. Desserts are artistic renditions of reliable favorites—a s'mores sundae or sugary apple crumble.

102 Pine Ave., Long Beach. ℭ 562/628-8866. www.madisonsteakhouse.com. Reservations recommended. Dinner main courses $18–$29; lunch $10–$22. AE, MC, V. Mon–Thurs 11am–11pm; Fri 11am–midnight; Sat 5pm–midnight; Sun 5–11pm. Valet parking $3.

Shenandoah Cafe ⋆⋆ AMERICAN/SOUTHERN   Here's a place where "American" food means regional home-style meals served in a high-ceilinged parlor equal parts New Orleans mansion and Grandma's house. It's not for vegetarians or light eaters; even fresh fish specialties are given rich, heavy Southern treatments, and meats take up most of the menu. Start by nibbling on fresh-from-the-oven apple fritters, and prepare for an enormous meal that includes soup or salad and sides. Specialties include Texas-sized chicken-fried steak with country gravy, Santa Fe–style baby-back ribs glazed with smoky chipotle, Cajun blackened fresh catch of the day, and Granny's deep-fried chicken.

4722 E. Second St. (at Park Ave.), Long Beach (Belmont Shore). ℭ 562/434-3469. www.shenandoah cafe.com. Reservations recommended. Main courses $13–$25. AE, DC, MC, V. Mon–Thurs 5–10pm; Fri 5–11pm; Sat 4:30–11pm; Sun 10am–2pm and 4:30–10pm.

Yard House ⋆ AMERICAN ECLECTIC   Not only does it have one of the best outdoor dining venues in Long Beach, the Yard House also features one of the *world's* largest selection of draft beers. The keg room houses more than 1,000 gallons of beer, all visible through a glass door where you can see the golden liquids transported to a signature oval bar via miles of nylon tubing to the dozens of taps. The restaurant takes its name from the early Colonial tradition of serving beer in 36-inch-tall glasses—or yards—to weary stagecoach drivers. Customers are encouraged to partake in this tradition and can drink from the glass yards, as well as half yards and traditional pint glasses. Signature dishes range from the tortelike California Roll to the Crab Cake Hoagie and an impressive selection of steaks and chops. There's also an extensive list of appetizers, salads, pasta, and rice dishes, as well as sandwiches and individual pizzas (the Thai Chicken Pizza is excellent). On sunny days be sure to request a table on the deck overlooking the picturesque harbor.

401 Shoreline Village Dr., Long Beach. ℭ 562/628-0455. www.yardhouse.com. Reservations not accepted. Main courses $10–$30. AE, DC, MC, V. Mon–Thurs 11:30am–midnight; Fri, Sat 11am–2am; Sun 11am–midnight.

2 Santa Catalina Island

22 miles (35km) W of mainland Los Angeles   *by Trisha Clayton*

After an unhealthy dose of the mainland's soupy smog and freeway gridlock, you'll appreciate an excursion to Santa Catalina Island with its clean air, crystal clear water, and the blissful absence of traffic. In fact, there isn't a single traffic light on the entire island. Conditions like these can fool you into thinking that you're miles away from the hustle and bustle of the city, but the reality is that you're only 22 miles (35km) off the Southern California coast and *still* in L.A. County.

Because of its relative isolation, out-of-state tourists tend to ignore Santa Catalina—which everyone calls simply Catalina—but those who do make the crossing have plenty of elbow room to boat, fish, swim, scuba, and snorkel. There are also miles of hiking and biking trails, plus golf, tennis, and horseback riding.

Catalina is so different from the mainland that it almost seems like a different country, remote and unspoiled. In 1915, the island was purchased by William Wrigley Jr., the chewing-gum magnate, who had plans to develop it into a fashionable pleasure resort. To publicize the new vacation land, Wrigley brought big-name bands to the Avalon Ballroom and moved the Chicago Cubs, which he owned, to the island for spring training. His marketing efforts succeeded and Catalina soon became world-renowned playground, luring such celebrities as Laurel and Hardy, Cecil B. DeMille, John Wayne, and even Winston Churchill.

In 1975, the Santa Catalina Island Conservancy—a nonprofit operating foundation organized to preserve and protect the island's nature habitat—acquired about 88% of Catalina Island, protecting virtually all of the hilly acreage and rugged coastline that make up what is known as the interior. In fact, some of the most spectacular outlying areas can only be reached by arranged tour (see "Exploring the Island," below).

ESSENTIALS

GETTING THERE   The most common way to get to and from the island is via the **Catalina Express** ferryboat (© **800/481-3470** or 562/519-1212; www.catalinaexpress.com), which operates up to 30 daily departures year-round from San Pedro and Long Beach. The trip takes about an hour. Round-trip fares are $40 for adults, $36.50 for seniors 55 and over, $30.50 for children ages 2 to 11, and $2 for infants. In San Pedro, the Catalina Express departs from the **Sea/Air Terminal,** Berth 95; take the Harbor Freeway (I-110) south to the Harbor Boulevard exit, then follow signs to the terminal. In Long Beach, boats leave from the **Queen Mary Landing;** take the Long Beach Freeway (I-710) south, following the QUEEN MARY signs to the Catalina Express port. Call ahead for reservations. *Note:* Luggage is limited to 50 pounds per person; reservations are necessary for bicycles, surfboards, and dive tanks; and there are restrictions on transporting pets. You can leave your car at designated lots at each departure terminal; the parking fee is around $8 per 24-hour period.

Island Express Helicopter Service, 900 Queens Way Dr., Long Beach (© **800/2-AVALON** or 310/510-2525; www.islandexpress.com), flies from Long Beach or San Pedro to Avalon in about 15 minutes. The expense is definitely worth the thrill and convenience (particularly if you're prone to seasickness) from

---

Fun Fact Cart Culture

One of the first things you'll notice when you arrive in Avalon is the abundance of golf carts in a comical array of styles and colors. Since Avalon is the only city in California authorized by the state legislature to regulate the number of vehicles allowed to drive on city streets, there are no rental cars and only a handful of privately owned vehicles.

---

either Long Beach or San Pedro. It flies on demand between 8am and sunset year-round, charging $67 each way. The weight limit for luggage, however, is a mere 25 pounds. It also offers brief air tours over the island; prices vary. The heliport is located a few hundred yards southwest of the Queen Mary.

Tip: **Elite Airport Transportation** (© 310/831-1369) offers shuttle service from LAX to the Catalina Express ferry and Island Express Helicopter Service.

VISITOR INFORMATION The **Catalina Island Chamber of Commerce and Visitors Bureau,** P.O. Box 217, Avalon, CA 90704 (© **310/510-1520;** fax 310/510-7606), located on the Green Pleasure Pier, distributes brochures and information on island activities, hotels, and transportation. Call for a free 100-page visitors' guide. Its colorful website, **www.catalina.com**, offers current news from the *Catalina Islander* newspaper in addition to updated activities, events, and general information.

ORIENTATION The picturesque town of **Avalon** is both the port of entry for the island and the island's only city. From the ferry dock, you can wander along Crescent Avenue, the main road along the beachfront, and easily explore adjacent side streets.

Northwest of Avalon is the village of **Two Harbors,** accessible by boat or shuttle bus. Its twin bays are favored by pleasure yachts from L.A.'s various marinas, so there's more camaraderie and a less touristy ambiance overall.

GETTING AROUND Once in Avalon, take a taxi **Catalina Cab Company** (© **310/510-0025**) from the heliport or dock to your hotel and enjoy the quick and colorful trip through town (don't blink or you'll miss it). Only a limited number of cars are permitted on the island; visitors are not allowed to drive cars on the island, and most residents motor around in golf carts (many of the homes only have golf-cart–size driveways). Don't worry, though—you'll be able to get everywhere you want to go by renting a cart yourself or just hoofing it, which is what most visitors do.

If you want to explore the area around Avalon beyond where your feet can comfortably carry you, try renting a mountain bike or tandem from **Brown's Bikes,** 107 Pebbly Beach Rd. (© **310/510-0986**). If you'll be doing a lot of exploring, you'll want to rent a gas-powered golf cart from **Cartopia Golf Cart Rentals** on Crescent Avenue at Pebbly Beach Road (© **310/510-2493**), or **Island Rentals** (© **310/510-1456**) across from the boat terminal. Both companies offer a detailed map of town for a self-guided tour. Rates are about $30 per hour.

EXPLORING THE ISLAND
ORGANIZED TOURS The Santa Catalina Island Company's **Discovery Tours** (© **800/626-7489** or 310/510-TOUR; www.scico.com) has a ticket and

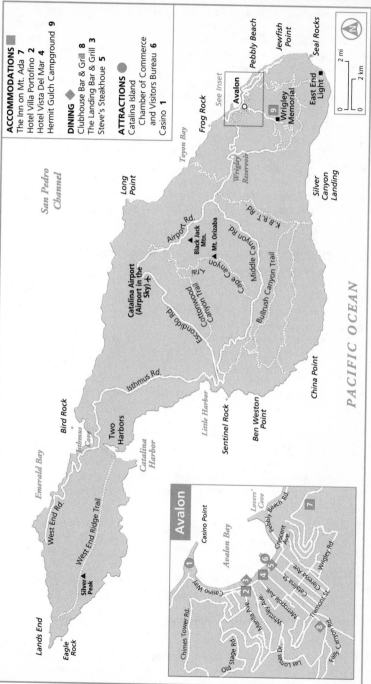

Santa Catalina Island

ACCOMMODATIONS ■
The Inn on Mt. Ada **7**
Hotel Villa Portofino **2**
Hotel Vista Del Mar **4**
Hermit Gulch Campground **9**

DINING ◆
Clubhouse Bar & Grill **8**
The Landing Bar & Grill **3**
Steve's Steakhouse **5**

ATTRACTIONS ●
Catalina Island
Chamber of Commerce
and Visitors Bureau **6**
Casino **1**

San Pedro Channel

PACIFIC OCEAN

Pebbly Beach
Jewfish Point
Seal Rocks
See Inset
Avalon
Wrigley Memorial
East End Light
2 mi
2 km

Frog Rock
Toyon Bay
Wrigley Reservoir

Long Point

Silver Canyon Landing

Airport Rd.
Black Jack Mtn.
Mt. Orizaba
K.B.R.T. Rd.
Catalina Airport (Airport in the Sky)
Cape Canyon Rd.
Middle Canyon Trail
Bullrush Canyon Trail

Escondido Rd.
Cottonwood Canyon Trail

Isthmus Rd.
China Point

Bird Rock
Two Harbors
Isthmus Cove
Little Harbor
Sentinel Rock
Ben Weston Point

Emerald Bay
Catalina Harbor

West End Rd.
West End Ridge Trail

Silver Peak

Lands End
Eagle Rock

Avalon

Casino Point
Lovers' Cove
Avalon Bay
Pebbly Beach Rd.
Crescent Ave.
Wrigley Rd.
Casino Way
Manila Ave.
Whittley Ave.
Metropole Ave.
Catalina St.
Clarissa Ave.
Tremont St.
Falls Canyon Rd.
Chimes Tower Rd.
Old Stage Rd.
Las Lomas Dr.

information office on Crescent Avenue across from the Green Pier. It offers the greatest variety of excursions from Avalon; many last just a couple of hours, so you don't have to tie up your whole day. Tours are available in money-saving combo packs; inquire when you call.

Noteworthy excursions include the **Undersea Tour,** a slow 1-hour cruise of Lover's Cove Marine Preserve in a semisubmerged boat that allows you sit 5 feet under the water in a climate-controlled cabin where you comfortably observe Catalina's kelp forests by day or night ($21 for adults and $13 for kids); the **Casino Tour,** a fascinating 1-hour look at the style and inventive engineering of this elegant ballroom (see "Catalina's Grand Casino" sidebar below; $8.50 adults, $4.25 kids); nighttime **Flying Fish Boat Trips,** a 70-minute Catalina tradition in searchlight-equipped open boats ($8.50 adults, $4.25 kids); and the **Inland Motor Tour,** a 32-mile (52km), 4-hour jaunt through the island's rugged interior, including at stop at the **Airport-in-the-Sky, Little Harbor** on Catalina's west coast (our favorite locale for camping, hiking, and swimming), and Wrigley's **El Rancho Escondido,** a working ranch where some of America's finest Arabian horses are raised and trained ($30 adults, $15 kids).

VISITING TWO HARBORS   If you want to get a better look at the rugged natural beauty of Catalina and escape the throngs of beachgoers, head over to Two Harbors, the quarter-mile "neck" at the island's northwest end that gets its name from the "twin harbors" on each side, known as the Isthmus and Cat Harbors. An excellent starting point for campers and hikers, Two Harbors also offers just enough civilization for the less-intrepid traveler.

The **Banning House Lodge** (© 310/510-2800) is an 11-room bed-and-breakfast overlooking the Isthmus. The clapboard house was built in 1910 for Catalina's pre-Wrigley owners, and has seen duty as on-location lodging for movie stars like Errol Flynn and Dorothy Lamour. Peaceful and isolated, the simply furnished but comfortable lodge has spectacular views of both Isthmus harbors. Rates range from $77 to $201 (Apr–Oct), and they'll even give you a lift from the pier.

Everyone eats at **Doug's Harbor Reef** (© 310/510-7265), down on the beach. This nautical- and tropical-themed saloon/restaurant serves breakfast, lunch, and dinner, the latter consisting of hearty steaks, ribs, swordfish, chicken teriyaki, and buffalo burgers in summer. The house drink is sweet "buffalo milk," a potent concoction of vodka, crème de cacao, banana liqueur, milk, and whipped cream.

WHAT TO SEE & DO IN AVALON   Walk along horseshoe-shaped Crescent Avenue, past private yachting and fishing clubs, toward the landmark **Casino** building. You can see the Art Deco **theater** for the price of a movie ticket any night. Also on the ground floor is the **Catalina Island Museum** (© 310/510-2414), which features exhibits on island history, archaeology, and natural history. The museum has a contour relief map of the island that's

Fun Fact

The 1-square-mile town of Avalon is populated by about 3,200 full-time residents, but on sunny summer weekends the body count nearly triples to more than 10,000.

C   **Catalina's Grand Casino**

No trip to Catalina is complete without taking the **Casino Tour** (see "Organized Tours," above). The Casino Building, Avalon's world-famous Art Deco landmark, is not—and never was—a place to gamble your vacation money away (*casino* is an Italian word for a place of entertainment or gathering). Rather, the incredibly ornate structure (the craftsmanship inside and out is spectacular) is home to the island's only movie theater and the world's largest circular ballroom. Virtually every big band in the '30s and '40s played in the 158-foot-diameter ballroom, carried over CBS radio since its grand opening in May 1929. Today it's a coveted venue for elaborate weddings, dances, gala dinners, and the Catalina Jazz and Blues Festivals. **The Blues Festival** (© **888/25-Event;** www.catalinablues.com) takes place in May and the 3-week **Jazz Trax Festival** (© **888/330-5252;** www.jazztrax.com) takes place every October. Both are extremely popular and make finding hotel rooms nearly impossible. To experience either festival, be sure to book your tickets and accommodations as far in advance as possible.

helpful to hikers. Admission is $1.50 for adults, 50¢ for kids; it's included in the price of Discovery's Casino Tour (see above).

Around the point from the Casino lies **Descanso Beach Club** (© **310/510-7410**), a mini–Club Med in a private cove. While you can get on the beach year-round, the club's facilities (including showers, restaurant/bar, volleyball lawns, and thatched beach umbrellas) are only open from Easter to September 30. Admission is $1.50.

About 1½ miles (2.5km) from downtown Avalon is the **Wrigley Memorial and Botanical Garden** (© **310/510-2288**), an invigorating walk or short taxi ride. The specialized gardens, a project of Ada Wrigley, showcase plants endemic to California's coastal islands. Open daily from 8am to 5pm; admission is $1.

DIVING, SNORKELING & SEA KAYAKING ✪

Snorkeling, scuba diving, and sea kayaking are among the main reasons mainlanders head to Catalina. Catalina Island's naturally clean water and giant kelp forests teeming with marine life have made it a renowned diving destination that attracts experts and beginners divers alike. **Casino Point Marine Park**, Southern California's first city-designated underwater park established in 1965, is located behind the Casino. Due to its convenient location, it can get outrageously crowded in the summer (just like everything else at that time of year).

Catalina Divers Supply (© **800/353-0330;** www.diveinfo.com/cds) offers a full-service dive shop from a large trailer that sits right at the Casino's edge. For guided half-day to 2-day snorkel and scuba tours with certified instructors, as well as equipment sales and rentals, try **Scuba Luv** (© **800/262-DIVE** or 310/510-2350; www.scubaluv.com) on Catalina Avenue. The three best locations for snorkeling are **Lover's Cove Marine Preserve, Casino Point Marine Park,** and **Descanso Beach Club. Catalina Snorkeling Adventures,** at Lover's Cove (© **877/SNORKEL**), offers snorkel gear rental. Snorkeling trips that take you outside of Avalon depart from **Joe's Rent-a-Boat** (✆ 310/510-0455) on the Green Pier.

At Two Harbors, stop by **West End Dive Center** (✆ 310/510-2800). Excursions range from half-day introductory dives to complete certification courses to multiday dive packages. It also rents snorkel gear and offers kayak rental, instruction, and excursions.

HIKING & BIKING

When the summer crowds become overwhelming it's time to head on foot for the peacefulness of the interior, where secluded coves and barren rolling hills soothe frayed nerves. Visitors can obtain a free **hiking permit** at the Conservancy Office (125 Claressa Ave.; ✆ 310/510-2595; www.catalinaconservancy.org), where you'll find maps, wildlife information, and friendly assistance from Conservancy staffers who love to share their knowledge of the interior. It's open daily from 9am to 5pm, weekends closed for lunch. Among the sights you may see are the many giant buffalo roaming the hills, scions of movie extras that were left behind in 1929 and have since flourished.

Mountain biking is allowed on the island's designated dirt roads, but requires a $50-per-person permit ($75 family) that must be purchased in person at the Conservancy Office.

BEACHES

Believe it or not, Avalon's beaches leave much to be desired. The town's central beach, located off on Crescent Avenue, is small and completely congested in the busy season. Be sure to claim your spot early in the morning before it's full. **Descanso Beach Club** offers the best beach in town but also gets crowded very quickly. Your best bet is to kayak out to a secluded cove where you have the beach virtually to yourself.

WHERE TO STAY

If you plan to stay overnight, be sure to reserve a room in advance, because most places fill up pretty quickly during the summer and holiday seasons. There are only a handful of hotels whose accommodations and amenities actually justify the rates that they charge. Some are downright scary, so be sure to book as far in advance as possible to get a room that makes the trip worthwhile. Don't stress too much over your accommodations as you'll probably spend most of your time outdoors. Keep in mind that the best time to visit is in September or October when the water is warm, the crowds have somewhat subsided, and hotel occupancy is easier to find. If you're having trouble finding a vacancy, try calling the **Convention and Visitors Bureau** (✆ 310/510-1520); they keep tabs on last-minute cancellations. **Catalina Island Accommodations** (✆ 310/510-3000) might be able to help you out in a pinch; it's a reservations service with updated information on the whole island. When booking, ask the hotel agent about money-saving packages that offer discounted room rates, boat or helicopter fare, and tours.

EXPENSIVE

The Inn on Mt. Ada ★★ When William Wrigley, Jr. purchased Catalina Island in 1921, he built this ornate hilltop Georgian colonial mansion as his summer vacation home; it's now one of the finest small hotels in California. The opulent inn—considered to be the best in town for its luxury accommodations and views—has several ground-floor salons, a club room with fireplace, a deep-seated formal library, and a wickered sunroom where tea, cookies, and fruit are always available. The best guest room is the Grand Suite, fitted with a fireplace and a large private patio. Amenities include bathrobes and the use of a golf cart during your stay. TVs are available on request, but there are no phones in the rooms. A hearty full breakfast, a light deli-style lunch, and a beautiful multicourse dinner complemented by a limited wine selection are included in the tariff. *Tip:* Even if you find that they're sold out or too pricey to fit your budget, make a lunch reservation and enjoy amazing views from the Inn's spectacular balcony.

398 Wrigley Rd. (P.O. Box 2560), Avalon, CA 90704. © **800/608-7669** or 310/510-2030. Fax 310/510-2237. www.catalina.com/mtada. 6 units. Nov–May Mon–Thurs $280–$350 double, $350–$455 suite; June–Oct and Fri–Sun year-round $300–$475 double, $475–$620 suite. Rates include 3 meals daily. DC, MC, V. **Amenities:** Courtesy car. *In room:* TV, hair dryer, iron. No phone.

MODERATE

Hotel Villa Portofino ★   European flair sets this hotel apart from the rest along with its efficient, friendly staff, and recently renovated rooms with beautiful marble bathrooms and fantastic views overlooking the bay from the hotels suite's private balconies. There's a rooftop deck overlooking the harbor, and some rooms have luxurious touches like fireplaces and deep soaking tubs. Just outside the front door is all of Avalon Bay's activity.

111 Crescent Ave. (PO Box 127), Avalon, CA 90704. © **310/510-0555.** Fax 310/510-0839. www.hotelvilla-portofino.com. 35 units. May–Oct $85–$209 double, from $245 suite; winter $75–$105 double, from $140 suite. Rates include continental breakfast. AE, MC, V, DC. **Amenities:** Award-winning restaurant; adjacent art gallery. *In room:* A/C, TV, refrigerator, coffeemaker, hair dryer.

Hotel Vista Del Mar   Located smack dab in the middle of town, there's nothing fancy about this well-maintained 15-room hotel, but its open-aired atrium garden courtyard, huge fish tank, freshly baked cookies and milk each evening, and friendly staff make it an island favorite. The ocean-view suites are fantastic but hard to secure, as there are only two and booked by regulars almost year-round.

417 Crescent Avenue. (P.O. Box 1979), Avalon, CA 90704. © **310/510-1452.** www.hotel-vistadelmar.com. 15 units. May–Oct $125–$350 double; Nov–Apr $105–$300 double. Winter discounts and midweek rates available. Rates include continental breakfast and freshly baked cookies and milk in the evening. AE, MC, V, Discover. **Amenities:** Garden atrium courtyard with sitting area and balcony with a huge fish tank and views of the harbor. *In room:* A/C, cable TV w/ VCR, Jacuzzi, fireplace, wet bar with refrigerator, coffeemaker.

INEXPENSIVE

Our recommended choices for inexpensive lodgings are: the **Pavilion Lodge** (© **800/414-2754** or 310/510-2500), whose rooms are extremely basic but affordable and clean (a great alternative when budgets and availability are tight); **Hotel Catalina** (© **800/540-0184** or 310/510-0027) a well-maintained Victorian-style hotel just a half block from the beach with tons of charm, family cottages, a courtyard with beautiful stained glass, and large verandas with bay views; **Zane Grey** (© **310/510-0966**), a Hopi-style pueblo built in 1926 and former home of American author Zane Grey, situated above town and equipped with a cozy living room with fireplace and piano, free shuttle service, and a swimming pool; **Hermit Gulch Campground** (℃ 310/510-7254), Avalon's only campground, which can be crowded and noisy in peak season. Campsites can be tough to secure, especially when hotels are booked, so it's a good idea to make reservations in advance. The walk to town and back can be draining, so hop on the green and white tram that runs you back and forth to town for a dollar each way.

WHERE TO DINE

Along with the choices below, recommended Avalon options include **The Busy Bee** on Crescent Ave. (℃ 310/510-1983), an always-crowded waterfront diner with a heated and wind-protected patio. On the Two Harbors side of the island, **Doug's Harbor Reef** is the place to eat; see "Exploring the Island," above.

EXPENSIVE

Clubhouse Bar & Grille ☆ CALIFORNIA   You'll find some of Avalon's most elegant meals at this landmark Catalina Country Club, whose stylish Spanish-Mediterranean clubhouse was built by William Wrigley, Jr. during the 1920s. Recently restored, it exudes a chic and historic atmosphere; the menu is peppered with archival photos and vintage celebrity anecdotes. Sit outdoors in an elegant tiled courtyard, or inside the intimate, clubby dining room. Much of the menu is served throughout the afternoon, including gourmet pizzas, international appetizer samplers, and soups (fisherman's bisque or French onion, both available in a sourdough bowl). Dinner offerings follow a fusion style, such as New Zealand lamb accented with a piquant mango-mint chutney; cioppino and pad Thai both appear on the menu. The club is a few blocks uphill, so shuttle service is available from Island Plaza (on Sumner Ave.) on weekends.

1 Country Club Dr. (above Sumner Ave.). ℃ 310/510-7404. Reservations recommended. Main courses $10–$30. AE, DISC, MC, V. Daily 11:30am–2:30pm and 5–9pm (closing hours will vary seasonally).

MODERATE

The Landing Bar and Grill AMERICAN   With a secluded deck overlooking the harbor, The Landing is generally agreed to be the most romantic dining spot in Avalon. It boasts beautiful Spanish-style architecture located in the historical El Encanto Center that manages to attract as many jeans-clad vacationers as dressed-up islanders. The menu is enticing, with local seafood offerings, pasta, Mexican cuisine, and gourmet pizzas that can be delivered to your hotel room if you wish.

Intersection of Crescent and Marilla ℃ 310/510-1474. Reservations recommended. Main courses $11–$22. AE, DISC, MC, V. Lunch daily 11am–3pm and dinner daily from 4–10pm year-round (subject to changes in winter).

Steve's Steakhouse AMERICAN   Step up above the busy bay-side promenade into a fantastic collage of murals that tribute film classic *Casablanca*. This setting overlooking Avalon Bay feels just right for the hearty menu of steaks, seafood, and pasta. Catalina swordfish is their specialty along with excellent cuts of meat. You can also make a respectable repast from the many appetizer selections, especially the fresh oysters.

417 Crescent Ave. (directly across from the Green Pier, upstairs). ℃ 310/510-0333. Reservations recommended on weekends. Main courses $7–$15 lunch; $15–$25 dinner. AE, MC, V, DISC. Lunch daily 11am–3pm. Dinner daily 5–10pm. Full bar.

INEXPENSIVE

Note: Street addresses are pretty much useless in a town as small as Avalon, so they are not listed here. All these restaurants are within a stone's throw of each other on the main strip.

Our three favorite places for a low-bucks meal in Avalon are: **Rosie's Fish and Chips** (℃ 310/510-0197), an Avalon classic located on the Green Pier that serves fresh seafood favorites like fish and chips and seafood cocktails; **Casino Dock Café** (℃ 310/510-2755), because nothing beats the cafe's live entertainment, marina views from the sun-drenched deck, and delicious breakfast burrito loaded with homemade salsa and a Bloody Mary (or wait till the outdoor bar opens and the lunch menu rolls out with fresh burgers and addictive fish tacos); and **Lori's Good Stuff** (℃ 310/510-2489), a tiny restaurant that serves the best sandwiches, smoothies, and milkshakes around. Their fresh and healthy fare is a nice alternative to the heavy burgers, burritos, and pizza offered elsewhere.

BARHOPPING

Note: Since there are no listed street addresses in Avalon, they are not listed here. Not that it matters, as all these bars are within a stumbling distance of each other.

Avalon's bar scene offers a slew of watering holes to choose from, most with good food and live entertainment. The **Chi Chi Club** (℃ 310/510-2828), the "noisy bar in Avalon" referred to in Crosby, Stills and Nash's song "Southern Cross," is the island's only dance club and quite a scene on summer weekend evenings—the DJ spins an eclectic mixture of dance tunes for the islanders and tourists get their mai tai cocktail groove on. **Luau Larry's** (℃ 310/510-1919) is Avalon's signature bar that everyone must visit; its tacky tiki theme kicks you into island mode as soon as you step inside and stumble out. Many a tourist has gotten his "Wicky Wacked" (the bar's signature drink) in Luau's famous cave. Don't leave without the straw hat sitting lopsided on your head and a Wicky Wacker bumper sticker proudly affixed. Go where the locals go and swill beers at **The Marlin Club** (℃ 310/510-0044), Avalon's eldest drinking hole, catch the Dodgers game at **J.L.'s Locker Room** (℃ 310/510-0258), and recover from your hangover with a spicy Bloody Mary at the rustic bar inside **The Busy Bee** (℃ 310/510-1983).

SHOPPING

Don't worry—you won't have any trouble finding that must-have Catalina key chain or refrigerator magnet, as Crescent Avenue is lined with a myriad of schlocky souvenir shops. There are, however, a few stores that do offer unique and tasteful items. **CC Gallagher** (℃ 310/510-1278) carries high-end gifts as well as a flower and coffee shop; they're best for finding beautiful art, music, and jewelry created by local artists. For colorful handmade Catalina pottery, stop by **Chet's Hardware** (℃ 310/510-0990) in The Arcade—an arched shopping annex that connects Sumner and Metropole Avenues. **Latitude 33** (℃ 310/510-0802) is the place to get your vintage aloha shirts, shorts, hats, and sandals. **Buoys and Gulls** (℃ 310/510-0416) offers men's and women's wear such as Nautica, Reyn Spooner islander shirts, Hurley, and Billabong. **The Steamer Trunk** (℃ 310/510-2600) is loaded with unique gifts to take home to the dogsitter or neighbor who collected your mail. **Leo's Drugstore** (℃ 310/510-0189) is the obvious spot to pick up the sunscreen that you forgot to pack. **Von's**, located on Metropole Avenue in the center of town, is Avalon's main grocery store where you'll find all your food staples.

3 The Orange Coast

Seal Beach is 36 miles (58km) S of Los Angeles; Newport Beach, 49 miles (79km); Dana Point, 65 miles (105km)

Whatever you do, don't say "Orange County" here. The mere name evokes images of smoggy industrial parks, cookie-cutter housing developments and the staunch Republicanism that prevails behind the so-called "orange curtain." We're talking instead about the Orange Coast, one of Southern California's best-kept secrets, a string of seaside jewels that have been compared with the French Riviera or the Costa del Sol. Here, 42 miles (68km) of beaches offer pristine stretches of sand, tide pools teeming with marine life, ecological preserves, charming secluded coves, quaint pleasure-boat harbors, and legendary surfers carving nectar waves. Whether your bare feet want to stroll a funky wooden boardwalk or your gold card gravitates toward a yacht club, you've come to the right place.

ESSENTIALS

GETTING THERE   See "Getting There," in chapter 2, for airport and airline information. By car from Los Angeles, take I-5 or I-405 south. The scenic, shore-hugging Pacific Coast Highway (Calif. 1, or just PCH to the locals) links the Orange Coast communities from Seal Beach in the north to Capistrano Beach just south of Dana Point, where it merges with I-5. To reach the beach communities directly, take the following freeway exits: **Seal Beach,** Seal Beach Boulevard from I-405; **Huntington Beach,** Beach Boulevard/Calif. 39 from either I-405 or I-5; **Newport Beach,** Calif. 55 from either I-405 or I-5; **Laguna Beach,** Calif. 133 from I-5; **San Juan Capistrano,** Ortega Highway/Calif. 74 from I-5; and **Dana Point,** Pacific Coast Highway/Calif. 1 from I-5.

VISITOR INFORMATION   The **Seal Beach Chamber of Commerce,** 311 Main St., #14A, at Electric (✆ 562/799-0179; www.sealbeachchamber.com), is open Monday through Friday from 10am to 4pm.

The **Huntington Beach Conference & Visitors Bureau,** 417 Main St., Suite A-2 (✆ 800/SAY-OCEAN or 714/969-3492; fax 714/969-5592; www.hbvisit.com), enthusiastically offers tons of information and personal anecdotes. Open Monday through Friday from 9am to 5pm.

The **Newport Beach Conference & Visitors Bureau,** 3300 W. Coast Hwy. (✆ 800/94-COAST or 949/722-1611; fax 949/722-1612; www.newportbeach-cvb.com), distributes brochures, sample menus, a calendar of events, and the free *Visitor's Guide.* Call or stop in Monday through Friday from 8am to 5pm (plus weekends in summer).

The **Laguna Beach Visitors Bureau,** 252 Broadway (✆ **800/877-1115** or 949/497-9229; www.lagunabeachinfo.org), is in the heart of town and distributes lodging, dining, and art gallery guides. It's open Monday through Friday from 9am to 5pm and on Saturday from 10am to 4pm (plus Sun in summer).

The **San Juan Capistrano Chamber of Commerce,** Franciscan Plaza, 31781 Camino Capistrano, Suite 306 (✆ **949/493-4700;** www.sanjuancapistrano.com), is within walking distance of the Mission and offers a walking tour guide to historic sites. Open Monday through Friday from 8:30am to 4pm.

The **Dana Point Chamber of Commerce,** 24681 La Plaza, Suite 120 (✆ **800/290-DANA** or 949/496-1555; www.danapoint-chamber.com), is open Monday through Friday from 9am to 4:30pm and carries some restaurant and lodging information as well as a comprehensive recreation brochure.

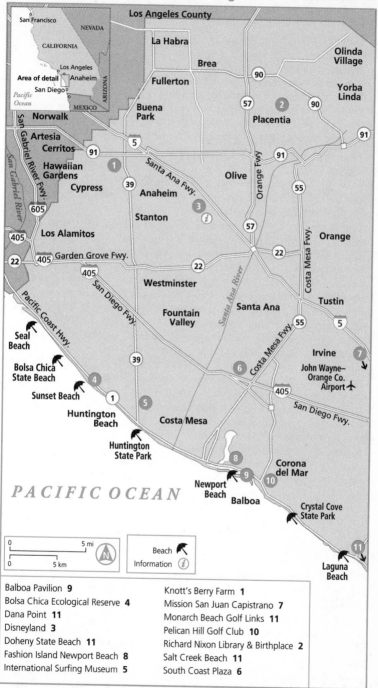

The Orange Coast & Inland Areas

Los Angeles County

San Francisco

NEVADA

CALIFORNIA

Los Angeles
Area of detail · Anaheim

Pacific
Ocean

San Diego

MEXICO

ARIZONA

La Habra

Brea

Olinda
Village

Fullerton

Yorba
Linda

Placentia

Norwalk

Buena
Park

Artesia
Cerritos

Hawaiian
Gardens

Olive

Cypress

Anaheim

Los Alamitos

Stanton

Garden Grove Fwy.

Orange

Westminster

Tustin

Santa Ana

Fountain
Valley

Irvine

John Wayne–
Orange Co.
Airport

Seal
Beach

Bolsa Chica
State Beach

Sunset Beach

Huntington
Beach

Costa Mesa

Huntington
State Park

PACIFIC OCEAN

Corona
del Mar

Newport
Beach

Balboa

Crystal Cove
State Park

Laguna
Beach

San Gabriel River Fwy.

San Gabriel River

Santa Ana Fwy.

Orange Fwy.

Costa Mesa Fwy.

Santa Ana River

Pacific Coast Hwy.

San Diego Fwy.

San Diego Fwy.

Costa Mesa Fwy.

0   5 mi
0   5 km

Beach
Information

Balboa Pavilion **9**

Bolsa Chica Ecological Reserve **4**

Dana Point **11**

Disneyland **3**

Doheny State Beach **11**

Fashion Island Newport Beach **8**

International Surfing Museum **5**

Knott's Berry Farm **1**

Mission San Juan Capistrano **7**

Monarch Beach Golf Links **11**

Pelican Hill Golf Club **10**

Richard Nixon Library & Birthplace **2**

Salt Creek Beach **11**

South Coast Plaza **6**

Tips A Special Arts Festival

A tradition for 60-plus years in arts-friendly Laguna, the **Festival of Arts and Pageant of the Masters** is held each summer throughout July and August. It's pretty large now, and it includes the formerly "alternative" Sawdust Festival across the street. See the "Los Angeles–Area Calendar of Events" in chapter 2 for details.

DRIVING THE ORANGE COAST

You'll most likely be exploring the coast by car, so we cover the beach communities in order, from north to south. Keep in mind, however, that if you're traveling between Los Angeles and San Diego, the Pacific Coast Highway (Calif. 1) is a fantastic scenic detour that adds less than an hour to the commute—so pick out a couple of destinations and go for it.

Seal Beach, on the border between Los Angeles and Orange counties and a neighbor to Long Beach's Naples Harbor, is geographically isolated by both the adjacent U.S. Naval Weapons Station and the self-contained Leisure World retirement community. As a result, the charming beach town appears untouched by modern development—it's Orange County's version of small-town America. Take a stroll down Main Street for a walk back in time, culminating in the Seal Beach Pier. Although the clusters of sunbathing, squawking seals that gave the town its name aren't around any more, old-timers still fish, lovers still stroll, and families still cavort by the seaside, enjoying great food and retail shops or having a cold drink at Hennessey's tavern.

Huntington Beach or "Surf City" as it's known, is probably the largest Orange Coast city; it stretches quite a ways inland and has seen the most urbanization. To some extent this has changed the old boardwalk and pier to a modern outdoor mall where cliques of gang kids coexist with families and the surfers who continue to flock here, drawn by Huntington's legendary place in surf lore. Hawaiian born George Freeth is credited with bringing the sport here in 1907, and some say the breaks around the pier and Bolsa Chica are the best in California. The world's top wave riders flock to Huntington each August for the rowdy but professional **U.S. Open of Surfing.** If you're around at Christmas time, try to see the gaily decorated marina homes and boats in Huntington Harbor by taking the **Cruise of Lights,** a 45-minute narrated sail through and around the harbor islands. The festivities generally last from mid-December until Christmas; call © **714/840-7542** for schedules and ticket information.

The name **Newport Beach** conjures comparisons to Rhode Island's Newport, where the well-to-do enjoy seaside living with all the creature comforts. That's the way it is here too, but on a less grandiose scale. From the million-dollar Cape Cod–style cottages on sunny Balboa Island in the bay to elegant shopping complexes like Fashion Island and South Coast Plaza (an übermall with valet parking, car detailing, limo service, and concierge), this is where fashionable socialites, right-wing celebrities, and business mavens can all be found. Alternatively, you could explore **Balboa Peninsula's** historic Pavilion and old-fashioned pier or board a passenger ferry to Catalina Island.

Laguna Beach, whose breathtaking geography is marked by bold elevated headlands, coastal bluffs, and pocket coves, is known as an artists' enclave, but the truth is that Laguna has became so *in* (read: expensive) that it's driven most of the true bohemians *out*. Their legacy remains with the annual **Festival of**

Arts and Pageant of the Masters (see "A Special Arts Festival," above), as well as a proliferation of art galleries mingling with high-priced boutiques along the town's cozy streets. In warm weather, Laguna Beach has an overwhelming Mediterranean-island ambience, which makes *everyone* feel beautifully, idly rich.

San Juan Capistrano, in the verdant headlands inland from Dana Point, is defined by Spanish Missions and its loyal swallows. The Mission architecture is authentic, and history abounds. Consider San Juan Capistrano a compact, life-size diorama illustrating the evolution of a small western town from Spanish-Mission era to secular rancho period, into statehood and the 20th century. Ironically, Mission San Juan Capistrano (see "Seeing the Sights," below) is once again the center of the community, just as the founding friars intended 200 years ago.

Dana Point, the last town south, has been called a "marina development in search of a soul." Overlooking the harbor stands a monument to 19th-century author Richard Henry Dana, who gave his name to the area and described it in *Two Years Before the Mast.* Activities generally center on yachting and Dana Point's lovely harbor. Nautical themes are everywhere, particularly the streets named for old-fashioned shipboard lights—a hodgepodge that includes Street of the Amber Lantern, Street of the Violet Lantern, Street of the Golden Lantern, and so on. Bordering the harbor is Doheny State Beach (see "Beaches & Nature Preserves," below), which wrote the book on seaside park and camping facilities.

ENJOYING THE OUTDOORS

BEACHES & NATURE PRESERVES   The **Bolsa Chica Ecological Reserve,** in Huntington Beach (© **714/840-1575**), is a 300-acre restored urban salt marsh that's a haven to more than 200 bird species, as well as a wide variety of protected plants and animals. Naturalists come to spot herons and egrets as well as California horn snails, jackknife clams, sea sponges, common jellyfish, and shore crabs. An easy 1½-mile (2.5km) loop trail begins from a parking lot on the Pacific Coast Highway (Calif. 1) a mile south of Warner Boulevard; docents lead a narrated walk the first Saturday of every month. The trail heads inland, over Inner Bolsa Bay and up Bolsa Chica bluffs. It then loops back toward the ocean over a dike that separates the Inner and Outer Bolsa bays and traverses a coastal sand-dune system. This beautiful hike is a terrific afternoon adventure. The Bolsa Chica Conservancy has been working since 1978 on reclaiming the wetlands from oil companies that began drilling here 70 years ago. It's an ongoing process, and you can still see those "seesaw" drills dotting the outer areas of the reserve.

Huntington City Beach, adjacent to Huntington Pier, is a haven for volleyball players and surfers; dense crowds abound, but so do amenities like outdoor showers, beach rentals, and rest rooms. Just south of the city beach is 3-mile-long (5km) **Huntington State Beach.** Both popular beaches have lifeguards and concession stands seasonally. The state beach also has rest rooms, showers, barbecue pits, and a waterfront bike path. The main entrance is on Beach Boulevard, and there are access points all along the Pacific Coast Highway (Calif. 1).

Newport Beach runs for about 5 miles (8km) and includes both Newport and Balboa piers. It has outdoor showers, rest rooms, volleyball nets, and a vintage boardwalk that just may make you feel as though you've stepped 50 years back in time. **Balboa Bike and Beach Stuff** (© **949/723-1516**), at the corner of Balboa and Palm near the pier, rents a variety of items, from pier fishing poles to bikes, beach umbrellas, and body boards. The **Southwind Kayak Center,** 2801 W. Pacific Coast Hwy. (© **800/768-8494** or 949/261-0200; www.south-windkayaks.com), rents sea kayaks for use in the bay or open ocean at rates of $10 to $14 per hour; instructional classes are available on weekends, with some midweek classes in summer. It also offers winter bird-watching kayak expeditions into the Upper Newport Bay Ecological Reserve at rates of $40 to $65.

Crystal Cove State Park, which covers 3 miles (5km) of coastline between Corona del Mar and Laguna Beach and extends into the hills around El Moro Canyon, is a good alternative to the more popular beaches for seekers of solitude. (There are, however, lifeguards and restrooms.) The beach is a winding, sandy strip, backed with grassy terraces; high tide sometimes sections it into coves. The entire area offshore is an underwater nature preserve. There are four entrances, including Pelican Point and El Moro Canyon. For information, call © **949/494-3539.**

Salt Creek Beach Park lies below the palatial Ritz-Carlton Laguna Niguel; guests who tire of the pristine swimming pool can venture down the staircase on Ritz-Carlton Drive to wiggle their toes in the sand. The setting is marvelous, with wide white-sand beaches looking out toward Catalina Island (why do you think the Ritz-Carlton was built here?). The park has lifeguards, restrooms, a snack bar, and convenient parking near the hotel.

Doheny State Beach in Dana Point, just south of lovely Dana Point Marina (enter off Del Abispo St.), has long been known as a premier surfing spot and camping site. Doheny has the friendly vibe of beach parties in days gone by: tree-shaded lawns give way to wide beaches, and picnicking and beach camping are encouraged. There are 121 sites for both tents and RVs, plus a state-run visitor center featuring several small aquariums of sea and tide pool life. For more information and camping availability, call © **949/492-0802.**

BICYCLING Biking is the most popular beach activity up and down the coast. A slower-paced alternative to driving, it allows you to enjoy the clean, fresh air and notice smaller details of these laid-back beach towns and harbors. The Newport Beach visitor center (see "Visitor Information," above) offers a free *Bike Ways* map of trails throughout the city and harbor. Bikes and equipment can be rented at **Balboa Bike & Beach Stuff,** 601 Balboa Blvd., Newport Beach (© **949/723-1516**); **Laguna Beach Cyclery,** 240 Thalia St. (© **949/ 494-1522**); and **Dana Point Bicycle,** 34155 Pacific Coast Hwy. (© **949/ 661-8356**).

GOLF Many golf course architects have used the geography of the Orange Coast to its full advantage, molding challenging and scenic courses from the rolling bluffs. Most courses are private, but two outstanding ones are open to the public. **The Links at Monarch Beach,** 33033 Niguel Rd., Dana Point (© **949/ 240-8247**), is particularly impressive. This hilly, challenging course, designed by Robert Trent Jones Jr., offers great ocean views. Afternoon winds can sneak up, so accuracy is essential. Weekend greens fees are $145 ($115 weekdays).

Another challenge is the **Pelican Hill Golf Club,** 22651 Pelican Hill Rd. S., Newport Beach (© **949/760-0707** starter, 949/640-0238 pro shop; www.peli-canhill.com), with two Tom Fazio–designed courses. The Ocean North course is heavily bunkered, while the Ocean South course features canyons and ravines; both have large, multitier greens. Weekend greens fees are $250; weekdays $175. And remember—when putting near the ocean, the break is always toward the water.

SEEING THE SIGHTS

Beyond the sights listed below, an excellent attraction is **Balboa Island.** The charm of this pretty little neighborhood isn't diminished by knowing that the island was man-made—and it certainly hasn't affected the price of real estate. Tiny clapboard cottages in the island's center and modern houses with two-story windows and private docks along the perimeter make a colorful and romantic picture. You can drive onto the island on Jamboree Road to the north or take the three-car ferry from Balboa Peninsula (about $1.50 per vehicle). It's generally more fun to park and take the ferry as a pedestrian, since the island is crowded and lacks parking and the tiny alleys they call streets are more suitable for strolling. **Marine Avenue,** the main commercial street, is lined with small shops and cafes that evoke a New England fishing village. Refreshing shaved ices sold by sidewalk vendors will relieve the heat of summer.

Balboa Pavilion ⭐ *Kids*   This historic cupola-topped structure, a California Historical Landmark, was built in 1905 as a bathhouse for swimmers in their ankle-length bathing costumes. Later, during the Big Band era, dancers rocked the Pavilion doing the "Balboa Hop." Now it serves as the terminal for Catalina Island passenger service, harbor and whale-watching cruises, and fishing charters. The surrounding boardwalk is the Balboa Fun Zone, a collection of carnival rides, game arcades, and vendors of hot dogs and cotton candy. For Newport Harbor or Catalina cruise information, call ☎ **949/673-5245;** for sportfishing and whale-watching, call ☎ **949/673-1434.**

400 Main St., Balboa, Newport Beach. ☎ **949/673-5245.** From Calif. 1, turn south onto Newport Blvd. (which becomes Balboa Blvd. on the peninsula); turn left at Main St.

International Surfing Museum   Nostalgic Gidgets and Moondoggies shouldn't miss this monument to the laid-back sport that has become synonymous with California beaches. You'll find gargantuan long boards from the sport's early days, memorabilia of Duke Kahanamoku and the other surfing greats represented on the "Walk of Fame" near Huntington Pier, and a gift shop where a copy of the *"Surfin'ary"* can help you bone up on your surfer slang even if you can't hang 10.

411 Olive Ave., Huntington Beach. ☎ **714/960-3483.** www.surfingmuseum.org. Admission $2 adults, $1 students, free for kids age 6 and under. Mid-June to late Sept daily noon–5pm; rest of the year Wed–Sun noon–5pm.

Laguna Art Museum   This beloved local institution is working hard to position itself as the artistic cornerstone of the community. In addition to a small but interesting permanent collection, the museum presents installations of regional works definitely worth a detour. Past examples include a display of surf photography from the coast's 1930s and 1940s golden era, and dozens of plein-air Impressionist paintings (ca. 1900–30) by the founding artists of the original colony. The museum is also open during Laguna Beach Artwalk, the first Thursday each month, when all are admitted free.

307 Cliff Dr., Laguna Beach. ☎ **949/494-8971.** www.lagunaartmuseum.org. Admission $5 adults, $4 students and seniors, free for kids under age 12. Tues–Sun 11am–5pm.

Mission San Juan Capistrano   The seventh of the 21 California coastal Missions, Mission San Juan Capistrano is continually being restored. The mix of old ruins and working buildings is home to small museum collections and various adobe rooms that are as quaint as they are interesting. The intimate Mission chapel with its ornate baroque altar is still used for religious services, and the Mission complex is the center of the community, hosting performing arts, children's programs, and other cultural events year-round.

This Mission is best known for its **swallows,** which are said to return to nest each year at their favorite sanctuary. According to legend, the birds wing their way back to the Mission annually on March 19, St. Joseph's Day, arriving at dawn; they are said to take flight again on October 23, after bidding the Mission farewell. In reality, you can probably see the well-fed birds here any day of the week, winter or summer.

Ortega Hwy. (Calif. 74), San Juan Capistrano. Ⓒ 949/234-1300. www.missionsjc.com. Admission $6 adults, $5 seniors, $4 children. Daily 8:30am–5pm.

SHOPPING

Just as the communities along the coast range from casually barefoot summer playgrounds to meticulously groomed yacht-clubby enclaves, so the shopping scene stretches to both ends of the spectrum. **Seal Beach,** indifferent to tourists, has appealing low-tech shops designed to service the year-round residents, while **Huntington Beach** offers a plethora of surf and watersports shops, reflecting its sporty nature. Both Huntington and Balboa have more than their share of T-shirt and souvenir stands, while **Newport Beach** has been called "Beverly Hills South" because of the many European designer boutiques and high-priced shops there. **Laguna Beach** is art-gallery intensive, with more than 100 at last count; you'll do well to pick up an expanded gallery guide at the Laguna Beach Visitors Bureau (see "Visitor Information," earlier in this chapter). Most galleries are clustered along Pacific Coast Highway, particularly at the northern end of town—a stretch that's historically been known as Gallery Row. There's little shopping in **Dana Point** and mostly Mission-themed souvenirs in **San Juan Capistrano.**

Shoppers from all over the Southland flock to the two excellent malls listed below. If that isn't to your taste, a drive along the Pacific Coast Highway will yield many other opportunities for browsing and souvenir purchases.

Fashion Island Newport Beach   It's actually *not* an island, unless you count the nearly impenetrable sea of skyscrapers that border this posh mall, designed to resemble an open-air Mediterranean village. Anchored by Neiman Marcus, Bloomingdale's, and Macy's, the mall is lined with outdoor artwork, upscale shops, and specialty boutiques including Allen Allen women's casual wear and the trendy Optical Shop of Aspen; 12 different restaurants offer something for everyone. They're at 401 Newport Center Dr., Newport Beach (Ⓒ **949/721-2000;** www.fashionisland-nb.com).

South Coast Plaza   South Coast Plaza, one of the most upscale shopping complexes in the world, is so big that it's a day's adventure unto itself. This beautifully designed center is home to some of fashion's most prominent boutiques, including Emporio Armani, Chanel, Alfred Dunhill, and Coach; branches of the nation's top department stores such as Saks Fifth Avenue and Nordstrom; and outposts of the best high-end specialty shops like Williams Sonoma, l.a. Eyeworks, and Rizzoli Booksellers. The multidimensional mall is also home to many impressive works of modern art, and snacking and dining options are a cut above as well—among the 40 or so restaurants scattered throughout are Wolfgang Puck Cafe, Morton's of Chicago, Ghirardelli Soda Fountain, and Scott's Seafood Grill. It's located at 3333 Bristol St. (at I-405), Costa Mesa (Ⓒ **800/782-8888** or 714/435-2000; www.southcoastplaza.com).

Artistic Laguna: A Guide to Gallery Hopping

Within moments of entering town, you might realize you can't turn a corner without encountering one of Laguna's more than 100 galleries. We highlight some of the best below. You can also pick up an expanded gallery guide at the Laguna Beach Visitors Bureau (see "Visitor Information," earlier in this chapter). *Local Arts* is a slick, colorful, free quarterly that covers all of Orange County, with a particularly good emphasis on the Laguna galleries.

As a general rule, we suggest skipping those galleries offering national or internationally recognized artists in favor of those specializing in local artists. One of the main pleasures of gallery hopping in Laguna is discovering its homegrown talent.

Most of the area's galleries line Coast Highway; they're easy to spot, clustered together throughout town. At the northern end of town lies historic **Gallery Row** (where you'll also find the Laguna Art Museum; see "Seeing the Sights," above), dating from the founding of Laguna's original artists' colony. **Laguna North Gallery,** 376 N. Coast Hwy. (© 949/494-4324; open Wed–Fri 11am–5pm), showcases 12 local artists, with an emphasis on watercolorists. Many of these originals are quite affordable, and the artists often hang around this friendly gallery and will discuss their work with visitors. Down the street is **California Art Gallery,** 305 N. Coast Hwy., Suite A (© 949/494-7270; open Wed–Sat 11am–5pm, Sun noon–5pm), which showcases early California oil and watercolor artists, plus the work of eight contemporary plein air painters; it also offers Arts and Crafts furniture and pottery. **Gallery McCollum,** 206 N. Coast Hwy. (© 949/497-4027), is will appeal to anyone with a tropical yen. It features vivid scenes of Hawaii and the South Pacific, in addition to works by local oil painters.

Most of the town's galleries primarily feature paintings, but there's one notable photography studio. **Bill Agee Studio & Gallery,** 1275 Glenneyre St. (at Cress St.; © 949/494-9948), displays black-and-white photographs in the classic style, from silver gelatin prints to large-scale works on paper. Many are hand-colored, lending an old-fashioned, painterly air. Agee excels in treating architectural subjects from around the world. Open by appointment, or call for weekend schedule (usually open in the afternoon).

Farther south along Coast Highway, across the street from the Surf & Sand Hotel, is the **Art Center,** a collection of around a dozen galleries. While quality (and prices) vary widely, even casual browsers should stop into the **Redfern Gallery,** 1540 S. Coast Hwy. (© 949/497-3356; open Wed–Sun 10am–5pm), which has specialized for more than 20 years in the California Impressionist School. This school, active from the 1890s to the 1940s, was the primary focus of Laguna's founding artists. Many of the gallery's pieces are museum quality, and they often carry fascinating stories of former owners.

WHERE TO STAY

Also consider the **Seal Beach Inn** (© **800/HIDEAWAY** or 562/493-2416; fax 562/799-0483; http://sealbeachinn.com), a romantic 23-room bed-and-breakfast inn 1 block from the beach in a charming residential neighborhood.

VERY EXPENSIVE

Ritz-Carlton Laguna Niguel ★★★   The Old World meets the Pacific Rim at this glorious hotel, set among terraces and fountained gardens on a 150-foot-high bluff above a 2-mile-long (3km) beach. There's a beautiful marble fireplace in the silk-lined lobby, and lush foliage abounds throughout the interior. A ravishingly arched lounge is perfect for watching the sun set over the Pacific. The service, in Ritz-Carlton style, is unassuming and impeccable. The spacious rooms are outfitted with sumptuous furnishings and fabrics, and all come with a terrace, an Italian marble bathroom equipped with double vanity, three phones (with voice mail), and a shoe polisher. Some suites even have fireplaces.

1 Ritz-Carlton Dr., Dana Point, CA 92629. © 800/241-3333 or 949/240-2000. Fax 949/240-0829. 393 units. From $325 garden/pool-view double; $475 ocean-view double; from $525 suite. Children age 17 and under stay free in parents' room. Midweek and special packages available. AE, DC, DISC, MC, V. Parking $25. **Amenities:** 4 restaurants; 2 lounges; 4 outdoor tennis courts; health club; whirlpool; sauna; children's programs; concierge; business center; 24-hour room service; in-room massage; babysitting; dry-cleaning/laundry service; executive-level rooms; regular shuttle to/from the beach and the golf course. *In room:* A/C, TV w/ pay movies, minibar, hair dryer, iron, safe, bathrobes.

St. Regis Monarch Beach Resort & Spa ★★★   Let's cut to the chase: The St. Regis Monarch Beach Resort is the finest luxury hotel I have ever had the pleasure of reviewing—and I've reviewed a *lot* of luxury hotels. They nailed it with this one, setting a standard for all other resort hotels to follow. Everything oozes with indulgence here, from the stellar service to the striking artwork, high-tech electronics, absurdly comfortable beds, four-star restaurant, and a spa that will blow your mind. The $240 million, 172-acre resort opened on July 30, 2001, with a massive star-studded gala, and has since been wooing the wealthy with its gorgeous Tuscan-inspired architecture and soothing ocean views.

Perfection is all in the details, and the St. Regis is full of them: a three-lane lap pool with an underwater sound system; a yoga, spinning, and "movement" studio; a full-service Vogue salon; private poolside cabanas; star chef Michael Mina's Aqua restaurant; couples spa treatment rooms with whirlpool baths and fireplaces; an 18-hole Robert Trent Jones, Jr., golf course; even a private beach club. Then there's the guest rooms, each loaded with beautiful custom-designed furniture, 32-inch Sony Wega flat-screen TVs with CD-DVD audio systems and a 300-DVD library, huge marble-laden bathroom with glass shower door that must weigh 100 pounds, and the most comfortable bathrobe I've ever worn. Even if it's a bit beyond your price range, give yourself one heckuva birthday present this year and book a room and spa treatment at the gorgeous new St. Regis resort.

1 Monarch Beach Rd., Dana Point, CA 92629. © 800/325-3589 or 949/234-3200. Fax 949/234-333. www.stregismonarchbeach.com. From $355 resort-view double; from $496 ocean-view double; from $1,000 suites. Golf and spa packages available as well. AE, DC, DISC, MC, V. Valet parking $23. **Amenities:** 4 restaurants; lounge; wine cellar tasting room; 3 pools; 2 hot tubs; 3 tennis courts (lit for night play); spa and fitness center; 18-hole golf course; 24-hour butler service; 24-hour room service; concierge; 24-hour business center; in-room massage; babysitting; dry-cleaning/laundry service; executive-level rooms; complimentary local shuttle; retail shops; morning paper. *In room:* A/C, TV w/ DVD library, minibar, high-speed Internet access, 3 telephones, CD-DVD, hair dryer, safe, bathrobes.

Surf and Sand Resort ★★   One of the finest hotels in Laguna Beach, the Surf and Sand has come a long way since it started in 1948 as a beach-side motor lodge with 13 units. Still occupying the same fantastic ocean-side location, it now features 165 top-of-the-line rooms that, despite their simplicity and standard size, feel enormously decadent. They're very bright and beachy; every one is done entirely white and has a private balcony with a limitless ocean view, a marble bathroom accented handsomely with granite, and plush cotton terry robes. Some units have whirlpool tubs. My advice: Try getting a deluxe corner room, each of which affords an expanded 90-degree view of the California coastline—well worth the additional $40.

Opened in early 2002, the new Mediterranean-styled **Aquaterra Spa** offers a tantalizing array of personalized massage, skincare, and body treatments. You'll find the requisite ocean-inspired treatments, but personal choice is the rule here: the menu features eight different specialty massages, each with your choice of four aromatherapy oils. The spa's four Couples Rituals each offer a themed body treatment followed by a bubble bath for two (the tub has an ocean view), and a massage to finish. **Stunning Splashes** restaurant serves three meals daily in a beautiful oceanfront setting; the rich Mediterranean cuisine is perfect against a backdrop of sunlight and crashing waves.

1555 S. Coast Hwy. (south of Laguna Canyon Rd.), Laguna Beach, CA 92651. © **888-869-7569** or 949/497-4477. Fax 949/494-2897. www.surfandsandresort.com. 165 units. Jan 3–Mar 28 $290–$485 double; $475–$780 suite; Mar 29–Jun 27 $295–$375 double; $395–$1085 suite; Jun 28–Oct 5 $385–485 double; $475–$1125 suite. AE, DC, DISC, MC, V. **Amenities:** Restaurant; bar; outdoor heated pool; full-service spa; fitness room; whirlpool; summer children's programs; concierge; business center; room service (6:30am–10pm); in-room massage; babysitting; dry-cleaning/laundry service; concierge-level rooms. *In room:* TV w/ pay movies, video games, CD, minibar, hair dryer, iron, safe, bathrobes.

EXPENSIVE

Portofino Beach Hotel ★   This oceanfront inn, built in a former seaside rail station, is steps away from the Newport Pier, along a stretch of bars and equipment-rental shacks; the beach is across the parking lot. The place maintains a calm, European air even in the face of the midsummer beach frenzy. Although it can get noisy in summer, there are advantages to being at the center of the action. The hotel has its own enclosed parking, and sunsets are spectacular viewed from a plush armchair in the upstairs parlor. Guest rooms, furnished with antique reproductions, are on the second floor—the first is occupied by a guests-only bar and several cozy sitting rooms—and most have luxurious skylit bathrooms.

2306 W. Ocean Front, Newport Beach, CA 92663. © **800-571-8749** or 949/673-7030. Fax 949/723-4370. www.portofinobeachhotel.com. 20 units. $159–$279 double. Rates include continental breakfast. Free parking. AE, DC, DISC, MC, V. **Amenities:** Whirlpool; coin-op laundry; dry-cleaning/laundry service. *In room:* A/C, TV.

MODERATE

Blue Lantern Inn ★   A three-story New England–style gray clapboard inn, the Blue Lantern is a pleasant cross between romantic B&B and sophisticated small hotel. Almost all the rooms, which are decorated with reproduction traditional furniture and plush bedding, have a balcony or deck overlooking the harbor. All have a fireplace and whirlpool tub. You can have your breakfast here in private (clad in the fluffy robe provided), or go downstairs to the sunny dining room that also serves complimentary afternoon tea. There are an exercise room and a cozy lounge with menus for many area restaurants. The friendly staff welcomes you with home-baked cookies at the front desk.

34343 St. of the Blue Lantern, Dana Point, CA 92629. © **800/950-1236** or 949/661-1304. Fax 949/496-1483. www.foursisters.com. 29 units. $150–$500 double. Rates include full breakfast and afternoon wine and hors d'oeuvres. AE, DC, MC, V. **Amenities:** Whirlpool; exercise room; complimentary bicycles; dry-cleaning/laundry service. *In room:* A/C, TV/VCR, minibar, coffeemaker, hair dryer.

Casa Laguna ★ Once you see this romantic terraced complex of Spanish-style cottages amid lush gardens and secluded patios—which offers all the amenities of a B&B *and* affordable prices—you might wonder: What's the catch? Well, the noise of busy PCH wafts easily into Casa Laguna, which might prove disturbing to sensitive ears and light sleepers. Still, the Casa has been a favorite hideaway since Laguna's early days, and now glows under the watchful eye of a terrific owner, who's been upping the comfort ante. Some rooms—especially the suites—are downright luxurious, with fireplace, kitchen, bathrobes, CD player, VCR, and other in-room goodies. Throughout the property, Catalina tile adorns fountains and bougainvillea spills into paths; each room has an individual charm. Breakfast is served in the sunny morning room of the Craftsman-style Mission House, where a cozy living room also invites relaxation and conversation.

2510 S. Coast Hwy., Laguna Beach, CA 92651. © **800/233-0449** or 949/494-2996. Fax 949/494-5009. 21 units. $120–$195 double; $195–$295 suite. Rates include breakfast, afternoon wine, and hors d'oeuvres. Off-season and midweek discounts available. AE, DISC, MC, V. **Amenities:** Heated outdoor pool; whirlpool. *In room:* TV.

Doryman's Inn Bed & Breakfast The rooms at Doryman's Inn are both luxurious and romantic, making this one of the nicest B&Bs to be found anywhere. The rooms are outfitted with French and American antiques, floral textiles, beveled mirrors, and cozy furnishings. Every room has a working fireplace and a sunken marble tub (some have whirlpool jets). King- or queen-size beds, lots of plants, and good ocean views round out the decor. The location, directly on the Newport Beach Pier Promenade, is also enviable, though some may find it a bit too close to the action. Breakfast includes fresh pastries and fruit, brown eggs, yogurt, cheeses, and international coffees and teas.

2102 W. Ocean Front, Newport Beach, CA 92663. © **949/675-7300.** www.DorymansInn.com. 10 units. $175–$295 double; from $325 suite. Rates include continental breakfast. AE, MC, V. Free parking. **Amenities:** Restaurant. *In room:* A/C, TV.

WHERE TO DINE
Options in Seal Beach are limited, but a good choice for seafood is **Walt's Wharf,** 201 Main St. (© **562/598-4433**), a bustling, polished restaurant featuring market-fresh selections either plain or with Pacific Rim accents.

EXPENSIVE
5'0" (Five Feet) ★★ CALIFORNIA/ASIAN While 5'0" may no longer break culinary ground, the kitchen still combines the best in California cuisine with Asian technique and ingredients. The restaurant has a minimalist, almost-industrial decor that's brightened by a friendly staff and splendid cuisine. Menu selections run the gamut from tea-smoked filet mignon topped with Roquefort cheese and candied walnuts to a hot Thai-style mixed grill of veal, beef, lamb, and chicken stir-fried with sweet peppers, onions, and mushrooms in curry-mint sauce. The menu changes daily, but you can always find the house specialty, whole braised catfish.

328 Glenneyre, Laguna Beach. © **949/497-4955.** Reservations recommended. Main courses $18–$30. AE, DC, DISC, MC, V. Sun–Thurs 5–10pm; Fri–Sat 5–11pm.

Roy's of Newport Beach ★ HAWAIIAN REGIONAL/PACIFIC RIM   Any foodie who's been to Hawaii in the past decade knows the name Roy Yamaguchi, father of Hawaiian Regional Cuisine (HRC) and the islands' answer to Wolfgang Puck. Roy's empire expanded to Southern California in 1999, with the opening of this dinner-only restaurant on the fringe of Fashion Island shopping center. Yamaguchi developed a menu that represents his groundbreaking East/West/Polynesian cuisine but can be reliably executed by chefs in far-flung kitchens. Most of each night's specials are fresh Pacific fish, given the patented HRC touch with Japanese, Thai, and even Latin accents. Signature dishes include island-style *ahi poke,* spicy Mongolian-glazed rack of lamb, and blackened yellowfin tuna in soy-mustard-butter sauce. The bar whips up "vacation" cocktails in tropical colors, and there's a to-die-for chocolate soufflé dessert.

453 Newport Center Dr., Fashion Island. © **949/640-ROYS.** Reservations suggested. Main courses $16–$29. AE, DC, DISC, MC, V. Mon–Thurs 5–10pm; Fri–Sat 5–11pm.

MODERATE

Crab Cooker SEAFOOD   Since 1951, folks in search of fresh, well-prepared seafood have headed to this bright-red former bank building. Also a fish market, the Crab Cooker has a casual atmosphere of humble wooden tables, uncomplicated smoked and grilled preparations, and meticulously selected fresh fare. The place is especially proud of its Maryland crab cakes; clams and oysters are also part of the repertoire.

2200 Newport Blvd., Newport Beach. © **949/673-0100.** Dinner main courses $10–$25; lunch $8–$19. AE, MC, V. Sun–Thurs 11am–9pm; Fri–Sat 11am–10pm.

Harbor Grill SEAFOOD/STEAK   Located in a business/commercial mall right in the center of the pretty Dana Point Marina, the Harbor Grill is enthusiastically recommended by locals for mesquite-broiled, ocean-fresh seafood. Hawaiian mahimahi with a mango-chutney baste is on the menu, along with Pacific swordfish, crab cakes, and beef steaks.

34499 St. of the Golden Lantern, Dana Point. © **949/240-1416.** www.harborgrill.com. Reservations recommended. Main courses $10–$20. AE, DC, DISC, MC, V. Mon–Sat 11:30am–10pm; Sun 9am–10pm.

Las Brisas *Moments* MEXICAN SEAFOOD   Las Brisas's breathtaking view of the Pacific (particularly at sunset) and potent margaritas are a surefire combination for a *muy romantico* evening. In fact, it's so popular that it can get pretty crowded during the summer months, so be sure to make reservation. Affordable during lunch but pricey at dinner, the menu consists mostly of seafood recipes from the Mexican Riviera. Even the standard enchiladas and tacos get a zesty update with crab or lobster meat and fresh herbs. Calamari steak is sautéed with bell peppers, capers, and herbs in a garlic-butter sauce, and king salmon is mesquite broiled and served with a creamy lime sauce. Although a bit on the touristy side, Las Brisas can be a fun part of the Laguna Beach experience.

361 Cliff Dr. (off the PCH north of Laguna Canyon), Laguna Beach. © **949/497-5434.** Reservations recommended. Main courses $10–$24. AE, DC, DISC, MC, V. Mon–Sat 8am–10:30pm; Sun 9am–10:30pm.

INEXPENSIVE

Ramos House Cafe ★★ REGIONAL AMERICAN   Hidden away in the historic Rios district next to the train tracks, this converted 1881 cottage brings the flavor of a simpler time to busy Orange County. The small seasonal menu of regional American favorites uses garden-grown herbs, house-baked breads, and hand-turned ice cream. The all-purpose breakfast/lunch menu (dinner only for special events) features warmly satisfying cinnamon-apple beignets, wild mushroom and sun-dried tomato omelets, fried green tomatoes sauced with goat cheese, southern fried chicken salad bathed in pumpkin seed–buttermilk dressing, shrimp and sourdough bread pudding, an always changing but always superb fresh soup, and more comfort food faves with a Southern flair. Seating is outside, on a tree-shaded brick garden patio that invites leisure.

31752 Los Rios St. (off Del Obispo St.), San Juan Capistrano. © 949/443-1342. Main courses $5–$10. AE, DC, DISC, MC, V. Tues–Sun 8am–3pm.

4 Santa Barbara

92 miles (148km) NW of Los Angeles

Situated between palm-lined Pacific beaches and the sloping foothills of the Santa Ynez Mountains, this prosperous resort community presents a mosaic of whitewashed stucco and red-tile roofs and a gracious, relaxed attitude that has earned it the sobriquet "American Riviera." It's ideal for kicking back on white-sand beaches, prowling the shops and galleries that line the village's historic streets, and relaxing over a meal in one of many top-notch cafes and restaurants.

Downtown Santa Barbara is distinctive for its Spanish-Mediterranean architecture. But it wasn't always this way. Santa Barbara had a thriving Native American Chumash population for hundreds, if not thousands, of years. The European era began in the late 18th century, around a Spanish *presidio* (fort) that's been reconstructed in its original spot. The earliest architectural hodge-podge was destroyed in 1925 by a powerful earthquake that leveled the business district. Out of the rubble rose the Spanish-Mediterranean town of today, a stylish planned community that continues to enforce strict building codes.

Visit Santa Barbara's waterfront on a Sunday, and you're sure to see the weekly **Arts and Crafts Show,** one of the city's best-loved traditions. Since 1965, artists, craftspeople, and street performers have been lining grassy Chase Palm Park, along Cabrillo Boulevard.

ESSENTIALS

GETTING THERE   By car, U.S. 101 runs right through Santa Barbara; it's the fastest and most direct route from north or south (1½ hr. from Los Angeles, 6 hr. from San Francisco).

By train, **Amtrak** (© **800/USA-RAIL;** www.amtrak.com) offers daily service to Santa Barbara. Trains arrive and depart from the **Santa Barbara Rail Station,** 209 State St. (© **805/963-1015**). Fares can be as low as $40 (round-trip) from Los Angeles's Union Station.

ORIENTATION   State Street, the city's primary commercial thoroughfare, is the geographic center of town. It ends at Stearns Wharf and Cabrillo Boulevard; the latter runs along the ocean and separates the city's beaches from touristy hotels and restaurants. Electric shuttles provide frequent service along these two routes if you'd rather leave the car behind.

VISITOR INFORMATION   The **Santa Barbara Visitor Information Center,** 1 Garden St. (off Cabrillo Blvd., across from the beach), Santa Barbara, CA 93101 (© **800/927-4688** to order a free destination 96-page guide, or 805/965-3021; www.santabarbaraca.com). The center distributes maps, brochures, an events calendar, and information. It's open Monday through Saturday from 9am to 5pm and Sunday from 10am to 5pm.

Be sure you pick up a copy of *The Independent,* Santa Barbara's free weekly, with articles and events listings; and *Explore Santa Barbara,* a compact visitor's

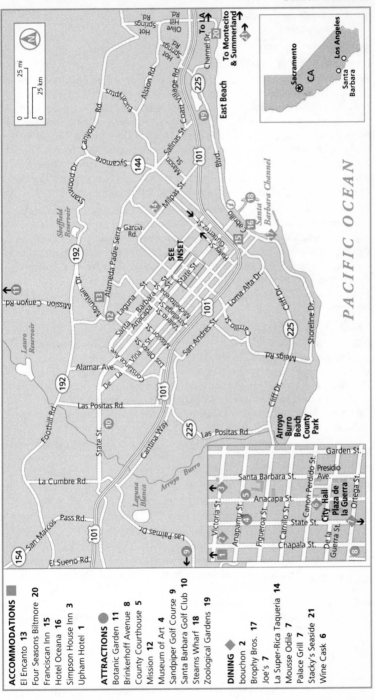

Santa Barbara

ACCOMMODATIONS ■
El Encanto **13**
Four Seasons Biltmore **20**
Franciscan Inn **15**
Hotel Oceana **16**
Simpson House Inn **3**
Upham Hotel **1**

ATTRACTIONS ●
Botanic Garden **11**
Brinkerhoff Avenue **8**
County Courthouse **5**
Mission **12**
Museum of Art **4**
Sandpiper Golf Course **9**
Santa Barbara Golf Club **10**
Stearns Wharf **18**
Zoological Gardens **19**

DINING ◆
bouchon **2**
Brophy Bros. **17**
Joe's **7**
La Super-Rica Taqueria **14**
Mousse Odile **7**
Palace Grill **7**
Stacky's Seaside **21**
Wine Cask **6**

guide published by the local paper, *New-Press.* Both are also available at shops and sidewalk racks throughout town.

SEEING THE SIGHTS
HISTORIC DOWNTOWN

Following a devastating 1925 earthquake, city planners decreed that all new construction would follow codes of Spanish and Mission-style architecture. In time, the adobe-textured walls, rounded archways, glazed tile work, and terra-cotta rooftops came to symbolize the Mediterranean ambience that still characterizes Santa Barbara. The architecture also gave a name to the **Red Tile Tour,** a self-guided walking tour of historic downtown. The visitor center (see "Visitor Information," above) has a map/guide of the tour, which can take anywhere from 1 to 3 hours, including time to visit some of the buildings, and covers about 12 blocks in total. Some of the highlights are destinations in their own right.

Santa Barbara County Courthouse ⭐ Built in 1929, this grand "palace" is considered the local flagship of Spanish Colonial Revival architecture. It's certainly the most flamboyant example, with impressive facades, beamed ceilings, striking murals, an 85-foot-high observation clock tower, and formal sunken gardens. Free guided tours are offered on Monday, Tuesday, and Friday at 10:30am and Monday through Saturday at 2pm.

1100 Anacapa St. ℂ 805/962-6464. Free admission. Mon–Fri 8am–5pm; Sat, Sun, and holidays 10am–4:45pm.

Santa Barbara Museum of Art ⭐ This little jewel of a museum feels more like the private gallery of a wealthy collector. Its leaning is toward early-20th-century Western American paintings and 19th- and 20th-century Asian art, but the best displays might be the antiquities and Chinese ceramics. In addition, there are often visiting exhibits featuring small but excellent collections from other establishments. Free docent-led gallery tours are given Tuesday through Saturday at 1pm, and exhibition tours are given Wednesday, Thursday, and Saturday at noon.

1130 State St. ℂ 805/963-4364. www.sbmuseart.org. Admission $66 adults, $4 seniors 65 and over, $3 students and children ages 6–17, free for children under age 6. Free for everyone Thurs and the 1st Sun of each month. Tues–Thurs and Sat 11am–5pm; Fri 11am–9pm; Sun noon–5pm.

ELSEWHERE IN THE CITY

Santa Barbara Botanic Garden *Finds* The Botanic Garden is devoted to indigenous California plants. More than 5½ miles (9km) of meandering trails on 65 acres offer glimpses of cacti, redwoods, wildflowers, and much more, many arranged in representational habitats or landscapes. The gardens were established in 1926. You'll catch the very best color and aroma just after spring showers. Docent tours are offered daily at 2pm, with additional tours on Thursday, Saturday, and Sunday at 10:30am.

1212 Mission Canyon Rd. (a short drive uphill from the Mission). ℂ 805/682-4726. www.sbbg.org. Admission $5 adults, $3 children 13–18 and seniors 60 and over, $1 children 5–12, free for children under 5. Mon–Fri 9am–5pm; Sat–Sun 9am–6pm.

Santa Barbara Mission ⭐⭐ Established in 1786 by Father Junípero Serra and built by the Chumash Indians, this is a rare example in physical form of the blending of Indian and Hispanic spirituality. This hilltop structure is called the "Queen of the Missions" for its twin bell towers and beauty. It overlooks the town and the Channel Islands beyond. Brochures are available in six languages.

Laguna and Los Olivos sts. (C) 805/682-4149. www.sbmission.org. Admission $4 adults, free for children under 12. Daily 9am–5pm.

Santa Barbara Zoological Gardens *(Kids)*   When you're driving around the bend on Cabrillo Boulevard, look up—you might spot the head of a giraffe poking through the palms. This zoo is an appealing, pint-sized place, where all 700 animals can be seen in about 30 minutes. Most live in natural, open settings. There are also a children's Discovery Area, a miniature train ride, and a small carousel. The picnic areas (with barbecue pits) are underused and especially recommended.

500 Ninos Dr. (off Cabrillo Blvd.). (C) 805/962-5339, or 805/962-6310 for a recording. www.santabarbara zoo.org. Admission $8 adults, $6 seniors and children 2–12, free for children under 2. Daily 10am–5pm; last admission is 1 hr. before closing. Closed Thanksgiving, Christmas.

Stearns Wharf   California's oldest working wharf attracts visitors for strolling, shopping, and snacking. There's also a Sea Center with aquariums, an outdoor touch-tank, and other exhibits. Although the wharf no longer functions for passenger and freight shipping as it did when built in 1872 by local lumberman John C. Stearns, you might still see local fishing boats unload their daily catch. You could also take a narrated sunset harbor cruise aboard the *Harbour Queen* at **Captain Don's** ((C) **805/969-5217**). Public parking is available on the wharf; it's free with merchant validation.

At the end of State St.

BEACHES

East Beach is Santa Barbara's favorite beach, stretching from the Zoological Gardens to Chase Palm Park and the wharf. Nearer the pier you can enjoy manicured lawns, tall palms, and abundant facilities; to the east are many volleyball courts, plus the Cabrillo Pavilion, a recreational center, bathhouse, and architectural landmark dating from 1925. Picnic areas with barbecue grills, showers, and clean, well-patrolled sands make this beach a good choice for everyone.

On the other side of Santa Barbara Harbor is **Leadbetter Beach,** less sheltered than those to the south, and popular with surfers. It's reached by following Cabrillo Boulevard after it turns into Shoreline Drive. This beach is also a great place to watch pleasure boats entering or leaving the harbor. Leadbetter has basic facilities, including restrooms, picnic areas, and a metered parking lot.

Two miles (3km) west of Leadbetter is secluded but popular **Arroyo Burro Beach County Park,** also known as "Hendry's Beach." This gem has a grassy park beneath the cliffs and a white crescent beach with great waves for surfing and bodysurfing. There are volleyball nets, picnic areas, restrooms, and a free parking lot.

OUTDOOR ACTIVITIES

BIKING & SURREY CYCLING   A relatively flat, palm-lined 2-mile (3km) coastal pathway, perfect for biking, runs along the beach. More adventurous riders can pedal through town (where painted bike lanes line many major routes, including one up to the Mission). These routes and many more are outlined in the Santa Barbara County Bike Map, a free and comprehensive resource available at the Visitor Center or by calling Traffic Solutions at (C) **805/963-7283.**

Wheel Fun Rentals, 22 State St. ((C) **805/966-6733**), rents well-maintained six-speed cruisers for $7 an hour and mountain bikes for $8 an hour. It also has tandem bikes and surrey cycles that can hold as many as four adults and two children; rates vary. The place is open daily from 8am to dusk. Several other operations on the same block rent similar equipment at similar prices.

BOATING   The **Santa Barbara Sailing Center,** in Santa Barbara Harbor (© **800/350-9090** or 805/962-2826; www.sbsailctr.com), rents sailboats from 21 to 50 feet in length, as well as paddleboats, kayaks, and motorboats. Both skippered and bareboat charters are available by the day or hour. Sailing instruction for all levels of experience is also available. Coastal, island, whale-watching, dinner-cruise, and adventure tours are offered on the 50-foot sailing catamaran *Double Dolphin.* Open daily 9am–5pm.

GOLF   At the **Santa Barbara Golf Club,** 3500 McCaw Ave., at Las Positas Road (© **805/687-7087**), there are a great 6,009-yard, 18-hole course and a driving range. Unlike many municipal courses, the Santa Barbara Golf Course is well maintained and presents a moderate challenge for the average golfer. Greens fees are $28 Monday through Friday and $37 on weekends ($30 for seniors). Optional carts rent for $24 for 18 holes, $14 for 9.

The 18-hole, 7,000-yard course **Sandpiper,** at 7925 Hollister Ave. (© **805/968-1541**), a scenic ocean-side course, has a pro shop and driving range. Greens fees are $118 daily, $130 with cart.

HIKING   The foothill trails in the Santa Ynez Mountains above Santa Barbara are perfect for day hikes. In general, they aren't overly strenuous. Trail maps are available at **Pacific Travelers Supply,** 12 W. Anapamu St. at State Street (© **805/963-4438**), at the visitor center (see "Visitor Information," above), and from **Traffic Solutions** (© **805/963-7283**).

One of the most popular hikes is the **Seven Falls/Inspiration Point Trail,** an easy trek that begins on Tunnel Road, past the Mission, and skirts the edge of Santa Barbara's Botanic Garden (which contains some pleasant hiking trails itself).

SKATING   The paved beach path that runs along Santa Barbara's waterfront is perfect for skating. **Wheel Fun Rentals,** 22 State St. (© **805/966-6733**), located near the path, rents both inline and conventional roller skates. The fee ($7 for the first hr., $10 for 2 hr.) fee includes wrist and knee pads.

WHALE-WATCHING   Whale-watching cruises are offered between late December and late March, when Pacific gray whales pass by on migratory journeys from their breeding lagoons in Baja California, Mexico, to their Alaskan feeding grounds. **Shoreline Park,** west of the harbor, has high bluffs ideal for land-based whale-spotting. Sea excursions are offered by both **Captain Don's Harbor Tours** (© **805/969-5217**), on Stearns Wharf, and **The Condor** (© **888/77-WHALE** or 805/963-3564; www.condorcruises.com), located on Cabrillo Boulevard at Bath Street.

SHOPPING

State Street from the beach to Victoria Street is the city's main thoroughfare and has the largest concentration of shops. Many specialize in T-shirts and postcards, but there are a number of boutiques as well. If you get tired of strolling, hop on one of the electric shuttle buses (25¢) that run up and down State Street.

Also check out **Brinkerhoff Avenue** (off Cota St., between Chapala and De La Vina sts.), Santa Barbara's "antiques alley." Most shops here are open Tuesday through Sunday from 11am to 5pm. **El Paseo** (814 State St.) is a picturesque shopping arcade reminiscent of an old Spanish street. It's built around an 1827 adobe home and is lined with charming shops and art galleries. **Paseo Nuevo,** on the other side of State Street, is a modern outdoor mall, featuring familiar chain stores and cafes, and anchored by a Nordstrom department store.

WHERE TO STAY

Before you even begin calling around for reservations, keep in mind that Santa Barbara's accommodations are expensive—especially in summer. Then decide whether you'd like to stay beachside (even more expensive) or downtown. Santa Barbara is small, but not small enough to happily stroll between the two areas.

The Convention and Visitors Bureau's one-stop reservations service, **Hot Spots** (② **800/793-7666** or 805/564-1637), keeps an updated list of availability for about 90% of the area's hotels, motels, inns, and B&Bs. The service will have the latest information on who might be looking to fill last-minute vacancies at reduced rates. Reservationists are available Monday through Saturday from 9am to 9pm and Sunday from 9am to 4pm. There's no charge for using the service.

VERY EXPENSIVE

Four Seasons Biltmore ★★★   This gem of the "American Riviera" manages to adhere to the most elegant standards of hospitality without making anyone feel unwelcome. It's easy to sense the ghosts of golden-age Hollywood celebs like Greta Garbo, Errol Flynn, and Bing Crosby, who used to play croquet or practice putting on the hotel's perfectly manicured lawns and then head over to the private Coral Casino Beach & Cabana Club—because that's exactly what today's privileged guests are *still* doing! The Four Seasons company acquired this Spanish-style hacienda (ca. 1927) in 1987 and restored the 20-acre property without spoiling a bit of its historic charm. Rooms have an airy feel, heightened by white plantation shutters, light wood furnishings, and full marble bathrooms with all the modern amenities. Guests can amuse themselves with a putting green, shuffleboard courts, and croquet lawn. In addition to two acclaimed dining rooms, the Biltmore offers a no-holds-barred Sunday brunch that draws folks from 100 miles (161km) away. The hotel's most recent addition is The Spa, a multimillion-dollar, 10,000-square-foot new Spanish-style annex that houses numerous treatment rooms, a swimming pool and two huge whirlpool baths, a state-of-the-art fitness center, and for the big spenders 10 ocean-view deluxe suites with fireplaces, in-room bars, changing rooms, and twin massage tables (essentially your own private treatment room).

1260 Channel Dr. (at the end of Olive Mill Rd.), Santa Barbara, CA 93108. ② **800/332-3442** or 805/969-2261. Fax 805/565-8323. www.fourseasons.com. 217 units. $295–$620 double; from $1,050 suite. Extra person $35. Free for children age 18 and under in parents' room. Special midweek and package rates available. AE, DC, MC, V. Valet parking $17; free self-parking. **Amenities:** 4 restaurants and 2 lounges; 2 outdoor heated pools; 3 lit tennis courts; health club; salon/spa services; whirlpool; complimentary bicycles; salon; 24-hour room service; dry-cleaning/laundry service. *In room:* A/C, TV/VCR w/ pay movies, high-speed dataport, complimentary morning paper, minibar, hair dryer, iron, safe, bathrobes.

EXPENSIVE

El Encanto Hotel & Garden Villas ★   This romantic hillside retreat, whose very name means "enchantment," was built in 1915 and is made up of Craftsman cottages and Spanish bungalows. Uphill from the Mission and surrounded by an exclusive older residential community, El Encanto features a spectacular view, secluded nooks, gardens and lily ponds, and lush landscaping. The hotel's discreetly attentive service has made it a favorite among privacy-minded celebs. The spacious rooms are decorated in a European country style and feature bathrobes and refrigerators; many have fireplaces, balconies, or patios.

1900 Lasuen Rd., Santa Barbara, CA 93103. ℂ **800/346-7039** or 805/687-5000. Fax 805/687-3903. www.elencantohotel.com. 85 units. $229–$269 double; from $349 suite. AE, DC, MC, V. Take Mission Rd. past the Mission, forking right and then turning left onto Lasuen Rd. **Amenities:** Restaurant; lounge; outdoor heated pool; 1 outdoor tennis court; concierge; room service (6am–10pm); in-room massage. *In room:* TV, minibar, hair dryer, iron.

Simpson House Inn Bed & Breakfast ★★ Simpson House is truly something special. Rooms within the 1874 Historic Landmark main house are decorated to Victorian perfection, with extras ranging from a claw-foot tub and antique brass shower to skylight and French doors opening to the manicured gardens; romantic cottages are nestled throughout the grounds. The rooms have everything you could possibly need, but most impressive are the extras: the gourmet Mediterranean hors d'oeuvres and Santa Barbara wines served each afternoon; the enormous video library; and the full gourmet breakfast (delivered, for detached cottages, on delicate china). Fact is, the Simpson House goes the distance—and then some—to create the perfect stay. Although this property is packed into a relatively small space, it still manages an ambience of country elegance and exclusivity—especially if you book one of the cottages. *Note:* Some rooms don't come with a TV/VCR, but you can have one by request.

121 E. Arrellaga St. (between Santa Barbara and Anacapa sts.), Santa Barbara, CA 93101. ℂ **800/676-1280** or 805/963-7067. Fax 805/564-4811. www.simpsonhouseinn.com. 14 units. $215–$435 double; $525–$550 suite and cottage. 2-night minimum on weekends. Rates include full gourmet breakfast, evening hors d'oeuvres and wine. AE, DISC, MC, V. **Amenities:** Complimentary bicycles; concierge; in-room massage. *In room:* A/C, TV/VCR, minibar, hair dryer, iron, bathrobes.

MODERATE

Hotel Oceana ★★ If you're going to vacation in Santa Barbara, you might as well stay in style and on the beach. Ergo, the Hotel Oceana, a "beach chic" hotel with an oceanfront setting and an L.A. makeover. The 2.5-acre Spanish Mission-style property consists of four adjacent motels built in the 1940s that have been merged and renovated into one sprawling hotel. The result is a wide range of charmingly old-school accommodations—everything from apartments with real day beds (great for families) to inexpensive courtyard rooms and deluxe ocean-view suites—with bright modern furnishings. Each guest room, decorated by renowned interior designer Kathryn Ireland, is smartly appointed with soft Frette linens, down comforters (the beds are fantastic), ceiling fans, CD players, cozy duvets, and Aveda bath products. Along with the size and location of your room, you also get to choose between four color schemes—soothing blue or green, racy red, and a cheery yellow (our preferred choice). The beach and jogging path are right across the street, and there's a huge lawn area that's perfect for picnic lunches. A Spa & Wellness Center offering various massage and facial treatments should be completed by the time you read this.

202 West Cabrillo Blvd, Santa Barbara, CA 93101. ℂ **800/956-9776** or 805/965-4577. Fax 805/965-9937. www.hoteloceana.com. 122 units. $175–$350 double; from $325 suite. 2-night minimum for weekend reservations. AE, DC, DISC, MC, V. **Amenities:** Denny's restaurant adjacent; fitness room; spa; 2 swimming pools; whirlpool; large lawn area; sundeck. *In room:* A/C, TV, CD player, high-speed wireless Internet access, refrigerator, hair dryer, iron.

The Upham Victorian Hotel and Garden Cottages This conveniently located inn combines the intimacy of a B&B with the service of a small hotel. Built in 1871, the Upham is the oldest continuously operating hostelry in Southern California. Somewhere the management made time for upgrades, though, because guest accommodations are complete with all the modern comforts. The hotel is constructed of redwood, with sweeping verandas and a Victorian cupola on top. It has a warm lobby, a cozy restaurant, and a resident cat named Henry.

1404 De La Vina St. (at Sola St.), Santa Barbara, CA 93101. ✆ **800/727-0876** or 805/962-0058. Fax 805/963-2825. www.uphamhotel.com. 50 units. $155–$235 double; from $275 suite and cottage. Rates include continental breakfast and afternoon wine and cheese. AE, DC, MC, V. **Amenities:** Restaurant; dry-cleaning/laundry service. *In room:* TV.

INEXPENSIVE

All the best buys fill up fast in the summer months, so be sure to reserve your room—even if you're just planning to stay at the decent, reliable **Motel 6,** 443 Corona del Mar Dr. (✆ **800/466-8356** or 805/564-1392), near the beach.

Franciscan Inn   The Franciscan is nestled in a quiet neighborhood just a block from the beach, near Stearns Wharf. This privately owned and meticulously maintained hotel is an affordable retreat with enough frills that you'll still feel pampered. The small but comfy rooms feature a country-tinged decor and finely tiled bathrooms. Services include morning newspaper and free local calls. Most second-floor rooms have unobstructed mountain views, and some suites feature fully equipped kitchenettes. The inn stacks up as a great family choice that's classy enough for a romantic weekend too.

109 Bath St. (at Mason St.), Santa Barbara, CA 93101. ✆ **805/963-8845.** Fax 805/564-3295. www.franciscan inn.com. 53 units. Summer (mid-May to mid-Sept) $95–$134 double, $145–$250 suite; winter $75–$120 double, $110–$200 suite. Extra person $8. Rates include continental breakfast and afternoon refreshments. AE, DC, MC, V. Free parking. **Amenities:** Heated outdoor pool; whirlpool; dry-cleaning/laundry service; coin-op laundry. *In room:* A/C, TV/VCR, dataport, coffeemaker, hair dryer, iron.

WHERE TO DINE
EXPENSIVE

bouchon ★★ CALIFORNIA   You can tell this warm and inviting restaurant is passionate about wine just from the name—*bouchon* is the French word for "wine cork." And not just any wines, but those of the surrounding Santa Barbara County. There are 50 different Central Coast wines available by the glass; have some fun by enhancing each course with a glass (or half-glass) of wine—knowledgeable servers help make the perfect match. The seasonally composed—and regionally inspired—menu has included dishes such as smoked Santa Barbara albacore "carpaccio," deliciously arranged with a tangy vinaigrette and shaved imported Parmesan; luscious sweetbread and chanterelle ragout cradled in a potato-leek basket; local venison sliced and laid atop cumin spaetzle in a shallow pond of green peppercorn-Madeira demi-glace; or monkfish saddle fragrant with fresh herbs and accompanied by a creamy fennel-Gruyère gratin. Request a table on the patio, and don't miss the signature chocolate soufflé for dessert.

9 West Victoria St. (off State St.) ✆ **805/730-1160.** www.bouchonsantabarbara.com. Reservations recommended. Main courses $18–$29. AE, DC, MC, V. Daily 5:30–10pm.

Wine Cask ★★ CALIFORNIA/ITALIAN   Take an 18-year-old wine shop, a large 1920s landmark dining room with a big stone fireplace, and outstanding Italian fare, and mix them with an attractive staff and clientele, and you've got the Wine Cask—the most popular upscale dining spot in Santa Barbara. Here you'll be treated to such heavenly creations as lamb sirloin with twice-baked au gratin potatoes. Other options include potato and prosciutto-wrapped local halibut in cioppino sauce; or grilled marinated chicken breast in a red-wine reduction with prosciutto, wild mushrooms, fresh rosemary, and sage. The wine list reads like a novel, with more than 1,000 wines (ranging from $14–$1,400), and has deservedly received the *Wine Spectator* award for excellence. There's also a happy hour at the beautiful maple bar from 4 to 6pm daily.

In El Paseo Center, 813 Anacapa, Santa Barbara. (℃) 805/966-9463. Reservations recommended. Dinner main courses $18–$29; lunch $8–$12. AE, DC, MC, V. Mon–Thurs 11:30am–9pm; Fri 11:30am–10pm; Sat 5:30–10pm; Sun 5:30–9pm.

MODERATE

Brophy Bros. Clam Bar & Restaurant ★★ SEAFOOD   This place is most known for its unbeatable view of the marina, but the dependable fresh seafood keeps tourists and locals coming back. Dress is casual, portions are huge, and favorites include New England clam chowder, cioppino, and any one of an assortment of seafood salads. The scampi is consistently good, as is all the fresh fish, which comes with soup or salad, coleslaw, and pilaf or french fries. A nice assortment of beers and wines is available. *Be forewarned:* The wait at this small place can be up to 2 hours on a weekend night.

119 Harbor Way (off Cabrillo Blvd. in the Waterfront Center). (℃) 805/966-4418. Reservations not accepted. Main courses $9–$16. AE, MC, V. Sun–Thurs 11am–10pm; Fri–Sat 11am–11pm.

Joe's Cafe AMERICAN   When they say "Eat at Joe's," they're talking about this Santa Barbara institution, going strong for 60-plus years. Friendly and loud, it's a meat-lover's haven. Its walls are loaded with faded photographs, local league sports trophies, and deer antlers. It's famous for serving stiff drinks, and crowds line the bar and pile into comfy booths. The menu features prime rib, steaks, chops, potatoes, and a few salads for the noncarnivores. Joe's is at the heart of lower State Street, which hasn't become quite as snooty as the stretch to the north; it's also in a convenient location for shoppers.

536 State St. (at Cota St.), Santa Barbara. (℃) 805/966-4638. Reservations recommended. Main courses $9–$17. AE, DISC, MC, V. Mon–Thurs 11am–11:30pm; Fri–Sat 11am–12:30am; Sun 4–11pm.

Mousse Odile FRENCH   Lately *everyone* seems to have learned about this romantic restaurant just off bustling State Street. Thankfully, even though they've started packing picnic baskets and bottling their vinaigrette (*mon Dieu!*), this classic French dining room with a casual contemporary attitude has changed little. *Pâté Maison* is served with chewy bread and plenty of tart *cornichons* (small sour pickles); filet mignon arrives in green peppercorn–cognac sauce; a selection of mushrooms are sautéed in cream and served *en croute* (wrapped in pastry); and desserts, of course, are to die for. If you're in the mood for a Gallic breakfast, come for rich, saucy omelets served with applesauce and potatoes au gratin, plus puff pastry breakfast specialties and picture-perfect espresso.

18 E. Cota St. (½ block off State St.), Santa Barbara. (℃) 805/962-5393. Reservations suggested. Main courses $14–$18. AE, MC, V. Mon–Sat 8am–2:30pm and 5:30–9pm.

Palace Grill ★ CAJUN/CREOLE   Strolling by this restaurant, just a stone's throw from State Street, you'll see why descriptions like "rollicking" and "atmosphere as hot as the food" are applied to the Palace Grill. The scene extends to the sidewalk, where waiting diners thirst after Mason jar Cajun martinis and Caribbean rum punch. Inside, you'll find yourself part of the loud and fun atmosphere; this is not the place for meaningful dinner conversation. Try a platter of spicy blackened steak and seafood, a rich crawfish étouffée, or a Creole jambalaya pasta. Save room for the renowned Southern desserts, including sweet potato–pecan pie, Florida Key lime pie, and the superstar Louisiana bread pudding soufflé, laced with Grand Marnier and accompanied by whiskey cream sauce.

8 E. Cota St., Santa Barbara. ℂ 805/963-5000. www.palacegrill.com. Reservations suggested; not accepted Fri–Sat. Dinner main courses $9–$25; lunch $5–$13. AE, MC, V. Daily 11am–3pm and 5:30–10pm (until 11pm Fri–Sat).

INEXPENSIVE

La Super-Rica Taqueria ★★ MEXICAN   Looking at this street-corner shack, you'd never guess it's blessed with an endorsement by Julia Child. The tacos here are no-nonsense, generous portions of filling piled onto fresh, grainy corn tortillas. Try *bistec* (steak), *adobado* (marinated pork), or *gorditas* (thick corn *masa* pockets filled with spicy beans). A dollop of homemade salsa is the only adornment required. You might catch Julia lining up for Sunday's special, *pozole*, a stew of pork and hominy in red chili sauce. On Friday and Saturday, the specialty is freshly made tamales. *Tip:* Be sure to ask for extra tortillas.

622 N. Milpas St. (between Cota and Ortega sts.), Santa Barbara. ℂ 805/963-4940. Most menu items $3–$7. No credit cards. Sun–Thurs 11am–9pm; Fri–Sat 11am–9:30pm.

Stacky's Seaside SANDWICHES   Stacky's is an ivy-covered shack filled with fishnets, surfboards, and local memorabilia. The menu of sandwiches is enormous, as are most of their pita pockets, hoagies, and club sandwiches. A sign proudly proclaims HALF OF ANY SANDWICH, HALF PRICE—NO PROBLEM, and Stacky's has made a lot of friends because of it. Choices include the Santa Barbaran (roasted tri-tip and melted jack cheese on sourdough), the Rincon pita (jack and cheddar cheeses, green Ortega chilis, onions, and ranch dressing), and a hot pastrami hoagie with Swiss cheese, mustard, and onions. Stacky's also serves breakfast, featuring scrambled egg sandwiches and south-of-the-border egg dishes. An order of crispy fries is enough for two.

2315 Lillie Ave., Summerland (5 min. on the freeway from Santa Barbara). ℂ 805/969-9908. Most menu items under $6. AE, DISC, MC, V. Mon–Fri 6:30am–7:30pm; Sat–Sun 7am–7:30pm.

5 Palm Springs

120 miles (193km) E of Los Angeles

Palm Springs had been known for years as a golf course–loaded retirement mecca, annually invaded by raucous hordes of libidinous college kids at spring break. Well, nowadays the city of Palm Springs is attracting a whole new crowd. Former mayor (later U.S. Congressman) Sonny Bono's revolutionary "anti-thong" ordinance in 1991 put a lightning-quick halt to the spring-break migration by eliminating public display of the bare female derrière, and the upscale fairway-condo crowd has decided to congregate in the outlying resort cities of Rancho Mirage, Palm Desert, Indian Wells, and La Quinta.

These days, the city fancies itself a European-style resort with a dash of good ol' American small town thrown in for good measure—think *Jetsons* architecture and the crushed-velvet vibe of piano bars combined with the colors and attitude of a laid-back Aegean island village. Also, Hollywood's young glitterati are returning to "the Springs." One thing hasn't changed: Swimming, sunbathing, golfing, and playing tennis are still the primary pastimes in this convenient little oasis.

ESSENTIALS

GETTING THERE   Several airlines serve the **Palm Springs Regional Airport**, 3400 E. Tahquitz Canyon Way (ℂ 760/318-3800), including **Alaska Airlines** (ℂ 800/426-0333; www.alaskaair.com), **America West** (ℂ 800/ 235-9292; www.americawest.com), **Delta/Skywest** (ℂ 800/453-9417;

www.delta.com), **United Express** (✆ **800/241-6522;** www.ual.com), and **US Airways Express** (✆ **800/428-4322;** www.usairways.com). Flights from Los Angeles International Airport (see chapter 2) take about 40 minutes.

If you're driving from Los Angeles, take I-10 east to the Calif. 111 turnoff to Palm Springs. You'll breeze into town on North Palm Canyon Drive, the main thoroughfare. The trip from downtown L.A. takes about 2 hours.

VISITOR INFORMATION Pick up *Palm Springs Life* magazine's free monthly **"Desert Guide."** It contains tons of visitor information, including a comprehensive calendar of events. Copies are distributed in hotels and newsstands and by the **Palm Springs Desert Resorts Convention & Visitors Bureau,** in the Atrium Design Centre, 69930 Calif. 111, Suite 201, Rancho Mirage, CA 92270 (✆ **800/41-RELAX** or 760/770-9000). The bureau's office staff can help with maps, brochures, and advice Monday through Friday from 8:30am to 5pm. They also operate a **24-hour information line** (✆ **760/ 770-1992**) and a website (**www.PalmSpringsUSA.com**).

Another website worth browsing is **www.inpalmsprings.com**, which contains a wealth of information designed for locals as well as visitors.

The **Palm Springs Visitors Information Center,** 2781 N. Palm Canyon Dr. (✆ **800/34-SPRINGS;** fax 760/323-3021; www.palm-springs.org), offers maps, brochures, advice, souvenirs, and a free hotel reservation service. It's open Monday through Saturday from 9am to 5pm and on Sunday from 8am to 4pm.

ORIENTATION The downtown area of Palm Springs stretches along **North Palm Canyon Drive.** The street is one way through the heart of town; its otherway counterpart is **Indian Canyon Drive,** 1 block east. The mountains lie directly west and south, while the rest of Palm Springs is laid out in a grid to the southeast. **Tahquitz Canyon Way** creates North Palm Canyon's primary intersection, tracking a straight line between the airport and the heart of town.

GOLF

The Palm Springs desert resorts are world-famous meccas for golfers. There are more than 85 public, semiprivate, and private courses in the area. If you start polishing your irons the moment you begin planning your vacation, you're best off staying at one of the valley's many golf resorts (most outside of Palm Springs), where you can enjoy the proximity of your hotel's facilities as well as smart package deals that can give you a taste of country-club membership. Some of the best golf resorts are **Marriott's Desert Springs Resort** in Palm Desert (✆ **760/341-2211**), **Marriott's Rancho Las Palmas** in Rancho Mirage (✆ **760/568-2727**), the **Hyatt Grand Champions** in Indian Wells (✆ **760/ 341-1000**), and **La Quinta Resort & Club** in La Quinta (✆ **760/346-2904**).

Palm Springs has courses at all levels open to the general public; call ahead to see which will rent clubs or other equipment to the spontaneous player.

Beginners will enjoy **Tommy Jacobs' Bel-Air Greens,** 1001 El Cielo, Palm Springs (✆ **760/322-6062**), a scenic nine-hole, par-32 executive course that has some water and sand-trap challenges but also allows for a few confidence-boosting successes. Generally flat fairways and mature trees characterize the relatively short (3,350 yd.) course. Greens fees are $17 and drop to $14 after 4pm. The complex also has an 18-hole miniature golf course.

More advanced amateurs will want to check out the **Tahquitz Creek Golf Resort,** 1885 Golf Club Dr., Palm Springs (✆ **760/328-1005**), whose two courses appeal to midhandicappers. The wide, water-free holes of the "Legend"

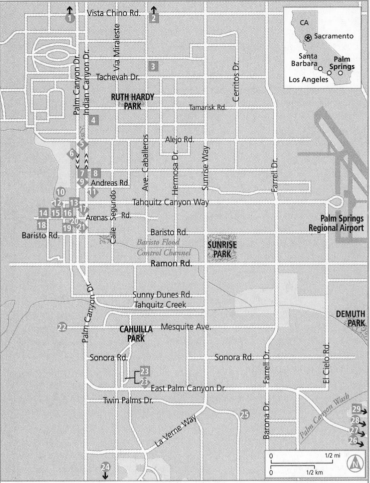

ACCOMMODATIONS ▪

Ballantine's Movie Colony **4**
Casa Cody **15**
Estrella Inn **16**
Holiday Inn
   Palm Mountain **13**
Hyatt Regency Suites **7**
Korakia Pensione **18**
La Mancha Resort Village **3**
La Quinta Resort & Club **29**
The Orbit Inn **14**
Orchid Tree Inn **19**
Spa Hotel & Casino **8**
Two Bunch Palms **2**
Villa Royale **23**

DINING ◆

Blue Coyote Grill **6**
Edgardo's Café Veracruz **5**
Europa Restaurant **23**
La Provence **17**
Las Casuelas Terraza **21**
Le Vallauris **12**
Mykonos **11**
Palmie **9**
Palm Springs Chop House **21**
Pomme Frite **21**
St. James at the Vineyard **20**

ATTRACTIONS ●

Indian Canyons **24**
The Living Desert **28**
Palm Springs
   Aerial Tramway **1**
Palm Springs
   Desert Museum **10**
Palm Springs
   Oasis Waterpark **26**
Shields Date Gardens **27**
Smoke Tree Stables **25**
Tahquitz Canyon **22**

Finds **Here's the Rub**

Since the time of the Native American Cahuilla, who knew how great it felt to soak in the Coachella Valley's natural hot springs, this desert has drawn stressed-out masses seeking relaxation, rejuvenation, and the pure sigh-inducing pleasure only a health spa can deliver.

Our number-one we-can't-recommend-it-enough choice is heavenly **Two Bunch Palms** 🔴🔴, annually voted one of the world's "Top Ten" by *Travel & Leisure* magazine. Posh yet intimate, this spiritual sanctuary in Desert Hot Springs (about 20 min. north of Palm Springs) has been drawing weary city dwellers since Chicago mobster Al Capone hid out here in the 1930s. Two Bunch Palms later became a playground for the movie community, but today it's a friendly and informal haven offering renowned spa services, quiet bungalows nestled on lush grounds, and trademark lagoons of steaming mineral water.

Service is famously—and excellently—discreet; and legions of return guests attest that the outstanding spa treatments (nine varieties of massage, mud baths, body wraps, facials, salt glo, and more) and therapeutic waters are what make the luxury of Two Bunch Palms irresistible. Room rates start at $175 (including breakfast) in the high season, with midweek and substantial seasonal discounts available. Spa treatments average between $75 and $100 per hour, and money-saving room/meal/spa packages are always offered. Don't want to stay over? Then book one of Two Bunch's 6-hour Day Spa packages. The resort is located off Palm Drive (Gene Autry Trail) at 67425 Two Bunch Palms Trail (© 800/472-4334 or 760/329-8791; www.twobunchpalms.com).

If you don't have the time to venture outside of town, you can still liberate your body, mind, and spirit at **Bonne Sante** 🔴. Specializing in a holistic approach to spa services and featuring custom plans for detoxifying the body, this soothing spa reminds you of a luxurious French Villa. It's the only place in the valley that uses "Endermologie," a non-invasive technique to rid the body of cellulite. This 35-minute treatment uses suction and motorized rollers to massage your skin and increase circulation, thus fighting the appearance of cellulite. They also offer colon hydrotherapy and body treatments such as herbal wraps and facials. Of course, if you simply want massage, you've come to the right place. Swedish, deep tissue, Shiatsu, Traditional Thai and even reflexology are among the many offerings. The owner, Gus Mendoza, has run some of the biggest spas in the desert and has created a soothing environment for healing and wellness. His focus on individual attention and customer satisfaction makes visiting a special treat. Massage treatments range from $75 to $100 for an hour or $100 to $150 for 90 minutes. Bonne Sante is located at the south end of town at 1000 South Palm Canyon Drive, Suite 103. (© 760/327-3880; www.bonnesantespa.com).

course will appeal to anyone frustrated by the target courses popular with many architects, while the Ted Robinson–designed "Resort" course offers the accuracy-testing bells and whistles more common to lavish private clubs. Greens fees, including cart, range from $60 to $95 depending on day of week.

The **Palm Springs Country Club,** 2500 Whitewater Club Dr. (© 760/
323-8625), is the oldest public-access golf course in the city of Palm Springs,
and it is popular with budget-conscious golfers, as greens fees are only $30 for
residents and $40 for nonresidents, including the required cart. The challenge
of bunkers and roughs can be amplified by the oft-blowing wind along the
5,885 yards of this unusually laid-out course.

A complete golfer's guide is available from the Palm Springs Desert Resorts
Convention & Visitors Bureau (see "Visitor Information," above).

The Palm Springs desert is truly a playground, and what follows a mere sampling of the opportunities to enjoy the abundant sunshine during your vacation
here.

A FAMILY WATER PARK   Knott's Soak City U.S.A.-Palm Springs, off
I-10 south on Gene Autry Trail between Ramon Road and East Palm Canyon
Drive (© 760/325-7873; www.knotts.com), is a water playground with 10
water slides, bodysurfing and board surfing, an inner tube ride, and more. Visitors must me a minimum of 40 inches tall to experience most rides, and at least
48 inches for the Tidal Wave Tower, which offers two seven-stories tall, high-
speed water slides. There are two kids' water slides for children under 48 inches
tall. Dressing rooms, lockers, and beach cabanas (with food service) are available. General admission is $21.95, $14.95 for kids from 3 to 11, and free for
kids under 3 ($11 for seniors). The park is open from mid-March to Labor Day,
daily from 10am to 6pm, plus weekends all of September and October.

BICYCLING   The clean, dry air just cries out to be enjoyed—what could be
better than to pedal your way around town or into the desert? **Adventure Bike
Tours** (© 760/328-0282) will outfit you with a bike, helmet, souvenir water
bottle, and certified guide; tours start at about $40, and bike rentals are $10 per
hour or $28 for the day. The **Bighorn Bicycle Rental & Tour Company,** 302
N. Palm Canyon (© 760/325-3367) has hourly ($7) and daily ($27) rental
rates in addition to guided bike treks (a 4-hr. guided ride/hike is $45 per person
including all equipment and snacks can be had with a 24-hr. advance reservation and at least three people in your party).

GUIDED JEEP & WAGON EXCURSIONS   Desert Adventures (© 888/
440-JEEP or 760/324-JEEP; www.red-jeep.com) offers four-wheel-drive eco-
tours led by experienced naturalist guides. Your off-road adventure may take you
to a replica of an ancient Cahuilla village, the rugged Santa Rosa Mountain roads
overlooking the Coachella Valley, or ravines on the way to the San Andreas Fault.
Tours range in duration from 2 to 4 hours and from $59 to $99. Advance reservations are required. The company's trademark red Jeeps depart from the Desert
Adventures Ranch on South Palm Canyon near the entrance to the Indian
Canyons, but most of the longer excursions include hotel pickup and return.

Covered Wagon Tours (© 800/367-2161 or 760/347-2161; www.covered
wagontours.com) embraces the pioneer spirit with a 2-hour ride through the
Coachella Valley Nature Preserve followed by a barbecue and live country music.
The tours take place 7 days a week from October to mid-May; the cost is $50 for
adults, $30 for children ages 7 to 16, and free for kids age 6 and under. Without
the "grub," the charge is $36 per adult and $20 per child. Advance reservations
are required.

HIKING   The most popular spot for hiking is the nearby **Indian Canyons**
(© 760/325-5673 for information). The Agua Caliente tribe made their home
here centuries ago, and remnants of their residency can be seen among the

streams, waterfalls, and astounding palm groves in Andreas, Murray, and Palm canyons. Striking rock formations and herds of bighorn sheep and wild ponies will probably be more appealing than the "Trading Post" in Palm Canyon, but it does sell detailed trail maps. This is Indian land, and the Tribal Council charges admission of $6 per adult, with discounts for seniors, children, students, and those in the military. The canyons are closed to visitors from late June to early September.

Don't miss the opportunity to explore the **Tahquitz Canyon** (500 W. Mesquite, west of Palm Canyon Drive), also an Agua Caliente territory. This incredibly scenic canyon, which features the waterfall filmed for the classic *Lost Horizon,* was closed to the public for nearly 30 years after it became an all-night party zone for thoughtless visitors, who vandalized land considered sacred— serious injuries also plagued careless canyon squatters. But now the vegetation is renewed and decades' worth of trash cleaned up, and in 2001 the tribe began offering 2-hour ranger-led hikes into their most spiritual and beautiful place. The canyon is open daily from 8am to 5pm, with hikes departing every hour until 3pm. The fee is $12.50 for adults and $6 for kids under 12; call ℂ **760/ 416-7044** for information and reservations.

HORSEBACK RIDING   Equestrians from novice to advanced can experi- ence the natural solitude and quiet of the desert on horseback at **Smoke Tree Stables** (ℂ **760/327-1372**), south of downtown. Guided rides, ideal for explor- ing the nearby Indian Canyon trails, cost $30 per hour. But don't expect your posse leader to be primed with information on the nature you'll encounter—this is strictly a do-it-yourself experience.

TENNIS   Virtually all the larger hotels and resorts have tennis courts, but if you're staying at a B&B, you might want to play at the **Tennis Club,** 1300 Baristo Rd., Palm Springs (ℂ **760/325-1441**). It has nine courts and offers day and evening clinics for adults, juniors, and seniors, as well as ball machines for solo practice. USPTA pros are on hand.

If you'd like to play free, the night-lit courts at **Palm Springs High School,** 2248 E. Ramon Rd., are open to the public on weekends, on holidays, and dur- ing the summer. There are also eight free lit courts in beautiful **Ruth Hardy Park** at Tamarisk and Caballero streets.

EXPLORING THE AREA

The Living Desert Wildlife and Botanical Park ☆   This 1,200-acre desert reserve, museum, zoo, and educational center is designed to acquaint visitors with the unique habitats that make up the southern California deserts. You can walk or take a tram tour through sectors that re-create life in several distinctive desert zones. See and learn about a dizzying variety of plants, insects, and wildlife, including bighorn sheep, mountain lions, rattlesnakes, lizards, owls, golden eagles, and the ubiquitous roadrunner.

Tips **Don't Dry Out in the Desert**

The strong sun and dry air that are so appealing can sneak up on you in the form of sunburn and heat exhaustion. Especially during the summer, but even in milder times, always carry and drink plenty of water and use generous amounts of sunscreen.

47900 Portola Ave., Palm Desert. © **760/346-5694.** www.livingdesert.org. Admission $8.50 adults, $7.50 seniors age 62 and over, $4.25 children ages 3–12, free for kids under age 3. Daily 9am–5pm (last entrance 4:30pm); summer (June 16–Aug) 8am–1pm. Closed Christmas Day.

Palm Springs Aerial Tramway ★★ To gain a bird's-eye perspective on the Coachella Valley, take this 14-minute ascent up 2½ miles (4km) to the top of Mount San Jacinto. While the Albert Frey–designed boarding stations retain their 1960s ski-lodge feel, the Swiss funicular cars—installed in 1999—are sleekly modern and rotate during the trip to allow each passenger a panoramic view. There's a whole other world once you arrive: alpine scenery, a ski-lodge-flavored restaurant and gift shop, and temperatures typically 40°F cooler than the desert floor. The most dramatic contrast is during the winter, when the mountaintop is a snowy wonderland, irresistible to hikers and bundled-up kids with saucers. The excursion might not be worth the expense during the rest of the year. Guided mule rides and cross-country ski equipment are available at the top.

Tramway Rd. off Hwy. 111, Palm Springs. © **888/515-TRAM** or 760/325-1391. www.pstramway.com. Tickets $20.80 adults, $18.80 seniors, $13 children ages 3–12, free for kids 2 and under. Ride 'n' Dine combination (available after 2:30pm, dinner served after 4pm) $27.80 adults, $18 children. Mon–Fri 10am–8pm; Sat–Sun 8am–8pm. Free parking. (If you have your AAA card you can get a 10% discount.)

Palm Springs Desert Museum ★ Unlikely though it may sound, this well-endowed museum is a must-see. Exhibits include world-class Western and Native American art collections, the natural history of the desert, and an outstanding anthropology department, primarily representing the local Cahuilla tribe. Traditional Indian life as it was lived for centuries before the white presence is illustrated by tools, baskets, and other relics. Check local schedules to find out about visiting exhibits (which are usually excellent). Plays, lectures, and other events are presented in the museum's Annenberg Theater.

101 Museum Dr. (just west of the Palm Canyon/Tahquitz intersection), Palm Springs. © **760/325-7186.** www.psmuseum.org. Admission $7.50 adults, $6.50 seniors 62 and over, $3.50 military and children ages 6–17, free for children under age 6, free for everyone the 1st Fri of each month. Tues–Sat 10am–5pm; Sun noon–5pm.

Shields Date Gardens *Finds* In a splendid display of fanciful thinking and clever engineering, the Coachella Valley has been developed into a rich agricultural region, known for grapefruit, figs, and grapes—but mostly for dates. The fascination of 1920s entrepreneurs with Arabian lore, fueled by the Sahara-like conditions of the desert around Indio, led to the planting of date palm groves, started with just a few parent trees imported from the Middle East. The groves now produce 95% of the world's date crop. The trees are hand-pollinated by farmers, a process detailed in *The Romance and Sex Life of the Date,* a film running continuously (its racy title is the best part). Also housed in the splendid 1930s modern building is a lunch counter (date shake anyone?), as well as a store selling an endless variety of dates and date-related goodies.

80225 Calif. 111, Indio. © **760/347-0996.** www.shieldsdates.com. Free admission. Daily 8am–6pm.

Windmill Tours ★ Travelers through the San Gorgonio Pass have for years been struck by an awesome and otherworldly sight: never-ending windmill fields that harness the powerful force of the wind gusting through this passage and convert it to electricity to power air conditioners throughout the Coachella Valley. If you get a charge from them, consider splurging on this guided tour offering a look into this alternative energy source. Learn how designers have improved the efficiency of wind turbines (technically they're not windmills, which are used in the production of grain) and measure those long rotors against the average human height (about 10 people could lie along one span). *Bargain-hunter's tip:* Summer visitors save 50% with Windmill Tours twofer deals, from June to September 15.

Interstate 10, Indian Ave. exit, Palm Springs. ℂ **877/449-WIND** or 760/251-1997. www.windmilltours.com. $23 adults, $20 seniors, $15 students, $10 kids under 14. Tours Tues–Thurs 10am and 2pm (can vary seasonally).

SHOPPING

Downtown Palm Springs revolves around **North Palm Canyon Drive;** many art galleries, souvenir shops, and restaurants are located here, along with a couple of large-scale hotels and shopping centers. This wide, one-way boulevard is designed for pedestrians, with many businesses set back from the street itself— don't be shy about poking around the little courtyards you'll encounter. On Thursday nights from 6 to 10pm, the blocks between Amado and Baristo roads are transformed into **VillageFest,** a street-fair tradition. Crafts vendors and aromatic food booths compete for your attention with wacky street performers and even wackier locals shopping at the mouthwateringly fresh produce stalls.

The northern section of Palm Canyon is becoming known for vintage collectibles and is touted as the "Antique and Heritage Gallery District." Check out **John's Resale Furnishings,** 891 N. Palm Canyon Dr. (ℂ 760/416-8876), for a glorious collection of mid-century modern furnishings; **Bandini Johnson Gallery,** 895 N. Palm Canyon Dr. (ℂ 760/323-7805), a cramped warren of eclectic treasures; and the **Antiques Center,** 798 N. Palm Canyon Dr. (ℂ 760/323-4443), a discriminating mall-style store whose 35 dealers display wares ranging from vintage linens to handmade African crafts to prized Bakelite jewelry.

WHERE TO STAY

Palm Springs offers a wide range of accommodations. We particularly like the inns that have opened in the fabulous, newly renovated 40- to 60-year-old cottage complexes in the wind-shielded "Tennis Club" area, west of Palm Canyon Drive. Remember that the rates given below are for high season (winter, generally Oct–May). During the hotter summer months, it's common to find $300 rooms going for $99 or less as part of off-season packages. Even in season, midweek and golf packages are common, so always ask when making your reservation.

VERY EXPENSIVE

La Quinta Resort & Club ✿✿ Located 19 miles southeast of Palm Springs, the sprawling LaQuinta Resort is the kind of place you might have seen on an episode of "Lifestyles of the Rich and Famous," featuring award-winning golf and tennis facilities, a luxurious spa, and gourmet dining. Opened in 1926, it was a popular destination among such Hollywood celebrities as Frank Capra, Greta Garbo, and Clark Gable. These days, the resort tends to attract golf enthusiasts and families, giving it more the air of a private country club than playground of the stars. Looking for nightlife? You may want to stay closer to town.

In contrast to the arid Santa Rosa Mountains that rise up around the property, the resort's grounds are lush green with blooming gardens. Neat pathways wind among pools and Spanish-style casitas, which house the guestrooms. Rooms are spacious, averaging 500 square feet, and feature Southwestern decor. Spacious bathrooms are adorned with rosy Spanish tile and have separate shower and bathtub. All rooms have patios, some more secluded than others. One or two of the oldest casitas have screened-in porches, and second-floor rooms have private terraces for sunning or stargazing. Many units feature fireplaces. Those planning long stays can opt for accommodations with fully-furnished kitchenettes and even washer-dryers.

Golf fans have hit the jackpot at La Quinta, with access to five courses: the resort's own Mountain and Dunes courses, as well as the TPC Stadium Golf, Jack Nicklaus Tournament, and Greg Norman courses at the nearby PGA West facility. The resort and the individual courses are consistently awarded top honors by *GOLF Magazine* among others. *Tennis Magazine* has ranked the La Quinta one of the nation's best tennis resorts. Tennis lovers have 23 courts at their disposal and can choose from hard, clay, or grass surfaces. The fitness center also schedules a variety of exercise classes, and Camp La Qunita offers daily activities for kids enrolled in the camp.

Spa La Qunita opened in 1998, with 35 treatment rooms and a host of relaxing and rejuvenating scrubs, wraps, masks, massages, and private open-air baths and showers. The **Yamaguchi Salon** within the spa handles hair, makeup, manicure, and pedicure appointments with a Feng Shui approach to beauty. Of the five restaurants on the property, the most notable is **Azur by Le Bernardin,** featuring a French seafood menu. Maguy Le Coze and Eric Ripert, co-owners of New York's renowned Le Bernardin, opened the restaurant's latest incarnation at La Quinta in 2001.

49-499 Eisenhower Drive (P.O. Box 69), La Quinta, CA 92253. ✆ **760/564-4111.** Fax 760/564-7656. www.laquintaresort.com. 800 units. Winter $405–$650 double, from $675 and way up for suites; spring and fall $345–$555 double, from $595 and way up for suites; summer $185–$395 double, from $415 and way up for suites. Golf, tennis, spa, and other packages available. AE, DC, DISC, MC, V. Valet parking $15; free self-parking. From the I-10, take the Washington St. exit and turn right onto Washington, then turn right on Eisenhower Drive and follow it 3/4 of a mile; the resort is on the right. **Amenities:** 3 restaurants (French, Mexican, American), spa bistro, clubhouse, cafe; 42 outdoor heated pools; 2 golf courses on site, access to 3 additional courses; 23 tennis courts, 10 lit for night play; fitness center, exercise classes and personal trainers available; full-service spa; 54 outdoor heated whirlpools; bike rental, electric bikes available; children's programs; video arcade; concierge; tour desk; business center; salon; 24-hour room service; massage, in-room appointments available; babysitting. *In room:* A/C, TV w/pay movies, dataport, minibar, coffeemaker, hair dryer, iron, safe, robes.

EXPENSIVE

Hyatt Regency Suites ✦   A perfect blend of location, service, and resort ambience, the Hyatt is a good choice if you plan on spending most of your trip perusing the shops and restaurants on Palm Canyon Drive. The staff is friendly and efficient and each room has a pool, golf course, or mountain view. All units are either one- or two-bedroom suites with TVs and phones in every room along with other amenities such as a wet bar and private balcony. They have superb food in two cafes located on the premises and have a casual lounge that is an ideal spot for an early evening cocktail. Tennis courts and a championship golf course make it enjoyable for sports enthusiasts.

285 North Palm Canyon Drive, Palm Springs, CA 92262. ✆ **800/55-HYATT** or 760/322-9000. http://palm-springs.hyatt.com. 192 units. $125–$300 double; from $425 suite. AE, DC, DISC, MC, V. Free parking. **Amenities:** 2 restaurants; lounge; outdoor heated pool; whirlpool; tennis courts; fitness center with spa; limited room service; valet service. *In room:* A/C, TV, fridge, coffeemaker, hair dryer, iron, safe.

La Mancha Resort Village ✦   The security-gated entry makes La Mancha look like a private community. Once you're inside, a warmly respectful staff will pamper you, just the way they've coddled the countless celebrities who've lent their names to the brochure. What distinguishes La Mancha from other resorts is its quiet elegance and service, not its modern but unoriginal furnishings. Most units are suites with TV/VCRs and phones in every room (they'll even provide

Fun Fact **Gay Life in Palm Springs**

The local chamber of commerce certainly recognizes that the Palm Springs area is currently one of the top three American destinations for gay and lesbian travelers. After just a short time here, you'll see that the gay tourists are courted as aggressively as straights. Real-estate agents cater to gay shoppers for vacation properties, and entire condo communities are marketed toward the gay resident. Advertisements for these and scores of other proudly gay-owned businesses can be found in *The Bottom Line,* the desert's free biweekly magazine of articles, events, and community guides for the gay reader; it's available at hotels, newsstands, and select merchants.

Be sure to visit **Village Pride,** 214 E. Arenas Rd. (© 760/323-9120), a coffeehouse and local gathering place. Besides offering a selection of gay- and lesbian-oriented reading material, Village Pride also serves as the lobby for the **Top Hat Playhouse.** This short block of Arenas is home to a score of other gay establishments, including **Streetbar** (© 760/320-1266), a neighborhood gathering spot for tourists and locals alike.

A few blocks away is a cozy neighborhood of modest homes and small hotels, concentrated on Warm Sands Drive south of Ramon. Known simply as **Warm Sands,** this area holds the nicest "private resorts"—mostly discreet and gated B&B-style inns. Locals recommend the coed **El Mirasol,** 525 Warm Sands Dr. (© 800/327-2985 or 760/326-5913), a historic resort; or **Sago Palms,** 595 Thornhill Rd. (© 800/626-7246 or 760/323-0224), which is small, quiet, and affordable. **The Bee Charmer,** 1600 E. Palm Canyon Dr. (© 888/321-5699; www.beecharmer.com), is one of the few all-women resorts in town.

Gay nightlife is everywhere in the Valley, and especially raucous on holiday weekends. Pick up *The Bottom Line* for the latest restaurant, nightclub, theater, and special-events listings.

Nintendo for the kids). Many guests opt for the villas, which have private pools, fireplaces, and wet bars. Fruit baskets welcome arrivals. A private fleet of rental cars stand ready should you want to venture the half mile into town, or you can simply relax the days away—how about a massage on your personal patio?

444 Avenida Caballeros, Palm Springs, CA 92262. © 888/PRIVACY or 760/323-1773. www.la-mancha.com. 66 units. $159–$245 double; from $295 villa. AE, DC, DISC, MC, V. Free parking. Dogs allowed with $200 fee. **Amenities:** Restaurant; lounge; outdoor heated pool; whirlpool; 5 outdoor tennis courts (lit for night play); fitness center with spa; in-room massage; complimentary bicycles; room service (7am–11pm). *In room:* A/C, TV/VCR, fridge, coffeemaker, hair dryer, iron, safe.

The Orbit In ✦✦ This much-hyped renovation of a classic 1950s motel gets our vote as grooviest digs in town, exceeding everyone's expectations with a mix of streamlined mid-century style, cocktails-by-the-pool Rat Pack aesthetic, and almost scholarly appreciation of the architects and designers responsible for Palm Springs's reign as a mecca of vintage modernism. Connoisseurs of interior design will find a museum's worth of furnishings, each of which adheres to its theme (Martini Room, Bertoia's Den, Atomic Paradise, and so on) down to customized lounge-music CDs for your in-room listening pleasure. The rest of us just enjoy tripping down memory lane with amoeba-shaped coffee tables, glowing rocket ship lamps, Eames recliners, kitschy Melmac dishware, and strappy vintage chaises on each room's private patio. Contemporary comforts are impeccably provided, from cushy double-pillow-top mattresses to poolside misting machines that create an oasis of cool even during midsummer scorchers. Kitchenettes all boast charming restored fixtures, as do the candy-pink-tiled original bathrooms, which have only stall showers, but make up for the lack of tubs by being surprisingly spacious—and naturally sunlit. Guests gather at the poolside "boomerang" bar, or in the Albert Frey lounge (homage to the late, great architect whose unique home sits midway up the mountain backdrop); a central "movies, books, and games" closet encourages camaraderie amid this chic atmosphere.

562 W. Arenas Rd., Palm Springs, CA 92262. ✆ 877/99-ORBIT or 760/323-3585. Fax 760/323-3599. www.orbitin.com. 10 units. $189–$249 double. Midweek and off-season discounts as low as $149. Rates include deluxe continental breakfast and evening hors d'oeuvres. AE, DISC, MC, V. Free parking. **Amenities:** Outdoor heated pool with adjacent honor bar; whirlpool with adjacent fire pit; complimentary cruiser bicycles. *In room:* A/C, TV/VCR, dataport, Internet access, CD player, fridge, coffeemaker, hair dryer, iron, safe, bathrobes.

Spa Hotel & Casino ✪ This is one of the more unusual choices in town. It's located on the Indian-owned land containing the original mineral springs for which Palm Springs was named. The Cahuilla claimed that the springs had curative powers. Today's travelers still come to pamper body and soul by "taking the waters," though now the facility is sleekly modern. There are three pools: One is a conventional outdoor swimming pool; the other two are filled from the underground natural springs brimming with revitalizing minerals. Inside the hotel's extensive spa are private sunken marble pools fed by the springs. After your bath, you can avail yourself of the many other pampering treatments offered. The adjoining Vegas-style casino features the familiar hush of gaming tables and clanging of video poker and slot machines. Despite that contemporary addition, the Cahuilla have managed to integrate modern hotel comforts with the ancient healing and Indian spirit this land represents.

100 N. Indian Canyon Dr., Palm Springs, CA 92263. ✆ 800/854-1279 or 760/325-1461. Fax 760/325-3344. www.spahotelandcasino.com. 230 units. $159–$239 double; $219–$279 suite. AE, DC, MC, V. Free parking. **Amenities:** 2 restaurants; 2 bars; 3 outdoor heated pools; full-service spa; fitness center; concierge; car-rental desk; 24-hour room service. *In room:* A/C, TV, minibar, hair dryer, iron, bathrobes.

MODERATE

Ballantine's Movie Colony ✪✪ Take one classic 1930s hotel designed by prolific and renowned area architect Albert Frey, add a warehouse's worth of barely used mid-century furnishings and repro classics (cleverly grouped to create minitheme rooms), sprinkle generously with stylish vacationers and flavor-of-the-month celebs, and you've got Palm Springs's grooviest digs. Situated off the town's main drag in a neighborhood once favored by golden-age celebrities (hence the name), Ballantine's offers a quietly hip, highly personalized experience in a setting marked by scrupulous detail and tantalizing colors: the swimming pool is edged in brilliant lime, the "Sinatra" room is boldly orange (Frank's favorite color), and the made-to-look-old dial phones are jelly-bean bright.

The same owners have a similarly outfitted property a few blocks away. **Ballantine's Original** (1420 N. Indian Canyon Dr., Palm Springs; ✆ 760/320-2449) has fewer rooms and a more discreet facade (Is there a hotel here?), while still boasting the same fabulous amenities. There's a pool with fire pit and outdoor bar, meticulous mid-century furnishings, personal service, and the usual luxury perks.

726 N. Indian Canyon Dr., Palm Springs. © **800/780-3464** or 760/320-1178. Fax 760/320-5308. www. ballantinehotels.com. 18 units. High season $139–$260 double. Rates include continental breakfast and evening cocktail. Midweek and summer discounts available (as low as $79). AE, MC, V. Free parking. **Amenities:** Outdoor heated pool; whirlpool. *In room:* A/C, TV, fridge, hair dryer, iron, bathrobes.

Estrella Inn ⚐ Once the choice of Hollywood celebrities, this outstanding historic hotel is quiet and secluded, yet wonderfully close to the action. It's composed of three distinct properties from three different eras, all united by a peachy desert color scheme and uniformly lavish landscaping. Guest rooms vary widely according to location, but all include pampering touches—some have fireplaces and/or full kitchens, others have wet bars or private balconies. The real deals are the studio bungalows, even though they have tiny 1930s bathrooms. The Estrella has an outdoor barbecue, plus a lawn with games equipment. Ask about attractive golf packages that include play at one of several nearby courses.

415 S. Belardo Rd. (south of Tahquitz Way), Palm Springs, CA 92262. © **800/237-3687** or 760/320-4117. Fax 760/323-3303. www.estrella.com. 63 units. $150 double; $225–$275 1- or 2-bedroom suite; $250–$350 1- or 2-bedroom bungalow. Rates include continental breakfast. Monthly rates available. AE, DC, MC, V. Free parking. Pets allowed in tile-floored units for $20 fee. **Amenities:** 3 outdoor heated pools (including 1 children's pool); 2 whirlpools; coin-op laundry. *In room:* A/C, TV, fridge, coffeemaker, microwave, hair dryer.

Korakia Pensione ⚐⚐ If you can work within the Korakia's rigid deposit-cancellation policy (see below), you're in for a special stay at this Greek/Moroccan oasis just a few blocks from Palm Canyon Drive. This former artist's villa from the 1920s draws a hip international crowd of artists, writers, and musicians. The simply furnished rooms and unbelievably spacious suites are peaceful and private, surrounded by flagstone courtyards and flowering gardens. Rooms are divided between the main house, a second restored villa across the street, and surrounding guest bungalows. Most have kitchens; many have fireplaces. All beds are blessed with thick feather duvets, and the windows are shaded by flowing white canvas draperies in the Mediterranean style. You also get a sumptuous breakfast served in your room or poolside. *Korakia* is Greek for "crow," and a tile mosaic example graces the pool bottom.

Note: You must pay a deposit when booking a room, and you have to give at least 2 weeks advance cancellation notice or you lose your deposit. For holidays it's 45 days advance notice or lose deposit.

257 S. Patencio Rd., Palm Springs, CA 92262. © **760/864-6411.** Fax 760/864-4147. www.korakia.com. 22 units. $119–$279 double. Rates include breakfast. MC, V. Free parking. **Amenities:** 2 outdoor heated pools; In-room massage. *In room:* A/C, fridge, coffeemaker, safe.

Villa Royale ⚐ This charming inn, 5 minutes from the hustle and bustle of downtown Palm Springs, evokes a European villa, complete with climbing bougainvillea and rooms filled with antiques and artwork. The main building was once home to Olympic and silver screen ice skater Sonja Henie. Villa Royale's reputation had been suffering due to indifferent management, but new ownership has brought renovation and a renewed dedication to service. Uniform luxuries (down comforters and other pampering touches) appear throughout. Rooms vary widely in size and ambience; large isn't always better, as some of the inn's most appealing rooms are in the smaller, more affordable range. Many rooms have fireplaces, private patios with whirlpools, full kitchens, and a variety of other amenities. A continental breakfast is served in an intimate garden setting surrounding the main pool. The hotel's romantic restaurant, **Europa,** is a sleeper, offering some of Palm Springs's very best meals (see "Where to Dine," below).

1620 Indian Trail (off East Palm Canyon), Palm Springs, CA 92264. © 800/245-2314 or 760/327-2314. Fax 760/322-3794. www.villaroyale.com. 31 units. High season (Oct–May) $125–$175 double; $230–$275 suite. Summer $87–$125 double; $165–$195 suite. Rates include full breakfast. Extra person $25. AE, DC, DISC, MC, V. Free parking. Small pets accepted with $50 deposit. **Amenities:** Restaurant; outdoor heated pool; whirlpool; concierge; in-room massage. *In room:* A/C, TV, hair dryer, iron, bathrobes.

INEXPENSIVE

Casa Cody ★ Once owned by "Wild" Bill Cody's niece, this 1920s *casa* with a double courtyard (each with swimming pool) has been restored to fine condition. It now sports a vaguely Southwestern decor and peaceful grounds marked by large lawns and mature, blossoming fruit trees. You'll feel more like a house guest than a hotel client at the Casa Cody. It's located in the primarily residential "Tennis Club" area of town, a couple of easy blocks from Palm Canyon Drive. Many units here have fireplaces and full-size kitchens. Breakfast is served poolside, as are complimentary wine and cheese on Saturday afternoons.

175 S. Cahuilla Rd. (between Tahquitz Way and Arenas Rd.), Palm Springs, CA 92262. © 760/320-9346. Fax 760/325-8610. www.palmsprings.com/hotels/casacody. 23 units. $79–$99 double; $99–$159 studio; $149–$259 suite; $299–$359 2-bedroom adobe. Rates include expanded continental breakfast. AE, DC, DISC, MC, V. Pets accepted for $10 fee per night. **Amenities:** 2 outdoor heated pools; whirlpool; in-room massage. *In room:* A/C, TV, fridge.

Holiday Inn Palm Mountain Resort *Kids* Within easy walking distance of Palm Springs's main drag, this Holiday Inn (like most in the chain) welcomes kids under 18 free in their parents' room, making it a terrific choice for families. The rooms are in the two- or the three-story wing, and many have a patio or balcony, with a view of the mountains or the large Astroturf courtyard. Midweek and summer rates can be as low as $59.

155 S. Belardo Rd., Palm Springs, CA 92262. © 800/622-9451 or 760/325-1301. Fax 760/323-8937. www.palmmountainresort.com. 122 units. High season $89–$169 double. Children under 18 stay free in parents' room. For the best rates, book online or ask for "Great Rates." AE, DC, DISC, MC, V. Free parking. **Amenities:** Restaurant; lounge; poolside bar; heated outdoor pool. *In room:* A/C, TV, fridge, coffeemaker, microwave.

Orchid Tree Inn Billed as a "1930s desert garden retreat," the Orchid Tree is a sprawling complex of buildings dating from the 1920s to 1950s, located a block from Palm Canyon Drive in the historic "Tennis Club" district. Dedicated family ownership ensures that the place is impeccably maintained. The inn truly feels like a retreat. The grounds are rich with flowering shrubs, citrus trees, and multitudes of hummingbirds, sparrows, and quail drawn by bird feeders and birdbaths. The rooms are nicer than you'd expect at this price, in keeping with the overall grace and excellence of the neighborhood. Room types range from simple, hotel-style doubles to charming bungalows to pool-front studios with sliding-glass doors.

261 S. Belardo Rd. (at Baristo Rd.), Palm Springs, CA 92262. © 800/733-3435 or 760/325-2791. Fax 760/325-3855. www.orchidtree.com. 40 units. Nov–May $110–$185 double; $150–$395 suite. Summer $65–$125 double; $105–$285 suite. Extra person $15. Rates include expanded continental breakfast (Nov–May only). AE, DC, DISC, MC, V. **Amenities:** 3 swimming pools; 2 whirlpools. *In room:* A/C, TV, hair dryer.

WHERE TO DINE
EXPENSIVE

Europa Restaurant ★★ CALIFORNIA/CONTINENTAL Located in the Villa Royale and long advertised as the "most romantic dining in the desert," Europa is a sentimental favorite of many regulars among an equally gay and straight clientele. This European-style hideaway exudes charm and ambience.

Whether you sit under the stars on the garden patio, or in subdued candlelight indoors, you'll savor dinner prepared by one of Palm Springs's most dedicated kitchens and served by a discreetly attentive staff. Standout dishes include deviled crab fritters on mango-papaya chutney, filet mignon on a bed of crispy onions with garlic butter, and a show-stopping salmon baked in parchment with crème fraîche and dill. For dessert, don't miss the chocolate mousse—smooth and addictive.

1620 Indian Trail (at the Villa Royale). © 760/327-2314. Reservations recommended. Main courses $18–$32. AE, DC, DISC, MC, V. Tues–Sat 5:30–10pm; Sun 11:30am–2pm and 5:30–10pm (also open Tues–Sat noon–2:30pm Oct–May only).

Le Vallauris ✦ FRENCH   Named after the small village in the south of France where Picasso made his ceramics, Le Vallauris is the creation of owner/chef Paul Bruggemans, who specializes in elegant cuisine from that same region. Housed within a unique historical abode with several individual dining rooms, it's currently one of the most popular restaurants in Palm Spring. Recommended dishes include the main lobster ravioli, the grilled jumbo tiger prawns with jasmine rice with Anaheim chili and coconut sauce, and the mallard duck "Two Ways" with orange and chili chutney. Request a table at the outdoor patio/garden where at night the trees are lit with twinkling white lights.

385 W. Tahquitz Canyon. © 760/325-5059. Reservations required. Main courses $18–$29. AE, DC, DISC, MC, V. Daily 11:30am–2:30pm and 6–11pm.

Palm Springs Chop House ✦✦ CALIFORNIA/TRADITIONAL   Owned by local father and son restaurateurs Kaiser and Lee Morkus, this modern update of the classic steak and chophouse combines mouthwatering food and great service with an impressive wine list from a 3,000-bottle wine cellar. An elegant dining room offers views of passerby's on Palm canyon or spacious booths with elegance and privacy. The decor is warm yet modern with unique lighting and a wonderfully intricate Sumerian relief adorning the back wall. Upstairs at **The Deck,** the more casual diner can enjoy appetizers and cocktails around the fire pit while listening to a swinging jazz band. The menu offers choice cuts of beef like their signature porterhouse and the filet mignon that literally melts in your mouth. Colorado lamb chops and fresh fish are available for non-beef eaters in the crowd. The sauces are cooked on the premises and add rich flavor to the quality cuts of meat. If you have room for desert the crème brûlée is outstanding.

262 S. Palm Canyon Dr. © 760/320-4500. Reservations recommended. Main courses $18–$49. AE, DC, DISC, MC, and V. Daily 4:30–11pm (upstairs opens at 11:30am).

Palmie ✦ CLASSIC FRENCH   You can't see Palmie from the street, and once you're seated inside its softly lit, lattice-enclosed dining patio, you won't see the bustle outside anymore, either. Martine and Alain Clerc's cozy bistro is filled with Art Deco posters of French seaside resorts. Chef Alain sends out masterful traditional French dishes such as bubbling cheese soufflé, green lentil salad dotted with pancetta, steak *au poivre* rich with cognac sauce, and lobster raviolis garnished with caviar; in fact, every carefully garnished plate is a work of art. To the charming background strains of French chanteuses, hostess/manager Martine circulates between tables, determined that visitors should enjoy their meals as much as do the loyal regulars she greets by name. Forget your cholesterol for one night and don't leave without sampling dessert. Our favorite is the trio of petite crème brûlées, flavored with ginger, vanilla, and Kahlúa.

276 N. Palm Canyon Dr. (across from the Hyatt). © 760/320-3375. Reservations recommended. Main courses $12–$26. AE, DC, MC, V. Mon–Sat 5:30–9:30pm.

St. James at the Vineyard ☆ INTERNATIONAL   This one-of-a-kind restaurant is located in the center of town and redefines the term *world cuisine.* Very popular and the bar on a Friday night is without a doubt one of *the* places to be in Palm Springs. This marvelously exotic venue dabbles in a bit of Thai here to a bit of "down under" there, while courses such as the rack of lamb encrusted with macadamia nuts and their special selection of fresh fish make it a one-of-a-kind dining experience. Savor the New Zealand Mussels steaming in a coriander and coconut broth. Or try the Bouillabaisse Burmese filled with lobster, clams, mussels, tuna, scallops, and shrimp in a wonderfully fragrant concoction of pineapple juice, coconut milk, lime juice, ginger, lemon grass, and cardamom. If you still have room, their scrumptious dessert selections include: chocolate crème brûlée with caramelized banana; flourless chocolate cake; poached pears; tiramisu; and assorted ice creams and sorbets.

265 South Palm Canyon Dr. ℂ 760/320-8041. St. James toll-free line: 866/365-6500; Reservations recommended. Main courses $18–$49. AE, DC, DISC, MC, and V. Daily 5:30–10pm. The bar is open until 1:30am Fri–Sat.

MODERATE

Blue Coyote Grille ☆ SOUTHWESTERN   This popular cantina features a series of roomy outdoor patios with red-tile floors and bright blue iron railings overlooking Mexican patios with flowing fountains. The kitchen puts a unique spin on the traditional Mexican fair, offering unique dishes such as *pollo cilantro* and Yucatán lamb. Best of all, the bar features muy strong yet flavorful margaritas.

445 N. Palm Canyon ℂ760/327-1196. Reservations recommended. Main courses $7–$12. AE, DC, DISC, MC, V. Mon–Sun 11am–10pm; dinner menu starts at 4pm.

La Provence ☆☆ COUNTRY FRENCH   The casually elegant La Provence is a favorite of locals and often gets recommended by knowledgeable innkeepers. This restaurant eschews heavy traditional French cream sauces in favor of carefully combined herbs and spices. The second-story terrace filled with tables sets a romantic mood on balmy desert evenings. The menu offers some expected items (escargots in mushroom caps, bouillabaisse, steak *au poivre*) as well as inventive pastas, like wild mushroom ravioli in a sun-dried tomato and sweet onion sauce.

254 N. Palm Canyon Dr. (upstairs). ℂ 760/416-4418. Reservations recommended. Main courses $14–$29. AE, DC, DISC, MC, V. Tues–Sun 5–10:30pm.

Las Casuelas Terraza CLASSIC MEXICAN   The original Las Casuelas, a tiny storefront several blocks away, is still open, but the bougainvillea-draped front patio here is a much better place to people-watch. You can order Mexican standards like quesadillas, enchiladas, and mountainous nachos, as well as supersize margaritas. Inside, the action heats up with live music and raucous happy-hour crowds. During hot weather, the patio and even sidewalk passersby are cooled by the restaurant's well-placed misters, making this a perfect late-afternoon or early evening choice.

222 S. Palm Canyon Dr. ℂ 760/325-2794. Reservations recommended on weekends. Main courses $7–$13. AE, DC, DISC, MC, V. Mon–Thurs 11am–10pm; Fri–Sat 11am–11pm; Sun 10am–10pm.

Pomme Frite ☆ BELGIAN/FRENCH   Set up like a traditional French bistro, this small (only 10 tables) yet charming restaurant serves good French cuisine without the European pomp. The mussels in garlic cream are as good as you get in Paris, and the California bouillabaisse is magnificent. Great wines by the glass as well. Try to get there early and sit in the small sidewalk patio.

256 S. Palm Canyon Dr. ✆ **760/778-3727.** Reservations recommended. Main courses $7–$18. AE, DC, DISC, MC, V. Mon–Fri 5:30pm–11pm; Sat–Sun 11:30am–2:30pm.

INEXPENSIVE

Edgardo's Café Veracruz ★ *Value* MEXICAN The pleasant but humble ambience at Edgardo's is a welcome change from touristy Palm Springs. The menu features authentic Mayan, Huasteco, and Aztec cuisine. The dark interior boasts an array of colorful masks and artwork from Central and South America, but the postage stamp–sized front patio with a trickling fountain is the best place to sample Edgardo's tangy quesadillas, desert cactus salad, and traditional poblano chilis rellenos—and perhaps even a oyster/tequila shooter from the oyster bar.

494 N. Palm Canyon (at W. Alejo Rd.). ✆ **760/320-3558.** Reservations recommended for weekend dinner. Main courses $3.50–$15. DISC, MC, V. Mon–Fri 11am–3pm and 5:30–9:30pm; Sat–Sun 8am–10pm (sometimes later). Free parking.

Mykonos GREEK Locals have been enjoying authentic Greek specialties at this family run spot for 10 years. Mykonos is supercasual, offering simple, candlelit tables (with vinyl tablecloths and the like) in an off-street brick courtyard, but it's a pleasant treat. Traditional lamb shanks over rice, dolmades (stuffed grape leaves), salad tangy with crumbled feta cheese, and sweet, sticky baklava are among the best items.

139 Andreas (just off Palm Canyon). ✆ **760/322-0223.** Most items under $10. MC, V. Wed–Mon 11am–10pm.

PALM SPRINGS AFTER DARK

Every month a different club or disco is the hot spot in the Springs, and the best way to tap into the trend is by consulting *The Desert Guide, The Bottom Line* (see the box "Gay Life in Palm Springs," above), or one of the many other free newsletters available from area hotels and merchants. **VillageFest** (see "Shopping," earlier in this chapter) turns Palm Canyon Drive into an outdoor party each Thursday night.

The **Fabulous Palm Springs Follies,** at the Plaza Theatre, 128 S. Palm Canyon Dr., Palm Springs (✆ **760/327-0225;** www.psfollies.com), a vaudeville-style show filled with lively production numbers, is celebrating its 11th year in the historic Plaza Theatre in the heart of town. With a cast of energetic retired showgirls, singers, dancers, and comedians, the revue has been enormously popular around town. Call for show schedule. Tickets range from $35 to $65.

Costa's, located at the Desert Springs Marriott, 74855 Country Club Drive, Palm Desert (✆ **760/341-**2211), is a dance club/bar where young singles go to get their groove on and meet and greet. Open daily from 8pm to 2am, there's a $10 cover on Friday and Saturdays.

Appendix:
Useful Toll-Free Numbers
& Websites

MAJOR HOTEL & MOTEL CHAINS

Best Western
✆ 800/528-1234
www.bestwestern.com

Clarion Hotels
✆ 800/CLARION
www.hotelchoice.com

Comfort Inns
✆ 800/228-5150
www.hotelchoice.com

Courtyard by Marriott
✆ 800/321-2211
www.courtyard.com

Days Inn
✆ 800/325-2525
www.daysinn.com

Doubletree Hotels
✆ 800/222-TREE
www.doubletreehotels.com

Econo Lodges
✆ 800/55-ECONO
www.hotelchoice.com

Embassy Suites
✆ 800/EMBASSY
www.embassy-suites.com

Fairfield Inns by Marriott
✆ 800/228-2800
www.fairfieldinn.com

Hampton Inns
✆ 800/HAMPTON
www.hampton-inn.com

Hilton Hotels
✆ 800/774-1500
www.hilton.com

Holiday Inn
✆ 800/HOLIDAY
www.basshotels.com/holiday-inn

Howard Johnson
✆ 800/I-GO-HOJO
www.hojo.com

Hyatt Hotels & Resorts
✆ 888/591-1234
www.hyatt.com

La Quinta Motor Inns
✆ 800/531-5900
www.laquinta.com

Marriott Hotels
✆ 888/236-2427
www.marriott.com

Motel 6
✆ 800/4-MOTEL6
www.motel6.com

Omni Hotels
✆ 800/THE-OMNI
www.omnihotels.com

Quality Inns
✆ 800/228-5151
www.hotelchoice.com

Radisson Hotels
✆ 800/333-3333
www.radisson.com

Ramada Inns
✆ 888/298-2054
www.ramada.com

Red Roof Inns
✆ 800/RED-ROOF
www.redroof.com

Renaissance Hotels and Resorts
✆ 800/HOTELS-1
www.renaissancehotels.com

Residence Inn by Marriott
✆ 800/331-3131
www.residenceinn.com

Rodeway Inns
✆ 800/228-2000
www.hotelchoice.com

Sheraton
✆ 888/625-5144
www.sheraton.com

Super 8 Motels
✆ 800/800-8000
www.super8motels.com

Travelodge
✆ 888/515-6375
www.travelodge.com

Vagabond Inns
✆ 800/522-1555
www.vagabondinns.com

Wyndham Hotels & Resorts
✆ 800/822-4200
www.wyndham.com

CAR-RENTAL AGENCIES

Advantage
✆ 800/777-5500
www.arac.com

Alamo
✆ 800/GO-ALAMO
www.goalamo.com

Avis
✆ 800/230-4898
www.avis.com

Budget
✆ 800/527-0700
www.budgetrentacar.com

Dollar
✆ 800/800-3665
www.dollarcar.com

Enterprise
✆ 800/325-8007
www.enterprise.com

Hertz
✆ 800/654-3131
www.hertz.com

National Car Rental
✆ 800/CAR-RENT
www.nationalcar.com

Payless
✆ 800/PAYLESS
www.paylesscar.com

Rent-A-Wreck
✆ 800/944-7501
www.rent-a-wreck.com

Thrifty
✆ 800/THRIFTY
www.thrifty.com

AIRLINES

Aer Lingus
✆ 800/IRISH-AIR
✆ 01-886-8888 in Dublin
www.aerlingus.ie

Aeromexico
✆ 800/237-6639
www.aeromexico.com

Air Canada
✆ 888/247-2262 in Canada
   & the U.S.
www.aircanada.ca

Air New Zealand
✆ 800/262-1234
✆ 0800/737-000 in New Zealand
www.airnewzealand.com

Alaska Airlines
✆ 800/252-7522
www.alaskaair.com

America West
✆ 800/235-9292
www.americawest.com

American Airlines/American Eagle
✆ 800/433-7300
www.aa.com

American Trans Air (ATA)
✆ 800/I-FLY-ATA
www.ata.com

British Airways
✆ 800/AIRWAYS
✆ 0845/77-333-77 in Britain
www.british-airways.com

Continental Airlines
✆ 800/525-0280
www.continental.com

Delta Air Lines
✆ 800/221-1212
www.delta.com

Frontier Airlines
✆ 800/4321-FLY
www.frontierairlines.com

Hawaiian Airlines
✆ 800/367-5320 in the
   Continental U.S. & Canada
✆ 800/882-8811 in Hawaii
www.hawaiianair.com

Japan Airlines
✆ 800/JAL-FONE
✆ 0120/25-5971 in Japan
www.japanair.com (in the U.S.
   and Canada)
www.jal.co.jp (in Japan)

JetBlue Airlines
✆ 800/JET-BLUE
www.jetblue.com

Midwest Express
✆ 800/452-2022
www.midwestexpress.com

Northwest Airlines/Northwest Airlink
✆ 800/225-2525
www.nwa.com

Qantas
✆ 800/227-4500
✆ 13-13-13 in Australia
www.qantas.com.au

Skywest Airlines
✆ 800/453-9417
www.skywest.com

Southwest Airlines
✆ 800/435-9792
www.southwest.com

United Airlines/United Express
✆ 800/241-6522
www.united.com

US Airways/US Airways Express
✆ 800/428-4322
www.usair.com

Virgin Atlantic Airways
✆ 800/862-8621
✆ 01293/747-747 (in Britain)
www.fly.virgin.com

Index

See also Accommodations and Restaurant indexes, below.

ACCOMMODATIONS

TRAVEL LIKE AN EXPERT
WITH THE
UNOFFICIAL GUIDES

For Travelers Who Want More Than the Official Line!

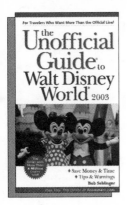

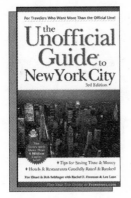

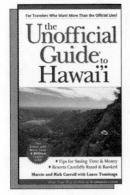

The Unofficial Guides®

Beyond Disney
Branson, Missouri
California with Kids
Chicago
Central Italy
Cruises
Disneyland®
Florida with Kids
Golf Vacations in the
  Eastern U.S.
The Great Smoky &
  Blue Ridge Region
Inside Disney
Hawaii
Las Vegas
London
Mid-Atlantic with Kids
Mini Las Vegas
Mini-Mickey
New England & New York
  with Kids
New Orleans
New York City

Paris
San Francisco
Skiing in the West
Southeast with Kids
Walt Disney World®
Walt Disney World®
  for Grown-Ups
Walt Disney World®
  with Kids
Washington, D.C.
World's Best Diving
  Vacations

Bed & Breakfasts and
Country Inns in:
  California
  Great Lakes States
  Mid-Atlantic
  New England
  Northwest
  Rockies
  Southeast
  Southwest

The Best RV & Tent
Campgrounds in:
  California & the West
  Florida & the
    Southeast
  Great Lakes States
  Mid-Atlantic States
  Northeast
  Northwest &
    Central Plains
  Southwest & South
    Central Plains
  U.S.A.

Frommer's Portable Guides
Complete Guides for the Short-Term Traveler

HIT THE ROAD WITH FROMMER'S DRIVING TOURS!

Frommer's Britain's Best-Loved Driving Tours
Frommer's California's Best-Loved Driving Tours
Frommer's Florida's Best-Loved Driving Tours
Frommer's France's Best-Loved Driving Tours
Frommer's Germany's Best-Loved Driving Tours
Frommer's Ireland's Best-Loved Driving Tours
Frommer's Italy's Best-Loved Driving Tours
Frommer's New England's Best-Loved Driving Tours
Frommer's Northern Italy's Best-Loved Driving Tours
Frommer's Scotland's Best-Loved Driving Tours
Frommer's Spain's Best-Loved Driving Tours
Frommer's Tuscany & Umbria's Best-Loved Driving Tours

Available at bookstores everywhere.

FROMMER'S® COMPLETE TRAVEL GUIDES

Alaska
Alaska Cruises & Ports of Call
Amsterdam
Argentina & Chile
Arizona
Atlanta
Australia
Austria
Bahamas
Barcelona, Madrid & Seville
Beijing
Belgium, Holland & Luxembourg
Bermuda
Boston
Brazil
British Columbia & the Canadian
  Rockies
Budapest & the Best of Hungary
California
Canada
Cancún, Cozumel & the Yucatán
Cape Cod, Nantucket & Martha's
  Vineyard
Caribbean
Caribbean Cruises & Ports of Call
Caribbean Ports of Call
Carolinas & Georgia
Chicago
China
Colorado
Costa Rica
Denmark
Denver, Boulder & Colorado
  Springs
England
Europe
European Cruises & Ports of Call
Florida

France
Germany
Great Britain
Greece
Greek Islands
Hawaii
Hong Kong
Honolulu, Waikiki & Oahu
Ireland
Israel
Italy
Jamaica
Japan
Las Vegas
London
Los Angeles
Maryland & Delaware
Maui
Mexico
Montana & Wyoming
Montréal & Québec City
Munich & the Bavarian Alps
Nashville & Memphis
Nepal
New England
New Mexico
New Orleans
New York City
New Zealand
Northern Italy
Nova Scotia, New Brunswick &
  Prince Edward Island
Oregon
Paris
Philadelphia & the Amish Country
Portugal
Prague & the Best of the Czech
  Republic

Provence & the Riviera
Puerto Rico
Rome
San Antonio & Austin
San Diego
San Francisco
Santa Fe, Taos & Albuquerque
Scandinavia
Scotland
Seattle & Portland
Shanghai
Singapore & Malaysia
South Africa
South America
South Florida
South Pacific
Southeast Asia
Spain
Sweden
Switzerland
Texas
Thailand
Tokyo
Toronto
Tuscany & Umbria
USA
Utah
Vancouver & Victoria
Vermont, New Hampshire &
  Maine
Vienna & the Danube Valley
Virgin Islands
Virginia
Walt Disney World® & Orlando
Washington, D.C.
Washington State

FROMMER'S® DOLLAR-A-DAY GUIDES

Australia from $50 a Day
California from $70 a Day
Caribbean from $70 a Day
England from $75 a Day
Europe from $70 a Day

Florida from $70 a Day
Hawaii from $80 a Day
Ireland from $60 a Day
Italy from $70 a Day
London from $85 a Day

New York from $90 a Day
Paris from $80 a Day
San Francisco from $70 a Day
Washington, D.C. from $80 a Day

FROMMER'S® PORTABLE GUIDES

Acapulco, Ixtapa & Zihuatanejo
Amsterdam
Aruba
Australia's Great Barrier Reef
Bahamas
Berlin
Big Island of Hawaii
Boston
California Wine Country
Cancún
Charleston & Savannah
Chicago
Disneyland®
Dublin
Florence

Frankfurt
Hong Kong
Houston
Las Vegas
London
Los Angeles
Los Cabos & Baja
Maine Coast
Maui
Miami
New Orleans
New York City
Paris
Phoenix & Scottsdale

Portland
Puerto Rico
Puerto Vallarta, Manzanillo &
  Guadalajara
Rio de Janeiro
San Diego
San Francisco
Seattle
Sydney
Tampa & St. Petersburg
Vancouver
Venice
Virgin Islands
Washington, D.C.

FROMMER'S® NATIONAL PARK GUIDES

Banff & Jasper
Family Vacations in the National
  Parks
Grand Canyon

National Parks of the American
  West
Rocky Mountain

Yellowstone & Grand Teton
Yosemite & Sequoia/ Kings Canyon
Zion & Bryce Canyon

FROMMER'S® MEMORABLE WALKS

Chicago	New York	San Francisco
London	Paris	Washington, D.C.

FROMMER'S® GREAT OUTDOOR GUIDES

Arizona & New Mexico	Northern California	Vermont & New Hampshire
New England	Southern New England	

SUZY GERSHMAN'S BORN TO SHOP GUIDES

Born to Shop: France	Born to Shop: Italy	Born to Shop: New York
Born to Shop: Hong Kong, Shanghai & Beijing	Born to Shop: London	Born to Shop: Paris

FROMMER'S® IRREVERENT GUIDES

Amsterdam	Los Angeles	San Francisco
Boston	Manhattan	Seattle & Portland
Chicago	New Orleans	Vancouver
Las Vegas	Paris	Walt Disney World®
London	Rome	Washington, D.C.

FROMMER'S® BEST-LOVED DRIVING TOURS

Britain	Germany	Northern Italy
California	Ireland	Scotland
Florida	Italy	Spain
France	New England	Tuscany & Umbria

HANGING OUT™ GUIDES

Hanging Out in England	Hanging Out in France	Hanging Out in Italy
Hanging Out in Europe	Hanging Out in Ireland	Hanging Out in Spain

THE UNOFFICIAL GUIDES®

Bed & Breakfasts and Country Inns in:
California
Great Lakes States
Mid-Atlantic
New England
Northwest
Rockies
Southeast
Southwest
Best RV & Tent Campgrounds in:
California & the West
Florida & the Southeast
Great Lakes States
Mid-Atlantic
Northeast
Northwest & Central Plains

Southwest & South Central Plains
U.S.A.
Beyond Disney
Branson, Missouri
California with Kids
Chicago
Cruises
Disneyland®
Florida with Kids
Golf Vacations in the Eastern U.S.
Great Smoky & Blue Ridge Region
Inside Disney
Hawaii
Las Vegas
London

Mid-Atlantic with Kids
Mini Las Vegas
Mini-Mickey
New England and New York with Kids
New Orleans
New York City
Paris
San Francisco
Skiing in the West
Southeast with Kids
Walt Disney World®
Walt Disney World® for Grown-ups
Walt Disney World® with Kids
Washington, D.C.
World's Best Diving Vacations

SPECIAL-INTEREST TITLES

Frommer's Adventure Guide to Australia & New Zealand
Frommer's Adventure Guide to Central America
Frommer's Adventure Guide to India & Pakistan
Frommer's Adventure Guide to South America
Frommer's Adventure Guide to Southeast Asia
Frommer's Adventure Guide to Southern Africa
Frommer's Britain's Best Bed & Breakfasts and Country Inns
Frommer's Caribbean Hideaways
Frommer's Exploring America by RV
Frommer's Fly Safe, Fly Smart
Frommer's France's Best Bed & Breakfasts and Country Inns
Frommer's Gay & Lesbian Europe

Frommer's Italy's Best Bed & Breakfasts and Country Inns
Frommer's New York City with Kids
Frommer's Ottawa with Kids
Frommer's Road Atlas Britain
Frommer's Road Atlas Europe
Frommer's Road Atlas France
Frommer's Toronto with Kids
Frommer's Vancouver with Kids
Frommer's Washington, D.C., with Kids
Israel Past & Present
The New York Times' Guide to Unforgettable Weekends
Places Rated Almanac
Retirement Places Rated

America Online Keyword: Travel
Booked seat 6A, open return.
Rented red 4-wheel drive.
Reserved cabin, no running water.
Discovered space.
n over 700 airlines, 50,000 hotels, 50 rental car companies and
0 cruise and vacation packages, you can create the perfect get-
y for you. Choose the car, the room, even the ground you walk on.
Travelocity.com
A Sabre Company
Go Virtually Anywhere.
Travelocity,® Travelocity.com® and the Travelocity skyline logo are trademarks and/or servicemarks of Travelocity.com L.P.,

You can't get any closer to the real Hollywood

Universal Studios Hollywood™ puts you so close, you can hear the cameras rolling. Take a revealing inside look at the sets and uncover the secrets of today's biggest films. Then, ride into the thrilling worlds of your favorite movies as you take the monster plunge of Jurassic Park®—The Ride. Venture into The Mummy Returns: Chamber of Doom, and more. Plus, visit Universal CityWalk®, featuring L.A.'s hottest entertainment, dining and shopping. It can only happen in Hollywood—Universal Studios Hollywood.

UNIVERSAL STUDIOS
HOLLYWOOD

WORLD'S LARGEST MOVIE STUDIO AND THEME PARK™